Globalization and
Business Practice

To William Nichols with boundless thanks for your
enthusiasm and encouragement

Globalization and Business Practice

Managing Across Boundaries

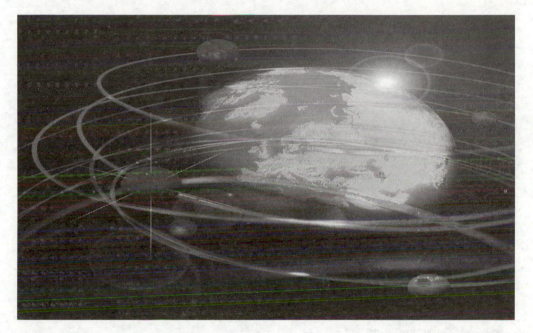

Barbara Parker

SAGE Publications
London · Thousand Oaks · New Delhi

First published 1998

 SAGE Publications Ltd
6 Bonhill Street
London EC2A 4PU

SAGE Publications Inc
2455 Teller Road
Thousand Oaks, California 91320

SAGE Publications India Pvt Ltd
32, M-Block Market
Greater Kailash - I
New Delhi 110 048

British Library Cataloguing in Publication data

A catalogue record for this book is available from the British Library
ISBN 0 7619 5693 X
ISBN 0 7619 5694 8 (pbk)

Library of Congress catalog card number 98-60535

Typeset by Type Study, Scarborough, North Yorkshire
Printed in Great Britain by Butler & Tanner Ltd, Frome and London

Contents

List of Tables
and Figures

Tables

Figures

Preface

MANAGING ACROSS BOUNDARIES

The world increasingly resembles a global marketplace where integration across 'traditional' borders is evident in almost every dimension of life. The daily news demonstrates growing worldwide integration across boundaries like time or national borders that once seemed immutable, and in academic fields the boundaries between disciplines like management, finance, marketing and other fields also have become more fluid. These and other global shifts described in this book have resulted in re-evaluation of business academics and also of business practice. Increasingly, a world with fewer boundaries calls for organizations able to transcend vertical and horizontal boundaries and create hybrids that are both cost effective and responsible to local, regional, domestic, international, and global communities of interest. Unlike other books that purport to map the 'one best way' to approach a topic of study, this book argues that globalization requires thoughtful combinations of management tradition with emerging business practices. Further, it raises many questions about globalization to be answered as today's students make business decisions.

TEXT FEATURES

This text is unique because it presents national, business, and human opportunities and challenges in the context of growing globalization in six spheres: culture, economics, politics, industries, technology, and the natural environment, to pose important questions about life, work, and management in an interdependent world. This is the first book to look at all of these environments at the global level, and one of a handful of books to link global activities with business management practices. Following the first three introductory chapters, each chapter provides an intensive examination of one of the six global environments listed above; each raises important questions about globalization; and each describes ways business managers operate in global environments. For example, Chapter 4 (a) examines the topic of cultural globalization, (b) raises issues associated with worldwide cultural globalization, and (c) describes how business managers develop globally competent people, processes, and structures. The wide range of global and managerial topics covered in chapter descriptions of people, processes, and structures offers great teaching and learning flexibility. Those most interested in strategic management can concentrate their reading on processes like strategy and structural issues associated with globalization in each chapter, whereas teachers and students of organizational behavior may devote their energies to understanding how globalizaation affects people in terms of hiring, development, training, teamwork, and leadership. Additionally, chapters subsequent to the first need not be read in sequence, although the first three chapters help to set the context for consideration of global environments in Chapters 4–10.

The text draws from tradition and current research generated by academicians and practitioners in multiple fields within and outside schools of business, and in doing so crosses disciplinary boundaries. The multidisciplinary scope of the book not only reinforces the global nature of the text, it also provides many ways to show how diversity of worldwide business extends far beyond activities of firms from postindustrial and developed economies. The introductory case for each chapter outlines concepts reinforced throughout the chapter, and each chapter contains examples and cases based on the experiences of firms other than those based in the US and other advanced economies, including the experiences of small- to medium-sized firms in the global arena. Finally, each chapter concludes with a summary of key chapter concepts and a set of discussion questions.

TEACHING AND LEARNING AIDS

Evidence of global integration surrounds us, but confirmatory data can be elusive or contradictory. When the latter occurred, I relied most often on data produced by nongovernmental agencies, particularly those with an established reputation. Most of the latter provide periodic electronic updates, and can be reached at websites accessible through my homepage.

Internet resources, particularly the World Wide Web, provide a particularly rich source of data on globally active businesses and research. At the same time, printed library resources should not be overlooked in the search for insight into the theory and management of global business activities. Valuable print and electronic resources have been collected and appear in a comprehensive students' web page developed in support of this text.

The author wishes to refer readers to her students' homepage at http://www. seattleu.edu/~parker where she makes regularly updated material available. All material contained in that site is the author's, and has no connection whatever with Sage Publications, who disclaim all responsibility for the site and its contents.

Acknowledgements

The global scope of this book produced challenges made less daunting by opportunities to field test content with Seattle University students from around the world. First and foremost they earned my gratitude and thanks for their patience, encouragement, and helpful insights. Tom Thompson particularly helped by drafting Chapter 9. Colleagues and friends at Seattle University and the University of Auckland also contributed ideas and personal support for which I am very grateful, and I particularly applaud James Tallerico, Barbara Di Ferrante, and David Ackerman for their efforts. The Executive Committee at the Albers School of Business and Economics and the Seattle University Summer Faculty Fellowship Committee provided summer grant funds that helped immeasurably.

Many thanks also to the people at Sage Publications who worked so hard with me on this project, including: Sue Jones who originally committed to the text; Rosemary Nixon and Hans Lock, Commissioning Editors; Vanessa Harwood, Production Editor; Justin Dyer, Copyeditor; Andy Esson, Designer.

Thanks also go to the following reviewers who provided wonderful ideas and helpful feedback: Peggy Golden, Florida Atlantic University; Robert Moran, American Graduate School of International Management (Thunderbird); Cynthia Hardy, McGill University and the University of Melbourne; and Nancy Napier, Boise State University.

Finally, I thank my family. The contents of this book span multiple boundaries and transcend more than one academic tradition to describe globalization. My desire to forge new connections surely comes from my parents Robert N. and Charlotte Bush who long ago confounded the boundaries of local tradition by raising their three little daughters abroad. Thank you. Thanks also to my husband and partner William Nichols whose patience is astounding. My children Katherine Parker and Gabriel Parker are among the many seeking world justice and to them I offer encouragement and say 'good on ya'.

PERMISSIONS

The author and publishers wish to thank the following for permission to use copyright material:

Academy of Management for **Figure 6.6** from Quinn et al. (1996) 'Leveraging intellect', *Academy of Management Executive*, 10: 3, p. 21; **Table 2.2** from Oviatt & McDougall (1995) 'Global start-ups: Entrepreneurs on a worldwide stage', *Academy of Management Executive*, 9: 2, pp. 30–43; **Box 10.1** from Gladwin et al. (1995) 'Shifting paradigms for sustainable development: Implications for management theory and research', *Academy of Management Review*, 20: 4, p. 877; **Figure 8.4** from Ghoshal and Bartlett (1990) 'The multinational corporation as an interorganizational network', *Academy of Management Review*, 15:4, p. 605.

Brigham Young University, The David M. Kennedy Center for International Studies, for **Figure 3.3** from Spencer (1991) *Understanding Latin American Underdevelopment and Tension with the United States: A Question of Applying the Right Paradigm*. Copyright (c) 1991.

Business Horizons for **Figure 7.6** adapted from Kreitner (1982) 'Personal wellness: It's just good business', *Business Horizons*, 25, Figure 2 p. 32. Copyright (c) 1982 by the Foundation for the School of Business at Indiana University.

Business Week for **Table 4.9** from 'Diversity, making the business case', *Business Week*, 9.12.96, Special Advertising Section, Exhibit 6.

The Economist for **Table 6.2** from 'Sliding scales', *The Economist*, 2.11.96, p. 17; **Figure 5.4** from *The Economist*, 21.6.97, p. 108; **Figure 7.3** from 'More-or-less European Union', *The Economist*, 26.8.95, p. 46; and **Table 5.4** from *The Economist*, 12.4.97, p. 71. Copyright (c) *The Economist*, 1996, 1997, 1995, 1997.

Elsevier Science Ltd for **Table 9.1** from Makridakis (1989) 'Management in the Twenty First Century', *Long Range Planning*, 22: 2, 37–53.

The Free Press, a Division of Simon & Schuster, for **Figure 8.1** from Porter (1980) *Competitive Strategy: Techniques for Analyzing Industries and Competitors*, Fig. 1.1, p. 4. Copyright (c) 1980 by The Free Press.

Richard H. Hall for **Table 3.4** for Hall and Xu, 'Research Note: Run silent, run deep – cultural influences on organizations in the Far East', *Organization Studies*, 569–576.

The Haworth Press, Inc. for **Table 4.5** from Hassan and Katsanis (1994), 'Global market segment strategies and trends' in Hassan and Kaynak, eds. *Globalization of Consumer Markets: Structures and Strategies*, p. 58.

Hazel Henderson for **Figure 5.5** from Henderson (1996, 1997) *Building a Win-Win World: Life Beyond Global Economic Warfare*, Berrett-Koehler Publishers, p. 154 (original appeared in Henderson (1981, 1988) *The Politics of the Solar Age: Alternatives to Economics*, Anchor/Doubleday).

Jossey-Bass Publishers for **Table 4.10** from O'Hara-Devereaux and Johansen (1994) *Globalwork*, p. 106.

The New York Times for **Table 8.5** from Tagliabue, 'This business club is the real old boys' network', *The New York Times*, 30.10.94, p. 4; and **Figure 5.8** from Brooke, 'South America's big trade strides', *The New York Times*, 10.12.94.

Nortel plc for **Figure 9.7** and **Table 9.7** from Monty (1997) 'Northern Telecom: The anatomy of a transformation', pp. 4, 24.

Oxford University Press, Inc. for **Figure 6.7** from Nonaka and Takeuchi (1995) *The Knowledge-Creating Company: How Japanese Companies Create the Dynamics of Innovation*. Copyright (c) 1995 by Oxford University Press, Inc.; and **Figure 6.1** from World Bank (1995) *World Development Report 1995: Workers in an Integrating World*. Copyright (c) by The International Bank for Reconstruction and Development/The World Bank.

Routledge for **Figure 8.3** from White and Poynter (1990) 'Organizing for world-wide advantage', p. 97 and **Figure 3.6** from Nonaka (1990) 'Managing globalization as a self-renewing process', p. 70, in Bartlett, Doz and Hedlund, eds. *Managing the Global Firm*.

Sage Publications, Inc. for **Figure 10.2** from Stead and Stead (1996) *Management for a Small Planet*, 2nd ed., p. 22.

Seattle Times Co. for **Figure 6.4** from *The Seattle Times*, 26.11.92.

Sloan Management Review for **Table 7.7** from Greenhalgh (1986) 'Managing conflict' *Sloan Management Review*, 27: 4, pp. 45–51.

Sandra Thiedemann for **Table 4.1** adapted from Thiedemann (1991) *Bridging Cultural Barriers for Corporate Success*, Lexington Books.

Time Inc. for **Table 10.4** from Bylinsky, 'Manufacturing for reuse', *Fortune*, 6.2.95, pp. 103–12. Copyright (c) 1995 Time Inc.; **Table 8.2** from 'Global 500 list', *Fortune*, July 1996. Copyright (c) 1996 Time Inc.; Merrifield, 'Wharton School', *Fortune*, 4.4.94, p. 75. Copyright (c) 1994 Time Inc.; **Table 8.3** for data from 'Global 500', *Fortune*, 4.8.97. Copyright (c) 1997 Time Inc.; and **Figure 9.3** and **Table 9.4** for data from Martin, 'When info worlds collide', *Fortune*, 28.10.96, pp. 130–33. Copyright (c) 1996 Time Inc.

UNCTAD for **Tables 5.7** and **6.4** for data from (1994) *World Investment Report 1994*, Sales No. E94.II.A.14.

John Wiley & Sons Ltd for **Table 5.9** from Melin (1992) 'Internationalization as a strategy process', *Strategic Management Journal*, 13, p. 100; and **Table 8.1** from Kobrin (1991) *Strategic Management Journal*. Copyright (c) John Wiley & Sons Ltd.

John Wiley & Sons, Inc. for **Figure 7.4** from Badiru (1995) *Industry's Guide to ISO 9000*; and **Table 4.2** from Bangert and Pirzadas (1992) 'Culture and negotiation', *The International Executive*, 34: 1, pp. 43–64.

The World Bank for **Figure 6.5** from (1995) *World Development Report 1995*; **Table 3.2** from (1996) *World Development Report 1996*; and **Figures** 5.7 and 6.1 from (1996) *World Bank Policy and Research Bulletin*, Aug.–Oct. 1995, April–June 1996.

Every effort has been made to trace the copyright holders, but if any have been inadvertently overlooked the publishers will be pleased to make the necessary arrangement and acknowledgement at the first opportunity.

Chapter 1

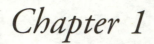

Introduction

CHANGES IN CHINA SHAPE WORLDWIDE OPPORTUNITIES AND THREATS

China's industrial output between 1990 and 1995 grew at an average annual rate of 22.8%, attracting interest from foreign investors and native Chinese alike. Many of the latter abandoned traditional agricultural work to search for jobs in urban areas, and perhaps, like busy city-dwellers everywhere, they found it easier and more desirable to substitute more meat, eggs, and milk for their traditional grain-based diet of the past.

Urbanization and economic development as well as changes in diet provided new opportunities for business. Dietary change, for example, has yielded business opportunities both within and outside China. For example, farmers in China are shifting their production from grain by building ponds for farm-raised fish or grain-fed livestock. Additionally, with migration from the country to China's cities, there is growing need for urban housing and business services such as telecommunications and freight delivery. Importers of grain see an opportunity to enter China's still large market for rice. To date, China's demand for grain imports has made Vietnam the third largest exporter of rice in the world. Increased imports of grain from Vietnam, as well as increased industrial production throughout China, have provided entrepreneurs all over Asia with business opportunities that make them more interdependent with business activities throughout the world. Within the agricultural industry, Chinese and Vietnamese farmers now find their prices are closely linked to world commodity prices rather than to the Communist world alone. Further, firms like Motorola, Siemens, and General Motors are providing foreign direct investment (FDI) amounting to billions of dollars fueling economic growth in manufacturing as well as agricultural and service sectors, creating jobs and further stimulating exodus from rural to urban areas. One example of a foreign direct investor is the Anglo-Dutch firm Unilever, which committed £100 million to seven joint *ventures in China ranging from detergents in Shanghai, ice cream in Beijing, and toothpaste production to serve all of China. Intel, Motorola, Sony, Matsushita Electric Industrial, General Motors, Procter & Gamble, have committed hundreds of millions of dollars to building production facilities in China, and global retailers like Carrefour and Royal Ahold NV have announced plans to expand their holdings in China. In 1996, business investments in China totalled $52 billion, making it the second biggest recipient of FDI that year (the US was the first).*

At the same time that these events provide increased local and global opportunities for business, Communist Chinese leaders are concerned that China's long-standing ability to feed its 1.2 billion citizens will evaporate. China's grain output has averaged annual growth of less than one-tenth of 1% since 1990, and from being a net exporter, China has become a net grain importer. J.P. Morgan & Co. economist Guocang Huan describes the mixed blessing of globalization for China: China could face chronic food shortages in the years ahead as its citizens substitute industrial production for agricultural production and increasingly turn to a protein-based diet. While some view China's industrialization and new grain import status as a business opportunity, Chinese farmers may well view these events in terms of threats to their livelihood, and political leaders may similarly see more threat than opportunity in this aspect of globalization. The Worldwatch Institute sees yet another threat: China's growing demand for food could drive up grain prices worldwide, making grain less accessible in much of the world. Rising grain prices in the industrialized world are unlikely to affect most people, but for the 1 billion people worldwide who live on the equivalent of one US dollar per day, global food shortages resulting in higher prices could mean disaster.

This simple example of a dietary shift in China shows that few things are simple in a global world. Further, tracing the real and potential effects of this dietary shift illustrates several of the key elements of globalization. First, the effects of events occurring within national borders have the capacity to cross those borders; in doing so their effect is global as well as local. Second, the global impact of an event creates interdependence not only among individuals, organizations, and industries, but also among political, economic, and other systems worldwide. Third, the results of global interdependence and interaction are difficult to control or predict. Finally, this example illustrates that globalization generates opportunities and threats for governments, small and large businesses, and indeed for all humankind.

Sources: Benjamin, Robert. (1994, Feb. 28). Revolutionary changes in diet challenge China. *The Seattle Times*, p. A8. Brown, Lester, R. (1995). *Who will feed China?* London: Earthscan.

The twenty-first century could well become the 'global century', even if rapid globalization of people, products, and markets slows from its blazing mid-1990s pace. Increasingly, organizational participants are urged to 'act global, think local' or become part of the 'global village,' but definitions, descriptions, and visions of globalization vary widely, making it quite difficult to know what it means to be 'global.' Additionally, it is not at all clear what the costs and benefits of globalization are or are likely to be for the future. It is, therefore, important to begin our exploration of globalization by defining the term.

GLOBALIZATION VARIOUSLY DEFINED
Definitions affect business responses

Author Jan Pieterse (1995) asserts there are almost as many conceptualizations of globalization as there are disciplines in the social sciences; this also may be true for the many fields assembled under the business umbrella, including marketing, management, finance, accounting, and economics. Globalization is popularly described as the absence of borders and barriers to trade between nations (Ohmae, 1995), but also has been viewed as shifts in traditional patterns of international production, investment, and trade (Dicken, 1992), and as interconnections between overlapping interests of business and society (Brown, 1992; Renesch, 1992). These definitional differences are more than semantic; each shapes assumptions about organizational actions that can or should be taken in response to globalization. Whereas a business leader who believes national borderlessness is the essence of globalization will guide organizational energy toward monitoring national and foreign political/economic change, one who views globalization as convergence between business and other societal interests would devote more attention to examining social changes. But boundarylessness is elsewhere described as more than a question of nations and economics; it refers to an ability to cross other traditional borders of time, space, scope, geography, functions, thought, cultural assumptions, and understanding of the self in relation to others (Rhinesmith, 1993) and to permeating boundaries *within* organizations as vertical boundaries of level and rank and horizontal boundaries of function and discipline also dissolve (Ashkenas, Ulrick, Jick, and Kerr, 1995). In their differences, these various approaches to thinking about globalization seem to point organizational attention in different directions.

Permeable borders of globalization

For purposes of exploring the concept in this introductory chapter, globalization is defined broadly as increased permeability of traditional boundaries of almost every kind, including physical borders such as time and space, nation-states and economies, industries and organizations and less tangible borders such as cultural norms or assumptions about 'how we do things around here.' This broad definition of globalization guides this chapter to show how concepts of border permeability arose from global events that may not have seemed global initially because they appeared to be occurring in isolation and in different spheres. Nevertheless, these events can shape activities worldwide. For example, the dietary shift in China with which we opened the chapter illustrates how a trend in one country has ramifications for the world. As the impacts of seemingly isolated events like these expand to affect activities in different realms – as political events shape cultural events – their global impact is clarified, and they provide evidence of the amorphous borderlessness characteristic of globalization. A high rate of change, the growing number and diversity of participants, and rising complexity and uncertainty also are features of globalization and all have implications for business managers.

Organizations shape globalization and its definition

Organizations are not simply affected by globalization: the combined activities of organizations pursuing profit, social, political, personal, family, or other goals stimulate, facilitate, sustain, and extend globalization. In the search for new products and markets, business enterprises spread not only consumer goods but ideas concerning wealth creation; ideals concerning how people should live and work; ideologies concerning political and business governance. Nor are the parameters of business in the global world easily controlled: a telephone link to the Internet yields tips on guerilla tactics or access to kiddie porn almost as readily as it provides the latest Dow Jones Index; mafia organizations and drug cartels operate in a worldwide arena with as much expertise as Royal Dutch Shell, Imperial Chemical Industries, Sony, Pemex, or Coca-Cola. Global business is not, then, just about business: it has cultural, legal, political, and social effects as much as economic ones. These are the topics to be explored in this text.

ORGANIZATION OF THE TEXT

The practical experiences of going global in an increasingly integrated world are new for most businesses, and studying them is difficult because global change has been rapid, constant, and non-linear. This book gathers theory and practice that has thus far emerged from global business experience and research. While the book's major emphasis is on examining *management* principles applicable in a global world, the multidisciplinary nature of globalization also calls for a look at principles of economics, political science, marketing, and international business. All are examined in the context of a global and interdependent world more than an international (nation-to-nation) world to see how worldwide integration in many spheres is affecting business practices. Those accustomed to a linear, cause/effect approach to business management will occasionally be frustrated by the discontinuous nature of global events described by interrelated circles more than straight lines, and for demands that call for global managers able to think in process-oriented as well as linear ways. Finally, the results of current experiments with global theories and practices are not yet known, and students of global business must be prepared to cope with the resulting ambiguity. The text is structured as follows:

1 A current case opens each chapter to introduce important chapter concepts; business examples for each chapter are incorporated in the text and in boxed examples further to illustrate concepts and demonstrate ways businesses are going global.

2 An introductory outline of each chapter's purpose is followed by a brief review of chapter topics and theories explored; some of these theories may have been ones to which readers have already been exposed, in which case this section of the chapters provides a review for students who have completed prior business studies and an introduction for those new to business studies.

3 The first three chapters establish premises of globalization; Chapters 4–10 then concentrate on a single global environment, e.g., global culture, global politics, or global economics; evidence of globalization in each sphere is presented in Part I of each chapter.

4 In Part II of each chapter subsequent to this one the focus shifts from evidence of globalization to show how managers are shaping people, processes, and structures in response to or anticipation of globalization; international and domestic management theories are examined for applicability to global practice, and managerial competencies required for the global arena also appear in Part II of each chapter.

5 Each chapter concludes with a review of key chapter concepts, a set of review and discussion questions, and current references to direct future reading.

6 Each chapter is supported by a separate section on the text's homepage (http://www.seattleu.edu/~parker); this homepage is updated on a quarterly basis and it is organized around contents of each chapter to lead readers to sources of information on each chapter's content.

Figure 2.1 (p. 74) presents a visual outline of topics explored in the text. Activities internal to the firm and of most immediate concern to business managers are located within three inner circles; these interrelated organizational activities include: (a) managing the *people* (P) who populate the organization; (b) organizing the *processes* (P) that accomplish organization purposes; and establishing the *structures* (S) that support them in their work. The outer circle in the figure shows that in addition to internal concerns (PPS), global managers and their enterprises also face external challenges and external opportunities. Increasingly, these external concerns are global as well as local, domestic, regional, and international. This increasingly interdependent global world requires that organizational leaders also look beyond domestic and international environments to examine the potential impact on them from global events that may, at best, seem distant. The figure demonstrates this fact, but what it cannot show are that a change in one global environment almost necessarily involves a change in others because they are interrelated at the world level. These interdependencies are dynamic and complex, requiring people to adopt two levels of analysis: the firm and the external environment. A clearer understanding of each can help decision-makers understand, analyze, and anticipate interactions *among* global environments and *between* firms and a globalizing world for business.

A brief review of chapter contents

To this point, *Chapter 1* has defined globalization, and later in this chapter we look at the six global environments examined in the text. An integrative or 'big picture' view of globalization is recommended because only from this perspective can we evaluate options for creating a world that is better than, worse than, or similar to the past. Describing and evaluating global integration is an important goal for this book; various views on the reality and potential of globalization are introduced later in this chapter and explored throughout the text. A second goal is to present theoretical and practical examples of options available to businesspeople when managing globally.

The first three chapters of the text frame global challenges; in turn they define globalization and views of it worldwide, what globalization has meant for businesses, and how and why globalization is changing the essential nature of business management. An important example of this change is growing public demand for business accountability and social responsibility, a topic implicit throughout the book that is introduced in Chapter 3, and explored in greater depth in Chapters 6 and 10. The introductory chapters pose questions also explored in greater depth throughout the book, such as: Will political globalization improve resource distribution or restrict it? Will global culture lead to more variety or less? Will a global economy create better quality of life or emphasize financial gains that divide the world into fewer 'haves' and many 'have nots'? The general and introductory information on globalization provided in these three chapters becomes a springboard for Chapters 4–10, which explore each of the six global environments in greater depth. Chapters 4–10 can be read in any order, depending upon personal interests and preferences.

The first half of each of these later chapters (4–10) presents evidence for and separate concerns about globalization posed by each environment, such as diversity, economic and social equity, business responsibility and ethics, and political and personal risk, to name a few. The second half of each chapter then explores how fundamental global questions and challenges for the selected environment, e.g., culture, technology, or politics, affect the theory and practice of managing global organizations. Management themes explored include theories and practices associated with organizational behavior such as motivation, leadership, stress management, career and skills development, teamwork, and human resource management, e.g., selection, compensation, training, development. Focus at the individual level shows how people transcend boundaries and develop professional and career skills important to the global manager, or motivate, lead, develop, and compensate a diverse workforce. Structural boundaries to be bridged include creating systems that control and are flexible, are dynamic and stable, are autonomous and interrelated. Examples include networks, alliances, and horizontal and virtual organizations. The portfolio approach to processes suggested in Chapter 3 is reinforced throughout the text, providing a framework for understanding processes such as renewal, learning, innovation, creativity, sustainable advantage, organizational culture, and core competencies, to name a few. Readings in this book introduce the student of global management to existing theories of management and international business and to emerging theories of both. Examples from actual global organizations in each chapter show how many are combining tradition with new ideas.

In *Chapter 2* we look at how an expanding global perspective creates a different context for business organizations than does cross-border international business. This expanding perspective has created interdependencies and shaped the focus and energies of business organizations. The chapter defines the global enterprise that pursues an integrative approach, and identifies four challenges of globalization any organization faces: there are problems that cannot be solved; organizations increasingly depend on intangibles; diversity must be managed at all levels; and dominant business traditions have not prepared us for the future we face. This chapter then looks at how organizations operate globally, returning to Figure 2.1 to show how attention may be focused simultaneously on internal organizational challenges and on external global challenges.

Chapter 3 further explores the organizational effects of globalization by assessing the boundaries of business traditions and theories in a globalizing world. Traditions reviewed include those now dominant, e.g., US, Japanese, Western European, and those emerging, e.g., South American, Vedantic, women in business. Blurring boundaries between sectors like business and politics enlarges traditional boundaries for businesses, creating new challenges for businesses to be members of communities of interest as well as profit-seeking entities. For example, where once businesses were viewed primarily as instruments for creating economic wealth, increasingly business is expected to serve social goals that improve quality of life *and* create economic wealth within the increasingly global communities in which they operate. Chapter 3 describes the demand for a community-based view of organizations to show why organizations must cross both external and internal boundaries of business traditions to be both socially responsible and economically successful in global business. This both/and approach enlarges the scope of management theory as well, creating challenges for both theory and practice. The chapter concludes with a look at structural, process, and managerial boundaries organizational participants transcend to go global, outlining the challenges this creates not only for managers but also for all employees.

Global culture is the subject of *Chapter 4*. The chapter defines culture and its function, describes global influences on culture such as entertainment and travel, provides evidence of global cultural convergence, and weighs two conflicting views of cultural globalization. The second half of the chapter explores boundaries of national and organizational tradition that shape culture in organizations, looking particularly at how issues of cultural diversity affect global organizations.

Chapter 5 compares closed and open economies before looking at how wealth creation is variously defined; comparative measures of wealth useful in a global world are presented. Evidence of growing global trade in goods and services, foreign direct investments, and global currency show that many conditions of market-based economics are not well met by economic globalization. This creates challenges for the firm which are explored in practice and application of structural theories such as product life cycle, structuring wholly owned subsidiaries and strategic alliances, process theories such as cultures of capitalism and decision-making, and personnel issues such as motivation and vision development.

Chapter 6 examines a fourth component of global economics: globalization of labor. Work hours and compensation, work conditions, global human migration, and job migration are four among the specific topics explored. Business organizations have played a role in globalizing labor and they are increasingly asked to play roles in structuring human rights and ethical codes. The challenges this creates for organizations are explored to show how organizations structure complex problems into organizational and global codes of ethics, and manage them with processes like organizational learning.

The global political and legal environment is the subject of *Chapter 7*. Domestic political roles have been reshaped by global politics, resulting in integration among governments and between business and government. Pressures toward more global forms of governance are contrasted with national self-interests, and global alliances are explored. The growing role of nongovernmental organizations in defining the political and business agenda also is reviewed to show that worldwide integration reduces national sovereignty and challenges business autonomy. The effects of these constraints on business are explored to show how they shape business practices, and particularly management of risks, ranging from corruption to workplace stress, conflict, and personal safety for the manager.

Chapter 8 looks at globalization of industries, explaining how industries have been viewed and how globalization alters these views. Many types of organizations participate in global business, and the likely effects on industry globalization are reviewed. Challenges of industry globalization include envisioning the future and considering whether it is firms or nations that compete globally. Management tools useful for industry globalization include developing sustainable advantage, managing strategically, and structuring for global presence by means of internal networks and horizontal structures.

Chapter 9 explores global technological issues, particularly those related to information technology. A comparison between the Industrial Revolution and what has been called the Information Revolution shows that these two revolutions share similarities but also differ in important ways. The World Wide Web provides one example of the challenge of an information revolution: information overload. Demands for constant innovation in the many industries driven by information have led to new ways of thinking about information management and to methods for stimulating creativity and teamwork.

Finally, *Chapter 10* concludes with a look at the natural environment. Earth is a closed system, and some believe population growth and economic development are straining this system beyond its capacity. Proponents of sustainable development believe this approach to managing growth provides an option that ensures a liveable quality of life for future generations, but others believe any problems caused by unbridled growth will be offset by technological breakthroughs. These frameworks are the basis for examining globalization of the natural environment. Global commons of air and water, globalization of disease and of natural disasters, and global population growth are only a few of the concerns explored in this last chapter. We return to the concept of organizations in community with others to examine effective, low-cost business options for a sustainable future. Throughout the book, it is important to remember that a global event classified, for example, as 'political' or 'economic' rarely occurs without affecting or being affected by its interdependence with other events. These interrelationships and interdependencies are the primary reason why global events have worldwide repercussions. Similarly, organizations experience interdependencies both internally, characterized by relationships among people, processes, and structures, and externally, as, for example, global cultural change affects industry or economic opportunities. Managers in a global enterprise who identify these relationships and forge links among them will be those best able to cross boundaries and barriers to organizational success in a global world. The following section examines both practical and academic perspectives on the sources of globalization.

SOURCES OF GLOBALIZATION
Technology

Changes in the technological environment clearly are one source of globalization. According to John Naisbitt's *Global paradox* (1994), telecommunications is *the* driving force powering economic globalization. Telecommunications and similar technologies provide opportunities for far-flung business interactions, and people from Bulgaria to Buenos Aires seize, rethink, and retool them to create more business opportunities. With little more than a computer, a modem, a telephone line, and fax capability, it now is possible to establish, maintain, and expand a business reaching outside traditional boundaries, borders, and barriers, including barriers of economies of scale and scope that previously restricted worldwide business to larger firms. For many small businesses, technological access has extended their reach worldwide. Technological breakthroughs in medicine, in television broadcasting, and in most other fields of endeavor also combine to make the world a smaller place where in-person or electronic access to people and other resources around the world is almost as great as to next-door neighbors. This access to information, opportunity, products, and markets is a reason to argue that globalization is a product of a technological revolution.

William Knoke (1996) argues that in the face of technological change, particularly the 'fourth dimension' of computerization, nation-states will lose sovereignty, and physical place will become almost irrelevant. According to Knoke, the impact on business is to create companies that use these linking technologies to quickly assemble and disassemble project teams throughout the world. Others similarly argue that technological breakthroughs of every kind are changing traditional assumptions as organizations become virtual (Davidow and Malone, 1992), as the gap between the 'haves' and 'have nots' becomes evident (Green and Ruhleder, 1996), as relationships between large and small organizations in a global sphere alter and enable small firms to compete globally (Naisbitt, 1994), and as jobs and work roles adapt to an information-driven world.

Economy

Others trace the roots of globalization to economic events, and considerable evidence can be assembled to support contentions that economic globalization powers world growth: growing world gross domestic product (GDP) reached approximately \$29 trillion in 1997, but is expected to increase to \$48 trillion by 2010 (A dynamic new world economy, 1994). Furthermore, global shifts in where growth is occurring and how wealth is reinvested are changing the face of this global economy. For example, rapid growth is occurring in many developing economies, although sometimes growth can be volatile. In Asia, where 1995 growth rates ranged from 5.7 to 11.3%, the growth picture has changed. Although the Organization for Economic Cooperation and Development (OECD) predicted Asian economic growth would remain high through 1998, a slowdown following economic and currency crises in 1997 subsequently lowered economic growth estimates for Malaysia, South Korea, Indonesia, Thailand and their neighbors.

TABLE 1.1   Asian GDPs

Nation	Annual percentages of GDP growth				
	1970–1979	1980–1989	1990–1996	1997	1998*
Hong Kong	9.2	7.5	5.0	5.4	2.1
Singapore	9.4	7.2	8.3	7.4	3.0
Taiwan	10.2	8.1	6.3	6.6	4.0
South Korea	9.3	8.0	7.7	5.8	1.0
Malaysia	8.0	5.7	8.8	7.4	0.2
Thailand	7.3	7.2	8.6	0.9	−4.1
Indonesia	7.8	5.7	7.2	6.3	−7.5
China	7.5	9.3	10.1	9.3	8.7
Philippines	6.1	1.8	2.8	4.9	2.0
Industrial countries	3.4	2.6	2.0	2.9	3.2–4.0

*1998 estimates are averages from multiple forecasters.
Source: Adapted from: Is it over? (1997, Mar 1). *The Economist*, p. 23; OECD; http://www.asiarisk.com; World Bank.

Newly industrialized countries (NICs) such as those of South Korea, Taiwan, Thailand, and Singapore contributed 25% to world GDP in the early 1990s as compared to 4% in the 1960s (Farrell, 1994). China alone is expected to account for a quarter of world GDP by 2015 (Wolf, 1997). The highest economic producers in the future are expected to be China, Israel, Japan, Korea, and Singapore (Quick, name, 1993), a future realized already in Singapore, which has been ranked the first or second most competitive among the more than 40 countries so ranked from 1994 to 1998 (International Institute for Management Development, 1990: http://www.imd.ch/wcy.html; *World Competitiveness Report*, 1994, 1995). The phenomenal pace at which NICs have grown is found in Table 1.1.

As data found in Table 1.1 would suggest, Asian economic expansion has occurred very rapidly, doubling per capita income in 10 years for China and in 11 years for South Korea. The adjustments necessary to match the volume and velocity of change are considerable, especially when one recognizes that the same doubling of per capita income took 58 years in Britain, 47 years in the US, and 34 years in Japan (A game, 1994). Nations experiencing rapid economic growth often face an equally rapid demand to adapt their social, political, legal and other systems. For example, Thailand's prosperity makes it possible for many to purchase their first automobile, but traffic jams routinely lasting one to two hours in Bangkok demonstrate that road systems and other infrastructure provided by governments often cannot keep pace with change. Labor strife in South Korea described in Box 1.1 illustrates how rapid economic change stimulated by global events also can alter the nation and its social culture.

BOX 1.1:   RAPID ECONOMIC GROWTH AFFECTS SOUTH KOREA

South Korean labor laws passed in 1953 provided generous worker benefits includ-ing near guarantees of lifetime employment. This and other benefits – combined with annual 15% increases in wages for the last decade – made South Korean workers among the best paid in the world. For example, Daewoo Electronics pays its South Korean factory workers more than it pays the same workers in their British factory, even though Britain is a wealthier country. Hyundai Group supervisor Kang Jo Wang, for example, earns an annual salary of almost $47,000 and enjoys bene-fits ranging from automobile discounts to school fees and apartment subsidies.

By 1996, a 15% growth in wages and benefits had outpaced the 6% rate of domestic economic growth, and worried legislators passed laws to make it easier to dismiss workers to achieve cost efficiencies. National strikes followed the new law's passage, and union leaders garnered worldwide support with endorsements from the International Labor Organization and other labor and rights groups.

According to some analysts, President Kim Young Sam passed these laws because he believed the public was more concerned about the economy's future than about workers' rights. Companies like Daewoo have moved many operations to lower wage regions in Asia and in Eastern Europe, and labor-intensive indus-tries like footwear that once were located in South Korea now have closed, locat-ing direct investments elsewhere. Mr Kang and others at Hyundai refused to join the national strikes, concluding that their companies need more hiring and firing autonomy to operate globally. The combined forces of job migration, strikes, alliances with global organizations, and business choice affect the economy, but they also affect lives of millions of South Koreans as they weigh interactions between economic downturn and wage increases in an increasingly complex global world.

Source: Pollack, Andrew. (1997, Jan. 12, p. A8). South Korean strikes expand. *New York Times*; Schuman, Michael. (1997, Jan. 20). Split in union ranks at Hyundai reflects shift by Korean workers. *The Wall Street Journal*, p. A12. Schuman, Michael (1997, Jan. 16). Economic reforms begin to irk Koreans. *The Wall Street Journal*, p. A11.

Economists Klaus Schwab and Claude Smadja (1995) believe the pace of economic growth in Asia is an 'economic revolution' that will make Asia the new center of gravity for the world economy, with the following results:

(a) a worldwide delocalization of industrial production as more goods are produced around the world;

(b) a decrease in the rate of job creation in service sectors most relevant to the industrial world where reliance on service sectors is highest;

(c) trade tensions between the West and emerging markets; and

(d) a desynchronization of economic cycles in Western Europe, North America, and East Asia.

Economic growth is booming in South America as well. For example, according to the OECD, GDP growth for Chile is likely to be 7% in 1997 and 1998; Mexico is a close second at 7 and 4.3% growth in the same two years. Whether growth in these nations creates economic revolutions remains to be seen. For example, economist Paul Krugman (1994) has argued that East Asia will not displace other regions in economic development.

What is clear is that mature industrial economies like Canada, Germany, France, Japan, Italy, Britain, and the US now contribute less in relative terms to world growth than they once did. Thus, as compared to many Asian countries, these economically developed economies are growing at an averaged rate of 2%. For example, in 1994, most of the mature industrial economies listed above experienced GDP growth of less than 5%, and according to the World Bank's 1996 world economic outlook, their average growth will remain below 3% through most of 1997. US projections are for GDP growth between 2 and 2.9% in 1997 (despite a 1997 first quarter pace double that). After several years of almost no growth, Japan's GDP is expected to grow, although estimates vary. According to the International Monetary Fund (IMF), Japan's GDP could grow as much as 3.1% in 1997 (IMF, 1996, *World Economic Outlook*), but Japan's Economic Planning Agency estimates GDP growth will grow only 1.9% through March 1998. European Union projections for 1997 similarly set growth at or below 3% for these nations in Western Europe.

Preceding examples show the source of world economic growth has altered, and the following sections show the direction of economic flows also has changed. Whereas once the direction of foreign direct investments (FDI) in the form of new buildings and equipment or acquisition of existing firms went primarily from one industrialized country to another and secondarily to developing economies, recent activity shows industrialized economies now invest in each other *and* in the developing world. Further, developing economies increasingly invest in the industrialized world and in each other.

UN *World Investment Reports* show that the $70 billion of 1993 FDI that went to the developing world increased to $97 billion in 1995. And developing economies are more than recipients of investment; they are major FDI contributors as well. Mergers and acquisitions on a worldwide scale also are a source of global economic shifts. A record $866 billion in global mergers and acquisitions was recorded in 1995, a figure representing a 51% increase over 1994 (Lipin, 1996). In 1996, a stunning $1.4 trillion in

TABLE 1.2   Sample acquisitions for 1996 and 1997

Buyer	Acquisition	Transaction type	Value (billion $US)
WorldCom	MCI Communications	Stock and cash	37.0
Grand Met	Guinness	Stock swap	22.0
Boeing	McDonnell Douglas	Stock swap	14.0
US West	Continental Cablevision	Stock and cash	11.4
NationsBank	Boatmen's Bancshares	Stock swap	9.5
Gillette	Duracell Batteries	Stock swap	7.9
Dun & Bradstreet Investors	Cognizant	Stock spinoff	5.4
IMC Global Inc.	Freeport-McMoran	Sale	1.2

Source: These data are from a table that appeared alongside Lipin, Steven. (1997, Jan. 2). Gorillas in our midst. *The Wall Street Journal*, p. R8.

global mergers was announced, including: the merger of Swiss pharmaceutical giants Ciba-Geigy and Sandoz in a $30 billion deal; and Gillette's acquisition of Duracell Batteries for the relatively small comparative amount of $7.3 billion; the total for 1997 was $1.63 trillion. Examples of important mergers and acquisitions during 1996 and 1997 appear in Table 1.2. Many acquisitions and mergers differ from past transactions because whereas many were paid in cash in the past, now they are more likely to be the result of stock swaps and spinoffs, and those stock investments create long-term cross-border links. One result is that stock distribution disperses firm ownership beyond a select group of nations or individuals and into a worldwide pool of people and institutions who may hold divergent views about how firms should be managed.

Worldwide electronic communication networks make it possible to trade on stock exchanges night and day, and this as well as a desire to raise funds within nations has fueled development of stock exchanges all over the world. Time is no longer the constraint it once was, and as the time barrier falls, yet another traditional border becomes permeable. Increased permeability along economic borders has led others to suggest that economics more than national politics will be a deciding factor in economic prosperity (Ohmae, 1995). Economist Robert Reich (1991) believes that globalization will cause business leaders to think of themselves less as autonomous actors and more as participants inextricably linked to one another in global industries and in global economies, as economics more than other factors drives world development.

Politics

Others point to numerous and recent political events to support a hypothesis that politics and legal issues are fueling globalization. The World Trade Organization – 1995 successor organization to the General Agreement on Tariffs and Trade (GATT) – is a worldwide membership organization established for the purpose of defining worldwide commercial relationships. Establishment of the WTO resolved key trade issues that had long plagued GATT progress, led to a fairly comprehensive set of commercial rules for the 126 member nations, and provided a viable mechanism for resolving trade disputes in the global arena. Interestingly, the first ruling made by the WTO was in favor of Venezuela and Brazil in their dispute against US gasoline import regulations. In ruling against the US, the WTO demonstrated that commitment to worldwide fair trade may supersede traditions of bowing to a nation's political or economic clout.

The retreat from Soviet-style Communism in 1989 as well as eased government restrictions on capitalist activities in China, Vietnam, and Cuba are evidence of important change in political spheres. In these economies, political changes have resulted in increased privatization of all types of industries. Growth in privatization in developing economies – defined by the World Bank in 1994 as those economies where per capita GDP is less than $8,955 US – has been nothing short of phenomenal. Prior to the fall of the Berlin Wall, there were few privatizations in developing economies, but the number of sales grew from 28 in 1988 to 775 in 1994 with a total sales volume of $21.8 billion (Fredman, 1996). Interestingly, the greatest volume of privatization in 1994 was in telecommunications, power utilities, energy, tobacco, and banking (What is privatization anyway?, 1995).

Privatization also is occurring throughout the industrialized world as governments divest themselves of entities established to provide goods and services in industries ranging from airlines to telecommunications, energy, banking, steel, education, and even prisons. Accordingly, the greatest volume of privatization (47.5%) from 1988 to 1993 was in Western Europe as firms like British Airways, San Paolo Bank in Italy, and Koninklijke PTT Nederland were wholly or partially sold to private investors. A banner year for privatization in Western Europe was 1996, led by the Deutsche Telekom sell-off for $13 billion, sales of Italy's Societa Finanziaria Telefonica per Azioni (Stet), 20% of France Telecom, and Italy's Ente Nazionale Idrocarburi SpA (ENI). Privatization represents more than a transfer of ownership from government to private hands. This shift represents a managerial challenge for new owners who inherit employees, processes, and structures originally organized to serve public needs more than business goals.

Government roles worldwide also are increasingly played by citizen groups, showing evidence of a 'global associational revolution' (Salamon, 1994), and they provide further evidence to argue that globalization is powered by political shifts. In some cases, organizations outside the government sphere – referred to as nongovernmental organizations (NGOs) – are taking on roles governments have more typically played. Examples of NGOs or global associations with growing clout in the global political arena include environmental protection and preservation groups such as Greenpeace and the

Worldwatch Institute, human rights groups such as Oxfam and Amnesty International, and charitable organizations such as CARE and UNICEF. Many hundreds of thousands of groups like these provide information and intervention to resolve global issues, variously serving to perform roles government cannot or will not perform. Some of these are clearly social service roles, but others are more nearly aligned with roles businesses play. For example, many NGOs in developing countries such as Bangladesh, India, and in some parts of Latin America provide seed money to women who then establish small businesses. In doing so, these NGOs assume traditional governmental roles in stimulating development and allocating resources, and they also play roles more frequently played by banks and other lending institutions. Possible effects are changes in assumptions about sectoral work, and enterprise practices that merge business and social service habits and norms. The results may well be changing assumptions about how work is accomplished, who is credit-worthy, or how profits can be generated. In turn, political power shifts also lead to shifts in assumptions about how the political game is or can be played.

Culture

A number of events are lightning rods for the issue of globalization of culture. First, products ranging from cola beverages to denim blue jeans are consumed throughout the world. Many of these products are staples for the 1.37 billion global teenager market who adopt the same modes of dress, jargon, music, entertainment preferences, and even converging values for environmental stewardship (Tully, 1994) and individualism (Fraedrich, Herndon, and Ferrell, 1995; Rohwedder, 1994). English is increasingly used as a business language, spread via Internet connections, face-to-face connections facilitated by business, tourism, study abroad, immigration, and by many forms of mass-market entertainment.

Whether a truly global culture is possible – in terms of either common habit or business-inspired materialism – is unclear, but its potential is a subject of considerable debate. Some see cultural merging occurring, calling it a form of neo-imperialism capable of eliminating cultural variety (Tomlinson, 1991); and others predict cultural pressures to merge leading to destructive forms of conflict (Huntington, 1993). Yet others (Swimme, 1984) suggest that scientific discovery tracing the beginnings of time, space, and life provide a common 'origin' story for all of civilization, and that this common story is the basis for thinking of human community as a single entity that transcends communities of nations and other identity groups. The argument for global community traced to a common origin sounds a hopeful note for addressing common and global problems. Less hopeful is evidence of a growing cult of violence among young men fostered by video images (Appadurai, 1990), or Barber's (1992) view that McDonaldization or Jihad are the likely outcomes of cultural merging.

Others challenge arguments for cultural merging, arguing that the cultural borrowing associated with 'creolization', '*mestizaje*', 'orientalization', and the like, enhance, but do not redefine, culture (Pieterse, 1995). 'Glocalization', or loose connections between what is local and what is global, may instead be forged (Robertson, 1995), leading to the multiplication of cultural differences through globalization rather than their reduction (Kahn, 1995). Instead of the globalization of a predominantly Westernized culture, where business language, values, and behaviors are standardized and homogenized on a worldwide basis, Robertson (1995) argues that cultural influences *from* East *to* West have been seriously underestimated. Availability of products and services in the West like Hong Kong action films, 'world' music, ethnic food, and consumer products produced from Japan to India bolster this argument. Thanks to satellite technology and a growing worldwide appetite for the diversion of entertainment, television's reach is growing, reaching 800 million homes in 1995 to convey fantasy images like *Mighty Morphin Power Rangers* and *Dynasty* as readily as CNN reports. It is impossible to guess if these influences are temporary or will have a lasting effect on shaping and defining national or global cultures. Nor is it clear that a truly global business culture will emerge. What is clear is that as similar cultural messages are distributed worldwide, they provide reason to argue that cultural exposure can be a powerful source of globalization.

Natural environment

The natural environment often is viewed only in the context of preserving the integrity of natural resources like air, water, and trees, but these natural resources include more than the air we breathe or the water we consume. As inhabitants of the same earth, people everywhere are likely to be similarly affected if any one or a group of nations or businesses degrade or alter commonly held resources. Raw materials of every type also are important parts of what can be thought of as the earth's 'natural' environment, and the contribution of each to business activities makes them important topics for consideration. Access to and use of raw materials, e.g., oil, is important to survival and to industrial production.

Oil spills, nuclear disasters, and similar accidents destroy natural resources, while industrialization consumes or depletes them. For example, water consumed during industrial production can pollute water worldwide just as air-borne emissions reduce air quality or reduce the ozone layer. By 2000, anticipated ozone reductions and global warming are expected to displace 95 million people who live at sea level, cause ecosystems to disappear, deserts to expand, and storms to become more violent and frequent (UN Framework, 1995). While industrialization creates jobs and a standard of living that individuals as well as nations seek, it also gathers people into densely populated areas where urban problems of garbage and water treatment as well as noise pollution further affect the environment. Industrialization is a mixed blessing in that it improves world prosperity at the same time that it increases the potential for ecological disruption. Ecological disruption also can occur as business activities transport plants and animals greater distances, and diseases that afflict both people and plants also are going global. Even natural disasters occurring in one part of the world have worldwide implications because of global connections. For example, floods in Europe and an earthquake in Japan in early 1995 disrupted world trade flows because so many goods bound for foreign markets travel through either Rotterdam or Kobe.

Some argue that economic development along free market lines must be replaced with principles of sustainable development that ensure a viable future for succeeding generations (Gore, 1992; Hawken, 1993). Proposals for sustainable development call for fundamental changes. For example, while markets sustain divisions between rich and poor, sustainable development calls for a greater degree of world economic equity. This is not to say that the world's wealth will be redistributed, but that long-standing inequities between richer and poorer nations must be overcome, and particularly that poorer nations must have better economic opportunities than in the past. According to authors of the United Nations 1994 *Human Development Report*, 'the concept of one world and one planet simply cannot emerge from an unequal world. . . . Global sustainability without global justice will always remain an elusive goal.' (p. 21).

Ironically, even as some argue that lifestyles in the rich nations must be reduced to consume less, many in developing countries advocate the opposite change as they adopt habits of materialism and consume more. Resources are consumed, forests and water evaporate, and desertification grows. Given a competitive business environment, and a world population anxious or forced to join the world economy, business organizations unwilling to compromise the natural environment may lose opportunities. Those organizations taking active steps to preserve the environment may be accused of imposing their own values on host countries anxious to develop economically. Thus, one of the challenges of sustainable development is to manage the balance between economic growth and protection of the natural environment and the people who live in it. In summary, pressures on natural resources are leading many to argue that this sphere is a source for globalization.

Business activities in global industries

Evidence of economic globalization presented earlier showed that industrial development spanning something more than 100 years in North America and Western Europe has occurred in newly industrialized nations in as few as 10 years. This pace has been powered by an array of firms, ranging from small to large, from publicly held to family-owned, or sponsored by 'overseas' or 'nonresident' groups of people who retain ties with their nations of origin. The business practices important to globalization also change when the scope of analysis includes firms like these whose names or products are little known. The opening case named many well-known firms investing in China, but more than two-thirds of the money that has flowed into China came from Taiwan and Hong Kong, often from firms that are not household names.

MULTI- OR TRANSNATIONAL CORPORATIONS

Proliferation of consumer goods like Coca-Cola, Levi's, Nestea, Walkman, and Here Kitty tend to focus global attention on consumer product industries and producers of brand name goods. The world's top 10 branded goods include many of these. In turn, this focus might lead one to conclude that global business is shaped by well-known, large, and often publicly held firms from industrialized countries like Germany, the US, the UK, France, and Japan. Variously called multinational enterprises or corporations (abbreviated as MNEs or MNCs) or called transnational corporations (TNCs), the world's largest 40,000 MNEs consistently attract most research and practical attention. Counted among these firms are ABB Brown Boveri, Daimler–Benz, Hanson, Glaxo, McDonald's, Siemens, Saint Gobain, Sony, Itochu, Amoco, Michelin, Samsung, and Grand Met. These firms are identifiable, and their control over 206,000 affiliates world-wide and combined assets in the trillions make them important to economic growth and development around the world. That alone is sufficient reason to study their experiences, but another reason is that many are the forces behind products known throughout the world; this point is demonstrated by brands appearing in the table of the world's top 10 branded goods (Table 1.3).

With globalization has come the opportunity for other firms to enter world markets, and they bring with them new reason to study smaller, less well-known, and privately owned firms as they too operate globally. One reason to expand the study of global business to firms throughout the world is that despite claims that MNEs are dominating the world of global business, according to a US National Bureau of Economic Research working paper, in 1990 MNEs accounted only for about 22% of world output and that percentage is about the same as at the beginning of the 1980s (Lipsey, Blomstrom, and

TABLE 1.3   World's top 10 branded goods, 1996

1	McDonald's	6	Gillette
2	Coca-Cola	7	Mercedes-Benz
3	Disney	8	Levi's
4	Kodak	9	Microsoft
5	Sony	10	Marlboro

Source: Interbrand and Kochon, Nick. (1997). *The world's greatest brands*. Washington, NY: New York University Press.

Ramstetter, 1995). Our examination below of organizations other than publicly held MNEs reveals different practices that may well be reshaping the nature of business.

PRIVATELY HELD ENTERPRISES

Privately held firms – those that are owned in forms other than publicly held equities – may operate globally for reasons other than or in addition to profits: to generate an economic base for the family; to provide jobs within a community; to realize a dream. The Swiss-based Family Business Network (FBN) declares that family-owned firms are difficult to define, but available evidence suggests they are important entities and they do not always operate as public firms do. According to *The Economist* staff, 'family firms account for 40% of America's GDP and 60% of its workforce; 66% of Germany's GDP and 75% of its workforce; and around 50% of Britain's workforce' (The family connection, 1996, p. 62). Objectives that sustain the family-owned firm can lead to a business vision and decisions less usual among firms primarily seeking highest economic returns to shareholders. For example, a member of Britain's wealthy Hindujas family described their business orientation as follows: 'We are following the Vedic tradition that the world is a family and that if everything is in good shape, then every businessman has a cut of the cake' (Going home, 1995, p. 81). What it might mean to conduct business as part of a world family is not clear, although we might guess it means something other than conducting business on the basis of short-run efficiencies more commonly found among for-profit enterprises. At the same time that comments like these define one generation, young managers educated in Western business schools appear to be taking a different position. For example, New York University MBA graduate Emma Marcegaglia believes that 'firms are more important than families,' even though she runs a family-owned Italian steel and engineering group with a turnover of $2 billion per year (Italy's young tycoons, 1996).

THE EXTENDED FAMILY IN GLOBAL BUSINESS

Examples of other business motives are found among 'overseas' or 'nonresident' nationality groups of Chinese, Indians, Hungarians, Burmese, and others, who have been among the first to invest in China, India, Hungary, and other developing economies. These investments include a mind to profits, but also may be intended to develop or renew cultural links, to make a difference for people in the home country, or to fulfill perceived obligations to help the home country develop. Whatever the reasons, overseas groups have fueled many economies, particularly China and India. The overseas Chinese generate an annual economic output equivalent to $500 billion US, comparable to mainland China's 1993 gross national product (GNP). As individuals, most of the billionaires in Southeast Asia are ethnic Chinese living outside China. Peter Drucker (1994) notes that these highly visible individuals constitute only a portion of the wealth of the overseas Chinese, most of whom are nearly invisible in the public sphere but who nevertheless control many mid-sized firms with worldwide sales of several hundreds of millions of dollars. Because many ethnic Chinese depend on personal ties to conduct business over the longer run, they tend to invest much more faith in personal trust than in written agreements when making a deal. Additionally, since personal and family ties tend to endure over the lifetime of the firm, profit-taking on each deal is less important than firm survival based on profits over the long run. Nonresident Indians number about 10 million globally, with a combined annual income in 1994 equivalent to India's $340 billion GDP; some, like Raj Bagri, chairman of the London Metal Exchange, invest in India because they have cultural attachments there, and others feel their family connections or patience will facilitate business opportunities (Passage back, 1995).

Obligations to family and other relationships in the business sphere extend well beyond Asia and the subcontinent, and they too show business practices vary widely worldwide. When Fiat automotive needed a cash infusion in 1993, family and friends of chairman Gianni Agnelli not only provided the necessary capital, they also agreed that Mr Agnelli could decide how much of a dividend to pay on these investments (Che non si, 1995). Arrangements like these in family businesses are found all over the world where small businesses are concentrated, including Italy, Germany, Portugal, and other Western European nations, Latin America, and most of Asia. As each plays a larger or more evident role in the global business sphere, the question is: How do their habits affect business practices for any firm? According to Adrian Slywatzky (1996), smaller companies are enjoying success worldwide because they are playing by new rules that are redefining their industries.

GLOBAL GANGS

An entirely different type of organization also plays a role in globalizing business activities. Global gangs based in Russia, China, Hong Kong, Japan, Colombia, Italy, and the US, for example, transport heroin, cocaine, and other illicit drugs throughout the world, traffic in human cargo, and use the global banking system and computer technology to launder billions in income. Worldwide trade in humans is estimated to generate $5–7 billion US per year (The trade, 1995), and Interpol estimates annual illegal drug sales at $400 billion. According to a report released by the UN International Drug Control Program in June 1997, illegal drugs equal 8% of world trade, which makes illegal drugs a bigger business than all exports of automobiles and about equal to worldwide trade in textiles. This industry begins with poor farmers in Asia and South America, and includes drug laboratories, runners to transport the drugs, sellers, and at the top of the hierarchy those who reap major profits. Thus, the reduction of national barriers not only makes it easier for business activities to cross borders efficiently, but also makes it easier for gangs to extend their reach. The brutal operating practices of these organizations challenge not only tenets of civil society, but also circumscribe business practices by putting new emphasis on issues of bribery, corruption, and personal safety for global managers and employees alike.

THE CHANGING LANDSCAPE OF MANAGEMENT

The boundaries of business assumptions reshaped by looking at legitimate activities of family businesses, nonresident groups, or small businesses and illegal but no less real activities of global gangs also are altered by changes in business practices by giant South Korean *chaebols*, Japanese *keiretsu*, Western European and US firms alike. Business changes reported in the trade press include layoffs and downsizing contrasted against norms for lifelong employment, new blends of individual and team efforts, and a preference for ethics over opportunism. Hermann Simon's (1996) look at 500 of the world's 500 best *unknown* companies provides still more evidence that global businesses can operate in ways other than the scientific management model most frequently taught in Western business schools. The firms Simon examined are as likely to have authoritative leaders as participative leaders, they are unlikely to divide work into functions and rarely even have a marketing group, and they pursue aggressive globalization within narrow markets. According to Simon, these firms succeed because they go their own way, following procedures quite different from those taught by modern management. According to one source, these changes may result in business organizations that rely on 'Western-style accounting and financial controls, yet stress Japanese-style teamwork. [These organizations] will value ethnic diversity. . . . [They] will be centrally directed by multicultural, or at least cosmopolitan, executives who will set overall tone and strategy but give entrepreneurial local managers a long leash' (Dwyer, 1994, p. 80).

These various examples of enterprises operating in a global business world suggest that models of business historically provided by those firms we learn most about may not be the only models for globalization. Moreover, they provide reason to look not just at the consumer products industries that are most immediately visible as global, but also at the extent to which firms from chemicals to electric motors to temporary labor services also can be thought of as global. The combined experience and learning of firms of every size and type operating in diverse industries is shaping global business and global industries. To the extent that global markets are characterized by multiple competitors of varying size and shapes operating with differing competitive motives, international and global management may be said to be both more complex and less certain than when market competitors share similarities of size and motives.

As business activities cross or recross established borders or boundaries, these boundaries shift, reshape, and even dissolve to assume new shapes. In turn, these shifts create challenges for businesses operating in the global sphere; challenges that increase the need to understand the separate and combined effects of dissolving barriers on the world, and

TABLE 1.4   Blurring boundaries

Advertising	In the spring of 1995 AT&T sponsored a special technology issue of *Time* magazine where ad copy and article copy appeared to be the same.	Most of music television content is advertisements for performing artists.
	Television's most popular commercial in 1994 was a Coca-Cola advertisement created and produced by a talent agency rather than by an advertising agency.	Seagrams advertises 'hard' liquor on US television, breaking a decades-old tradition.
Medicine	Telelink connections and special 'sniffers' make it possible for physicians to diagnose illnesses by telephone.	SatelLife uses e-mail networks to connect Sub-Saharan hospitals and malaria research sites. This violates assumptions that telecommunications will benefit only those in the developing world.
	Computer virus safeguards use medical science models to create new software. IBM offers a software 'disinfectant' modeled after the human immune system.	
Education	Distance-learning links teachers and learners worldwide, challenging assumptions for how learning may be organized.	The Internet provides access to resources all over the world, reducing boundaries to information access.
Airlines	Airlines issue ticketless tickets.	The 'Singapore Airline Girl' is from Beijing, and had never been on an airplane before joining the airline.
	Swissair expects to become the first big air carrier to convert long-haul aircraft into flying casinos by installing a $80 million in-flight gambling system; travelers can pay with their credit cards.	
Entertainment	The boundaries of entertainment and information industries blurred to shape an 'infotainment' industry.	Educational publishing and video/CD-ROM technologies combined to create the 'edutainment' industry.

TABLE 1.4   Continued

Business across sectors/borders	Long-distance telephone links can be made through the Internet.	Mergers between conservative merchant banks and higher risk investments banks generate hybrids that break with tradition by taking on risky loans and competing for customers worldwide.
	European shareholder protests limited executive compensation in 1996. US shareholder complaints resulted in the ouster of top executives in 1996.	The Vatican Library has launched a mass-licensing program to put images from the library's art collection, manuscripts and architecture on T-shirts, ornaments, and other products.
	Instinet, a computerized stock-trading system, bypasses brokers to let traders negotiate their own trading prices 24 hours a day.	Not-for-profit environmental groups and insurance agencies collaborate in efforts to halt global warming.
Government	L-carnitine is a stimulant found in the Chinese herb ma huang. When Sigma-Tau Spa. introduced a drug containing l-carnitine in the US at a cost of millions, they found that health food stores can sell the same product without licensing or FDA approval. The boundary between natural dietary supplements and drugs is blurred.	On-line casinos and sports betting establishments are springing up on the Internet, evading regulations against gambling. In the same way, pornography evades Iranian governance. This alters assumptions that nations are sovereign and the final arbiters of what citizens can and cannot do.
Academic study	Bioethics combines philosophy, sociology, psychology, and the law.	Globalization of business crosses disciplinary boundaries of anthropology, sociology, political science, economics, ethics, business fields and beyond.
Jobs and titles	sustainable architecture socially responsible investment counselor corporate network administrator ecological accountant forensic accountant	Chief Knowledge Officer Chief Diversity Officer Office of Corporate Philanthropy

particularly on world business practices. A look at Table 1.4 demonstrates that in many fields of endeavor, traditions of how work was to be accomplished, where boundaries were drawn, even what jobs are available now are subject to new interpretations. The very fact that these changes are occurring more in combination than in isolation creates conceptual and practical demands for interpreting any isolated aspect of global change. These demands multiply when rapid and simultaneous change occurs in many sectors, interacts, and changes again. As the economic fortunes of individuals, organizations, and nations are linked to one another, new interdependencies of many kinds also are created.

Having looked at each of these sources of globalization, and examples of how each has shifted boundaries and caused them to be more permeable, conclusions that can be reached are as follows: globalization is occurring in all spheres of activity; globalization is occurring rapidly; globalization is drawing more diversity into business practices; globalization is creating uncertainties; and business enterprises no less than other organizations are affected by the resulting uncertainties. In view of the dynamic and important results of globalization in every sphere, it is important to look not only at individual sources of globalization but to view global events as part of an integrated system. This simultaneous look at the whole and each of its parts creates a potential to see points of similarity and difference that studies of individual business disciplines and individual events may not reveal.

A SECOND LOOK AT 'CHANGES IN CHINA'

A second look at dietary changes in China illustrates how a seemingly simple event is far more global than local in its results. The introductory case described two ways citizens of mainland China are becoming more global. First, China is industrializing to become more interdependent with the world economy, and Chinese people are substituting traditional grain-based dietary habits for the meat, eggs, milk, and farm-raised fish consumed more in the industrialized world. In isolation, this change in the Chinese diet does not seem like an event of monumental importance to the rest of the world, but its global importance becomes clearer when we look at this event in the context of the various global environments we will study.

The cultural environment: people alter two traditions: they move to urban areas to work, and they eat less grain and more protein

Results: changes in work habits and practices
China contains one-fifth of the world's population; they become more like others worldwide.
One hundred million Chinese are migrants within China and immigrants elsewhere.
For the first time since 1947, China's people can be divided into groups of economic 'haves' and 'have nots.'

Businesses opportunities shift worldwide as investment in China grows.
Other habits also change; women now smoke tobacco products.
Health care problems associated with smoking increase worldwide.

The economic environment: China's economy shifts to higher value crops and industrial production and service

Results: China was the world's fastest growing economy in 1996 and is expected to grow from 8–10% GDP in 1997 and 1998.
More than a half of 1996 FDI going to developing economies went to China. Although most Chinese firms remain partly or fully state-owned, stocks in many are publicly traded. Citizen enthusiasm for these stocks has been high, even leading to riots at the Shanghai stock exchange on opening day.
Jobs created have moved many people from the informal sector, where work is largely unpaid, and into the formal sector, where jobs earn disposable income. Many of the companies producing in China are not themselves Chinese. For example, the largest sneaker manufacturing plant in China is owned by Yue Yuen Industrial Holdings, which obtained start-up capital from Goldman, Sachs and Company, employs Taiwanese managers, and fulfills contracts for Adidas, Nike, and Reebok. Although it is possible to measure the economic impact of Yue Yuen, it is less possible to allocate exports in arriving at a balance of trade.

Global politics: China's government must absorb $12–40 billion per year to import grain for livestock, reducing spending on other government priorities, and forcing the country to abandon its traditional self-sufficiency

Results: Greater interdependence with the world increases political pressure on China.
NGOs pressure China to improve the human rights agenda.
The UN Conference on Women held in Beijing in the summer of 1996 illustrated how the Chinese government tries to control freedom of speech; detention of Henry Wu illustrates government control over freedom of movement. China's refusal to participate in nuclear arms treaties illustrates reluctance to conform to worldwide norms and practices.
China applies for WTO membership; human rights and nuclear arms practices become reasons to bar China from entry.

Natural resources: World consumption of grain and highest energy growth is in China

Results: The Worldwatch Institute, an environmental group, argues that China's rising demand for feed grain comes at a time when the world is less able to produce sufficient food to feed the world's people (Brown, 1995).

World grain stocks now stand at 13% of annual consumption and this represents the lowest grain food reserve since these figures were first recorded.

The dwindling world population of giant pandas is starved out as eucalyptus trees yield to China's industrialization.

Industry environment: Agriculture, like many other industries, is global. Competitors from around the world now vie to buy and sell grain as well as agricultural equipment and chemicals to support this industry. Additionally, new opportunities such as the following develop:

Tobacco firms find new opportunities in China.

Increases in disposable income draws in additional industry; China is the fastest growing market for films, other forms of entertainment, cosmetics, and similar goods.

Foreign companies control about three-quarters of China's exports, and many of these companies are owned by nonresident Chinese.

Technological improvements: Those available globally include 'miracle' fertilizers, standardized seeds, and machinery that improves the process of planting and harvesting, as well as processes that hasten sale and distribution of agricultural products.

Results: Bioengineered products that might provide needed grain are held in low esteem in Europe where many fear their development will have unintended consequences.

Weather patterns in the natural environment disrupt grain harvests.

Internet connections make it possible for Chinese dissidents to communicate externally.

In summary, the example of a dietary change in China shows that an event that may have seemed unimportant or isolated to a particular nation can take on global importance in every sphere. The interdependencies among these global environments are many and they provide business enterprises with critical opportunities worldwide even as they pose attendant threats to businesses and to life as we know it. For example, interrelationships make these global shifts complex, and complexity calls for re-examination and possible revision of 'traditional' business practices.

EXAMINING BUSINESS TRADITIONS

Some believe that bureaucracy in its various forms is, or ought to be, dead, but there is also evidence to show that principles of bureaucracy may have as much currency today as they have ever had. Perhaps these principles will take on a new form and coexist alongside newer organizational principles, some of which are distinctly counter-bureaucratic. This expands choices for organizations, choices likely to result in more complex, hybrid organizational structures and processes better able to help organizations survive and thrive in the global marketplace. These hybrids call for managers who are able to think 'outside the box' of tradition – whatever that tradition may be. In some cases, these hybrids are consistent with traditional theories as practiced in home nations, and in others they challenge existing theory. An example from the US Samsonite Corporation illustrates the latter point (Box 1.2).

BOX 1.2: SAMSONITE GIVES IT A GO

Many US theorists from fields ranging from cultural anthropology to political science to strategic management argue that cross-cultural preferences worldwide require different features for consumer products, and Samsonite accordingly had created different types of luggage for its US and Western European customers. However, in 1997, Samsonite went global with a single brand that combined product features from its most popular US and European models. This choice to 'go global' on a consumer product may seem counter-theoretical, but it may reflect a change in buying habits from local to national. Samsonite's leaders did not stop at combining product features; they also dumped peripheral businesses, restructured into hard-sided and soft-sided luggage lines, and reorganized personnel to create a strong focus on customers. These latter activities are consistent with theories on strategic focus, divisionalization, and customer service.

Source: Bigness, Jon. (1996, Dec. 26). Why Samsonite is dumping the gorilla. *The Wall Street Journal*, pp. B1, B12.

As compared to simpler 'either/or' options, this example shows that the challenges for global businesses and their managers focus on how to adopt, blend, or manage complex sets of alternatives into a cohesive global whole. Managers at Samsonite recognized a need to change what they were doing, and these changes meant a blend among theories and practices reflective of the past, a perceived present, and an anticipated future.

As businesses increasingly go global, managers of all kinds of businesses similarly are forced to rethink theory previously applied to a world where business was more international and between nations rather than global and across nations. In this more complex context, there may be few universal or uniform recipes to management (Hu, 1992), nor are the various recipes proposed likely to come from the same source. According to Scott Cowan in his 1996 address as outgoing President of the American Assembly of Collegiate Schools of Business (AACSB), for the first time management theory is lagging management practice because practitioners more than academics are at the leading edge of management. For those schooled in competition, the fact that practitioners lead theorists might appear to be a threat. But for those engaged in an increasingly cooperative world of global business and global business theory, the important thing may not be who is first at any given time, but rather how academics and practitioners jointly learn more about survival and success in global business.

PERSPECTIVES ON GLOBALIZATION

Globalization was earlier defined as increased permeability of traditional boundaries, a permeability created by increased numbers of or awareness of global events. Global events are themselves defined as those events that may or have affected the planet as a whole. These events, which are well outside the control of most nations and organizations, not only shape opportunities but also create threats of many kinds. Which represents a threat and which an opportunity may very well depend on the perspective of the person or organization affected. The opening case represents this conflict, showing how China's growth is a boon for would-be investors, and a challenge for world grain supplies or for centralized political control of China. To others, these events may have no immediate meaning. These differences of opinion about any aspect of globalization are a matter of perspective, a theme introduced in the following section and explored throughout the text.

Globalization: nothing new?

Some assert that globalization is, in a world, 'globaloney,' arguing that business interdependence is no greater in the 1990s than it was in the nineteenth century. According to one source, 'Trade in goods and services is only slightly larger now, as a fraction of gross world product than it was before 1914. Measured against GDP, U.S. imports are only slightly bigger now (11%) than they were in 1880 (8%)' (Farnham, 1994). Economic historians point to several similarities between what is now called globalization and earlier events: prior to the war of 1914–18 national economies had increased their links; investments were flowing from the new world into the old; and immigration was growing. The Ford Motor Company exported the fourth automobile ever manufactured, becoming a boon to worldwide travel and a carrier of cultural information from one nation to another. The five autos that completed the 1907 Peking to Paris cross-continental race were traveling illustrations of an outside world moving across the vast continent. Even Worcestershire sauce can be used to argue that globalization of products is nothing new. Developed in 1834 and used around the world, Worcestershire sauce is based on an Indian sauce that contains vinegar, molasses, sugar, Spanish anchovies, black Calcutta tamarinds, Dutch shallots, Chinese chiles, Madagascar cloves, French garlic, and secret ingredients.

According to Jeffrey Williamson (1996), current increases in economic inequalities in rich countries and decreased economic inequalities in poor countries also occurred in the nineteenth century. The 'nothing new' argument can be bolstered with business evidence showing that many firms involved in global business today remain as firmly rooted within national cultures and practices as in the past. For example, membership on boards of directors, even for corporations that operate worldwide, is drawn almost exclusively from a company's headquarters (Hu, 1992), and despite recent changes, stock ownership remains concentrated largely in country of origin, often in the hands of just a few families or a few large interlinked networks of owners. These conditions support contentions that globalization of economics or culture or politics, or worldwide impact of any event, is nothing new, and globalization of business is simply business as usual.

The New World Order and neo-colonialism

A different perspective is that globalization is something more than business as usual; it is consolidation of business and political power to create a powerful and abusive 'New World Order.' First given voice by Mikhail Gorbachev in a 1988 speech, the concept of a New World Order was popularized by then-US President Bush when used to explain US retaliation against Iraq in the 1990–1 Gulf War. Since then, many have given thought to the meaning of a New World Order, and many conclude it is consolidation of power among already powerful business and governmental interests. Richard Falk (1993) characterizes business roles in the New World Order as 'globalization-from-above,' arguing that nations and organizations with economic and political power will pool their clout to advance their common economic interests by disseminating consumerism worldwide. Worldwide proliferation of branded products like Coca-Cola or Pepsi and growing distribution of information and entertainment media are but two of the ways consumerism is spread. As the message of consumption spreads and leads to still more purchases, power is further consolidated among global product and service powerhouses. This point can be illustrated by means of the quiz 'Who Owns What?' which asks you to match well-known products with some known and not-so-well-known global businesses that own them (answers appear at the end of the chapter).

Who Owns What?

A	L'Oréal Cosmetics	Unilever, Anglo-Dutch
B	Stouffer Hotels	Sony, Japan
C	American NuKEM Waste Mgmt	Grand Metropolitan, UK
D	Harrods Department Store	Nestlé, Switzerland
E	Euro-Disney part-owner	RWE, Germany
F	Johnnie Walker Scotch Whisky	Al Fayed family, Egypt
G	Burger King	Michael Otto, Germany
H	Gerber Baby Foods	Kuala Lumpur Kepong Bhd, Malaysia
I	Columbia Pictures	Luxottica, Italy
J	Crabtree and Evelyn	Hong Kong's Cheng family
K	Calvin Klein Perfume	Guinness, UK
L	Spiegel Catalog Sales	Prince Al Waleed, Saudi Arabia
M	US Shoes	Swiss merger of Ciba-Geigy and Sandoz

If you looked at quiz answers appearing at the end of this chapter, you could conclude that many well-known products are owned by firms that are less well-known or even unknown outside their home bases. Lea and Perrins' Worcestershire sauce, for example, is owned by France's Danone Group. These examples suggest that the consolidation of power that many fear from the New World Order represents a worldwide consolidation among the already wealthy, including those that are well and little known. MacEwen (1994) also argues that globalization has moved power from the hands of political leaders and concentrated more and more power in the hands of business entities. According to MacEwen, this could lead to (a) greater inequality, (b) restricted social programs, and (c) new threats for the natural environment.

Another voiced concern about the New World Order version of globalization is that it can become a new name for imperialism as stronger economic entities use their economic clout to exact concessions from weaker entities, whether they be workers, other companies, or even nations. Jude Wanniski (1995) believes that the threatened 1995 trade war between Japan and the US represented this form of imperialism with the US bullying Japan until it showed favor to US exporters, particularly auto exporters. By the same token, China has threatened to close its markets to the US if the latter assists Taiwan with political memberships, and still other nations rule out trade relationships with firms based in countries that have staked out territory as 'enemies.'

Among those who also view the New World Order with suspicion are Steingard and Fitzgibbons (1995), who argue that management literature and management educators are to blame for promoting myths of globalization like 'Globalization leads to one healthy world culture,' 'Globalization brings prosperity to person and planet,' or 'Global markets spread naturally.' Instead, and consistent with the neo-colonial view of globalization, these authors argue that globalization ideals represent primarily Westernized perspectives. They further assert that management educators have given little thought to the fact that not everyone wants to be a member of a global village. These authors argue for the importance of scholars and citizens to balance unbridled enthusiasm for capitalism with evidence of its results, and they call for establishing an open and egalitarian dialogue among those who promote globalization and those who are least well able to defend themselves against negative consequences of globalization.

Attacks on the purported New World Order are many. In the book titled *When corporations rule the world*, David Korten (1995) asserts that rapid economic growth since the 1950s has led to 'accelerating social and environmental disintegration in nearly every country of the world – as revealed by a rise in poverty, unemployment, inequality, violent crime, failing families, and environmental degradation' (p. 11). In face of such evidence, information overload and a sense of powerlessness might cause 'globosclerosis' to set in and paralyze individual and organizational activities. And yet, the same information overload that can paralyze also can empower. Without denying any of Korten's assertions, it also can be argued that within the last 20 years economic development has: distributed sufficient riches to create a growing middle class in many countries, particularly Asian and Latin American countries; distributed more jobs globally; and provided opportunities worldwide that never existed before. For example, according to International Labor Organization statistics, between 1985 and 1991 in 39 of 41 countries surveyed, women's opportunities had increased to include a greater number of them in managerial jobs with higher pay and status, and more authority over decisions made. The point is that 'easy' either/or, good/bad characterizations of globalization are incapable of capturing the complexity of the phenomenon. The rubric for globalization as a 'New World Order' is very scary indeed. Fears of globalization are high worldwide, including advanced economies as well as developing ones. For example, although US firms were among the first to go global, according to a *Wall Street Journal* poll (Opinions diverge, 1997), an estimated 48% of all US citizens view globalization as bad, and 40% believe it will create more divisions between people. However, the New World Order described does not tell all we need to know about globalization or the role businesses can or should play in the process. An additional concern about attacks on the New World Order is the tendency to generalize in two ways that may be counterproductive. First, although large firms have the potential to abuse their economic power, not all do nor will they. Second, the conflict-oriented nature of this argument reinforces win/lose approaches to managing challenges of worldwide scope, suggesting that globalization can produce only winners or only losers.

Transformative social forces

Falk's characterization of the New World Order as globalization-from-above is complemented by 'globalization-from-below.' Businesses and powerful nations are the 'above' forces, but social forces come from 'below.' Working toward a vision of human community driven less by consumption than by caring 'animated by environmental concerns, human rights, hostility to patriarchy, and a vision of human community based on the unity of diverse cultures' (Falk, 1993, p. 39), these organizations and people work to achieve social justice, even though they work from a less powerful and less well-funded position than do the firms and nations believed to be part of the New World Order. While much of globalization-from-below has come from transnational groups that are voluntary in nature, a more inclusive view also acknowledges that business organizations of every size also can be forces for what Falk called globalization-from-below for the common good. Growing awareness of the need for corporate philanthropy as well as increased business emphasis on personal concern for others, reflected in published titles like *Leading with soul* (Bolman and Deal, 1995), *Servant leadership* (Greenleaf, 1978), and *Reawakening the spirit at work* (Hawley, 1993), suggest that at least some believe businesses have a role to play in transforming society in positive ways. If and how they will play this transformative role is an important decision for organizational participants in a global world.

In valuative terms, these views on globalization suggest three scenarios: globalization is business as usual; globalization is creating a world that benefits only a few; globalization is developing the capacity to create a just world that benefits many. Which becomes reality for the global century or beyond is a matter for action, action involving not just a few but all who stand to gain and lose from globalization.

Businesses as countervailing forces

The inclusive view of globalization adopted here is that businesses and voluntary organizations as well as other organizations do not divide neatly into opposing camps, but that they cross boundaries and borders as voluntary or governmental organizations take on business roles and business organizations play social roles. In providing the model for globalization-from-above and globalization-from-below, Falk helps us understand that countervailing forces for globalization exist. These forces can be and are being pursued by social organizations, business organizations, national politicians, and individuals. Further, this notion can be expanded to reflect the underlying complexity of globalization by suggesting that these same opposing forces for globalization are found *within* organizations, and *between* organizations from every sector. That is, some in the same government doubtless seek to consolidate their power while others want to distribute it;

in organizations there also are likely to be those who share power by empowering others and those who hoard it. The dilemma of managing with globalization is that it is very difficult to separate one from another, particularly since most claim a desire for social justice even when they thwart it. Thus, the boundaries between differing motives are unclear, and this makes it far more difficult for leaders to move their organizations toward common purpose of any sort.

Nevertheless, having played a role in generating many more economic opportunities globally, businesses have increased their importance to and interdependence with other sectors. This shift also generates new expectations for and social responsibilities from business organizations, and many people worldwide look to businesses to provide models for the future. In a world that does not think or act as one in response to any global event, businesses are affected by the very complexity of globalization that their activities helped create. Expectations for businesses are greater and they are more closely scrutinized for decisions made, even as those decisions occur against a backdrop that is complex, dynamic, and uncertain. In this global sphere of interrelatedness and interdependence, it is important to recognize that business activities result from human activity, and it is people who generate positive or negative outcomes. As individuals, as organizational participants, and as citizens of nations and an emerging global world, we need not make or become victims of globalization, but developing the potential and avoiding the threats of globalization demand attention and action. Both are the compelling reasons for this book; we cannot afford to remain ignorant, even though global complexity is difficult to understand and creates decision-making ambiguities for citizens and for business leaders. A compelling reason to learn about and involve ourselves in globalization is that global decisions made without our participation may lead to outcomes that serve few interests – outcomes that could realize the worst qualities of the New World Order many fear. According to William Greider, author of *One world, ready or not* (1997), globalization is a form of 'creative destruction' made more destructive by ignorance.

KEY CHAPTER CONCEPTS

Global Events: Global events and issues are those activities or decisions that have affected or could affect the planet and its people as a whole. An increasing number of these events are stimulated by business activities.

Globalization as a Stage of Business Development: Globalization represents a new stage of world development – a development process that is having a profound effect on business activities. In this stage of development, the world has for all intents and purposes become a single marketplace for buying and selling where goods, capital, and people increasingly are able to move more freely in response to global supplies and global demands.

Globalization Defined: Because it represents a new stage of world development, globalization is not well defined, and so it is difficult to say with certainty what globalization means or is likely to mean in the future. Here, globalization is defined as increased permeability of traditional boundaries such as nations, time, and space.

Characteristics of Globalization: Boundary permeability or transcendence, a high rate of change, the growing number and diversity of participants, and rising complexity and uncertainty are principal features of globalization.

Sources of Globalization: Many writers have argued that globalization emanates primarily from one source; the argument in this text is that a distinctive feature of globalization is that it emanates from multiple sources. The interrelationships and interdependencies among these disparate sources converge to power globalization.

Global Business Participants: Large publicly owned multinational enterprises (MNEs), particularly those from the industrialized world, tend to attract most public attention. Accordingly, much of what we know about global business has been based on the experiences of these firms. In view of evidence showing that many firms other than MNEs have contributed to and benefited from globalization, it is important to include the experiences of these enterprises in accounts of globalization.

Perspectives on Globalization: Globalization is alternatively viewed as 'business as usual,' as a force for evil, or as a force for improved social justice, and all three scenarios are potentially achievable.

A New World Order: Some argue that powerful businesses and governments have colluded to create a New World Order, the negative effects of which are greater inequalities, restriction of social programs, threats to the natural environment, and greater concentration of power in the hands of a small number of very large corporations. Privacy and autonomy also may be threatened.

Transformative Social Forces: Businesses are viewed as having the potential to change the world for the better or for worse. Through their decisions and activities, business people and members of civil society will be those who decide which scenario will be realized.

The Impact of Globalization on Management Thought: Globalization has meant more opportunities for businesses to operate on a worldwide basis, and the experience of operating globally has caused many business managers to rethink the basic assumptions of how their firms are organized and operated. This results in choices that combine management traditions from many sources to create a 'both/and' mentality creating managerial hybrids.

The Impact of Globalization on People: Rapid change suggests that individuals must monitor global activities and take an active role in shaping their outcomes. Knowledge of globalization may be the only way individuals can understand and anticipate global activities that affect their lives.

The Impact of Globalization on Managers: Decisions and activities consistent for building a just world depend on the ability to analyze complex and rapidly changing global conditions, to see interrelationships, and to visualize a future characterized by greater diversity and a rapid pace of change.

REVIEW AND DISCUSSION QUESTIONS

1 Three perspectives on globalization were presented: it's nothing new; it's power consolidation among those with power; it's a fundamental shift toward worldwide social justice. Select the perspective that is closest to your own beliefs and provide arguments to support your point of view.

2 What does your answer to no. 1 suggest about how you should prepare yourself for global business? What courses should you take? What academic interests should be your specialty? What skills will be most important to you?

3 Select a news event reported in the last month and provide at least one example to link this event with each of the six global environments introduced in this chapter, e.g., culture, economics, politics, industries, technology, natural environment.

4 Does globalization make it more or less likely that small- to medium-sized businesses will compete worldwide?

5 In what ways do entities other than businesses, e.g., families or global gangs, also share global business activities?

6 Almost all opportunities associated with global business are emerging very rapidly. Those who are 'selling' the change, or those who discover its advantages, may be inclined to focus on the positive aspects of potential change rather than explore the negatives as well. What examples of this are evident to you? Analyze the problems you see with adopting these perspectives without questioning them.

7 Draw a line horizontally. Place the following examples above and below that line to examine the value of thinking about organizations as being above or below the line on globalization:

- DuPont voluntarily agrees to phase out carbofluorocarbons.
- An environmental group bombs the railroad tracks on which nuclear arms are to be shipped.
- AT&T offers every employee a paid day off per year to serve as volunteers.
- Sara Lee requires every top executive to serve on the board of an organization that represents the interests of people 'not like them'.
- Anti-fur activists mass outside symphony halls to argue with those wearing fur.
- Hitachi establishes the Hitachi Foundation to encourage corporate philanthropy.
- Canon pays postage for consumers to return copier cartridges.
- An anti-abortion activist in the US shoots and kills employees at an abortion center.
- Textile firms respond to consumer protests by withdrawing production from El Salvador; people formerly employed lose their jobs.
- Fur traders club baby seals.
- By treaty, fishing vessels release dead, unwanted fish back into the sea.

8   Think of an event that recently occurred in another country. A war? An economic recession? Discovery of a new drug? A natural disaster? How did this event affect your daily life? After reading this chapter, describe the indirect effects this event might have had on your life.

Answers to the Who Owns What? quiz:

A   L'Oréal Cosmetics is owned by Nestlé, Switzerland.

B   Stouffer Hotels are owned by Hong Kong's Cheng family.

C   American NuKEM Waste Mgmt is owned by RWE, Germany.

D   Harrods Department Store is owned by the Al Fayed family, Egypt.

E   Euro-Disney's part-owner is Prince Al Waleed, Saudi Arabia.

F   Johnnie Walker Scotch Whisky is owned by Guinness, UK, which merged with Grand Met in 1997 under the name Diageo Plc.

G   Burger King is owned by Grand Metropolitan, UK which merged with Guinness in 1997 to become Diageo Plc.

H   Gerber Baby Foods is owned by Novartis, the 1996 merger of Swiss pharmaceutical giants Ciba-Geigy and Sandoz.

I   Columbia Pictures is owned by Sony, Japan.

J   Crabtree and Evelyn is owned by Kuala Lumpur Kepong Bhd, Malaysia.

K   Calvin Klein Perfume is owned by Unilever, Anglo-Dutch.

L   Spiegel Catalog Sales is owned by Michael Otto, Germany.

M   US Shoes is owned by Luxottica, Italy.

REFERENCES

Appadurai, Arjun. (1990). Disjunctures and difference in the global cultural economy. In M. Featherstone (Ed.), *Global culture*, pp. 295–310. Newbury Park, CA: Sage.

Ashkenas, Ron, Ulrich, Dave, Jick, Todd, and Kerr, Steve. (1995). *The boundaryless organization*. San Francisco, CA: Jossey-Bass.

Barber, Benjamin. (1992, Mar.). Jihad vs. McWorld. *The Atlantic Monthly*, pp. 53–61. (See also *Jihad vs. McWorld*, 1996. New York: Ballantine Books.)

Bolman, Lee G., and Deal, Terence E. (1995). *Leading with soul*. San Francisco, CA: Jossey-Bass.

Brown, Juanita. (1992). Corporation as community: A new image for a new era. In John Rensch (Ed.), *New traditions in business*, pp. 123–139. San Francisco, CA: Berrett-Koehler.

Brown, Lester. (1995). *Who will feed China? Wake-up call for a small planet*. New York: W.W. Norton/Worldwatch Institute.

Che non ci sera. (1995, Apr.). *The Economist*, pp. 75–76.

Davidow, William and Malone, Michael. (1992) *The virtual corporation*. Burlingame, NY: Harper.

Dicken, Peter. (1992). *Global shift* (2nd ed.). New York/London: Guilford Press.

Drucker, Peter. (1994, Dec. 20). The new superpower: The overseas Chinese. *The Wall Street Journal*, p. A16.

Dwyer, Paula. (1994, Nov. 18). Tearing up today's organization chart. *Business Week*, Special Issue: 21st century capitalism, pp. 80-90.

A dynamic new world economy. (1994, Nov. 18). *Business Week*, Special Issue: 21st century capitalism, pp. 22–23.

Falk, Richard. (1993). The making of global citizenship. In Jeremy Brecher, John Brown Childs, and Jill Cutler (Eds), *Global visions*, pp. 39-50. Boston, MA: South End Press.

The family connection. (1996, Oct. 5). *The Economist*, p. 62.

Farnham, Alan. (1994, June 27). Global – or just globaloney? *Fortune*, pp. 97–100.

Farrell, Christopher. (1994, Nov. 18). The triple revolution. *Business Week*, Special Issue: 21st century capitalism, pp. 16–25.

Fraedrich, John, Herndon, Neil C., Jr, and Ferrell, O.C. (1995). A values comparison of future managers from West Germany and the United States. In Salah S. Hassan and Erdener Kayak (Eds), *Globalization of consumer markets*, pp. 303–325. New York: International Business Press.

Fredman, Albert J. (1996). The mutual fund route to the growth potential of emerging markets. *AAII Journal*, 18(4): 22–26.

A game of international leapfrog. (1994, Oct. 1). *The Economist*, Survey: The Global Economy, pp. 6–9.

Going home. (1995, Sept. 30). *The Economist*, p. 81.

Gore, Al. (1992). *Earth in the balance: Ecology and the human spirit*. Boston, MA: Houghton Mifflin.

Green, Carolyn, and Ruhleder, Karen. (1996). Globalization, borderless worlds, and the Tower of Babel. *Journal of Organizational Change*, 8(4): 55–68.

Greenleaf, Robert K. (1978). *The leadership essays: The servant as leader*. Newton, MA: Robert K. Greenleaf Center.

Greider, William. (1997). *One world, ready or not*. New York: Simon & Schuster.

Hawken, Paul. (1993). *The ecology of commerce*. New York: HarperBusiness.

Hawley, Jack. (1993). *Reawakening the spirit at work*. San Francisco, CA: Berrett-Koehler.

Hu, Yao-Su. (1992). Global or stateless corporations are national firms with international operations. *California Management Review*, pp. 107–126.

Human Development Report. (1994). New York: Oxford University Press.

Huntington, Samuel. (1993, Summer). The clash of civilizations. *Foreign Affairs*, pp. 22–49.

IMF. (1996, May). *World economic outlook*. Washington, DC: International Monetary Fund.

Italy's young tycoons. (1996, Aug. 3). *The Economist*, p. 57.

Kahn, Joel S. (1995). *Culture, multiculture, and postculture*. Beverly Hills, CA: Sage.

Knoke, William. (1996). *Bold new world*. New York: Kodansha Intl.

Korten, David C. (1995). *When corporations rule the world*. San Francisco, CA: Berrett-Koehler.

Krugman, Paul. (1994). The myth of Asia's miracle. *Foreign Affairs*, 73(6): 62–78.

Lipin, Steven. (1996, Jan. 2). Let's do it: Disney to diaper makers push mergers and acquisitions to record high. *The Wall Street Journal*, p. R8.

Lipsey, Robert E., Blomstrom, Magnus, and Ramstetter, Eric D. (1995). Working paper. Washington, DC: National Bureau of Economic Research.

MacEwan, Arthur. (1994, Sept./Oct.). Markets unbound: The heavy price of globalization. *Real World International* (2nd ed.), Somerville, MA: Dollars and Sense.

Naisbitt, John. (1994). *Global paradox*. New York: William Morrow.

Ohmae, Kenichi. (1990). *The borderless world: Power and strategy in the interlinked economy*. London: Collins.

Ohmae, Kenichi. (1995). *The end of the nation state*. New York: Free Press.

Opinions diverge on globalization. (1997, Jun. 27). *The Wall Street Journal*, American Opinion, A quarterly survey of politics, economics, and values, p. R6.

Passage back to India. (1995, July 17). *Business Week*. pp. 44–46.

Pieterse, Jan N. (1995). Globalization as hybridization. In Mike Featherstone, Scott Lash, and Roland Robertson (Eds), *Global modernities*, pp. 45–68. London: Sage.

Quick, name the top five nations of the future. (1993, Oct. 11). *Business Week*, p. 26.

Reich, Robert. (1991). *The work of nations: Preparing ourselves for 21st Century capitalism*. New York: Alfred A. Knopf.

Renesch, John. (Ed.). (1992). *New traditions in business*. San Francisco, CA: Berrett-Koehler.

Rhinesmith, Stephen H. (1993). *A manager's guide to globalization*. Homewood, IL: Business One Irwin.

Robertson, Roland. (1995). Glocalization: Time–space and homogeneity–heterogeneity. In Mike Featherstone, Scott Lash, and Roland Robertson (Eds) *Global modernities*, pp. 25–44. London: Sage.

Rohwedder, Cacilie. (1994, Oct. 18). Youths in Germany put individualism ahead of politics. *The Wall Street Journal*, p. A12.

Salamon, Lester M. (1994, July/Aug.). The rise of the nonprofit sector. *Foreign Affairs*, pp. 109–122.

Schwab, Klaus, and Smadja, Claude. (1995). Power and policy: The new economic world order. In K. Ohmae (Ed.), *The evolving global economy.* pp. 99–111. Cambridge, MA: Harvard Business School Press. (The article first appeared in *Harvard Business Review,* Nov./Dec. 1994.)

Simon, Hermann. (1996). *Hidden champions: Lessons from 500 of the world's best unknown companies.* Cambridge, MA: Harvard Business School Press.

Slywatzky, Adrian. (1996). *Value migration.* Boston, MA: Harvard Business School Press.

Steingard, David S., and Fitzgibbons, Dale E. (1995). Challenging the juggernaut of globalization: A manifesto for academic praxis. *Journal of Organizational Change Management,* 8(4): 30–54.

Stoll, Clifford. (1995). *Silicon snake oil: Second thoughts on the Information Highway.* New York: Doubleday.

Swimme, Brian. (1984). *The universe is a green dragon.* Sante Fe, NM: Bear and Company.

Tomlinson, John. (1991). *Cultural imperialism.* Baltimore, MD: Johns Hopkins University Press.

The trade in humans. (1995, Aug. 5). *The Economist,* pp. 45–56.

Tully, Sean. (1994, May 16). Teens, the most global market of all. *Fortune,* pp. 90–96.

UN Framework Convention on climate change. (1995). *International Legal Materials,* 34: 1671–1710.

Wanniski, Jude. (1995, July 6). The new American imperialism. *The Wall Street Journal,* p. A8.

What is privatization anyway? (1995, Oct. 2). *The Wall Street Journal,* p. R4.

Williamson, John G. (1996, Mar.). Globalization and inequality: Then and now. Working Paper 5491. Cambridge, MA: National Bureau of Economic Research.

Wolf, Charles, Jr. (1997, Mar. 20). Asia in 2015 [Rand Report summary], *The Wall Street Journal,* p. A16.

World Competitiveness Report. (1994, 1995). Geneva: International Institute for Management and Development and the World Economic Forum.

Chapter 2

Global Enterprises

DOC MARTENS RULE! (UNTIL FASHIONS CHANGE)

Over 225 million global teens from the Pacific Rim, Europe, Latin and North America share tastes and habits. To prove this point, New York City ad agency BSB Worldwide videotaped teenagers' rooms in 25 countries to reveal similarities that made it difficult to know just where each tape was made. Closets contained baggy Levi's or Diesel jeans, Nike shoes, NBA jackets, and shoes from Timberland and Doc Martens; tabletops held Macintosh PCs, Pepsi, Coca-Cola; the television blared MTV; Sega and Nintendo videogames whirred; and recordings from grunge and hip-hop bands dominated.

So just how does a firm tap into this global teen market? There must be many pathways, one of which leads by the store for Doc Martens shoes, those ubiquitous boots showing up on teens and young adults all over the world, first as steel-toed black boots and later in a rainbow of colors. Global teens might be surprised to learn this standard issue for their generation was fashioned originally from auto tires and other products sealed to cushion the foot. The patented model created by Bavarian doctor Claus Maertens (who suffered from foot pain) and his partner Dr Herbert Funck was a postwar favorite for German women with bunions. The first pair sold in England adopted the Anglicized name Dr Martens, and they were marketed by the small, privately held firm of R. Griggs Group Ltd beginning in 1960. The shoes were intended for postal carriers or police, but they were an immediate hit among Britain's early skinheads. The Griggs group adapted quickly to this countercultural shift, and by watching how buyers customized the shoes, they have kept up with the fashion demand.

R. Griggs has never advertised the product, finding that their best business comes from those who adopt the boots. Calvin Klein sent model Kate Moss down the fashion runway wearing nothing but underwear and her Docs, and rock star Madonna also has posed in her

boots. The company's market research also is limited, and includes observing how buyers cus-
tomize the shoes they purchase.

By 1995, Griggs produced 150 styles of the boot in 3,000 versions, including a 'vegan'
version manufactured from leather-like material. Griggs sells the shoes for $62 to $135 US
per pair and hopes to cash in on the strong brand image with a new clothing line introduced
at Dr Martens' department store overlooking London's Covent Garden. R. Griggs sales have
increased steadily since 1991, going from $88 million then to over $263 million in 1995.

Sources: Morais, Richard C. (1995, Jan. 16). What's up, doc? *Forbes*, pp. 42–43; Tully,
Shawn. (1994, May 16). Teens, the most global market of all. *Fortune*, pp. 90–96.

PART I   EXPANDING BOUNDARIES OF BUSINESS

DEFINING THE GLOBAL ENTERPRISE

Doc Martens' universal appeal to the teen market was the primary reason this product went global. Our look at this organization's global appeal above and to follow will provide insight into the central question for this first section of the chapter: what defines global enterprises? Subsequent sections examine challenges that global enterprises face, and provide a glimpse of what they are doing to meet these challenges. Finally, this chapter concludes with a visual model that illustrates the relationships between internal concerns and external demands in a global organization.

The example of Doc Martens shows that *au courant* trendiness has helped this firm from an industrialized country become known globally, but there are many other boot-makers in England whose products remain local. Further, unlike Doc Martens, other products and firms are global even though they have little name recognition, and many come from nations that are newly industrializing. For example, many firms from developed economies like the US, Japan, and nations of Western Europe are known worldwide, including Kelloggs, Unilever, Nestlé, Sony, Honda, and the like. But Asian and Latin American companies are well known within their own nations and regions, and many also are participating in global markets, including Pemex, Sime Darby, Telekom Malaysia, and Telebras.

According to George Yip (1995), author of *Total global strategy*, it is difficult for these or any firms to remain totally unaffected by global conditions because globalization is affecting 'virtually every industry.' Some of these industries, like automotives or aerospace, are well known to us by virtue of their size: the industry for motor vehicles and parts generated revenues in excess of $1 trillion US in 1995, aerospace production contributed $122 billion to world revenues. But other industries also are global, and they take on varying degrees of importance to each of us. For example, the porcelain toilet industry is global, and the $7.6 million industry in human hair swatches also has gone global – hair purchased from women in India, China and elsewhere in Asia is cleaned and processed in Hong Kong and travels to Chicago to be made into weaves sold in the US, Europe and Japan. Even the local restaurant that relies primarily on local supplies is reliant on some products that are traded globally. But, while virtually all organizations are affected by globalization of business, and many industries are global, this is not to say that every firm is a global one. The following outline of characteristics for the global enterprise helps make distinctions between global and international enterprises.

A distinction between international and global enterprises

The global enterprise is both associated with different activities and brings a different approach to its larger market than the international enterprise, and these differences are embedded in the following view of non-domestic business activities:

> . . . internationalization connotes expanding interfaces between nations sometimes implying political invasion or domination. Internationalization of business, therefore, is a concept of an action in which nationality is strongly in people's consciousness. It means the flow of business, goods or capital from one country into another. Globalization, by contrast, looks at the whole world as being nationless and borderless. Goods, capital, and people have to be moving freely. . . . (Sera, 1992, p. 89)

At its most basic and by definition, the international firm can be defined as one engaged in business activities that cross national boundaries, or simply as one that involves itself in business in two or more countries. According to Hordes, Clancy, and Baddaley (1995), the international firm is rooted within its own nation: its headquarters are almost always based in a single country, although it might establish partial or complete operations in others. Its culture and organizational structure are consistent with the practices and norms of the home or headquarters country. It adopts standardized technologies and business processes throughout its operations, regardless of where they are located, and it relies on similar policies, especially regarding human resources, worldwide. In summary, the international firm remains firmly rooted in a national base.

By contrast, the global enterprise is less place-bound and less tied to the traditions of a single nation. The break with national traditions can result from geographic separation that occurs when a firm operates largely outside national borders, or, as in the case of Doc Martens boots, it can be a symbolic break. Because their popularity stemmed from countercultural youth rejecting the values of a particular national culture, Doc Martens' boots were less associated with a particular sense of space or nation than a symbol of disaffected youth worldwide. The boots were more than boots, they were an iconoclastic symbol. This is one way to slip the bounds of tradition of place. A second way is to become a 'stateless' organization, one that is known for its products but whose national links are less clear. Organizations like Nestlé and Sara Lee earn most of their profits outside their home countries, but because they acquire and develop existing brands, the fact of their ownership usually is not known widely. They make the world rather than a single country 'home.' For example, oil and natural-gas giant Unocal remains headquartered in California, but no longer considers itself a US company; describes itself as a global energy company; and in April 1997 opened a 'twin' headquarters in Malaysia to serve as the base for several senior executives. According to Yao-Su Hu (1992), the stateless corporation often is more rhetorical than real. Hu proposes the following questions as the true measure of the extent of statelessness:

1 Where are the bulk of assets and people found?
2 In which nation is firm ownership located and who owns and controls foreign subsidiaries?
3 What are the nationalities of senior executives at headquarters and decision-makers in subsidiaries abroad?
4 What is the legal nationality of the firm and to what nation does it turn for political or diplomatic protection?
5 Can tax authorities in a nation choose to tax corporate earnings worldwide? (p. 121)

Inasmuch as corporate taxation lies primarily within the political sphere, and global taxation is not yet viable, the answers to the last two questions may be ones that allow limited organizational autonomy. However, an assessment of firms listed in Table 2.1 shows that many have made at least some progress toward meeting the first three criteria.

In 1997, the United Nations Conference on Trade and Development (UNCTAD) created an index of transnationality by averaging the following ratios of company performance: foreign assets to total assets; foreign sales to total sales; and foreign employment to total employment. According to this measure, Nestlé is highest on transnationality followed by Canada's Thomson Financial Services, Switzerland's Holderbank Finacière, Canada's Seagram, and Belgium's Solvay Pharmaceuticals (cited in Economic indicators, 1997). According to the UNCTAC 1997 list, global giants Coca-Cola and McDonald's rank 31st and 42nd on transnationality.

Inconsistent use of terms 'blurs' distinctions between international and global business activities

Evidence presented in the previous section shows there are differences between the global enterprise and the international enterprise, but the exact nature of the former and its distinction from, say, the multinational enterprise is far less clear. This occurs in part because descriptions of global business use different terms to mean the same thing and the same terms to mean different things. Inconsistent use of the term 'global' has led to misconceptions and confusion about global enterprises. In the following section, some of these inconsistencies will be described, and used to develop definitions that clarify the essential nature and characteristics of the global enterprise. Bartlett and Ghoshal (1989) provide one framework for distinguishing among organizations:

TABLE 2.1   Stateless organizations, 1997

Organization/ homepage	Productive assets	Evidence of diversity
ABB abb.com	209,000+ employees; 1,300 companies operating in 140 countries	Established the Asia Pacific Business School to educate 200 managers a year; top managers are Swiss, Swedish, German, US
Acer acer.com.tw	Operates in 38 countries with dealers in 100 nations	Acer was among the first Chinese firms to break with hiring/retention traditions
Citicorp citicorp.com	Operates in 96 countries with 85,300 employees	Shaukat Aziz is head of business for all of Asia except Japan; 8 non-Americans are among 15 executive VPs
DuPont dupont.com	50% sales are international; 105,000 employees, one-third outside US; operating in 50 nations	Middle- and upper-level management positions for women and minorities have increased 64% and 37%; over 3,000 employees with disabilities
Ford Motor Company ford.com	346,000+ employees; active manufacturing or sales in 200 countries	CEO is from Scotland; several division heads are non-US
Hanson	58,000 employees worldwide	Managers believe a company with a sense of world diversity is more responsive to world markets
Hoechst AG hoechst.com	150,000 workers worldwide, but only 30% in Germany	Chairman Jürgen Dormann is the first non-engineer in his position; the nine-member management board includes a manager from Brazil and one from the US
Merck merck.com	45,200 employees, half outside the US; manufacturing facilities in 30 nations	Host country nationals control interests in operating units from Chile to Romania to the PRC
Motorola motorola.com	63% of sales are foreign; 142,000 employees worldwide	Established executive succession plan to develop female and minority managers
Nomura Securities nomurany.com	150 domestic and 62 overseas offices; 16,000 employees worldwide	Max Chapman, Jr became 1st co-chair of the NY subsidiary; Wong Kok Sieu heads Singapore operations
Philips NV philips.com	265,000+ employees worldwide	Traded on 16 stock exchanges; 60% of shares are owned abroad
Sara Lee saralee.com	Manufacturing operations in 40 nations; branded products in 140 nations; 135,300 employees worldwide	Of 14 outside directors, half are women, African Americans, or foreign nationals
SBC Warburg sbcwarburg.com	10,000 employees in 40 nations	Hire and train worldwide with recruiting centers on the Internet, in the US, Britain, Switzerland, Singapore, Japan, and Hong Kong
Seiko-Epson epson.co.jp	12,000 domestic, 15,000 overseas employees	North and South America, Asia Pacific, and Japanese zones operate autonomously
Unilever unilever.com	Production in 90 countries; sales in 150 countries; 308,000 employees worldwide	50 Indian expatriate managers work worldwide among 1,700 managers from 50 different nations

1 *The international organization* is defined as a coordinated federation in which the parent company transfers knowledge and expertise to foreign markets.
2 *The multinational organization* is defined as a 'decentralized federation of assets and responsibilities' (p. 49) that allows foreign operations to respond to local differences.
3 *The global organization* is a centralized hub where most assets and decisions are centralized.
4 *The transnational organization* is characterized by an integrated network where efficiency can be balanced against local responsiveness to obtain both global competitiveness and flexibility in an organization dedicated to organizational learning and innovation.

In their research, Bartlett and Ghoshal found that neither international, multinational, nor global organizations were managing globalization well, but they believed the transnational organization they described would operate most successfully in a complex world.

In other quarters, however, transnational corporations are viewed as 'synonymous with multinational enterprises' (Daniels and Radebaugh, 1992, p. G-21), simply as those that see the world as a single market (Ohmae, 1989), or as one among many firms worldwide whose activities are monitored by the United Nations Centre on Transnational Corporations. Established in 1975, this Centre uses the term 'transnational' as an umbrella term to describe firms that could fit any of the four definitions proposed by Bartlett and Ghoshal above.

Global companies also have been variously defined. For example, some see global firms as those with global strategies where economies of scale are realized from worldwide integration and standardization (Hout, Porter, and Rudden, 1982; Levitt, 1983). For example, worldwide integration of design groups as well as other restructuring at Ford Motor Company led to production of a 'world car' able to enjoy scale economies and earning Ford the sobriquet of a global company (Kerwin, 1994). However, as Yip (1995) notes, a global strategy so defined is not necessarily synonymous with a global firm since the latter can sustain an integrated standard for one business line and be locally responsive in other business lines. This suggests that the global enterprise might be more or less global depending on the amount of its business that has a worldwide presence.

Efforts to balance worldwide standards with demands for the localization of products and services have also been called a global strategy (Hamel and Prahalad, 1985), although Yip (1995, p. 8) describes this approach as *multilocal*, and Phatak (1992) and Ashkenas et al. (1995) call it *glocal*. In summary, different uses of the word 'global' may be diluting any specific meaning it has in describing a strategy (Yip, 1995, p. 8) or a business. Such definitional differences are perhaps one unavoidable result of the rapid pace of global change, but they are a compelling reason to define the various forms of international and global enterprises. Accordingly, in this text international enterprises will be viewed as those drawing resources primarily from a domestic base to operate beyond national borders. In contrast, the multinational firm operates from more than its domestic base, readily drawing resources of people and knowledge from sources throughout the world. Finally, the global enterprise views the world as its base, and although it typically operates from one or more geographic locations, it could just as readily be a virtual organization operating from no fixed place.

CHARACTERISTICS OF A GLOBAL ENTERPRISE
The world as home

Drawing resources from the world and viewing the entire world as its home are two characteristics of the global enterprise. Three additional characteristics further define the global enterprise and distinguish it from the one that simply responds to changes in global markets.

The global enterprise establishes a worldwide presence

Global enterprises are those that by chance (as occurred for R. Griggs) or by design establish *and* seek to maintain a *worldwide presence* in one or more businesses. Firms like PepsiCo, CNN ('the global news network'), and Benetton can be readily identified as global enterprises because they purposefully established a global presence in virtually all their businesses. Additionally, firms like Daimler–Benz, Hanson, Glaxo, McDonald's, Siemens, Saint Gobain, Sony, Itochu, Amoco, Michelin, and Grand Met are most frequently viewed as 'global' because their names or products are well known worldwide. Privately held firms such as Sainsbury, Henkel, Porsche, Heineken, Vuitton, Salim Group, Peugeot, Gudan Garam, and Thomson Financial Services also are global, but they may or may not be known globally.

It is clear that R. Griggs never intended or expected to establish a global presence with Doc Martens boots. However, having established a presence, they now seek to maintain that position, and firms like this and others demonstrate that small firms also can be global enterprises. Smaller, less well-known firms like Israel's VocalTech (developer of software facilitating long-distance telephone calls over the Internet) or Dutch Digicash (developer for the digital equivalent of cash for electronic purchases) also can be described as global enterprises because they are committed to establishing a worldwide presence in a product line. A new breed of small firms called global start-ups are established for the very purpose of being global in their focus.

GLOBAL START-UPS, ENTREPRENEURS ON A WORLDWIDE STAGE

Successful global start-ups are a growing form of international new venture, and they are most often found outside the US. According to Benjamin Oviatt and Patricia Phillips McDougall (1995), Logitech Inc., a manufacturer of computer mice, represents a prototypical global start-up. Founded by a Swiss and two Italians, the firm was established in 1982 and headquartered from the start in both California and Switzerland. Research and development as well as manufacturing also were conducted in California and Switzerland, but soon expanded to include Taiwan and Ireland. By 1989, Logitech had revenues of $140 million US and held 30% of the world market for computer mice. Based on research examining Logitech and other global start-ups, Oviatt and McDougall concluded these entities are characterized by several common attributes (see also Table 2.2):

1 A global vision exists from inception.
2 Managers are internationally experienced.
3 Their entrepreneurs have strong international business networks.
4 They exploit preemptive technology or marketing.
5 They have a unique intangible asset, e.g., tacit knowledge.
6 Product or service extensions are closely linked.
7 The organization is closely coordinated worldwide.

Large firms like Nestlé and Unilever also have a significant global presence, although not in every business line; just as independent Washington-state fruit growers from the US often sell one but not all branded fruit lines worldwide. Thus, it is not size so much as establishing a global presence in one or more product or service businesses that is part of becoming a global enterprise. This definition of the global enterprise encompasses not just business organizations but also other types of worldwide organizations as well, including transnational organizations committed to social goals. It becomes clear that the potential to engage in global activities is not confined to large business organizations, but that many different types of organizations are 'going global.' This diversity is illustrated in Table 2.3.

The global enterprise adopts a global strategy

The examples appearing above demonstrate that organizations of any size can establish a global presence, and also show it is possible to establish a global presence in one, many, or all product or service businesses. We can, then, think of 'global' business organizations as those that take a purposeful worldwide view of business markets, using descriptors such as *multilocal* to refer to strategies that firms employ when they combine worldwide

TABLE 2.2   Success characteristics for global start-ups

Global start-up & headquarters	Success characteristics							Current status
	Global vision	International experience	Strong network	Preemptive technology or marketing	Unique intangible asset	Linked product extension	Tight coordination	
Ecofluid Ltd Brno, Czech Republic	**	*	*	*	**		*	Operating
EEsof, GmbH Munich, Germany	***	**	***	***			***	Acquired
Heartware International Atlanta, GA, USA	*	**		*	*			Failed
International Investment Group Atlanta, GA, USA	***	***	***	***				Failed
IXI Ltd Cambridge, UK	**		**	***	**		*	Acquired
Momenta Corp, Mountain View, CA, USA	***	***	***	***			***	Failed
OASIS Group Plc Berkshire, UK	*		*				***	Acquired
Oxford Instruments Oxford, UK	**	**	**	*	***	***	***	Operating
SPEA Starnberg, Germany		***	**	**	***	*	**	Operating
Techmar Jones International Indus. Atlanta, GA, USA	***	***	**				***	Ceasing operation
Technomed International Lyon-Bron, France	***	***	*	**	***	***	**	Operating
Wave Systems New York, USA	***	***	***	*			*	Operating

*** = Characteristic is strongly present; ** = Characteristic is somewhat present; * = Characteristic is present; Blank = Characteristic is not present.

Source: Oviatt, Benjamin and McDougall, Patricia Phillips. (1995, May). Global start-ups: entrepreneurs on a worldwide stage. *Academy of Management Executive*, 9(2): 30–43.

TABLE 2.3   Size and ownership of global enterprises

	Large	Small
Public	Most MNEs Global 1,000 or 500 Stateless organizations Government-owned entities	Global start-ups Franchises, licenses, distributors, local agents Transnational not-for-profits
Private	Some MNEs Family-owned enterprises Resident or overseas enterprises Global gangs	Individual entrepreneurs Family-owned business Private not-for-profits

standards with local responsiveness, or *worldwide standardization* when referring to integration and standardization of products and services on a worldwide basis. For business firms with a global presence, either of these strategies is a measure of the degree to which a firm is global. Additionally, since many smaller firms can be global enterprises, a niche strategy, defined as specialization within a narrow product or service line, also is possible. Firms selecting a niche strategy then must decide how to leverage this strategy, whether as a multilocal or by adopting a worldwide standard.

The global enterprise transcends external and internal boundaries

The global enterprise also can be described according to its abilities to transcend three kinds of existing boundaries. First, global enterprises cross external boundaries of nations (Ohmae, 1995), space and time, or responsibilities (Brown, 1992) that are in some sense measurable. Additionally, some boundaries internal to the global organization have to be bridged. Some of these boundaries are amorphous and difficult to measure or change. For example, when Whirlpool acquired Philips European appliance divisions, there was a need to change 'attitudes' from engineering-driven to customer-driven. But attitudes like these are difficult to measure and therefore difficult to change. Third, less tangible boundaries like culture, thought, or the relationship between individual or organizational self and others (Rhinesmith, 1993) must also be crossed to seize global opportunities. Below we look at some of those tangible and less tangible boundaries.

TRANSCENDING EVIDENT EXTERNAL BOUNDARIES
The previous chapter established that global boundaries to be crossed are not only national, but also involve crossing time, space, and similar external boundaries.

According to Ashkenas et al., authors of *The boundaryless organization* (1995), there are two forms of external boundaries. These are:

(a) boundaries between the organization and its suppliers, customers and regulators;

(b) boundaries between nations, cultures, and markets.

Boundaries like these are perceived to be barriers to global organizations because they assume and reinforce historical traditions that may not yield to globalization. According to Ashkenas and his colleagues, boundaryless behavior is necessarily fluid and external borders like these accordingly must become more permeable. This permeability is enhanced when boundaries of time and space also can be bridged, a possibility realized via worldwide telecommunications links from and to suppliers, customers, and others.

TRANSCENDING EVIDENT INTERNAL BOUNDARIES

Ashkenas et al. also believe two internal boundaries are particularly important to cross. These are:

(a) vertical boundaries between levels and ranks of people; and

(b) horizontal boundaries between functions and disciplines.

Vertical boundaries pertaining to task or rank (Ghoshal and Bartlett, 1995) rarely yield readily to change, particularly when people occupy the jobs that represent higher and lower levels of organizational rank, authority, or compensation. Not surprisingly, those already occupying positions with greater benefits are loath to give them up; resistance is likely. These levels and ranks go beyond what is evident because in many organizations these vertical barriers are embedded in the culture of the firm or in national practice. For example, veneration for age in Japan makes it difficult for experienced engineers to make way for innovation among the young in the computer industry. The vertical structures in place have promoted people on the basis of tenure with the company, yet in the fast-paced computer industry it is not age so much as innovation that wins the day. In Toshiba, for example, older engineers are finding it difficult to acknowledge innovative ideas coming from computer scientists not only because computer information is perceived as something other than engineering, but because the computer wizards are young.

Most organizations worldwide are organized around the same functions most students of business or commerce study: marketing, management, accounting, engineering, finance, or production. Each of these functions is a discipline unto itself with a distinctive jargon and belief system introduced when one 'majors' in one or another of them in school or university, and reinforced at work by the sense that 'we' in our function are different from 'they' in their function. Thus, crossing a functional boundary not only violates organizational tradition, it also violates educational and professional traditions. Crossing these functional and disciplinary boundaries also is difficult because in most organizations one of these functions is viewed as most important. In the highly competitive fast-food industry, for example, the most important function in the last decade has been marketing, whereas in the aircraft industry the most important function has been engineering. Historical emphasis on engineering and design created internal boundaries at the Boeing Corporation, a point illustrated in Box 2.1.

BOX 2.1: CHANGE IS MORE THAN A DECISION

The Boeing Corporation found that a sense of engineering primacy was an impediment to it in its attempt to streamline design and new aircraft manufacture. In the past, Boeing engineers created aircraft designs without consulting manufacturing. Thus, they rarely knew if their designs could be built. When faced with a need to collaborate with manufacturing in the design phase, many engineers objected and were little prepared to accommodate the ideas of nonengineers. At the same time, lack of experience meant that manufacturing personnel were initially unable to contribute fully to the collaborative process. Thus, organizational leaders recognized that crossing these functions required more than a decree: it meant training in teamwork; it meant recognizing assumptions and perceptions of what was most and least important to the organization and why; it meant changing the way people viewed themselves relative to others. Crossing functional boundaries between design and manufacturing took time and effort at the Boeing Corporation, but the expected benefits are improved teamwork for other challenges to come in the global market for airplane design and production.

Source: Yang, Dori Jones. (1994, Jan. 17). When the going gets tough, the tough get touchy-feely. *Business Week*, pp. 65–67.

TRANSCENDING LESS EVIDENT EXTERNAL AND INTERNAL BOUNDARIES

From the discussion above, it should be clear there are many challenges to crossing traditional boundaries. The greatest of these challenges occurs when trying to traverse boundaries that are intangible, immeasurable, and less evident to organizational participants. These boundaries are less evident because they are embedded in rarely examined and long-established value systems. Existing beliefs in a link between age and wisdom or a belief that one function is 'better than' another are difficult to change because many are unaware of these beliefs, and many more are unwilling to acknowledge them even as they become aware. In some cases, failure to acknowledge an existing belief may result from acting in 'politically correct' ways, whereas, in other cases, individuals may be embarrassed to express their beliefs or afraid their views will not find a welcome audience. Further, since belief systems tend to emerge from a larger cultural milieu, there may be a fear that a change in one aspect of the firm culture will lead to changes in the national culture. This has particular relevance because organizations with a worldwide presence usually are staffed with people grounded in a single culture. How, then, does the global organization fashion unity from growing diversity? These reasons suggest that belief systems and the intangibles of organizational life that are most difficult to measure will be the most difficult to change in organizations.

BOX 2.2:   MANAGING INTANGIBLES AT NISSAN DESIGN INTERNATIONAL

Traditional practice in many organizations is to hire new employees who will work well and 'fit' in with existing employees. This has been particularly true among Japanese firms where collective values are held in high regard and individualism often is avoided. So when Nissan Design International began to hire people in contrasting pairs the company was not only violating principles of Japanese business harmony, it was violating principles of national culture and collectivity. Motivating this change was a desire for 'creative abrasion' among employees sufficient to stimulate new ways of thinking and new ways to design Nissan products. Employees were asked to cross boundaries of behavior and boundaries of thought. The creativity the company sought is an intangible believed to be stimulated by difference and even conflict. For existing employees long-schooled in conflict avoidance, crossing boundaries of behavior must have been difficult. Moreover, since creativity is not easily assessed, positive results were not measurable. How, then, can organizational leaders convince employees that these changes are worthwhile? In some cases, they can't and organizational changes lead to voluntary departures. Leaders then must weigh and perhaps defend the benefits of intangibles like hoped-for creativity against measurable losses experienced when seasoned employees leave.

Belief systems like how creativity can be stimulated, or how conflict operates, or even how one should spend work time are intangibles, and their intangibility makes them difficult to describe and to measure. Even when acknowledged, belief systems may be hard to alter if people find it difficult to view themselves objectively relative to others. However, an ability to view others relative to oneself involves an underlying ability within organizational leaders to be reflective about the organization and about themselves as leaders. According to Stephen Rhinesmith (1993), author of *A manager's guide to globalization*, the careful thought and consideration characteristic of reflection is a key personal characteristic of the successful global manager:

> Reflection . . . enables one to weave some sense of development and progress into the fabric of one's life and the life of the organization and the people with whom one works. Lifelong learning and education drive most successful global managers, because they recognize that they can never know enough to deal with the world around them. (p. 31)

Knowing oneself and understanding what is valuable and important and why to organizational participants and to people who consume the organization's products or services is a critical task because it provides a way to get beyond one's own assumptions and recognize competing assumptions being made in the market and in the organization.

Thus, in addition to developing a worldwide presence, the global enterprise crosses traditional boundaries, perhaps breaking through national borders and nationalistic thinking to reconceptualize its activities or internal barriers that impede its ability to gain or sustain a global position. Each firm is likely to have different priorities for reshaping these internal and external boundaries because firms vary according to size, industry, strategy, leadership or other factors. For example, a start-up in an Internet-dependent industry might place highest priority on leveraging knowledge technology, whereas an established firm might see a greater need to break down internal barriers to diversity in order to leverage knowledge. In this context, diversity would include visible differences between people like gender or ethnicity, and also differences in rank, functional assignments, role, or behavior.

BEYOND 1945: MANAGEMENT PRACTICES AND RESEARCH IN CONTEXT

To this point, the global enterprise has been defined as one that views the world as its home, establishes a worldwide presence in one or more businesses, adopts either a worldwide standardization or multilocal strategy within broad or niche lines, and is able to cross targeted external and internal boundaries. Leaders of these firms face similar demands which are to create effective organization-wide processes and structures and hire people from the global marketplace to support global commitment. The following review of contemporary business history shows that aligning internal demands of people with processes and structures is a historical challenge, differing over time according to activities that attract most organizational attention.

Contemporary organizations operating outside domestic spheres

Writing in 1981, Richard Robinson classified non-domestic business into four post-World War II periods:

1 The Postwar Decade (1945–1955).
2 The Growth Years (1955–1970).
3 Time of Troubles (1970s).
4 The New International Order (1980 and beyond).

The following analysis of these time periods shows that each created different challenges for decision-makers who chose to operate outside domestic borders. Because extra-territorial challenges were similar in each historical context but different from the one preceding it, new managerial practices, and innovations on existing practices were developed to address them. Additionally, managerial practice and changes in those practices were complemented by research developed to explore and explain what worked and what did not.

REASONS FOR EFFICIENCY IN THE POSTWAR DECADE

Following the conclusion of World War II, organizations that had survived the war intact became suppliers of needs that were almost universal. Most of the firms that could respond to these needs were based in the US, where business energies concentrated primarily on internal mechanisms to improve production and distribution efficiencies. In practice as in research, firms were viewed primarily as closed systems with clear borders between the firm and its environment (Wright and Ricks, 1994). In this time period, concepts of scientific management arguing for 'one best way' were brought to bear on decisions made as to whether firms operated strictly in a domestic sphere or beyond. Ideas of bureaucracy and efficiency proposed earlier in the century by the likes of Max Weber, Henri Fayol, and Frederick Taylor were used to centralize decisions, routinize work, rationalize production, and reinforce efficiencies by implementing ideas that clarified chain of command, limited span of control, and created tall, fairly inflexible hierarchical structures. The rigid nature of these structural arrangements created a need for what became known as the 'organization man,' so-called because managerial employment in the US was almost the exclusive domain of men, and because what was required of these men was a will to put organizational needs ahead of personal needs.

The drive toward efficiency resulted in research examining coordination and control issues for the international firm, and the efficient transfer of resources from home to host country. Senior managers tended to come from the home country and were transferred to various international operations. Heenan and Perlmutter (1979) described this kind of staffing as ethnocentric because it put home country interests first. Henry Luce had characterized the twentieth century as 'the American century,' a characterization that seemed to be borne out by post-1945 events. Research in the organizational sciences at the time was characterized by 'American researchers focused on American firms, American perspectives, and those questions most salient to American managers' (Boyacigiller and Adler, 1991, p. 264). Economic success and both public and academic reinforcement doubtless confirmed an impression that bureaucratic management practices as developed by US firms were superior.

ACHIEVING SYSTEMS CONGRUENCY IN THE GROWTH YEARS AND THROUGH TIMES OF TROUBLE

Except for 1975 and 1982, world manufacturing and trade began to increase after the early 1960s; between 1976 and 1990 alone foreign direct investment tripled worldwide from under $50 billion to more than $150 billion (*World Investment Report*, 1993). As trade and direct investment increased globally, US-based firms grew in number and geographic scope worldwide, and more of them established a significant presence in multiple countries. As they expanded and grew in size, their assets increased until many were greater than the countries in which they operated. Further, their economic clout often was equated with real or perceived political clout.

Robinson (1981) described the 1970s as watershed years for large international and multinational enterprises (MNEs) because host countries began to reject the dominant role multinationals played. Some industries and businesses were nationalized to constrain or expel business interests from developing economies. At the same time, following postwar reconstruction, business interests in Western Europe and Japan had begun to grow, spilling out into international business where US firms now faced new or revived competitors. Research followed to examine links between the firm and its political environment; to analyze political risk; and to create competitive strategies for firms within the same industry (Porter, 1980, 1985). Growing competition for international opportunities focused attention on culture and national interests followed by studies of cultural traits (Hofstede, 1983). Japanese success in auto, television, and consumer electronics industries attracted interest in firms and business techniques unique to Japan, particularly total quality concepts and their implications for non-Japanese firms.

Explorations of the interface between an organization and its environment took on a new urgency in these eras as turbulence, uncertainty, and discontinuities became reality for international and multinational firms. The developing link between organizations and their international environments fostered a new level of complexity in the practice and study of international businesses, with organizations increasingly viewing international business as a process by which firms increased their awareness of how international activities would affect their future (Beamish et al., 1991). This process had become more complex; there was increased interdependence between organizations and their environments; and it suggested that there was no 'one best way' to conduct international business. Businesses could not conduct business as usual in the international sphere, and the pressure was on them to find new ways to operate in a newly complex environment. Whereas the earlier era of international business initiated in the postwar years emphasized the strategy/structure 'fit,' the greatest practical concern for firms operating in the increasingly complex 1970s was achieving congruence among strategy, structure, and systems (Bartlett and Ghoshal, 1995). Achieving congruency among systems did not displace internal efficiency goals; they too were believed to be enhanced by this new attention to strategy and integrative systems.

AN EMPHASIS ON PROCESSES AND PEOPLE FOR A NEW INTERNATIONAL ORDER

As firms moved into the 1990s and prepared for the decades beyond, the international era reached a more global stage that resulted in yet another shift in managerial emphasis. In this stage, the structural mechanisms and systems thinking important in earlier years are being reconsidered in light of a new emphasis on organizational processes and human skills and abilities to manage them. Bartlett and Ghoshal (1989) indicate these challenges will be quite distinct from earlier ones, with the strategy/structure/systems concerns of the 1970s and 1980s being supplemented with a concern for processes, with *how* links within firms and between firms and their constituents can best be managed to overcome boundaries of thought and action.

Hordes, Clancy, and Baddaley (1995) describe how the global firm might create links around processes: it is organized around a few core values; although it has a headquarters, it is most often managed by a team operating in diverse locations; it adopts an organizational culture that values diversity; except for a few standardized policies, its processes, policies, and technologies are diverse. Others suggest that a combination of mission, vision, education, and training is combined with an emphasis on processes of global corporate culture (Evans, Doz, and Laurent, 1990) or that knowledge (D'Aveni, 1995; Senge, 1990) and diversity among people, processes, or structures (Hoecklin, 1995; Rhinesmith, 1993; Trompenaars, 1994) are essential to sustain flexibility and adapt quickly to opportunities and threats in a rapidly globalizing world.

Although the processes suitable for the global firm today appear to vary widely, an underlying theme is that they take their strength less from structures and systems and more from people and processes. Second, their success depends on tangible assets and on intangibles like knowledge, vision, and mission. Managing these intangibles is one of many challenges the global firm faces. Third, the mix of intangibles with tangibles creates a need for systems and processes capable of managing diverse needs. Responding to diversity on this and other fronts is another challenge global organizations face. Finally, organizational adjustments intended to achieve flexible efficiencies for the dynamic and competitive global business world add to rather than displace other concerns like efficiency and systems thinking. This results in tradeoffs difficult to balance in view of continuous change. In the following section we examine these challenges more specifically to frame common concerns for virtually all global enterprises.

COMMON CHALLENGES OF GLOBALIZATION

Writing in *The age of paradox*, Charles Handy (1994) identified nine paradoxical challenges affecting mature economies like the UK and the US. Throughout this book we see evidence that these same paradoxes are affecting businesses and individuals beyond the industrialized world. Paradox can be defined as a statement or proposition that seems self-contradictory. Organizational participants increasingly face situations that can be defined as paradoxes: these situations just do not seem to be resolvable. At the individual level, an apparent paradox is expressed by the statement 'The more I do, the less I get done.' For students, the paradox often comes from realizing that the more one learns, the more questions one has. At the global level, one of many paradoxes is how all nations can benefit economically from competitive business activities since competition usually implies that there will be winners and losers. At the level of national governments, paradox includes balancing between global interests and domestic interests. At the organizational level, paradoxes might include cooperating to compete, and managers might see profitability as a tradeoff between their own interests and the interests of a larger society. Individuals also face a number of paradoxical challenges when they are encouraged to think in linear and process-oriented fashions; to be autonomous and yet to be team members; to have a full life and to devote all free time to the organization.

A Center for Creative Leadership Conference created a list of these and similar paradoxes organizational participants face, and these are listed in Table 2.4

TABLE 2.4   Dimensions of paradox

Individual achievement vs teamwork
Competition vs cooperation
Hands-off management vs hands-on management
A focus on people vs a focus on the bottom line
An emphasis on process vs an emphasis on results
Organizations as engines of economic development vs organizations as contexts for human development

Source: Center for Creative Leadership Conference, reported by Walter W. Tornow. (1994). *Issues and Observations*, 14(2): 7.

In personal lives and professional worlds, many are taught to look at paradoxes and other challenges as problems that need solving. However, according to Charles Handy, a major managerial challenge of paradox is to get beyond trying to resolve paradox and learn how to live with it and the attending uncertainties. This suggests the first global challenge all organizations face: there are problems that cannot be solved immediately with either traditional or developing responses; some problems may not yield to solutions at all but only be manageable.

Challenge 1: Organizations face problems that cannot be solved

Few certainties characterize globalization, but it is certain that it has increased the number of multiple and competing objectives every person and organization – governmental, business, or not-for-profit – faces. In view of cultural, political, economic, and other differences throughout the world, it is currently impossible to reconcile many of these objectives. Thus, one of the primary challenges associated with globalization is balancing conflicting and/or competing objectives such as the apparent tradeoff between profits and social responsibility, individual and collective interests, autonomy and collaboration, innovation and order, heterogeneity and homogeneity. In many chapters to follow, we explore how firms live with these and other ambiguities. The examples in Box 2.3 provide a range to show the type of challenges organizations face but may not be able to solve.

Challenge 2: Organizational success increasingly is derived from intangibles organizations cannot own

Rapid growth in knowledge-based industries has drawn attention to the roles intellect and knowledge play in organizations. Each information technology breakthrough clarifies that knowledge is critical to organizational achievement. 'The ability to link and leverage knowledge is increasingly the factor that differentiates the winners and the losers and the survivors,' claim Bartlett and Ghoshal (1989, p. 12), and many argue that knowledge is the critical variable for organizational success.

Unlike important productive factors such as land, capital, and equipment that contributed to early industrialization, intelligence does not belong to the organization: it cannot be taken, redistributed, owned, accurately measured, or monopolized (Handy, 1994). Organizations cannot redistribute intelligence nor can they prevent others from acquiring it, and they cannot preserve it. Finally, although organizations depend heavily upon knowledge as a critical resource, they cannot value it, and so most of the resources of an organization are not reflected in public valuations of the enterprise.

The critical importance of knowledge to success creates a unique challenge for

---

BOX 2.3:   CHALLENGES MANAGED BUT UNRESOLVED

Global pharmaceutical firms invest in research and development that cannot be recaptured in many markets because few have the financial resources to purchase them. Yet, growing networks for medical information make it impossible to withhold knowledge about useful remedies, often the formulae are copied with no reimbursement to the originator, and no worldwide legal conventions provide universal protection.

SmithKline Beecham was chosen to handle drug testing at the 1996 Olympics, but found that competitors found ways to circumvent the tests faster then the firm could develop new ones. By the end of events, the firm had been forced to acquire new machines to conduct hundreds of different drug tests, and to bring in many specialists to manage the lab work.

Unilever's global growth has outstripped its supply of managers experienced to handle it. According to Unilever's Chair in 1994, the company could not find enough qualified managers in developing markets to manage available growth.

The Nestlé Group derives income from so-called 'junk' food like candy and snacks, but questions its own and world ability to provide enough wholesome and healthy food for everyone.

The Swiss Banking Corporation acquired Warburg Investments to create a worldwide investment bank, but found that retaining Warburg customers meant allowing Warburg to retain its own identity.

Merck's product Crixivan has been shown effective against AIDs, but neither Merck nor its subcontractors can produce sufficient supplies worldwide to keep up with the spread of this disease.

---

organizations and theorists. Unlike other raw materials, information is not a scarce resource (Henderson, 1996). Thus, business enterprises could well emerge from countries where intelligence and education already are held in high regard, such as Mexico or Brazil, and the latter could thereby create a 'natural' advantage over enterprises coming from countries where tangible resources are more highly valued.

Knowledge frequently is leveraged via means of intangible processes such as relationship-building or trust enhancement. Strategy is based less on a tangible plan and more on core values and culture; work is performed through the power of teams; decisions are made via intuition and inspiration; and management is conveyed through vision, and achieved via trust and empowerment. Intangibles like these are difficult to measure, assess, or implement. Rosabeth Kanter (1995) believes these knowledge-based intangible assets are of three kinds:

1 Concepts are leading-edge ideas, designs or formulations for products or services that create values for customers.
2 Competence is the ability to translate ideas into applications for customers.
3 Connections are alliances among businesses to leverage core capabilities, create more value for customers, or simply open doors and widen horizons (p. 152).

Knowledge is important to any organization, and throughout this book we will explore theories and practices of knowledge creation in the global firm.

Challenge 3: Organizations increasingly manage many forms of diversity

Diversity of people – their color, their nationality, their gender – appeared to emerge as an issue almost simultaneously around the globe, fostered by global economics and immigration, government regulations, and transnational human rights mandates. Whether couched in humanitarian, legalistic, or moralistic terms, incorporating unaccustomed heterogeneity in organizations was initially viewed in most quarters as a problem, and many around the world first viewed it as an 'American' one because it was most evident there in civil rights struggles beginning in the 1960s and 1970s. Initial business responses to the 'problem' of diversity often followed national legislation based on differences of color, gender, or nationality. Many firms assumed that assimilation was the most desirable response to diversity. In other words, early business efforts involved training women, ethnic minorities, and/or immigrants to act and look more like existing employees.

As will be explored in later chapters, organizational managers soon discovered the impracticalities of assimilation, and in an increasingly heterogenous and global world began to discover that diversity of experience is exactly what is required. In an interdependent global world – one where businesses operate not just domestically but globally – many firms have found that successful business decisions are most likely to be reached when relevant and diverse perspectives on global choices are incorporated into the decision-making process. Incorporating diverse perspectives becomes possible with increased understanding of the ways in which the world is currently understood or may change, and how those perspectives are affecting business roles. The boundaries of diversity, like other boundaries, also have expanded to show a great range of human difference as well as similarities where differences had been assumed. Organizations house not only diverse people, but diverse systems, diverse structures, diverse ways of thinking and acting, and all these are aspects of managing diversity. The challenges associated with managing these many forms of diversity also will be explored throughout subsequent chapters, but some examples appear in Box 2.4.

BOX 2.4: MANAGING DIVERSITY

In 1996, sexual harassment charges were leveled at Mitsubishi Motors in Normal, Illinois, leading to a law suit, to widespread claims of racial and sexual discrimination at Mitsubishi Motor Manufacturing of America, and to a national US boycott of Mitsubishi products.

Release of taped discussions among Texaco managers in 1996 were interpreted as evidence of anti-African–American sentiment in the firm; the firm subsequently settled a racial discrimination lawsuit for $176 million and introduced a diversity program expected to increase minority-owned suppliers by 50% and increase the number of minorities on the payroll from 23 to 29%.

Just as the examples above show managing diversity poorly can threaten the firm, managing diversity well can provide benefits and opportunities.

Challenge 4: Business managers and organizations assume new roles for which the past has not prepared them

Business research necessarily looks at the past and the present more than at the future, but global firms face a future that is by no means guaranteed to look like the past. For example, most research on MNEs is derived from studies of the manufacturing sector, even though many service industries, including banking, telecommunications, tourism, or education, have become important global industries. One application of the manufacturing framework for research in service industries revealed that globalization may require different strategic capabilities in the service sector than those used in manufacturing (Campbell and Verbeke, 1994). This suggests that research assumptions may need revision. Assumptions in practice also are undergoing reevaluation today. Mitsubishi Motors and Sweden's Astra both have come under fire in the US for allowing sexual harassment, some Japanese and South Korean firms have discontinued lifetime employment practices, and some US firms have gained media attention with humanitarian moves that suggest a change from profit-oriented 'business as usual.' For example, AT&T announced in late 1996 that all employees would be paid for one day of community volunteer work per year.

Adapting to global integration may well mean different roles for managers in both their external and internal relationships. The examples of sexual harassment charges against Astra and Mistubishi described above show that managerial behaviors that might be acceptable or ignored in one or more countries can have a negative affect on the firm globally when media reports illustrate them. Learning how to be a global manager may involve new skills that essentially change the role of management as well as relationships between managers and subordinates. For example, having instituted 'open-book' management by making financial details available to all employees, Sara Lee managers realized a first step would be to teach employees how to read these books. Once training occurred, managers found that employees were just as adept as they in recognizing gains and losses, and perhaps more adept in finding ways to balance them (Lee, 1994). This sudden empowerment among employees meant that managers had to share roles previously reserved only to them; further, managing an open-book financial system also can mean that it is managers as well as employees who are expected to explain expenditures. Thus, many managerial and organizational roles and responsibilities bear reexamination and some are revised in a global context. The examples in Box 2.5 introduce only a few of these challenges, but many more are presented throughout the text.

This section opened with the concept of paradox to outline the types of challenges managers face for which there may not be ready solutions, and it closes on this same point to illustrate the challenges of assuming roles for which organizations and individuals are ill prepared. The following four paradoxes described by Charles Handy (1994) illustrate the paradox of justice in the world, the paradox of riches among nations, the paradox of the organization, and the paradox of the individual. The exploration of each begins with the challenge of managing world justice.

THE PARADOX OF JUSTICE

The paradox of justice is that unjust societies earn little citizen loyalty but the very basis of capitalism is to provide most rewards to those who achieve most. The problem of justice in the world today is that by providing more rewards to those who achieve most in an economic sense is to ignore the needs of those who contribute in other ways, e.g., home labor, or to overlook those who for one reason or another cannot achieve economically. The latter are unlikely to be loyal to their society, but may respond to perceived inequities by working to subvert the society. Organizations face this same paradox, particularly as they strive to find ways to reward intelligence, an ability that is rarely seen and difficult to measure. People who perform measurable labor may well perceive that thinkers do nothing and deserve lower rather than higher wages. Handy believes that the paradox of justice may be one of the more crucial paradoxes of our time as the lives of those who have resources are increasingly exposed to scrutiny from those who have little in the world today. Because much wealth is concentrated in business organizations, it is businesses that are increasingly asked to participate in achieving a just world. The form of wealth and well-being that justice can provide differs significantly from the fiscal wealth many businesses have traditionally sought to amass.

BOX 2.5:   REEXAMINATION AND REVISION OF BUSINESS PRACTICES

Privatization at Deutsche Telekom and for many other telecommunications companies is forcing managers and employees to make the transition from providing a government benefit to providing a profit-generating business. As organizational purpose changes, so will the roles organizational employees are expected to play.

Many firms long accustomed to relative autonomy from public scrutiny now face shareholder scrutiny and increased demands for accountability. This suggests that managers accustomed to making decisions in private will increasingly be asked to reveal and explain their decisions to the public.

US leaders schooled in 'lean and mean' fiscal management are increasingly asked to be socially accountable by withdrawing from nations whose political regimes are perceived to be oppressive, e.g., PepsiCo withdrew from Myanmar (Burma) in response to student protests and threatened boycotts.

Japanese students attending Tokyo University are no longer guaranteed jobs after graduation; Japanese employers less frequently endorse lifetime employment. The result is that young people in Japan increasingly look for work among smaller firms, and older employees are being laid off.

Worldwide, many larger firms are finding their newer competitors to be the women, minorities, or immigrants they themselves wouldn't hire or didn't promote. The fastest-growing small businesses in the US, Western Europe, and Japan are those established by women. The result is that managers in these firms still must learn how to work with people 'not like them.'

THE PARADOX OF RICHES

Maintaining economic growth means that business enterprises must create an ever-increasing demand for products, but growth is less feasible in the developed world where people have sufficient wealth to buy products and services. Birth rates in the industrialized countries have been falling for many years, and the aging population has resources but fewer needs for many products. Conversely, among the growing populations in developing economies, few have wealth. World growth and world wealth, then, depend on making the poor nations richer, and this has implications for worldwide wealth distribution. At the business level, this paradox translates into enterprises taking on social goals to stimulate wealth, but by their very nature, businesses are profit-seeking entities with little experience in meeting social goals.

THE PARADOX OF THE ORGANIZATION

Trying to meet social and profit goals reflects part of the paradox of organizations. They are asked to be many and different things to all or many people simultaneously. Organizations going global need to be simultaneously global and local, act small when they are big and big when they are small, centralize and decentralize, operate within an industry yet prepare to shift as industry boundaries shift, and remain stable but constantly redefine the organization. Doing all this simultaneously necessarily creates challenges at the firm level, particularly for scientific managers trained to think in terms of 'one best way.'

THE PARADOX OF THE INDIVIDUAL

The paradox of the individual is to operate in systems, work for organizations, and live in families that have differing expectations of them. For example, supporting oneself or a family creates a desire for job security, but organizations prefer the hire/fire mode most responsive to dynamic change. The creativity essential to innovation often comes via individual activity; yet organizations frequently endorse teamwork. Encouraging both simultaneously may mean developing hybrid reward systems that can acknowledge the need for different skills, and training workers who can shift easily from one set of skills to another. For the individual, this paradox may generate some degree of uncertainty and confusion over changing roles; it requires individuals to anticipate and prepare for the future; and it often shifts training costs to the individual who can foresee future job demands perhaps better than can organizational leaders. Moreover, even willing workers find it difficult to change habits developed over a lifetime, and some are unwilling to change.

In summary, change and the increased complexity brought about by global change reduces the reliability of managerial tradition and increases the need to develop a more dynamic and complex view of the organization in global contexts. The model introduced in Chapter 1 provides one view for how this can be accomplished, and the following sections show how this model can be used.

PART II   A DYNAMIC MODEL OF GLOBAL ENVIRONMENTS

INTERNAL CONCERNS: STRUCTURE, PROCESSES, AND PEOPLE

Managing organizations becomes much more complex as the 'one right way' of scientific management becomes many right and many wrong ways and as Japanese firms and South

Korean firms and European firms join enterprises from around the world and re-evaluate their traditions. As events occurring worldwide interact to alter more traditional or well-accepted operating assumptions, these and other firms from all over the world adapt, and in doing so they contribute to a changing base of practice that necessarily alters the base of management knowledge. Changes occur in practice and research, and thus it becomes even more important to examine these changes as a first step towards making sense of them. A suggested format appears in Figure 2.1. As the figure demonstrates, managerial attention tends to begin with internal concerns focused on three related but distinguishable organizational components: (a) managing organizational structure; (b) managing processes, such as organizational strategy or culture; and (c) managing people. These three beacons for managerial attention can be distinguished from each other by looking at tasks associated with each.

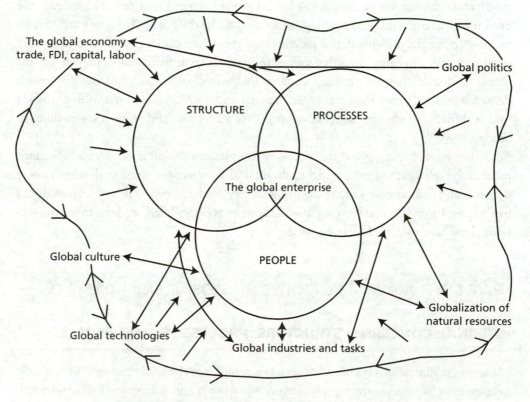

FIGURE 2.1 *Managing globalization of business*

Managing organizational structure

As shown in Table 2.5, structures provide a framework for action, and are analogous in some ways to the human skeleton. Bones in the human skeleton connect to permit upright locomotion for most, but a different configuration for other mammals means they move in different ways. So it is with organizations: the unseen structure defines relationships which in turn shape how the organization appears and how it functions. Sometimes an organization's formal structure is made visible in an organizational chart showing reporting relationships, but charts do not capture informal relationships that also shape structure. A classic example is the secretary to the CEO, who often has considerable power even though secretarial jobs rarely appear on the organizational chart. Organizational charts also are difficult to draw as relationships become more complex. In this text we will examine both simple and complex structures in use today. Alterations in an organization's structure often are a reason for changes in organizational processes and in the people who contribute to organizational success; the Whirlpool example (Box 2.6) illustrates this point.

BOX 2.6:   STRUCTURAL CHANGES ALSO AFFECT PEOPLE AND PROCESSES

Whirlpool Corporation's transformation into the world's number one appliance manufacturer shows relationships between structures, processes, and people. Efforts to transform Whirlpool Corporation into a global appliance firm led CEO David Whitman first to alter structure by acquiring N.V. Philips' ailing European appliance business. Instead of leaving the US and European divisions as they were before acquisition, Whitman unified them, turning them into one customer-driven enterprise rather than two margin-driven firms. Introducing a customer-driven philosophy meant a change in the processes by which employees dealt with others. Finally, because too many managers were running their businesses as regional fiefdoms, Whitman made personnel changes to enhance the drive toward customer satisfaction. In summary, although the original change began with structure, becoming a global enterprise meant that Whirlpool had to make alterations in people and processes as well.

Source: Maruca, Regina Fazio. (1989, Mar./Apr.). The right way to go global: An interview with Whirlpool CEO David Whitman. *Harvard Business Review*, pp. 134–145.

TABLE 2.5 Internal focus of managerial attention

Structures	Processes	People
The framework or skeleton that describes relationships between jobs and functions	Systematic or continuous activities to accomplish the organization's specific tasks	Human resources including managers and all other employees needed to achieve purpose
Examples/terms used		
Hierarchy; bureaucracy	Strategy	Human resource planning/ development
Reporting relationships	Vision; mission; objectives	
Communications flows	Knowledge transfer	Selection
Job design	Change	Diversity
Centralization	Policies; codes; audits	Employee rights/responsibilities
Organizational form	Information systems	Managing
Stand alone vs alliances	Organizational culture	Teams
Keiretsu; *chaebol*	Operations/service mgmt	Compensation; incentives
Formalization (rules)	Learning organization	Careers and jobs
Division of labor	Efficiency/effectiveness	Staffing; full-time; part-time
Line of authority	Birth/growth/stability/decline	Resistance; conflict; violence
Departmentalization	Ethics; social responsibility	Balance: work/family
Chain of command	Functional management; marketing; finance; budgeting processes	Substance abuse
Organic vs mechanistic	Quality or total quality	Organized labor; co-determination
Flat; pyramid; family structures	Innovation	Attitudes; values; behaviors
Control	Renewal	Leaders/coaching
Networks; spiderwebs	Entre- or intrapreneurship	Thinking/doing
Shamrock		Jobs/projects/contract work
Virtual organizations	Core competencies	
	Re-engineering; outsourcing	Motivation; satisfaction
	Empowerment	Portfolios of skills
	Loyalty; trust	Contract work
		Job security

Note: Each column contains examples that are not matched by row.

Often, but not always, the experience of Whirlpool is the experience of the global firm. Organizations are cohesive entities where a change in one part of the entity is almost bound to affect other parts of the entity. The whole organization often is affected by what seem simple or isolated changes, just as the whole world of business can be changed by what seem like single events. The popularizing of Doc Martens boots among teens in Malaysia might seem an isolated occurrence, but when combined with the same purchases among teens worldwide, it represents a trend that has ramifications for global buying habits and global culture. Similarly, the event of a structural change within an organization may seem isolated, but often results in many associated changes in processes and people worldwide.

Managing organizational processes

Processes are systematic or continuous activities intended to accomplish the organization's purposes. Unlike programs which can be added or deleted to meet temporary needs, processes tend to be long term and embedded within the organization via structural means and human memory. In most firms, for example, the strategic management process is periodic or continuous, and entails systematic examination of firm competencies and external demands to find an appropriate match between the two. Creating a strategy, developing a vision, or managing a culture are three processes all organizations develop, but how they develop, what they are called, and why they are introduced can vary from one firm to the next. This partially explains why statements of company objectives are couched in different terms ranging from vision to mission to values to commitments. The success and retention of processes depends on how well they fit with each other and with structure and people in the organization. According to James Champy (1995), many process re-engineering attempts failed when people viewed them as a prelude to job losses they had reason to resist. In other words, a perception that re-engineering would cost them their jobs caused people to resist them.

Managing people

Organizations exist because people create and sustain them. More than either of the other two dimensions of organizations, human resources from workers to managers are the factors that make or break organizations. Much of the emphasis in the field of human resources has been on how to select, develop, train, compensate and otherwise manage human resources efficiently. These are the definable dimensions of managing people. Another dimension looks at the intangibles that people bring to organizations like diversity, intellect, skills, abilities, or attitudes toward work. In the global sphere, differences in culture make it difficult to unite human resources to achieve common purpose. Differences in how people think, the time they are willing to devote to organizations, the skills and abilities they have or can acquire, or the compensation they expect vary widely. Managing people globally creates many challenges for managers, often because people create challenges for each other. The global manager balances among these challenges to structure an organization capable of action. With respect to people, a question to ask is: what people do we need to hire and where do they need to be located to achieve current and future goals? While the two parts of this question might once have been addressed by hiring males from the dominant domestic culture, today the answers are less clear-cut.

Achieving fit among, within, and between these three categories of internal environment is an important and demanding task for managers, who more than most are responsible for increasing the overlap between people, processes, and structures shown in Figure 2.1. Box 2.7 illustrates how difficult it is to achieve congruency or overlap among these three. The example of Ford in this box shows that in order to achieve 'fit' within the rather small window of opportunity provided in global environments, organizational leaders must not only recognize interdependencies within the internal environment of the firm, but they also must look beyond the firm to understand the external environment.

In summary, people, processes, and structures are the internal concerns of managers. A purposeful change in one of these three often brings about changes in the other two, and together these multiple changes create complexity for managers. This complexity is considerable even when the firm is domestic, but it increases exponentially as the firm goes global because global change is more difficult to recognize and to monitor than is domestic change. Further, because globalization is a new phenomenon, managers often do not have a well-spring of experience from which to draw. Finally, research is limited on global change and what it means for managers.

EXTERNAL CONCERNS

Research on externalities provides a useful approach to thinking about managing in a global environment. As was mentioned earlier in this chapter, one result of strategic thinking developed in World War II was to see interconnections and relationships among separate events. Applying this concept to businesses meant seeing organizations in a context or external environment where factors outside organizational control nevertheless shaped organizational choice. Many different concepts of external environment were put forward, but most agree that a first step toward understanding externalities is to understand how each operates. This is important because each environment is complex and firms differ in their purposes; therefore external events can affect them in different ways. The relative effect each environment has on a firm in part depends on the organization itself. Managers of a small organization with few operating rules might find it easier to exploit information technology than a larger firm with a steep bureaucracy, but the latter firm may have financial resources that the smaller firm does not have. The industry or industries in which the firm operates also can affect the firm. For example, globalization is occurring in both banking and burial industries. For both industries, globalization has meant consolidation and a wave of mergers and acquisitions among existing firms. In banking, it is possible to move funds across borders of every kind almost instantly, but in the burial industry the work itself remains mostly local even though management of the firm can be global. Thus, bankers have the option of advertising globally but this opportunity is less likely for the funeral home, whose advertisements are more likely to be local in character due to cultural differences in how death is managed. In summary, the impact of global events occurring in a single environment such as economic change can be different for firms because

BOX 2.7:   ACHIEVING FIT: FORD'S 'WORLD CAR'

In 1994 the Ford Motor Company reorganized its internal structure. Ford previously had a regional divisional structure that created a separate division for Europe, another for North America, another for Latin America, and another for the Asia-Pacific region, but these regional divisions created national barriers inside the company which were costly because engineering and product development functions were not shared. Ideas often were unknowingly developed simultaneously in two or more places. In one instance, a similar four-cylinder automotive engine was developed in both Europe and North America, but neither engine shared a single component with its counterpart. Needless duplication like this no doubt had an effect on costs, and consequently on profits. Accordingly, Ford restructured to merge its North American and European auto operations into one division that will share manufacturing, sales, and product development. Eventually, the division also will include Latin America and Asia, with expected savings of $3 billion or more a year. The overall plan to create Ford 2000 includes a global car known as the Contour in the US and the Mondeo in Europe.

Although it might seem that $3 billion is well worth reorganizing for, restructuring in this way is much easier said than done, for several reasons. First, making changes in an existing organization can be difficult. Ford's regional divisions have product development teams. What happens to individuals when reorganization occurs? The people holding those jobs doubtless recognize that only some will be retained. This may result in employees spending more time worrying than working, or in internal strife among Ford's employees. Additionally, this restructuring represents a shift in Ford's strategy, which requires a redefinition of Ford's vision and mission. Transcending internal borders and barriers to change have proved difficult at Ford. Below-industry average profits for Ford remained a source of analysts' reorganization concerns, but Ford's changes may be paying off. In second-quarter operations reported in June 1997, Ford posted record profits, due in part to boundary-crossing cost reductions in materials, marketing, and design and engineering that led to manufacturing and other efficiencies. Analysts expect record profits to continue into 1998 as the company's long-running global reorganization begins to pay off.

Source: Reitman, Valerie. (1997, June 3). Ford is steering toward a record profit. *The Wall Street Journal*, p. A3; Simison, Robert L. (1998, Jan. 14). Ford's profit is expected to top GM's. *The Wall Street Journal*, p. A3.

the firms differ. Box 2.8 further illustrates that the same global event can affect firms in different ways.

BOX 2.8:   THE ECONOMY SURGES!

For many firms, economic growth represents an opportunity because it creates more jobs, more disposable income, more opportunity for sales. But for organizations that thrive in economic hard times such as bill collection agencies or mobile home producers, a good economy can bring bad times to their businesses. In a global economy, however, the latter firms identify growth opportunities worldwide by looking at other global environments. Observation of increased credit sales in response to cultural changes creates an attendant need for bill collectors. Industry shifts leading to job growth and a demand for new housing can produce an opportunity for mobile home production and sales in still other locations. Having identified global events within each category relevant to them, firm leaders are better able to assess worldwide opportunities or threats associated with 'a good economy.'

In a global world, it also is important for managers to look at interactions among global events and assess their impact not just on the firm, but on how they create potential change that could reshape culture, technology, industries, or other environments. Experts rarely agree on which external environment is most or least important, and few agree as to what each environment should be called.

Six global factors or external environments are examined in this text; each is shown in Figure 2.1. These are: (a) globalization of culture; (b) economic globalization of trade, foreign direct investment, capital, and labor; (c) globalization in the political/legal sphere; (d) increasing globalization of task and industry environments; (e) the globalization of technology, particularly information technologies; and (f) globalization in the natural environment. As Figure 2.1 shows, these factors are at the perimeter of organizations where they operate largely beyond direct control of individual organizations. Connecting arrows between each of the global factors shows that events of global significance in a single sphere tend to influence events in other spheres, with a change in one aspect followed, caused, or concurrent with still other changes. These interrelationships were made evident in the review of a change in Chinese dietary habits in Chapter 1.

Just as it is difficult to draw complexity and dynamism in our figure, it also is difficult to talk about environments simultaneously until we have first established the critical characteristics of culture, or of the political/legal environment, or of the economy. The balance of this chapter introduces the six environments of greatest concern to global managers, and briefly identifies what managers look for to anticipate or interpret global change in each environment. Later chapters examine each of these environments in much greater depth, and in these later chapters we also look at interdependencies among these environments.

Globalization of culture

According to Terpstra and David (1991), 'culture is a learned, shared, compelling, interrelated set of symbols whose meanings provide a set of orientations for members of a society.' (p. 6). This shared set of meanings provides a way for people in cultural groups to address common problems and challenges. Cultural groups can be a family, an organization, a society, a civilization, the world. Every cultural group creates stories, habits, and practices that reinforce its beliefs and values. A story of Uncle's triumph against adversity reinforces perseverance among family members, and Benetton advertisements call for tolerance and world unity. Stories and advertisements are only two among many ways a cultural group reinforces beliefs about how life is or ought to be organized. Cultural habits and behaviors appropriate to those values are reinforced by language, by nonverbal behaviors, and in all other ways people communicate expectations. An important observable aspect of culture is behavior, including how people look and act, how they communicate, what seems important to them. Many features of culture are not visible.

Worldwide, people have common survival needs for water, air, and food, and basic needs like shelter and safety also must be met. Formerly a family or a tribe was sufficient to meet survival needs, but today these are more often met by nation-states. Organized as sovereign entities, most national cultures share a common language, a common form of government, a common economic system, and a shared orientation of how to think, act, and behave to remain a member of the nation-state. These characteristics are, as the definition of culture suggests, learned, shared, and interrelated, with each reinforcing the other. When looking at national culture, the challenge is to examine these interrelationships by asking how each reflects beliefs held by most in the nation. These beliefs shape behavior in terms of products and services consumed, in terms of behavior and expectations of business organizations.

There are also cultural differences within nations that create diverse cultural groups. The preferences and tastes of these groups also are important to examine when looking at national culture. Singapore's population, for example, is composed of Malays, Indians, and Chinese with different habits, and the business practices appropriate in dealing with each may vary even though all are Singapore citizens. In his book *The nine nations of North America*, Joel Garreau (1992) observed that US regions are different enough to have their own cultures; the Ecotopia of the Pacific Northwest is distinct from the Breadbasket of the middle US and Canada and both differ from Dixie, which contains most of the Southern states. These examples illustrate that subgroups within nations may create habits and values different from the parent culture. The values and habits of subcultures organized around families, religion, age, race, or national origin within and across nations also should be considered when examining global culture because they represent segmented markets within nations and may signal a global market. Countercultural youths provided an opportunity for sales of Doc Martens boots, but this focus on youth revealed existence of a global teen with similar values worldwide.

Cross-cultural comparisons also yield insight into global business potential and challenges. We gain insight into similarities and differences by looking at where cultural globalization is occurring: English increasingly is a global language for business; food habits are merging; travel is global; artifacts of popular culture from television and film are viewed worldwide; and business activities increasingly are viewed as modes of distributing resources and knowledge across the world. In the chapter examining global culture, we observe the global business language has taken many forms, that business habits shared worldwide do not necessarily mean shared business values.

Our study of cultural globalization looks at how differences between cultures and similarities among them emerge to shape global business behaviors and values. As the activities of businesses and other global enterprises transcend barriers of every type, these activities shape and reshape cultural beliefs not only within the organization but among the individuals, groups, and nations that interact with these organizations. Many cultural clashes between conflicting value sets also are taking place against the backdrop of the global enterprise. Religious habits, language standards, operating assumptions concerning bribery, learning styles, sex roles, cultural diversity, and even the purpose of work are only a few among many issues for global enterprises.

Finally, today we face global challenges to answering questions of survival, of resource distribution, of reproduction, individual freedom, economic opportunity, and the role of faith and religion in life. Business activities shape those decisions as well, and they are increasingly asked to operate in roles with which they are unfamiliar.

Globalization of the economy

The global economy continues to develop at a rapid pace, characterized by increased interdependencies among national fiscal and monetary systems as well as emergence of worldwide capital and equity markets that only recently were more closely aligned with nations. The sheer size of the stakes in the global economy increases the uncertainty associated with managing these markets. A Canadian official observed in 1994, 'With one trillion dollars flowing through the markets daily, there's little governments can do except stop the momentum for one day, one hour – or more like 10 minutes' (quoted in Gumbel and Davis, 1994). Globalization of the economy has not only disrupted some traditional economic roles, e.g., the role of central banking, but also brought more participants into the global economy. Both small and large enterprises from all parts of the world find it attractive and possible to participate in global economics because capital can move easily across borders.

In this global economy, dynamic changes are increasing the size of world trade and altering its shape. The less tangible nature of services makes them more difficult to measure even as they become more important measures of economic globalization. Funds available on global markets search for greater returns on investments to create 'hot' money that enters or flees a domestic economy within seconds. Business activities that transfer funds quickly to virtually all parts of the world have produced opportunities and posed challenges for financial markets and the institutions that manage them, and many ponder the value of traditional institutions such as the World Bank. Equity and bond markets are springing up around the world; trade and foreign direct investment have increased; and there is increasing need for a common global currency. In summary, foreign direct investments, currency fluctuations, and national debts are intertwined; capital and equity markets are globalized; and increasingly business activities are affecting and affected by globalization of economy. Changes like these create business challenges of decision-making under uncertainty, appropriate foreign direct investment strategies, and managing information.

Labor also contributes to wealth creation, and a look at the economic consequences of labor globalization focuses attention on compensation, job and human migration, safety, and other work conditions. There are new demands for organizations to participate in achieving job and human equities. Global staffing, leveraging and accounting for knowledge, and managing intellectual capital are only a few among many organizational challenges for managing a global workforce.

Globalization of political/legal environments

The political/legal environment of global business is increasingly characterized by shifts to regional and worldwide arrangements that reduce national autonomy. These shifts put less emphasis on legal and political mechanisms within domestic environments, such as how a country is governed or how resources are distributed internally, and put more emphasis on how government actors participate in worldwide resource distribution systems, and on how common business rules can be established or regulated at a global level. Societal decisions on how to distribute resources, how to divide labor, where to allocate power, or how to manage reproduction are all moving outside national borders to become issues of global concern. These become organizational concerns tied to equity, opportunity, organizational democracy, and work/family issues.

Taxes, tariffs, and rules and regulations vary widely worldwide, but it has become clear to some that worldwide business efficiency can result from standardization and harmonization of commercial rules. Ironically, politicians who are helping to shape worldwide commercial codes do so by reducing their own ability to govern autonomously. Globalization in the political/legal sphere has created concerns over how the governance structure of any given country interacts with other countries in the global environment. The latter relationships often are regulated by trade agreements that cover growing regional groups and even global compacts. The growing frequency and importance of regional and worldwide trading entities have contributed substantially to globalization of political initiatives, and examination of how these affect firms is one way to look at political globalization. Just as governmental organizations are reshaping the political/legal landscape, so too nongovernmental organizations are acting globally to reshape assumptions about how business is conducted and by whom. Similarly, professional groups acting outside the government sector influence rules and regulations as they harmonize and standardize business practices ranging from manufacturing and environmental standards to accounting rules. Finally, having introduced terrorism, kidnapping, and murder to the global business scene, global gangs and cartels also are players in the global political environment. All of these political/legal factors are reshaping conditions for global business, and from the perspective of a business they also reshape workplace practices to reduce political, economic, intellectual property, and personal risk.

Globalization of industries

Because they focus on different tasks, firms within specific industries tend to share similarities with one another but differ from firms in other industries. For this reason, many who study task or industry environments use Michael Porter's (1980) model of industry structure. The five forces affecting an industry are buyers, suppliers, substitute products, barriers to new entrants, and competitive rivalry. Because it focuses more specifically on an individual industry – and possibly on the core competencies of a particular firm within that industry – the task environment and industry environments may seem somewhat different from other global environments. Unlike changes in culture, which may be difficult to discern, changes in the industry environment usually are immediately evident when customers withdraw support or when suppliers are unhappy. Thus, because they are more involved with the day-to-day operations of the firm, elements in the task environment tend to attract more regular managerial attention than do events in environments that seem more distant. Additionally, because the industry environment is likely to be somewhat different for each industry, there is some tendency for managers to think of this environment also as different from other global environments.

However, as industries globalize, many changes pertinent to individual industries occur at some distance from the focal firm. Those who focus attention exclusively on current buyers or suppliers within narrow or domestic markets may miss seeing global change in the industry that has occurred or could occur. Moreover, inattention to global interactions between the industry environment and other aspects of global change may catch organizations unaware of change occurring around them. For example, global competitors such as Citibank were able to woo customers from German banks because the latter had not kept pace with global introduction of telephone banking, cash dispensers, and other improvements that make it easier for consumers to conduct banking outside so-called 'banker's hours.' This example demonstrates the danger of exclusive focus on a domestic or static task and industry environment. The nature of the task and the structure of an industry will alter with global change in industries and interaction among those changes and other aspects of global environments. The strategies, structures, and practices appropriate to thinking about tasks and competitors within and across industries should be monitored in a global world. Finally, assumptions of a competitive environment for business consistent with many task and industry analyses may be changing as nations and firms consider concepts of collaboration and competition.

Globalization of technology

The technological environment of global business necessarily focuses on those processes and products with greatest global impact. Many associate technological progress with development of new *products* and services because it is relatively easy to observe new products. The technological breakthrough that produced the compact disc player was more evident than the production processes that made it possible to produce them. Frozen yogurt, squeeze bottle condiments, microwave cooking, and virtual reality video games are all examples of product developments due to technological breakthroughs occurring in the past decade. Certainly one of the most profound technological changes in the last decade has been the introduction of telecommunications sufficient to link the whole world, and computers that use those links. In addition to very visible products and services, it is important to recognize that less evident *processes* associated with work also are part of the global technological environment. Many breakthroughs in process technologies are reshaping the nature of work no less than products. For example, both organizational learning and total quality management processes capitalize on the knowledge every employee brings to the organization. Although these two processes are explored in greater detail in Chapters 6 and 9 respectively, each chapter offers a section for exploring processes important to global firms. Whether they reshape products or processes, technological breakthroughs have the capacity to change the nature of work and business assumptions. Computerization and telecommunications can be used to restructure work by allocating human tasks to computers, jobs by introducing telecommuting, and organizations by creating virtuosity. The sheer size and stakes of technological breakthroughs have been motivators for structuring alliances and partnerships managed in ways that differ from autonomous organizations. Technological breakthroughs have made it possible to hire people all over the world, even as they demonstrate that motivation schemes are culture-bound; and they generate new questions about haves and have nots, privacy, and the organization's ability to stimulate creativity at arm's length.

Globalization of natural resources

The natural environment for global business examines the raw materials and resources needed for business production. Geographic features such as water can separate a country from other countries or, in the case of the Philippines – a nation of 8,000 islands – can separate national inhabitants from one another. Distance from trading partners can increase the cost of global business participation, while distance from one's country people can create cultural divisions between groups of people living within the same nation. A country's topography also can affect distribution systems. For example, a paramount problem for the former Soviet Union was to transport goods across vast land masses, but this was difficult because of mountain ranges, freezing temperatures, and other impediments to rail or truck transport. Organizational decisions to sell products in Russia today are doubtless affected by these same geographic impediments.

Nations also have greater and lesser deposits of raw materials such as wood, rubber, minerals, ores, or oil, but as one world there is a finite amount of these resources available to all of us. Additionally, there are a number of natural resources that already are owned on a global basis. One example is the marine resources found in oceans as well as the water itself; another is the air we breathe. Often extraction or exploitation of natural resources, and the use of common resources such as air and water, lead to issues associated with preserving the environment or environmentalism. Natural disasters like floods and earthquakes can have global impact; diseases like AIDs have spread unimpeded worldwide; population growth has destroyed natural habitat; and animals and plants are affected by global change.

The relationship between environmentalism and business is an issue of increasing importance worldwide with some firms restructuring their accounting practices to include resource depletion as a cost of doing business. Dutch computer consulting firm BOS/Beheer BV was one of the first companies to develop an ecological accounting system to calculate costs such as ozone depletion with the firm's use of styrofoam cups, pollution caused by an employee's plane trip, and even how much sewage employees contribute per year (Pope, 1995). Environmental accounting requires accountants trained in new skills. The role organizations must play in training and educating their own employees as well as issues of sustainable development are business challenges to consider when studying the globalization of environmental issues.

ACHIEVING FIT BETWEEN ORGANIZATIONS AND GLOBAL ENVIRONMENTS

Achieving fit between organizations and the global world where they increasingly operate depends not just on the will to manage well, but also on an ability to juggle among multiple and sometimes competing interests represented by forces both internal and external to the firm. The environmental complexity of global business together with the many uncertainties fueled by a rapid pace of change may make it difficult for organizational participants to keep up with the effects of multiple and sometimes conflicting political, cultural, economic, and competitive events occurring on a global scale. It may be difficult for managers to collect, interpret, and act on available global information.

In order to operate in this global environment, organizations and their managers must become more aware of and adaptive to changes in their environment. They can do this by constant boundary spanning not only on their own part but on the part of multiple organizational players. This learning can be used to position the organization in the global business environment.

Many Westernized firms once articulated their strategy as profit-seeking, and established stand-alone hierarchical structures, but few in the global sphere find it possible solely to pursue profits, and many are experimenting with flatter organizational structures and joining forces to establish joint ventures and other strategic alliances. Proliferation of options generated among global environments is complemented by a proliferation in the options available to organizations with respect to people, processes, and structures. Western traditions of scientific management, Japanese traditions of lifetime employment, Chinese traditions of family ownership, and many other traditions are under review. Under similar review are high wage rates and quality of life issues in German firms, ethics of work in Eastern Europe and other former communist countries, and the relationship between global business and global society. Global firms may mix and match old principles with newly developed ones that borrow best practices worldwide. In this way, management practices undergo some amount of globalization as well. The challenges of global environments argue for a move away from traditional management principles to look at these principles in a global sphere. Similarly, managerial competencies needed for a more global world encompass but also go beyond those traditionally proposed: leading, planning, organizing, and controlling.

MANAGERIAL COMPETENCIES FOR A GLOBAL WORLD: A GLOBAL MINDSET

According to a 1993 survey of global managers and a review of over 1,000 books and articles published between 1987 and 1993, the global manager must draw on 12 organizational and individual competencies to make globalization work (Moran and Riesenberger (1994), including:

1 A global mindset.
2 An ability to work as an equal with persons of diverse backgrounds.
3 A long-term orientation.
4 The ability to facilitate organizational learning.
5 The ability to create learning systems.
6 The ability to motivate employees to excellence.
7 Skill in negotiation and an ability to approach conflict in a collaborative mode.
8 Skillful choices and assignments for managers worldwide.
9 The ability to lead and participate effectively in multicultural teams.
10 An understanding of one's own cultural values and assumptions.
11 An ability to profile the organizational and national culture of others with accuracy.
12 Avoidance of cultural mistakes and ability to behave in an appropriate manner in all countries (p. 191).

A look at these attributes and competencies shows that the action components of traditional management skills such as controlling or leading are increasingly complemented in a global world by more reliance on less easily measured managerial intangibles such as attitudes and values. Self-reflection, interpersonal interaction, and awareness of one's own operating assumptions also are critical to the global manager. Sometimes these less tangible attributes are difficult to describe, but many view them as essential to global managers. Stephen Rhinesmith (1993) argues that the global mindset will differ profoundly from mindsets based on domestic environments (see Table 2.6). For example, whereas Western firms have traditionally hired from functional areas, generated decisions in a step-by-step fashion, created hierarchical structures, and encouraged individual initiative, a more global mindset calls for generalized and broad expertise, a less clear set of decision rules, and an emphasis on processes as much as structures. Global mindsets call for teamwork and partnerships, creating a challenge for the 'go it alone' individual and challenges for the global enterprise. For example, rewards and compensation in firms characterized by Rhinesmith's domestic mindset are likely to be based on individual action, and will need to be revised to create team as well as individual rewards. Clearly, a key challenge is for the global manager to achieve balance among competing and even conflicting interests to reach organizational objectives. These and similar challenges may result in alterations of processes, structures and people because these are the decisions over which managers have control. Throughout this book, we will look at how these challenges are reshaping the role of organizations and focus on importance competencies required of managers.

TABLE 2.6   A comparison of domestic and global mindsets

Domestic mindset	Global mindset
1 Expertise in a function, e.g., marketing, accounting, finance	1 Expertise needs to be general, based on a broad view
2 A need to prioritize in a step-by-step fashion	2 Need to balance contradictions and recognize paradoxes and challenges
3 Hierarchical structure is usual	3 Emphasis on processes
4 Individual responsibility is encouraged	4 Emphasis on diversity and teamwork
5 Eliminate surprises	5 View change as an opportunity

Source: Adapted from Rhinesmith, Steven H. (1993). *A manager's guide to globalization.* Homewood, IL: Business One Irwin.

As national economies, political systems, cultures, technologies, resources, and industries increasingly converge – perhaps to meld, perhaps to take shape in new forms – global business and management skills are likely to become more important to all organizations. These skills will be diverse, and blend traditional and emerging demands for learning, managing diversity, and managing ambiguity. Accordingly, learning about global environments is important even for those who never manage a global firm. The broad definition of globalization provided above suggests that increased permeability of traditional borders in all spheres of activity throughout the planet will mean that managing in any environment will be characterized by global challenges. Knowledge of globalization and its development should provide directions for action to individuals and the organizations of which they are a part, but the important task remains the human task of deciding who will benefit and in what ways from globalization. For the individual manager, the task is to prepare for projects, jobs, and careers in a future where direction is unclear. For organizations as well, the challenge is to anticipate change and learning to live with ambiguity. Challenges facing nations, organizations, and managers will be explored throughout succeeding chapters.

KEY CHAPTER CONCEPTS

The Difference Between International and Global Business: International business is defined as cross-border transactions involving companies from two or more countries, and it concerns the flow of business, goods, or capital from one country into another. Thus, internationalization of business is strongly defined by nationality. By contrast, globalization looks at the whole world as being nationless and borderless where goods, capital, and people move freely.

The Difference Between International and Global Enterprises: Evolution of understanding of domestic, international, and global business has brought new words into the business lexicon. It is by no means certain that terms like 'the multinational corporation' are used to describe the same entities. In this text international enterprises are those drawing resources primarily from a domestic base to operate beyond national borders. In contrast, the multinational firm operates from more than its domestic base, readily drawing resources of people and knowledge from sources throughout the world. International, multinational, and global enterprises also are distinguishable from one another because of differences related to where the firm is headquartered, the nationality of managers, values associated with diversity, and the extent to which policies, processes, and technologies are standardized.

Stateless Organizations: Statelessness is defined as an organizational process wherein the country of origin for the business enterprise is no longer central to organizational identity. Stateless organizations usually are known by their products and services rather than by their country of origin.

Globalization Defines Our Collective Future: Managing in global environments is no longer a matter of choice for most organizations or people as all of us are drawn inexorably into a global arena punctuated by events that affect not only the future of business, but also the business of how our futures will unfold.

Characteristics of the Global Enterprise: The global enterprise is one that views the world as its home, establishes a worldwide presence in one or more businesses, adopts either a worldwide standardization or multilocal strategy within broad or niche lines, and is able to cross targeted external and internal boundaries.

A Global Strategy Can Take More Than One Form: A global strategy is not necessarily synonymous with a global firm since the latter can sustain an integrated standard for one business line and be locally responsive in other business lines. In this text, multilocal strategy involves combining worldwide standards with local responsiveness; worldwide standardization strategy occurs when products and services are standardized and integrated on a worldwide basis. A firm also can adopt niche strategies that are multilocal or involve worldwide standardization.

Boundaries Global Enterprises Transcend: Global enterprises transcend three types of boundaries: external ones like nations, space, or time that are in some sense measurable; and both external and internal ones that are less tangible and less easily measured or changed. Every firm is likely to have different priorities for reshaping internal and external boundaries because of differences in size, industry, strategy, leadership, or other factors.

Managers Respond to Their Historical Context: Management practices and management research have changed over time because the context for business also has changed over time. At the very least, a globalizing world requires reevaluation of existing management traditions.

Internal Concerns for the Global Enterprise: In the context of global environments, internal firm issues are of three general types that concern (a) people, (b) processes, and (c) structures.

Six Global Environments Interact: Six global environments constrain organizational choice: global culture, global economy, global politics, globalizing industries, global technology, and globalization of the natural environment.

Globalization Challenges Management Traditions: Globalization has meant more opportunities for businesses to operate on a worldwide basis, and the experience of operating globally has caused many business managers to rethink the basic assumptions of how their firms are organized and operate. Global management may require mixing and matching among tools and techniques derived from a variety of cultures, perhaps to meld Western-style financial techniques with Eastern-style team-oriented work techniques. While it is relatively easy to think about altering systems and ways of thinking, it is much more difficult to alter the practices of a lifetime or of organizational generations.

Globalization Generates Paradoxes: Paradox is a statement or proposition that seems self-contradictory, but which can be explained as expressing a truth. Globalization is generating multiple paradoxes with which nations, organizations, and individuals must cope. One of the primary challenges associated with globalization is balancing conflicting and/or competing objectives.

Four Common Challenges for Global Enterprises: Global organizations face four common challenges: they face problems that cannot be 'solved' but must be managed; their success increasingly is derived from intangibles that the organization cannot own; leaders increasingly manage many forms of diversity; and business managers and organizations assume new roles for which the past has not fully prepared them.

Managerial Competencies Needed: Traditional managerial competencies such as leading, controlling, organizing, and planning are complemented in a global sphere by competencies that rely on intangibles like attitudes and processes like facilitation. Self-reflection also is an important competence for managing global enterprises.

REVIEW AND DISCUSSION QUESTIONS

1   Refer to the characteristics of the global enterprise to decide if the following firm is a global one. How is it the same as or different from R. Griggs, maker of Doc Martens boots?

Picture an assembly line containing a dozen 60-foot-long printing presses and 800 sewing machines. Your visual image will have captured a scene both from the early Industrial Revolution, which began around 1770 with mushrooming textile mill growth in towns like Manchester, England, and a scene that occurs today and every day in emerging and developing economies found in the Caribbean, Latin America, and Southeast Asia, as well as in most industrialized economies. The scene described is a daily occurrence for a factory north of Bangkok, Thailand, where 3,000 Thai women work around the clock to design, cut, sew, and ship cotton clothing depicting Mickey Mouse. The labels will show Austrian ownership, but the cotton comes from China, the sewing machines from Japan, and the financing from Europe; Mickey Mouse hails from the USA, but since 1983 and 1992 respectively the Mouse has maintained second homes at a Disney theme park outside Tokyo and Paris. And the products? They're targeted for sale to teenagers in Germany, Japan, and the US.

2   Ford Motor Company has restructured on a worldwide basis to produce a global automobile. Provide examples to show how this restructuring is likely to affect people and other processes within Ford. What are the problems and challenges associated with structural change?

3   Describe a paradox you face in your own life. What does this suggest to you about your ability to live with paradox?

4   Often individuals are the first to feel the impact of globalization as jobs are created and disappear. In terms of the job, the impact is experienced as organizations strive to become more adaptable, perhaps replacing traditional management principles with unfamiliar ones. Changes like these shape opportunities to work and the environment of work. For the individual, these changes may seem personal when in fact they reflect a much bigger force called globalization. What changes in job opportunities do you foresee in the next five years, and how will these affect your work options?

5   Many theories of management emerged from the study and experiences of US firms. In what ways has this influence shaped business expectations in a global world? Identify three concepts presented in this chapter and describe the ways they reflect US influence.

6   What advantages and disadvantages do you see for organizations becoming 'stateless' from the perspective of the enterprise, from the perspective of nations, and from the perspective of individuals employed by the 'stateless' firm?

7   If traditional domestic mindsets are the US norm, but the emerging global mindset

is the wave of the future, what will be the implications for you as a manager? What type of skills do you need to develop to think according to a more global mindset? What changes will you need to make in the way you currently think and work?

8　*The Global Enterprise Project*: Select a global enterprise to study throughout the course; you may find it a challenge to your own assumptions about how business should be conducted if you study a firm with headquarters located in a nation other than your own. Ideally, the firm would be one with a homepage (check the course homepage for ideas), and one whose annual report is accessible. Prepare a two-page report on the organization that includes an introduction to the firm and provide a *brief* history. Provide most recent specifics on firm size in terms of revenues, markets/nations served, and number of employees worldwide. Also include information to show how the firm is structured – refer to Table 2.5 for the words usual when describing organizational structure or design.

REFERENCES

Ashkenas, Ron, Ulrich, Dave, Jick, Todd, and Kerr, Steve. (1995). *The boundaryless organization*. San Francisco, CA: Jossey-Bass.

Bartlett, Christopher A., and Ghoshal, Sumantra. (1989). *Managing across borders: The transnational solution*. Boston, MA: Harvard Business School Press.

Bartlett, Christopher A. and Ghoshal, Sumantra. (1995, May/June). Changing the role of top management: Beyond systems to people. *Harvard Business Review*, pp. 132–142.

Beamish, Paul, Killing, J. Peter, Lecraw, Donald J., and Crookell, Peter. (1991). *International management*. Burr Ridge, IL: Irwin.

Boyacigiller, Nakiye A., and Adler, Nancy J. (1991). The parochial dinosaur: Organizational science in a global context. *Academy of Management Review*, 16(2): 262–290.

Brown, Juanita. (1992). Corporation as community: A new image for a new era. In J. Rensch (Ed.), *New traditions in business*, pp. 123–139. San Francisco, CA: Berrett-Koehler.

Campbell, Alexandra, and Verbeke, Alain. (1994, Apr.) The globalization of service multinationals. *Long Range Planning*, 27(2): 95–102.

Champy, James. (1995). *Reengineering management: The mandate for new leadership*. New York: HarperBusiness.

Daniels, John D., and Radebaugh, Lee H. (1992). *International business* (6th ed.). Reading, MA: Addison-Wesley.

D'Aveni, Richard A. (1995). *Hypercompetitive rivalries*. New York: Free Press.

Economic indicators. (1997, Sept. 27). *The Economist*, p. 119.

Evans, Paul, Doz, Yves, and Laurent, André. (Eds). (1990). *Human resource management in international firms: Change, globalization, innovation*. New York: St Martin's Press.

Garreau, Joel. (1992). *The nine nations of North America*. New York: Avon.

Ghoshal, Sumantra, and Bartlett, Christopher. (1995, Jan./Feb.) Changing the role of top management: Beyond structure to processes. *Harvard Business Review*, pp. 86–96.

Gumbel, Peter. (1994, Nov. 29). German bankers get busy catching up. *The Wall Street Journal*, p. A21.

Gumbel, Peter, and Davis, Bob. (1994, July 11). G-7 countries show limits of their power. *The Wall Street Journal*, pp. A3, A4.

Hamel, Gary, and Prahalad, C.K. (1985, July/Aug.). Do you really have a global strategy? *Harvard Business Review*, pp. 139–148.

Handy, Charles. (1994). *The age of paradox*. Cambridge, MA: Harvard Business School Press.

Heenan, David A., and Perlmutter, Howard V. (1979). *Multinational organization development*. Reading, MA: Addison-Wesley.

Henderson, Hazel. (1996). *Building a win-win world: Life beyond global economic warfare*. San Francisco, CA: Berrett-Koehler.

Hoecklin, Lisa. (1995). *Managing cultural differences: Strategies for competitive advantage*. Wokingham: Addison-Wesley.

Hofstede, Geert. (1983). The cultural relativity of organization practices and theories. *Journal of International Business Studies*, 14(2): 75–90.

Hordes, Mark W., Clancy, J. Anthony, and Baddaley, Julie. (1995). A primer for global start-ups. *Academy of Management Executive*, 9(2): 7–11.

Hout, Thomas, Porter, Michael E., and Rudden, Eileen. (1982, Sept./Oct.). How global companies win out. *Harvard Business Review*, pp. 98–108.

Hu, Yao-Su. (1992). Global or stateless corporations are national firms with international operations. *California Management Review*, 34(2): 107–126.

Kanter, Rosabeth Moss. (1995, Sept./Oct.). Thriving locally in the global economy. *Harvard Business Review*, pp. 151–160.

Kerwin, Kathleen. (1994, Nov. 18). Getting 'two big elephants to dance.' *Business Week*, Special Issue: 21st century capitalism, p. 83.

Lee, Chris. (1994). Open-book management. *Training*, 31(7): 21–27.

Levitt, Theodore. (1983, May/June). The globalization of markets. *Harvard Business Review*, pp. 92–102.

Moran, Robert T., and Riesenberger, John R. (1994). *The global challenge.* London: McGraw-Hill.

Ohmae, Kenichi. (1989, Mar./Apr.). The global logic of strategic alliances. *Harvard Business Review*, pp. 143–154.

Ohmae, Kenichi. (1995). *The end of the nation state.* Cambridge, MA: Free Press.

Oviatt, Benjamin M., and McDougall, Patricia Phillips. (1995). Global start-ups: Entrepreneurs on a worldwide stage. *Academy of Management Executive*, 9(2): 30–43.

Phatak, Arvind V. (1992). *International dimensions of management* (3rd ed.). Boston, MA: PWS-Kent.

Pope, Kyle. (1995, July 7). Hip Dutch computer consulting concern bets merger would make it global player. *The Wall Street Journal*, pp. B1, B4.

Porter, Michael E. (1980). *Competitive strategy.* New York: Free Press.

Porter, Michael E. (1985). *Competitive advantage.* New York: Free Press.

Rhinesmith, Stephen H. (1993). *A manager's guide to globalization.* Homewood, IL: Business One Irwin.

Robinson, Richard. (1981, Spring/Summer). Background concepts and philosophy of international business from World War II to the present. *Journal of International Business Studies*, pp. 13–21.

Senge, Peter. (1990). *The fifth discipline: The art and practice of the learning organization.* New York: Doubleday.

Sera, Koh. (1992). Corporate globalization: A new trend. *Academy of Management Executive*, 6(1): 89–96.

Terpstra, Vern, and David, Kenneth. (1991). *The cultural environment of international business* (3rd ed.). Cincinnati, OH: South-Western Publishing.

Trompenaars, Alfons. (1994). *Riding the waves of culture*. Burr Ridge, IL: Irwin.

World Investment Report. (1993). New York: United Nations.

World Investment Report. (1997). Geneva: UNCTAO.

World Trade Organization. (1998, Jan. 12). After two outstanding years, world trade growth returned to earlier levels. www.wto.org/wto/intltrad/introduc.htm. Also see World Trade Organization. (1997, Dec. 19). WTO Annual Report. Geneva: WTO.

Wright, Richard W., and Ricks, David A. (1994). Trends in international business research: Twenty-five years later. *Journal of International Business Studies*, 25(4): 687–701.

Yip, George S. (1995). *Total global strategy*. Englewood Cliffs, NJ: Prentice Hall.

Chapter 3

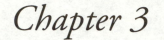

The Global Role of Business

A TALE OF TWO GLOBAL TITANS: ROYAL DUTCH/SHELL GROUP AND GREENPEACE

In both 1994 and 1995, Anglo-Dutch giant Royal Dutch/Shell Group led the Fortune Global 500 list, turning in 1995 profits of $6.9 billion. By the end of 1996, Shell had announced a drop in profits, layoffs, a restructuring plan likely to eliminate 30,000 people in management positions, and a new determination to focus on refining operations. Although Shell predicted that world energy demand could grow by 70% for the next 30 years, it had also become aware that global survival may depend on acquiring new skills, implementing new processes, and restructuring. Two factors may have contributed to this realization.

    First, like other firms in the oil production and refining industries, Shell leaders realize that growth depends on a global workforce and on a capacity to meet global demands, particularly in developing economies where energy growth is greatest. Headquarters staff is expected to be reduced by about 25% to around 3,700, and re-engineering of businesses also has meant downsizing and readjustments. For example, in 1995 the matrix structure formerly used at Shell headquarters was judged to be too bureaucratic and slow for a global market, and it was replaced with a centralized structure that assigns executives oversight for worldwide divisions. Shell Chemical introduced a five-member business management team to coordinate strategy with leaders of operating units worldwide. Low-profit divisions like chemicals are being sold, high-end businesses like refining are garnering more headquarters attention, and plans include new plants in Nanhai, China, and other developing economic areas.

    Competitive pressures on costs and profits are only one of the challenges created by globalization. Royal Dutch/Shell also faced increased scrutiny for its actions and inactions, and was called to public account on two decisions. In both cases, the not-for-profit organization Greenpeace claimed responsibility for calling public attention to Royal Dutch/Shell. The two stories and their aftermath shed considerable light on global shifts in business practices, they demonstrate growing demands that businesses take on social roles, and they show that organizations other than businesses are acting business-like.

In February 1995, Royal Dutch/Shell quietly announced a government-approved plan to sink the Brent Spar, an oil platform in the North Sea. Installed in the 1970s and subsequently made obsolete by an underwater pipeline, the Brent Spar served no useful purpose. Shell proposed to sink the platform and the 100 tons of oil sludge it could not remove, reasoning that the rig would be so far below the surface of the water that it wouldn't affect much sea life. Alerted to the plan, Greenpeace commissioned its own study, arguing that more marine life would be damaged than had been estimated and questioning Shell's claim that dismantling the rig on land would be impossibly difficult and costly. When their plan was ignored, Greenpeace activists escalated their approach, boarding the Brent Spar in April and taking along a satellite feed and video equipment that allowed them to televise pictures of the rig, Shell's forceful ejection of the activists, and water-cannons that kept a Greenpeace helicopter from landing on the rig. Shell leaders' adamant refusal to meet with environmentalists, and escalating commitments to chosen courses of action for both Shell and Greenpeace, attracted ever-wider television audiences, an informal boycott that spread from Germany to the Netherlands and Denmark, internal dissent at Shell, and Shell's eventual decision to retreat from the Brent Spar plan. According to some, this conflict had proved a public relations fiasco for Shell and a bonanza for Greenpeace.

An analysis of Greenpeace shows it is not without business acumen. The study it commissioned, the economic boycott, and its ability to attract worldwide attention by providing satellite videos of an environmentally conscious David fighting eco-insensitive Shell were all part of a plan. Like Shell, Greenpeace is global in scope; it maintains offices in 30 countries and a presence in many more. With an annual income of $130 million, Greenpeace has turned to business practices to realize operating efficiencies. Because it suffered from bureaucracy that demotivated volunteers and paid employees, Greenpeace – like Shell – restructured, downsized, and outsourced. Its decision-making process delegates decisions to nations and regions, but it can coalesce around issues of worldwide concern like the Brent Spar. Long-term strategy and planning at Greenpeace is complemented by structural and operational mechanisms that permit rapid response to emerging crises. For example, Greenpeace installed a worldwide computer network in 1986. This network proved useful in the Brent Spar incident and it was used again to galvanize public opinion against Shell in November of 1995 when Ken Saro-Wiwa and eight other pro-democracy campaigners were hanged in Nigeria. Greenpeace International executive director Thilo Bode claimed the hangings were retaliation for protests against environmental damage in the Niger delta region, damage opponents claimed was caused by Shell. Further, Greenpeace activists felt Shell's importance to the Nigerian economy could have been used to save Saro-Wiwa had the company interceded. Moreover, the publicity tried Shell in the court of public opinion and the results were financial as well as social.

Toronto, Canada, rejected a contract with Shell Canada, the International Finance Corporation canceled its planned participation with Shell to open a $4 billion liquefied natural gas project in Nigeria, and Saro-Wiwa's heirs filed a lawsuit against Shell charging it with complicity in the hangings.

According to an editorial that later appeared in the Oil and Gas Journal, *accusations against Shell and their aftermath made it evident that international oil companies were increasingly being held accountable for misdeeds committed by host country governments. Evidence provided in this chapter suggests that the Shell experience is indicative of growing public expectations that global businesses have a different role to play than 'business as usual.'*

In summary, the Shell examples illustrate a growing call for social, political, and environmental accountability on the part of business organizations. The Greenpeace examples demonstrate a desire on the part of a not-for-profit global organization to use business tactics to resolve challenges that are more nearly global than local or regional. This blending of roles blurs sectoral responsibilities, and seems to suggest that many organizations will be called to greater accountability for their actions in a globalizing world.

Sources: Adapted from: A new political risk. (1996, Feb. 5). *The Oil and Gas Journal*, 94(6): 25; Giant outsmarted. (1995, July 7). *The Wall Street Journal*, pp. A1, 4; Greenpeace means business. (1995, Aug. 19). *The Economist*, pp. 59–60; Layman, Patricia L. (1996, July 29). *Chemical & Engineering News*, 74(31): 25–28; Still sparring. (1996, July 20). *The Economist*, p. 52.

PART I BUSINESS TRADITIONS AND CHALLENGES

Chapter 1 outlined how externalities such as the global economy, technology, culture, politics, environment, and globalization of industries increasingly shape business practices. Chapter 2 examined how these externalities shape structures, processes, and people important to the firm; it also defined the global enterprise, and looked at how global enterprises anticipate or respond to global shifts outside their immediate control. In this chapter, we take a closer look at changes occurring in relationships between external, global events and more internal, firm-specific events to examine how business leaders conceptualize and act on global interdependencies. This chapter opens with three important changes in business/government/society relationships to show why various members of the global community expect new social responsibilities from global businesses. A later section explores what this type of boundary-crossing of sectors means for management traditions practiced according to scientific management, Japanese-style management, and Western European business traditions. Emerging business practices and existing traditions among groups that have attracted limited business attention also are examined to provide a broader perspective on the many engaged in global business. The parallel examination of existing and emerging theories of management and business adopted for this chapter illustrates the additive quality of globalization. This chapter emphasizes that new demands on organizations do not displace traditional demands for profits, for managing tangibles, or for managing straight-forward challenges. Finally, the chapter concludes with a general introduction to theories and practices organizations are using to shape structures, processes, and people responsive to a global world, and takes a look at the functional skills and abilities and self-knowledge required of global managers and employees.

THE GROWING CENTRALITY OF BUSINESS ACTIVITIES

Since their inception, businesses have played important roles in the societies where they operate and many view business, government, and society as the three major components of a civilization. The interactions among these three sectors have varied from nation to nation. Although the degree of separation varies from nation to nation, the Western tradition has been to view these three sectors as separate. In the US, for example, separation between religious and governmental sectors is legally mandated. Conversely, in Saudi Arabia and many other Islamic nations the government is structured around religious law and the state conforms to society's religion. Consistent with the rapid shifts of globalization, the boundaries among existing sectors whether in Saudi Arabia or the West have begun to blur, and as they blur the role of business has taken on more importance in governmental and social sectors, just as roles formerly allocated to business are increasingly played by social, governmental, and religious organizations. Greenpeace's adoption of business practices is but one illustration of the latter point. Many believe role shifts at organizations like Greenpeace and among business enterprises are making business practices more central to life as we know it; this occurs for many reasons, three of which are described below.

Business initiatives

BUSINESSES ARE WELL KNOWN WORLDWIDE

Names like Nestlé, ICI, Unilever, Sony, and Hanson are known throughout the world because these and similar organizations are major players in manufacturing, exporting, and/or investing throughout the world. These practices are pursued by firms headquartered in both the industrialized and the economically developing world, and their combined economic clout is significant. According to Barnet and Cavanagh (1994), 300 companies own an estimated 25% of the world's productive assets. *Business Week's* list of the 'top 100 companies' shows these firms come from large and small countries, e.g., Switzerland and Singapore, and represent many industries including automotives, pharmaceuticals, software, consumer products, commodities, banking, and investment, and health care (see Table 3.1).

BUSINESSES OUTSTRIP GROSS DOMESTIC PRODUCT (GDP)

Additionally, some of the world's largest business organizations generate annual sales greater than the GDP of many nations. Using world GDP and company sales figures for 1995, Sarah Anderson and John Cavanagh (1997) of the Institute for Policy Studies calculated that 51 of the 100 largest economies in the world are global corporations. As shown in Table 3.2, Mitsubishi Corporation is the twenty-second largest economy in the world, leading all but 21 nations in its economic size. The example in Box 3.1 shows how a company's economic clout can shape a nation's policies.

CONTRIBUTIONS TO JOB GROWTH

In addition to their absolute size and financial clout, firms operating on a global scale also are major employers and count 61 million employees in developed countries, and 12 million in the developing world (You ain't seen, 1994). Large, publicly held firms are significant contributors to job growth in the developing world, and for that reason as well as their access to capital resources, they are likely to have considerable economic and political clout in the countries where they operate. Enterprises appearing on published lists of publicly held firms are by no means the only participants in business activities around the globe, however. For example, Chapter 1 showed that private and family-held

TABLE 3.1 The top 50 companies from the *Business Week* 100

Rank 1997	1996		1997 Market value (billions US$)	1996 Revenues (millions US$)
1	1	General Electric	198.09	79,179
2	4	Coca-Cola	169.86	18,546
3	2	Royal/Dutch Shell	168.99	128,174
4	3	Nippon Telegraph & Tele.	151.57	78,320
5	12	Microsoft	148.59	8,671
6	6	Exxon	147.15	119,434
7	15	Intel	124.08	20,847
8	8	Toyota Motor	108.67	108,702
9	10	Merck	108.49	19,828
10	9	Philip Morris	106.58	54,553
11	42	Novartis	93.48	29,310
12	18	Procter & Gamble	93.39	35,284
13	20	IBM	85.91	75,947
14	11	Roche Holding	83.51	12,915
15	5	Bank of Tokyo – Mitsubishi	80.90	46,451
16	40	HSBC Holdings	80.71	28,859
17	13	Johnson & Johnson	79.91	21,620
18	32	Bristol-Myers Squibb	73.38	15,065
19	16	Glaxo Wellcome	70.85	13,025
20	19	Wal-Mart Stores	67.68	106,147
21	25	British Petroleum	67.34	69,851
22	27	Pfizer	64.38	11,306
23	29	American Intl Group	63.57	28,205
24	28	DuPont	61.45	39,689
25	*	Deutsche Telekom	60.97	41,910
26	7	AT&T	59.71	74,525
27	24	PepsiCo	56.31	31,645
28	35	Walt Disney	55.28	18,739
29	30	Mobil	55.03	72,267
30	82	Lloyds TSB Group	53.85	20,372
31	65	SBC Communications	53.64	13,898
32	49	Berkshire Hathaway	52.98	10,500
33	48	Unilever	52.64	52,067
34	39	Citicorp	52.56	32,605
35	23	Hewlett–Packard	52.53	38,420
36	52	Eli Lilly	51.65	7,346
37	77	Gillette	49.52	9,697
38	31	Nestlé	48.93	48,932
39	56	American Home Products	48.92	14,088
40	54	Abbott Laboratories	48.73	11,013
41	47	Allianz	47.96	56,577
42	72	SmithKline Beecham	47.32	12,375
43	57	Fannie Mae	46.42	25,054
44	43	Chevron	45.74	38,691
45	53	British Telecom	45.55	23,695
46	38	BellSouth	44.98	19,040
47	63	Cisco Systems	44.96	4,096
48	33	Ford Motor	44.66	146,991
49	51	Amoco	44.17	32,726
50	16	Sumitomo Bank	43.40	22,810

*Deutsche Telekom was created in 1996.
Source: Rankings and market value from The Top 100 Companies. (1997, July 7). *Business Week*, p. 53; revenues from Fortune Global 500. (1997, Aug. 4); homepages for Microsoft, AIG, Eli Lilly & Cisco Systems.

BOX 3.1:   BHI CORPORATION, BELIZE

Englishman Michael Ashcroft holds a 65% stake in BHI, Belize's largest trading company and full or partial owner of Belize Bank (100%), Belize Telecommunication (26%), Belize Electricity (20%), Belize International Services (50%), Belize Food Holdings (27%), and Great Belize Productions (38%). Together, these firms manage 40% of Belize's commercial bank deposits, 50% of Belize's frozen orange and grapefruit juice concentrates, and all of Belize's telecommunications, commercial electric power, and television stations. In Belize, Mr Ashcroft is alternately viewed as a hero who created jobs for Belize's population of 200,000 and as a behind-the-scenes manipulator who shaped government policy to favor his own interests in creating an offshore financial services industry.

Source: De Cordoba, José. (1996, Sept. 19). Sometimes it's hard to be top banana in a small republic. *The Wall Street Journal*, p. A14.

---

firms as well as smaller firms called global start-ups also have taken initiative to become global participants. In Table 3.3, we find evidence of growing knowledge of little-known but large firms and concentrated business/family interests (other than real estate) throughout Asia. The sources from which these data are drawn list hundreds of Asian individuals and families whose wealth is estimated at over $1 billion; this wealth is fueling industries ranging from banking to manufacturing to real estate and retailing.

The rush to capitalism

The fall of the Berlin Wall in 1989 touched off a worldwide rush to capitalism that has left few unaffected. The resulting emphasis on consumerism, entrepreneurism, and their conceptual cousins has turned world attention to entities established for the purpose of generating wealth: businesses. Symptoms of worldwide embrace of business are increasing enrollments in schools of business, growth in business formation among women and members of minority groups, and business activities on the part of organizations that are not businesses. In fall 1996, England's Oxford University welcomed its first class of MBA students; the number of women-owned businesses in the US, Europe, Japan, and in the developing economies is increasing; and in June 1996, the Catholic Church launched a mass-licensing program to sell reproductions of Vatican art and other holdings. Commenting on the latter, Kevin Locke, SJ, confirmed the goal is to make money and 'use appropriate business techniques for a pastoral purpose' (Gucci, Armani, and . . ., 1996).

TABLE 3.2   World's top 100 economies, 1995

	Country/Corporation	GDP/sales ($million)		Country/Corporation	GDP/sales ($million)
1	United States	6,648,013	51	*Daimler–Benz*	72,253
2	Japan	4,590,971	52	*IBM*	71,940
3	Germany	2,045,991	53	Malaysia	70,626
4	France	1,330,381	54	*Matsushita Electric*	70,454
5	Italy	1,024,634	55	*General Electric*	70,028
6	United Kingdom	1,017,306	56	Singapore	68,949
7	Brazil	554,587	57	*Tomen*	67,809
8	Canada	542,954	58	Colombia	67,266
9	China	522,172	59	*Mobil*	64,767
10	Spain	482,841	60	Philippines	64,162
11	Mexico	377,115	61	Iran	63,716
12	Russian Federation	376,555	62	*Nissan Motor*	62,618
13	Korea, Rep.	376,505	63	*Volkswagen Group*	61,487
14	Australia	331,990	64	*Siemens Group*	60,673
15	Netherlands	329,768	65	Venezuela	58,257
16	India	293,606	66	*British Petroleum*	56,992
17	Argentina	281,922	67	*Bank of Tokyo-Mitsubishi*	55,243
18	Switzerland	260,352	68	*Chrysler*	53,195
19	Belgium	227,550	69	*Philip Morris*	53,139
20	Austria	196,546	70	*Toshiba*	53,089
21	Sweden	196,441	71	Ireland	52,060
22	*Mitsubishi*	184,510	72	Pakistan	52,011
23	*Mitsui and Co.*	181,661	73	Chile	51,957
24	Indonesia	174,640	74	*Nichimen*	50,882
25	*Itochu*	169,300	75	New Zealand	50,777
26	*General Motors*	168,829	76	*Tokyo Electric Power*	50,343
27	*Sumitomo*	167,662	77	Peru	50,077
28	*Marubeni*	161,184	78	*Kanematsu*	49,878
29	Denmark	146,076	79	*Unilever*	49,638
30	Thailand	143,209	80	*Nestlé*	47,767
31	*Ford Motor*	137,137	81	*Sony*	47,619
32	Hong Kong	131,881	82	*Fiat Group*	46,467
33	Turkey	131,014	83	*VEBA Group*	46,278
34	South Africa	121,888	84	*NEC*	45,593
35	Saudi Arabia	117,236	85	*Honda Motor*	44,090
36	*Toyoto Motor*	111,139	86	*UAP-Union des Assurances*	43,929
37	*Royal Dutch/Shell*	109,853	87	*Allianz Worldwide*	43,486
38	Norway	109,568	88	Egypt	42,923
39	*Exxon*	107,893	89	Algeria	41,941
40	*Nissho Iwai*	97,963	90	*Elf Aquitaine Group*	41,729
41	Finland	97,961	91	Hungary	41,374
42	*Wal-Mart*	93,627	92	*Philips Group*	40,146
43	Poland	92,580	93	*Fujitsu*	39,007
44	Ukraine	91,307	94	*Indust. Bank of Japan*	38,694
45	Portugal	87,257	95	*Deutsche Bank Group*	38,418
46	*Hitachi*	84,233	96	*Renault Group*	36,876
47	*Nippon Tel and Tel*	82,002	97	*Mitsubishi Motors*	36,674
48	*AT&T*	79,609	98	*du Pont de Nemours*	36,508
49	Israel	77,777	99	*Mitsubishi Electric*	36,408
50	Greece	77,721	100	*Hoechst Group*	36,407

Note: Company sales figures are for 1995; country GDP figures are for 1994. Corporations are *italicized*.
Source: Anderson, Sarah, and Cavanagh, John. 1997. *The top 200: The rise of global corporate power*. Washington, DC: Institute for Policy Studies, calculated from data in *Forbes* magazine and World Bank, *World Development Report 1996*.

TABLE 3.3   Asia's billionaires in the $5 billion club

Name	Nation	Industry/business example
Sultan of Brunei	Brunei	Oil and gas/Brunei Investment Agency
Dhanin Chearavanont	Thailand	Diversified/TelecomAsia
Chung Ju Yung	South Korea	Diversified/Hyundai
Robert Kuok	Malaysia	Diversified/Kerry Group
Yoshiaki Tautsumi	Japan	Diversified/Seibu Railway
Li Ka-shing and family	Hong Kong	Diversified/Cheung Kong Holdings
Suharto family	Indonesia	Diversified/Satelindo
Tsai Wan-lin and family	Taiwan	Insurance/Cathay Life
Eka Tjipta Widjaja	Indonesia	Diversified/Sinar Mas
Wonowidjojo family	Indonesia	Cigarettes/Gudang Garam
Wang Yung-ching	Taiwan	Diversified/Formosa Plastics

Sources: At a crossroads: Asia. (1997, July 28). *Forbes*, pp. 106–115; Hiscock, Geoff. 1997. *Asia's wealth club*. London: Allen and Unwin; How to become a billionaire (1997, Aug.) *Asian Business Review*, pp. 33–49; The *Forbes*, 1998 list of global billionaires can be searched on-line at: http://www.forbes.com

Nongovernmental organizations loan funds to the disenfranchised who use it to start businesses, university faculties are enjoined to focus on customer service, and government entities are under pressure to provide objective evidence of successful service delivery. These examples demonstrate growing pressures for non-business organizations to adopt a myriad of practices formerly associated primarily with businesses. Thus, there is increased pressure to adopt business practices to settings that were not established to generate wealth.

Whereas firms in the developing economies once concentrated their energies on internal initiatives, increasingly they seek opportunities beyond national borders. Their success is evident in projections indicating that emerging nations will generate 50% of world GDP by 2010 as compared to 24% in 1994 (Farrell, 1994). Although this rush to consumerism and business activities has received most attention in the former Soviet Union and in developing economies in Asia such as China, Thailand, Malaysia, or Indonesia, it is important to note that Latin American countries similarly have joined the fray and many have undertaken reforms to facilitate market economics. Trade within Latin America increased from less than $4 billion US in 1990 to over $8 billion in 1993, providing new opportunities for firms in those countries, and making them an attractive market for foreign direct investment (FDI). As countries like these develop economically, the world business environment becomes more diverse, creating new or unaccustomed demands for businesses. As business opportunities increase among consumers and firms in the economically developing world, centrality of business activities also increases. This centrality has come with a price: increased expectations that businesses play a more active role in shaping the societies in which they operate.

BOX 3.2:   THE PEPSI CHALLENGE

In May 1992 Pepsi-Cola Products, Philippines, Inc. introduced a promotional campaign called 'Number Fever' offering to pay 1 million pesos (roughly $36,400 US) to those finding the numeral '349' stamped inside a Pepsi bottle cap. This must have seemed a small fortune to the 60% of Filipinos who live below the poverty line.

According to Pepsi representatives, a computer software flaw caused the number '349' to be stamped erroneously on quite a few bottle caps: five hundred thousand, to be exact. Pepsi was subsequently swamped with overjoyed holders of number 349, but calculated that potential claims could total $1.9 billion – equivalent to 8% of Pepsi's worldwide sales of $25 billion in 1993. Realizing the problem they had on their hands, organizational leaders rationally explained the error. But would-be prize-winners were not satisfied with the explanation and responded by forming the Alliance 349. Public rallies were held, lawyers hired, and Pepsi was pilloried in the press with claims of double-dealing. Public outrage and skepticism at Pepsi explanations escalated until Pepsi trucks were dynamited and the Manila Pepsi plant was set on fire. Interestingly, police accused Pepsi of having hired the saboteurs to discredit Alliance 349. Was Pepsi guilty of anything more than a colossal mistake? Filipinos thought so, and public censure of Pepsi continued, uniting Filipinos in a way few other events have been able to do. Pepsi's experience with this promotion is reflective of conditions organizations face in a globalizing world: change occurs rapidly, complexities have increased, and uncertainties are many.

Blurring sectoral boundaries

The rush to embrace market economics also is reflected in governmental action. Many governments have voluntarily transferred some part of their authority to the business sector via privatization – the transfer of ownership from government hands to private hands in service industries such as airlines, banking, utilities, or telecommunications and in manufacturing industries ranging from low-tech textiles to high-tech aircraft. According to Peter Drucker (1987), business ownership of these important services increases the power of business when the public depend upon them to get to work, manage their money, heat their homes, and communicate with one another. By creating business/government partnerships, governments further involve businesses in decisions formerly made by politicians. Government interests in facilitating business formation have led to evident willingness to blend business, government, and civic interests. For

---

BOX 3.3:   TAKE IT TO THE PUBLIC

Public reports of real or perceived business transgressions such as those Greenpeace identified at Royal/Dutch Shell increasingly come from insiders or 'whistle-blowing' on the part of employees. Often, these reports are carried globally where the firm then defends itself in the court of public opinion. The employee's role in the flap often becomes secondary to the firm's exposure.

For example, Morgan Grenfell's Asset Management group promoted and then suspended top fund manager Nicola Horlick, claiming she had engaged in a serious breach of confidence. In turn, Horlick resigned, but having changed her mind the next day, she brought the press with her to record her demand for reinstatement. Morgan Grenfell and parent company Deutsche Bank AG expressed reluctance to engage in a press battle, but may have had little choice. The press sometimes lionized Ms Horlick as a business superwoman raising five children, and the public seemed to sympathize because one of the children was very ill. Investors worldwide doubtless view this dust-up with alarm, wondering if their assets belong in a firm where real or perceived irregularities have occurred.

---

example, once the US trade embargo on Vietnam was lifted, the grounds of Hanoi's ancient university were used to paint Coca-Cola advertisements for display throughout the nation, and the steps of the Hanoi opera soon were occupied by a pair of two-story plastic bottles proclaiming Coke's legal return to Vietnam.

Increases in the numbers of businesses created, shifts of government roles to the private sector, and criss-crossing of external boundaries have led to real and perceived increases in the importance of business to society. This exacts costs from business organizations including greater public scrutiny of business activities, and growing demand for organizations to be responsive to the societies that support them. PepsiCo experienced this demand in a very concrete way, producing a different kind of 'Pepsi challenge' to the one advertisements usually portray (Box 3.2).

The Pepsi challenge is one challenge of globalization: organizations worldwide are frequently held accountable for real and perceived public transgressions even at a time when the potential for error has grown. As Chapter 9 demonstrates, public scrutiny of business and other activities has become possible because of improved modes of global communication. The example in Box 3.3 proves this point.

Finally, as the opening case for this chapter shows, nongovernmental organizations like Greenpeace intervene with public and governmental decisions to alert the global community to issues of political and legal note. These and similar activities occurring in all six global environments have expanded the roles businesses are expected to play globally, and increased demands for social responsibility from firms.

The following section explores how this expanding role is reshaping relationships between business and a larger global society, altering managerial habits, and leading to new theories of management for a global world. As indicated earlier, these changes have been additive rather than substitutes for existing theories of management. The challenges of merging theories and practices become clearer with consideration of the following questions central to business organizations: What is it businesses should do? To whom should they answer? And how should they function in society?

EXPANDING NOTIONS OF BUSINESS ROLES AND RESPONSIBILITIES

Organizations in a globalizing world are asked to take on social as well as business roles. This occurs for many reasons, one of which is that people believe they are the only entity capable of achieving social changes sought. Businesses too are increasingly aware of the environmental agenda. Rolf Gerling, of Germany's Gerling Group of Insurance Companies, claims that his organization, taking its lead from Greenpeace, is alive to the full consequences of environmental degradation. There is a growing belief even among transnational groups that it is businesses rather than environmental groups that will solve the world's problems.

Businesses as change agents

Businesses are encouraged to take on socially responsible roles because it is only they who have the collective clout to protect the natural environment and resolve global social problems (Hawken, 1993). Edward Simon, President of Herman Miller maintains that 'business is the only institution that has a chance, as far as I can see, to fundamentally improve the injustice that exists in the world.' Global businesses are enjoined to become community members (Brown, 1992), and even to become a type of global conscience (Roy and Regelbrugge, 1995). A number of these demands doubtless arise from evidence showing that business organizations shape more than businesses. Some of these efforts are purposeful, others are not. For example, the AT&T-sponsored Africa One project is intended to bring telecommunications services to all of Africa; it has the potential to change life for the many Africans who have never used a telephone, but changes in daily life in Africa are doubtless secondary to AT&T's business expansion goals. William Clay Ford, Jr, meanwhile, heir apparent at Ford Motor Company, frequently expresses deep concern over environmental issues, and according to a report appearing in the September 13, 1996, *Wall Street Journal*, he would like to find a way for Ford to play a role in developing schools, highways, and hospitals for nations that are moving toward industrialization.

Levels of social responsibility

Smith and Quelch (1992) assert that all people across all circumstances have three levels of duty: avoid causing harm, prevent harm, and do good. These individual levels of duty also are reflected in organizational action worldwide and are represented by the following philosophies of business:

(a) profit maximization and social irresponsibility;

(b) profit maximization and self-regulation where organizations observe a moral minimum;

(c) take profit as a necessary goal and strive to do some good as well;

(d) take profit as a necessary goal but aim to be the moral champion via active involvement in causes related and unrelated to the company's activities (Smith and Quelch, 1992).

This list suggests broad latitude for firms with regard to social responsibilities, but breadth of choice may be shrinking in a globalizing world. The three important challenges to businesses described below show how globalization of information technology, of culture, of political action, and of business reshape options for social responsibility.

According to Anthony Sampson, author of *Company Man* (1995), the forerunners of today's corporations were collaborative arrangements among European merchants who shared costs of foreign ventures during the Crusades. The charters of these and early seventeenth-century business organizations were to return profits to owners and other shareholders, and those that survived were successful in returning wealth to owners. The less successful fell prey: to pirates, to each other, to natives who could resist colonization, to global weather, or to other forces. According to John Keay, author of *The honourable company: a history of the English East India Company* (1991), at the height of its influence in the early nineteenth century, the English East India Company controlled nearly half of the world's trade in a business empire that stretched from England to India, and throughout Asia. In the same period, the Dutch East India Company established itself as a rival firm by concentrating its efforts on supplying spices and other valuables to a willing European market. Wealth creation remains an important business goal. However, as the following sections show, global changes are redefining wealth, the role of shareholders, and the degree of autonomy businesses and other types of organizations are allowed when engaged in wealth creation.

Measures of wealth

Wealth is often viewed narrowly as readily measurable and tangible assets such as money, real estate, gold, diamonds, etc. In the business world, success has often been measured

---

BOX 3.4:   ECONOMIC VALUE ADDED AT ELI LILLY

Success in the pharmaceutical industry often depends on technological break-throughs, particularly new drugs capable of reducing the discomfort of symptoms or cures for diseases that reduce the quality of human life. Like other drug companies, Eli Lilly invests considerable assets in research and development to discover these drugs, an expense of at least $500 million in 1996. The question EVA forces managers to ask is: To what extent are we creating shareholder wealth with this $500 million investment? This is examined by looking at the cost of capital and returns to it. Although this is not the case, the following hypothetical situation illustrates how this occurs:

If Lilly were to borrow the full $500 million from a bank at 10% interest, but provide returns to shareholders on that $500 million of 9%, then the firm would be destroying rather than creating wealth. In fact, the only way the firm could produce wealth at a 10% rate of investment is to provide returns on the borrowed money of more than 10%.

Lilly has encouraged top executives to calculate EVA on major capital investments by introducing a plan that pays bonuses when wealth is created, and expects to expand the plan to more managers as EVA becomes better understood as a measure of wealth creation.

Source: Eli Lilly is making shareholders rich. How? By linking pay to EVA. (1996, Sept. 9). *Fortune*, pp. 173–174.

against returns on investments (ROI) on sales (ROS), on assets (ROA), or similar measures that reflect success in generating tangible wealth. An emerging tangible measure of firm performance is called Economic Value Added (EVA), so-called because EVA is the operating profit of a company minus the cost of capital. The example of Eli Lilly (Box 3.4) shows how and why one firm uses EVA to measure wealth creation.

ZERO-SUM ASSUMPTIONS OF WEALTH CREATION

Whatever the financial measure used, the tradition in many profit-oriented businesses has been to assume that wealth creation requires engagement in what is called a 'zero-sum' game of business competition where gains almost necessarily must come with actual losses or failed gains for one's competitors. Put in more concrete terms, if wealth is viewed as a pie, we can readily see that there are a finite number of ways the pie can be sliced. The finite sum of the pie represents a zero-sum position because competitors carve up the pie leaving nothing for those that cannot compete at their level.

INFINITE-SUM ASSUMPTIONS OF WEALTH CREATION

In a globalizing world, wealth is increasingly and more broadly believed to include less tangible and less measurable assets such as quality of life, happiness, or human progress as well as the tangible yields such as ROI described above. When added to the pie of wealth, and unlike tangible forms of wealth that are finite, intangible forms of wealth can be infinite. Happiness, for example, is abundant and, in theory, it is available to all. Commitment to less tangible forms of wealth is evident among Western Europeans who are resisting longer work hours; among Asians struggling to sustain family relationships against the rationality of business; among US workers calling for balance between work life and personal life; among Africans who expect kinspeople to support extended families with profits rather than to reinvest them. In a world where wealth is defined in different ways, it is important to look at the role of tangible and intangible wealth in business, and according to Paul Hawken (1993), founder of gardening retailer Smith and Hawken, it has become important to ask: If business adds value, then what is the value it adds? One perspective is that business activities have a potential to add intangible as well as tangible wealth to communities.

COMBINING ZERO- AND INFINITE-SUM PROPOSITIONS FOR BUSINESS

Several challenges arise as intangibles become part of the business success equation. First, performance is more difficult to measure quantitatively than is a more concrete outcome measure such as ROI. Second, expanding the scope of their results to include intangibles forces managers to enter new territory. Finally, inasmuch as intangibles can be infinite, the nature of the competitive game changes with an expanded definition of wealth. What had been win/lose assumptions of zero-sum competitive position now can be complemented with win/win solutions where every party can gain and the total size of the gains is enlarged to define an 'infinite sum.' By returning to the analogy of the pie, we see that the infinite-sum approach assumes that the pie itself can be increased in size so that it serves more people. Additionally, the contents of the pie can be changed to enhance its flavor or richness such that a smaller slice is sufficient for more, or we might suggest a low- or no-cost alternative to the pie that proves more attractive to some consumers. For example, in the case of businesses, a possibility available when cash incentives are not available is to offer options like rewards or recognition or time that may be more important to people than money. The latter option is particularly useful in societies where people have money but little time available to enjoy it. Changes like these in the nature of the competitive 'game' also create challenges for managers, many of whom are ill equipped to develop win/win positions where there are multiple victors and no losers. A recent example of a win/win solution is evident in the United Auto Workers (UAW) 1996 contract with US auto makers (see Box 3.5).

Increased scrutiny of businesses and heightened desire for businesses to provide

BOX 3.5:   WIN/WIN SOLUTIONS FOR US AUTO MAKERS AND THE UAW

The most adversarial US union/business relationships traditionally are found in the auto industry. Increased competition from global firms are driving quality up and auto costs down. Among the highest for any US industry, auto labor costs were under review by auto makers. Auto workers, on the other hand, wanted job guarantees to protect jobs from plant shutdowns and outsourcing to other nations or non-union domestic shops. Restructuring at Ford and Chrysler had reduced their labor costs, but lagging productivity at General Motors led to pessimism that they would agree to job guarantees. However, following talks at GM, the firm and the United Auto Workers (UAW) reached an agreement billed as 'win/win' because GM gained more flexibility for remaining competitive in a global world and workers gained unexpected job guarantees. Contract renewals for GM workers reviewed in 1998 required additional efforts to find proposals acceptable to workers and management. GM currently uses 47 worker hours to produce a car compared to Nissan's 28 worker hours per car, and this raises the cost of a GM car to $700 more than Nissan – the industry's lowest-cost producer. By comparison, Chrysler produces a car in 38 work hours, and Ford produces it in 41 hours.

Source: Blumenstein, Rebecca, and Christian, Nichole M. (1996, Dec. 9). UAW contract appears to provide win-win situation. *The Wall Street Journal*, p. B6; Vlasic, Bill. (1997, June 23). GM can't afford to budge. *Business Week*, p. 46.

tangible and intangible returns to society come from groups like Greenpeace that perceive themselves to have a stake in organizational outcomes. Their activities have led organizations to look as much to external stakeholders as to stockholders for direction, a point explored more fully below.

Shareholders and stakeholders

Shareholders are investors who provide firm capital; they can be private shareholders or public ones. Although public shareholders typically hold their investments in the form of stocks or bonds in the company, this common form of ownership does not necessarily lead to similar shareholder behaviors. For example, US CEOs are rarely recognized by the public or their shareholders; an example from India (Box 3.6) demonstrates a different orientation there.

BOX 3.6:   RELIANCE INDUSTRIES OF INDIA

Shareholder response to Dhirubhai Ambani, head of Reliance Industries Inc. – India's fastest growing industrial organization – stands in sharp contrast to shareholder response to executives elsewhere. Mr Ambani is viewed as a hero to his 6.7 million shareholders, thousands of whom turn up to see him at annual meetings. According to Suman Dubey's (1994) account in *The Wall Street Journal*, Mr Ambani is 'almost a cult figure in India.'

Source: Dubey, Suman (1994, Nov. 28) India's Reliance sees vision shift to Ambani sons. *The Wall Street Journal*, p. A9A.

TRADITIONS AND TRENDS AMONG US SHAREHOLDERS

In contrast to India, individual US shareholders are more passive. Traditionally, they have liquidated shares in firms that do not perform according to expectations and purchased shares in financially successful firms. This tradition is undergoing change: increasingly, shareholders' activities in the US have escalated to include disrupting annual meetings, lobbying in office headquarters, and private or public campaigns to discredit the firm and/or intervene with managerial decisions. Institutional shareholders, particularly managers of large pension and mutual funds, also are increasingly voicing concerns over corporate governance, and according to a *Business Week* poll reported in December 1995, 45% of giant shareholders expected their influence to grow; none expected a decreased role. In the US, institutional shareholders of ITT, Baxter International, and United States Shoe are credited with pressuring those firms to restructure and replace top executives, and K-Mart CEO Joseph Antonini was demoted following years of shareholder agitation against him (Shareholder activists, 1995).

TRADITIONS AND TRENDS AMONG SHAREHOLDERS OUTSIDE THE US

In Europe, shareholders who could previously be counted on to remain silent now are calling for 'corporate governance' to reshape what they perceive to be overly generous executive pay packages, poor economic performance, and poor managerial performance (Viotzthum, 1995). As is true in the US, increased activism from both individual and institutional investors has had mixed results worldwide. Shareholder activist Ekkehard Wenger filed suit against Deutsche Bank in Germany, claiming a share-options plan for top managers was too generous; shareholders pressured Cie de Suez for corporate change and forced the resignation of Pierre Suard as chairman of Alcatel-Alsthom SA after he was indicted for misuse of corporate funds; and small shareholder groups sued Mario Conde of Banco

Espanol de Credito SA for bad management after a bank seizure in 1993, blocked a pay increase for board members at Cristalaria Espanola SA, and took control of Puleva SA dairy group to implement a new strategic plan (Corporate governance is bringing change, 1995). Corporate governance is under similar review in Britain, Japan, Italy, Portugal, and worldwide scrutiny of corporations is growing. In Japan, for example, where outside influences have had limited historical impact on firms, businesses are the subjects of greater stakeholder pressure (Steadman, Zimmerer, and Green, 1995). Tensions between shareholder and stakeholder interests are increasingly global; the example in Box 3.7 shows how.

BOX 3.7:   THE 'RHINE' MODEL VERSUS THE 'ANGLO-SAXON' MODEL

In November 1996, the Amsterdam Stock Exchange issued a report that clarified two models of company/shareholder relations. The 'Rhine' model puts shareholder interests secondary to larger interests of the company and its employees, but the 'Anglo-Saxon' model puts shareholder interests first. The report suggested that shareholders in the Netherlands prefer the latter model, and it calls for giving shareholders new rights such as influence over the agenda for annual meetings and input into membership for the company's board. Dutch firms cited shareholder interests when explaining decisions made. For example, Philips Electronics NV cited shareholder value as a reason to restructure the company, and paper and packaging firm KNP BT cited shareholder interests when it announced a decision to withdraw financial support from its money-losing KNP Leykam division.

Source: Schiffrin, Anya. (1996, Nov. 1). Dutch firms debate whether employees or shareholders should get priority. *The Wall Street Journal*, p. A7A.

STAKEHOLDERS

Improved technologies, especially telecommunications, facilitate almost unimpeded information flows across borders, making it possible for many to monitor and intervene in organizational decisions. Although the latter may not own stock, they often perceive themselves to have a stake in firm decisions, and hence they are more appropriately called 'stakeholders.' Broadly defined, stakeholders are those individuals and groups who have a direct stake in the firm, e.g., employees, labor unions, stockholders, and those whose stake is less direct but nonetheless perceived to be important. Stakeholders in a decision might include members of the immediate geographic community near a global firm, members of any community where the company's products are sold, and increasingly members of the global community affected by business activities.

Although stockholders can be expected to encourage organizations to yield profits, similar interest cannot be assumed among stakeholders. Stakeholder groups like Greenpeace mount costly product boycotts, demonstrations, and take illegal actions against firms whose operations are perceived to violate social norms. Demonstrating against military control in Myanmar (Burma), US university students organized by campus are credited with Pepsi's decision to abandon current efforts there, and other US firms like Amoco, Levi Strauss, Liz Claiborne, Eddie Bauer, and Reebok International have similarly avoided protests by withdrawing from the country. In view of improved access to information, we can reasonably expect that more stakeholders will find it possible to concern themselves with business activities. Moreover, cross-cultural differences in what is perceived as 'right' or 'good' are likely to generate additional complexity for organizations, even those that intend to be socially responsible.

BALANCING CONFLICTING DEMANDS

According to John Naisbitt in *Global paradox* (1994), convincing socially conscious stakeholders of responsible and ethical behavior is an important challenge for global firms. Moreover, business organizations may find it difficult to take on these roles. First, it may be difficult to discern what is appropriately responsible behavior in a global sphere. Naisbitt credits Joseph Badaracco, Jr with observing that the real challenge may come not from the choice between clear and evident rights and wrongs but among hierarchies of goods. As the example in Box 3.8 indicates, choosing among a hierarchy of goods is not new to business.

Similar dilemmas face global organizations, and they too arise when national norms

---

BOX 3.8: CADBURY'S DILEMMA

Writing for the *Harvard Business Review* in 1987, Adrian Cadbury, head of Cadbury Schweppes PLC, described a dilemma his grandfather faced. So strong was his opposition to the Boer War in South Africa, the senior Cadbury bought and financed the only British newspaper that opposed the conflict. Since he also was opposed to gambling, he eliminated horse racing information from the paper. Subsequent declines in circulation caused Cadbury to rethink his position. In pursuing what he felt were dual goods of active opposition to the war and opposition to horse racing, Cadbury faced the possibility that the paper would fail. The senior Cadbury reintroduced racing results, concluding it was better to indirectly endorse gambling than to let bankruptcy silence the paper's anti-war voice.

Source: Adapted from: Cadbury, Adrian (1987, Sept./Oct.). Ethical managers make their own rules. *Harvard Business Review*, pp. 69–73.

collide at a world level. Withdrawal from a country for political reasons costs employees jobs or provides opportunity for remaining competitors to build market share; refusal to hire children may force them to seek other work that is unsafe or abusive. Any transition to being both profitable and socially responsible will be more difficult for some firms than for others. For example, US-based consumer-products company Sara Lee is profitable, but leaders view it as a committed member of its communities: it gives away 2% of pre-tax profits (on about $18 billion in 1995 revenues); it sponsors a diversity program to ensure that women and members of ethnic minorities advance to managerial position; it applies US safety and environmental standards to its plants throughout the world; and it even expects its senior managers to engage in voluntary work.

CORPORATE PHILANTHROPY

Philanthropy is defined as a love of humankind manifested by actions that have a practical benefit for people, and corporate philanthropy includes providing cash or other services to projects ranging from education, parks, and the arts to improving the quality of life in local and global communities. As US firms have expanded abroad, they also have increased their rate of corporate giving abroad and over half of US Fortune 500 firms have or expect to increase philanthropic contributions abroad. The concept and practice of corporate philanthropy is new to many organizations, but growing involvement in the global community has encouraged many businesses to develop philanthropic as well as profit goals. For example, in Japan corporate philanthropy is unusual but by 1994 'about 400 Japanese companies reported an *average* of over $4 million in contributions abroad' (Roy and Regelbrugge, 1995, p. 10). The Hitachi Foundation was developed to encourage this type of community involvement among businesses worldwide. Its statement of purpose (Box 3.9) illustrates a growing commitment among firms to 'act global' by being philanthropic.

BOX 3.9:   THE HITACHI FOUNDATION

Hitachi Ltd of Tokyo founded the Hitachi Foundation in 1985 as a nonprofit, philanthropic organization with a mission to promote social responsibility through supporting efforts by individuals, institutions, and communities to participate effectively in a global society. It maintains a $2.3 million annual giving program, making grants . . . for projects in education, community development, and global citizenship.

Source: Hitachi Foundation, 1509 22nd St NW, Washington, DC, 20037-1073, USA.

The above examples of philanthropic giving illustrate changes in processes experienced by global firms: new demands that businesses become community members as well as autonomous business actors. Although firms like Shell Oil have long been aware that philanthropic programs can be less expensive than the time, money, and social image forfeited to social protest (Mescon and Tilson, 1987), the opening case demonstrates that this kind of learning is not always generalizable. However, according to a 1987 study reported by Wokutch and Spencer, philanthropy has a payoff even among firms engaged in perceived or actual social transgressions. This study of 130 large manufacturing firms showed that public perceptions of corporate social responsibility are influenced more by the philanthropic activities of the firm than by commission of illegal activities.

Autonomy and community

In his study of Western industrialized firms involved in international joint ventures, Janger (1980) found a bias toward autonomy that made it difficult for these firms to join forces with others in joint ventures. This finding is consistent with the fierce sense of individualism characteristic of the US, and with the tradition that suggests competition is a zero-sum game from which emerge clear winners and losers. Most businesses in and from the US still prefer to be autonomous and free-standing because they equate autonomy with the control believed to affect winning. According to Chris Brewster (1995), the 'frontier mentality' reflected in a 'private enterprise' culture is a belief in 'rights to manage' that vests most authority in management. Antagonism toward labor unions evident in the US is less usual in European countries where companies are less autonomous. Similarly, firms in Japan are interconnected with government and each other through *keiretsu* arrangements, as are South Korean firms involved in *chaebols*. While it remains important to recognize that the degree of organizational autonomy may vary according to national culture, it is also important to bear in mind that profit-seeking organizations usually command high degrees of decision-making autonomy. Threats to autonomy, to profit goals, and to corporate governance have relevance globally because they alter reasons for and ways of doing business. For example, having lost their battle with the government in Tiananmen Square, Chinese students and workers shifted their efforts to the business sector, demanding better wages and work conditions as well as a greater role in corporate governance (Lindorff, 1994).

Western firms emphasizing profit maximization are being moved toward greater social responsibility. At the same time, global forces also are encouraging greater profit-seeking behavior on the part of firms with a more traditional commitment to other, often social, goals. In some cases, family-oriented priorities among the overseas Chinese are giving way to profit-seeking; full employment in formerly communist countries is giving way to capital pursuits; and collective interests in communist China are caving in to private enterprise. An example of this rush to capitalism was business behavior following the death of Deng Xiaoping in February 1997. Deng initiated bold reforms in 1978 that catapulted China into the global economy, coining the phrase 'to get rich is glorious.' Chinese interest in getting rich was tested the day following Deng's death, which found most hard at work. Customers at Beijing Bank in Hong Kong continued to deposit money; after a short dip, stock exchanges in Hong Kong and Shanghai recovered to close higher the next day; and business in almost all sectors went on at its usual frenetic pace. Pressures to move away from traditions and toward market economics also are evident in India, where managers at Tata companies have traditionally displayed a high degree of social responsibility by providing lifetime employment, free housing, education, and medical care to employees or locating water wells and power plants in villages near their plants. But Ratan Tata faced a challenge to balance this degree of social responsibility against profits of 3.7% (India's Mr. Business, 1994).

In summary, to the extent that businesses accept or are forced to accept an enlarged role as global community members and leaders, become answerable to external stakeholders worldwide, or take on goals that include generating intangibles, these new roles increase dependencies and uncertainties for business, government, and society. The rapid pace of change may mean that no amount of experience with any of these challenges will ensure success. A concluding point is that all organizations are likely to see a reason to balance between profits and other more social roles prescribed for a global world. The section to follow demonstrates how the need to balance conflicting demands in a global world have the capacity to fundamentally alter every aspect of organizational life.

BUSINESS AND COMMUNITY MODELS OF ORGANIZATIONS
Dominant business practices in the US

The fundamentals of organizational life as defined by dominant practice in the US appear under the title 'the corporate business model' (Figure 3.1). Attributes of organization popularized in the early twentieth century – particularly in the US – emerged from theories of organizations meant to improve efficiencies. A legacy of Frederick Taylor's principles of 'scientific management' is that scientific method can be used to analyze and identify the single best way to accomplish work (Box 3.10). Once that 'one best way' is discovered, workers can be scientifically trained to repeat prescribed functions, and thus workers become – like the machines they operate – cogs in the industrial process.

Writing at the same time as Taylor, Henri Fayol also sought to uncover universal truths applicable to business settings, focusing his attention on the science of management. Fayol is credited with introducing the five managerial universals of planning, organizing, coordinating, controlling, and commanding, and suggested how these management functions could best be achieved. For example, the ability to command is

> **BOX 3.10: FEATURES OF BUREAUCRACY AND SCIENTIFIC MANAGEMENT AS 'ONE BEST WAY'**
>
> ---
>
> 1 Division of labor or specialization occurs – people are trained as experts in narrow areas.
> 2 Tasks are standardized to perform the same job in exactly the same way.
> 3 Hierarchy of authority is established.
> 4 Unity of command is established so no employee answers to more than one boss.
> 5 Span of control is limited to no more than seven for any one supervisor.
> 6 Line and staff responsibilities are divided – line makes decisions, staff advises.
> 7 Decentralization locates authority at the lowest level possible without losing control over critical issues.
> 8 Structure is established according to purpose, function, geography, or by customer served to organize work in logical groupings.
> 9 Activities of the manager include planning, organizing, leading, coordinating, controlling.

facilitated by a clear chain of command where orders to employees come from only one superior. Interestingly, Taylor and Fayol also viewed cooperation and teamwork as important to their theories, but both are remembered less for the latter ideas than for the specifics of a scientific work regime.

Max Weber's ideal for a bureaucratic organization complemented and expanded on the developing science of work rationality by showing how jobs could be organized into a cohesive whole. This bureaucratic ideal is the pyramid-shaped hierarchy that remains popular today; it is sustained by clear divisions of labor, authority and control, and supported by written rules and regulations.

What may be less evident from examining attributes of the corporate business model is that its features are largely measurable, principally tangible, and their underpinnings are largely known or at least well understood by those involved with them. The number of workers, their jobs, the centralized command of the leader, the pyramid shape defining chain of command and communication, and quarterly financial returns are all measurable. Most of the details for accomplishing this purpose are visually captured by an organizational pyramid. All of these attributes define clear boundaries for a stable world.

An analysis of Brown's corporate community model provides one view on how traditional theories of management must yield. The very stability provided by the corporate business model is threatened first by the dynamics inherent to a community model

The corporate business model

The corporation is a well-oiled machine

Shaped like a pyramid of individual boxes

Supported by written rules and regulations

Peopled by replaceable human capital

And managers who plan and execute aggressive attacks on competitors

Under the command of a Chief Executive Officer

To provide maximum quarterly financial returns to corporate stockholders

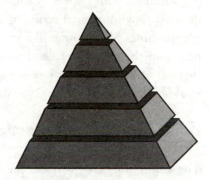

The corporate community model of business

The corporation is a dynamic community

Linked by networks of interdependent teams composed of

Self-managing people with diverse characteristics and talents

Guided by shared purpose

Leaders committed to continuous learning and improvement

In the service of maximum long-term customer satisfaction, employee and shareholder enrichment, and the health of the larger society

FIGURE 3.1 *The corporate business model and the corporate community model of business* (adapted from: Brown, Juanita. (1992). Corporation as community: A new image for a new era. In John Renesch (Ed.), *New traditions in business*, pp. 123–139. San Francisco, CA: Berrett-Koehler)

of organizations. Further, a comparison between corporate and community business models reveals that attributes for corporate business are primarily tangible and measurable, whereas attributes of community-oriented businesses often are intangible and difficult to identify, much less measure. Integrating these clear, objectively measurable, and fairly well-known attributes of organizations with those that are less clear, less tangible, and difficult to measure is a second common organizational challenge of globalization. Finally, inasmuch as the corporate model is a long-standing one, the theories and practices informing it are well understood and well articulated.

Community models of organization share none of these advantages. The boundaries established by clear and shared definitions of the terms and meanings of a corporate model have not been established for the community model whether between or across organizations with respect to concepts like 'networks' or attributes like 'diversity.' Practices like 'environmental scanning' are not clearly articulated for a global world, nor are the meanings of outcomes like 'enrichment' or 'health of the larger society.' This fuzziness, and the absence of definitional and conceptual boundaries, creates practical and theoretical challenges not just in the US but for business systems found throughout the world.

Dominant business practices in Asia

The community-based model presented above is believed to be one global firms will adopt to some degree. Having compared this model to traditions of formalization, specialization, and centralization found in the Westernized world, particularly in North America, it is important also to compare it to enterprises from industrial countries in Asia like Japan, South Korea, and Taiwan. Like US firms, these firms are difficult to characterize as members of an Asian 'group' because of regional differences in beliefs and practice. Many of the more easily identifiable traits of global firms were adopted from practices successful in globalizing Japanese firms, and a look at them is one way to examine how community needs for efficiency and flexibility, for adaptability and stability, and for social accountability are met by these firms.

In contrast to an emphasis on individualism dominant among US firms, a group or collectivist theme is dominant in much of Asia. According to Yasutaka Sai (1995), Japanese are socialized from early childhood to consider themselves members of groups. In the workplace, the group is reinforced by mechanisms like the following:

1 At the level of persons, permanent employees are hired once a year in a group; assigned to a work group rather than a job; function in and are evaluated on the basis of their team's work.
2 At the organizational level, Japanese firms operate as horizontally integrated industrial groups to join forces with companies in different industries or vertically integrated *keiretsu* to join forces with buyers and suppliers within the same industry. Intense rivalry between companies focuses less on vanquishing opponents than on winning skirmishes over price, product quality, or delivery.

Admiration for Japanese business success led many to adopt the seniority-based, consensus decision model dominant in Japanese firms. Taiwan's Eva Air, for example, adopted Japanese-style management, and South Korean firms also adopted a collectivist model reflected in *chaebols* or large industrial conglomerates dominating South Korean business. Although this model did not represent a perfect fit with Korean culture, it was consistent with a need for businesses and South Korean government to cooperate and direct national economic goals.

Orientation to the group is one of several core beliefs among Japanese businessmen; others proposed by Sai that also apply to the community model are as follows:

- Diligence includes a high priority for education and knowledge, a belief in work as the center of life, and a sense that one must be persistent and never give up: to show *gambaru* or perseverence against adversity.
- Aesthetic beauty and perfection are valuable; this makes Japanese customers demanding and causes Japanese businesses to strive for perfection and attend to detail.
- Curiosity and emphasis on innovation leads to *kaizen* or continuous improvement.
- Respect for form results in detailed expectations about business behaviors, and *hana yori dango* means that performance must come before rewards.
- A mind for competition is expressed internally between work groups, and externally through engagements with competitors, primarily over market share.

COLLECTIVISM

Geert Hofstede (1980) observes that the groupism evident in Japanese businesses is a phenomenon found throughout Asia; he calls this quality 'collectivism,' noting that as compared to the preference for acting independently reflective of North American individualism, collectivism reflects a greater preference to work in relationship with others. Many believe the roots of collectivism can be traced to Confucianism, and Hofstede and Bond (1988) attribute economic success in many Asian countries to what they call 'Confucian dynamism.'

CONFUCIANISM

According to the Christian calendar, the prophet Confucius lived in the fifth century before Christ. Confucius was a wise spiritual leader whose ideas about life were recorded in *The book of rites*, and have since been applied to personal and organizational life throughout Asia. Core beliefs include an emphasis on relationships, achieving harmony, doing what one is expected to do, leading by moral example rather than by brute strength, and accommodating others rather than calling attention to the self. The rules of social interactions are defined by five relationships: ruler and follower, father and son, husband and wife, brothers, and friends. In the context of an organization, the follower is the employee expected to show deference to the employer/owner at all times. These practices are found throughout the world, often spread by overseas Chinese who reinforce and practice virtues of thrift, discipline, industriousness, family cohesion, and reverence for education, even though decades and even centuries separate them from China (Tanzer, 1994). Contrasts between the Japanese and the Chinese versions of Confucianism shown in Table 3.4 demonstrate the variety of adaptive responses to Confucianism, despite their common roots.

Dominant business practices in Europe

Global firms from Europe have to date been based primarily in Western Europe. Although many of the nations from which they come are characterized by greater collectivism than found in the US and less collectivism than found in Asia, they are otherwise quite diverse in character. However, dominant traits can be identified among European firms and European managers. Groupism within Europe, once limited to pride of nationality, has evolved to include a sense of European citizenship. The underlying sense of group is uneasy and not well developed; it is least evident among the British, and more evident in smaller countries that have most to gain from union. Firms from Western Europe are practiced at working with collective bargaining units and other stakeholders, having gained practice via partnerships such as co-determination in Germany, cooperatives in Ireland or antagonism between French unions and the government. At the same time, the traditions of many European nations include features of hierarchy reflected in figurehead monarchies and to-the-manor-born attitudes. In France, for example, hierarchies remain tall, and formal controls are rampant; all are intended to reduce uncertainty and complexity (Sorge, 1993). This stands in sharp contrast to firms

TABLE 3.4 Confucian values evident in China and Japan

	Chinese values	Japanese values
Family	Blood-linked; family power increases with expanding branches of the family; closest relationship traditionally is father and son	Community-linked; one can adopt a son to head the family to ensure there is a male heir; based on loyalty and obedience to one's superior
Where one owes loyalty in a choice	To the family first; family and Confucianism extend into organizations to promote family interests	To the organization and one's superior; promote the organization and what is best for the organization; perform and be loyal
Five virtues	Greatest emphasis is on benevolence Righteousness Propriety Intelligence Faith	Greatest emphasis is on loyalty Propriety Courage Faith Honesty

Source: Hall, Richard H., and Xu, Weiman. (1990). Research Note: Run silent, run deep – cultural influences on organizations in the Far East. *Organization Studies*, 11(4): 569–576.

from more northerly countries such as Sweden, Denmark, or Norway where consensus and cooperation frequently guide organizational actions.

Links between business and government in Western Europe also are greater than those observed in the US, but less than those found in Asia. This is partially based on a general commitment among Europeans for long-run quality of life goals over organizational profit goals. Thus, Europeans expect the government to play an advocacy role in balancing their private interests with the less community-minded interests of business organizations. Figure 3.2 demonstrates differences in thinking that occur when profits or social responsibility are the starting points. Many Western European countries assume social responsibility motives as a starting point, as shown in the second figure, and presumably this national attitude is to some degree reflected in Western European businesses. Additionally, since many firms in Europe are small firms, e.g., the *Mittelstand* in Germany, local firms in Portugal, Italy, and Spain, they may be more likely to develop links with the government than in the US where small firms are viewed as secondary rather than central to economic development.

In summary, the preceding look at priorities, preferences, interests and practices

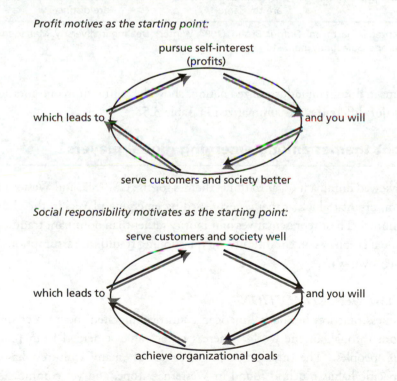

FIGURE 3.2 *The process ends where it begins* (Hampden-Turner, Charles, and Trompenaars, Alfons. (1993). *The seven cultures of capitalism*, p. 14. New York: Currency/Doubleday)

TABLE 3.5   US, Japanese, and Western European models of business

US model	Japanese model	Western European model
Emphasis on economic returns to shareholders	Emphasis on long-term growth; little or no influence by shareholders	Emphasis on cultural and humanistic values; stakeholders like government have more clout than shareholders
Product versus customer orientation	Quality orientation to customers' needs and continuous improvement	Customers to be satisfied include stakeholders
Compete universally for short-run economic returns	Compete externally and cooperate internally to achieve market share	Compete and cooperate globally and locally to balance short- and long-run objectives
Individualism expressed in organizational autonomy and individual actions	Collectivism and groupism creates primary loyalty to the firm and the work group over self	Obligation to sacrifice some economic gains for the community quality of life
Cultural diversity viewed as a legal challenge	Cultural diversity viewed as a threat	Cultural diversity viewed as business as usual
Personal and professional life interrelate	Personal and professional life are the same	Personal and professional life are distinct

Source: Adapted in part from: Dufour, Bruno. (1994, Winter). Dealing in diversity: Management education in Europe. *Selections*, pp. 7–15.

among firms in dominant industrialized nations show they differ from one another. Some of these major differences are summarized in Table 3.5.

Dominant themes among emerging global players

Having reviewed dominant organizational themes for the US, Asia, and Western Europe, it also is important to look at themes expressed by emerging players in the global business community. These representatives of minority rather than dominant traditions share organizational emphases on community, on questioning traditional assumptions, and on forging their own ways.

SOUTH AMERICAN TRADITIONS

Many business practices in South American countries migrated there via colonists and settlers from throughout the world, whereas other values emerged from practices of indigenous peoples. The melding and merging of many cultures has created country-specific habits much as found in Western Europe, and yet commonalities are identifiable. Among the values applicable to work are that destiny or fate outside individual control also guides life; veneration for tradition is reinforced by social and organizational hierarchies; work success is shaped by fate as well as by individual actions; results are predicated upon who one knows as much as upon what one knows; and it is important to avoid challenges to authority in order to preserve dignity and avoid losing 'face.' Family and friendship connections are central to obtaining jobs and promotions. Finally, families more than work define human existence, and so one owes greater loyalty to the latter than to the former (Harris and Moran, 1996). Relationships between personal and community members are shown in Figure 3.3. This figure shows the individual as one whose sense of values at work or elsewhere is embedded in a system of interlocking extended family and social community. Yet, as the example in Box 3.11 shows, these Latin American values also might be changing in a globalizing world.

VEDANTIC TRADITION

The 'overseas Indians' also are a growing economic force, enhanced by high literacy rates in India and a propensity for Indians to seek higher education at home and opportunity abroad (see Figure 3.4). Many of the nonresident Indians as well as most resident Indians are schooled in a Vedic tradition that Chakraborty (1995) indicates embodies the following business values and behaviors:

1 Striving for a pure mind is more important than sharpening the intellect because feelings more than intellect lead to decisions and behaviors.
2 Primary organizational reliance should be on humans rather than on systems or structures.
3 '[W]ork must be done without personal claims to egocentric results (i.e. rewards) as the primary driving force' (p. 10).
4 Ego-led decisions or acts return unfavorable results; this is the notion of karma.
5 Striving for unity and 'oneness' is true development.

Chakraborty believes that realizing this vision of unity would result in cooperative business relationships; decreased business efforts to grow via greed or manipulation; shifts to local rather than global approaches; and fewer changes simply for the sake of change (pp. 27–29).

TRIBES

Joel Kotkin (1993) believes that transnational ethnic groups or tribes like the overseas Indians or Chinese have the capacity to transcend national borders, arguing that, via common and shared values spanning the globe, these tribes have been instrumental in fostering global business and will remain a force for stability. According to Kotkin, tribes poised to span the globe in future include Filipinos, Lebanese, Palestinians, Mormons,

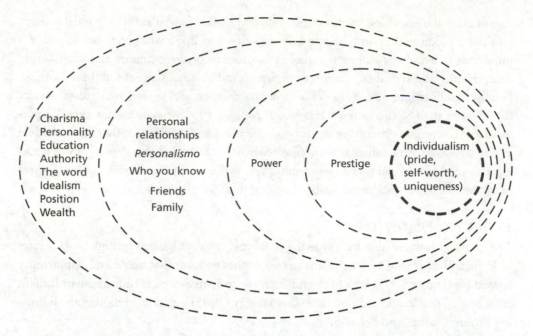

FIGURE 3.3 *Latin American values as illustrated in layers* (Spencer, Berkeley A. (1991). *Understanding Latin American underdevelopment and tension with the United States: A question of applying the right paradigm*, p. 6. Provo, UT: David M. Kennedy Center for International Studies, Brigham Young University)
Note: The core (circle) is the most important value, with each outlying layer being less important, but necessary to reach the next layer.

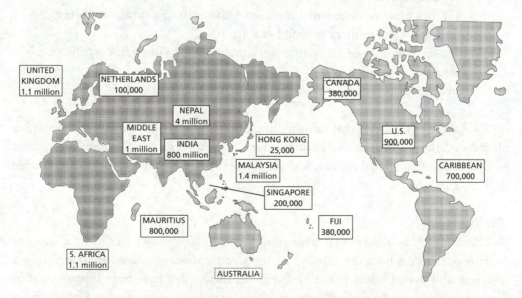

FIGURE 3.4 *Where the overseas (nonresident) Indians live* (*Business Week*. (1995, July 17), p. 45; http://www.littleindia.com)

BOX 3.11:   CISNEROS FAMILY VALUES

Venezuela's Cisneros family conglomerate is privately held, but generated over $3.2 billion in sales for 1995. The family has targeted its efforts toward international growth and this has meant changes in long-standing relationships. For example, in August 1996, bottler Hit de Venezuela abandoned its 50-year relationship with PepsiCo to align long-term growth interests with Coca-Cola. Overnight Pepsi products disappeared from Venezuelan store shelves, and thousands of Hit trucks were repainted as the 18 bottling plants switched to Coke products. The subsequent lawsuit filed by Pepsi was settled with fines against Coke and Cisneros, but allowed the Coke–Cisneros venture to continue. Pepsi struck a new venture with Empresas Polar, the country's major distributor of beer, and hopes to regain their national reputation and distribution capability. Six months later, the Cisneros family sold most of its newly acquired bottling interests to Panamco, part of a long-term strategy to move out of retail and consumer goods and into global telecommunications. Cisneros family decisions showed that traditions of business in Latin America such as developing and maintaining long-standing relationships may be undergoing change in a more global world.

Source: Vogel, Jr, Thomas T., and Deogun, Nikhil. (1996, Dec. 11.). Venezuela fines Coke, Cisneros; Allows Venture. *The Wall Street Journal*, p. A16.

---

and people from Eastern Europe. People from most of these groups come from nations least involved in global business, and appreciable entry of members of these tribes also may reshape business practices globally.

WOMEN IN BUSINESS

Although women do not in any sense constitute a cohesive 'tribe,' the management literature shows that the very presence of women is changing the face of business. Increased numbers of female employees in business worldwide have reshaped policies primarily affecting women such as maternity leave or child care provisions, but also reshaped opportunities for advancement. Women increasingly hold jobs in the paid labor force and they now are 40% of the global workforce. Often, women create new businesses. According to the US Census Bureau, the number of US businesses owned by women increased 40% from 1987 to 1992 to 6.4 million or one-third of all US businesses. Women-owned businesses jumped 18% from 1991 to 1994 and for the first time the number of people they employed in the US was greater than jobs provided globally by

TABLE 3.6   Women in positions of corporate authority, 1997 and 1998

	Company	Position
Jill Barad	Mattel	CEO
Lois Juliber	Colgate-Palmolive	Operations head in North America and Europe & Executive VP
Carol Bartz	Autodesk, Inc.	CEO
Christina Gold	Avon	Senior VP for North America
Ellen Marram	Seagram	Exec. VP and head of Tropicana Beverage Group
Karen Katen	Pfizer	Exec. VP of pharmaceuticals
Kathy Dwyer	Revlon	President, Revlon Consumer Products, USA
Linda Sapford	IBM	General Manager for Global Industries
Brenda Edgerton	Campbell Soup	VP Finance in soup division

Source: Primarily from White, Joseph B., and Hymowitz, Carol. (1997, Feb. 10). Broken glass: Watershed generation of women executives is rising to the top. *The Wall Street Journal*, pp. A1, A6.

all Fortune 500 companies (Women-owned businesses, 1995). According to 1995 reports from the National Foundation for Women Business Owners, the fastest-growing areas for business creation are in traditionally male industries like manufacturing, construction, transportation and finance. In Japan five out of six new businesses in 1993 were created by women (Fisher, 1993), in Europe women barred from established businesses are creating their own businesses, and entrepreneurship is credited with advances for even the world's poorest women (*Human Development Report*, 1995).

The management literature offers many examples of how women's management styles, interests, and business approaches differ from those of men throughout the world (Gibson, 1995; Rosener, 1990). A tendency toward entrepreneurial behavior is one indicator of difference, but others include a longer run profit horizon, participative management styles, and efforts to create structures and processes designed to meet human needs. Often rejected by more traditional systems of business, women show a will to shape their own firms around emerging issues as much as around tradition.

In the US as elsewhere, women also are advancing to positions of authority within large corporations. Some examples are given in Table 3.6.

Worldwide, there is no single model for female advancement. For example, efforts to diminish sex role stereotypes in the US and other Westernized countries are less in evidence in India and Japan where there is greater emphasis on motherhood as an exalted role. Further, equality of opportunity for men and women has been important in the US but it has not been a goal elsewhere. For example, many big companies in Japan created dual tracks for women to be managers or remain nonmanagers, but similar tracks are not an option for men. Box 3.12 with its profile of a woman in a leadership position at Shiseido Company – the leading Japanese cosmetics firm and a global competitor in the cosmetic industry – provides one example of how women have succeeded in setting new directions for corporations that employ them.

BOX 3.12:   SHISEIDO'S HISAKO NAGASHIMA

In contrast to the traditional image of Japanese woman as shy and deferential toward men, Hisako Nagashima – only the second female director in Shiseido's 125-year history – is far from retiring. She is credited not only with spearheading Shiseido's successful overseas expansion, but also with reviving many thousands of small family-owned businesses selling Shiseido cosmetics in Japan. In addition to boosting company presence in domestic and world markets, Ms Nagashima has proved herself a strong advocate for women. In the late 1970s she advocated better pay for women who work at cosmetics counters, and, finding that female employees at Shiseido could not get home-purchase loans equal to male employees, she also provided an impetus for change. Both policies were subsequently changed. This example suggests that despite the odds, women can be and have been advocates for justice at work.

Source: Shirouzu, Norihiko. (1997, May 19). How one woman is shaking up Shiseido. *The Wall Street Journal*, pp. B1, B6.

GLOBAL DEMANDS AND LIMITS OF TRADITION

Global challenges outlined above create more rather than fewer pressures to wrestle efficiencies from organizations; more rather than less need to value diversity; compelling reasons to develop skills useful for managing tangibles and intangibles; and evidently less room for error in accomplishing any objective. As examples in the following section show, traditional systems may create disadvantages as well as advantages in a global sphere, making it more important for firm leaders to weigh both when selecting processes, structures, and employees suitable for their organizations. The following sections explore both advantages and disadvantages of dominant practices.

Limits of dominant US theories in a global sphere

The pyramid of individual boxes representing organizational structure supports the order of scientific management. It visually demonstrates that information and decisions – almost as certainly as by force of gravity – are expected to move from top to bottom. Managers are expected to attack the competition in what is understood to be a zero-sum or win/lose world where options are limited to attack or be attacked. Finally, in service to quarterly financial returns, a manager's commitment is not so much to building a future but to making sure that this quarter's financial returns meet investor expectations. In this corporate business model, people as well as other organizational resources are viewed as interchangeable parts or cogs in the wheel of industrial progress to be commanded and controlled by leaders grounded in the competitive profit-seeking model outlined earlier in this chapter.

John Fernandez (1991) identified five reasons why it may be less possible to derive efficiencies from traditional hierarchical work arrangements:

1 Rules rarely address unanticipated events; they are not flexible.
2 Rules can stifle creativity and innovations.
3 Needs for thinking may be limited by specialization.
4 Bureaucracies rarely encourage cooperation, teamwork or open communication.
5 Bureaucracies tend to create a sense of internal competition leading to win/lose positions even within organizations.

The example of Eastman Chemical (Box 3.13) illustrates variations in how a particular system like scientific management is applied even within the same country, and it suggests diversity of business practice occurs within cultures as well as between them. Thus, it suggests that potential responses to global challenges may come from looking at practices near at hand as well as oceans away.

BOX 3.13:   EASTMAN CHEMICAL: THE PAST MEETS THE FUTURE

Eastman Chemical is a bastion of paternalistic tradition. Contrary to now-dominant US practices, the firm believes employees and communities are as important as shareholders. Their human assets can vacation at the company's campgrounds, attend free movies at the company theater, and take comfort that there has been no employee layoff in nearly 50 years. Efforts to cut $325 million in labor expenses by the year 2000 include retraining, transfers, and outsourcing as current employees retire, but no planned layoffs.

Source: Bleakley, Fred R. (1997, Jan. 16). A bastion of paternalism fights against change. *The Wall Street Journal*, p. B1, 2.

Limits of dominant Asian theories in a global sphere

Confucian ideals and collectivism, as well as mechanisms that support them at work, tend to emphasize processes that make it possible to share information, reach consensus, and accomplish work in teams. *Gambaru* and diligence create workers willing to work long hours for postponed rewards; striving for perfection results in continuous improvements and high-quality Japanese products; and paternalistic leadership generates high loyalty. Limitations of these and other processes include a tendency to follow the leader in an industry and/or within a work group; suppression of individual innovation and dissent; perfectionism that delays action; and focus on internal challenges. In some cases, entrenched practices associated with processes like collectivism can prove as inflexible as hierarchical structures can be in the US, and entrenched systems like seniority and compensation based on longevity discourage individual innovation. Firms like Toyota (see Box 3.14), Acer, and Nomura demonstrate efforts among Asian firms to alter their traditions in a global world. As president of Taiwan-based Acer, Stan Shih has laid-off employees and moved away from hiring family members, two practices that stand in sharp contrast to traditional Chinese management style. These newer practices are expected to improve productivity among employees and eliminate hiring based on affiliations rather than on abilities. Finally, at Nomura – a brokerage company plagued by scandals in the mid-1990s – incoming president Junichi Ujiie declared his intentions to make the organization flat and transparent so as to avoid the design flaws of past bureaucracy that kept senior managers from full awareness of activities that led to the scandals.

The family structure most typical of Chinese conglomerates also is under pressure to change in a global world, and some owners have moved to restructure their firms to improve

---

BOX 3.14: WHEN THE BEST ISN'T GOOD ENOUGH

In 1995, Hiroshi Okuda became the first non-Toyoda family member appointed president of Toyota Motor Company. His goals included making globalization a reality rather than just a slogan at Toyota. This has meant changes in traditions long-practiced at Toyota, including asking people to look less at Toyota's successes and more at the successes of others. Models include arch-rivals like Mercedes-Benz on design and General Motors for managing cash and other assets. The changes also include new behaviors; Mr Okuda is working to stimulate objections to his own views, and this includes talking to younger people with new perspectives.

Source: Changing gear at Toyota. (1996, Oct. 5). *The Economist*, p. 68.

global adaptability. An effective way to do this has been to carve out identifiable business units from the conglomerate and raise capital by selling shares of these entities to the public. This tactic reduces the number of disparate businesses held by the conglomerate but also raises capital for expansion in global businesses. For example, the Cheng family created a new company from its hotel, property, and telecommunications holdings to focus attention on interests in the Hong Kong property market. Focus in the conglomerate also improves as different businesses gain financial and managerial independence needed for rapid response to events in a global world. For similar reasons, the Hong Kong Tsui family spun off their profitable bus company Citybus to concentrate more on expanding their paint business, and the family owners of Tem Fat Hing Fung, a jewelry and property developer, sought a separate market listing for their gold-bullion business. Changes like these improve efficiencies for Chinese family businesses, but at the same time they threaten to reduce some degree of the family's control and its managerial reach.

Limits of dominant European theories in a global sphere

When the hierarchical form found in the US combines with the paternalistic attitude found among Asian managers, individual creativity often is stifled or suppressed to create a worst-case condition. At its best, this combination releases the power of teams operating under clear and known controls. Western European firms operating globally have witnessed both scenarios because among them they demonstrate so many different styles. The example in Box 3.15 illustrates that the challenge of change in Western Europe often is specific to the nation from which the firm emerges.

Many successful global enterprises have come from smaller countries like Switzerland and the Netherlands, perhaps because the size of the nation compelled companies from them to expand globally well before companies from larger countries. As a result,

---

BOX 3.15:   BOUNDARIES FOR GERMAN TRADITIONS

Large German firms, particularly in industries previously protected by German law, often find it difficult to adapt to global business. Hierarchical structures seven and eight layers deep make it difficult to respond to dynamic global events. The high cost of labor suggests a need to move some types of production out of Germany, but close ties between business and the German government make it difficult to reduce local labor forces, and traditional German attention to precision makes it difficult to put resources into marketing in place of research or engineering development.

firms from smaller countries may have the benefit of experience in shaping hybrids responsive to multiple markets. The description of Unilever's experience in Box 3.16 illustrates the challenge this company faced to become a global hybrid.

BOX 3.16: UNILEVER

Former Unilever PLC Chairman Sir Michael Perry believed that rapid shifts in world-wide economic opportunities required a change in Unilever's organizational structure. Accordingly, the firm eliminated its cumbersome executive body and product-coordination matrix structure in favor of a regional focus. This focus was expected to eliminate problems of coordinating headquarters, brand managers, and country managers in favor of developing products and marketing strategies for an entire region.

In conclusion, whether occurring for firms from the US, Asia, or Europe, principles of collectivity that enhance consensus decision-making can be impediments to innovation; principles of individualism that enhance innovation can be impediments to teamwork; principles of hierarchy lack flexibility, but more flexible systems can confuse responsibilities and may reduce profits. Simultaneous demands for efficiency and flexibility, adaptability and stability, independence and interdependence, or social accountability and profits make it almost impossible to operate globally according to existing tradition.

According to a study of 300 senior executives from five continents, globalization offers many challenges for which there are no clear rules except to be decisive (Ettorre, 1994). Thus, although some believe a new 'post' era, variously called post-Fordist, post-modernist, or post-Sloanist, has arrived, it may be more accurate to think of this as an era where the job of the manager is to identify the best elements of Fordism, modernism, and Sloanism and combine them with emerging theories of management. Combining elements of these theories is likely to produce organizational hybrids rather than 'pure' species of organizations. Because they will emerge from experimentation, some of these hybrids will be successful and others will fail. For example, combining the advantages of both hierarchies and horizontal organization may make it possible for employees to be both generalists and specialists, for organizations to take on characteristics of being both big and small, for strategies to be both global and local. At the same time, coordination can become more difficult since much depends on assumptions of shared understandings; hybrids can be difficult to create since processes are intangible and hard to describe; they are inherently 'messy' because they tolerate uncertainties; and at their worst they can incorporate the worst qualities of multiple systems rather than the best of each. When hierarchies and horizontal structures are combined, the worst case is distributed decision-making where no one has authority but everyone is held accountable.

PART II   THEORY AND PRACTICE OF GLOBAL CHANGE

Characteristics of globalization such as a rapid pace of change, increased complexity, and heightened uncertainties demand a degree of flexibility difficult to achieve with traditional structures, many processes, and most people. In view of an apparent need for organizational hybrids, it is important to review emerging theories and practices proposed for reshaping structures, processes, and people in global organizations. These are briefly introduced in the following section, and we will return to examine some of them in greater depth in later chapters.

STRUCTURAL CHALLENGES

A 1994 study of 778 major North American and European corporations revealed that half expected to alter their organizational structure within three to five years. According to the *Wall Street Journal* report of this study, the CEO for A.T. Kearney commissioned the study to show that 'complacency has been replaced by a fierce commitment to remake the competitiveness of the corporation in this new environment' (Schellhardt, 1994). Emerging structural hybrids are expected to address problems created with centralized and/or decentralized structures, but as noted earlier, these alterations may create new challenges.

Within the last decade, suggested alternatives to existing structural arrangements have been intended primarily to sustain efficiency while also introducing flexibility. Some of these suggestions address internal restructuring and others can more appropriately be thought of as external restructuring. All emphasize shorter, flatter visualizations than a pyramid; distribute decision-making; demonstrate multiple rather than one-way relationships among people; attempt to separate critical from less critical functions; and rely at least in part on information technologies. Internal forms of restructuring include flat or horizontal structures, inverted pyramids, networks, spiderwebs, shamrocks, and virtuality; structures that are described in greater detail in subsequent chapters. External forms of restructuring include strategic alliances, joint marketing campaigns, and alliances to create global codes of ethics or human rights statements.

It often is difficult to produce a visual representation of structural arrangements suggested for global firms. Further, the very dynamism of community models of organizations may lead to obsolescence before the ink has dried. Concepts such as spiderwebs or networks reflecting development of structural arrangements advancing from simple, to complex, to almost impossible to draw are shown in Figure 3.5.

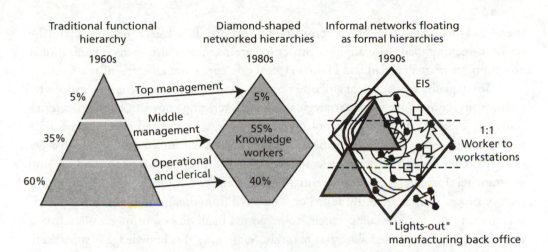

FIGURE 3.5 *Evolution of organizational structures* (Eccles, Robert G., and Nolan, Richard L. (1993). A framework for the design of the merging global organizational structure. In S.P. Bradley, J.A. Hausman, and R.L. Nolan (Eds), *Globalization, technology, and competition*, pp. 57–80. Boston, MA: Harvard Press; after Nolan, Richard L. (1992, Jan. 7). Unpublished presentation given at the 'CEO Symposium' at the Harvard Business School)

These few examples of alterations in internal and external structural arrangements provide new alternatives for structuring work, but when adopted they have in most cases been supplementary to rather than total replacements for organizational hierarchies. The latter remain the norm for most organizations, and organizations adopting new forms also may find reason to retain some aspects of traditional structures. For example, Ford's intention to produce a world car led to less rather than more autonomy for research, design, and production teams. Organizations pursuing a global integration strategy also are likely to achieve economies of scale and resulting efficiencies by centralizing rather than decentralizing worldwide functions.

PROCESSES

Dual needs for efficiency and for innovation lead to calls for flexibility and responsiveness to customers and for a simultaneous stable and dynamic posture; these demands are among the reasons behind greater emphasis on processes (Boynton and Victor, 1991). In some cases, processes become an important substitute for people made redundant as organizations downsize, re-engineer, and outsource to achieve efficiencies. It is simply impossible in such cases for managers to supervise all the people reporting to them and new processes like empowerment are introduced as a way to share the decision-making load. Alterations in structural arrangements also focus organizational attention on what Prahalad and Hamel (1990) call 'core competencies' of the firm.

Total quality management and other continuous improvement schemes, process re-engineering, core competencies, strategic thinking, leveraging knowledge and other terms found in Table 2.5 above are some of the major processes suggested for global organizations. Ideally, every organizational process is fully articulated and coordinated with every other to reinforce and improve on core competencies. This need for coordination and constant reinforcement is the differentiating feature between processes and either projects or programs that are easily added or subtracted from organizational life. In the US, it is not unusual for core competencies to be posted in all offices, printed on laminated cards workers carry, recited almost as mantras. Sometimes this knowledge is superficial, going little deeper than words on a page. To reach deep into the organization, core competencies must be supported by appropriate organizational processes.

Evidence taken from Pepsi's experience in the Philippines and Royal Dutch/Shell's experiences with the Brent Spar illustrate that organizations can be and have been held accountable for their activities. This accountability makes it difficult for them to achieve limited and articulated goals, much less unlimited and unclear goals. According to Acer's Stan Shih (1995), 'In a borderless business environment, each country and enterprise should not try to do everything. Instead, each company should focus only on its most effective and competitive areas and integrate them with the best of other companies.' Identification of core abilities or competencies provides one way to respond to increased global demands to be all things to all people at the same time, and it explains renewed interest in the strategic processes described below.

Strategic processes

In the 1980s, the strategy-making process was characterized primarily by business strategies in answer to the question: how shall we compete in the businesses we manage? In a global world, the competitive approach to strategy is expanding to emphasize broader questions about organizational purpose. As Box 3.17 illustrates, business organizations exist for diverse reasons, but in a global world where it is not possible to be all things to all people, it is increasingly important to be clear as to what that reason is. Organizational purpose can be defined as enterprise strategy because it examines the general role the organization plays in society; a firm's definition of enterprise strategy – whether made explicit or implicitly understood – should inform and flow into four other levels of organizational strategy and operations (Table 3.7).

Although leaders of every company make decisions at each of the five levels of strategy described in the table, they use different words when doing so. Additionally,

TABLE 3.7   Levels of strategy defined

Enterprise strategy: What is our purpose in society; why do we exist as an organization?

Corporate strategy: What businesses shall we be in now and into the future? What are our core competencies for each?*

Business strategy: How shall we compete/collaborate in the businesses we select?

Operational strategy: How shall we coordinate among processes, people and structures to meet enterprise, corporate, and business strategies?

Individual strategy: What must each individual do to meet organizational goals of the subunit, operations, business, corporate and enterprise strategy? For example, in Levi's pay-based Partners in Performance program, each employee forms a partnership with the company to align their objectives with the company's global business plan.

*The language of strategy reflects differences of opinion. The hierarchy of strategic questions provided accommodates any type of organization, from large conglomerate to small, single product firm. Although it is possible for a conglomerate or corporation with several divisions to identify a single set of core competencies for all their businesses, it is more usual for core competencies to be identified at the business level. Although some practitioners differentiate between the firm's vision and its mission, others do not. In either case, the suggested hierarchy shows that core beliefs about the purpose of the organization should be reflected at every organizational level.

implementation can be more implicit than explicit. This variety in choice of words and how strategy is articulated is evident in the words different organizations use when describing purpose, e.g., mission, vision, values, and research shows the meaning of these words also varies by country. For example, a comparison of company missions in a sample of British and French firms showed processes of mission development vary, reflecting major differences in how the mission is developed, its content, and even its impact (Brabet and Klemm, 1994). The consumer of organizational statements should be aware of this variety, and may find it necessary to draw inferences when seeking to identify distinctions between the five levels of strategy described. For example, each statement in Box 3.17 is a definition of enterprise strategy, but none are described in those terms.

As might be obvious, organizational leaders who articulate or reinforce enterprise-level strategy then are better able to hire the people they need to operationalize overall purpose and to develop structures that support the enterprise. The example in Box 3.18 illustrates this point, showing how Reinhard Mohn developed an enterprise strategy that shaped other processes and structures, and attracted employees whose individual objectives were consistent with enterprise strategy and objectives.

Portfolios of processes

Many of the processes reviewed above are intended to be part of integrative systems. Ghoshal and Bartlett (1995) argue that a one-world approach requires a portfolio of important processes to manage, and according to these authors the portfolio should

BOX 3.17: ENTERPRISE STRATEGY: WHAT IS OUR PURPOSE?

B.C. Forbes, founder of *Forbes* magazine

What are we in business for? We are in business to benefit others. If we are not, then our business won't prosper permanently. All business is a matter of reciprocity, of giving something in exchange for something else. Unless we give, we cannot receive. (Forbes archive)

Jeno Paulucci, founder of Chun King and Jeno's Pizza

No matter where you are, you really gotta contribute back to your community in order to justify, in my own mind, growth and progress and happiness. (Simon, 1994)

Ben and Jerry's, premium ice-cream manufacturers

It's a business that cares about people, that seeks to use its power to improve the quality of life within society. It seeks profits and tries to integrate spiritual and social concerns into day-to-day activities. Typical businesses tend to do everything in terms of narrow self-interest. They want to maximize profitability and quality. We add a third factor: impact on the community, on the consumer, on our employees. (Dreifus, 1994)

William I. Spencer, Citibank president

Our mission is: *To provide all financial services every place in the world where it is legal, moral and on which we can make a profit. (Dreifus, New York Times, Dec. 28, 1980, p. B22)*

W.T. Gore and Associates

The objective of the enterprise is to make money and have fun doing so. Feb. 1994*

Cargill, Inc.

We will be the best in improving the standard of living of the five billion people in the world. Cargill will pay the producer better prices and sell to the consumer for a little less. This vision will increase purchasing power and/or capital formation for the world population. from 'Cargill's Vision: A view to the future,' July 12, 1990*

Source: both of these statements of purpose, as well as many more, appeared in: Graham, John. (1994). *Mission statements: A guide to the corporate and nonprofit sectors*. New York: Garland. pp. 130, 522–523. Simon, Jane. (1994, Aug.). Are you hungry tonight? *Northwest Airlines World Traveler*, p. 19.

contain the entrepreneurial process, the competence-building process, and the renewal process. Among them, the entrepreneurial, competence-building, and renewal processes share the following organizational attributes:

BOX 3.18: FIVE LEVELS OF STRATEGY AT BERTELSMANN AG

Carl Bertelsmann founded Bertelsmann AG in 1835. His great grandson, Reinhard Mohn, served in World War II, returning home in 1947 to find family factories had been reduced to rubble. Fifty years later, the rebuilt firm had become the world's third largest media giant, including publishers like Bantam Doubleday Dell, record label RCA, and Europe's biggest broadcasting company. Bertelsmann employs 58,000 people, operates in 50 countries, and turned a net profit of $571 million (905 million Deutschmarks) in fiscal year 1996.

Reinhard Mohn rebuilt Bertelsmann around an *enterprise strategy* or purpose that puts contribution to society ahead of profit maximization. Since 1977, the Bertelsmann Foundation has contributed about $48 million to philanthropic interests, and today profits are shared with employees in the form of an annual dividend. *Corporate strategies* preserve the firm and protect employees by reducing risk: there is a mandatory 15% rate of return on any project to reduce costly mistakes that might lead to layoffs, and one result is that Bertelsmann has not acquired businesses it could well afford financially. Within the TV industry, Bertelsmann businesses have grown through cooperation rather than head-to-head competition, showing a preference for a *business strategy* characterized more by collaboration than competition. *Operational strategies* to achieve coordination among processes, people and structures include a structure that is decentralized and includes employees on the company's supervisory board, and decision-making processes that involve partnerships between managers and employees. At the level of *individual strategy*, executives are well aware they are expected to be servants to society and to their employees, and employees follow Mohn's dictates to be modest and share credit for work rather than focus on individual ambitions.

Source: Adapted from: Rohwedder, Cacilie. (1997, Jan. 15). Reinhard Mohn: The quiet media mogul. *The Wall Street Journal*, p. A10.

- an organizational culture that emphasizes abilities;
- an environment that is open and where trust is generated;

- a structure in which employees accommodate vertical and horizontal relationships;
- a structure that reduces reliance on formal controls – this does not mean there are no 'rules' but rather that people agree to abide by the ones that develop;

- people who are stimulated by creativity;
- people who have talent and knowledge, and will take responsibility for activities over which they have limited control;
- people who will challenge existing strategies and underlying assumptions;
- top managers willing to make hard choices and allocate resources to support them.

The self-renewal process may be initiated internally or result from pressures from external, global forces, but, according to Ikujiro Nonaka (1990), either impetus for self-renewal results in four phases for the Japanese firms he studied (see Figure 3.6). Chaos, or the introduction of fluctuation and uncertainties, generates tension because it challenges current abilities to cope with change. This activates an inflow of heterogeneous information, cooperation throughout the organization to find information and workable responses to chaos, and finally to restructuring of organizational knowledge. In the latter phase, employees not only learn what they need to know, but unlearn what is now redundant. Nippon Electric Company Ltd's (NEC) motto 'Stability in instability' indicates that self-renewal at NEC is a norm rather than an occasional intervention.

In summary, these proposed processes range from incremental to revolutionary, and they involve bridging vertical and horizontal boundaries within and outside the organization to create hybrids. Their introduction in firms also has been both incremental and profound. So many more processes than the preceding are repeated in the management lexicon that managers and theorists might well develop an attitude of 'another day, another theory.'

What about results?

According to 1993 results of a now annual study, 463 companies surveyed by Bain and Company and the Strategic Leadership Forum (Rigby, 1994), the most commonly used management tools were mission statements (used by 94% of respondents), and customer surveys (90%). Total quality management was third at 76%. Interestingly, the study showed no apparent relationship between the management tool introduced and

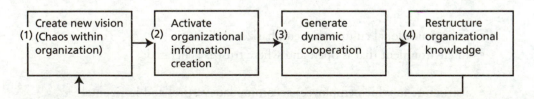

FIGURE 3.6 *The self-renewal process in Japanese firms* (Nonaka, Ikujiro. (1990). Managing globalization as a self-renewing process. In Christopher Bartlett and Sumantra Ghoshal (Eds), *Managing the global firm*, p. 70. London: Routledge)

BOX 3.19:   IMPORTED TECHNIQUES REQUIRE ADAPTATIONS

The Pennsylvania-based auto-parts supplier plant for Federal-Mogul was revamped in 1987 to include state-of-the-art automation ideas imported from Japan that included robots, computers, and other equipment. But the company never realized productivity gains, finding that the complex machinery required extensive maintenance and could not adjust quickly to production changes. By 1992, Federal-Mogul had introduced a newer process that fit better with their own needs to respond to customers' demands.

General Electric introduced Work-Out programs to replace quality circles after they realized that US workers favored radical change ideas over the incremental changes produced by many quality circles.

the company's financial performance, but did observe that the most important factor is finding the right technique for each company. The 1997 Bain and Company update further showed that firms from around the world, and especially US firms, are quick to adopt management fads that yield dissatisfying results. Both culture and globalization play a role in this phenomenon. First, US managers are under considerable pressure to do something at all times; management fads and reorganizations demonstrate activity and provide what Salancik and Meindl (1984) once called 'the illusion of management control.' At the same time, the rapid pace of globalization is calling leaders to find ways to accomplish work faster, cheaper, better. Newer concepts touting 'agile' strategies or 'fast companies' emphasize this point. However, according to Darrell Rigby, who conducts the Bain survey of management fads, the cost is that 'fads can waste energy and resources, create unrealistic expectations, and often prove divisive' (Byrne, 1997, p. 47).

In their book *Management redeemed: Debunking the fads that undermine our corporations* (1997), Frederick Hilmer and Lex Donaldson assert that management fads are not useless; rather, managers often adopt these fads without adapting them to their own situation. Although there is no 'one best way' for every firm, it is important for leaders to acknowledge unique organizational characteristics of the firm they manage when adopting new managerial techniques. In summary, these authors all reinforce an earlier point: leaders need to decide what is important to their organizations because there are no universal managerial 'givens'; and they must be efficient in their use of resources, including employee energy and enthusiasm.

In summary, management processes are increasingly important to global organizations, but processes newly introduced often do not succeed because they cannot be aligned with other parts of the organization. For example, the Japanese system of *kanban* or just-in-time inventories is difficult to achieve in the US because suppliers and buyers are not linked as closely as they are in Japan, and quality circles have had limited success in US workplaces because the underlying principles are not consistent with the autonomy US workers expect. Examples from companies described in Box 3.19 reinforce the need for managers to analyze proposed changes in processes, people, or structures for their fit with the existing organization.

Approaches adopted by global leaders like ABB's former leader Percy Barvenik, General Electric's Jack Welch, Jr, or Alex Trotman at Ford include a look at the entire organization to introduce entrepreneurial spirit and innovation more characteristic of a small firm into the large firms they manage. By the same token, smaller firms filled with entrepreneurial spirit seek the efficiencies afforded by being large. Changes like these take considerable resources and time, and they particularly require people capable of change.

PEOPLE

Global business leaders almost uniformly agree that processes as well as structures are developed, implemented, and sustained by people, and this has led to growing emphasis on the 'people' component of organizations. Consistent with US hierarchy, Asian paternalism, and European classism, the important people in the past were managers, particularly top managers. In a rapidly changing global world where flexibility is a critical variable, resources are less than abundant, and learning and thinking at all levels have become important, lower level employees also have become involved in all aspects of organizational change and development. The following sections look at how those changes are affecting employees at every level.

Top managers

Hierarchies delegate authority to top managers, who, by definition, are expected to be authoritarian. Today, this manager and the fear and trembling he might inspire is not necessarily a desirable leader. CEO Jack Welch, Jr believes the authoritarian leader cannot easily advance at General Electric, describing four types of leaders at GE as:

1 The leader who delivers on financial and other commitments and shares the values of the company will advance onward and upward in the company.
2 The leader who misses a commitment but shares company values gets a second chance, often with a different group or a new task.
3 The future of the leader who delivers on commitments but doesn't share company values, e.g., intimidates or suppresses others, is difficult to predict.

4 The future of the leader who misses commitments and does not share values lies with another company (G.E. is no place for autocrats, 1992).

Formerly alone in 'big picture' strategic thinking, top managers were among the first to observe sweeping global change. Proudfoot Change Management polled 400 US executives in 1993 who characterized change in the following ways:

- 79% noted rapid change in their companies
- 61% believed the pace of change would accelerate
- 47% viewed their companies as capable of coping with changes, and
- 62% had a conservative or reluctant approach to change

Part of the reluctance to change among the 62% who admitted to it may stem from the fact that global change continues to threaten roles and behaviors of top managers. In a multilingual survey of 1,500 senior executives in 20 countries, Lester Korn (1989) identified a shared belief that roles and behaviors of top managers will change as indicated in Table 3.8.

Few believe 'communicating' more frequently will displace traditional management functions of planning, delegating, coordinating, organizing, and controlling. According to a survey of CEOs in small businesses, the top five leadership skills needed are financial management, communication (including informing, listening, oral and written forms), motivation of others, vision, and motivating self (Eggers and Leahy, 1994). How these skills will be exercised also is a defining difference. Suggested practices like envisioning, teaming, unlearning, decoupling, and dreaming are expected to replace some practices of the autocratic leader.

Reporting on a study conducted by Assessment Circle Europe, Richard Hall (1994) found the most important qualities in EuroManagers – whom he defined as anyone with managerial responsibilities in a multicultural organization – to be language ability, communication and social skills, listening skills, a social personality and the ability to work in a team. Additionally, this EuroManager needs to develop initiative, independence and

TABLE 3.8 CEO roles and behaviors

Behavior of CEOs	1988	2000
Communicates frequently with employees	59	89
Communicates frequently with customers	41	78
Emphasizes ethics	74	85
Conveys strong sense of vision	75	98
Makes all major decisions	39	21

Source: Korn, Lester B. (1989, May 22). How the next CEO will be different. *Fortune*, pp. 157–159.

strong planning skills. These changes are evident in organizational choices such as Fiat's expenditure of $64 million in training at their $2.9 billion plant in Basilicata to create independent and multiskilled teams of workers and engineers.

In Asia, where envisioning has traditionally been part of managers' roles, there are pressures to step up the pace of doing. This change is represented by Toyota Motor Company's decision to replace aging patriarch Tatsuro Toyoda with president Hiroshi Okuda, whose physical demeanor, personal style, and organizational acumen more nearly resemble the outspoken, competitive, 'lean and mean' Westernized leader than the traditionally soft-spoken, retiring, and group-oriented manager traditional to Japanese firms in general and Toyota in particular. Both small and large firms throughout Asia also are finding it difficult to grow globally with traditional family-based practices, and many see the need for professional managers who can think beyond a family business paradigm. In Europe as well, there has been greater focus on abilities and attributes required from leaders. Hybrids in management also are emerging as firms adopt 'best' practices from around the world. For example, Taiwan's Eva Airlines combines quasi-Japanese personnel policies emphasizing attention to quality, politeness, and a personal touch with strong personal responsibility among managers, minimal paperwork, and frequent rotation among departments and headquarters/overseas offices.

Middle managers

Pressures to achieve financial results and manage external relations at the top are likely to trickle down to middle managers. This and organizational downsizing have increased the size and scope of the middle managers' role such that they play a more important role than in the past (Floyd and Wooldridge, 1994; Kraut et al., 1989). According to Harry Levinson (1988), middle managers, like top managers, will be both authoritative and participative, and it will take self-knowledge to play these dual roles. Challenges for these middle managers include: (a) closer involvement with subordinates over the periods of time necessary to create commitments; (b) understanding the personalities of subordinates; and (c) dealing with more significant personality differences and resolving more conflicts. Because of increased interdependence worldwide, all managers may become international managers to one extent or another, and more will manage organizations in a global context in the years ahead. What skills are needed?

MANAGERIAL COMPETENCIES FOR A GLOBAL WORLD: PEOPLE-CENTERED MANAGERS

Bartlett and Ghoshal (1995) believe a people-centered entrepreneurial management philosophy and style is essential to global participation, and Stephen Rhinesmith, author of *A manager's guide to globalization* (1993), indicates this style will be reflected in global managers with six competencies:

(a) knowledge to manage competitiveness;
(b) conceptualization to manage complexity;
(c) flexibility and trusting process over structure to manage adaptability;
(d) sensitivity to diversity as a way to manage teams;
(e) judgment and an ability to manage change and uncertainty;
(f) reflection and being open to managing learning.

Nancy Adler and Susan Bartholomew (1992) believe that global competence for managers will require skills that transcend those of managers in domestic or even in international markets. As shown in Table 3.9, these skills include a global perspective,

TABLE 3.9   Transnationally competent managers

Transnational skills	Transnationally competent managers	Traditional international managers
Global perspective	Understand worldwide business environment from a global perspective	Focus on a single foreign country and on managing relationships between headquarters and that country
Local responsiveness	Learn about many cultures	Become an expert on one culture
Synergistic learning	Work with and learn from people from many cultures simultaneously	Work with and coach people in each foreign culture separately or sequentially
	Create a culturally synergistic organizational environment	Integrate foreigners into the headquarters' national organizational culture
Transition and adaptation	Adapt to living in many foreign cultures	Adapt to living in a foreign culture
Cross-cultural interaction	Use cross-cultural interaction skills on a daily basis throughout one's career	Use cross-cultural interaction skills primarily on foreign assignments
Collaboration	Interact with foreign colleagues as equals	Interact within clearly defined hierarchies of structural and cultural dominance
Foreign experience	Transpatriation for career and organization development	Expatriation or inpatriation primarily to get the job done

Source: Adler, Nancy, J., and Bartholomew, Susan. (1992). Managing globally competent people. *Academy of Management Executive*, 6(3): 54.

local responsiveness, synergistic learning that makes it possible to work with and learn from people from many cultures, and an ability to collaborate with others on an equal basis.

According to Roland Calori and Bruno Dufour (1995), notwithstanding obvious differences throughout Europe, the European style of management can be differentiated from the US and Japanese on the basis of four characteristics that appear on most lists of what it takes to be a global manager. These are:

(a) a greater orientation toward people as individuals;
(b) a higher level of internal negotiations between superordinates and subordinates;
(c) greater skills at managing international diversity; and
(d) an enhanced ability to manage between extremes like short-run versus long-run goals.

In answer to questions like: 'Is there a global manager?' and 'Where would this manager come from?' (Taylor, 1991), Percy Barvenik former CEO of ABB replied:

Global managers have exceptionally open minds. They respect how different countries do things, and they have the imagination to appreciate why. . . . But they are also incisive, they push the limits of the culture. Global managers are made, not born. . . . You rotate people around the world . . . you encourage people to work in mixed-nationality teams. You *force* them to create personal alliances across borders [because] mixing nationalities doesn't just happen. (Taylor, 1991, pp. 67–68)

Employees

Employees in jobs traditionally defined as least managerial face perhaps the greatest role changes. Business initiatives like total quality management and concepts like learning organizations increasingly call on all employees to manage themselves or others. Those accustomed to teamwork now are encouraged to work and think as individuals and vice versa. Those accustomed to seniority-based promotions and compensation now face different expectations. In Japan, Korea, Taiwan, and among family-owned firms where age and seniority have been traditional paths to organizational and peer-group respect, employees now must consider the possibility of layoffs and being replaced with workers who are energetic and anxious to embrace global change. For example, beginning in 1992, Hitachi, Nissan Motor, Nomura Securities, and Sanyo Electric introduced layoffs and made personnel cutbacks among 'lifetime' employees.

Defining personal options

The enormity of a seemingly chaotic global world rather than a boundaried nation has special implications for the individual who perceives diminished capacity to identify appropriate options. Also, there is increased pressure on the individual to reach personal and organizational decisions quickly, wisely, and well. Futurist William Van Dusen Wishard (1995) believes there is no blueprint for success, but suggests the following options:

1 There is a need to discern what is permanent and immutable.
2 We must learn to make interconnections between people, events, and different categories of life because interdependence is an emerging condition of life.
3 We must learn to know ourselves.
4 We each need some understanding of how change and technology are affecting people and institutions.
5 We need to be open to dimensions of existence that are difficult to understand, value or control; within ourselves we need to value intuition.
6 There is a need to interact with people in a manner that will bridge racial and cultural differences.
7 There is a need to have a personal sense of creating something new for the future.

The 'soft' side of science represented by Van Dusen Wishard's list is not easily operationalized, but the need to do so is reinforced by growing interest in values-based management associated with self-renewal and development of full potential in others. This movement is reflected in Stephen Covey's emphasis on moral renewal, Peter Senge and others' application of concepts like servant-leadership (Spears, 1995), or Bolman and Deal's call for 'Leading with soul' (1995). These qualities also have value in Europe where an *International Management* survey (Brown, 1994) to identify the most admired senior executives in Europe placed Percy Barnevik at the top, describing him as humane, professional, determined, close to his employees, and an excellent communicator. Second and third most admired among European managers were Colin Marshall of British Airways and Bernd Pischetsrieder of BMW. In a study of perceptions of good leadership in Asian organizations (Selvarajah et al., 1995), top priority was on honesty, followed by strategic vision, and recognizing good work in others. These studies reinforce a sense that managers who can combine people skills with other skills are highly regarded worldwide. A desirable result of personal growth movements is to help people interact successfully with others who are different, to be more tolerant of uncertainty and irresolution, and to create organizations capable of playing multiple roles.

Examining self and examining organizations are critical to defining self and strategy in a global world.

In summary, changes affecting people have been as sweeping and have met with similar advantages and disadvantages as have changes in structures and processes for the global firm. Organizational leaders are creating hybrids to generate profits and remain welcome members of the global community. Although there are clear successes and failures, it is premature to conclude they represent truths. There may be no 'one best way' to globalize, but good practices include knowing self, firm, and employee competencies, incorporating flexibility and stability in organizations, valuing diversity and homogeneity, and otherwise balancing among the many tradeoffs and paradoxes facing the global enterprise. The topic of the chapter to follow returns us to the global environment to examine how rapid global changes in culture are driving organizational actions.

KEY CHAPTER CONCEPTS

Rising Expectations Generate Social Responsibilities: Expectations of powerful economic entities are rising, and many act on a belief that organizations of every size must be more responsible to those they serve. Mistakes are less frequently tolerated and organizations worldwide are more frequently held accountable for real and perceived public transgressions. Having stimulated global changes, business enterprises have been forced to assume some degree of responsibility for managing these changes.

Challenges of Social Responsibility: Among the important challenges of social responsibility for global businesses are achieving balance in three arenas: between tangible and intangible forms of wealth; shareholders and stockholders interests; and autonomy and community membership.

Creating Wealth Defined as More than Economy: The ability to contribute to intangible as well as tangible forms of wealth creation is reshaping views of business to incorporate zero-sum, competitive propositions and infinite-sum collaborative propositions in a world where multiple gains are possible.

Stakeholders and Stockholders: Organizational stakeholders include not only those individuals and groups who have a direct stake in the firm, e.g., employees, labor unions, stockholders, but also those whose stake is a little less direct but nonetheless perceived as important either by the organization or by those holding a stake. Both stockholder and stakeholder activism are on the rise worldwide, and together they increase pressure on business decisions.

Imperfect Business Traditions for a Global World: A comparison of business traditions in successful economies shows that none are perfectly suitable for the global community.

Business Hybrids Emerge: Creation of business hybrids suitable for global business involves experimentation that can yield the worst of multiple traditions rather than the best of many.

Hybrids of Structure: Multiple demands such as those for efficiency and creativity are likely to yield structures that blend elements of hierarchy and of flatter organizational forms that emphasize lateral connections. Structural hybrids responsive to a globalizing world are likely to be 'messy' and less easily drawn or described than traditional hierarchical types of structure.

Hybrids of Processes: Multiple demands globally enhance the need for a strategic management process that defines organizational purpose. Strategy is the most important process in what should be the portfolio of processes global enterprises develop. Other important processes include the process of entrepreneurship, of renewal, and of learning.

Levels of Strategy: Five levels of strategy are important to the business enterprise. The purpose of the enterprise or enterprise strategy should serve as the guide for corporate strategy, business strategy, operational strategy, and individual strategy.

The Growing Importance of Human Assets: Human assets are viewed as increasingly important to the global enterprise. Developing these assets requires top managers who can make decisions yet delegate responsibility.

Managerial Competencies: Those needed include both 'hard' and 'soft' skills, such as technical and functional skills and self-knowledge and an ability to interact well with others.

REVIEW AND DISCUSSION QUESTIONS

1   The argument in this chapter is that businesses affect their societies. Operationalize this concept by identifying the business in your community that employs the most people. What would be the immediate and long-term effects to your community if this employer were to close its operations tomorrow? How would these changes affect your life now and into the future?

2   Frederick Taylor and Henri Fayol viewed cooperation and teamwork as important to their theories, but they are remembered less for these ideas than for their contributions to rational, scientific management. What was the historical business context

that made scientific management principles more important to practice than ideas like teamwork that have only recently been adopted in the US?

3 According to a report appearing in a September 28, 1996 edition of *The Economist*, ('Tomorrow's second sex'), in North American and in Europe women dominate jobs that are growing and men are trapped in jobs that are declining. In rapidly growing Asian nations, women's job and educational opportunities also are growing, and in many developing economies, women increasingly are taking jobs in the paid labor force. Analyze how these changes are likely to affect work organizations. What are the likely impacts of these changes on social relationships between women and men? Overall, are these changes likely to prove positive or negative? Take a position and provide evidence to support it.

4 In February 1997, Royal Dutch/Shell Group announced a 23% increase over net income in the previous year, but analysts indicated these gains might be temporary. Shell Chairman John Jennings said global oil and natural gas output for Shell was expected to rise by about 7% annually between 1997 and 2001, but did not comment on crude oil growth potential, citing continuing expansion of non-OPEC production and resumption of Iraqi oil exports. Look at these events and those that opened the chapter to argue that a global world increases uncertainty for firms.

5 *The Global Enterprise Project*: For the enterprise you decided to study, find a statement of firm mission, vision, purpose, or ideals to answer the question: What is firm purpose and how does it accomplish purpose in the global marketplace? Concepts like core competencies or sustainable advantage also may help you answer this question.

REFERENCES

Adler, Nancy J., and Bartholomew, Susan. (1992). Managing globally competent people. *Academy of Management Executive*, 6 (3): 54.

Anderson, Sarah, and Cavanagh, John. (1997). *The top 200: The rise of global corporate power*. Washington, DC: Institute for Policy Studies.

Barnet, R.J., and Cavanagh, John. (1994). *Global dreams*. New York: Simon & Schuster.

Bartlett, Christopher, and Ghoshal, Sumantra. (1995, May/June). Changing the role of top management: Beyond systems to people. *Harvard Business Review*, pp. 132–142.

Bolman, Lee G., and Deal, Terrence E. (1995). *Leading with soul*. San Francisco, CA: Jossey-Bass.

Boynton, Andrew C., and Victor, Bart. (1991, Fall). The dynamically stable organization. *California Management Review*, pp. 53–66.

Brabet, Julienne, and Klemm, Mary. (1994). Sharing the visions: Company mission statements in Britain and France. *Long Range Planning*, 27(1): 84–94.

Brewster, Chris. (1995). Towards a 'European' model of human resource management. *Journal of International Business Studies*, 26(1): 1–21.

Brown, Andrew. (1994). Top of the bosses. *International Management*, 49(3): 26–29.

Brown, Juanita. (1992). Corporation as community: A new image for a new era. In John Renesch (Ed.), *New traditions in business*, pp. 123–139. San Francisco, CA: Berrett-Koehler.

Byrne, John. (1997, June 23). Commentary: Management theory – or fad of the month? *Business Week*, p. 47.

Calori, Roland, and Dufour, Bruno. (1995). Management European style. *Academy of Management Executive*, 9(3): 61–77.

Chakraborty, S.K. (1995). *Ethics in management: Vedantic perspectives*. Delhi: Oxford University Press.

Corporate governance is bringing change to the boardrooms of Europe. (1995, July 21). *The Wall Street Journal*, p. A5A.

Dreifus, Claudia. (1994, Dec. 18). Passing the scoop: Ben & Jerry. *New York Times Magazine*, p. 41.

Drucker, Peter. (1987). Social innovation: Management's new dimension. *Long Range Planning*, 20(6): 29–34.

Dubey, Suman. (1994, Nov. 28). India's Reliance sees vision shift to Ambani sons. *The Wall Street Journal*, p. A9A.

Eccles, Robert G., and Nolan, Richard L. (1993). A framework for the design of the emerging global organizational structure. In S.P. Bradley, J.A. Hausman, and R.L. Nolan (Eds), *Globalization, technology, and competition*, pp. 57–80. Boston, MA: Harvard Press.

Eggers, John H., and Leahy, Kim T. (1994). Entrepreneurial leadership in the US. *Issues and Observations* [Center for Creative Leadership publication], 14(1): 1–5.

Ettorre, Barbara. (1994). The experts rally: Tough leaders needed. *Management Review*, 83(9): 33–37.

Farrell, Christopher. (1994, Nov. 18). The triple revolution. *Business Week*, Special Issue: 21st century capitalism, pp. 16–25.

Fernandez, John. (1991). *Managing a diverse work force*. Lexington, MA: Lexington Books.

Fisher, Ann B. (1993, May 31). Japanese working women strike back. *Fortune*, p. 22.

Floyd, Steven W., and Wooldridge, Bill. (1994). Dinosaurs or dynamos? Recognizing middle management's strategic role. *Academy of Management Executive*, 8(4): 47–58.

G.E. is no place for autocrats, Welch decrees. (1992, Mar. 3). *The Wall Street Journal*, p. B1.

Ghoshal, Sumantra, and Bartlett, Christopher. (1995, Dec./Jan.). Changing the role of top management: Beyond structure to processes. *Harvard Business Review*, pp. 86–96.

Gibson, Cristina B. (1995, 2nd quarter). An investigation of gender differences in leadership across four countries. *Journal of International Business Studies*, pp. 255–279.

Gucci, Armani. . . and John Paul? (1996, May 13). *Business Week*, p. 61.

Hall, Richard. (1994). *EuroManagers and Martians*. Brussels: Europublications.

Harris, P R., and Moran, R.T. (1996). *Managing cultural differences* (4th ed.). Houston, TX: Gulf Publishing.

Hawken, Paul. 1993. *The ecology of commerce*. New York: HarperBusiness.

Hilmer, Frederick, and Donaldson, Lex. (1997). *Management redeemed: Debunking the fads that undermine our corporations*. Boston: Free Press.

Hofstede, Geert. (1980). *Culture's consequences*. Beverly Hills, CA: Sage.

Hofstede, Geert, and Bond, Michael H. (1988). The cultural connection: From cultural roots to economic growth. *Organizational Dynamics*, 16(4): 4–21.

Human Development Report. (1995). New York and Geneva: United Nations.

India's Mr. Business. (1994, Apr. 18). *Business Week*, pp. 100–101.

Janger, Allen R. (1980). *Organization of international joint ventures*. New York: Conference Board.

Keay, John (1991). *The honorable company: A history of the English East India Company*. London: HarperCollins.

Korn, Lester B. (1989, May 22). How the next CEO will be different. *Fortune*, pp. 157–159.

Kotkin, Joel. (1993). *Tribes*. New York: Random House.

Kraut, Allen I., Pedigo, Patricia R., McKenna, D. Douglas, and Dunnette, Marvin D. (1989). The role of the manager: What's really important in different management jobs? *Academy of Management Executive*, 3(4): 286–293.

Levinson, Harry. (1988). You won't recognize me: Predictions about changes in top-management characteristics. *Academy of Management Executive*, 2(2): 119–125.

Lindorff, Dave. (1994 , Nov. 18). Raised fists in the developing world. *Business Week*, pp. 130–132.

Mescon, Timothy S., and Tilson, D.J. (1987). Corporate philanthropy: A strategic approach to the bottom-line. *California Management Review*, 29(Winter): 49–61.

Naisbitt, John. (1994). *Global paradox*. New York: Easton Press.

Nonaka, Ikujiro. (1990). Managing globalization as a self-renewing process. In Christopher Bartlett and Sumantra Ghoshal (Eds), *Managing the global firm*, pp. 69–94. London: Routledge.

Prahalad, C.K., and Hamel, Gary. (1990, May/June). The core competence of the corporation. *Harvard Business Review*, pp. 79–91.

Rhinesmith, Stephen. (1993). *A manager's guide to globalization*. Alexandria, VA and Homewood, IL: American Society for Training and Development and Business One Irwin.

Rigby, Darrell K. (1994, Sept./Oct.). Managing the management tools. *Planning Review*, pp. 20–24.

Rosener, Judith. (1990, Nov./Dec.). Ways women lead. *Harvard Business Review*, pp. 119–125.

Roy, Delwin, and Regelbrugge, Laurie. (1995, Apr.). *Global citizenship: Gaining momentum and depth*. New York: Hitachi Foundation.

Sai, Yasutaka. (1995). *The eight core values of the Japanese businessman: Toward an understanding of Japanese management*. Binghamton, NY: Haworth Press.

Salancik, Gerald R., and Meindl, James R. (1984). Corporate attributions as strategic illusions of managerial control. *Administrative Science Quarterly*, 29(2): 238–245.

Sampson, Anthony. (1995). *Company man*. New York: Times Business.

Schellhardt, Timothy D. (1994, Oct. 28). Major firms in North America, Europe plan marketing changes, survey shows. *The Wall Street Journal*, p. A5B.

Selvarajah, Christopher T., Duignan, Patrick, Suppiah, Chandrseagran, Lane, Terry, and Nuttman, Chris. (1995). *Management International Review*, 35(1): 29–44.

Shareholder activists put CEOs on notice. (1995, Feb 20). *Fortune*, p. 16.

Shih, Stan. (1995, Nov. 3). On Asian competitiveness. *Asia Week*, 21(44): 30–32.

Smith, N. Craig, and Quelch, John A. (1992). *Ethics in marketing*. Homewood, IL: Irwin.

Sorge, Arndt. (1993). Management in France. In David J. Hickson (Ed.), *Management in Western Europe*, pp. 65–87. Berlin/New York: de Gruyter.

Spears, Larry. (Ed.). (1995). *Reflections on leadership*. New York: John Wiley.

Steadman, Mark E., Zimmerer, Thomas W., and Green, Ronald F. (1995). Pressures from stakeholders hit Japanese companies. *Long Range Planning*, 28(6): 29–37.

Tanzer, Andrew. (1994, July 18). The bamboo network. *Forbes*, pp. 138–144.

Taylor, William. (1991). The logic of global business. Reprinted in James Champy and Nitin Nohria (Eds), *Fast forward* (1996), pp. 61–88. Cambridge, MA: Harvard Business School Press.

Van Dusen Wishard, William. (1995). *We have crossed over the border of history*. Potomac, MD: Porter McGinn Associates.

Viotzthum, Carlta. (1995, July 21). 'Corporate governance' is bringing change to the boardrooms of Europe. *The Wall Street Journal*, p. A5A.

Wokutch, R.E., and Spencer, B.A. (1987). Corporate saints and sinners: The effects of philanthropic and illegal activity on organizational performance. *California Management Review*, 29(Winter): 62–77.

Women-owned businesses: Breaking the boundaries. (1995). New York: Dun and Bradstreet Information Services.

You ain't seen nothing yet. (1994, Oct. 1). *The Economist*, pp. 20–24, The Global Economy Survey.

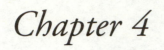

Chapter 4

Global Culture

I WANT MY . . . MTV

Founded with about $15 million US, Music Television (MTV) became a part of television and music history at its 12:01 am airtime on August 1, 1981. Its initial promotional image was a global one: an astronaut planting an MTV flag on the moon. Today's MTV images are similarly irreverent, reflective perhaps of a tendency among MTV's 18- to 24-year-old demographic group to question the status quo. Music Television is an organization with a strong internal culture whose icons are likely to be recognizable to music devotees throughout the world. Viewers not only learn about the culture MTV reflects but become part of an emerging global culture that is taking on a life of its own by melding words, music, and symbols across and between cultures.

MTV, together with new stations DD2 Metro in India, VH-1 in Britain, and MTV Asia, could reach from 250 to 500 million households by the turn of the century, and now include more viewers in the developing economies than in the US: according to Viacom, Inc., MTV's parent firm, 70 million households get MTV Brasil, Latin America, Mandarin, Asia, or India. While many of the video hosts, called vee-jays, use local dialects and languages, they make liberal use of a universal language that changes rapidly; where 'phat' and 'fly' can mean 'cool' one day and mean nothing the day after. And although MTV music videos came originally from the English-speaking world, they increasingly come from a global world of music. The growing influence of world music is reflected in Warner Music International's sales figures: less than a third of 1980 sales came from non-US artists, but in 1994 non-US acts provided 60% of Warner's sales, bringing in over $630 million. According to Tower Record's head of retail operations, even in the US 'foreign music is where all the hipsters are.'

MTV's stated mission is to be television's most powerful source of freedom, liberation, personal creativity, unbridled fun and hope for a radically better future. The reception desk in MTV's head office reflects some of the fun: it is a huge plastic rock symbolic of rock and roll. At the studios for the head office the monitors are always tuned to MTV, and among the staff it is considered uncool to ask someone to turn down their music.

College interns and production assistants populate MTV studios, and most are in MTV's demographic target group. Except for a very few, aging is synonymous with leaving MTV. Development of MTV programs or new formats for showing video music tapes often is in the hands of 24-year-old associate producers who can create an idea on Monday, 'sell' it to a producer on Tuesday, write it on Wednesday, shoot the video on Thursday, cut and edit on Friday, and air the show on Saturday. The organization has adopted a horizontal structure that enhances the speedy decision-making necessary to track fads and constantly evolving interests among young people. In summary, the mission, the language, the tangible symbols, and the behaviors of MTV employees underscore the solutions MTV has created to remain viable in a society where its audience is increasingly global.

Sources: La Franco, Robert, and Schuman, Michael. (1995, July 17). How do you say rock 'n' roll in Wolof? *Forbes*, pp. 102-103; Seabrook, John. (1994, Oct. 10). Rocking in Shangri-La. *The New Yorker*, pp. 64–78.

PART I   CONCEPTS OF CULTURE

The border crossings of time and space, of nation-states and economies, and of organizations and industries characteristic of globalization have focused increased attention on culture. Via emerging information technologies, people throughout the world are exposed to the cultural norms, values, and behaviors of many nations besides their own, and subsequently have the opportunity to think and even behave in ways that increasingly are described as global. Among adults, globalization of culture is particularly evident in widespread haste to engage in for-profit business activities. Microsoft Corporation's 1995 slogan 'Business is the engine of society' captures this dimension of globalization, suggesting that the world is a single society organized around for-profit business activities. As images like these and business activities go global, they not only are affected by but increasingly are having an effect on traditional cultural habits and beliefs within nations. Whether these habits and beliefs can lead to a truly global culture is a subject explored in this chapter.

DIMENSIONS OF CULTURE

Studies of culture once were the almost exclusive intellectual territory of cultural anthropologists, but with increasing world commerce throughout the 1970s and 1980s, business academicians recognized that concepts of culture could explain business activities in two ways. First, it became more usual to think of organizations as entities with separate 'cultures' made unique by the propensity of people within them to act, think, and develop common goals different from those found in other organizations. 'Strong' organizational cultures were expected to help organizations develop and implement common goals, while 'weak' organizational cultures were viewed as a drag on organizational purpose (Schein, 1992). The introductory case demonstrates that MTV's is a very strong and rich culture characterized by special habits, a specialized language reflected in words that originated in or are used only within MTV, and values shared by MTV employees.

Cultural concepts also were applied to businesses because of growing awareness of costs attributable to cross-cultural misunderstandings and culture 'clash.' In his book *Blunders in international business*, David Ricks (1993) described a great many business problems that resulted from cultural mismatches and misunderstandings. For example, Olympia tried to introduce a photocopier in Chile under the brand name ROTO. Poor sales of the copier may have been due to the fact that *roto* is the Spanish word for 'broken,' and is used to refer to lower socio-economic classes in Chile. Mistakes like these can be attributed not only to language differences, but to the fact that most of what we need to know about culture is hidden from us. Figure 4.1 shows how this occurs.

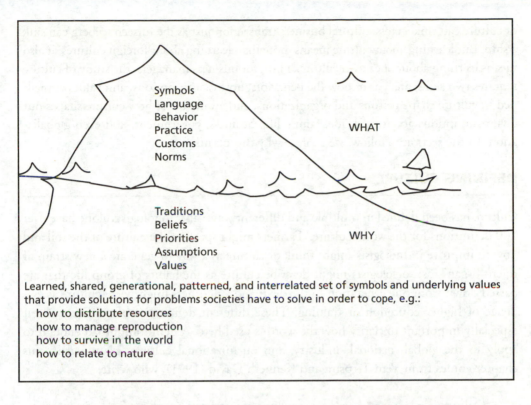

Symbols
Language
Behavior
Practice
Customs
Norms

WHAT

Traditions
Beliefs
Priorities
Assumptions
Values

WHY

Learned, shared, generational, patterned, and interrelated set of symbols and underlying values that provide solutions for problems societies have to solve in order to cope, e.g.:

    how to distribute resources
    how to manage reproduction
    how to survive in the world
    how to relate to nature

FIGURE 4.1 *Culture: what you see doesn't tell you why*

The cultural iceberg in this figure demonstrates that much of what we think we know about culture is embedded in behaviors or in 'what' we see. When people are part of the same culture, they generally derive the same meaning from the signs they read, words they hear, or behaviors they see. The same understanding is not assured when cultures mix; for the cultural sojourner 'what' is seen or heard may not explain 'why' it occurs. As a result, the newcomer's behavior may not be consistent with the host culture's norms and values. Often, culturally deviant behavior is viewed as evidence of abnormality, but before judging the international sojourner we should first go below the surface level of behavior to ask why that individual acts as she or he does. For example, it is not unusual for a Saudi Arabian to stare deeply into another's eyes because many in the Arab world believe eyes are a window on one's human qualities. In Nigeria, however, averting the eyes is a sign of respect, particularly where there are status differentials.

Differences in cultural beliefs explain why many behavioral differences occur. This 'why' of the cultural iceberg is less visible and below the cultural water-line, and it explains language, behaviors, economic systems, political systems, uses of technology, relationships with the natural environment, and other ways of being. The unseen and underlying values of culture can sink a cross-cultural business transaction just as the unseen iceberg can sink a ship. But learning about culture means more than learning about foreign cultures; it also means learning about one's own culture. Thus, for business managers, the study of culture requires two skills: analysis of how the behaviors, norms, assumptions, and values embedded in culture shape persons and organizations, and awareness of how culture shapes our own assumptions about work life, family life, business, government, and even globalization. In the section to follow, we analyze why this occurs.

DEFINING CULTURE

Culture has been defined in multiple and different ways; anthropologists alone have over 200 definitions for the word 'culture.' Farmers might speak of the culture of the soil and how to improve it; biologists might think of culture as a way to generate a new strain of micro-organisms; sociologists might describe culture as the habits of group life that are passed down from one generation to the next; and still others might view culture as evidence of higher education or training. These different definitions of culture make it especially important to clarify how the word is used here. A definition broad enough to apply to the global, national, industry, and organizational cultures examined in this chapter comes from Vern Terpstra and Kenneth David (1991), who write:

> Culture is a learned, shared, compelling, interrelated set of symbols whose meanings provide a set of orientations for members of a society. These orientations, taken together, provide solutions to problems that all societies must solve if they are to remain viable. (p. 6)

By definition, a society or culture is a group of people who associate with one another for some purpose. These purposes can vary widely, but societies tend to face similar problems and resolve them with similar mechanisms. For example, all societies need to find ways to feed their people. According to John Bennett and Kenneth Dahlberg (1993), five transitions occurred in cultural groupings as people developed societies to meet common needs.

- *Transition 1*: People living in family units as part of hunting and gathering societies *joined other families in larger groups* whose undertakings were directed and organized by group members.
- *Transition 2*: Nomadic group hunting became localized and *people settled in geographic territories* where they established one or more encampments.
- *Transition 3*: People began to raise plant foods and breed animals in *emerging village communities*.

- *Transition 4*: The rise of trade and craft manufacturing led to an urban revolution where people in groups began to *concentrate geographically in cities or towns*.
- *Transition 5*: Discovery of means to extract and concentrate energy and other resources in great quantities led to *the modern state* which balances between business interests and community interests.

A global world may represent a sixth transitional stage:

- *Transition 6*: Business activities make it possible for people to *transcend geographic and national loyalty barriers* to meet their needs.

Challenges that culture helps resolve

Linguistic, behavioral, and other cues to underlying values tend to reflect a cultural system in which people adopt similar priorities and belief systems. This commonality of thought and purpose assists cultural groups in generating common solutions for satisfying lower level needs for basic resources and higher level needs for human relationships and development. Its learned, shared, reinforced, and interrelated character makes culture something far more than a written list of rules. It is instead a dense network of behaviors, values, beliefs, and unarticulated assumptions. Untangling this web has been a life's work for many a social scientist and considerable insight into every aspect of human and organizational behavior has been gained from studying culture.

CULTURE ADDRESSES BASIC NEEDS

Abraham Maslow's (1954) hierarchy of human needs represents both basic and universal lower level physiological needs for food, water, shelter, and warmth; an intermediate need for safety; and higher level needs such as social needs for relationships and belonging, esteem needs for worth such as social or work status, and self-actualization or self-fulfillment needs (Figure 4.2). For most people living today, these needs – from the most basic and tangible needs to the least tangible – have been met by nations, but this may be changing.

Warfare in Rwanda and Eritrea demonstrate that a nation's inability to provide sufficient food and water can lead to insurrection, ethnic conflict, and even genocide. Through warfare, groups of people strive to develop new societies or new nations capable of providing the resources they need. Following its recent return to democracy, the island state of Haiti faced a similar cultural challenge: 'degraded by poverty, illiteracy, malnutrition, disease, violence, corruption, overpopulation, rapid urbanization, deforestation and soil erosion' (Rohter, 1994), Haitians found it difficult to cooperate in meeting basic

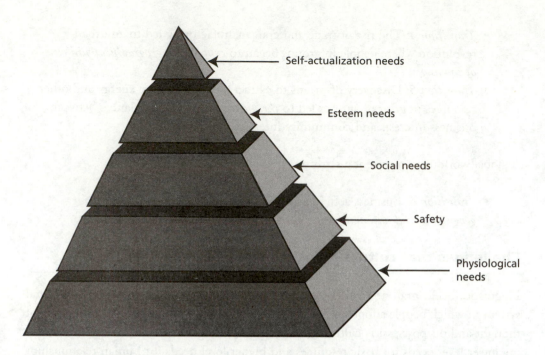

FIGURE 4.2 *Maslow's hierarchy of needs*

needs. Rwandan and Haitian responses to internal disunity have been to transcend national boundaries rather than reshape them. Haitian blacks look to African-Americans for development assistance, and Rwandans look to the human community for help.

Whether organized around nations or affinities, meeting basic needs is an important challenge a national culture resolves. Other challenges resolved by shared cultural norms include:

- protection from enemies and natural disasters with defense and emergency response systems;
- child raising and instruction;
- division of human labor;
- social controls against deviant behavior such as laws and prisons;
- providing ways to motivate people to do what they have to do;
- legitimizing and distributing power (Terpstra and David, 1991, p. 7).

CULTURE ADDRESSES HIGHER LEVEL NEEDS AND DEFINES VALUES

Cultural groups also create common answers to questions such as: Why am I here? What is the inherent nature of the human person? What should be the relationship between people and the natural environment? Answers to questions such as these provide people with a sense of values and give meaning to life, and they serve the 'higher order' needs in Maslow's hierarchy. The following sections examine how differences in national values have resulted in behavioral differences in the business world.

Values are the internalized rules people use to select and justify actions and to evaluate the self, other people, and events (Schwartz, 1992). Values tend to vary between nations. Table 4.1 shows that differences in values result in different beliefs and behaviors. For example, a valuative stance toward one's place in the greater scheme of things is demonstrated by polar opposites of FATALISM vs CONTROL. In a society where fatalism is prevalent, negative events at work or in personal life are attributed to the will of a supernatural force, to fate, or to luck. Since these events are perceived to be outside individual control, people most often acquiesce when they occur. Conversely, a cultural belief that people control their own destiny almost certainly will motivate individual efforts to alter negative outcomes. Follow the line of values down the middle of the table and you will see that underlying values shape assumptions, priorities, beliefs, and traditions as well as behaviors.

Among the many and varied cultural beliefs found in Table 4.1 is that some cultures affirm a belief that the past and present are more important than the future, whereas other cultures affirm a belief that the future is more important than what's past or even more important than the present. Planning is likely to be a more important business activity in a future-oriented society, while enjoyment of the present moment or friends – even if such enjoyment is not a business activity – is more likely in a present-oriented society. Recall, differences like these are not important when cultures are separate, but they have a profound impact on global and international business when the planner from a future-oriented culture perceives the present-oriented worker is playing instead of working. Similarly, the worker in a present-oriented society could easily conclude the future-oriented planner is rigid and overly serious about work. Neither behavior is wrong in its own society, but the two sets of cultural rules are in conflict. These cultural conflicts can lead to differences in behavior that result in misunderstandings and even personal conflict.

Researchers have explored value differences between nations to identify cultural attributes for nations. Some cross-cultural research efforts have examined which, if any, universal values apply across all or many cultures. The search for universals has been conducted for various reasons, with some seeking to explain why nations or cultures have developed economically and others satisfying interests in how people differ cross-culturally. An underlying interest for research on values is to understand the motivations that cause people to do what they do. If these values become clear, then from a business perspective it may be easier to motivate desired behavior.

TABLE 4.1 Cultural contrasts

Outcomes are influenced by fate or a higher authority	FATALISM VS CONTROL	Individuals control their own destiny
Humans should accommodate themselves to nature	HARMONY VS DOMINATION	Nature is a resource for people to use
Tradition is revered and reveals today's lessons	TRADITION VS CHANGE	Change is in most cases desirable
Live for today	PRESENT VS FUTURE	Plan for the future
Nurture the human spirit	PURPOSE OF LIFE	Create material wealth
Life is part of an independent whole	WAYS TO KNOW	Life is rational
Quality of life determines life success	DEFINITIONS OF SUCCESS	Wealth and status reflect success
Use time to build relationships	HOW TO USE TIME	Use time to acquire resources
Friendships are lifelong	THE ROLE OF FRIENDS	Friendships are quickly made and dissolved
Age is venerated	AGE VS YOUTH	Youth is valued; the old discarded
Identity is derived from group membership	SOURCE OF IDENTITY	Individual acts define the person
Depend on the group	SELF VS GROUP	Personal independence is paramount
Action results from compulsion and force	CAUSE FOR ACTION	Persuasion and reason direct action
Boasting disrupts harmony	MODESTY VS BOASTING	Self-aggrandizement is the only way to attract attention
Mistakes result in a loss of face	RISKS THAT FAIL	Mistakes show one is trying
Find ways to maintain harmony and save face for all parties	RESPONDING TO OTHERS	Tell it like it is, even if information criticizes
Cooperation leads to desired outcomes	COOPERATE OR COMPETE	Winning is the important outcome
Be indirect to avoid rudeness	HOW TO ASK QUESTIONS	Be direct; ask for what you want
Avoid conflict	HOW TO MANAGE CONFLICT	Confront conflict directly
Information is in the context and in the words	HOW MESSAGES ARE CONVEYED	Words embody meaning
Listen and memorize	WAY TO LEARN	Actively participate to learn

Source: Adapted from: Thiedemann, Sandra. (1991). *Bridging cultural barriers for corporate success.* Lexington, MA: Lexington Books.

NATIONAL VALUES

Hofstede's national cultural dimensions

Dutch researcher Geert Hofstede (1984) collected questionnaire responses on culture from what became a sample of 116,000 people in more than 50 countries. The research purpose was to identify values useful to cross-cultural management; average scores derived for 53 countries and regions are shown in Table 4.2. Hofstede described four dimensions of national cultural values as follows:

- *Individualism/collectivism*: This dimension reflects the relationship an individual is expected to develop with others. High individualism reflects a preference to act independently and high collectivism reflects a greater preference to work in relationship with others. In family life, individualism would be associated with nuclear families whereas collectivism would be associated more with extended families. In work life, individualism might manifest itself as a desire to work independently as compared to a desire to work in collective groups.

- *Power distance*: This dimension reflects the extent to which a society accepts that power is distributed unequally in society, its institutions and organizations. Inherent to a monarchy or caste system, for example, is a belief that some people are born to power and others are not. This inequality between persons is expected and accepted in a society high on power distance. In contrast, members of a low power distance society believe that status differences between individuals are associated with the roles they are playing. A preference for high power distance translates into behaviors that suggest one's position in life is determined, into a clear family hierarchy, and at work into a clear definition of who is to lead and who to follow. In a low power distance society, social inequities are minimized, there is substantial belief in equality among individuals, and a belief that hierarchies are convenient but not unalterable.

- *Uncertainty avoidance*: This dimension measures the extent to which people prefer certainty in their lives. Individuals high on uncertainty avoidance prefer formal rules and absolute truths, whereas individuals low on uncertainty avoidance enjoy lax rules and relative truths. Those low on uncertainty avoidance enjoy working with few rules. In contrast, uncertainty avoiders tend to prefer clear rules.

- *Masculinity/femininity*: This dimension of Hofstede's work is perhaps the least developed and the least well understood of those proposed. Part of the challenge is that words like masculine and feminine carry different sex-role expectations in various nations. As Hofstede defined them, these scales have little to do with sex roles *per se*, but rather reflect a society's preference for things versus people. In a masculine society, the emphasis is on valuing money and things; assertive acquisition of these things is reflective of a masculine society. Conversely, a feminine society is more likely to emphasize

TABLE 4.2 Scores on four national cultural dimensions for 53 countries or regions

Country	Power/distance		Individualism/collectivism		Masculinity/femininity		Uncertainty avoidance	
	Index (PDI)	Rank	Index (IDV)	Rank	Index (MAS)	Rank	Index (UAI)	Rank
Argentina	49	18–19	46	31–32	56	33–34	86	39–44
Australia	36	13	90	52	61	38	51	17
Austria	11	1	55	36	79	52	70	29–30
Belgium	65	34	75	46	54	32	94	48–49
Brazil	69	40	38	27–28	49	27	76	32–33
Canada	39	15	80	49–50	52	30	48	12–13
Chile	63	29–30	23	16	28	8	86	39–44
Columbia	67	37	13	5	64	42–43	80	34
Costa Rica	35	10–12	15	8	21	5–6	86	39–44
Denmark	18	3	74	45	16	4	23	3
Ecuador	78	45–46	8	2	63	40–41	67	26
Finland	33	8	63	37	26	7	59	22–23
France	68	38–39	71	43–44	43	18–19	86	39–44
Germany, FR	35	10–12	67	39	66	44–45	65	25
Great Britain	35	10–12	89	51	66	44–45	35	6–7
Greece	60	26–27	35	24	57	35–36	112	53
Guatemala	95	51–52	6	1	37	11	101	51
Hong Kong	68	38–39	25	17	57	35–36	29	4–5
India	77	43–44	48	33	56	33–34	40	9
Indonesia	78	45–46	14	6–7	46	23–24	48	12–13
Iran	58	24–25	41	30	43	18–19	59	22–23
Ireland	28	5	70	42	68	46–47	35	6–7
Israel	13	2	54	35	47	25	81	35
Italy	50	20	76	47	70	49–50	75	31
Jamaica	45	17	39	29	68	46–47	13	2
Japan	54	21	46	31–32	95	53	92	47
Korea, Rep. of	60	26–27	18	11	39	13	85	37–38
Malaysia	104	53	26	18	50	28–29	36	8
Mexico	81	48–49	30	22	69	48	82	36
Netherlands	38	14	80	49–50	14	3	53	19

TABLE 4.2 Continued

Country	Power/distance Index (PDI)	Rank	Individualism/ collectivism Index (IDV)	Rank	Masculinity/ femininity Index (MAS)	Rank	Uncertainty avoidance Index (UAI)	Rank
New Zealand	22	4	79	48	58	37	49	14–15
Norway	31	6–7	69	41	8	2	50	16
Pakistan	55	22	14	6–7	50	28–29	70	29–30
Panama	95	51–52	11	3	44	20	86	39–44
Peru	64	31–33	16	9	42	16–17	87	45
Philippines	94	50	32	23	64	42–43	44	10
Portugal	63	29–30	27	19–21	31	9	104	52
Salvador	66	35–36	19	12	40	14	94	48–49
Singapore	74	41	20	13–15	48	26	8	1
South Africa	49	18–19	65	38	63	40–41	49	14–15
Spain	57	23	51	34	42	16–17	86	39–44
Sweden	31	6–7	71	43–44	5	1	29	4–5
Switzerland	34	9	68	40	70	49–50	58	21
Taiwan	58	24–25	17	10	45	21–22	69	28
Thailand	64	31–33	20	13–15	34	10	64	24
Turkey	66	35–36	37	26	45	21–22	85	37–38
Uruguay	61	28	36	25	38	12	100	50
USA	40	16	91	53	62	39	46	11
Venezuela	81	48–49	12	4	73	51	76	32–33
Yugoslavia	76	42	27	19–21	21	5–6	88	46
Regions								
East Africa	64	31–33	27	19–21	41	15	52	18
West Africa	77	43–44	20	13–15	46	23–24	54	20
Arab countries	80	47	38	27–28	53	31	68	27

Source: Bangert, David C., and Pirzadas, Kahkashan. (1992). Culture and negotiation. *The International Executive*, 34(1): 43–64.

quality of life values, relationships, and nurturing behavior toward people in society.

Hofstede's significant contribution to understanding national values is not without its critics. Their views are summarized as follows:

- The value dimensions articulated in Hofstede's work are not exhaustive.
- Nationality in the various samples was limited to countries in which IBM had a subsidiary, so communist bloc countries weren't included.
- All data were drawn from one corporation, and results may have been influenced by IBM's corporate culture.
- Data were gathered from 1967 to 1973; major cultural changes have occurred since then and continue to do so.
- The dimensions are based on country means rather than individual means; there may be individual differences in culture that are lost by averaging scores within a country.
- Specific items for deriving cultural-level dimensions may not have the same meaning in each of the cultures (Bangert and Pirzada, 1992).

Trompenaars' dimensions of culture

Over a 10-year period, Alfons Trompenaars (1994) administered research questionnaires to over 15,000 managers from many countries, and based on at least 500 responses from each of 23 countries he proposed the following framework for comparing the cultural dimensions of a nation:

- *Universalism/particularism*: This is the belief that ideas and concepts can be applied everywhere vs the belief that circumstances dictate responses.
- *Individualism/collectivism*: Like Hofstede's scale, this represents the order of individual orientation; in an individualistic culture, the person would put his or her own interests first before group interests; the reverse is the case in a collectivist culture.
- *Neutral/affective*: Members of a neutral culture are expected to mask feelings whereas an affective culture considers it normal to show emotions and assumes emotions are a natural part of communication.
- *Specific/diffuse*: A specific culture supports large amounts of public space and small amounts of private space but a diffuse culture would support equal amounts of space for both public and private space; in a diffuse culture public space is more guarded because it provides entry into private space.
- *Achievement/ascription*: This orientation allocates status on the basis of

achievement or on the basis of accidents of birth such as year of birth, gender, ethnicity, nationality, birth order, etc.; this dimension is similar to Hofstede's power distance dimension.

Differences in cultural dimensions often are expressed in business behaviors that become the source of culture clash. For example, Table 4.3 illustrates that value differences lead to different behaviors throughout Western Europe. For example, higher relative collectivism in Germany results in group projects and decisions by committee whereas in the more individualistic Netherlands consensus is valued but individual decisions also are possible.

Trompenaars also concluded that cultures have different concepts of time that lead to sequential or synchronous preferences in the way time is used. A sequential preference focuses on the present or the future, with cultures that are sequential honoring appointments and schedules. The more synchronous approach to time puts a greater value on relationships of the past or the present, and time is seen as more flexible and less definite than in a sequential culture. Cultural orientations to the environment also generate different approaches to control. Defined as locus of control in much of the management literature, this dimension of culture includes an external locus of control for those who believe events are outside their control and an internal locus of control for those who believe they affect their environments with the decisions and actions they take. According to Trompenaars' data, locus of control is viewed as external in many nations where collectivism also is encouraged, including China, Singapore, Japan.

The dimensions of national culture produced by Trompenaars and Hofstede are useful tools for examining business behaviors and preferences for individuals from various nations. For example, nations with few management education programs tend to be those most likely to believe in ascription because training and education makes little difference for managers born to lead. An opposing belief in achievement in the US is one among many cultural reasons for management education programs intended to develop managerial skills and produce successful US leaders. For the most part, studies of national cultures tend to focus on what we might call the 'dominant' culture because it is the one most people know. This is not to say that nations are unified in terms of their cultural orientations. Within nations, we find subordinate cultures as well as dominant cultures. Additionally, there may be regional, organizational, familial, and other cultures in which an individual takes part. In this book, we focus primarily on the business culture.

INDIVIDUAL VALUES

Whereas Hofstede and Trompenaars focused on national values, Schwartz (1992) focused on universal individual values for people living in many nations. Based on his research, Schwartz concluded that there are four higher order value types that form two bipolar

TABLE 4.3 Country comparisons on six dimensions of culture

Country	Universalism vs particularism	Individualism vs collectivism	Neutral vs affective	Specific vs diffuse	Achievement vs ascription	Time concept
Germany	Universalistic: Focus on rules more than relationships 'A deal is a deal'	Collectivist: Decision by committee Group projects	Middle of the road May appear stuffy but warm under surface Devoted to order	Somewhat diffuse Formality is maintained at all times	Achievement: High status given achievement	Sequential: Future-oriented Honor appointments/ schedules
UK	Universalistic: Inner pride History of colonialism (universal rules) Common law	Individualistic: Quaint Eccentric Individual achievement emphasis Inventive	Neutral: Stoic and reserved Polite Gentlemanly Unflappable	Specific: Use of titles in formal settings Slow to form strong bonds	Achievement: Strong emphasis on business hierarchy Task orientation Goal-oriented	Sequential: Future-oriented Honor appointments/ schedules
Netherlands	Universalistic: History of colonialism Highly structured Proceduralized	Individualistic: Balance between knowledge and social factors Consensus also valued	Balanced, tending towards affective: Sociable once they know you Neighborhood orientation Enthusiastic with known entities	Specific: Long-term employment creates work/ home life bonds Loyal	Achievement: Often use aptitude testing to recruit Less careerist than some Tend to recruit from top echelon of schools	Sequential: Present- and future-oriented One activity at a time undertaken
Switzerland	Universalistic: Follow rules carefully Systematic	Balanced: Social contract is important	Affective: Outgoing Social	Specific: Tight inner circle of friends	Achievement: Personal achievement is important	Sequential: Present orientation Punctual and precise

TABLE 4.3 Continued

Country	Universalism vs particularism	Individualism vs collectivism	Neutral vs affective	Specific vs diffuse	Achievement vs ascription	Time concept
Denmark	Universalistic: Monarchy Highly structured Idealistic	Individualism: Individual responsibility for own actions Initiative rewarded Broad social support system	Neutral: Emotions controlled, but direct critique accepted	Diffuse: Long-term employment (work and private lives often closely related)	Achievement: Highly focused on education Small size but high quality, aggressive	Sequential: Keep appointments Act in present but look to future
Spain	Particularistic: Focus on relationships Personal systems Trust Duty to friends, family, etc.	Individualistic: Focus on individual achievement Personal responsibility Standing out is desirable	Affective: Physical contact more open and free Expressive, vocal Strong body language	Diffuse: Indirect Avoid direct confrontation More closed, introverted Link private and work lives	Ascription: Status based on position, age, schooling, or other criteria More homogenous workforce	Synchronous: Relationships most important, time not concern Flexible Present-oriented
Greece	Particularistic: Pride in own history, and ideas Not subject to others	Collectivist: Family and groups highly valued Church plays significant role in sense of community	Affective: Open and confident Expressive	Specific: Open/extroverted Private and tight inner circle	Balanced: Belief in experts and expertise Traditional family ties important	Synchronous: Long, distinguished history, time not definite

dimensions. As shown in Figure 4.3, one dimension of motivational values is labeled openness to change versus conservation while the other is labeled self-enhancement versus self-transcendence. These are explained as follows:

- *Openness to change versus conservation*: This dimension arranges values in terms of the extent to which they motivate people to follow their own interests in unpredictable and uncertain directions versus the extent to which they motivate people to resist change and preserve the status quo and existing relationships with others, institutions, and traditions.
- *Self-enhancement versus self-transcendence*: This dimension arranges values by the extent to which they motivate people to enhance their own interest – even if at the expense of others – as opposed to the extent that they motivate people to transcend selfish concerns in the interests of others' welfare. In this case, the welfare of others includes both close and distant relationships as well as a concern for the welfare of the natural environment.

One point of overlap between Hofstede and Schwartz is that what the former labeled uncertainty avoidance, the latter labeled openness to change versus conservation. Those who prefer to avoid uncertainties also are those who enjoy the status quo and seek security, tradition, and conformity. A second interesting point of overlap is that both

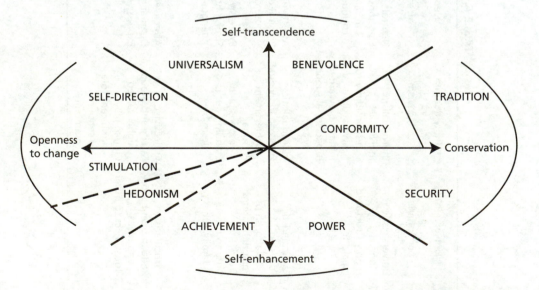

FIGURE 4.3 *Schwartz's two-dimensional model of motivational values* (Schwartz, Shalom H. (1992). Universals in the content and structure of values: Theoretical advances and empirical tests in 20 countries. *Advances in Experimental Social Psychology*, pp. 1–62)

authors view the conflict between self-interest and the welfare of others (individualism/collectivism) as universal.

Traditional sources of organizational culture

Like the larger societies from which they spring, businesses are collections of people who come together to resolve common problems, and just as national cultures provide answers to the problems societies face, organizational cultures provide answers to the challenges organizations face such as providing jobs, creating wealth, or surviving. Like nations, business enterprises develop symbols, behaviors, practices, customs, norms, values, assumptions, and even specialized language to achieve their objectives. Also like nations, organizations can house dominant and subordinate cultures; the latter can exist among professional groups, teams, or gender and ethnic groups, to name a few. Together, these above- and below-water-line aspects of the cultural iceberg define an organization's culture – what some think of as the organization's personality. The opening case demonstrates that MTV has a well-developed cultural personality reflected in cultural norms, behaviors, and widely shared values. For example, the practice of retiring older people reinforces the notion that MTV is for young people between 18 and 24. An organization with easily recognized symbols and habits like those described for MTV is considered one with a strong culture, a culture that describes how one is expected to behave both on and off the job. As with nations, organizational cultures may fail to meet participant needs, in which case they are forced to change or be changed. The BBC, for example, changed its mission to be more adaptive to listeners' demands and growing competition in a globalizing world (Box 4.1).

BOX 4.1:   THE EVOLVING MISSION AT THE BBC

The BBC was founded in 1922 to counter the growing influence of US mass culture. Broadcasting intent was to focus on self-improvement; symphony, opera, and chamber music were important features providing the public with what it ought to have rather than what it wanted. Under growing pressure to give people what they want and in the face of growing competition worldwide, the BBC expanded its mission by September 1996 'to remain the touchstone of quality in the new global multimedia environment.'

Sources: Dignam, C. (1995, Mar. 2). Media industry reels over BBC. *Marketing*, p. 9; LeMahieur, D.L. (1995). British Broadcasting Corporation. *Twenty-first century Britain: An encyclopaedia*, pp. 101–104. London: Garland.

FIGURE 4.4 *Traditional influences of culture on business organizations*

Like the BBC did when it was founded, business organizations operating solely within a domestic environment typically derive their cultural habits and values from their nation of origin. This relationship is illustrated in Figure 4.4, which shows that cultural values and beliefs within a nation usually have a common base reinforced by the people who populate those organizations. Workers throughout Asia are characterized as dedicated to their work – so much so in Japan that some die of overwork and the government mandates holidays. Thus, businesses in Japan and other nations with this Confucian work ethic encourage dedication to work and the organization. In this way attributes of national culture also become attributes of organizational culture.

Cultural congruence between organizational and national culture leads to organizational homogeneity, and when people within organizations are alike in appearance, thought, and action, they operate within a homogeneous organizational culture congruent with their own nation. However, organizations now increasingly operate across borders, and it may not be possible or desirable to remain homogeneous even within one's home culture.

GLOBALIZATION OF CULTURE
Changing business cultures

Efforts to be more heterogeneous often require a change in organizational culture, changes evident in organizations operating worldwide. IBM has abandoned its 'blue suit' mentality in favor of more chinos and 'casual' days to reduce formal relationships among themselves and between customers; the Mercedes-Benz label 'Made in Germany' that reflected national pride has been replaced with 'Made by Mercedes-Benz'; and the BBC has adapted to its more global world. Thus, going global either by chance or by choice may mean that organizations reflect their own cultures less than they once did. The example from Samsung in Box 4.2 shows how this may occur.

BOX 4.2:   CULTURAL CHANGE AT SAMSUNG

Samsung is the largest non-Japanese conglomerate in Asia with combined sales in 1996 of over $58 billion. Leader Lee Kun Kee sought to improve Samsung's competitive advantage with a change in organizational culture, asking employees for more flexible actions and new ways of thinking to develop a more creative and global outlook. Decision-making was moved from the hands of top-level Samsung managers to those most affected by the decision. To no one's surprise, wide-ranging changes like this one are difficult to implement in an organizational and national culture where conformity has more often been rewarded than individuality, and so Lee encouraged desired cultural changes by also changing Samsung structure, implementing rewards for individual success, and redesigning jobs and function. For example, meetings are limited to one hour, and reports to one or two pages. Changes like these that go against the grain of well-developed cultural norms for conformity and upward-oriented decision-making have had a spillover effect on other Korean firms, on Korean work habits, and even on government policy as South Korean politicians struggle to pass laws favoring firm autonomy in hiring, firing, and compensating employees.

Source: Kraar, Louis. (1994, Apr. 18). Korea goes for quality. *Fortune*, pp. 153–159.

Changes in organizational traditions necessarily create changes in organizational culture, but in the world of global business these changes also can be fed back to the parent culture. Focus on quality improvement initiatives among giant South Korean conglomerates like Samsung, Sunkyong, and Daewoo called for individual initiative and accountability instead of the deference to authority more traditional to Korean culture. Lee Kun Kee of Samsung, for instance, insists that employees leave work after eight hours. Changes like this presage a national change. As these large firms pursue an eight-hour day, smaller supplier firms also follow. This occurred in mainland China after Motorola introduced a 40-hour work week in 1995. In playing roles like these, business activities and enterprises become conduits for global culture as well as recipients of culture from many nations. Thus national culture is no longer the only source of culturally acceptable behaviors or beliefs as behaviors, norms, assumptions, and values begin to come from outside national boundaries. In this sense, culture has become 'boundaryless' as business activities increasingly transcend national boundaries. The nature of this relationship is shown in Figure 4.5.

A major source of cultural globalization today is business activities. As businesses

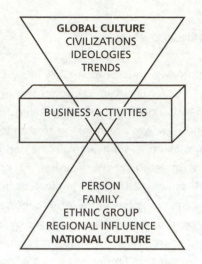

FIGURE 4.5 *Business activities in a global context*

find new markets for products, they transmit cultural messages of how people should look, talk, dress, think, and feel. More competitors provide alternative cultural messages to be weighed against existing norms and values, and combined they may produce individuals whose norms and values are more global than national. The process of cultural change is simultaneous with globalization in other spheres. Integration among market economies, more educated and sophisticated consumers, a growing middle class, and improved technologies of every sort create opportunities for cultural change. For example, reduced working hours, growing prosperity, and interest in Western life habits created an outlet for Western entertainment in China. By 2000 the entertainment industry is expected to invest $5 billion in Asia – a five-fold increase from 1994 (Darlin, 1994). The films, television programs, and music sold in China tell more than a story; they show a different way of life and suggest a different way of fulfilling life's needs. However unrealistic they may be to Westerners, when shown in another culture, these entertainment vehicles provide an ideal of market economics that people all over the world have begun to adopt. The culture of consumption displayed in entertainment media has, in effect, provided models for action copied not just in China but all over the world. Finally, global culture may be emerging because the cultural mechanisms found within nation-states are less well able to address or manage the problems and challenges societies face in a globally interdependent world.

Many business activities have the potential to shape worldwide cultural norms. This potential is explored in the following sections by looking at the cultural impact of two influential worldwide business activities: entertainment and travel.

Influences of entertainment

A major source of cultural globalization is entertainment media, including film, television, print media, games and human interactions, live and recorded performances, and other activities such as films, theme parks, and athletic performances. Unlike print media, electronic images and telecommunications are democratic, transmitted to a broad audience including the educated and the illiterate alike. Improvements in telecommunications and travel, the introduction of the Internet, and changes in work patterns are three factors fueling increased consumption of entertainment media, for which total worldwide sales and services were $132 billion in 1994 (Battle for the couch potato, 1995). The following examples show how entertainment media stimulate cultural globalization.

FILM

In the 1960s, former Indonesian president Ahmed Sukarno summarized cultural concerns about film in the following way:

> The motion picture industry has provided a window on the world, and the colonized nations have looked through that window and have seen the things of which they have been deprived. It is perhaps not generally realized that a refrigerator can be a revolutionary symbol – to a people who have no refrigerators. A motor car owned by a worker in one country can be a symbol of revolt to a people deprived of even the necessities of life. . . . [Hollywood] helped to build up the sense of deprivation of man's birthright, and that sense of deprivation has played a large part in the national revolutions of postwar Asia. (cited in McLuhan and Fiore, 1967)

Like other forms of entertainment media, film images convey cultural messages, and because the US produces 80% of worldwide movie box-office business (Auletta, 1993) many cultural images are Hollywood versions of life. Interestingly, many Hollywood special effects now are being filmed in India to take advantage of technical know-how and the lower relative cost of labor there. Bombay or 'Bollywood' is the second largest film producer in the world, followed closely by Hong Kong. Wherever produced, film images increasingly cross national borders, attracting US and European fans to Jackie Chan and John Woo as readily as other fans have been attracted to US films. In the third week of April 1997, *Return of the Jedi* – a film crossing borders of time, space, and nation – was simultaneous among the top three box-office hits in Brazil, Britain, Germany, Egypt, and the US.

TELEVISION

Television made it possible for 538 million people to watch the first person walk on the moon, an event symbolic of border transcendence in information and beyond geographic borders. US businesses were among the first to exploit advantage of reaching millions with a television message. Today over half of non-news television programming comes from the US, and television reaches over 800 million homes. In Asia alone, the number of TV households is expected to increase from 290 million in 1995 to 616 million in 2005. Hong Kong-based Star television was established in 1991, and it now sends its signals to 45 million viewers from Jordan to Japan. Potential growth is enormous since Star reaches 38 countries whose combined population is half the world or 2.7 billion people (Brauchli, 1994).

Television images beamed throughout the world attract many viewers, some of whom are making significant financial sacrifices to acquire this technology. People wringing out a scarce living on a *falucca* in Egypt, a *shakara* in Kashmir, or on a plot of land in Peru share priorities for television ownership. So pervasive is interest in television that those who cannot purchase their own often pool village or family resources to purchase a television.

Programming for children

Cartoons and fantasy tend to be fairly universal in their appeal, and children watch the same cartoons and fantasies worldwide. In the United States, children spend an average of 20 hours per week in television viewing, and much of what US children learn is via television. Many are believed to be influenced by activities of the Mighty Morphin Power Rangers, teenage characters developed in Japan who are forces for good against the world's evils. A program like this introduces egalitarian values since viewers tend to identify with the need to fight evil in the world. It also develops habits. The Mighty Morphin characters manage to kick, hit, and fight their way through most of every 30-minute television program. Children as young as pre-school reportedly 'skulk around kicking each other in the playground' (Caution, 1994), and otherwise mimic Power Ranger behavior so frequently that schools from New Zealand to Europe banned morphing activity. Children's programming not only sells values and demonstrates behaviors that children adopt worldwide, but also provides a forum for selling products, including an endless stream of toys from Power Rangers to Rug Rats. This early exposure may be a building block for a global society oriented toward consumption.

News

The concept for 'the world's only 24-hour global television news network' was pioneered by Cable News Network (CNN), which by 1993 reached 200 nations and more than 16% of all homes with televisions (Auletta, 1993). CNN views every citizen as a global citizen, but it took time to develop those citizens as viewers of a global news network.

When CNN was launched in 1980, it had only 1.7 million subscribers, but news broadcast worldwide began to foster the sense that events were occurring that concerned the whole world. CNN introduced the world to changes occurring in mainland China by covering Tiananmen Square events in 1989; through it we witnessed the fall of the Berlin Wall; and CNN's coverage of the Gulf War brought us live war. Perhaps mindful of potential CNN coverage, demonstrators worldwide frequently carry placards with their demands printed in English.

Globally telecast news events doubtless make them more real for people, bringing the world closer in knowledge if not in understanding. The success of CNN has attracted competitors from around the world, including the BBC, Reuters Holdings PLC, Australia Broadcasting's Asa-news channel, Euronews, and Sky News (Valente, 1994), suggesting that global news broadcasting is an emerging standard.

Music television

Perhaps more than any other form of popular culture, music television is most reflective of globalizing culture today. Not only does it reach an enormous audience worldwide, but its appeal transcends barriers of age and blurs what once was a clearer line between music and advertising. Further, where once being 'cool' was a spontaneous and local occurrence, now people can learn what is trendy elsewhere and adopt globally endorsed styles – providing they have the money. Thus music television has extended values associated with wealth creation and consumption. Music television also blurs the line between real life and fantasy life. For example, MTV broadcasts a program called *Real Life* which chronicles the experiences of a group of young people selected as roommates to be filmed for MTV. Is it life, or is it . . . MTV? Is there a difference?

The concept of music television was pioneered by MTV, which attracts viewers from every continent but Antarctica, and reaches 190 million households outside the United States. Whereas many European viewers have not embraced US television programming, they often will watch MTV or similar channels like VIVA music channel in Germany, or STAR – a growing music television force in Asia. The lively graphics and repeated themes in both advertising and performances on music television make it difficult to distinguish between content, advertisements, and music video. The distinction between music and ad may be irrelevant since the video is an advertisement for the performing artists. The music, the programs, and the advertisements all become part of the same package selling consumption. Branded products become not only a product but a lifestyle choice.

MUSIC

Perhaps because it is broadcast via the most developed global media, television and radio, music also has gone global. Sales in music recordings doubled in many nations from 1990 to 1995, including an increase of over 100% in Ireland, Hong Kong, Austria, Japan, and

Norway. Total global sales of music reached $35 billion in 1994 and topped $39.8 billion in 1996; according to the International Federation of the Phonographic Industry (http://www.ifpi.org), 70% of 1996 increases came from sales in less developed markets in Latin America and Asia. As the opening case indicated, music sales for non-US artists are growing exponentially throughout the world. This shift represents a radical departure from the early days of MTV, which featured primarily mainstream US and British artists. 'Indie' music produced by independent labels is an example of music outside the mainstream that migrated outward from Britain, while Europop music, also known as 'techno' or 'house', dominates the music scene in Europe. By 1997, techno – electronic dance music characterized by a strong beat, sound distortion, and occasional lyrics – found US popularity for the Chemical Brothers, the Prodigy, and Goldie, all of whom found initial fame in Europe. MTV responded to expanding music interests by introducing a techno show called Amp. In Taiwan music variety introduced from abroad has made it possible for local producers to expand their repertoire and offer Taiwanese recordings as well as Mandarin, US, Japanese, European, and other music. Globalization is altering the music industry by admitting new entrants worldwide. Table 4.4 illustrates the global reach of the music market and dominant business players in it.

Also indicative of globalization is that many more recording artists find audiences

TABLE 4.4   Globalization of popular music

Company name	Sales ($billion)	World market share (%)	Top talent
Polygram	4.7 (1994)	19	Bon Jovi, Boys II Men, Stevie Wonder (US); Ace of Base (Sweden), Jacky Cheung (Hong Kong), MC Solaar (France)
EMI Music	3.35 (1995)	15	Garth Brooks, Frank Sinatra, Janet Jackson (US); Roxette (Sweden), Yumi Matsutoya (Japan), Jon Secada (Cuba), Mamonas Assassinas (Brazil), Eric Moo (Taiwan)
Warner Music Group	4 (1994)	18	Madonna, Hootie & the Blowfish (US); Laura Pausini (Italy), Dadawa (China), Aaron Kwok (Hong Kong), Luis Miguel (Mexico)
Sony Music Entertainment	4.9 (1995)	17.5	Michael Jackson, Bruce Springsteen, Pearl Jam (US); TUBE (Japan), Harlem Yu (Taiwan), Patricia Kaas (France)
Bertelsmann Music Group	3.8 (1995)	13	Whitney Houston, Grateful Dead (US); Masaharu Fukuyama (Japan), Diego Torres (Argentina), So Pro Contrariar (Brazil)

Source: Dwyer, Paula. (1996, Jan. 15). The new music biz. *Business Week*, pp. 48–51.

among those without a shared language. Youssou N'Dour sings in his native language, Wolof – he is from Senegal – but still sold more than 1.5 million copies in the US, Europe, Asia, Africa, and Latin America; India's Daler Mehndi plays to huge audiences around the world; Ireland's Enya sings in Gaelic and has sold 8 million copies of her *Shepherd Moon* album; Eros Ramazotti from Rome sold 3.5 million of an album in Europe and Latin America; and Heroes Del Silencio sold more than half of their latest album in countries where Spanish is not the native language (La Franco and Schuman, 1995, pp. 102–103). Dangdut music produces a dreamy, throbbing beat, and while it originated in Indonesia, it has found listeners from Japan to the Middle East. Many of the songs have a strong Islamic theme, flavored by Indian movie themes and Middle Eastern pop music (Cohen, 1991). Similarly, the drumming, dancing music of Sikh banqara blended with rap, hip-hop, and other sounds has found listeners worldwide (Booth, 1997). Together, these examples illustrate the capacity for global business activities to cross national boundaries and reshape buying habits, listening habits, and even cultural values. Many fear these values will be based on mass-market tastes, but the experience described in Box 4.3 suggests the opposite also is possible.

BOX 4.3:   MARKETING PARADOX

Launched in 1992 by global media giant Time Warner and a British local-radio group, Britain's Classic FM posted an operating profit by 1995. Using advertising techniques pioneered by mass marketers, and a computer-based catalog of almost 33,000 pieces of music sortable by mood, composer and length, John Spearman tailors programs to specialty niches in the classical music market. The concept caught on first in Britain, then spread to the European continent and the US, benefiting from worldwide admiration for classical music and few language constraints. Technological breakthroughs, a global audience for classical music, globalization in the entertainment industry, and mass market advertising techniques applied in new ways produced a winner for Classic FM.

Source: Adapted from Marketing Mozart. (1995, Dec. 2). *The Economist*, p. 74.

Influences of travel

Travel also provides exposure to cultural norms other than one's own. Four sources of increased travel are particularly important to globalization of culture: business, education, tourism, and electronic travel. Many if not most of these activities are motivated by or responses to growing global business activities.

BUSINESS TRAVEL

Globalization of business has sent business travelers all over the world, including expatriates sent abroad by their companies and people who can be characterized as voluntary expatriates because they migrate on their own. Ease of travel and improved access to information has increased voluntary expatriate behavior among those who are not necessarily part of the professional class. For example, Filipinos working abroad as seamen, maids, cooks, and nurses now contribute almost 4% of GNP to the home country.

EDUCATION ABROAD

The relatively low cost and ease of air travel has increased tourist travel abroad, and a number of factors also have increased interest in higher education abroad, e.g., worldwide belief that education is a means for acquiring the knowledge necessary for economic development, low or no access to higher education in the home country, family connections in other lands, and better means of communication and travel that facilitate home country contact. In the US about 62% of engineering doctorates are awarded to foreign-born students, and the numbers are almost as high for doctorates earned in math, computer science, and the physical sciences. In 1996–97 the total contribution of international students to the US economy hovered around $7 billion per year (Institute of International Education, 1998). Confucian reverence for education, coupled with rising incomes among the Chinese middle class, and the limited number of higher education slots in Asia have led many overseas Chinese to send their children abroad for undergraduate and graduate study. Over 10% of US doctoral degrees in science and engineering in 1990 went to students from Taiwan, China, and South Korea. Many international students study business and economics. For example:

- Among the 453,000 international students enrolled in US colleges and universities in 1995, 20% studied business administration.
- Half of the 6,000 students at the London School of Economics are from outside the European Union.
- Many former students of economics at the University of Chicago have been central to economic planning in Latin America (see Box 4.4).

According to the *International Herald Tribune*, English public schools attract a growing number of secondary school students from Asia (British public schools, 1994) and many foreign leaders also are educated in England, including India's finance minister, Manmohan Singh, who was educated at Oxford. *Forbes'* list of billionaires contains dozens educated in countries other than their own. For example, following schooling at the University of California, Berkeley, Masayoshi Son built Softbank Inc. into Japan's biggest software wholesaler, and Marco De Benedetti of Olivetti studied at Wesleyan

---

BOX 4.4:   POLITICIANS EDUCATED IN THE US

Part of the free market revolution occurring in Latin America is attributed to US graduate study in economics (Moffett, 1994), particularly among 'Los Chicago Boys' who studied at the University of Chicago with Arnold Harberger who developed technically skilled policy makers with a penchant for free markets and low government intervention in business. Latin American leaders who studied in the US include Pedro Aspe, Mexico's former finance minister; Alejandro Foxley, former finance minister of Chile; and Domingo Cavallo, economic minister of Argentina.

Source: Moffett, Matt. (1994, Aug. 1). Key finance ministers in Latin America are old Harvard-MIT pals. *The Wall Street Journal*, pp. A1, A6.

University and completed an MBA at the Wharton School. By 1990 over 85,000 Japanese students were studying abroad, and this number was triple those studying abroad five years earlier. US students also increasingly study abroad, and it is more usual than not for university business students in Europe to spend some time in countries other than their own to acquire language and other cultural skills. In New Zealand, university students often consider their education incomplete without an 'overseas experience'.

Both tourists and to a greater extent students contribute to increased cultural convergence because they bring new habits to home cultures, encouraging local businesses to carry foreign products, seeking out international restaurants, starting their own businesses, and otherwise generating greater diversity within the home nation. Moreover, countries often are more responsive to cultural shifts generated by travelers when they are linked to economic gains. *New York Times* journalist Michael Specter (1994) describes how this looks in one part of Russia (Box 4.5).

TOURISM

Tourism is a global industry numbering 592 million travelers in 1996 and 540 million international arrivals in 1995 as compared to 321 million in 1994 (World Tourism Organization, 1997). Overall air travel is predicted to quadruple from 1.3 billion passengers in 1995 to 5.2 billion expected in 2010, equivalent to 90% of today's population of about 5.8 billion. International tourism receipts were $372 billion in 1995, representing 7% growth over 1994, and tourism receipts grew another 4.6% in 1996. Tourism is of growing importance to most economies. Tourism represents as much as 7.8% of annual GDP in Brazil, employing about 6 million people (Life's a beach, 1995); and the

---

BOX 4.5:   DATELINE . . . KHABAROVSK, RUSSIA

A popular Korean takeout place has opened at the corner of Leo Tolstoy and Kin Yu Chen Streets. Women are wearing cotton sundresses bought from Chinese salesmen who live across the border, 20 miles away. A visitor from Seattle has set up an espresso bar. And at the top of the city's Intourist Hotel, part of a chain that in most Russian cities still seems about as innovative as an old Communist Party boss, Japanese businessmen perform karaoke and eat Tokyo-quality sushi.

Source: Specter, Michael. (1994, Aug. 14). A Russian outpost now happily embraces Asia. *New York Times*, Section 1, p. 12.

Russian tourist trade is responsible for expansion of Istanbul's Aksaray district from 1,000 shops in 1993 to 40,000 in 1995. In the US, international tourism accounted for $75 billion in 1997.

In summary, business activities associated with tourism not only stimulate economies, but also stimulate cultural melding as travelers bring new products and new ideas to other cultures and return them to their own. With worldwide integration, and particularly increased human mobility, these activities contribute to cultural convergence, providing global opportunities and challenges that require global solutions. For example, according to a spokesperson for Human Rights Watch, 'there has been the clear emergence of a global market for child prostitution, both male and female, and that market is being fueled by tourists' (cited in Shoup, 1994). Nations like Sweden have taken the initiative to stop global child prostitution by prosecuting Swedish citizens who participate in it, and the same globalization of information that makes it possible to create a global market for child prostitution also is a resource for informing the world and galvanizing action against human exploitation.

ELECTRONIC TRAVEL

Part entertainment, part form of mind travel, the Internet is a hybrid mode of information exchange. Assuming that telephone lines and computers are available, this medium is inexpensive as compared to other media, it becomes easier to use each day, and access is improving to facilitate trade of electronic images, ideas, and information across traditional boundaries of time, convention, and national borders. It would be difficult to overestimate the potential effects on culture this form of information exchange provides, and some of these effects will be explored in Chapter 9. Other technological breakthroughs with a great impact on culture include improved telephone communication, which has enhanced information exchange; this too will be explored in greater depth as a part of global technology.

EVIDENCE OF GLOBAL CULTURAL CONVERGENCE

Entertainment, travel, and related industries demonstrate high potential for cultural convergence of visible behaviors – those that are above the water-line on the cultural iceberg. The following section provides evidence of global shifts in behaviors, examines their potential for reshaping underlying values, and outlines concerns associated with cultural globalization.

Global habits

Thirty-five years ago pizza was a new item in the heartland of the US, and Ricky's Russian restaurant was the closest Hong Kong came to serving Western food. In its many forms, pizza has become a global food; in Hong Kong alone it can be found as only one among many food offerings, including Western-style cookies, hamburgers, and hot dogs, Thai food, Japanese, French, and Southwestern cuisine. Introduction and adoption of similar eating habits throughout the world is stimulated by fads and by a globalizing workplace. Younger people like to try new tastes, and want to be like others their age worldwide. Throughout the world, more women work outside the home, and in many countries there are growing numbers of single-parent households. This leaves little time for daily shopping or cooking, and stimulates the number of households relying on fast foods, quick takeouts, and frozen meals. It also increases waste; one country's response to wasting food is featured in Box 4.6. Worldwide fast food sales per capita are highest in the US, where most women now work outside the home. In Japan, Kentucky Fried Chicken is more popular than it is in the US and in Britain home-delivered pizza is the fastest growth segment of the fast food market. In the US, many eat more like the rest of the world; cilantro, shiitake mushrooms, and sun-dried tomatoes are only a few *de riguer* foods scarcely known in the heartland of America a decade ago.

Global changes in economics, politics, and technology now appear to be fueling globalization of food habits and interests. As noted above, global teens spread fads and busy working women find little time for daily shopping. Growing concerns about health also are stimulating food convergence and so are technological and industry changes. Technological breakthroughs make it possible to produce specialty foods in quantities sufficient for retail, and domestic harvests create no barriers since preservation and distribution breakthroughs aid speedy delivery worldwide. Reflective of this are food sales in quality-conscious Japan where imports of US foods increased by almost $2 billion to $11 billion in 1995. Convergence in food preferences also has created business opportunities,

BOX 4.6:   SOUTH KOREA'S WAR ON LEFTOVERS

Rapid economic development in South Korea permits a cultural habit the govern-ment is trying to change: reducing the millions of tons of food South Koreans throw out each year. Thirty-two percent of all garbage in South Korea is food as compared to 25% in Canada or 28% in Germany. Cultural tradition and economic prosperity combine to produce meal tables overflowing with dishes including the rice bowl, soup, stew, a main dish and 5–6 side dishes. Government programs to reduce waste include regulations and incentives. Companies also are joining in, reducing waste at company-sponsored cafeterias, and even embarrassing workers into waste reduction. For example, a chemical company weighs employees' left-overs in full view of other workers. The reasons for conserving food are global as well as local: the world's food supplies are dwindling even as global economics stimulates the South Korean economy and makes it possible for people to act on cultural beliefs that 'more is better.'

Source: Jelinek, Pauline. (1997, Jan. 1). South Korea motto: Clean your plate. *The Seattle Times*, p. A12.

but as the example of Domino's Pizza shows (Box 4.7), those opportunities often require businesspeople to create food hybrids to bridge cultures.

Increased industry competition in grocery sales results in a search for interesting, new products for all consumers. Availability of options results in cultural mergers like moo goo tacos, sushi crêpes, and Taos-style paella. Changes in food habits have affected other cultural norms: the French now schedule the big meal of the day in the evening instead of at midday, Japanese and US women postpone home-style meals for weekends, and dining alone has become more nearly a worldwide norm. Food prices worldwide also are rising, spurred not by demand but by falling supplies created by interdependent global shifts in many sectors (Box 4.8).

In addition to these changes in food and dining habits, commercial holidays once found within a limited number of nations also have spread. For example, Valentine's Day is now celebrated in many nations. Style of dress and other consumption habits, e.g., use of cellular telephones and beepers, also are more global. Finally, sports also are con-tributing to changes in cultural habits: US-style football is gaining in popularity in Europe, and soccer is gaining adherents in the US. Sports globalization has come about because of shifts in the various global environments we are studying; this is illustrated with the example of soccer globalization in Box 4.9.

BOX 4.7:   DOMINO'S PIZZA IN JAPAN

Ernest M. Higa is a native of Hawaii who took the Domino's Pizza concept to Japan in 1984. Domino's corporate leaders were skeptical, and Higa's family members fearful that pizza would not fare well in Japan because of cultural preferences. Japanese were unaccustomed to eating without instruments, did not universally enjoy cheese, and tended to avoid foods that were not Japanese in character. As it turned out, young Higa had read his market correctly. Young Japanese were ready for changes, and willing to give pizza a try. Moreover, while it remains true that older Japanese are cautious about change, young people in Japan not only enjoy change, but have other cultural reasons for embracing change. Globalization is drawing more women and men into the workplace, and as has occurred in the industrialized countries this increases demand for easy meals, many of which are available from fast-food vendors operating franchises. The Domino's example shows how success can occur. Ten years after opening their first store in central Tokyo in 1985, Domino's has expanded to include 106 stores in Japan with $140 million in annual sales and over 4,200 Japanese employees. While the pizza product remains essentially the same, cultural adaptations in Japan include tuna and squid pizza toppings, and food preparation oriented to presentation in response to Japanese beliefs that 'one eats with one's eyes' first.

Source: Steinberg, Carol. (1995, Mar.). Millionaire franchisees. *Success*, p. 65.

BOX 4.8:   FOOD PRICES RISE

Growing demand for food in China is but one factor driving worldwide food price increases. Government alliances like the World Trade Organization have reduced farmer incentives and subsidies, poor harvests due to weather shifts have created lower yields, and export booms have reduced domestic supplies followed by a demand run-up in prices. Government stockpiles worldwide also are at their lowest historical points, winnowed by growing demand and by government decisions to get out of the food-subsidy business.

BOX 4.9:   SOCCER GOES GLOBAL

Technological breakthroughs in satellite transmissions have created worldwide opportunities for private broadcasters like BskyB of Britain, Canal Plus of France, Kirch Group of Germany, and Mediaset of Italy. These and other broadcasters now pay billions for the rights to televise soccer games, using soccer's popularity to gain new viewers. Governmental changes have relaxed rules on the number of non-locals who can play on national teams, resulting in mini-United Nations of team players selected from among the best in the world. Corporations are discovering the sponsorship value of soccer in reaching new audiences, and industries are altered as firms like Adidas and Disney produce merchandising tie-ins to link their products with soccer. With more viewers and more sponsors has come pressure on soccer teams and fans to tone down their language and behaviors, and players as well as managers increasingly view soccer as a business as well as a game. Further, proving that a change in one aspect of culture often produces another, interest in classical music surged following use of Pavorotti's 'Nessun dorma' as the theme song for the 1990 World Cup matches.

Source: Goodbye hoodlums, hello big money. (1996, Sept. 23). *Business Week*, pp. 66–68.

This example shows that as interests of sports, government, business, and technology all converge around soccer to expand business interests, they bring about changes in the game that have altered its essential nature and people's views of it. These behavioral changes also are reflected in the world of business.

Global business

In the world of global business, Western-style suits, business cards printed in different languages, and handshakes are usual. Punctuality and efficient use of time also are growing in universal appeal. Alvin and Heidi Toffler (1994) assert that in the accelerated system of wealth creation each unit of time saved is actually worth more than the last unit of time because one can create more value with each new minute of time. MTV demonstrates the speed of global business: an idea proposed on Monday is written and produced for Saturday's broadcast. The more social business style of meeting within 10 minutes to an hour or more of the appointed time traditionally practiced in France, Latin America, Spain, and many Pacific Rim countries has given way to punctuality, reinforcing

Western norms that 'time is money.' For example, Peruvian business meetings typically begin late, but if foreigners are present, the meeting begins on time.

Many of these alterations in business practices complement rather than replace prior custom. A handshake and a bow, a business card with different languages on reverse sides, and surrounding business meetings with social events are a few of many ways business practices have become hybrids reflecting both Western and non-Western norms. These behavioral changes are superficial, and as such they may not challenge home culture practices or norms. A Japanese in a Western-style suit remains Japanese beneath the suit. Real change comes not from the superficial or from behavior, but from shifts in underlying values of the culture. However, behavior and values are related and a change in one can bring about a change in the other. The following example illustrates this point.

A GLOBAL BUSINESS LANGUAGE

Scientists meeting at the American Association for the Advancement of Science in 1995 concluded there were about 6,000 languages, but predicted that over half of them were likely to die out in the twenty-first century (Haney, 1995). The demise of language variety is in part due to business globalization, particularly use of business English in many, if not most, international transactions, and English-language programming for many forms of entertainment. Further, the growing number of Internet users are almost forced to use English because that is the language of most World Wide Web sites. So, despite the fact that Chinese is the native tongue of the majority of the world's population, it is English that has become the global language. By one estimate, over 1 billion of the world's 5.3 billion people speak English, although most speak it as a second or foreign language (Newman, 1995). The pervasive reach of English is demonstrated in Box 4.10.

Many worry that business English will corrupt other cultures as concepts particular to the English-speaking world ride the vehicle of language to supplant existing cultural norms. For example, the English 'Program of Action' for the 1994 United Nations

---

BOX 4.10:   ENGLISH LANGUAGE IN USE

- Over 85% of World Wide Web sites are in English.
- Over 80% of information stored in all the world's computers is in English.
- English is the dominant or official language in over 60 countries, and is routinely used in 75 other countries.
- The world's largest language school, Berlitz International, reports that 70% of the 5 million lessons it gives per year are English.

population conference included words like 'empowerment,' 'reproductive rights,' and 'birth control' that were difficult to translate into other languages. The 'sexually active unmarried individuals' described in the Program of Action would, for instance, be criminals under Islamic law, and many languages contain no word for empowerment, much less female empowerment (Waldman, 1994).

The pervasive reach of English words into other languages, and the cultural concepts that underlie them often are unwelcome. The Academie Française, established in 1635 to legislate French language use, passed a law barring English words like *le weekend*, *le parking*, and *le cheeseburger*. This law was watered down by subsequent legislation, but it demonstrates the clear interrelationships the Academie Française sees between national culture and language use. In the US, a group calling itself English US has lobbied to make English the nation's official language, and they too operate in the belief that language erosion is cultural erosion.

Inasmuch as many who speak English today are learning it as a second language, mistakes are frequent. Repeated often enough, these mistakes can become the standard and further confuse cross-cultural communications. For example, in Russia the definitions for short-term government bills and longer term bonds somehow were transposed, raising both language and investment issues for would-be investors. Additionally, since many learn English via a specialized language, e.g., computer-speak, they may be acquiring a vocabulary that most of the English-speaking world does not share.

Global demographic groups

Global teens and global elites are two demographic groups identifiable worldwide. The characteristics of each group are shown in Table 4.5. The global elite, composed of the very wealthy who move in rarefied circles, probably do not represent a new phenomenon. There is little doubt that these elites spread habits of high-price quality and consumption worldwide, but for the most part their influence is contained within the group. Teens, on the other hand, represent a new phenomenon attracting global attention because this group is part of the middle class. Global teens are by definition 13- to 19-year-olds who share behaviors, interests, and values, and who are reached via similar mechanisms. Teens number about 228 million in Europe, Latin America, the Pacific Rim, and North America; in the US alone they spend over $109 billion annually on goods ranging from groceries to compact discs. Increasingly wealthy youths in China also are adopting the lavish spending habits of the West (Young Chinese, 1996). Global teens tend to develop and follow fads, favoring Black urban styles in 1995 and Fifth Avenue fashions in 1996. The global teen is well stocked with the same unisex clothes, Nike footwear, Levi's jeans, and Sega videogames. In addition, these teens share values: a desire to cure the world's ills, to be part of other cultures, and to communicate via the Internet

TABLE 4.5   Global demographic groups

	Name of global segment	
	Global elites	**Global teenagers**
Shared values	Wealth, success, status	Growth, change, future, learning, play
Key product benefits sought	Universally recognizable products with prestige image, high-quality products	Novelty, trendy image, fashion statement, name brands/novelty
Demographics	Very high income, social status and class/well traveled/well educated	Age 12–19, well traveled, high media exposure
Media/communication	Up-scale magazines, social selective channels (i.e. cliques), direct marketing, global telemarketing	Teen magazines, MTV, radio, video, peers, role models
Distribution channels	Selective (i.e., up-scale retailers)	General retailers with name brands
Price range	Premium	Affordable
Targeted by global firms such as:	Mercedes-Benz, Perrier, American Express, Ralph Lauren's Polo	Coco-Cola Co., Benetton, Swatch International, Sony, PepsiCo, Inc.
Related micro-segments/ clusters	Affluent women, top executives, highly educated professionals, professional athletes	Pre-adolescents, female teens, male teens, adolescents
Factors influencing the emergence of the segment	Increased wealth, widespread travel, advancement of communication, technology	Television media, international education, travel, music

Source: Hassan, Salah S., and Katsanis, Lea Prevel. (1994). Global market segment strategies and trends. In Salah S. Hassan and Erdener Kaynak (Eds), *Globalization of consumer markets: Structures and strategies*, p. 58. Binghamton, NY: International Business Press/Haworth.

(The universal teenager, 1994). The hopes and dreams expressed are global, but not all teens have access to this shared culture. Additionally, boys and girls are similar but not the same in terms of buying habits.

Existence of a global teen group provides business opportunities like the ones MTV exploit. Other firms also appear to be targeting their products and advertising to similar teen aspirations and challenges. For example, Benetton ads focus on two concerns shared by the world's teens: AIDS and world conflict. MTV's 'Free Your Mind' ad campaign similarly encourages viewers to embrace different races, religions, and lifestyles. In summary, the cultural phenomenon of the global teen provides business enterprises throughout the globe with an opportunity they exploit by adjusting advertising and production processes to appeal to young adults. But the fact that this group exists suggests that some type of cultural convergence is occurring as the result of business activities.

To this point we have reviewed cultural changes that are for the most part behavioral. Many of the greater challenges for globalization of business culture have arisen because behaviors and actions create challenges for the home culture that go below the surface to tap into less visible and far more enduring aspects of culture. The shared values of global teens represent one such set of changes, and other value-based cultural challenges are reviewed below.

Global values

Globalization of culture has come about in part because most people in the world have access to the same information, and to the same or similar forms of popular culture such as music, television, and films. One result of increased access to information has been increased global awareness of issues of individual opportunity, and increased aspirations, and these aspects of cultural globalization are having profound effects on global opportunities. The following section defines values to examine national values and individual values as compared to globalizing managerial values.

INDIVIDUALISM AND COLLECTIVISM

Much business research on the topic of individualism/collectivism focuses on the extent to which one polar opposite or the other fosters economic development or enhances business activities. An example from the airline industry shows how one business used this information. The Boeing Commercial Airplane Group observed that countries with high individualism had low airplane accident rates, and that countries with both high individualism and a low power distance index had accident rates 2.6 times less than those with low individualism and high power distance (Phillips, 1994). Although additional study is called for, one possible explanation for these findings is that pilots and other responsible personnel high on individualism avert accidents by responding rapidly to perceived problems; whereas, people from more collectivist cultures would more likely confer with others before taking action, perhaps losing time to avoid accidents. A study of business owners exploring the relationship between entrepreneurial behavior generated by individualism and collectivism suggested that the 'best' mix may come from balancing these two conflicting values. Entrepreneurship was found to be highest under conditions where there was a balance between individualism and collectivism, and declines in entrepreneurial behavior were observed for highly individualistic and more collectivist environments. The authors of the study concluded that entrepreneurship flourishes when there is a relative balance between individualism and collectivism (Morris, Avila, and Allen, 1993). Similar results also were found with a South African sample, with high levels of individualism or collectivism labeled as dysfunctional to entrepreneurial behavior (Morris, Davis, and Allen, 1994).

Values of individualism and collectivism appear to be blending, particularly among young people, but also as a natural extension of business activities. A poll conducted by the Emnid Institute for Germany's *Der Spiegel* magazine found that young Germans (14 to 29 years old) tended to prefer individualism and self-oriented pursuits over national politics, ideas, or values. A turn toward individualism affects not only German political life, but also business life. For example, leaders at German apparel manufacturer Hugo Boss AG restructured to move production outside Germany in an effort to extend its brands and appeal more to the individualistic and segmented marketplace of the 1990s. Similar deviations from nationalism and collective behavior also are observed among young people elsewhere. In Japan, for example, *shinjinrui* or 'new breed of humans' are opting out of salaried jobs to follow their own interests, and 'Generation X' in the US is believed to be more interested in balancing work and personal life interests than their parents, many of whom made personal sacrifices for their work. In summary, values among young people may be converging at least in terms of individualism.

MANAGERIAL VALUES

Converging global values were the topic of a 1991 study sponsored by the *Harvard Business Review* (Transcending business boundaries, 1991) that showed similar management tensions and conflicts were occurring worldwide. The survey itself contained 91 questions related to five themes; it appeared in publications in 25 nations on six continents; and almost 12,000 managers returned the completed questionnaire. The typical respondent proved to be a 40-year-old, married and bilingual male senior manager employed by an established, privately held, mid-size organization of several thousand workers.

Cultural affinity more than geographic proximity was a major determinant of managers' views. For example, there were similarities among English-speaking countries, Hispanic, and upper Western European countries. Findings related to tensions addressed by survey themes and responses appear below.

- *Social responsibility of business*: Managers throughout the globe agreed with one another that education and environmentalism both represent important social responsibilities for businesses.
- *Workplace factors*: These managers claimed more skills and reported being more motivated than employees of a decade earlier. Workers were seen as having an edge over managers in their ability to work well in teams, but managers were seen as increasing their cross-functional knowledge more than nonmanagers. It was observed that managerial loyalty worldwide had shifted from the organizational level to one's own profession.
- *Anxious alliances*: Many respondents indicated that blurring of external boundaries associated with globalization is happening faster than shifts in

internal organizational boundaries. Responses showed a general trend toward customer service and good supplier relationships. The more individualistic countries tended to generate inwardly focused organizations.

- *Productivity and parenting*: Many managers described needs for enhancing organizational productivity, but frequently felt stretched to meet both organizational and parenting demands.
- *International vs domestic patriots*: These responses showed how corporate and national interests conflict or coincide in a globalizing world. For example, most of the people responding to the survey described themselves as 'internationalists' in support of free trade without government favoritism or support for domestic business. At the same time, over a third did want businesses to pay a premium to support domestic markets.

This review of global business habits and values suggests some degree of cultural convergence has occurred to produce similar behaviors and some values for global businesses. Some of these changes, particularly behavioral changes, appear to be additions to rather than substitutes for national norms, but it is clear that changes in one aspect of culture do occasion changes in other aspects of culture. The example based on settlement of a claim against Kikkoman Corporation (Box 4.11) illustrates the point.

BOX 4.11:   KIKKOMAN CORPORATION

US attorneys for Japan's Kikkoman Corporation agreed to an out-of-court settlement with 72-year-old Japanese businessman C. Sugihara, who claimed he was entitled to part of the soy sauce empire's profits because of a verbal 1957 joint-venture agreement to establish Kikkoman in the US. The jury acknowledged that cultures differ in the forms of agreements made and the binding nature of those agreements, but that those agreements should be honored worldwide.

This and evidence brought to bear in our review of cultural dimensions shows that some values may be converging globally. In the following section, we explore anticipated results of combined changes in cultural behaviors and values.

CHALLENGES OF CULTURAL GLOBALIZATION

Many worry that cultural globalization in the form of English as a business language or the 'dumbing down' of popular culture constitute threats to nation-states and the people who populate them. For example, pub enthusiasts worry that the home-away-from-home ambience and local historical significance of the British pub will vanish as local owners sell to pub chains (Parker-Pope, 1995). Malaysian parents worry that a growing consumer culture is weakening control over their children (Richardson, 1994), and a new devotion to careers among Russians has disrupted many of the friendships that sustained people through Soviet times (Stanley, 1995). In view of disruptions such as these, there are concerns that cultural convergence on a global scale will reduce human variation and produce conflict.

Clash of cultures

Many take a bleak view of cultural globalization, focusing on rising evidence of a culture for violence, overt reactions to cultural imperialism, and growth of a consumer- and self-oriented society capable of displacing spiritual and community-oriented values worldwide. Terrorism, vigilantism, and extremism are three examples of violent responses to culture clash; they represent an either/or response to cultural change.

Samuel Huntington (1993) believes that culture is a dominant source of potential conflict among the seven or eight major civilizations he defines as: Western, Confucian, Japanese, Islamic, Hindu, Slavic-Orthodox, Latin American, and possibly African. According to Huntington, culture clashes between civilizations could arise from differences of cultural opinion on important social issues such as equality, individuality, and human rights. Increased access to and knowledge of each other could highlight value differences, and a growing need for common identity within civilizations could accelerate culture clashes, particularly in view of trends in economic regionalization that make cultural similarities seem important to economic prosperity. Benjamin Barber (1992) similarly argues that cultural polarization characterized by 'Jihad vs McWorld' will diminish civil behavior. These points of view also suggest that culture can contain only single messages.

Evidence of increased variety

Will national, regional, and affinity cultures such as religion be subsumed by global culture? Few are willing to give up their own values, and many fear traditional values will be corrupted. As television, Internet, and other influences skirt legal and value-based sanctions against them, they stimulate growing fear that global media rather than families and nations will shape the values of the next generation. Further, since much programming comes from the US, there are fears that US values will displace world variation in values and behaviors. Thus, the world will become homogeneous and Westernized.

Some of what we learned earlier is an argument against this concern. First, we observed that globalization of culture is producing some amount of business convergence,

but changes are largely superficial and represent additions to rather than outright replacements of traditions. Globalization of entertainment and travel provide examples of how
options have increased. Others also outline why homogeneity is an unlikely outcome of
globalization.

STEREOTYPES EXPOSED

In the not-so-recent past, popular culture exposed US people only to stereotypical images
of others as 'Japanese geishas, Latin Americans as drug dealers or men on burros selling
coffee beans, Dutch as braided skaters, and French women as a French Barbie doll dressed
in her . . . can-can outfit' (Finel-Honigman, 1993, p. 125). In turn, the image the US
projected of itself showed it to be a murderous, gun-toting society populated with thugs,
drug dealers, and sex-starved young people. With greater exposure to many sources of
popular culture, it becomes clearer that none of these stereotypes are accurate.

Forced to confront them, stereotypes are revised. For example, according to editors
at *The Economist*, Asian values of respecting elders and collectivism over individualism
are not particularly Asian because these same values are found in many countries, including many developing countries in and outside Asia (Japan and Asia, 1995). We can
further surmise that these values are espoused by some segment of the population in any
nation. Expanded knowledge like this provides hope that global markets create opportunities to expand the human body of knowledge. In learning about others, we find they
are more like us than the stereotypes suggest, and perhaps recognize that many differences and similarities are found within and across all cultures. At the same time, we learn
that we are more different than we realized within nations as the values of women,
minorities, or ethnic groups gain greater voice.

CULTURAL IMAGES MOVE IN ALL DIRECTIONS

Cultural images now come from multiple sources, and as many influences are going from
East to West as vice versa. International soccer has increased its US popularity because
of worldwide television broadcasts like the '94 World Cup; the Chinese Channel (CC)
in Europe attracts Europeans interested in acquiring Chinese language skills and cultural
knowledge; and rapid economic growth in the developing and newly developed
economies is increasing the influence enterprises from these countries have on an emerging global culture. Film-makers Zhang Yimou and Chen Kaige who began their careers
in mainland China have popularized images of China, Jackie Chan successfully crossed
over into US movie markets, John Woo found opportunities to direct Hollywood films,
and Taiwanese producers are finding worldwide audiences. For example, Edward Yang's
mixture of Chinese and Western values in work and personal life popularized *A Confucian Confusion* because this mix and match challenge is real for many people. The interactive effect of culture with other environments is demonstrated in Box 4.12.

BOX 4.12: GLOBAL TELEVISION ENTERTAINMENT

Satellite technology and changes in consumption patterns worldwide are two stimulants for a growing global entertainment market. Interestingly, the relaxation or removal of government controls on television programming outside the US provided a first-mover advantage to US firms. After regulatory holds on television entertainment were reduced, the number of television channels increased and only US producers could quickly fill the void: English TV channels increased from 4 to 33, and French from 3 to 22 between 1988 and 1993. These new outlets, however, produced an incentive for local production crews to create television programs for sale not only locally but worldwide. In turn, this created a shift in the global entertainment industry as US firms faced new competition and were forced to develop localized products. An example of this shift occurred in Germany: in the absence of local products, viewers were fond of US soap operas in the 1980s, but by 1997 the top three films in Germany were German-made, and US-made TV serials no longer were in prime-time viewing slots.

AFFILIATIVE OPTIONS GROW

The growing number of nations and affinity groups suggests affiliative options will increase rather than decrease. The number of nations could grow from 300 to over 1,000 in the twenty-first century (Outlook, 1994), and religion, gender, and color groups may find it possible to pool interests globally. Further, exposure to worldwide events has led to promising possibilities for a global civil society. Global news broadcasts motivate individuals to join nongovernmental organizations or lobby government entities to relieve suffering for war victims. The culture of violence reflected in video games or films has led to codes of conduct to direct these activities. For example, video game ratings generated from within the industry began to appear in 1994 on game boxes sold in Europe, while the US firm Wal-Mart provided external directions to the industry by insisting that video games sold in Wal-Mart stores contain ratings. Consumers in a global world have many choices, and thus globalization of culture has not only made us one, it has increased cultural difference and diversity (Kahn, 1995). Increasingly 'the awareness of the finitude and boundedness of the planet and humanity is not to produce homogeneity but to familiarize us with greater diversity, the extensive range of local cultures' (Robertson, 1995, p. 86).

The paradox and the challenge of global culturalization is there are growing pressures for homogeneity within cultures, but travel of persons and information has increased heterogeneity. As time and space compression bring us to a realization of one world, they also expose us to the infinite variety and diversity of the world. These tensions create opportunities and they exact costs for nations. Like nations, business organizations also must balance between tensions of homogeneity and heterogeneity. The need for a common culture to direct firm activities is offset by external demands for responding to many needs. Traditionally, organizations have been structured to program out or control diversity. Hierarchical systems, for example, regularize, standardize, and reinforce sameness. Differences in seeing and believing stimulate creativity in organizations at the same time they challenge order, structure, and 'the way we do things.' These tensions also exact costs and provide opportunities for organizations. Part II explores how organizations are managing these tradeoffs.

PART II   ORGANIZATIONS AND GLOBALIZING CULTURE

Evidence presented earlier in this chapter showed how global enterprises have influenced cultural globalization. For example, MTV's stated mission is to influence global culture. In this section, we examine how the process of cultural globalization also is changing organizations. For example, MTV's global audience responds to the images they see and competitor enterprises also respond, causing MTV to reshape its internal culture, processes, and people to produce new programs that stay current with global demand. One such demand is for local programming mixed with global music images. In making this and other adaptations, an organization like MTV becomes both the changer and the changed as external and internal cultural forces combine to reshape organizational and national culture and develop global business culture.

Developing an organizational culture around common and enduring themes that are at the same time flexible and adaptive to global markets can be difficult. After returning to profitability, Chrysler tried 'to portray itself as a "schizophrenic" company that's conservative with the balance sheet but is still run by creative car lovers' (Templin, 1995, p. B1). Portraying two values simultaneously represents a change in Chrysler's culture that affects people and structures. For example, where once design was an engineering task, now a focused platform team is used to develop a new car more quickly. This effort is led by Robert Lutz, who defied custom by staying with Chrysler after someone else was chosen for the chairmanship he sought. In staying as president, Lutz demonstrates that 'losing' a job can lead to new gains for the organization and for the individual. This example demonstrates that tradition can change, and in the following section we will look at the challenges for creating a common and global culture based on tradition combined with new practices.

Global organizations take shape by borrowing best practices and new ideas from among multiple cultures. As they blend differences, they also seek to instill unity and a sense of common direction. Common worldwide processes and structures often are introduced for this purpose, but their success depends on human willingness to make changes work. Human decisions to aid or subvert a new process or structure make or break the global organization as it struggles to learn and grow a culture responsive to the dynamics of global change.

Lynne McFarland, Larry Senn, and John Childress (1993) interviewed 100 top leaders of global organizations and academic institutions to identify some of the core values around which leaders rally their workforces. Integrity and honesty, openness and trust, teamwork, caring, customer focus, respect for the individual and diversity, innovation, social responsibility, and life balance were a few of the values these top leaders mentioned repeatedly. The authors compared core values like these with values more traditionally found in organizations, and their results are shown in Table 4.6. Whether they focus on customer service, innovation, diversity, integrity, or other values, statements of core values usually are simple, easy to remember, and direct action. These qualities are reflected in the following examples:

- McDonald's Corporation strives to achieve unity by placing primary emphasis on overriding attributes of culture like a customer-service orientation. This common value or orientation helps pull the organization together even when the norm for customer service differs.
- Global retailer Makro reinforces its culture by emphasizing core values of integrity and trust.

TABLE 4.6   Cultural barriers vs winning shared values

Cultural barriers	Winning shared values
Hierarchical leadership	Distributed leadership
Hidden agendas, dishonesty, and lack of openness	Open, honest, and flowing communication
Short-term and strictly bottom-line driven	Long-term quality, service, and excellence
Task-oriented and internally focused	Customer/market-oriented and externally focused
Prejudiced and judgmental	Embracing diversity and differences
Strict rules and rigid policies	Flexible, fluid, and rapidly responsive
Win/lose games	Win/win games and bigger wins for entire organization
Autonomous, responsibility to shareholders only	Social and community responsibility as well as to shareholders

Source: Adapted from: McFarland, Lynne Joy, Senn, Larry E., and Childress, John R. (1993). *21st century leadership*, p. 155. New York: The Leadership Press.

- Motorola's key beliefs include constant respect for people and uncompromising integrity.
- Guinness' five-point Star System reinforces quality, safety, people, productivity, and information as priorities.

Kenneth Chenault, President of the American Express Consumer Card Group, US, believes it is important to stand for something in the global society, thinks it essential for organizations to create shared values broad enough to support society, and finds it critical, 'given the diversity in our country and our world, that values bring order to our thinking and our conduct' (McFarland, Senn, and Childress, 1993, p. 130). In summary, shared values among employees appear to be important building blocks for worldwide organizational unity. Although the values themselves may be simple, the example from Bechtel in Box 4.13 illustrates that this is far from the case when it comes to implementing common organizational values.

Lisa Hoecklin (1995) notes that cultural differences affect how corporate values are

---

BOX 4.13:   BECHTEL CONSTRUCTS A GLOBAL VISION

In a document called *Toward 2001*, Riley Bechtel – Chairman of San Francisco-based construction firm Bechtel – articulated a global vision and core values to adapt his firm's corporate culture to one responsive to a global context. The emphasis was on process-oriented changes, and it began with a massive information-gathering task that asked 22,000 employees to answer a 102-question survey. This was followed with more information-gathering from over 200 focus groups, and resulted in a communication plan including a newsletter and other means for disseminating information to all levels of the organization. Having involved people and their perceptions from the start of the cultural change also resulted in structural changes, including removing a perceived barrier between the US operation and international operations. Work now is accomplished through project teams formed to accomplish specific tasks, and this as well as a decentralized structure make it possible for Bechtel employees to mobilize and respond quickly to new assignments. These examples of changes at Bechtel illustrate that a cultural change intended to fulfill a global vision often requires changes in structure and in how people organize and complete their work.

Source: Solomon, Charlene Marmer. (1993, Oct.). Transplanting corporate cultures globally. *Personnel Journal*, pp. 78–88.

interpreted worldwide, and outlines three ways organizations create global unity out of these differences:

1 by permitting local interpretations of values statements;
2 by incorporating local views when creating values statements;
3 by implementing a formal process to discuss how the values should be interpreted locally.

Earlier discussions of cultural learning showed that individuals learn about their culture via direct means such as language, and indirectly through behaviors and consequences, actions and events. Organizational participants also learn about organizational culture through direct and indirect means, what Nonaka and Takeuchi (1995) call explicit knowledge and tacit knowledge. Explicit knowledge about culture can be formalized and widely distributed in printed statements of values, beliefs, or mission. But much of what is known within organizations is not explicit; it is culturally implicit, passed along not according to what is stated but according to what is done. Organizational leaders are encouraged to 'walk the talk' because unless they do, organizational participants identify a gap between what is said and what really gets done in the organization. These types of norms or implicit forms of knowledge permeate the organization, also helping to shape organizational culture.

PEOPLE IN A GLOBAL CULTURE

In homogeneous organizations, it is implicitly understood that hiring involves identifying people 'just like us.' In the late 1980s, this homogeneity was reflected in many organizations and described as 'strong culture.' Interestingly, the book *In search of excellence* (Peters and Waterman, 1982) identified strong organizational culture as an important contributor to performance success, but only a few years later many of the firms Peters and Waterman viewed as having strong cultures were no longer performing well. This led many to conclude that the unifying strength of a strong culture also can be a weakness unless organizational culture is adapted to the larger, more global world in which many firms operate. IBM, for example, found that the strong culture and standards critical to early success required adaptation and more flexibility in a global world. Similarly, the Disney Corporation faced resistance to the corporate culture in their French theme park, even though the same culture had been enthusiastically received in Japan. French workers, it seems, were less willing to conform to corporate prescriptions covering personal appearance and work habits and practices.

The pressures on homogeneity due to proliferation of products and markets are mainly experienced via people, and the global organization has become the crucible for working out cultural differences in values, assumptions, and behaviors. Many of the management concepts expected to help organizations make this transition focus on maximization of human resources, including total quality management, the learning organization, process re-engineering, and diversity management. All argue that organizational futures depend on mobilizing all resources, and particularly human resources.

Changing organizational culture by hiring people with differences is only one step toward managing heterogeneity. It also is important that people within the organization be encouraged to view these changes as positive and useful to the organization and to their own future. Transcending implicit boundaries that include narrow definitions of 'who we are' makes this difficult, particularly if efforts to incorporate diversity occur only at the surface level. Like the previous culture, the new culture must be embedded in processes and structures such that people have an incentive to change their behavior and their thinking. Incorporating diversity in an organization is more than hiring; it includes recruiting, training, and reaching outside the organization to cultivate community relations and establish a reputation for being an organization that hires and promotes from diverse pools. Changes in culture that accommodate greater diversity also require changes in patterned thinking among managers and other employees.

From the person leading organizations to the shop floor, managing diversity begins first with knowledge and understanding of why culture is important. It is critical for people to understand their own national cultures and assess the strengths and weaknesses that culture offers in a globalizing world. Within the organization, it is important to make features of culture explicit, to ask, as is done in process re-engineering: Why do we do what we do in the way we do it?

Training

Training is used to stimulate cultural understanding, but the type, cost, and intensity of cross-cultural training varies widely. Having surveyed international management training programs in Europe, Japan, and the US, Rosalie Tung (1982) observed six types of training in use:

1 Environmental briefings typically provide descriptions of a nation, including information about climate, topography, infrastructure, population, and housing.
2 Cultural orientations typically provide information about cultural institutions, habits, or values of the nation – typically these orientations are to the dominant culture.
3 Cultural assimilators are used to expose participants to likely intercultural encounters.

4 Language training.

5 Sensitivity training helps the individual recognize how values affect behaviors.

6 Field experience is gained when the individual lives in the assigned country and experiences some of the challenges that lie ahead.

Lectures or briefings on country demographics or host country values and behaviors often are relatively inexpensive because many people can be exposed to the same information in a relatively short period of time. Cost and intensity escalate when training involves simulations, role plays, reflection, field trips and visits, or cultural immersion in another country for an extended period of training time, regardless of whether the training is for work abroad or to understand diversity within organizations. As the example from Intel shows (Box 4.14), some organizations use multiple forms of training to improve intercultural learning across nations and within the organization.

BOX 4.14: INTEL CORPORATION'S INTERCULTURAL TRAINING

- **Intercultural awareness**: Managers and employees are introduced to information about how workers from different cultures perceive the business structure, processes, and procedures.
- **Multicultural integration**: A series of workshops provide skill building and career development for foreign born professionals.
- **Culture-specific training**: When groups are to work with others from a specific culture, they receive training better to understand their own cultures and to learn about cultural nuances of the other group.
- **Training for international assignments**: Usually a training consultant who has lived and worked in the assigned country is brought in to orient the newly assigned person to the language, culture, and practices of the host country.
- **Intact team training**: Consultants are brought in to act as liaisons, translators or intervention providers to encourage positive ways for people from different cultures to work together.

Source: Odenwald, Sylvia. (1993, July). A guide for global training. *Training and Development*, pp. 22–31.

Informational forms of training enhance cognitive knowledge and improve awareness of behavioral differences, but more intensive (and expensive) cultural learning is needed to move below the surface level of culture. Often these more intensive forms of cultural learning such as sensitivity training are resisted because they ask people to reach a new level of awareness about themselves and examine both the positives and negatives of their own cultural values and behaviors when interacting with people from another culture.

MANAGERIAL COMPETENCIES FOR A GLOBAL WORLD: CULTURAL SENSITIVITY

The global manager can be someone who lives outside a home country, but more importantly this manager can put aside national allegiances at work. Kenichi Ohmae (1990) believes this person can be in different national cultures, but not 'of' them because she or he has an overriding commitment to the single, unified global mission and culture of the global organization. This global manager can be from any country, but typically speaks more than one language fluently and has lived and worked in more than one country. Often they have passports from more than one country, and frequently they are the children of parents who are from different nations. Global managers must have a broad nonparochial view of the company and its operations and at the same time an understanding of their own business, country, or functional tasks (Bartlett and Ghoshal, 1992; Reich, 1991). Third, global managers need to increase their cultural sensitivity, but some may find this easier than others. Those who are the product of two cultures or who have lived and worked in other countries or in culturally diverse communities within their own country may have an advantage over those who have no experience of cultural diversity.

Developing cultural sensitivity in people

According to Milton Bennett (1993), as a first step many deny there are differences cross-culturally. Denial is then followed by defense, often characterized by 'us versus them' thinking. The third stage of 'minimization' recognizes and accepts superficial cultural differences such as eating habits, but a belief in all people being the same remains strong. A fourth stage of cultural sensitivity is acceptance of differences, and, having accepted differences, one can then move to the fifth stage of adapting to differences. Finally, there is a sixth stage of cultural sensitivity, which is to integrate differences so they are internalized and understood. This model was developed with the expatriate or long-term sojourner in mind, but it is equally applicable to the global manager who operates within an organizational and world culture where diversity is the norm. Among the 12 important individual and organizational competencies appearing in Chapter 2 are several cultural ones, including an understanding of one's own cultural values and assumptions and an ability to avoid cultural mistakes. Both of these cultural needs can be addressed by managers able to assess and adapt their cultural sensitivities.

PROCESSES
Adapting behaviors, practices, customs, and norms

The frequency with which one bathes, food preparation and preferences, manner of dress, work habits, and responsiveness to criticism are all part of the cultural habits now important also at work. When assumptions about 'normal' behavior are violated, there is a tendency to judge them unfavorably. For example, the extraverted behavior dominant for US men often is viewed as brash and impulsive in France where the norm is introversion. The US manager is equally likely to take a dim view of thoughtful deliberation in the French person, seeing it as tentative and lacking in commitment. In other words, people who do not demonstrate cultural norms are not viewed as normal. They are instead perceived to be abnormal and hence can be rejected as fitting candidates for friendship, work, or other relationships. These assumptions can extend to external relationships with buyers and suppliers as well as internal relationships. For example, spending 30 minutes or so in friendly discussion is not unusual where friendship precedes business; this is reflected in an Arab attitude of 'Let us be friends, and we will do business forever,' versus a US attitude more akin to 'Let us do business – and then we may be friends' (Elashmawi, 1994). Because of these differences in attitudes toward time and work, friendly discussion for a US businessperson could well be perceived as a waste of that precious commodity – time.

Communication processes

As discussed above, English has become the common business language, and global enterprises tend to adopt English as their standard. Challenges for using English as a business language include the following:

- There is limited agreement on word use, spelling, or meaning. English slang for criticism is 'slagging'; in India and Britain 'give a tinkle' is a request to telephone; and Spanglish, Chinglish, and other adaptations of English have created diverse words and meanings.
- A *Wall Street Journal* article reported that an English woman who tried to use a voice recognition system could not make herself understood because the system was programmed for US pronunciations (Phillips, 1995). Thus, English language use is not standard.
- Also problematic for English is that it is a dynamic language containing much slang and many clichés and idioms inaccessible to the non-native speaker, and often to the native speaker as well. A short list of US idioms appears in Table 4.7.

TABLE 4.7   What you see is (not) what you get: terms understood in one language often lead to misunderstandings when translated into another language

Company slogan	What it means in original language	What it means in translation
COORS – 'Turn it loose'	Relax, enjoy yourself	Spanish – 'suffer from diarrhea'
BUDWEISER – 'King of Beers'	In a hierarchy, the top beer	Spanish – 'Queen of Beers'
PERDUE CHICKEN – 'It takes a tough man to make a tender chicken'	A tender chicken is the result of hard work on the part of real men	Spanish – 'It takes a sexually stimulated man to make a chicken affectionate'
BRANIFF – 'Fly in leather'	Leather seats are viewed as a step above cloth seats, suggesting a special luxury	Spanish – 'Fly naked'
PEPSI-COLA – 'Come alive with Pepsi'	Pepsi will make you feel lively and part of something important	German – 'Come out of the grave'

Source: Helin, David W. (1992, Feb.). When slogans go wrong. *American demographics*, 14(2): 14; and Ricks, David. (1983). *Big business blunders*. Homewood, IL: Dow Jones-Irwin.

Another challenge to using business English at work is legal, especially in the US where English-only rules have been challenged in court. Leaders at some organizations believe it is important to use the same language so that co-workers can understand one another and customers' needs can be met, and there are businesses where clear communication is essential such as medical work, chemical plants, or oil refineries. In some organizations, efforts to improve business efficiencies have removed many complexities from the English language, replacing language with pictographs or producing a highly specialized, albeit limited, language.

PICTOGRAPHS

- McDonald's Corporation employees worldwide ring up sales on machines that display symbols of Big Macs, french fries, or colas instead of words or numerals. Software links price and total items.
- Computer programs often operate with icons or symbols that are not universally understood. Apple Computer discovered the palm-forward, open-handed symbol that means 'stop' in the US conveys a different meaning in Greece. Eastern Europeans do not use file folders, and so the icon representing it has little meaning for many there.

Efforts to simplify computer use have led many companies to introduce pictographs or icons to guide users, but many firms discovered that these icons had different meanings not only across cultures but within them. Figure 4.6 will illustrate the point.

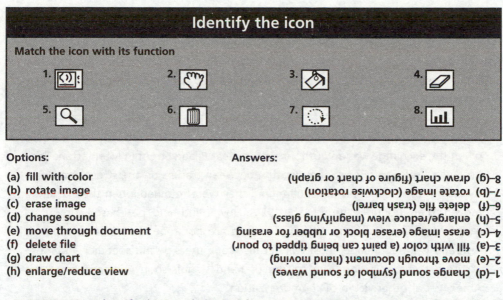

FIGURE 4.6 *Identify the icon* (adapted from: Kansas, Dave. (1993, Nov. 17). The icon crisis: Tiny pictures cause confusion. *The Wall Street Journal*, p. B1)

SPECIALIZED LANGUAGE

- Voice of America pioneered this concept almost forty years ago, using Special English to transmit to non-native English speakers.
- Caterpillar developed a system of printed communication called Caterpillar Fundamental English (CFE) – a condensed, simplified, and specialized form of English providing non-English speakers with a reading vocabulary of less than 1,000 words sufficient to service Caterpillar machinery.
- Edward Johnson at Cambridge University created an operational language for communications at sea, and is in the process of developing about 5,500 languages for global 'police speak.'

None of these approaches are ideal for communicating well in the business setting. First, a reduced form of language makes it difficult to express complex thoughts, but complexity is a part of the global organization and provides a means for creating knowledge in the global organization. Second, language often contains more information than the words convey; nonverbal dimensions of communications such as silences, pauses, body language, and facial expressions also convey meaning. Meaning also is conveyed through nonverbal means. As the example found in Box 4.15 shows, nonverbal signals in one instance are being replaced with computers, just as words have been replaced in some cases with pictographs. Interestingly, although computers make it possible to transmit more information, they also eliminate much of the nuance embedded in nonverbal communication. The importance of this form of communication varies cross-culturally for reasons described in the following section.

BOX 4.15: COMPUTERS REPLACE HANDSIGNALS AT THE AMERICAN STOCK EXCHANGE

Hand signals used at the American Stock Exchange were introduced in the 1880s when the exchange was an outdoor market near Broad Street in Manhattan. They proved a useful form of communication between traders on the street and clerks located in offices around the square, and they were retained when the exchange moved to an indoor location in the 1920s. Now, hand-held, pen-based computers can do the same job, and although traders are not required to use computers instead of sign language, most will because computers permit speedier and more accurate communication. The culture of hand signals soon will fade from the Amex, yet another victim of computerization.

Source: Davies, Erin. (1996, Oct. 28). The Amex's old hand signals give way to computers. *Fortune*, p. 52.

NONVERBAL COMMUNICATIONS

In Scandinavia, North America, Switzerland, and Germany, most of the information conveyed in communication is embedded in the words. According to Edward Hall (1976), these languages are 'low-context' because meaning equals words. For example, the business meaning of the low-context phrase 'time is money' is recognized as a belief that time is the critical resource available for making money. In contrast to English or German, 'high-context' languages like Mandarin Chinese and other tonal languages convey meaning that extends far beyond the words. In a high-context language, the vast majority of information is conveyed not only through words but also through the communication process: who speaks, who listens, how words are combined, inflections, and the like (Hall, 1976). Awareness of the communication setting, the relative status of speakers, past experiences, and historical background also are important in a high context culture.

SPEAKING AND LISTENING

The Japanese president of Mazda Motors Corporation estimated that 20% of the meaning communicated was lost between him and his interpreter during meetings with US representatives of partner firm Ford Motor Company. Another 20% was lost between the interpreter and the US representatives. This also can occur when people from different cultures are speaking the same language. Percy Barvenik, former CEO, of ABB indicates that he sometimes finds it difficult to listen, forgetting that many who work for him speak English as a second language. He admits that providing time to listen can make him impatient, and fears that being impatient will convey unintended messages.

People who speak English as a first language usually are from low-context cultures. When high- and low-context speakers communicate, cross-cultural miscommunications can be reduced when the low-context participant listens and observes more than is usual and the high-context speaker listens more for word meaning than for context. Providing a context for understanding culture and communicating well is one process global firms adopt.

Processes for managing diversity

For many organizational leaders, the first challenge of diversity is defining it. Organizations typically begin with a focus on visible dimensions of diversity such as gender, race, nationality, age, and physical abilities. Often, this emphasis on visible forms of diversity leads to a recognition that organizations house many less visible forms of diversity such as propensity for risk-taking, skills, entrepreneurship, veteran status, sexual orientation, family relationships, or values and beliefs. These as well as more visible evidence of diversity are important to organizations because they are important to employees. If, for example, an employee believes he or she is less valuable to the organization than others are, the potential exists for the employee to perform less well than employees perceived to be more valued. Table 4.8 illustrates the many forms of diversity found in organizations.

Many business leaders believe diversity is important to their future:

- Ford leaders believe that diversity will be the engine that drives the creative energy of the company in the twenty-first century, and the strength of the Ford 2000 alteration in organizational culture rests on fully utilizing the company's depth of human diversity.
- DuPont sees diversity management as a method for global competition.
- Avon leaders believe diversity management is a business issue rather than an issue of social responsibility. According to Avon's CEO, diversity isn't 'something to do because it's nice but because it is in our interest' (Dreyfuss, 1990, p. 168).

Defining diversity or believing that it is important to be diverse are only preliminary steps to leveraging diversity as an advantage. However, the advantages of diversity are sometimes difficult to achieve. Lisa Hoecklin (1995) believes that global leaders must

TABLE 4.8   Sources of workplace diversity

Visible or inferred differences	Less visible/less easily inferred differences
Age	Marital status
Gender	Education
Race, ethnicity, or color	Economic class
National origin, including	Religion
accent or mode of dress	Sexual orientation
Attractiveness	Values
Height/weight distribution	Personality
Organizational position	Veteran status
Physical abilities	Lifestyle
Intellectual abilities	Political affiliation
	Geographical origins

recognize that cultural diversity can simultaneously cause problems and provide benefits to organizations. Efforts to balance benefits against costs have yielded different approaches to managing diversity. According to a research project conducted by David Thomas and Robin Ely (1996), business leaders tend to adopt one of three different views to incorporate cultural diversity in their organizations.

1 *The discrimination and fairness paradigm* has been most used in US organizations; this approach assumes that prejudice has kept members of certain groups out of organizations and can be remedied by focusing on equal opportunity, fair treatment, and compliance with Equal Employment Opportunity laws. Remedies consistent with this paradigm favor assimilation and conformism, with newcomers becoming more like existing employees.

2 *The access and legitimacy paradigm* emerged from the competitive business climate of the 1980s and 1990s, relying more on acceptance and valuing of difference than the discrimination and fairness paradigm and often motivated by an awareness that diversity outside the organization required greater diversity within. Among the limitations of this paradigm is that it accepts diversity without really understanding how diversity can or does change the way work is accomplished. Although boundaries to acceptance can be transcended with this paradigm, boundaries to understanding remain.

3 *The emerging paradigm* has been found only in a few organizations. Its main feature is that it emphasizes understanding how to incorporate employees' perspectives into the main work of the organization. This perspective not only values diversity for its ability to reach new audiences or retain existing ones, but it also recognizes that differences in perspectives can change the

organization. This perspective on diversity involves organizational learning and integration of that learning throughout the organization. Like the discrimination and fairness paradigm, it promotes equal opportunity, and like the access and legitimacy paradigm, it acknowledges cultural differences, but it transcends both as learning creates an organization united because of its differences, not in spite of them.

SUCCESSFUL DIVERSITY INITIATIVES

According to Ann Morrison, author of *The new leaders: Guidelines for leadership diversity in business* (1992), successful diversity initiatives at the organizational level include the following:

1 Top managers intervene to establish the need for diversity.
2 Nonmanagers are recruited for managerial jobs to improve diversity in management.
3 Internal advocacy groups are established to provide champions for diversity.
4 Company profiles/statistics are developed to provide a baseline for diversity.
5 Appraisal is tied to diversity progress.
6 Promotion criteria and processes change.
7 Succession planning is modified to incorporate diversity goals.
8 Diversity training occurs.
9 Informal networks and support groups are developed.
10 Work/family policies are developed.

CREATING A CULTURE THAT VALUES DIVERSITY

A final suggestion for incorporating diversity throughout the organization is to take steps that give more than lip service to concepts of difference. Consistency in the walk and the talk affirms that leaders are serious about diversity, and it reinforces the unity important to the global organization. It is vital to recognize that being diverse in terms of organizational demographics or markets served is a necessary but not sufficient condition for making diversity a sustainable advantage because the advantage comes not from the diversity itself but from becoming an organization that honors difference as much as similarity. Doing this includes a clear statement of values and encouraging diversity across all vertical and horizontal boundaries. According to the Conference Board (Winterle, 1992), 'unless an organization develops a culture that understands, respects, and values differences, diversity is likely to result in decreased organizational effectiveness' (p. 19). Table 4.9 lists many of the ways company leaders attempt to enhance advantages from diversity. General recommendations for proceeding include the following:

TABLE 4.9 Corporate diversity initiatives

Communication	Education and training	Employee involvement	Career development and planning	Performance and accountability	Culture change
Speeches by CEO/ senior executives	*Classes/lectures/ seminars*	Task forces	Mentoring	Link diversity performance to other corporate objectives	Conduct internal diagnostic studies
Video by CEO	Diversity briefings for senior management	Task teams	Identification process for 'high potential' employees	Develop diversity performance measures	• glass ceiling audit
Teleconferencing	Diversity integrated into executive education	Issue study groups	Succession planning	• quantitative	• equity studies
Closed circuit television	Board of Trustees orientation	Focus groups	Expanded job posting up to VP levels	• qualitative	• culture audits
Executive forum	Awareness training	Diversity council	Career pathing	Incorporate diversity in management by objectives	Incorporate diversity items in employee attitude surveys
Corporate vision statement	• for managers	Corporate advisory committee	Individual development plans	Define and reward behaviors that reinforce diversity	Benchmark other companies
Diversity mission statement	• for employees	Corporate steering committee	Executive MBA programs	Monitor and report progress	Develop corporate diversity strategy
Diversity policy	Diversity skills training	Business unit steering committee	Developmental assignments	Evaluate business units' performance	Integrate diversity into total quality strategy
Diversity letter/memo from CEO	• for managers	Networking groups	• lateral	Evaluate managers' performance	Establish stand-alone diversity position
Senior management behavior modeling	• for employees		• rotational	Evaluate all employees' performance	Add diversity responsibilities to EEO/AA position
Diversity brochure	Sexual harassment training		• special short term	Tie diversity performance to:	Emphasize line management ownership
Employee handbook	New manager training		• task forces	• business unit head's compensation	Adopt flexible managerial style, not 'one size fits all'
Employee newspaper/ periodical articles	*Required core courses*		Internships	• business unit's compensation	Revise policies/ benefits to support diverse needs
Special diversity newsletters/status reports	Mainstreaming diversity into other training		Self development planning	• business unit's bonus pool	
Second language communication	Worldwide training		Networking directories	• individual incentive compensation	
New manager orientation	Train-the-Trainer programs		Development programs for 'nontraditional' employees	• direct compensation	
	Change-agent seminars		English as a Second Language (ESOL) courses	• other rewards and recognition	
	Cross-race/gender training teams		Remedial education		
	Partnering in-house trainer/external consultants				

Source: Reproduced from the Special Advertising Section, 'Diversity: Making the Business Case' appearing in the December 9, 1996 issue of *Business Week* by special permission, copyright © 1997 by The McGraw-Hill Companies, Inc.

(a) develop a diversity policy for all organizational levels that outlines what is meant by diversity;

(b) practice checking the assumptions behind decisions, and ask others to do the same;

(c) create a high-trust work environment that discourages disparaging jokes or comments, facilitates opportunities among workers, and incorporates people from all levels in projects and processes;

(d) get to know people as individuals to discover their points of view;

(e) expect to be a teacher as well as a learner about diversity;

(f) recognize that resistance and anger are likely responses to changing a homogeneous culture;

(g) reward small successes and progress;

(h) hire talented trainers or encourage people to enroll in training offered;

(i) encourage formation of interest groups and diversity learning inside and outside of work;

(j) embed the planned change in all processes and structures.

STRUCTURE
Teamwork

When able to combine the insights, abilities, and skills of several individuals, teams provide a means for maximizing the advantages of diverse thinking. Writing in *The wisdom of teams*, Jon Katzenbach and Douglas Smith (1993) acknowledge that many teams do not function well, but believe that the following specifications contribute to success:

(a) keep teams small, preferably to less than 10 members;

(b) mix people who have complementary skills in terms of technical expertise and ability to solve problems or manage interpersonal conflict;

(c) commit the team to a common purpose that is realistic and do-able;

(d) set specific performance goals.

A challenge for team members is to work as a team; for managers the challenge is to learn how to assemble a team with potential, to instruct them in team processes, and to facilitate the team's achievement. According to management scholars, virtually every successful project or team group progresses through five project stages:

1 *The forming stage* is characterized by hopeful uncertainty as individuals get to know one another and struggle to define the project and the role of each in it.

People are usually well disposed to work together, but some will be anxious to get on with the task and others will want to develop trust. Both sets of needs must be met at this stage, and so it is imperative to take the time to talk out individual interests and concerns; to be honest about constraints faced; to describe past experiences with groups to help the group pool prior learning. Most groups are composed of people who have the technical skills and abilities to succeed nicely in the assigned task, but projects fail when social needs go unmet.

2 In *the storming stage*, individuals work out differences in approach, opinion, interests, and personality. Many individuals are uncomfortable with conflict, and will try to smooth it out before it is resolved. Cross-cultural differences in resolving conflict need to be described and decisions made to ensure that all are able to contribute fully to the group.

3 In *the norming stage*, members of the group become a group, establishing explicit and implicit expectations of each other. In this stage, it is imperative for individuals to share their expectations of each other and create a performance appraisal system for group use. The latter is difficult to do but provides a mechanism for dealing with problems that may arise later. Rotating meeting leadership or other roles provides insight into the work others do.

4 In the *performing stage*, the group completes its tasks and achieves set objectives. It assesses its performance against standards established in the norming stage.

5 In *adjourning*, some people will feel elated at task accomplishments, others will feel sad because the group's work is done. The group should find ways to accommodate both.

The example from Sun Microsystems (Box 4.16) shows that much goes on in a team that transcends the obvious and explicit. Managing these dynamics requires a team leader with more than technical skills; also important are personal skills such as patience and persistence and work-related skills such as an ability to interpret cross-cultural business cues. Table 4.10 lists some of the personal, work-related, and intellectual/social skills a global team leader needs.

Reducing culture clash when organizations merge

Acquisitions, mergers, and joint ventures increased significantly in number throughout the 1990s, stimulated by a desire for rapid growth among would-be global enterprises. Firms in banking, telecommunications, entertainment, chemicals, and pharmaceuticals are a few among many that extended their global scope through these types of structural

BOX 4.16:   CULTURAL DIVERSITY IN TEAMS

There were few examples to guide Khanh Vu in managing 35 engineers from 11 nations in an engineering department of Sun Microsystem in 1993 (Lewis, 1993). All the engineers shared technical expertise, but few were fluent with US culture and fewer still with the free-wheeling culture of the Silicon Valley in California where Sun is headquartered. Accordingly, Vu and his group had to invent the future, and face challenges that arose because the pathway to the future was not cleared. For example, many of the engineers were from Asian cultures where conflict and criticism would not be tolerated in meetings. These people wondered how criticism of work could be anything other than criticism of a person's character. Vu himself wondered how people could shout at one another in a meeting, yet walk out the door and be friends. As a group, the engineers realized that certain topics were culturally sensitive and could not be discussed in casual conversation, including sex, religion, politics, money, and relationships.

Source: Lewis, Marilyn. (1993, Feb. 3). Multicultural companies invent the future as they go. *The Seattle Times*, p. E9.

TABLE 4.10   Characteristics of successful global team leaders

Personal	Work-related	Intellectual/social
Patient/persistent	Capable of systems thinking	Curious – intellectually and socially
Emotionally stable	Can make decisions in ambiguous situations	
Able to live with failure		Able to form personal relationships and build rapport
Open-minded	Capable of pushing cultural limits	
Sense of humor		Knowledgeable about historical and current social developments
Humble (as opposed to modest)	Able to model behavior valued in each cultural environment	
Strong imagination		Sensitive to the value of every person
	Able to read cross-cultural business cues	
	Able to adapt management style	Motivated to work cross-culturally
	Technically competent	

Source: O'Hara-Devereaux, Mary, and Johansen, Robert. (1994). *Globalwork*, p. 106. San Francisco, CA: Jossey-Bass.

rearrangements. Alterations in structures that cross external boundaries of nations often produce culture clash. The results from one study of national and corporate culture 'fit' in mergers and acquisitions showed that national culture is a more important force than organizational culture in predicting stress, negative attitudes toward the merger, and actual cooperation. Yaakov Weber, Oded Shenkar, and Adi Raveli (1996) also concluded that both national and corporate cultures are essential inputs in determining the outcomes of structural rearrangements in mergers and acquisitions. Box 4.17 illustrates how culture clash was managed in one merger.

BOX 4.17:   THE PHARMACIA/UPJOHN MERGER, 1995

These two drug companies merged in 1995 to leverage their combined size and synergies. Pharmacia was based in Sweden but had a significant presence in Italy, while Upjohn was based in the US. One of the key steps undertaken to create a unique corporate culture was to reduce nationalistic tendencies by placing corporate headquarters in London; business centers were maintained in Michigan, Stockholm, and Milan. Clear communication between employees based in the three national cultures proved difficult, and top executives decided to meet and talk with employees from cultures other than their own to improve their awareness of cultural differences.

Source: Flynn, Julia, and Naughton, Keith. (1997, Feb. 3). A drug giant's allergic reaction. *Business Week*, pp. 122–124.

The kind of cultural clash experienced at Pharmacia/Upjohn or at virtually any firm resulting from cross-cultural blending can be reduced or avoided when managers are sensitive to the impact culture has on the workplace. Thus, an active plan to manage culture clash may prove more useful than reaction when problems of culture arise.

Culture and virtual organizations

A final point to be made about structural change related to organizational culture concerns virtual corporations – organizations that exist more in electronic and occasional personal linkages than in geographic place. The concept of a virtual organization is borrowed from the term 'virtual memory,' describing configurations that cause a computer to act as if it has more storage capacity than it does (Byrne, 1993). As applied to organizations and their structures, it suggests an organization can be configured to appear to be something more than what objectively exists. Virtual organizations have been described in myriad ways as 'lean' or 'flat,' as a conglomeration of companies brought together to serve a temporary purpose, or as a vertically integrated entity (Davidow and Malone, 1992). IBM's experience demonstrates one way a virtual organization can be structured (Box 4.18).

BOX 4.18:   VIRTUAL AMBRAS

IBM's Ambras subsidiary adopted a virtual structure to market IBM personal computer clones. The firm drew on the core competencies of six independent companies to market a clone to almost any specification. Managers were in North Carolina, designers were in Singapore, but telemarketing, order taking, and final assembly were performed by other firms.

Source: Goldman, Samuel. (1994, July). Agile competitive behavior: Examples from industry. *Agility Forum Working* Papers, pp. 1–30.

The Ambras example shows the virtual organization need not exist in physical space, but there often needs to be a core group who focus on strategic priorities. Employees are contract workers, often working from home via telecommuting technologies to complete work independent of constraints like place and time. By integrating computers and communications technologies, these contract workers become part of an entity that can be assembled and disassembled almost instantly. When people are not in the same place or work in different time zones throughout the world, it can be difficult to create processes like culture that reinforce a common sense of organizational purpose. This cultural challenge is exacerbated by a structural challenge that is in turn likely to alter processes and people willing to be part of the virtual corporation. The emergence of organizational forms that blur traditional expectations also has created challenges for management scholars who describe them. This is illustrated by turning to the topic of how teams operate in a virtual organization.

Teamwork in virtual organizations

One benefit of virtual organizations is that people spread worldwide can contribute to the same project, but this advantage also creates challenges. Specifications for global teams listed earlier in this chapter are especially challenging when work is in the virtual organization. According to Michael Kossler and Sonya Prestridge (1996), these challenges are to communication, conflict resolution, decision-making, and to members' abilities to feel the sense of team unity valuable to success. These authors distinguish between virtual teams which they view as temporary, and geographically dispersed teams (GDT) which are relatively permanent. This distinction suggests that a virtual team suffers from the same problems any temporary team faces, i.e., lack of commitment to the team or divided interests, whereas the GDT might be more akin to permanent teams whose members become willing to commit to each other because they recognize the long-term nature of the commitment. One can conclude that virtual teams face special challenges, but that some of these challenges may be reduced when the teams are permanent rather than temporary. Other suggestions Kossler and Prestridge offer for GDTs include:

(a) hold an initial face-to-face start-up meeting;
(b) establish interdependency among team members;
(c) establish a schedule of periodic face-to-face meetings;
(d) agree on what, when, and how information will be shared and how team members are to respond to information that is shared;
(e) establish clear norms and protocols for surfacing assumptions and conflicts;
(f) clarify need for GDT members to nurture each other and credit relationships;
(g) recognize and honor diversity of cultures.

In conclusion, this chapter has reviewed concepts of culture to argue that globalization causes organizations to play a greater role in transmitting cultural habits and norms on a worldwide basis. Playing these roles necessarily involves a change in organizational culture, and the same pain and problems evident in changing national culture also are evident in firms. Unlike nations, firms are forced to alter their cultures rapidly in response to globalization and this creates anxiety among employees and difficulties for managers who have limited experience in creating mechanisms to facilitate cultural change. The example of diversity management alone demonstrates how difficult it is for employees to transcend borders of thought and practice in creating an organizational culture responsive to global demands.

We can conclude that globalization of culture provides options of every sort, ranging from the mundane choices of what food we will eat to the more important challenges of choosing the people who enrich our lives and the jobs we perform. Most importantly, this chapter argues that people have options with respect to the cultural norms they adopt and that it is possible to live comfortably in both local and global cultures. Just as it is now possible for individuals to live within sometimes conflicting cultures of home, family, religion, subgroup, region, or nation, it is also technically possible to operate reasonably well within organizational, national, and global cultures. However, since global culture is emerging rapidly, many may feel they do not have the knowledge they need, and for others the transition to yet another new culture may be painful.

KEY CHAPTER CONCEPTS

Culture Affects Business Practices and Organizations: Increased importance of international business led academicians and business leaders to explore two aspects of culture. First, organizations have their own cultures, and, second, unresolved differences in cultural assumptions and practices can disrupt business transactions between and among firms from different nations.

Culture Provides Solutions to Common Problems: One purpose of culture is to provide solutions to the problems societies need to solve. Examples of the types of problems societies face are obtaining and distributing resources, protecting citizens, or maintaining order.

National Culture Helps People Meet Basic and High-Level Needs: Societies organized around nation-states develop culture to resolve problems people face in meeting basic needs for food, water, shelter, and warmth, and higher level needs for relationships and for finding meaning in life.

Culture Defined: Culture has been defined in many ways, but a recurring theme is that culture represents a highly integrated and intensely interrelated set of learned symbols and values. Interrelationships among sets of cultural symbols and norms are important because they serve to reinforce the values, beliefs, and behaviors expected from individuals.

Stimuli for Cultural Change: Although culture does not change quickly, it begins to change when prior solutions to social problems no longer work. One result is that individuals and organizations begin to operate in new or unaccustomed ways as a means of finding a new way to resolve social challenges. Global culture is emerging because the cultural mechanisms found within nation-states are less well able to address or manage the problems societies face in a globally interdependent world.

Societies Organized as Nation-States Have Different Cultures: Most societies are organized as nation-states. The culture of each of these societies is reflected not only in how individuals act and react, but also in how political and economic systems are structured, how natural resources are allocated, how technology is used, and how industries and task environments are structured.

Nations Contain Dominant Cultures and Subcultures: Most nations have dominant cultures as well as subordinate cultures, and most people learn to operate efficiently and well in the various cultures – national, regional, organizational, familial – of which they are a part.

Cultural Change Results from Border Transcendence: Where once cultural groupings resulted primarily from influences in nation-states, the ease of transcending those borders increasingly has led to a global business language, global habits, norms, behaviors, and values and to organizations that are more nearly global than domestic.

Global Businesses Are Cultural Conduits: Global business activities have altered the traditional relationship between organizations and nation-states. Whereas the values of nation-states traditionally were the major influence on organizations based there, today business activities and the organizations that stimulate them are conduits for global culture more than they are recipients of national culture.

The Impact of Popular Culture: Popular culture in the form of sports, entertainment parks, television, film, and video games are important global business activities affecting cultural change worldwide. Music television is perhaps the most global of popular culture media. It blurs the distinction between content, ad, and music, it appeals to young and old, it blurs the line between fantasy and real life, and it makes it possible for young people worldwide to feel part of the same trends.

Culture and Politics Are Interdependent: Concerns about US cultural imperialism are based on evidence that many of the media that convey popular culture are produced in the US. However, there is evidence that with deregulation of broadcasting, companies located throughout the world have new incentives to participate in global entertainment production. As these companies enter the market, the evidence shows that they too influence the market and cultural change becomes reciprocal.

Cultural Imperialism: Cultural imperialism differs from political imperialism because it is motivated toward winning an audience rather than conquering one. The evidence shows that, given a choice, people do not always choose Western media.

Organizations as Crucibles for Cultural Change: Among the challenges organizations face in a global world are that they have become the crucible for working out cultural differences in values, assumptions, and behaviors; melding cultures is challenging and difficult; and the path is not clear as to what is going to work and what is not. Thus, organizational leaders may feel more vulnerable than they did when organizations operated according to the cultural rules of only one nation.

Culture Clash: Among the general challenges people within and across nations feel in managing changes in culture are that cultures clash – sometimes violently – the rules of change are unclear, and some are better able to adapt to global culture's demands than are others.

Avoiding Culture Clash: Adaptive organizations identify opportunities associated with globalization of culture that include a growing consumer society, experiments that lead to organizational innovations, and combining traditional and nontraditional management techniques in new ways to manage structures, processes, and people for a global market.

Cultural Change Offers Opportunities: The advantages people and nations may derive from globalizing culture include the ability to identify with new affinity groups, enhanced knowledge and understanding, and an awareness of options that did not previously exist.

People and Organizations Operate Successfully in More than One Culture: Just as people find it possible to live within the same nation and subscribe to different cultural rules of family, religion, ethnic group, and nation, so too should it be technically possible for people to live comfortably with global business culture and national culture.

Managers Must be Sensitive to Culture: Cultural sensitivity and adjustment tend to follow a pattern leading from denial of differences to integration of differences. Making this transition improves self-awareness and helps managers avoid cultural mistakes.

REVIEW AND DISCUSSION QUESTIONS

1 Think of your 'work ethic' or how you orient to work. Trace this work ethic to your own cultural experiences with family, friends, organizations. Use this example to support the assertion that culture is learned, shared, and interrelated.

2 Describe behaviors, practices, customs, and norms for work as you have experienced it (your own experience or observations of others' experiences). Explain how these overt expressions of culture are associated with the values of yours or another culture.

3 Whether through reading or personal experience, describe an organization's structure, processes, and people practices that show the organization is consistent with the culture of the nation where it is located *or* globally.

4 What are the additional problems and opportunities of cultural globalization beyond those described in the chapter?

6 In the summer of 1992, the global teen seemed at home in Britain, the Netherlands, Hungary, and the US, where many young people dressed in the same type of jeans and the ubiquitous T-shirt. The T-shirt often was emblazoned with words that are not always socially acceptable. Boys even wore the same type of earrings (a small loop) in only one ear. Compare and contrast these findings with evidence available to you

in the countries you visit. Is there such a thing as a 'global' teen? How widespread is this phenomenon?

7 This chapter argues that people live in different cultures, including the dominant culture and subcultures of family, friendships, ethnic groups, religious groups, or regional groups. Make a case for or against the importance of dominant cultures and parallel subcultures.

8 According to the text, global business culture is emerging because the cultural mechanisms within nation-states are less well able to address and manage the problems societies face in a globally interdependent world. What national cultural mechanisms have failed? What are the problems societies face in a globally interdependent world? How and why are businesses involved in solving these problems?

9 *The Global Enterprise Project*: This chapter covered some of the central themes facing global organizations: problems that cannot be solved, measuring intangibles, valuing diversity, addressing new issues for which managers and organizations are ill prepared. Provide two examples from your readings on the global enterprise you chose to study to illustrate how the organization faces at least one of these common challenges. You can select two examples to illustrate two of these four challenges.

10 *The Global Enterprise Project*: Find examples of cultural globalization that reinforce concepts presented in this chapter or that show how the global enterprise you are studying is shaped or shaping cultural values.

11 If class members are expected to produce a team project, the following format can be used to help them prepare a plan of action:

The main challenge for a team/group is to specify their task and how they will go about it. Join a group to prepare a written plan that includes the following:

(a) an overall vision/mission statement outlining your joint purpose and its expected outcome, e.g., in terms of the product and the process, what you hope to learn about the topic and about working in teams, the contributions you will make, and the grade you are trying to achieve.

(b) Outline specific and measurable objectives for the project: how and when you will pass through each of the five stages of group performance; what steps you will take to achieve each.

(c) Decide on logistics and roles: who is to do what, when, where, in what format, e.g., Word or Powerpoint?

(d) Develop a set of common commitments and a method for evaluating input and output for each individual's work.

REFERENCES

Auletta, Ken. (1993, Dec 13). TV's new gold rush. *The New Yorker*, p. 84.

Bangert, David C., and Pirzada, Kahkashan. (1992). Culture and negotiation. *The International Executive*, 34(1): 43–64.

Barber, Benjamin. (1992, Mar.). Jihad vs. McWorld. *The Atlantic Monthly*, pp. 53–61. (See also *Jihad vs. McWorld*. New York: Ballantine Books, 1996).

Bartlett, Christopher, and Ghoshal, Sumantra. (1992, Sept./Oct.). What is a global manager? *Harvard Business Review*, pp. 124–132.

Battle for the couch potato. (1995, Jan. 9). *Business Week*, p. 91.

Bennett, John W., and Dahlberg, Kenneth A. (1993). Institutions, social organizations, and cultural values. In *The earth as transformed by human action*, pp. 69–85. New York: Cambridge University Press.

Bennett, Milton. (1993). Towards ethnorelativism: A development model of intercultural sensitivity. In Michael R. Paige (Ed.), *Education for the intercultural experience*, pp. 21–71. Intercultural Press.

Booth, Gregory D. (1997, Aug. 21). World comes to a rockin' Punjabi party. *New Zealand Herald*, p. B5.

Brauchli, Marcus W. (1994, May 16). Star-struck. *The Wall Street Journal*, pp. A1, A7.

British public schools start to look East. (1994, Nov.). *International Herald Tribune*, p. 5.

Byrne, John. (1993, Feb. 8). The virtual corporation. *Business Week*, pp. 98–103.

Caution: 'Morphing' may be harmful to teachers: Teen rangers have the power to transform tykes. (1994, Dec. 7). *The Wall Street Journal*, pp. A1, A8.

Cohen, Margot. (1991). The whole archipelago's doing the dangdut. *The Wall Street Journal*, p. A14.

Darlin, Damon. (1994, Dec. 19). Hollywood with a Confucian touch. *Forbes*, pp. 110–120.

Davidow, William, and Malone, Michael. (1992). *The virtual corporation: Structuring and revitalizing the corporation for the 21st century*. Burlingame, NY: Harper.

Dreyfuss, J. (1990, Apr. 23). Get ready for the new work force. *Fortune*, pp. 165–181.

Elashmawi, Farid. (1994, Sept./Oct.). Managing culture conflict in the Arab world. *Trade and Culture*, pp. 48–49.

Farney, Dennis. (1995, Apr. 27). Emergence of extremist groups reflects changing U.S. society, researcher says. *The Wall Street Journal*, p. A4.

Finel-Honigman, Irene. (1993). Popular culture in the global economy: Antithesis or reconciliation? In Ronald R. Sims and Robert F. Dennehy (Eds), *Diversity and differences in organizations*, pp. 123–133. Westport, CT: Quorum.

Fuller, Thomas. (1994, Nov.). Chinese channel beamed to Europe. *International Herald Tribune*, p. XV.

Hall, Edward T. (1976). *Beyond culture*. New York: Doubleday/Anchor.

Haney, Daniel Q. (1995, Feb. 19). Experts say world may lose half its languages. *The Seattle Times*, p. A1B.

Hoecklin, Lisa. (1995). *Managing cultural differences*. Reading, MA: Addison-Wesley.

Hofstede, Geert. (1984). *Culture's consequences*. San Francisco, CA: Sage.

Huntington, Samuel. (1993, Summer). The clash of civilizations. *Foreign Affairs*, pp. 22–49.

Institute of International Education. (1998, Jan. 9). Open doors 1996/97: Foreign students in the US. http://www.iie.org/opendoors/forstud1.htm

Japan and Asia, A question of balance. (1995, Apr. 22). *The Economist*, pp. 21–23.

Kahn, Joel S. (1995). *Culture, multiculture, and postculture*. Beverly Hills, CA: Sage.

Katzenbach, Jon R., and Smith, Douglas K. (1993). *The wisdom of teams*. Cambridge, MA: Harvard Business School.

Kossler, Michael E., and Prestridge, Sonya. 1996. Geographically dispersed teams. *Issues and Observations*, 16(2/3): 9–11 (a publication of the Center for Creative Leadership, Greensboro, North Carolina, USA – http://www.ic.ncs.com/cds).

La Franco, Robert, and Schuman, Michael. (1995, July 17). How do you say rock 'n' roll in Wolof? *Forbes*, pp. 102–103.

Life's a beach. (1995, Apr. 8). *The Economist*, pp. 59–60.

Maslow, Abraham. (1954). *Motivation and personality*. New York: Harper & Row.

McFarland, Lynne Joy, Senn, Larry E., and Childress, John R. (1993). *21st century leadership*. New York: The Leadership Press.

McLuhan, Marshall, and Fiore, Quentin. (1967). *The medium is the massage*. New York: Bantam.

Morris, Michael H., Avila, Ramon A., and Allen, Jeffrey W. (1993). Individualism and the modern corporation: Implications for innovation and entrepreneurship. *Journal of Management*, 19(3): 595–612.

Morris, Michael H., Davis, Duane L., and Allen, Jeffrey W. (1994, 1st quarter). Fostering corporate entrepreneurship: Cross-cultural comparisons of the importance of individualism versus collectivism. *Journal of International Business Studies*, pp. 65–89.

Morrison, Ann M. (1992). *The new leaders: Guidelines for leadership diversity in business*. San Francisco, CA: Jossey-Bass.

Newman, Barry. (1995, Mar. 27). Global chatter. *The Wall Street Journal*, pp. A1, A18.

Nonaka, Ikujiro, and Takeuchi, Hirotaka. (1995). *The knowledge-creating company*. New York: Oxford University Press.

O'Hara-Devereaux, Mary, and Johansen, Robert. (1994). *Globalwork*. San Francisco, CA: Jossey-Bass.

Ohmae, Kenichi. (1990). *The borderless world: Power and strategy in the interlinked economy*. New York: HarperBusiness

Outlook '95. (1994). *The Futurist Magazine*, p. 7.

Oviatt, Benjamin, and McDougall, Patricia Phillips. (1995). Global start-ups: Entrepreneurs on a worldwide stage. *Academy of Management Executive*, 9(2): 30–43.

Parker-Pope, Tara. (1995, July 10). God save the pub: Lather over names has Britain foaming. *The Wall Street Journal*, pp. A1, A6.

Peters, Tom, and Waterman, Robert, Jr. (1982). *In search of excellence*. New York: Harper & Row.

Phillips, Michael M. (1995, Feb. 7). Voice recognition systems work, but only if you speak American. *The Wall Street Journal*, p. B1.

Phillips, Don. (1994, Aug. 22). Culture may play role in flight safety. *The Seattle Times*, pp. E1, E3.

Reich, Robert. (1991, Fall). The stateless manager. *Best of Business Quarterly*, pp. 84–91.

Richardson, Michael. (1994, Nov.). With more money, fewer values? *International Herald Tribune*, p. 4.

Ricks, David. (1993). *Blunders in international business.* Cambridge, MA; Blackwell. (See also *Big business blunders*, Homewood, IL: Dow-Jones-Irwin, 1983.)

Robertson, R. (1995). Glocalization: Time–space and homogeneity–heterogeneity. In M. Featherstone, S. Lash, and R. Robertson (Eds), *Global modernities*, pp. 25–44. London: Sage.

Rohter, Larry. (1994, Aug. 14). Haiti is a land without a country. *New York Times*, Section 4, p. 3.

Schein, Edgar H. (1992). *Organizational culture and leadership.* San Francisco, CA: Jossey-Bass.

Schwartz, Shalom H. (1992). Universals in the content and structure of values: Theoretical advances and empirical tests in 20 countries. *Advances in Experimental Social Psychology*, 1–62.

Shoup, Mike. (1994, Sept. 18). Tourism's ugly side: Child prostitution. *The Seattle Times*, pp. K10–11.

Stanley, Alexandra. (1995, Jan. 1). A toast! To the good things about bad times. *The New York Times*, pp. E1, E4.

Templin, Neal. (1995, Apr. 4). Passed over for the No. 1 job at Chrysler, he parked his pride and thrives as No. 2. *The Wall Street Journal*, B1.

Terpstra, Vern, and David, Kenneth. (1991). *The cultural environment of international business.* Cincinnati, OH: Southwestern Publishing.

Thomas, David A., and Ely, Robin J. (1996, Sept./Oct.). Making differences matter: A new paradigm for managing diversity. *Harvard Business Review*, pp. 79–90.

Toffler, Alvin, and Toffler, Heidi. (1994). *Creating a new civilization.* Atlanta, GA: Turner Publishing.

Transcending business boundaries: 12,000 world managers view change. (1991, May/June). *Harvard Business Review*, pp. 151–164.

Trompenaars, Alfons. (1994). *Riding the waves of culture.* Burr Ridge, IL: Irwin.

Tung, Rosalie. (1982). Selection and training procedures of US, European, and Japanese multinationals. *California Management Review*, p. 62.

Tuttle, Alexandra. (1993, Oct. 5). Steamy Russian soap with a capitalist message. *The Wall Street Journal*, p. A14.

The universal teenager. (1994, Apr. 4). *Fortune*, p. 14.

Valente, Judith. (1994, Aug. 19). Global TV-new races heats up – but is payoff there? *The Wall Street Journal*, pp. B1, B2.

Waldman, Peter. (1994, Sept. 13). Lost in translation: How to 'empower women' in Chinese. *The Wall Street Journal*, pp. A1, A8.

Weber, Yaakov, Shenkar, Oded, and Raveli, Adi. (1996). National and corporate cultural fit in mergers/acquisitions: An exploratory study. *Management Science*, 42(8): 1215–1227.

Winterle, Mary J. (1992). *Work force diversity: Corporate challenges, corporate responses.* New York: Conference Board.

World Tourism Organization. (1997, Feb.). Global overview. http://www.12world-tourism.org/ESTA/highlights/prelres.htm

Young Chinese loosen the purse strings. (1996, July 15). *The Wall Street Journal*, p. A8.

Zha, Jianying. (1995). *China pop.* London: New Press.

Chapter 5

The Global Economy: Trade, FDI, Capital

SO MUCH DATA, SO LITTLE INFORMATION: BARINGS BANK

Barings Bank's first foray into derivatives was part of a 1993 joint venture. Peter Baring, chair of conservative bank Baring Brothers, was quoted as saying at the time, 'Derivatives need to be well controlled and understood, but we believe we do that here.' By spring 1995, Barings PLC was bankrupt. This is a story of 'unauthorized' trading in derivatives on the part of one man that led to the demise of the organization he represented. According to the many perspectives taken on the Barings bankruptcy, it is also a story of dangers with derivatives, of rapid industry change that is outpacing the abilities of some to keep up, and of how financial markets have become global. In sum, it is the story of opportunities and challenges in worldwide financial markets.

Until spring 1995, 28-year-old Nick Leeson was a Singapore-based trader in the Barings Futures (Singapore) Pte Ltd division of Britain's Barings PLC. According to published reports, Leeson had been successful in futures trading for Barings, and was sent out to the Singapore office in 1992 to head up the settlements department. In 1995, he was supposed to be arbitraging between Japanese- and Singapore-based derivatives, which in this case involved simultaneous buying of Nikkei-225 futures contracts in Japan and selling them on the Singapore Monetary Exchange. In reality, he was engaged in different activities. Between 1992 and 1995, he had been made head of trading while retaining his role as head of settlements; playing these dual roles simultaneously made it possible for him to cover evidence that he was buying derivatives, betting on a healthy Japanese stock market by trading in futures contracts and options contracts on the Nikkei Exchange. For Neeson's bet to pay off, the Japanese stock exchange had to stay in the 18,500–19,500 range. On January 17, a disastrous earthquake in Kobe rocked Japan and a few days later the effects were felt in Tokyo: the Tokyo stock market fell 1,000 points to under 17,800. Mindful of Barings' generous bonuses to be allocated on

February 24 – from which Leeson stood to gain about £450,000 – Leeson's efforts to recoup his losses and shore up a sinking market led to more investments in Nikkei futures. He failed; Barings' losses eventually totaled about £900 million ($1.3 billion US), and after 223 years, England's oldest merchant bank was bankrupt. The question that remains is: What made it possible for Leeson to take on so much risk without alerting Barings officials?

Some facts are clear, and they shed light on global changes in the banking industry that may have made the Barings collapse possible. First, while Barings was well known as a banking institution, its reputation depended on cautious and conservative banking practices such as corporate finance and asset management. Further, as the banking industry changed in response to global opportunity, like other banks, Barings began to lose some of its traditional sources of income since customers often could find better loan terms through other institutions. Hence, Barings – also like other banks – began to expand. The more conservative merchant bank had been merged with Barings Securities, taking on riskier opportunities for return with which Barings' existing staff had little experience. Derivatives, a financial contract whose value is linked to or derived from some underlying asset, were one such opportunity. Options, swaps, and futures contracts are derivatives on which huge bets can be made with small amounts of capital. While the pay-off is good, so too is the potential for losses.

As compared to traditional bankers, derivatives managers often are more risk-tolerant. Additionally, they tend to be youthful like Leeson and have or pretend to have knowledge their managers do not claim. These differences in style and knowledge may make it difficult for traditional bankers to understand or manage derivatives managers. Certainly, Barings as well as Leeson were motivated to take risks by the tremendous gains that were possible. Barings also had increased its worldwide staff by 30% between 1993 and 1995, and this sudden growth spurt may have spread people too thin, so that too few were supervising too many others worldwide. Additionally, there were clearly problems with Barings' internal controls. Only a few months before bankruptcy, Barings' head of treasury had complained to his chief executive that it was 'a struggle to get hard information,' and 'it is becoming much clearer that our systems and control culture are distinctly flaky' (Seeger, 1995). According to the Bank of England report on the collapse, Barings officials regularly remitted significant amounts to Barings Singapore without any clear understanding among Barings' managers on whose behalf those monies were to be applied. At the time of the bank's collapse, the amount sent to Singapore was approximately equal to the bank's entire share capital and reserves. Barings officials could not have missed knowing how much they had sent to Singapore, and further must have known exactly what those funds were equal to in assets, yet they did not know that Nick Leeson was engaged in unauthorized gambling on derivatives.

Worldwide response to Barings' collapse was immediate. Some feared Barings' losses would cause chaos in financial markets or lead to other bank failures; others saw a need for regulation; still others felt the British government should intervene to save the bank; and some saw these events as a clear indicator that derivatives are dangerous. In the end, derivatives remained, with few willing to close out a market that traded over $22 trillion in 1994. The British government did not intervene to save Barings, and the lesson to the world's bankers was clear: live with the consequences of your actions. It is likely that individual banks worldwide immediately began reviews of their own financial control systems. Finally, no other banks failed and there was no chaos in financial markets. But in view of how quickly opportunity outpaced Barings, one has to wonder if it isn't possible to have a great deal of data, but no real information.

As for Leeson, having realized his mounting losses would not be covered, he fled Singapore the day before the news of his losses broke, making it only to Germany before border police escorted him to a Frankfurt prison. His first official comments were made in – what else? – a television interview where he said he had gotten away with unauthorized trading because Barings' key executives in London did not understand the business he was engaged in. He admitted to being glad he was in jail since it meant he no longer had to live with the uncertainties and pressures of trading in derivatives.

From his jail cell in Singapore, where he is serving a six and a half year term for fraud, Leeson regards Barings managers as greedy and inept. The Bank of England report on Barings' losses blamed executives for failing to supervise Leeson, but one of those executives in turn claims a conspiracy among his colleagues prevented Leeson's exposure. Barings was taken over by Dutch banking and insurance giant Internationale Nederlanden Groep (ING) in March 1995, meanwhile Coopers & Lybrand and Deloite & Touche face allegations of negligence in Singapore; the Singapore International Monetary Exchange has revised its risk management procedures; and the Bank of England report blamed Baring's managers. Leeson's staggering losses of $1.3 billion now seem relatively small in the wake of Daiwa Bank losses of $1.1 billion in September 1995, Sumitomo Corporation's $2.6 billion losses in unauthorized copper trading, and Yamaichi Securities $24 billion bankruptcy. The various finger-pointing and blaming exercises provide little clarity as to what really happened at Barings, proving that data do not necessarily yield information.

Sources: Bank of England report on Barings. (1995, July 18). London: Bank of England; Bray, Nicholas. (1996, July 22). Ex-boss of Barings' Leeson fights back. *The Wall Street Journal*, p. A8; The collapse of Barings. (1995, Mar. 4). *The Economist*, pp. 19–21; Leeson, Nick with Edward Whitley. (1996). *Rogue trader*. New York: Little, Brown; Seeger, Charles M. (1995, Aug. 8). How to prevent future Nick Leesons. *The Wall Street Journal*, p. A15; Who lost Barings? (1995, July 22). *The Economist*, p. 16.

The Barings case demonstrates the challenges of keeping pace with rapid change. In a globalizing economy, rules that once seemed reasonably robust in explaining economic events now seem less well able to explain global occurrences, and blurring boundaries of every type contribute to greater complexity and fewer certainties for every aspect of the global economy. In this emerging global economy, many markets have become global, and most organizations and individuals are affected by global economic events and trends as well as national ones. This chapter begins with a look at domestic economies to provide a context for the later examination of the global changes producing strains within and among nations. As existing mechanisms falter and fail, assumptions about how economies and firms operate bear reexamination.

PART I   A GROWING GLOBAL ECONOMY CREATES NEW CHALLENGES

Economic systems provide the means for generating and distributing resources within a society. These economic systems are supported by distribution systems that transfer goods to satisfy demand; by currency systems that provide a medium for exchange; and by banks and other businesses that facilitate resource generation and distribution. Until the twentieth century, most national economies were more closed than open, and within these economies people used the same currency, the same distribution systems, the same institutions, and relied upon domestic businesses to generate economic wealth. In a closed system like this, the economic indicators to watch are those that reflect the health of domestic activities.

As a result of industrialization, many domestic economies became more open to economic interactions with others, and this marked the beginning of an active international trading era that required international solutions to the problems of payment, resource acquisition, and distribution. For example, payment for goods acquired in trade was made difficult because there was no commonly recognized currency, and firms were reluctant to trade without it. Thus, new – more international – systems developed to manage exports and imports, to calculate the balance of trade when trade between countries was unequal, to set currency exchange rates, and to foster direct investments abroad. These systems evolved to manage international commerce and continue to evolve to facilitate global commerce in a changing world. This evolution also requires a change in how we think and talk about economy. For example, nations once referred to as industrialized now are deindustrializing and often are described as 'advanced' economies, whereas nations striving toward industrial or postindustrial status are described as newly industrialized countries (NICs) and as developing economies.

MARKET ECONOMICS

Global commerce has been stimulated by almost worldwide embrace of market economics. By definition, market-based economies are a forum for people to come together to exchange ownership of goods and services. Assumptions of free markets include the following: economic decisions are made by markets rather than by governments; buyers and sellers can freely enter markets; and all have full access to knowledge of prices, quantities, and the activities of others. Market capitalism further assumes economic rationality from market participants whose decisions are presumably based on economic self-interests. In theory, individuals or individual households, together with many organizational entities, make independent spending decisions, creating a supply and demand market responsive to collective wants and needs. If independent decisions lead individuals to stop purchasing a good, then producers respond by lowering prices or cease production. Conversely, if all want the same goods, this creates a scarcity that permits producers to raise prices. As prices go up, ardor for the desired product decreases and alternatives are sought. This up and down movement in availability and price is the law of supply and demand, but it is difficult to predict with any certainty, and that is one reason it often is referred to as the 'invisible hand.' Markets are governed largely by costs, prices, and profits, but the underlying factors for those markets are rarely visible and therefore difficult to predict.

Many dominant and enduring maxims of market economics were outlined by Adam Smith in 1776. Leonard Silk (1978) paraphrases Smith, writing:

> Economics is about wealth creation, and wealth-creating choices are (or should be) made by comparing the amount of time, labor, resources, and capital invested in a project with the return on that investment – and with alternate investments and organizations of production. (p. 40)

Creation of economic wealth via free market economics is a driving force for globalization of economies. According to 1997 Heritage House calculations, the nations with greatest economic freedoms are those with the highest living standards, and lowest living standards are found in nations with the fewest economic freedoms. The Heritage House-sponsored comparison of GDP growth in more and less economically free nations between 1980 and 1993 revealed that most free nations added real per capita GDP growth of 2.88% as compared to negative per capita GDP growth of –1.44% in the most repressed economies. An abbreviated list of most and least free economies appears in Table 5.1; bear in mind that this report measures economic freedoms but not political freedoms.

Economies tend to be organized around nation-states. The combined economic

TABLE 5.1 Index of Economic Freedom, selected 1997 rankings

Free	Mostly free	Mostly unfree	Repressed
1 Hong Kong	9 Bahamas Netherlands	73 Djibouti, South Africa	140 Myanmar (Burma)
2 Singapore	15 Canada Belgium, UAE	85 Honduras, Poland	142 Azerbaijan
3 Bahrain	27 Norway, S. Korea, Sri Lanka, Sweden	87 Fiji, Nigeria	143 Iran, Libya, Somalia, Vietnam
4 New Zealand	43 Belize, Jordan, Uruguay	94 Brazil, Ivory Coast, Mexico, Moldova	147 Iraq
5 Switzerland USA	64 Hungary, Peru, Uganda	115 Albania, Lesotho, Russia	148 Cuba, Laos, North Korea
7 UK Taiwan		123 Congo, Ukraine	

Source: 1997 Index of Economic Freedom, New York: Heritage House and the *Wall Street Journal*.

activities of all actors operating within a nation define a national economy; those that operate according to free markets then depend on the independent decisions of a great many economic actors, including businesses, individuals, households, and governmental entities. The following look at closed and open participation in the global economy identifies important economic measures and shows why a more open global economy reduces national economic autonomy.

MEASURES OF NATIONAL ECONOMIC PERFORMANCE
A closed economic system

Indicators for a domestic economy measure economic health within the nation. These indicators include microeconomic activities such as personal income or business investments in capital equipment, and they include macroeconomic activities that reflect the economy as a whole, including overall employment rates or national inflation. In addition, national economic measures reflect activities sponsored by the public sector or government including fiscal policies that extract assets from the system in the form of taxes and redistribute assets in the form of transfer payments or subsidies. Additionally, government actors in market economies tend to shape individual economic decisions by pursuing monetary policy – those decisions that generate the supplies of money that influence interest rates.

Assume that the national system of supply and demand described above is a closed national system; nothing comes in and nothing goes out except what is generated from within the system. Figure 5.1 illustrates this closed system in a market economy;

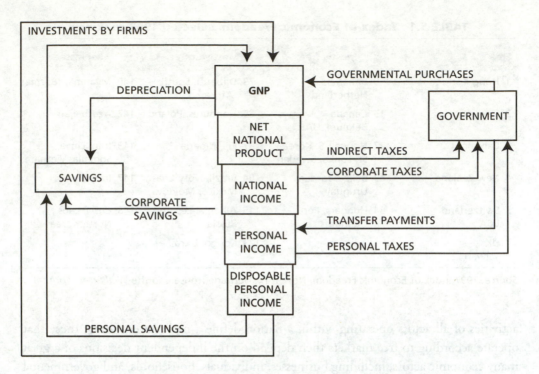

FIGURE 5.1 *A closed national economic system*

indicators also appear in Box 5.1. Gross national product (GNP) measures the total value of all finished goods and services generated by producers in or from the nation. In this closed system, investments on the part of organizations must go into either domestic investments or savings, and individual income can only go into domestic savings, investments, taxes, or spending. In view of early international trading between countries, the closed economic system represented by this figure is not very realistic, but it makes a useful point which is that prosperity in a closed domestic system depends almost entirely on internal economic activity.

An open economic system

The 1997 Index of Economic Freedom mentioned above evaluated 150 countries from Albania to Zimbabwe, examining links between living standards and economic freedom. Among the 10 key areas examined were trade policy, taxation, government intervention, monetary policy, capital flows and foreign investments, banking policy, wage and price controls, property rights, regulations, and black market activities. This study led to the following conclusions:

BOX 5.1:   ECONOMIC INDICATORS FOR A CLOSED ECONOMY

The overall measure of national output appropriate to a closed system is gross national product (GNP); this measure includes goods produced in the nation (except by foreign firms) and by domestic firms operating abroad. National income is measured by:

domestic transactions:
- personal income;
- household income;
- disposable income;
- savings rates for individuals and organizations;
- investments;
- construction of new housing;
- industry investments, new equipment orders;
- productivity rates;
- employment and unemployment rates;
- government activities;
- government expenditures;
- money supply changes, interest rates;
- federal surplus/deficit;
- government (central, regional, community) expenditures;
- defense expenditures.

- Only 9 nations were judged to be free economically. An additional 72 nations were judged to be mostly free, 78 were judged mostly unfree or repressed, and 18 were judged to be repressed.
- A comparison among scores for 1997 and earlier assessments of economic freedom suggested that as countries become richer, government adds welfare and other social programs that did not exist when the country was poorer.
- Examples taken from Western Europe suggested that national economic freedoms rise and fall with prosperity, with government instituting controls and social programs during economic prosperity and curtailing them when prosperity declines.

In view of the link between free markets worldwide and economic prosperity within nations, a more realistic view of domestic economies is the one represented by Figure 5.2.

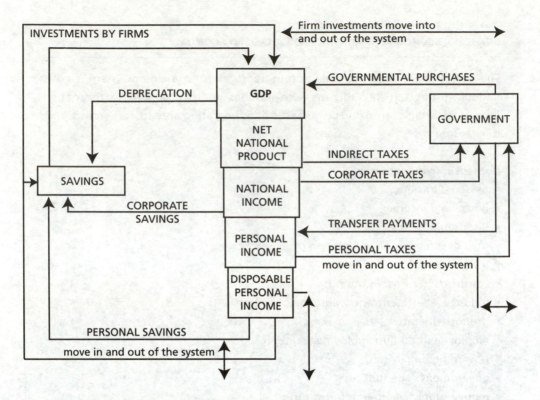

FIGURE 5.2 *An open system view of national economies*

This figure shows the clean, crisp border around the national economy has become blurred as factors of production, e.g., people, capital, equipment, flow freely into and out of the system from and to other nations. These factor flows include transfer funds from government to retirees living abroad or taxes gained from individuals working abroad, but for the most part the movement of productive factors is related to business activities associated with trade and direct investments both into and out of a nation. This includes trade activities measured by exports and imports, the annual balance of trade when imports are reconciled with exports, direct investments into the country, and currency exchange rates. Adding GDP and the list of international transactions to domestic measures creates a set of indicators reflective of economic health for a nation operating in an international sphere. The economic indicators usual to international transactions are listed in Box 5.2 and an explanation of how each functions follows.

TRADE AND THE BALANCE OF TRADE

International trade figures include components of trade that are tangible and visible as well as intangible services. Merchandise traded includes jeans, cola beverages, and other highly visible consumer products, as well as less publicly visible but no less tangible

BOX 5.2:   ECONOMIC INDICATORS FOR AN OPEN ECONOMY

First, the best overall measure of output becomes gross domestic product (GDP); this measures all finished goods and services produced within the nation, including those of foreign producers. It does not include what domestic firms produce elsewhere.

   Second, add:
- international transactions;
  - trade in exports and imports;
    - trade in manufactured goods;
    - trade in services;
  - balance of trade;
  - foreign direct investments;
    - investments in equities like stock or funds;
    - investments in fixed, productive assets like plant and equipment;
  - currency exchange.

commodities like silver, gold, sugar, many agricultural products, and merchandise ranging from aircraft to machine tools to furniture. Trade in visible merchandise is a major source of international revenue and expenditures for many countries. Trade also includes services ranging from accounting to travel to personal services; total commercial services reached $1.2 trillion in 1996, and worldwide trade in goods totalled $5 trillion the same year. In all, about 70% of world trade traditionally has been conducted by and among industrialized countries. These forms of trade require payments, and an imbalance in payments between countries creates the nation's balance of trade.

   The balance of trade results when a country subtracts the cost of imports for goods and services from the income gained from exports in the same period, e.g., quarterly or annually. A negative number indicates the value of goods imported to the nation is greater than the value of goods exported; this results in a negative balance of trade. A positive balance results when the value of exports is greater than the value of imports. National reports of trade balances often state a single figure to show that the country has a positive or negative balance of trade, but country-by-country trade balances also are used to demonstrate trading inequalities between nations. For example, the US/Japan trade balance is calculated to show that the US buys more from Japan than Japan buys from the US, and this chronic imbalance then provides evidence for politicians to use when calling for fewer Japanese trade barriers.

FOREIGN DIRECT INVESTMENTS

Foreign direct investment (FDI) is broadly defined as investments in firms located abroad. Individuals and institutional investors make foreign direct investments when they purchase stocks for their portfolios and their activities are counted as part of worldwide FDI; indeed, the growing number of individual and institutional investors is one reason for increased worldwide FDI. But another and more important reason for increases in FDI is business activities. In this context, FDI is defined more narrowly as *control* of a company in another country with minimum ownership of 10–25% of the voting stock, and it may involve partial or full ownership of productive factors abroad such as plant and equipment. Thus, a firm can foreign direct invest by buying a foreign firm's stock or by buying its productive capacity. Reasons for business direct investment abroad in either of these two ways vary widely, but could include a firm's desire to expand to new markets, to acquire foreign resources, to enhance a global position via acquisition, or even to attain political influence in the host country.

CURRENCY EXCHANGE RATES

Exchange rates are the number of units of one currency paid to acquire a unit of another currency. Variations in currency exchange rates have price implications for firms and for individuals, and most of these are manifest not only when we exchange currency but also when we purchase goods that involve currency transactions. Global price comparisons prepared by Runzheimer International illustrate this point. Table 5.2 shows that the price of 100 aspirin tablets ranges from a high of $35.93 in Tokyo to a low of $1.16 in Mexico City. Travelers have little choice but to pay the current price for aspirin when in Tokyo, but doing so reduces the amount available to purchase other goods and services. Cost variations resulting from exchange rate variations have similar implications for the firm caused by price and cost differences over time. These fluctuations make it difficult to plan costs and they necessarily affect profits. For example, when the Japanese yen was at a peak relative to the US dollar in April 1996, Japanese automakers initiated construction of auto manufacturing plants in the US because each yen bought more real estate, more plant and equipment, and more labor than in the past. In 1985 the yen to dollar ratio was ¥258 to $1; by April 1996, it was ¥79 to $1. In effect, the dollar could be bought for fewer yen in 1996 as compared to 1985 and so each yen bought more goods in the US than in earlier years. But the reverse also occurs. As the dollar strengthened against the yen through late 1996 and 1997, commitments made to build plants in the US then had to be paid in more yen per dollar because by March 1997 the dollar could be exchanged for ¥121. The rollercoaster ride of yen/dollar exchange rates is evident in Figure 5.10 below. In the following section, we examine historical events affecting exchange rates.

TABLE 5.2   Global price comparison of selected goods and services (dollars)

Location	Apples (1 lb)	Aspirin (100 tab.)	Candy bar (1)	Snack food (8 oz)	Toothpaste (6.4 oz)
Hong Kong	.72	9.61	.71	2.15	2.57
London	.80	9.69	.35	2.22	3.63
Los Angeles	.83	7.69	.48	1.56	2.42
Mexico City	.69	1.16	.45	.97	1.08
Paris	.77	7.91	.75	1.42	3.54
Rio de Janeiro	1.32	7.23	.63	2.28	2.91
Sydney	.89	7.43	.58	2.70	2.08
Tokyo	3.96	35.93	1.06	2.62	4.24
Toronto	.94	5.00	.60	1.33	1.88

Source: All research is conducted by Runzheimer International the Rochester Wisconsin-based management consulting firm specializing in travel and living costs. Based on Runzheimer analyzes goods and services worldwide. (1996, July 22). Rochester, MN: Runzheimer International press release.

The Bretton Woods agreements

In the 150 years prior to the Bretton Woods agreements, the world's exchange rate system had operated on a gold standard managed by a private bank: the Bank of England. This system was disrupted by two devastating world wars. The representatives of the 44 nations who gathered for the Bretton Woods agreement feared the consequences of economic instabilities that had contributed to world war, and in their historic 1944 meeting, they moved to establish a monetary system intended to stabilize exchange rates worldwide. This stability was viewed as crucial to trade and economic revitalization. Delegates 'fixed' currencies to a standard valuing gold at $35 per ounce.

Seventy percent of the world's gold reserves in 1947 were held in the US as a guarantee for the currencies of Bretton Woods participants. Accordingly, member currencies were denominated in gold and in US dollars. Because it was far easier to trade in paper assets than in gold, governments as well as business organizations bought and sold dollars rather than gold on the assumption that the US government would pay gold for dollars should the need ever arise. This fixed rate system was altered in 1971 because a dwindling US trade surplus and a devalued dollar made it less desirable to peg the world's economy on the strength of the US dollar. Nevertheless, the US dollar remains an important form of global currency. Its suitability for this role is explored later in the chapter.

The three most frequently used approaches to setting currency exchange rates are to peg currency rates by fixing them to one or several other currencies according to the comparative value of the same basket of goods, to allow currency rates to fluctuate around some relatively stable currency standard, or to allow currency exchange rates to float freely in response to the market. Globalization has witnessed a move away from the relative safety of pegged exchange rates which were the norm (63.5%) as recently as 1984. By the end of 1994 pegged rates were found in only 39.9% of 178 countries as compared to 32.6% of freely floating currencies. This change is represented in Figure 5.3.

Central bankers establish pegged exchange rates, but free-floating currency exchanges are determined by market factors, and the market can be fickle, wrong, and opportunistic when buyers and sellers of currency operate on world markets. According to Gregory Millman (1995), currency speculators play the central role in determining the value of currency as their collective bets lead to currency fluctuations. Their role in futures and options markets can sometimes outstrip the role of central banks and cause currency panics that have little to do with the underlying strength of the affected economy. While panic did not ensue from the Barings Bank disaster described in the opening case for this chapter, many feared that Leeson's failed bets on derivatives would touch off a global panic and a run on bank assets. Millman maintains that traders rather than central bankers provide financial discipline in world markets, and this marks a departure from international business where central banks exercised control over currency exchange rates by buying and selling the currency in international markets.

Our current concern is: What happens as the world globalizes and outstrips the ability of any individual country to control the economic events affecting its own prosperity? A look at the experiences of the past decade or so yields insight. The worldwide

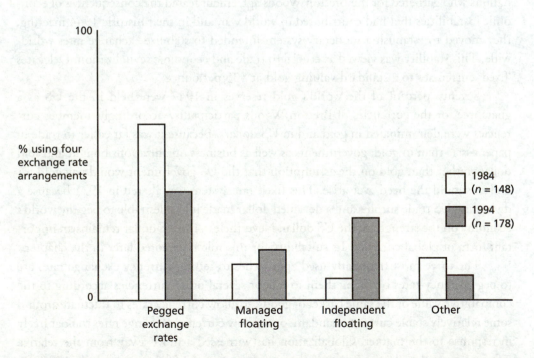

FIGURE 5.3 *Floating away* (adapted from: Fixed and floating voters. (1995, Apr. 1). *The Economist*, p. 64)

balance of economic power changed as former and current communist countries increased their economic interrelationships with the rest of the world, and these inter-relationships created dependencies that make it more difficult for individual nations to manage their own economies. An example is the 1988 US–Canada Free Trade Pact which made each more vulnerable to the other's fate. In 1994, Canada's economy grew on the strength of US orders for lumber, computers, and automobiles, but when the US Federal Reserve Board raised interest rates to slow the US economy, Canada's economy also cooled. Thus, with increased economic interdependency comes loss to some degree of control over national economies. It also becomes more difficult to measure and compare national economic progress, a point illustrated by a look at GDP use in a global economy.

GDP IN A GLOBAL ECONOMY

As an indicator of a society's well-being, GDP measures all finished goods and services produced within a nation, whether produced by domestic or foreign capital. These calculations are based on final goods and services. For example, a loaf of bread is counted as part of GDP only when it is purchased; its price is assumed to be the value added by the wheat grower, the miller, the manufacturer, the distributor, and all others who contributed to the final product. When making foreign investment decisions, organizational leaders aim to invest in nations where growth is evident or has great potential.

World GDP in 1997 totalled approximately $29 trillion and is expected to grow at about 2–4% into the 2000s. According to most estimates US GDP amounted to about $7.5 trillion in 1997 (almost one-quarter of world GDP), and this and other reasons, such as many buyers, has attracted more direct investments to the US than to any other nation. But, the US is finding it more difficult to track economic data. According to US Commerce Department figures, accurate statistics are available only for about 30% of the measures used in calculating GDP (Mandel, 1994). The US government changed its methods for calculating GDP in 1995, but rapidly changing economic conditions world-wide may make it difficult for the US or any nation to achieve high degrees of accuracy when compiling and comparing worldwide economic data. Additionally, measures available may not reflect the true extent of global economic activity. These points are explored below.

There are several impediments to measuring global GDP and other economic activities. First, many activities that reflect national economic health are not counted as such. For example, United Nation estimates are that unpaid labor worldwide amounted to about $16 trillion in 1995, but unpaid labor is almost never included in economic analyses. Were unpaid labor included, the size of both the global economy and some national economies most reliant on it, e.g., developing economies, would be much greater than currently reported. Transfer payments like social security or pensions, gifts, and many other indicators of economic activity also are purposefully excluded from GDP. Additionally, national GDP is inflated by activities that do not necessarily increase the standard of living. For example, the cost of criminal defense is part of US GDP calculations. Additionally, it is difficult to track the global economy because nations prepare and report economic data in different ways; comparisons then are difficult to make.

A third challenge to measuring global economic activity is that even if economic reports are standardized, nations and economic actors may be motivated to provide inaccurate reports. The following examples illustrate this can occur for many reasons.

- In Russia, GDP was estimated to be as much as 40% higher than official Goskomstat figures in 1994 not only because reporting mechanisms developed under the communist system are inadequate to track activities for a market economy, but because many Russians are reluctant to report real economic activity. For example, in 1993 Russia reported $27 billion in imports but its trading partners put exports at $33 billion. The missing $6 billion may not have been reported to the government. Misha Belkindas, a World Bank statistical advisor, described the problem as a breakdown in the old statistical system without having a new system in place (Rosett, 1994).
- In Angola, the size of the underground economy is estimated to be larger than reported GDP.
- The Ukraine reported GDP of about $32 billion in 1995, but the World Bank estimates another $30 billion is generated in unreported cash.
- A 1994 investigation by Chinese officials identified 60,000 cases of falsified and mistaken figures, many of which are directly related to GDP reports.
- GDP measures differ; some are infrequently reported, not measured, or reflect national differences in accounting practices and national priorities.

Finally, GDP and other economic reports can tell different stories. For example, if we rely on absolute GDP, the US would appear to be the strongest economy, but if the comparative measure is per capita GDP, then other nations would come in 'first.' As Table 5.3 shows, absolute and per capita GDP ratings create different impressions of a nation's prosperity. For example, France ranked fourth in overall GDP in 1996, but GDP rankings according to unadjusted earnings averages placed France sixth after Switzerland, Japan, Norway, Denmark, and Germany.

Further examination of per capita GDP also show these can themselves be flawed measures of a nation's internal prosperity. According to Ibbotson and Brinson (1993), per capita gross product calculations are averages and do not reflect the fact that countries can have richer and poorer regions within them. Additionally, these authors argue

TABLE 5.3   How they stack up

	1996 per capita GDP	Per capita GDP, adjusted for PPP	GDP in billions $US, 1996 current prices	Population estimates 1997 (millions)	Population growth est 1995–2000
Switzerland	43,233	24,800	292.9	7,277	.67
Japan	40,726	21,795	4,578.2	125,638	.22
Norway	33,535	22,672	156	4,364	.35
Denmark	33,144	21,529	174.3	5,248	.19
Germany	29,542	20,497	2,354.2	82,190	.27
France	26,445	19,939	1,544.7	58,543	.33
United States	26,348	26,438	7,263.2	271,648	.79
Netherlands	25,597	19,782	392.5	15,661	.50
United Arab Emirates	NA	20,654[a]	29[b]	2,308	2.01
Canada	18,915	21,031	577.9	29,942	.85
United Kingdom	18,777	17,756	1,140.2	58,201	.09

[a] 1994 data.

[b] Based on constant 1985 US$.

Source: Data from 1997 OECD National Accounts; UN indicators on population; *Fortune*, Global economy, 1995.

that money income may not be the best indicator of real wealth, which also might include the extent to which one enjoys or is able to enjoy life. We will return to the latter point after looking at how to adjust for over- or under-stated comparative measures of GDP.

Purchasing power parity

It is usually more costly to live in an advanced or industrialized economy than a developing economy, and it is important to look at differences like these when comparing national GDPs. To make sound investment decisions, we want to compare apples to apples when using GDP, but looking at raw data without cost of living adjustments would make our comparisons more akin to comparing apples to oranges. Accordingly, GDP comparisons often are adjusted statistically. The best known adjustment is purchasing power parity (PPP). The guiding assumption for PPP is that the underlying value of goods is the same, even if costs of living vary. The 'hamburger index' makes this point. If the Big Mac is $2.42 in the US, and the ingredients are exactly the same in Japan, then the Biggu Macku in Japan should cost about the equivalent of $2.42 in yen. This is rarely the case, and variations in Table 5.4 show where over- and under-valuations occur. Thus, PPP makes it possible to see where costs would be higher or lower than expected; this information is not reflected by raw GDP figures. The advantages of PPP are offset by

TABLE 5.4 The hamburger standard

	Big Mac prices in local currency	in dollars	Implied PPP[a] of the dollar	Actual $ exchange rate 7/4/97	Local currency under(−)/over(+) valuation,[b]%
United States[ttc]	$2.42	2.42			
Argentina	Peso2.50	2.50	1.03	1.00	+3
Australia	A$2.50	1.94	1.03	1.29	−20
Austria	Sch34.00	2.82	14.0	12.0	+17
Belgium	BFr109	3.09	45.0	35.3	+28
Brazil	Real2.97	2.81	1.23	1.06	+16
Britain	£1.81	2.95	1.34[tt]	1.63[tt]	+22
Canada	C$2.88	2.07	1.19	1.39	−14
Chile	Peso1,200	2.88	496	417	+19
China	Yuan9.70	1.16	4.01	8.33	−52
Czech Republic	CKr53.0	1.81	21.9	29.2	−25
Denmark	DKr25.75	3.95	10.6	6.52	+63
France	FFr17.5	3.04	7.23	5.76	+26
Germany	DM4.90	2.86	2.02	1.71	+18
Hong Kong	HK$9.90	1.28	4.09	7.75	−47
Hungary	Forint271	1.52	112	178	−37
Israel	Shekel11.5	3.40	4.75	3.38	+40
Italy	Lire4,600	2.73	1,901	1,683	+13
Japan	¥294	2.34	121	126	−3
Malaysia	M$3.87	1.55	1.60	2.50	−36
Mexico	Peso14.9	1.89	6.16	7.90	−22
Netherlands	F15.45	2.83	2.25	1.92	+17
New Zealand	NZ$3.25	2.24	1.34	1.45	−7
Poland	Zloty4.30	1.39	1.78	3.10	−43
Russia	Ruble11,000	1.92	4,545	5,739	−21
Singapore	S$3.00	2.08	1.24	1.44	−14
South Africa	Rand7.80	1.76	3.22	4.43	−27
South Korea	Won2,300	2.57	950	894	+6
Spain	Pta375	2.60	155	144	+7
Sweden	SKr26.0	3.37	10.7	7.72	+39
Switzerland	SFr5.90	4.02	2.44	1.47	+66
Taiwan	NT$68.0	2.47	28.1	27.6	+2
Thailand	Baht46.7	1.79	19.3	26.1	−26

[a] Purchasing power parity; local price divided by price in the United States.
[b] Against dollar.
[tt] Average of New York, Chicago, San Francisco, and Atlanta.
[c] Dollars per pound.
Source: *The Economist*. (1997, Apr. 12). p. 71, using data from McDonald's.

some limitations. For example, some argue that PPP theory works only in an ideal or abstract world without trade barriers and without real differences, and that labor, rents, and inflation can and do change all the time, so PPP figures can over- or under-state GDP. Nevertheless, PPP remains a better comparative measure of economic performance than raw, unadjusted GDP figures.

Sources of world GDP

As recently as 1993, North America, Western Europe, and Japan – also known as the Triad – accounted for about 65% of world GDP. These nations will account for 55% of GDP by 2010 because industrial or advanced economies are at or near stable growth. In 1994 their economies grew at an average rate of less than 3%, including .8% in Japan and 4.3% in Canada. Growth predictions for these advanced economies in 1996 and 1997 are projected at between 1 and 4% per year (Richman, 1995). In contrast, many developing economies are witnessing strong economic growth. Many nations in East Asia grew at 5–11% GDP from 1994–1996. Despite 1997 slowdowns, most Asian nations still anticipate GDP growth in 1998 and beyond. Interestingly, just as fast-growth economies like Thailand, Indonesia, and Malaysia began to slow in 1997, many developing economies in Latin America showed unexpectedly high growth. Thus, overall world growth continued (Table 5.5 and Table 1.1)

The preceding review of GDP measures described how these figures reflect national economic wealth and how they are calculated. They also show shifts in where GDP growth is concentrated, and we reviewed some reasons to exercise caution when using GDP to assess absolute or relative national prosperity. The following section suggests additional reasons to exercise caution when using GDP to measure world wealth and prosperity.

EXPANDED DEFINITIONS OF WEALTH

Gross domestic product reflects economic activity, and, as we saw above, world economic activity in many nations can be seriously under-reported or inaccurate for other reasons. Further, GDP does not measure future costs of economic activities. Although the present costs of consuming natural resources are counted as part of GDP, the cost of

TABLE 5.5   Real GDP growth, in annual average (%)

	1974–1993	1994–2003
World	3.0 or less	4.2
Advanced and industrialized economies	2.9	2.7
Developing economies	3.0	4.8
East Asia	7.5	7.6
South Asia	4.8	5.3
Latin America	2.6	3.4
E. Europe and former USSR	1.0	2.7
Sub-Saharan Africa	2.0	3.9
Middle East and N. Africa	1.2	3.8

Sources: World Bank, 1994; IMF World Economic Outlook, 1997.

nonrenewable resources, e.g., polluted rivers or land erosion, are not factored into GDP. The absence of these inputs in economic figures understates the actual cost of producing the good, and there is little reason for organizations to view them as a cost of doing business. Another concern is that economic activity is only one among many measures of wealth and human prosperity.

The Human Development Index

In 1990 the United Nations Development Program developed an alternative scale of wealth called the Human Development Index (HDI). The HDI measures five basic components: life expectancy, adult literacy, average years of schooling, educational attainment, and adjusted income, and it is based on this philosophy:

> . . . human choices extend far beyond economic well-being. Human beings may want to enjoy long and healthy lives, drink deep at the fountain of knowledge, participate freely in the life of their community, breathe fresh air and enjoy the simple pleasures of life in a clean physical environment. (*Human Development Report*, 1994, p. 15)

Comparisons between 1993 HDI and adjusted GDP show similarities, but the two were not identical, with human development higher than GDP in developing economies such as Malaysia, Turkey, South Africa, and Indonesia. By 1994, only a few had a higher HDI than GDP. The comparison of HDI and GDP for 1994 (Figure 5.4) shows the gap is closing between HDI and GDP, but like earlier years it continues to demonstrate that the gap is least in advanced economies and greatest in developing economies. An interesting 1993 finding is that the advanced economies have a Human Development Index only 1.6 times more than developing economies, even though GDP gaps can be more than five times as high. From this we might infer that GDP is an incomplete measure of wealth when wealth is viewed as a concept accommodating considerable diversity of experience and values; high GDP and high human development are compatible; and many developing countries have sufficient human resources to develop economically.

Compatibility between human and economic development may be possible, but this does not mean the two move together. The 1996 *Human Development Report* showed that quality of life for humans has improved by 44% since 1980: people eat better, get cleaner water, more children survive, and educational opportunities are growing. In the same time period, economic conditions grew worse than they had been in 1970 for people in 43 countries. The 1997 *Human Development Report* reported a loss on the HDI for 30 countries – mostly due to drops in life expectancy or per capita

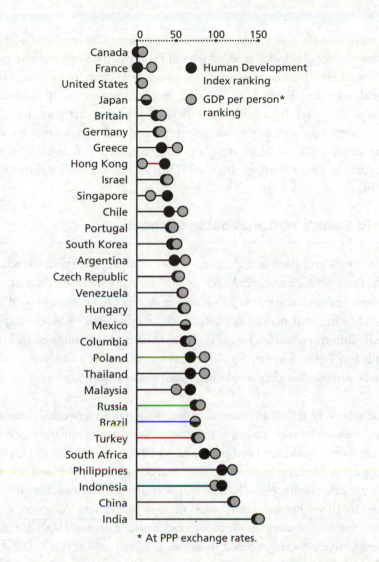

FIGURE 5.4 *Human Development Index: country ranking (selected countries), 1994* (*The Economist*. (1997, June 21). p. 108, using UNDP data)

GDP – and this occurred as most of the world experienced buoyant economies. In 1997 the United Nations Development Program created a second measure further to explore human development, and particularly to examine the dimensions of poverty rather than income alone. The HPI used reflects three variables: lifespan as measured by the percentage of the population in each nation expected to survive to age 40; basic education measured by the percentage of population illiteracy; and access to public and private resources which is a composite measure for the percentage of population without access to health services, safe water, and reasonable nutrition. Comparisons of HDI results with the Human Poverty Index revealed overall HDI progress in developing economies, but also showed that human poverty varies widely within these nations. For example, although Pakistan and Egypt have reduced income poverty to 20% (measured at a poverty line of $1 a day), their HPIs are at 35%. This means that fewer poor have access to safe water, health services, and reasonable nutrition, and it shows that income poverty and human poverty do not move together. To summarize, just as GDP is a less-than-prefect measure of national prosperity, the HDI is an incomplete measure of the quality of human life.

The World Bank's national balance sheet

In fall 1995, the World Bank issued its first report on a proposed plan to include natural, physical, human, and social capital such as income equality or democracy on national balance sheets. Incorporating these forms of wealth alters the picture viewed through the GDP lens, showing that natural resources such as minerals or forests catapult Canada and Australia into top positions on the national balance sheet, followed by Luxembourg, Switzerland, and Japan. Sweden and Iceland were ranked six and seven on the national balance sheet scheme, but they would be ranked twentieth and twenty-first on the basis of GDP.

These relatively recent alternatives to assessing national 'wealth' demonstrate that the flaws evident with GDP measures and comparisons are stimulating new alternatives to measuring global wealth and prosperity. As we have seen, the flaws in GDP make this measure less than ideal for measuring national economic wealth and when trying to compare economic wealth globally. The implications for business are the same: GDP may not tell us all we need to know when making investment decisions, and it creates uncertainties for business expansion in a global world. Futurist Hazel Henderson takes another perspective on market-based measures of development like GDP. As shown in Figure 5.5, Henderson believes that market economics represent a very early 'stage' in human development that emerged because it reinforces boundary-based identification of people living in groups and nations. She argues that long-held beliefs about money, wealth, productivity, and efficiency of market economics are 'rooted in immature, often infantile states of mind – easily manipulated by politicians and advertisers' (Henderson, 1996, p. 153). Further, she suggests that as people expand the calculus of human interest to include social objectives, the species will evolve to transcend divisive, boundary-based loyalties and reach fully integrated planetary identity. Although it is almost impossible to imagine how a planetary identity will transcend markets, equity and survival issues are challenging business leaders and politicians to rethink market assumptions.

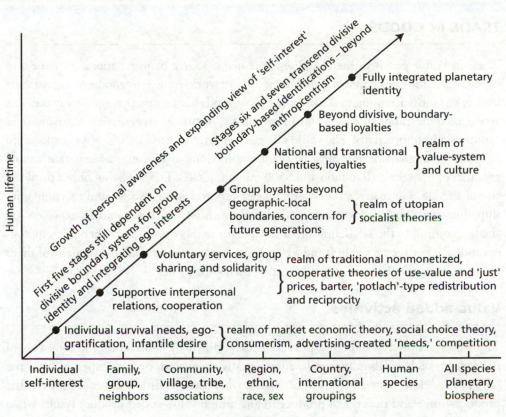

FIGURE 5.5 *Expanding calculus of self-interest* (Henderson, Hazel. (1996). *Building a win-win world*, p. 154. San Francisco, CA: Berrett Koehler Books; original appeared in Henderson's *The politics of the solar age: alternatives to economics* (1981, 1988). Garden City, NY: Anchor/Doubleday.

Assessing global economics

In summary, the business decision-maker faces multiple challenges when assessing global economic opportunities, such as: (a) trade in goods and services, including those where personal contact with the ultimate consumer is essential, such as in banking or health care, and those that deal with information, such as entertainment, computers, and higher education; (b) global flows of investments; (c) global flows of currency; and (d) the global movement of labor. Labor issues are the subject of Chapter 6. This chapter concentrates on globalization of trade in goods and services, foreign direct investment, and global flows of capital to illustrate challenges and opportunities faced in those segments of a global economy.

TRADE IN GOODS

Trade in visible goods or merchandise is the major source of international revenue and expenditures for most countries, and about 70% of world trade is in goods. Many national leaders pay most attention to statistics on visible goods because their tangibility makes this aspect of trade easier to count and more reliable. Virtually every nation is involved in export and import activity. The world's biggest exporter is the US; 70% of US exports are supplied by large firms and 30% by small and medium-size firms that generate annual revenues of between $10 million and $500 million in sales. Despite being only a third the size of the US, Germany is the second biggest exporter in the world, and its companies ship almost as many goods abroad as do US firms. Many of these German exporters are small according to the US definition of small firms as those with fewer than 500 employees and sales between $500,000 and $10 million. Table 5.6 lists small firms, many of them German, that have become global 'giants' in their own niches.

Value-added activities

The value a company adds to a product is determined by subtracting the total cost of production such as labor, materials, administrative overhead, or sales expenses from the sales price. A low value-added product results when there is little difference between the product's price and the cost to produce it; and a high value-added product results when a product's price far exceeds its actual costs. When firms from developing economies initiate trade relationships, traditionally they have done so with exports of low value-added goods such as textiles or agricultural products. Today, firms from developing economies also operate in high value-added industries, and in some cases nations are leapfrogging intermediate stages of national development and industrial production to compete in high value-added business activities such as aircraft, heavy equipment, electronics,

TABLE 5.6   Hidden champions

Company	Primary product	Sales (millions US$)	Employees	World rank in niche
Brähler	Rental of conference translation systems	45	390	1–2
Carl Jager	Incense cones, sticks	3	10	1
Soring	Ultrasonic dissectors	3	20	1
Grenzebach	Computer controlled management of float-glass production	67	450	1
Carl Walther	Sports guns	17	200	1

Source: Simon, Hermann. (1996). *Hidden champions*, pp 20–21. Boston, MA: Harvard Univ. Press.

automobiles, and computers. Exports almost doubled Samsung's electronics sales between 1989 and 1993; Taiwan's Mitac and Acer have become major world producers of inexpensive but reliable personal computers sold throughout the world (Kraar, 1994); and Industri Pesawat Terbang Nusantara's (IPTN) final assembly and sales of turbo-prop aircraft in the US are intended to be partially assembled in Indonesia.

According to the World Bank, the share of world exports accounted for by developing economies expanded from 5% to 22% between 1970 and 1993. Data from 1985–96 show developing economies accounted for 217% of real growth in exports as compared to only 69.6% of real export growth from industrialized economies (Emerging nations win, 1997). This shift in world exports resulted in more imports to the industrialized world from the developing economies. From 1981 to 1990, North America, the European Union, and Japan increased the amount of manufacturing imports purchased from developing economies. For example, North American manufactured goods imported from developing economies rose to total 42% of consumption in 1991 over 22% in 1981. Developing economies are expected to contribute 38% of growth in world output in 1995-2010, compared with 22% in the 1980s, and they could account for 55% of global consumption and capital formation by 2010. Further, by 2010 more than one billion consumers in developing countries could have per capita incomes exceeding those of Greece and Spain today (Reverse linkages, 1995).

With greater economic wealth, developing economies have increased their import activity as well. Between 1990 and 1993 developing economies' imports grew by 37%, an amount that exceeds total world increases in imports (The missing link, 1994). These goods come from the industrialized world whose economies depend on exports for 2% to 50% of GDP, but they also come from other developing economies. Latin American countries now trade more with each other than they once did, and ASEAN countries also trade more with each other than with advanced economies. For example, Thailand's exports to the six other members of ASEAN increased 34% in 1995.

TRADE IN SERVICES

Trade in services such as travel, transportation, entertainment, advertising, equities, and telecommunications is growing; additional evidence of these phenomenon are found in examples appearing in Chapters 4 and 9. Less evident service growth also comes from consultants, janitorial services, engineering, tax and accountancies, and myriad business activities listed by Peter Dicken (1992) in Figure 5.7.

From 60 to 70% of advanced economies now are based on services, and as more people in industrialized economies join the paid labor force, they generate even more demand for time-saving services like restaurants, child-care, personal shopping, or laundry. International trade in services now are about 26% of world exports. The US sold $178

CONSTRUCTION SERVICES
Site preparation
New constructions
Installation and assembly work
Building completion
Maintenance and repair of fixed structures

COMMUNICATION SERVICES
Postal services
Courier services
Telecommunications services
(telephone, telegraph, data transmission,
telemetrics, radio, TV, etc.)
Film distribution and related services
Other communications services
(incl. news and press agency, library and
archive services)

TRANSPORTATION SERVICES
Freight services
Passenger transport services
Charter services
Services auxiliary to transport
(incl. cargo handling, storage)
Travel agency and tour operator services
Vehicle rental

INSURANCE SERVICES
Insurance on freight
Non-freight insurance
(incl. life insurance, pensions, property,
liability)
Services auxiliary to insurance
(incl. brokerage, consultancy, acturial)
Reinsurance

FINANCIAL SERVICES
Banking services (commercial and retail)
Other credit services (incl. credit cards)
Services related to administration of
financial markets
Services related to securities markets
(incl. brokerage, portfolio management)
Other financial services
(incl. foreign exchange, financial consultancy)

EDUCATION SERVICES

BUSINESS SERVICES
Rental/leasing of equipment
Real estate services
Installation and assembly work
Professional services
(incl. legal services, accountancy, management
services, advertising, market research, design
services, computer services)
Other business services
(incl. cleaning, packaging, waste disposal)

HEALTH-RELATED SERVICES
Human health services
(incl. hospital services, medical and dental
services)
Veterinary services

RECREATIONAL AND CULTURAL SERVICES

TRADE SERVICES; HOTEL AND RESTAURANT SERVICES
Wholesale trade services
Retail trade
Agents fees/commissions related to distribution
Hotel and similar accommodation services
Food and beverage serving services

PERSONAL SERVICES
(not included elsewhere)
e.g. house cleaning/maintenance; nursing,
day-care services

FIGURE 5.6 *Service industries* (Dicken, Peter. (1992, 2nd ed.). *Global shift*, p. 351. New York/London: Guilford Press)

billion in services in 1994, or almost 17% of world totals; France was the second biggest exporter of services followed by the Netherlands, Italy, the UK, and Japan (After two outstanding years, 1998). Growth in the service component of trade is an ever-larger chunk of the trade equation: the World Trade Organization estimates that the value of global trade just in commercial services like accounting, consulting, engineering, and other professional services, as well as travel, communications, and banking, expanded 14% in 1995 to just less than $1.2 trillion, or a quarter of trade in goods. These invisible forms of trade are less easily counted and are difficult to isolate. As the example in Box 5.3 demonstrates, factoring service into the trade equation shows a different picture than is revealed by looking at trade in goods alone.

BOX 5.3: JOBS SUPPORTED BY TRADE

In 1995, the US Department of Commerce estimated that the average number of jobs supported by every $1 billion of goods exported was 14,200. When services were factored in, the total number of jobs supported by exports in goods and services was 11 million or more than 10% of total employment.

The same rapid development in visible trade in Asia also has occurred with less visible global services. Taiwan-based EVA Airways and Singapore Airlines are growing contenders in commercial air travel, and Singapore's Y.Y. Wong is only one among many Asian entrepreneurs selling telecommunications and family entertainment services globally. Further, growing awareness of and desire for branded products worldwide also is increasing service trade activities associated with franchising, licensing, fees and royalties in selling tangible goods.

As these examples indicate, the amount of trade, its direction, and activities of businesses have undergone significant changes in the last quarter century. Between 1985 and 1994, the ratio of world trade to GDP rose at triple the rate of growth in the preceding decade. Trends appearing in Figure 5.7 show that, except for Sub-Saharan Africa, every region of the world has experienced significant growth in trade in less than a decade.

FOREIGN DIRECT INVESTMENTS

Direct investment activities include equity investments in businesses, e.g., stocks, and purchase or development of production facilities abroad. Both these forms of FDI are surging throughout the world, causing FDI to double as a share of world GDP between 1985 and 1994. Among the developing economies, South, East, and Southeast Asia have attracted most direct investments, followed by Latin American and the Caribbean.

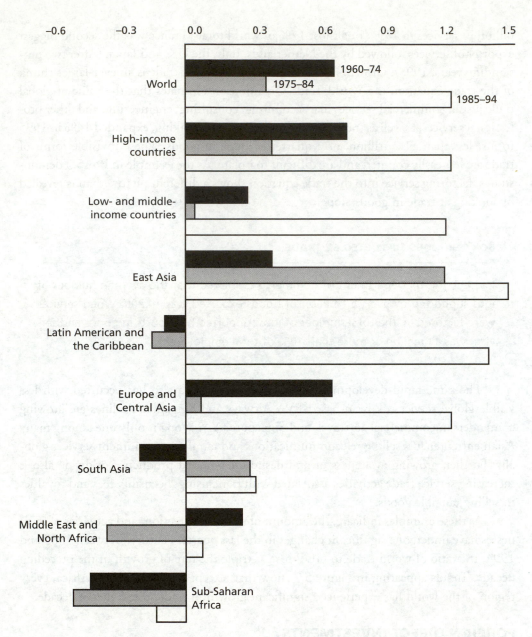

FIGURE 5.7 *Changes in ratio of real trade to real GDP, 1960–1994 (%)* (Disparities in global integration and in growth. *World Bank and Policy Research Bulletin.* (1996, Apr.–June). pp. 1–4, after World Bank (1996) *Global Economic Prospects and the Developing Countries 1996.* Washington, DC: World Bank)

Despite trade liberalization, Africa has yet to attract significant amounts of direct investment, and annual FDI flows of about $3 billion to all of Africa is less than went to Malaysia per year in the early 1990s (*World Investment Report*, 1994). The direction and size of these FDI flows between 1981 and 1993 appear in Table 5.7, showing a clear trend of increasing inflows and outflows of direct investments among developing economies. Developing countries received about 40% of global FDI inflows between 1992 and 1994, compared with 23% in the early 1980s. Additionally, FDI in the developing countries has increased because returns on FDI flows between 1991 and 1994 averaged about 21% as compared to an 8% rate of returns on FDI flows from the US to six other major industrial economies (Reverse linkages, 1995). These 'reverse linkages' between developing and industrialized economies represent business challenges as companies learn how to do business in new locations.

FDI in plant and equipment

According to the 1995 *World Competitiveness Report*, of the total $226 billion in foreign direct investment in 1994, the largest recipient for foreign direct investment was the US

TABLE 5.7   World direct investment flows (billions of dollars)

Country	Annual average[a]							
	1981–1985	1986–1990	1988	1989	1990	1991	1992	1993[b]
Developed countries								
Inflows	37	130	131	168	176	121	102	109
Outflows	47	163	162	212	222	185	162	181
Developing countries								
Inflows	13	25	28	27	31	39	51	80
Outflows	1	6	6	10	10	7	9	14
Central and Eastern Europe[c]								
Inflows	0.02	0.1	0.015	0.3	0.3	2	4	5
Outflows	0.004	0.02	0.02	0.02	0.04	0.01	0.03	..
All countries								
Inflows	50	155	159	196	208	162	158	194
Outflows	48	168	168	222	232	192	171	195

[a] Compounded growth rate estimates, based on a semi-logarithmic regression equation.
[b] Based on preliminary estimates.
[c] Former Yugoslavia is included in developing countries.
Note: The levels of worldwide inward and outward FDI flows and stock should balance; however, in practice, they do not. The causes of the discrepancy include differences between countries in the definition and valuation of FDI; the treatment of unremitted branch profits in inward and outward direct investment; treatment of unrealized capital gains and losses: the recording of transactions of 'offshore' enterprises; the recording of reinvested earnings in inward and outward direct investment; the treatment of real estate and construction investment, and the share inequity threshold in inward and outward direct investment.
Source: *World Investment Report* 1994: Transnational corporations, employment and the workplace. An executive summary. (1994, Aug.). *Transnational Corporations*, pp. 73–113, after UNCTAD, Division on Transnational Corporations and Investment, *World Investment Report 1994: Transnational Corporations, Employment and the Workplace* (United Nations publication, Sales No. E.94.II.A.14).

with a total direct investment of $49 billion. By 1993, foreign multinational corporations produced one-fifth of total US output (Kogut and Gittelman, 1994), representing a tremendous increase over the 4% FDI contributed to US output as recently as 1977. This 20% figure puts the US about equal to most countries in Europe, where foreign multinationals generate between 20 and 25% of manufacturing output (Chetwynd, 1994). Reasons to manufacture in the US in the past were to circumvent tariffs or import quotas and reduce currency exchange risk, but more recent reasons to manufacture in the US include moving closer to customers and competitors, and to be part of technology development. For example, Samsung Electronics Corporation built a $1.3 billion semiconductor plant in Texas to improve proximity and responsiveness to the US market. According to corporate planning manager Chanhee Joe, 'we would like to set up a kind of American company, using American labor, American equipment and American facilities to be competitive in the US' (cited in Foreign executives see, 1997, p. A1).

Advanced, industrialized, and developing economies have contributed to FDI growth in the US. Asian, Latin American, and Eastern European firms are initiating foreign direct investments to spread their risks, reduce costs, and otherwise benefit from a world economy. As we saw with trade, developing economies also are investing more in each other to stimulate growth. According to a 1994 Arthur Andersen survey, executives throughout Latin America believe that the most attractive foreign markets include not only the industrialized countries where economic links already exist, but also other Latin American countries as they continue to grow in economic strength. The magnitude of these expectations is represented in Figure 5.8.

FDI in equities

The preceding discussion of FDI focused primarily on investments in productive plant and equipment, but FDI also is represented by mergers and acquisitions and stock purchases. A look at just the latter component of FDI illustrates global integration as well. A look at global integration in stock purchases illustrates growth and a changing source of growth. For example, total worldwide value of listed stocks and bonds was only $5 trillion in 1980, but had grown to $35 trillion by the end of 1992 (Edmunds, 1996). According to Edmunds, savings generated by a growing middle class have poured into equities because they offer good rates of returns and high liquidity. By 1997 the daily volume of trading in stocks approached $1,260 billion, and more than ever before is generated in developing economies. For example, in 1970, 66% of the world's equity capitalization was in US stocks; by 1995 the US share was 38%. This becomes possible because many non-US companies now are listed on US exchanges either in direct, dollar-denominated sales or as ADRs (American Depository Receipts). The latter are dollar-denominated certificates issued for foreign stocks held in a US depository. Over 1,300

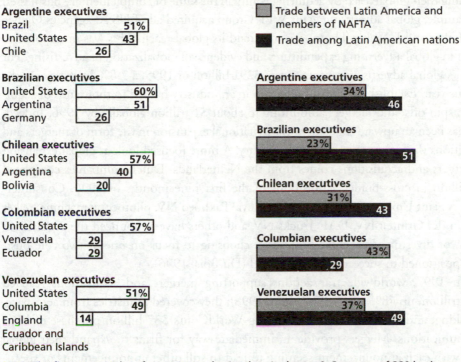

The foreign markets that respondents said were the most important for international operations (multiple responses)

Argentine executives
Brazil — 51%
United States — 43
Chile — 26

Brazilian executives
United States — 60%
Argentina — 51
Germany — 26

Chilean executives
United States — 57%
Argentina — 40
Bolivia — 20

Colombian executives
United States — 57%
Venezuela — 29
Ecuador — 29

Venezuelan executives
United States — 51%
Columbia — 49
England — 14
Ecuador and Caribbean Islands

The trading relationship that respondents said will be the most important for Latin America in five years

□ Trade between Latin America and members of NAFTA
■ Trade among Latin American nations

Argentine executives
34%
46

Brazilian executives
23%
51

Chilean executives
31%
43

Columbian executives
43%
29

Venezuelan executives
37%
49

Note: The figures are taken from a survey by Aurthur Andersen & Company of 280 businessmen in eight nations, 35 from each country. In addition to the countries listed, executives from countries in NAFTA were also interviewed.

FIGURE 5.8 *Latin America looks inward* (Brooke, James. (1994, Dec. 10). South America's big trade strides. *The New York Times*, pp. Y1, Y27)

ADRs are available on US stock exchanges. Bank of New York – the leading manager of ADR programs – reported that in the first half of 1996, 62 non-US companies and 11 governments raised about $6.7 billion through ADR programs, representing an increase of 75% over the previous year. Many companies sell equity shares worldwide, shifting a company's dependency from a nation to the world. As early as 1985, Volvo's Pehr Gyllenhammer campaigned to get more individuals outside Sweden to hold Volvo stock; today it is traded on multiple exchanges and 15% of the owners are outside the country; 48% of Olivetti shares, meanwhile, are owned abroad. Over 600 foreign stocks are traded on the New York stock exchange, and electronic trading has made it even easier for individual investors and companies to purchase an equity position in publicly traded firms located anywhere in the world.

Another approach to FDI is for a company to purchase stocks in other firms, and thereby grow by full or partial acquisition. Many multinational enterprises (MNEs) are extending their global reach by acquiring equity in the same or complementary businesses. For example, global advertising giant WPP Group acquired all of US ad agencies Ogilvie and Mather and J. Walter Thompson to extend its global reach. This was in response to growth in global advertising expenditures and evidence of globalization of advertising. For example, global advertising revenues were $291 billion in 1995, a 7.8% increase over the previous year. Establishing global leadership in an industry has led to thousands of acquisitions, spin-offs, and mergers amounting to about $1 trillion globally by 1996. Indeed, there has been an upward trajectory of international expansion in the form of mergers and acquisitions throughout the twentieth century. A more focused look at global expansion via mergers and acquisitions comes from the Netherlands. Dutch companies completed $11 billion in cross-border acquisitions in the first nine months of 1996. Consumer-products giant Unilever, storage company Royal Pakhoed NV, photocopy machine maker Oce-van der Grinten NV, DAF Trucks NV, and others have announced the acquisition, merger, or divestment of whole businesses, choosing to focus on one or two core businesses positioned to succeed at a global level (Du Bois, 1996).

In 1997, worldwide transactions supporting mergers and acquisitions reached $1.63 trillion, up 48% over 1996 (Lipin, 1998); they covered industries from aerospace, to banking, and communications including WorldCom's $37 billion purchase of MCI Communications. Mergers provide an immediate way for firms to expand their global reach, with each announcement seeming to lead to still other announcements or speculation over the next, even bigger merger. For example, accounting giants KPMG Peat Marwick and Ernst & Young announced their merger plans on the heels of a similar announcement from Coopers & Lybrand and Price Waterhouse. The creation of a mammoth United Bank of Switzerland from Swiss Bank and Union Bank of Switzerland gave rise to speculation of additional European bank mergers, just as $60 billion merger discussions between SmithKline Beecham and others touched off a flurry of speculation around future plans for pharmaceutical firms such as Eli Lilly, Warner-Lambert, Schering-Plough, and American Home Products.

Stock offerings have proved useful as a way to privatize a firm, and tremendous growth in privatization around the world has put more non-US equities on the market. Stock exchanges have emerged worldwide to extend the trading day from Tokyo to London and New York. By June 1996, the International Finance Corporation of the World Bank prepared daily stock market reports in 27 countries, and expected to add Russia, Morocco, and Egypt. It also tracks 58 'frontier' stock markets like Lithuania and Botswana on a monthly basis, bringing the total of stock markets it covers to 85. According to Figure 5.9, these various stock markets had varying levels of success in 1997. Nevertheless, these exchanges have made it possible for many more people in the world

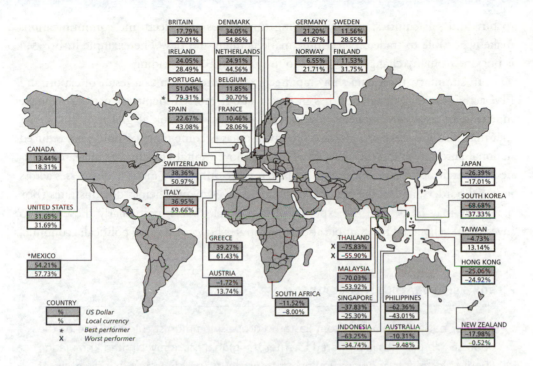

FIGURE 5.9 *Performance of the Dow Jones World Stock Market Indexes* (Stock investors had their fill of the good, the bad, and the ugly. (1998, Jan. 2). *The Wall Street Journal*, p. R10).

BOX 5.4: TWENTY-FOUR-HOUR TRADING

The New York Stock Exchange operates only during weekdays, but the 'after hours' market increasingly provides trading opportunities to some. According to *The Wall Street Journal*, millions of shares are routinely traded after the markets close, even seven days a week. For example, a Florida jury verdict against a tobacco company drove Philip Morris to a $102 close on Friday's market, but after hours trading resulted in a Monday morning opening price of $95. Because after hours trading results are not reported widely, only some buyers and sellers were aware of the price drop over the weekend. Those relying on published results from Friday's market close must have been surprised to learn their investments in Philip Morris had lost over $7 in market value over the weekend.

Source: Kansas, Dave. (1996, Aug. 12). Nicked at night: Even after the market closes, stock prices can take wild swings. *The Wall Street Journal*, pp. A1, A8.

to buy and sell equities, and overlapping time zones and electronic communications make it possible to trade on electronic markets night and day. The example in Box 5.4 is but one of many changes brought about by global equity trading.

In summary, these data show rapid economic integration as a result of export and FDI activities. This integration has in turn made it more difficult for nations to make independent fiscal and monetary decisions. The following look at global capital shows that this third indicator of a global economy also has become more complex, has reduced national autonomy, and the constant ability to move capital globally has increased business uncertainties. These uncertainties make it more difficult to manage businesses across national borders, and as the example of pyramid investment schemes demonstrates (Box 5.5), they may be beyond the expertise of individual traders, particularly those new to investment vehicles. This example also demonstrates how converging political, economic,

---

BOX 5.5:   PYRAMIDS FALL IN ALBANIA

The last nation to emerge from Eastern Europe's communist rule and one of the poorest, Albania was ill prepared to enter the global economy. Limited knowledge about investments and unscrupulous entrepreneurs combined to rob individuals of about $1 billion by 1997, an amount equal to about 43% of Albania's GDP. Promising extraordinary investment interest, pyramid schemes were offered and high rates of return promised in short periods of time. Initial investors receive the promised returns, which they then reinvest even as they are telling family and friends about the pyramid opportunity. As more and more people join the scheme, the pyramid grows in size, allowing its operator to return wealth to still more until the inevitable day when too many are due returns that cannot be paid. Typically the pyramid operator then absconds, often as the only profiteer. Albanians were convinced to invest not only because of the success of earlier investors, but because many wanted to get rich like other capitalists, few understood how stock exchanges work, and most were deceived by slick sales pitches and sophisticated television advertisements. As pyramid schemes throughout Albania began to crumble, the government stepped in to arrest pyramid operators and freeze bank accounts. For most Albanians it was too late; their meager savings were gone, victims of greed, naivety, and limited understanding of capital markets. Riots followed, resulting in the *de facto* collapse of the government and the collapse of Albanian civil society.

Source: Wood, Barry D. (1997, June). A tidal wave of anger sweeps over Albania. *Europe*, pp. 30–31.

---

cultural, and technological interests create opportunities for global bandits and costs for the naive.

MONEY AND FINANCIAL MARKETS

In 1991, the world's economic wealth was held in: (a) equities (25.5% or $11,163 billion US); (b) bonds (18.6% or 8,284 billion); (c) real estate 48.8% or $32,411 billion); (d) cash (3.9% or $1,700 billion); and (e) precious metals (3.8% or $1,307 billion). Among these factors of wealth, probably the most important in the global marketplace is liquid capital or cash because it funds growth. Demand and competition for liquid capital worldwide is keen.

Capital in the form of cash or currency is especially easy to move globally. Investors in many parts of the world – particularly US baby boomers looking toward retirement – are willing to take on higher global risks in return for higher potential returns; retirement funds are bulging with capital seeking investments somewhere in the world; and technology makes it possible to trade easily by modem or telephone any time of night or day. Thus, trading in global capital crosses not only national boundaries but also traditional barriers of time. The market for capital or for equities need never stop so long as there are mechanisms for moving capital. The example of Globex illustrates how mechanisms have sprung up to accommodate non-stop demand, and it also demonstrates how cultural habits and practices of trading have responded to this new technology (Box 5.6).

Both Globex and CBOT's Project A demonstrate the potential for trading in equities, futures, options, or other instruments day and night. The challenges faced in implementing systems to support constant trading are illustrated in the following section, which examines some of the organizations already involved in the all-day, every-day capital market.

Global currency

Funds can be transferred worldwide electronically and instantly via computer technology. The equivalent of about $2 trillion is traded daily in the world currency market and as much as 60% of this currency is denominated in US dollars. In 1995 Citibank alone moved over $500 billion US per day through electronic transfers.

THE US DOLLAR

The US dollar accounts for about 61% of foreign-exchange reserves; roughly half of global private financial wealth; and two-thirds of world trade invoices (That damned dollar, 1995). Worldwide use of the US dollar in these ways inextricably links the US economy with the world economy. For example, two-thirds of $360 billion in US currency is held outside the US. As the examples in Box 5.7 show, the US derives some benefits from the

BOX 5.6: GLOBEX

Developed jointly by the Chicago Mercantile Exchange and Reuters Holdings PLC, Globex became the first computer-trading system. It was heralded as the 'exchange of the future' because it facilitated 24-hour cross-border computer trading. In 1997, Paris-based futures and option exchange Marché à Terme International de France (Matif) announced it would withdraw from Globex to return to auction-style open-outcry trading pits where traders shout out buy and sell prices. The traders favor open-outcry over electronic trading, and cross-border trading at Matif never amounted to more than 2% of total Globex trades. The technology is there, but the culture of trading and traditional practices of trading have proved more powerful in France than the lure of 24-hour trading. Meanwhile, back at the Chicago Board of Trade (CBOT), open-outcry trading at night may be replaced with electronic trading. The Project A graphically enhanced network that matches customer orders and trader positions during an afternoon and overnight session has mushroomed, growing by 33% in 1996 alone. Electronic trading on futures and options exchanges worldwide rose from 7% in 1989 to 18% of all trades worldwide by 1996. These examples show increased pressure to use electronic trading balanced by cultural preferences among traders and within nations to remain with a 'known' system of open-outcry trading.

Source: Lucchetti, Aaron. (1997, Feb. 27). Some traders cry, but CBOT after dark is high-tech. *The Wall Street Journal*, pp. C1, C17.

dollar's utility as a world currency, but at the same time, the dollar's importance to the world keeps the US economy under close scrutiny. Further, this attention may make it more difficult for US policy-makers to pursue longer run monetary or fiscal policies, particularly if they involve short-term problems affecting the strength of the US economy. Since many sales are invoiced in dollars, most of the world is directly or indirectly affected by strength or weakness in the dollar. Effects become keener in a dynamic global marketplace where the number and size of worldwide transactions can be completed at almost lightning speed. For example, as Figure 5.10 demonstrates, dollar fluctuations against the yen between 1992 and 1998 resemble a rollercoaster. These fluctuations make it particularly difficult for businesses to avoid currency exchange losses and they make it hard to make *a priori* decisions favoring exporting, importing, or FDI strategies. Following IMF bailouts of Thailand and South Korea in 1997, currency fluctuations against the dollar became a particular concern to Indonesia, concerns that emerged from political, cultural, and economic sources. On the

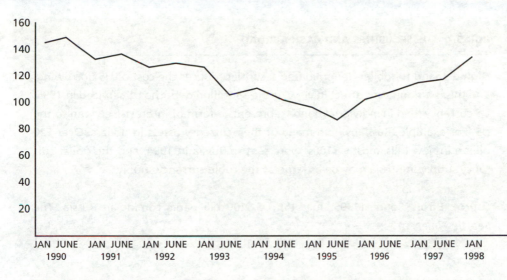

FIGURE 5.10 *Dollar/yen fluctuations, 1990–1998* (OANDA Inc. (1998, Jan. 5). 164 currency converter. http://www.oanda.com/cgi-bin/ncc)

economic front, Indonesian growth through the 1990s had been fueled by low interest rate investment funds from abroad. Prior rupiah stability encouraged business people to take on this debt, even though it was to be repaid in US dollars. When the rupiah began to fall against the dollar, businesses faced conversion losses to repay their loans. Additionally within the nation, there was a propensity to think in dollar rather than rupiah terms. Many goods, most hotels, tours, and travel for Indonesians are priced in dollars, even though they are paid in rupiahs. This cultural practice meant that even the simplest puppet maker became aware of Indonesia's currency woes, and many individuals began to speculate by buying and selling dollars. Finally, there was the upcoming March election. Aging President Suharto intended to run, but he had not chosen a running mate, an important decision to the many who feared he would die in office. Panic rose, fueled by economic problems and by rumors over Suharto's health, anti-Chinese sentiment, and feared abandonment by the IMF and the foreign investment communities. In nearby Malaysia where transactions are quoted in ringgits, the currency slide against the dollar was much smaller but more importantly, there was far less panic than in Indonesia.

The centrality of the US dollar and its volatility in global markets are both a vestige of history and an indicator of the need for a global currency. In other words, the dollar now stands in as a form of global currency, a role it was not intended to play. As global events unfold, the problems associated with the dollar's role as a global currency become more evident. Transactions worldwide would be facilitated by a global currency. Accounting for paper or actual gains and losses due to exchange rates would all but disappear; organizations could more readily gain access to payments; and tourists could throw away

BOX 5.7: US SECURITIES AND CASH ABROAD

High demand for dollar-denominated securities reduces the cost of US borrowing, and this is a significant effect in view of the $5 trillion debt the US serviced in 1995. US currency held in individual hands represents a form of interest-free loan to the US. For example, Russians hold many of their currency assets in dollars. Over $20 billion in new bills, mostly $100s, were sent to Russia in 1994, and the dollar currency supply in Russia may be as large as the ruble currency supply.

Source: Efron, Sonni. (1995, July 15). US $100 bill panic coming in Russia. *The Seattle Times*, p. A2.

their conversion charts and calculators. This same advantage would be a plus for businesses whose leaders are just as easily surprised by exchange rate variations, and just as vulnerable as the tourist to exchange rate risk, although on a much larger scale.

THE EURO

In the absence of a true global currency, the US dollar is the most bankable common currency around the world. Emerging supranational currencies include the 'euro' proposed by the Economic Monetary Union and a yen bloc proposal. The common currency of the euro is to be available widely in 1999, although currency coins and notes are not expected to be introduced until 2002, but the first proposed versions showed the borderless approach to currency the EU hopes to take. The front face of 1, 2, and 5 euro coins showed Europe situated on a globe against a background of stars; the 10, 20, and 50 euro coins depicted EU countries as a collection of nations; and the 1 and 2 euro coins showed a borderless Europe. Problems with introducing the euro as well as its ultimate design are largely political because a common currency would reduce the fiscal and monetary autonomy of member nations. As introduced, a single European currency would make it easier for consumers to compare prices and remove exchange rate risk for businesses operating within the EU. At the same time, the euro would almost eliminate foreign exchange operations in banks, put pressure on profits as consumers within Europe find it easier to compare prices, and generate administrative costs as accounting, information, and control systems are revised.

THE YEN BLOC

Another proposal is to establish a yen bloc wherein member nations using the yen as an international currency could reduce their exposure to dollar volatility. According to

C.H. Kwan (1996), a yen bloc is needed because traditional reasons to use the dollar no longer apply. For example, Asian countries are less dependent on the US and more dependent on each other for economic growth. Impediments to introduction of a yen bloc or a euro-currency are impediments to every other suggested form of global currency: the players cannot agree on the rules by which they will play.

In the absence of a single global currency, we may be moving into an era where the world moves from a currency system dominated by a single currency (the role that US currency now plays) to a multiple-currency system where the German mark and the Japanese yen will play bigger roles than they now do. Others call for a return to the gold standard (Shelton, 1994), but this may be problematic since new production of gold adds only about 2% annually to the existing supply, and the global economy is moving much faster than a 2% rate. In brief, the perceived need for a global form of currency is unmet by gold, the US dollar, or any other existing currency.

Financial institutions

Advertising in 1995, the investment firm Merrill Lynch noted that the difference between crossing borders and barriers has been that while crossing borders has required little effort for some time, what has been more important to global business opportunities – and more particularly to the global flow of capital – has been revolutionary and evolutionary reductions in cultural, economic, and political barriers worldwide (Merrill Lynch advertisement, 1995). Crossing all of these barriers has created worldwide competition in banking and security industries, and made it more difficult for financial institutions to fulfill their charters. The opening case looking at Barings PLC demonstrates only some of the difficulties the private sector has had in keeping up with the rapid pace of change in global financial markets.

Global changes affecting sources and uses of capital have made it difficult for financial institutions of an earlier era to keep pace, and this is no less true for business organizations than for other institutions established to manage international flows of currency, equities, and debt. The following descriptions of central banks, of the World Bank and the IMF, and of private market makers show that, as currently chartered, none are perfectly well suited to the demands of a global economy.

CENTRAL BANKS

Central banks such as the US Federal Reserve Bank, the Bank of England, the German Bundesbank, and the Bank of Japan were chartered to manage monetary policy within nations. In this role, central banks determine and adjust money supply and may intervene to buy currency on open markets to manipulate exchange rates. Their ability to manage either increasingly is undermined by the sheer size of global investments. Central banks no longer operate in the relative stability of a regulated environment and some may feel they operate in a frontier environment where little can be taken for granted. Increasingly, if central banks are to have an impact, it must come from cooperating with one another to create a super central bank. Even then, success is not assured. For example, to shore up the sinking dollar between January and May 1995, central banks in Japan, Germany, and the US simultaneously purchased dollars ($24.7 billion, $3.6 billion, and $1.4 billion respectively), but the dollar fell almost 17% against the yen and more than 11% against the mark (Sesit, 1995). Even when acting in concert, activities on the part of central banks may not be sufficient to counteract the force of independent traders who trade over $1 trillion per day.

This world market threatens to overwhelm the ability of central banks to manage the world money supply and exchange rates, and for some the challenge of finance on a global sphere is whether central bankers will prevail in maintaining orderly markets, or whether fickle, interest-seeking global traders will prevail in making and breaking financial markets around the world. Many fear that financial markets will be far too volatile without central banks; accordingly, they argue for increased authority for central banks (Solomon, 1995). The description of 'hot money' in Box 5.8 shows why some argue against uncontrolled capital movement.

The world's first supranational central bank is expected to emerge when the Maastricht proposal for Economic Union is implemented. Located in Frankfurt, this supranational central bank called the European Central Bank would replace or weaken central banks of individual EU nations. The Maastricht Treaty provided that four to six people would be appointed to a European Central Bank board by heads of member-state nations who would collaborate with governors of former national central banks to set monetary policy for the EU. However, it is not yet clear how this supranational bank will operate in practice, and throughout Europe there are evident concerns that national differences in culture, politics, and economic policy may be impediments to common monetary policy, to implementation of the euro, and to establishing a European central bank.

THE WORLD BANK AND THE INTERNATIONAL MONETARY FUND

The World Bank and the International Monetary Fund (IMF) were chartered to manage global debt and wealth creation. Both were part of the Bretton Woods agreements. The World Bank was meant to foster economic stability worldwide by financing postwar reconstruction and the IMF to manage controls on what were then a fairly rigid set of world currency exchange rates. The global challenge to these institutions is twofold. First, capital demands increasingly can be and are met with funds from private rather than institutional sources, and in the developing economies private capital is displacing the need for capital from the World Bank or control from the IMF. Second, politicians in developing countries chafe under rules designed for other cultures and for other modes

BOX 5.8: 'HOT' MONEY

According to Ron Kwan, author of 'Footloose & country free' (1996), free capital movement should be controlled to provide pre-1980s protections. He argues that when central banks and private sector banking controlled capital assets they followed fiscally conservative policies. Today's capital markets are increasingly dominated by US mutual and hedge-fund investors who control about $3 trillion in assets. These investors are far from conservative and instead pursue a quick-return strategy to create 'hot' money held in private retirement accounts that is constantly and instantly tradeable on global markets. According to Kwan, hot money puts national debt into foreign hands and reduces national autonomy, it artificially inflates prices for popular stocks and bonds, and it increases volatility by flooding or draining national markets. Many believe that Mexico's economic contraction in 1994 and 1995 was more severe because the money that had rapidly entered Mexico was just as quickly withdrawn. The 'hot' withdrawal of funds from Mexico was not an isolated occurrence. Global money managers withdrew funds from currencies, stocks and bonds in nearly every economy that had either weak national finances or heavy foreign debt, causing each to experience a downturn as a result of Mexico's woes. Attracted by rapid recovery from the 1994–95 economic crisis, hot money was back in Mexico by early 1997, contributing to a strengthening peso.

Source: Kwan, Ron. (1995). Footloose & country free. In Marc Brewlos, David Levy, Betsy Reid and the Dollars and Sense Collective (Eds), pp. 18–22. *Real World International*, 2nd ed. Somerville, MA: Dollars and Sense.

of economic development. In an article titled 'Reign of errors: The World Bank's wrongs', Walden Bello and Shea Cunningham (1994) claim that structural adjustment programs (SAPs) in developing countries have contributed to economic stagnation and instability in the world economy because SAP criteria reduce national autonomy and undo much of the good local politicians can do. In addition to their 'one economic policy fits all' proclivity, World Bank officials have been criticized for timidity in helping countries move from socialist to market economies, have shown limited interest in funding projects in riskier less-developed economies, and have invested little in development projects such as education for girls, family planning, and aid to small enterprises (It's time, 1994).

Although there seems to be general agreement that the IMF and the World Bank have outgrown the roles established for them at Bretton Woods, it is not clear what roles they can or should play in future. Suggested roles for the IMF include: a watchdog to prevent economic disasters (Why can't a country, 1995); a central bank for the world; a global Securities and Exchange Commission to exert pressure on governments to disclose their full financial health (Foust, 1995); and to serve as a sort of permanent staff for the G-7 (Magnusson, 1994). Following the 1995 economic collapse of Mexico, the IMF provided about $19 billion to aid in recovery, loaned $10 billion to Russia and the Ukraine in 1995 and another $10 billion to Russia in 1996. In 1997 the IMF loaned a total of $114 billion to Thailand, South Korea, and Indonesia to stabilize the latter economies. In all cases, these loans have come with strings attached which include restructuring to eliminate existing business inefficiencies, and greater transparency of business transactions.

Global activities suggested for the World Bank include programs to develop quality of life. An alternative is to privatize the World Bank (Eberstadt and Lewis, 1995). The changing world economy may need new approaches to economic development management, but it is not clear that these approaches can come from current World Bank or IMF protocols.

PRIVATE MARKET MAKERS

Business transactions that cross national borders require currency exchanges and foreign exchange and commercial banking are two functions traditional to private institutions like banks. Commercial banks or foreign exchange brokers facilitate most currency exchanges and banks also provide loans, trade in securities, and handle commercial and business as well as individual accounts.

Factors that began to stimulate growth in banking and investments industries in the 1980s included global mergers and acquisitions, increased equity trading on both new and existing stock markets, growing levels of foreign direct investment, and expanding speculation, particularly in currencies. All these factors create opportunities and threats for banking and investment industries, and Barings Bank is only one among many banks to fail in a constantly changing industry. Investment houses also have experienced constant change, and one product of changes are experiments that range from the successful to the questionable and unethical. The Triangle Corporation scandal (see Box 5.9) demonstrates that ethics also are to be unbordered.

Post hoc analyses of this and other investment activities reveal many violations of ethical and legal codes: in Britain a Morgan Grenfell employee was indicted for illegal merger activity; in the US the Bank of Boston was caught laundering money; in Germany an official at Deutsche Bank was linked to insider trading; in Japan the Industrial Bank of Japan Ltd was linked to fraudulently obtained loans; in Australia a former managing director of a merchant bank was charged with insider trading (Vogel, 1992). These ethical breaches may have occurred for several reasons besides the obvious one of corruption. The global industry for banking is not yet well defined, and practices standard or

> **BOX 5.9:   THE TRIANGLE CORPORATION**
>
> Investors in France, Luxembourg, and Switzerland bought more than 200,000 shares in the Triangle Corporation shortly before the firm was acquired by Pechiney, the French state-owned aluminum company. The stock purchases had been made in the United States and had been brought to the French Government's attention by the US Securities and Exchange Commission.
>
> *Source*: Vogel, David. (1992, Fall). The globalization of business ethics. *California Management Review*, p. 32.

acceptable in one nation may be less acceptable in a globalizing world. Other breaches resulted from the error component of a natural trial and error process to test the parameters of the emerging global investment industry. Daniel Fischel (1995), a University of Chicago law professor, argues that financier Michael Millken became a victim because he forged new rules of business in global investments. Fischel argues that Millken went to jail not because he committed crimes, but because the US public and its government sought a scapegoat for the financial greed played out in the 1980s. Because of new activities made possible by globalization of investments, the industry was transformed almost overnight, providing opportunities for many to define new territory and for others to remap traditional terrain. The rapid pace of change in investment banking has led to many more 'experiments' that are changing the traditions of the industry. For example, to meet its goal of global market penetration, Credit Suisse broke with conservative Swiss banking tradition to invest in risky ventures in China and Russia, and became the first bank in the Swiss industry to be involved in a hostile takeover. Often unregulated because new opportunities develop faster than regulations to govern them, these experiments have led to successes and to failures and financial crises in some cases. One result is that the G-30 group of international banks announced plans in 1997 to draft global standards for regulating multinational banking groups as a way for national regulators to cope with globalization in the banking industry.

CHALLENGES TO A CAPITALIST VIEW OF MARKET ECONOMICS

The preceding review of trade in goods and services, FDI, and capital shows that these three components of a global economy create fiscal challenges for firms that include greater volatility, increased complexity, and heightened uncertainty. There may be a sense that economic integration on a global scale resembles a free-for-all where the invisible hand of markets makes it almost impossible to plan for or predict events. This market volatility is in part due to global transformations in market assumptions. In view of the many changes occurring in a globalizing economy, economists also are under pressure to rethink economic assumptions of markets and trade. According to Peter Drucker (1989), current economic theory no longer describes transnational markets, businesses, or relationships and different theories are needed. The following review is consistent with Drucker's argument, and shows why it may be difficult for firms to operate as perfectly rational actors in the global economy.

Information is available

Information is abundant, and in many ways information is more freely available than ever before. However, as we saw in our review of trade figures, GDP reports and other market data, available information often is inaccurate. Information flows are constrained for other reasons as well. Barings' managers in London, for example, had data but their knowledge base did not cover derivatives. Nick Leeson's requests for funds far outstripped Barings' reserves, yet top managers in London continued to send funds. Leeson is one example of many who violate market assumptions by controlling information flows. Even when information flows freely, it may not inform because there are too few mechanisms available to process or interpret vast amounts of information.

Behavior is economically rational

Economist and Nobel prize winner Douglass North believes economic choices are a function not only of rational self-interest, but also of membership in a cultural group. The cultural attributes of that group direct behavior, and this behavior is not always consistent with economic self-interest or wealth maximization. The example of communitarian values (Box 5.10) illustrates this point.

Having made the choice to give away his profits, Mr Koffi (in Box 5.10) is demonstrating that economic rationality in the Ivory Coast involves a trade-off with community membership. The choice he makes may not be in his best economic interests, but it does serve his interests to remain a member of his own family group. This behavior shows that cultural norms and economic behavior are related. North and others who examine these so-called 'irrational' economic choices are called behavioral economists because they examine economic behavior in a context that admits complexity and dynamism. When examining more complex reasons for economic choices, economists move closer to management theorists in trying to explain economic activities. These efforts mark a departure from traditional economic calculations where conditions of *ceterus paribus* or 'other conditions being equal' are assumed. As economists from other

---

BOX 5.10:   WHAT PRICE WEALTH?

Ivory Coast tailor Lazare Koffi said he might have opened two or three businesses or even a real store except for his obligation to give whatever is left from rent and personal needs to his family. Refusal to help family carries the risk of being cursed, and one is therefore obligated to share wealth.

Source: French, Howard W. (1995, Jan. 14). Does sharing wealth only promote poverty? *The New York Times*, p. A4.

---

than the developed nations participate in global economic theory, these opportunities for insight will grow.

Markets are open

The theory of free markets is that they are open to all potential buyers and sellers and operate in relative freedom without government influence. However, in all but a few nations, government does interfere with market mechanisms to correct inherent market defects such as the following:

1 Markets may not adequately protect future rights and interests.
2 Markets do not provide certain types of public goods such as roads or clean air.
3 Markets create spillovers and externalities which can be positive or negative; a positive spillover occurs when business research and development (R&D) benefits society, and a negative externality occurs when producers do not pay full costs of air pollution.
4 Markets may not guarantee a high level of employment, price stability, or a socially desirable rate of growth.
5 Market outcomes may violate social values about justice and equality (Marcus, 1993, pp. 215–218).

Subsequent chapters on global politics and on globalization of the natural environment look at how governments and other entities intercede to correct these and similar market defects. The important point to be made here is that markets do not operate without encumbrances.

Buyers and sellers spread throughout the world live under different national regimes and regional alliances that also affect market entry and exit; all are not altogether free to enter this global market. Many decisions made in the global market come more from the countries most adept with market capitalism, creating potential entry problems for firms from transitional economies like Poland or Argentina. Finally, our review of new measures of national prosperity reveals that presumptions of economic rationality are not applicable worldwide. These violations of market assumptions make it difficult for the world to adopt a market system, and the result may be worldwide variations on that system. This point is illustrated by a look at varied cultures of capitalism.

Cultures of capitalism

Global economic integration relies on market economics as a global standard. This form of economic arrangement appears to be less than monolithic. Capitalism has developed in different ways within nations and regions and it is organized around culture, political arrangements, and national heritage more than around emerging global markets. Organizations trading with or investing in transitional economies and others formerly closed or unattractive to them will need to acknowledge distinctions between the various forms of capitalism.

FRONTIER CAPITALISM

In a 1994 special issue of *Business Week* titled '21st century capitalism,' Christopher Farrell (1994) argues that capitalism has taken new form in formerly closed economies. The 'frontier capitalism' found in Russia and mainland China is characterized by a three-stage evolutionary process. First, following alteration or collapse of a state-run economy, black marketeers and even gangsters gain enormous profits, and government corruption spreads. In the second phase of frontier capitalism, independent businesspeople and entrepreneurs with limited capital begin to flourish. Because commercial laws have not yet developed, these entrepreneurs develop operating standards that can become commercial rules. Finally, in the third stage of frontier capitalism, economic growth is brisk, particularly as financial markets begin to evolve. This attracts foreign investors who demand higher returns in lieu of certainty which in turn creates an incentive for a clearer legal code.

ASIAN CAPITALISM

According to the editors of *The Economist*, two forms of capitalism operate in Asia. The Southeast model practiced by early 1990 economic powerhouses such as Singapore, Thailand, Malaysia, and Indonesia are exporting not only goods but also ideas, with three unusual practices for Northeast Asian countries like Japan and South Korea: they are open to foreign direct investment; they are much less likely than South Korea and Japan to establish government-directed industrial policies; and they have allowed financial markets to develop (Asia's competing capitalisms, 1995). Singapore, for example, is where Barings' Nick Leeson executed his infamous derivatives orders. An unanswered question for much of Asia today is whether sleeping giants like China and India and smaller Asian nations like Vietnam will follow the Northeast or the Southeast model of capitalism.

TRIAD CAPITALISM

Economist Lester Thurow (1996) believes that the strongest capitalist economies face crises in the years ahead that will transform them. In the US, falling real wages of hourly workers in the last 20 years combined with gains for the top 20% of earners have led to blaming, scapegoating, and extremism. Japan's prosperity has been based on running a positive trade balance, but there is growing world demand for Japan to open its doors and develop its internal economy. In Western Europe, persistent unemployment and high wages relative to the rest of the world have shifted investments out of Europe and away from the industries of the future. These crises must be addressed by the Triad nations in Western Europe, Japan, and the US if their forms of capitalism are to survive. Thurow believes none of the Triad nations will become the dominant economic, political, or military power, but that remains to be seen.

COOPERATIVE CAPITALISM

US business stresses competitive and individualistic forms of capitalism, but Margaret Sharp (1992) believes the world needs more cooperative forms of capitalism that stress group harmony and consensus like in Japan, Germany, and Sweden. According to Sharp, cooperative capitalism

> embraces new forms of collaboration, particularly vertical collaboration between makers and users, customers and contractors, 'just in time' relationships and quality control. . . . It calls for a new approach to accounting standards to give recognition to the long-term value of investments made by the firm in R&D, education and training. (pp. 25–26)

The cooperative form of capitalism Sharp suggests is consistent with the corporate community model of business presented in Figure 3.1 of Chapter 3, but stands in sharp contrast to the corporate model most US organizations bring to the global market. At the same time, firms patterned on Japanese-style management practices and those based in Western Europe may find it difficult to put their own or even world economic interests ahead of national economic interests, or may face criticism when they do.

In summary, globalization of these economic factors requires institutions and economic entities capable of responding to different and varying challenges, and because these challenges are diverse and sometimes conflicting, questions of economic and social justice also are being raised. Among major global challenges are whether the world economy must be played according to a self-interest agenda, and how resources are to be allocated when some number of people are satisfying wants, while the basic needs of others go unmet. Globalization of the economy is creating the same challenges for economists as are created for central bankers, business leaders and managers, and for students of global business activities. The complexity and uncertainty of a global market combined with unexpected experiences and a combination of both traditional and emerging business theories and practices is making it quite difficult to develop a cohesive theory of business management for a global world. At the same time, the fact of globalization in the economy makes it imperative to discover ways to be both effective and efficient when managing globally. For firms, the challenge is to organize for a global market and also be responsive to market variations affecting business decisions.

PART II   ORGANIZATIONAL ACTION

Trade, GDP, and similar reflections of economic growth are relevant to business decisions because they show where overseas expansion opportunities are greatest. At the same time, businesses that diversify into the many countries offering opportunities find they then face different conditions. Motorola, for example, has a significant investment in China, where growth rates have been in excess of 10% per year, but the company maintains a strong presence in the US, where economic growth is less than 4%. Increasingly, companies like Motorola find that in crossing national boundaries to conduct business, they adapt US management practices abroad and bring successful management practices from elsewhere to the US. Motorola's Olympic-style internal quality event encourages transfer of management practices when worldwide teams compete for gold medals by explaining how they eliminated defects, hastened product speed to market, and achieved goals. At the same time, the economic fortunes of this and other companies become tied not only to the economic fortunes of these two countries but to modes of economic development throughout the world. As new and existing companies engage in business throughout the world, business practices formerly contained within specific countries or companies are exposed to global scrutiny, and their differences and similarities become more evident.

Our earlier review of economic theories that revolve around market economics and cultures of capitalism as defined in the Westernized world may not be sufficient to explain global economic activities. Economic needs differ, measures of economies differ, and as the review of cultures of capitalism to follow shows, even capitalist motives differ throughout the global economy. These differences have implications for the firm.

PROCESSES
Operationalizing cultures of capitalism

In their book *The seven cultures of capitalism*, Charles Hampden-Turner and Alfons Trompenaars (1993) outline how the unique cultural values of the US, Japan, Germany, France, Sweden, the Netherlands, and the United Kingdom have resulted in different approaches to wealth creation. Hampden-Turner and Trompenaars argue that the question 'How shall wealth be created?' can be answered by looking at seven dilemmas societies manage when creating wealth:

1. *Universalism versus particularism*: When no law, code, or rule applies to an exceptional case, shall the most relevant rule be applied (universalism) or should the case be decided on its unique merits (particularism)?

2. *Analyzing versus integrating*: Are managers more effective when they analyze data by breaking them into component parts or when they do not segregate information but rather try to find a pattern or unifying whole capable of explaining the data?

3. *Individualism versus communitarianism*: Should wealth creation focus on the individual or the group/community/nation?

4. *Inner-directed versus outer-directed orientation*: Should economic choices be subject to inner-directed values or in response to a constantly changing world?

5. *Time as sequence versus time as synchronization*: Is it more important to achieve as much as possible in a limited time or to synchronize efforts such that completion of a job is coordinated?

6. *Achieved status versus ascribed status*: This involves a tradeoff for employees' status, with achieved status focusing on rewards for performance and ascribed status focusing more on other characteristics that may be important to organizations, such as education, position, strategic role.

7. *Equality versus hierarchy*: This is the balance or tradeoff between treating people as equals or emphasizing an existing hierarchy.

Decision-making

The different ways nations resolve these dilemmas explains why work traditionally has been organized and managed in different ways worldwide. This chapter opened with an example of information management, and we return to the example to look at how different nations might manage information. As shown in point 2 above, Barings managers evidently were unable to find a pattern or unifying whole capable of explaining the data they had in hand. Instead, they appeared to analyze data by segregating one set from another, managing information sequentially in a step-by-step fashion. This analytical style of thinking is most often associated with Westernized firms. Many of the assumptions important to rational decision-making are violated in the global sphere: problems are ambiguous; many alternatives are not known; preferences are unclear or dynamic; and there are time constraints.

Thus, assumptions of rationality such as unitary decision-making, an exhaustive search for alternatives, a quantifiable approach to weighing costs and benefits, or top-down control over plans and implementation (Table 5.8) stand in contrast to what might more legitimately be found globally. Where political processes are the business norm, decisions are more likely to be distributed among multiple powerful groups; alternatives are limited to those that can be negotiated; and the existence of self-interested groups de-emphasize rules over interests. According to Herbert Simon (1955), who defined 'bounded rationality' as behavior rational within a simplified framework of any problem, in most organizations decision-making is distributed, access to information is limited, and decision-makers tend to pursue acceptable rather than perfect alternatives to 'satis-fice' in an environment where market information is not perfect. When governments play a role in shaping business decisions, political processes may be more relevant to decision-making in the firm than rational economic decision models. The comparison of these three decision-making styles presented in Table 5.8 shows that each style of decision-making makes different assumptions about who makes decisions, the search for available alternatives, the basis for alternative selection, and methods of implementing decisions made.

Information represented by raw data is abundant globally, but transforming it into knowledge has proved difficult in a dynamic and uncertain global world. Thus, linear and rational decision-making may not be universally useful; more process-oriented think-ing capable of discovering relationships among and between information bits may be needed as well, and awareness of political realities associated with choices also is impor-tant. The latter two approaches to decision-making may depend less on technical forms of knowledge and more on skills or abilities that are subjective. Organizations may need human insight and intuition to transform data into meaningful knowledge. Bolman and Deal (1991) believe that expanded management thinking might include the following:

(a) a holistic framework that encourages inquiry into a range of issues rather than focusing on single issues one at a time;
(b) awareness of a set of options that range from dependence on skills to dependence on abilities like bargaining;
(c) creativity and a willingness to risk;
(d) an ability to ask the right questions more than to find the right answers;
(e) an ability to remain flexible to external events.

TABLE 5.8   Approaches to decision-making

	Rational	Organizational process	Political process
Decision-maker	Unitary at the top of a steep hierarchy	Distributed among process participants	Distributed among dominant coalitions
Search for alternatives	Exhaustive search for single best alternative	Search for acceptable alternatives (bounded rationality)	Might makes 'right'; dominants prevail
Basis for alternative selected	Quantifiable: maximize benefits; minimize costs	Satisfice important actors in the environment	Satisfy important participants
Methods of implementing	Rules; top-down hierarchy; formal planning and performance reviews	Provide inducements sufficient to motivate desired contributions	Appeal to self- or group interest; de-emphasize rules

STRUCTURING THE GLOBAL ENTERPRISE
Modes of foreign market entry

A business decision to expand outside domestic markets involves many choices, including mode of market entry. For many firms, franchise or licensing arrangements prove useful. A licensing arrangement usually covers a particular geographic area with the parent company taking a fee allowing the licensee to produce, market, or use a product brand name. For example, US retailer JC Penney has expanded to the United Arab Emirates, Singapore, Portugal, Greece, and Mexico by licensing others to run Penney's stores, capitalizing on sharing firm strengths such as appealing merchandise presentation and low cost private labels. Sometimes, a licensing agreement protects existing brands. In the 1980s, Gucci chose to license its brand name in Mexico as a defense against the many unlicensed Gucci knock-offs then available in Mexico.

McDonald's and other fast food companies provide good examples of how franchising rapidly expands firm growth. For a fee and typically a percentage of future profits, franchisors often provide a facility that meets parent company standards, and supply products, information, marketing, or other support to encourage franchisee success. Like a licensing agreement, the franchise agreement allows the parent firm to expand with limited investments of fiscal resources and it provides an opportunity to the franchisee. Both of these arrangements preserve parent company resources and provide a means for the parent company to control operations, advertising, or other important sources of reputation. Although companies like McDonald's have pursued global expansion via franchising, they also have the option of direct investment in company-owned stores, productive facilities, or service centers. McDonald's Corporation, for example, has many franchisees, but they also own many of their restaurants outright and share ownership through joint ventures in yet other restaurants. These direct investment decisions give rise to related decisions about how to structure overseas entities.

Product cycles and globalism

The structure appropriate to an overseas facility is at least partially associated with firm strategy and leaders' views of future potential in overseas markets. Writing in the 1960s, Raymond Vernon (1966) argued that limits on domestic growth would motivate US firms to follow a linear pattern for overseas expansion based on stages of the product cycle.

1 At the product's introductory stage when sales growth is uncertain and production runs limited, the firm uses excess productive capacity domestically to produce and export to similar industrialized economies.
2 At the product's growth stage, firms will increase exports to developing economies to further expand their markets and ease growing competition in the domestic market.
3 As the product matures and competition mounts, costs become more important and the firm may then use improved process technologies discovered during the growth cycle to produce more abroad and export less; manufacturing abroad often occurs first in other industrialized countries for export to developing economies.
4 At the decline phase of the product life cycle, almost all production moves to lesser developed economies for worldwide distribution.

Many well-known firms expanded their scope from industrialized to developing economies by following the process Vernon described, but globalization may create new challenges for implementing this theory. First, improved communication creates almost simultaneous worldwide demand for new products, reducing opportunities to extend product life cycles through sequential introductions. At the same time, refinements or innovations can be introduced incrementally to extend the product's life cycle. Gillette is able to enjoy this advantage with some of its consumer products, and also extends the life of manufacturing equipment by shifting it from country to country. Some firms even shift the headquarters for products to countries where they are most in demand. For example, IBM moved its networking systems from the US to the UK; Siemens moved its ultrasound business to the US; DuPont moved its electronics business to Japan; and Hyundai Electronics moved its personal computer business to the US.

World business opportunities associated with services like television, engineering, and communication may be more difficult to introduce on a country-by-country basis, although delayed introduction is possible, especially for entertainment products. For example, the television show *Dallas* appeared first in the US and later in Europe and in Asia. Films typically open in their home market and subsequently in venues abroad, and this too is an example of delayed service introduction. A third challenge for applying product life cycle theories in a global world is that a growing number of firms based in Asia and Latin America by-pass domestic economies to produce first in the advanced economies. For example, Indonesia's IPTN set out to manufacture mid-size aircraft in the US. In summary, application of the product life cycle theory to global exporting and production finds the theory in practice, but firms also take different routes to exporting and production abroad. Thus, the relevance of this theory may be specific to a particular set of circumstances rather than universal, and it is imperative that global leaders consider its relevance to their own businesses.

Stage models of multinational structuring

According to Leif Melin (1992), the linear type of thinking reflected in product life cycle theory also appeared in studies of multinational structuring. The 'stage' models of the 1960s and 1970s explained expansion at early stages of internationalization and most were prescriptive, like Vernon's product life cycle model. These were followed by studies emphasizing the strategy/structure link, and more recently by research Melin calls *management process models*. Melin believes that US research overlooked early efforts to incorporate non-linear types of thinking in strategy. For example, he observed that Stopford and Wells' 1972 study of the strategy/structure relationship was remembered more for the tight link between strategy and structure than for observations that a grid or matrix type of structure reduces boundaries, introduces blurred relationships, and depends more on management skills and abilities than on the structural arrangement of the firm. As Table 5.9 illustrates, coordinating mechanisms used to pursue global strategies differ according to whether activities cross internal organizational borders or external borders between organizations. The reason for this is explored in the section to follow.

Structuring FDI

The decision to expand abroad raises questions centered on coordination and control of relationships between the parent company and its offspring. Some firms centralize control, making most important decisions at headquarters; others decentralize, expecting managers abroad to make important decisions. Global firms like Makro and Eva Airlines have decentralized decisions because top managers believe local managers are in a better position to make decisions. For example, Makro's Paul Van Vlisingen has

TABLE 5.9   Activities across borders

Activities	Organizational boundaries	
	Within organizations – across borders	Between organizations – across borders
Entry modes	A Internationalization stage models	B
Transactions	Internationalization; transaction costs Intraorganizational trade; transfer prices	C International trade International marketing Foreign direct investments International business networks	D
	Transfer of technology	
	E Global strategies	F
Coordination mechanisms	Structural forms Formal control systems Informal/social integration and coordination	Alliances and joint ventures Host government relationship

Source: Melin, Leif. (1992). Internationalization as a strategy process. *Strategic Management Journal*, 13: 100.

decentralized this retail giant, allowing local managers daily control over decisions without having to ask for approval from headquarters. Sweden's IKEA also is radically decentralized, depending mostly on in-person communication and other media to exchange information. Ford, on the other hand, has centralized decisions to better achieve a worldwide integration strategy. NV Philips has done both: decentralized and then centralized to improve coordination and control as it reduced the workforce. The choice of whether to centralize or decentralize depends in part on the strategy the firm pursues, and it depends on the type of entity established abroad. In the following section, we see that entering a foreign market with a wholly owned subsidiary abroad allows decision-making choices – choices more constrained when the choice of entry mode is a strategic alliance. The choice of structural form appropriate for these two types of entities demonstrates tensions between linear and more process-oriented decision-making as well as tensions between centralization and decentralization.

Wholly owned subsidiary structures

A wholly owned subsidiary is established when the parent company fully owns and controls subsidiary decisions. This has traditionally been the most popular form of FDI. The structural or design frameworks suggested for expanding abroad by means of wholly owned subsidiaries are several, including functional, divisional, and matrix-type structures. For all, the purpose of structure is to coordinate and control the subsidiary organization, but because there is no 'perfect' structure, each has its advantages and disadvantages.

GLOBAL FUNCTIONAL STRUCTURE

A functional structure manages coordination and control by organizing tasks around principal functions such as marketing, accounting, operations, or research and development (Figure 5.11). Advantages of this approach globally are several: the top executive or leader can coordinate among functional areas to reduce overlap; everyone knows her/his function so there is limited confusion over responsibilities; and it makes good use of technical people and/or their specialized skills and knowledge. However, the functional form also has disadvantages when taken abroad. For example, it becomes more difficult for a single coordinating leader to manage all concerns; specialization can lead to jealousies, particularly if resources are disproportionately allocated; and it may be difficult to coordinate among units, particularly if they are at great distances or when practices differ on a global scale. For example, costing practices are difficult to coordinate globally because nations impose different requirements and allow different accounting practices.

GLOBAL DIVISIONAL STRUCTURE

Organizations can be divisionalized in several ways, including product lines, geographic area, e.g., North America, South America (Figure 5.12), or customers served such as commercial users, consumers, government. Advantages of divisionalization may include the following: having functional specialties where they are needed rather than organized in some central location; spotlighting those divisions most important to the firm and

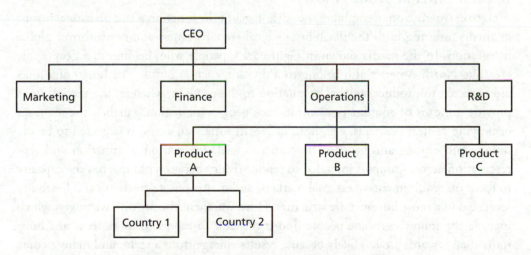

FIGURE 5.11 *Global functional structure*

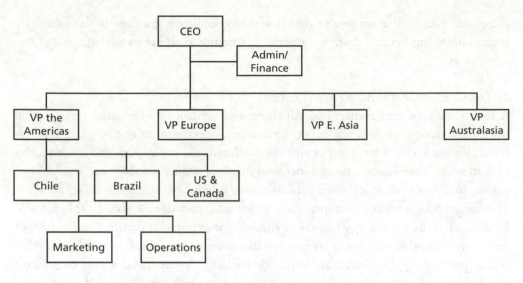

FIGURE 5.12 *Global divisional structure*

providing a good way to remain focused on what is important; and measuring performance by division. However, as is true for any form of structure, the divisional form has disadvantages as well as advantages. The disadvantages are as follows: often a large staff is needed for purposes of coordination; there may be duplication, particularly if each division has its own functional areas, such as personnel; and divisions may become too independent, particularly if the division's competencies are distinctive or if it is difficult for the home office to communicate with the division because of geographic distance.

GLOBAL MATRIX STRUCTURES

A matrix structure often combines the advantages of the functional and divisional forms, in theory offering both the flexibility of local responsiveness and control over global integration. In the matrix shown in Figure 5.13, people who 'belong' to a geographic area like North America also belong to a division such as autos. The horizontal links are expected to produce a global orientation to the product; whereas, the vertical links provide a means of coordination within each geographic region. Further, the manager occupying central positions, e.g., head of North American autos, is expected to be the linking pin among and between functions as well. Integration of function and representation across groups is intended to reduce rivalry between groups; has the capacity to focus on requirements of external markets; and may promote creativity and flexibility less usual in a more bureaucratic structure. However, there also are disadvantages, which include the following: some people find it difficult to report to more than one boss; individual rewards are less likely because results emerge from a team; and many people prefer stability and control over their own destiny. Efforts to create hybrids have resulted

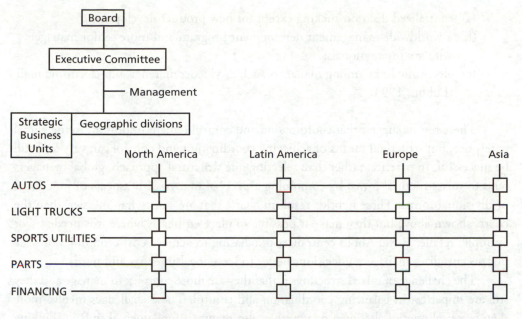

FIGURE 5.13 *Global matrix structure*

in experimentation with hybrid structures where some measure of control might be bureaucratic and another measure more flexible. For example, frequent visits and both telephone and e-mail messages between people in headquarters and the subsidiary provide a means of informal communication that improves flexibility without giving up bureaucratic controls. Perhaps because they offer a way to manage the complexity usual to global enterprises, matrix structures have been used by many global giants, including Ford and ABB. However, after several years of managing complex matrices, both Ford and ABB reduced the number of components in their matrix designs. Interestingly, the complexities of a matrix grow as companies themselves grow via merger and acquisition.

One recommended structure for a global organization has been to adopt centralized decision-making within a worldwide product division structure. This recommendation might encourage would-be global firms to restructure, but according to a 1993 McKinsey & Company study of the relationship between success and changes, alterations in structure were not critical to superior performance. Neither were creation of global divisions, centers of excellence, international business units, cross-border task forces, or globally integrated management information systems. According to this study of 43 large US consumer companies, among those activities that do lead to higher performance are the following:

(a) centralized decision-making except for new product development;
(b) a worldwide management development program and more senior managers who are internationals;
(c) electronic links among managers such as videoconference and electronic mail (Lublin, 1993).

These results suggest that coordination and control remain important to the global enterprise, but structural means of achieving coordination and control can vary and still be successful. In practice, rather than selecting one structural approach, global managers tend to mix structural forms by combining aspects of matrix with aspects of functional or divisional forms. These hybrids result in charts that are somewhat 'messier' than the charts shown above but they make it possible to place emphasis where it is needed. For example, retailer Royal Ahold centralizes purchasing to achieve cost economies of scale but decentralizes managerial decisions better to serve local interests and needs.

The challenge of mixed structures is that they are more complex to manage and they still are imperfect in balancing coordination and control. These challenges involve more than practical ones of altering a design; they also require a fundamental shift in thinking about coordination and control that cuts across all organizational concerns. According to Robert Moran and John Reisenberger (1994), this shift in thinking includes the following:

1 Strategic focus centralizes key decisions but permits local autonomy when appropriate.
2 Corporate vision continually evolves and must be communicated worldwide.
3 Cooperation improves as all employees share and accept global strategic vision.
4 Subsidiary/parent and subsidiary/subsidiary knowledge transfer and learning must occur.
5 Decision-making becomes more shared and more complex (pp. 170–176).

Moran and Reisenberger also believe that changes in strategic focus, cooperation, and decision-making necessarily alter the firm's structural orientation. They argue that the 'old' paradigm for achieving worldwide competitive advantage was centralization and economies of scale; whereas, a newer paradigm involves simultaneous and coordinated centralization together with local adaptability. The 'both/and' approach they suggest is consistent with a belief that the challenges of globalization must be met with more a 'one best way' approach to structuring. In summary, globalization gives us many reasons to alter structural designs but these alterations in structure involve concomitant alterations in thinking. The following section examining strategic alliances as another approach to global expansion also shows this arrangement creates control issues for the global firm and demonstrates how organizational vision is thereby altered.

Strategic alliances

Within the last 15 years, strategic alliances have emerged to structure decisions when ownership and control are blended. James and Weidenbaum (1993) describe strategic alliances as 'cooperative, flexible arrangements, born out of the mutual need of firms to share the risks of an often uncertain marketplace by jointly pursuing a common objective' (p. 61). Growth and expansion is costly not only because of fiscal concerns, but because expansion into new nations carries learning costs associated with culture, local conditions, politics, economics, and human resources management. Both economic and learning costs are reasons for firms to form strategic alliances. According to Farok Contractor and Peter Lorange (1988, p. 9), other reasons for structuring cooperative relationships include:

(a) risk reduction;
(b) economies of scale and/or rationalization;
(c) technology exchange;
(d) co-opting or blocking competition;
(e) overcoming government-mandates, trade, or investment barriers;
(f) facilitating initial international expansion of inexperienced firms;
(g) vertical quasi-integration advantages of linking the complementary contributions of partners in a value chain.

According to Pekar and Allio (1994), a strategic alliance can include a myriad of non-equity as well as equity arrangements ranging from an independent entity in the form of an international joint venture to collaborative advertising, research and development partnerships, and cross-manufacturing, to name a few.

Perhaps because of inexperience with them, organizations face many challenges in structuring and managing alliances. Assessing internal needs and abilities of an alliance, partner selection, relationship building, planning, and evaluating are alliance challenges. Implementation also is problematic because partners with different national or organizational cultures produce managers with different views of what is normal, natural, or 'right.' Issues of control often are difficult to resolve, and cultural values can lead to different points of view on how people and processes should be managed. The success of alliances frequently depends on qualitative factors like trust and relationship building, but both are difficult to create when national or organizational cultures differ. Thus, forming an alliance by no means guarantees success. Further, success in strategic alliances appears to depend more on the 'soft' side of management such as managing culture than on 'hard' skills like financial acumen or technical expertise. Thus, the linear types of bottom-line decision-making that can more easily be made in a wholly owned subsidiary are complemented by cultural processes and less linearity in problem-solving in cross-national strategic alliances. The example in Box 5.11 demonstrates how cultures clashed in one strategic alliance.

BOX 5.11:   CULTURE CLASH AT TRIAD

Siemens AG of Germany, Toshiba Corp. of Japan, and IBM of America joined forces as Triad to create a revolutionary computer memory chip, but culture clash among engineers and scientists has impeded progress. Cultural groupings by nation created an 'us versus them' atmosphere; imposing English as the common language was less comfortable for some than for others; and work habits differed. For example, Japanese were accustomed to working in open spaces and Germans were accustomed to windows, but Triad workers were assigned individual space without windows. This was more usual for US workers, but problematic for others. Communication styles also differed and were a barrier for information exchange. Thus, the structure selected affected work processes that in turn affected how people felt about the work; the results were not the desired ones.

Source: Browning, E.S. (1994, May 3). Computer chip project brings rivals together, but the cultures clash. *The Wall Street Journal*, pp. A1, A11.

The now-famous NUMMI GM/Toyota venture (New United Motor Manufacturing Inc.) was intended to blend the best of Japanese and US manufacturing practices in a car sold under both firm's names. The reality was that GM was unable to correct its weaknesses by venturing. The car produced by NUMMI still sells six times as many cars in the US under the Toyota name as with the GM name. Corning, on the other hand, has successfully created and sustained alliances, defining itself as a network of organizations. Part of Corning's success with alliances may be that executives view alliances as long-term commitments. Corning seeks partners with compatible values and cultures, encourages 50/50 ownership, and clearly distinguishes the alliance from parent firms. In other words, alliances may be more successful when they are part of a longer term vision than when they are viewed as a temporary contributor to short run financial returns.

This section has suggested that workable approaches to managing structures in a global setting include mixing and matching principles of management or international business by borrowing some practices from traditional concepts and some from less traditional schemes. For example, the efficiency emphasis traditional to scientific management principles would discourage systems that centralize all but one set of decisions, yet as the McKinsey study showed, performance success is associated with centralizing all but new product development. This mix and match recipe for success suggests that managing in a global economy is difficult because it is complex and requires managers who can coordinate among conflicting objectives. Further, it requires managers who are able to demonstrate skills in both linear and process-oriented modes of decision-making. In the following section, attention turns to decision-making at the individual and managerial level.

PEOPLE
Motivation

Motivation is willingness to work hard to achieve a desired goal, and organizations attempt to channel employees' energy in productive ways by matching rewards to the goals people want and will work hard to achieve. Tangible rewards such as money often are the basis of performance incentives in the US, a practice based on assumptions of economic rationality. However, researchers have shown that tangible rewards may not have the same relevance in other settings. For example, in a study of Russian workers, Welsh, Luthans and Sommer (1993) found that consumer goods from the West were better motivators than roubles because the consumer goods were unavailable. The goals people will work hard to achieve also vary cross-culturally. Among family-owned businesses, it is often more important to please one's family than to achieve highest economic returns. In countries of Latin America, where affiliation with family and community are important norms, helping a friend gain employment may be more important than what he or she contributes to the organization. According to Robert Moran and John Reisenberger (1994), the problems of motivating excellence among global employees occur because borders are blurring and employees are challenged to know where home is or to decide where they will place their loyalties. They argue this problem will be overcome when employees are motivated by empowerment, believing it is the CEO's job to see that all employees are empowered. However, a desire to be empowered may be more relevant to nations that encourage autonomy and less relevant where the individual is less important than the collective group. National and individual motivational differences suggest managers balance among a wide variety of needs and desires when managing employees. Work/family balance, loyalty exchange, values, beliefs, and priorities – all are among the challenges managers face in managing people globally. Recognizing these and other variations in work orientation is more demanding than assuming workforces are homogeneous, and recognizing variations and creating skills for working with them is but another of the many challenges the global manager faces.

A 1995 Gallup Poll sponsored by *Inc* magazine (Seglin, 1996) showed that among

US employees, satisfaction and job performance depend not only on employees having the opportunity to do what they do best, but also on having opportunities for personal growth, a sense of importance to the job and as an individual, a belief that personal opinions matter, and a 'family-friendly' workplace. Interestingly, two different studies showed that Japanese employees are less happy with their jobs and less loyal to them than are US or Western European employees. Results from a study conducted by International Survey Research showed that of 8,600 Japanese respondents, only 44% answered favorably to the question: Taking everything into account, how satisfied are you with your company as an employer? In the same study, satisfaction with employers was 82% for the Swiss, 72% for Mexicans, 66% for Germans, and 65% for US workers. A study of company loyalty revealed that Japanese workers are less loyal than Canadian, Finn, Spanish, US, and South African employees (Worldreports, 1997).

MANAGERIAL COMPETENCIES FOR A GLOBAL WORLD: RATIONALITY AND INTUITION

Global managers must use all the resources available to them to manage global challenges. Like managers at Barings in 1993, global managers are confronted with reams or megabytes of data, but the accuracy of these data is difficult to verify. Electronic databases are particularly vulnerable to rumors and even purposefully fraudulent data reporting. To the extent that business decisions are based on these data, those decisions are themselves faulty. The rapid pace of global business may discourage verification or encourage managers to ignore symptoms until presented with tangible evidence of problems. For Barings, concrete information came too late to save the firm.

Intuition represents another way of knowing, and it can be defined as the process of knowing that does not rely consciously on rational or linear thought processes. In the US, managers tend to use intellect more than they use intuition when problem-solving. Yet, according to Daniel Isenberg (1984), intuition plays an important role for managers because it can help them:

(a) sense when a problem exists;
(b) perform well-learned behaviors and patterns rapidly;
(c) synthesize isolated data into an integrated picture;
(d) rein in over-reliance on rationality.

Willis Harmon (1993) believes the assumptions of scientific rationality so useful to exploring an external, physical world are less suitable for exploring the inner experiences from which humans and societies have traditionally derived meaning and value. Further, he asserts that reliance on rationality has led to organizational decisions that squander irreplaceable resources, foul the environment, threaten the Earth's life-support systems, inhumanely use our fellow citizens, create chronic poverty and hunger, and imperil the future of civilized society on the planet – decisions that individual humans in those institutions know are unwise. (p. 226)

Harmon believes there is awakening emphasis on intuition in organizations and he views this trend as very positive both for organizations and for society. According to him, this approach to decision-making can improve decisions because it uses more of human knowledge, it provides a way for businesses to reassess the role of business in the world, and it may have global implications for changing the assumptions that have shaped life to this point. He points to global problems such as terrorism and extinction of species as interrelated consequences of having put our faith in science to the exclusion of values.

Managers at Barings PLC seemed unable to synthesize data, and apparently did not recognize the magnitude of the threat that bankrupted them. Rationality may have functioned to shape their assumptions, leading them to believe that with 223 years of history, Barings would persist. In Japan, by contrast, there is a tendency to over-rely on qualitative data and a disinclination to use computers or develop policy-capturing systems that rationalize some part of decision-making. For example, Sumitomo Bank suffered massive losses of about $2.6 billion from an employee's unauthorized copper trades. Outside observers believe these losses were partially the result of computer-aversion among Sumitomo headquarters personnel; the paper trail they preferred came too late to undo damage already done. These examples suggest that rationality and intuition are important partners in global decision-making. Again, we see that the challenge is combining ideas rather than replacing old theories with new.

This look at the global economy has examined some of the challenges associated with managing global trade, FDI, and capital. The economic rationality presumed to be operating in the US was shown to operate in other ways worldwide, creating demands for hybrid ways of structuring, decision-making, and motivating people worldwide. In the next chapter on globalization of labor, we look at economic challenges as they assume a human face.

KEY CHAPTER CONCEPTS

The Purpose of Economic Systems: Economic systems provide the means for generating and distributing resources within a society. These economic systems are supported by distribution systems that transfer goods to satisfy demand; currency systems that provide a medium for exchange; and banks and businesses to facilitate resource generation and distribution.

Market-based Economics Defined: Market-based economies are a forum for people to come together to exchange ownership of goods and services. Assumptions of free markets include the following: economic decisions are made by markets rather than by governments; buyers and sellers can freely enter and exit markets; and all have full knowledge of prices, quantities, or others' activities. The combined economic activities of all actors operating within a nation define a national economy, and they include microeconomic activities and macroeconomic activities.

GNP and GDP: Gross national product (GNP) measures the total value of all finished goods and services generated by national producers whether they are located in the nation or not. Gross domestic product (GDP) measures all finished goods and services produced within the nation, including that of foreign producers. It does not include goods domestic firms produce elsewhere.

Indicators of National Economic Wealth: Trade in goods and services, trade balances, foreign direct investments, and currency exchange all become more important indicators of national wealth with increased worldwide economic integration.

Reasons Global Economic Activities Are Difficult to Measure: Economic activity is difficult to measure in a global economy because economic conditions change rapidly, and many existing measures of these activities are incomplete.

Alternative Measures of Wealth: According to some, economic activity is only one among many measures of true wealth and human prosperity. They argue that other measures of wealth combined with economic wealth provide a better picture of the investment potential within and among nations.

World Trade in Goods and Services Defined: Trade in visible goods or merchandise is the major source of international revenue and expenditures for most countries, and about 70% of world trade is in goods, but trade in services such as travel, transportation, entertainment, and telecommunications is a growing component of the global economy.

World Foreign Direct Investments Defined: Foreign direct investments in the form of both equity and capital investments are growing, and there is a clear trend of increasing inflows and outflows of direct investments among developing as well as among already industrialized economies.

Managing Investment Capital Worldwide: Competition for investment capital is keen worldwide. The efforts of financial institutions like the World Bank and the IMF, central banks, and private lending institutions show that managing this competition on a global scale creates unaccustomed opportunities and challenges.

Global Currencies: In the absence of a true global currency, the US dollar is the bankable currency around the world. Demand for a more global currency has fostered interest in the euro and suggestions for a yen bloc.

Market Assumptions Tested by a Global Economy: In a global economy, assumptions of free markets such as information availability, economic rationality, and free and unimpeded market entry and exit are met only with great difficulty.

Capitalist Approaches to Markets Vary: Capitalist approaches to free market economics vary from the competitive model dominant in Triad nations to include frontier capitalism, Asian capitalism, and cooperative capitalism.

Linear Decision-Making in a Global World: Decision-making according to linear, rational models dominant in the US is expanding to accommodate more process-oriented modes of thinking.

Structures Suggested for Global Business: The range of structures available to the global enterprises is expanding to accommodate both the hierarchical model consistent with autonomous and rational decision-making and strategic alliances that depend more on distributed and shared decision-making.

Motivations Needs Differ Cross-Culturally: Motivation of a heterogeneous global workforce with differing needs and values requires a manager adept at understanding cultural differences in motivation.

Managerial Competencies: People who manage global enterprises increasingly rely on intuition as well as economic rationality and an understanding of political processes to reach decisions.

REVIEW AND DISCUSSION QUESTIONS

1   In view of economic globalization, weigh the relative effects of a nation's economic downturn against a global business downturn. How does a global economy create national interdependencies?

2   How are global events in the economic and other environments affecting business practices of investment bankers? What traditions of banking are changing and how do these reflect an era of global banking versus banking within nation-states?

3   Provide arguments for establishing a global form of currency. What are the current and potential impediments to its establishment?

4   Weigh the reasons most likely to lead to a decision to establish a wholly owned subsidiary abroad. How do these reasons compare to the decision to go abroad via a strategic alliance?

5   What are key sources of global economic convergence? How and why does one calculate PPP? What are the differences between GDP and GNP?

6   When the business leader uses GDP figures to compare opportunities for expansion abroad, what concerns should be raised when comparing GDP on national and per capita bases? If these data cannot be compared, what other sources of information are available to support informed decisions?

7   *The Global Enterprise Project*: Demonstrate ways it is evident that the firm you are studying is responsive to a globalizing economy. If it is traded on a stock exchange, track its current stock values for the past year. (Calculate values by translating them into your own currency; use current data and provide the source of your exchange ratio.) What are its practices relating to managing in a global economy, e.g., direct investments, export/import behavior, sourcing patterns, accounting for profits and costs abroad. What models of decision-making are evident?

REFERENCES

After two outstanding years, world trade growth returned to earlier levels. (1998, Jan. 12). http://www.wto.org/wto/intltrad/introduc.htm

Asia's competing capitalisms. (1995, June 24). *The Economist*, pp. 16–17.

Bello, Walden, and Cunningham, Shea. (1994, Sept./Oct.). Reign of errors: The World Bank's wrongs. *Real World International*.

Bolman, Lee, and Deal, Terrence. (1991). *Reframing organizations*. San Francisco, CA: Jossey-Bass.

Chetwynd, Josh. (1994, Dec. 1). Foreign firms produced 20% of '93 U.S. output. *The Wall Street Journal*, p. A8.

The collapse of Barings. (1995, Mar. 4). *The Economist*, pp. 19–21.

Contractor, F.J., and Lorange, Peter. (1988). Why should firms cooperate? The strategy and economics basis for cooperative ventures. In F.J. Contractor and Peter Lorange (Eds), *Cooperative strategies in international business*, pp. 3–30. Lexington, MA: Lexington Books.

Dicken, P. (1992, 2nd ed.). *Global Shift*. New York/London: Guilford Press.

Drucker, Peter. (1989). *The new realities*. New York: Harper & Row.

Du Bois, Martin. (1996, Oct. 22). Cross border deals boom in Netherlands as Dutch firms seek global leadership. *The Wall Street Journal*, p. A19.

Eberstadt, Nicholas, and Lewis, Clifford, M. (1995, June 26). Privatize the World Bank. *The Wall Street Journal*, p. A12.

Edmunds, John C. (1996, Fall). Securities: The new world wealth machine. *Foreign Policy*, pp. 118–134.

Emerging nations win major exporting roles. (1997, Feb. 24). *The Wall Street Journal*, p. A1.

Farrell, Christopher. (1994, Nov. 18). The triple revolution. *Business Week*, Special issue: 21st century capitalism, pp. 16–25.

Fischel, Daniel. (1995). *Payback: The conspiracy to destroy Michael Millken and his financial revolution*. New York: HarperBusiness.

Foreign executives see US as prime market. (1997, Feb. 3). *The Wall Street Journal*, p. A1.

Foust, Dean. (1995, Feb. 20). What the IMF needs is a good alarm system. *Business Week*, p. 55.

Hampden-Turner, Charles, and Trompenaars, Alfons. (1993). *The seven cultures of capitalism*. New York: Doubleday.

Harmon, Willis. (1993). Intuition in managerial decision-making: Codeword for global transformation. In Brenda Sutton (Ed.), *The legitimate corporation: Essential readings in business ethics and corporate governance*, pp. 224–235. Cambridge, MA: Blackwell Business.

Henderson, Hazel. (1996). *Building a win-win world: Life beyond global economic warfare*. San Francisco, CA: Berrett Koehler Books.

Human Development Report. (1994). New York: Oxford University Press.

Human Development Report. (1996). Cary, NC: Oxford University Press.

Human Development Report. (1997). Cary, NC: Oxford University Press.

Ibbotson, Roger G., and Brinson, Gary P. (1993). *Global investing*. New York: McGraw-Hill.

IMF. (1997, Oct.). *World economic outlook*. Washington, DC: International Monetary Fund.

International Survey Research. (1996). Reported in International morale watch. (Jan. 13), *Fortune*, p. 142; and Satisfaction at work. (June 24), *Business Week*, p. 28.

Isenberg, Daniel J. (1984, Nov./Dec.). How senior managers think. *Harvard Business Review*, 62(6): 81–90.

It's time to redefine the World Bank and the IMF. (1994, July 25). *The Wall Street Journal*, p. A1.

James, H.S., and Weidenbaum, M. (1993). *When businesses cross international borders*. Westport, CT: Praeger Publishers.

Kogut, Bruce, and Gittelman, Michelle. (1994, Nov.). *The largest foreign multinationals in the United States and their contribution to the American economy*. Philadelphia, PA: The Wharton School.

Kraar, Louis. (1994, Aug. 8). Your next PC could be made in Taiwan. *Fortune*, pp. 90–96.

Kwan, C.H. (1996). A yen bloc in Asia. *Journal of the Asia Pacific Economy*, 1(1): 1–21.

Lipin, Steven. (1998, Jan. 2). Murphy's Law doesn't apply. *The Wall Street Journal*, p. R6.

Lublin, Joann S. (1993, Mar. 22). Study sees US businesses stumbling on the road toward globalization. *The Wall Street Journal*, p. A7B.

Magnusson, Paul. (1994, Oct. 3). The IMF should look forward, not back. *Business Week*, p. 108.

Mandel, Michael. (1994, Nov. 7). The real truth about the economy. *Business Week*, pp. 110–115.

Marcus, Alfred A. (1993). *Business and Society*. Homewood, IL: Irwin.

Melin, Leif. (1992). Internationalization as a strategy process. *Strategic Management Journal*, 13: 99–118.

Merrill Lynch advertisement. (1995, June 12). *Fortune*, p. 49.

Millman, Gregory. (1995). *The vandals' crown: How rebel currency traders overthrew the world's central banks*. Cambridge, MA: Free Press.

The missing link. (1994, Oct. 1). *The Economist*, The global economy survey, pp. 10–14.

Moran, Robert, and Reisenberger, John. (1994). *The global challenge: Building the new world enterprise*. London: McGraw-Hill Europe.

Pekar, Peter Jr, and Allio, Robert. (1994, Aug.). Making alliances work: Guidelines for success. *Long Range Planning*, pp. 54–65.

Reverse linkages – Everybody wins. (1995, May). *Development Brief*. (Additional information appears in World Bank (1995). *Global economic prospects and the developing economies 1995*. Washington, DC: World Bank.)

Richman, Louis S. (1995, Mar. 20). Global growth is on a tear. *Fortune*, pp. 108–114.

Rosett, Claudia. (1994, July 1). Figures never lie, but they seldom tell the truth about Russian economy. *The Wall Street Journal*, p. A6.

Seglin, Jeffrey L. (1996, May 21). The happiest workers in the world. *Inc.*, Special Issue: The state of small business, pp. 62–64, 66, 68, 70, 72, 74, 76.

Sesit, Michael R. (1995, Apr. 25). Central Bank's efforts to bolster the dollar spur mostly decline. *The Wall Street Journal*, p. C1.

Sharp, Margaret. (1992). Tides of change: The world economy and Europe in the 1990s. *International Affairs*, 68(1): 17–35.

Shelton, Judy. (1994). *Money meltdown: Restoring order to the global currency system*. Cambridge, MA: Free Press.

Silk, Leonard. (1978). *Economics in plain English*. New York: Simon & Schuster/Touchstone.

Simon, Herbert E. (1955). A behavioral model of rational choice. *Quarterly Journal of Economics*, 69: 99–118.

Solomon, Steven. (1995). *The confidence game*. New York: Simon & Schuster; also see Deane, Marjorie, and Pringle, Robert. (1995). *The central banks*. New York: Viking; or Millman, Gregory. (1995). *The vandals' crown*. Cambridge, MA: Free Press.

Stopford, J.M., and Wells, L.T., Jr. (1972). *Managing the multinational enterprise*. New York: Basic Books.

That damned dollar. (1995, Feb. 25). *The Economist*, pp. 17–18.

Thurow, Lester. (1996). *The future of capitalism: How today's economic forces shape tomorrow's world*. New York: William Morrow.

Vernon, Raymond. (1966, June). International trade and international investment in the product cycle. *Quarterly Journal of Economics*, pp. 190–207.

Vogel, David. (1992, Fall). The globalization of business ethics. *California Management Review*, p. 32.

Welsh, Dianne, Luthans, Fred, and Sommer, S.M. (1993). Managing Russian factory workers: The impact of US based behavioral and participative techniques. *Academy of Management Journal*, 36(1): 58–79.

Why can't a country be like a firm? (1995, Apr. 22). *The Economist*, p. 79.

World Investment Report 1994: Transnational corporations, employment and the workplace. An executive summary. (1994. Aug.). *Transnational corporations*, pp. 73–113.

Worldreports. (1997, Jan./Feb.). *World business*. New York: KPMG Peat Marwick (ceased publication in spring 1997).

Chapter 6

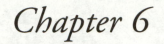

The Global Economy: Labor

MOTOROLA'S LEARNING ORGANIZATION

Motorola Incorporated's manufacturing plants and sales and service outlets throughout the world facilitate success in global markets, and its satellite system Iridium promises to extend those markets into space as well as across national boundaries. Numbered among the largest semiconductor producers in the world, Motorola may be best known to the public for its tele-communications products, particularly pagers, two-way private radios, and cellular phones. With annual sales approaching $30 billion (63% of them in foreign markets) and over 142,000 employees worldwide, Motorola also is known as a company committed to total cus-tomer satisfaction; as a company providing superior company-wide management of quality processes and winner of the 1988 Malcolm Baldridge National Quality Award; as a firm that identifies human resources as the critical strength and contributor to total customer satisfac-tion; and as a firm that puts money and effort into learning.

Motorola's training programs are considered a model for other firms because they link training to corporate strategy, but for the firm they represent good business sense. Motorola's emphasis on education and training began in the early 1980s when then-chairman Robert Galvin founded Motorola University to bolster global competitiveness. Originally located at firm headquarters in Schaumberg, Illinois, Motorola University now operates in 14 locations around the world with a budget that equals about 4% of Motorola's annual payroll – over $150 million in 1995. In comparison, the average US firm allocates about 1% of payroll to training.

Motorola requires every employee throughout the world to take at least 40 hours of classes per year. The type of training offered ranges widely, reflected in over 600 classes from English as a second language to creativity and innovation. Often, the type of training selected is the employee's option. Top managers, for example, typically focus on skills needed for their own business areas or their job responsibilities. For example, one course is a computer-based strategy game full of external disasters like bankrupt customers and factory fires and internal shocks including a fired CEO. Middle managers might focus on interpersonal skills like team building; one offering is a program for managers who want to know how to work with difficult employees. Specialists in functional areas like engineering or marketing might take classes to keep current in their own fields or learn the rudiments of other fields so that they can cross disciplinary boundaries of thought and expertise. Employees at entry levels who have not previously acquired skills they need to contribute to Motorola's success also train in basic skills, particularly math computations that include how to read graphs or solve algebraic problems. More recently, Motorola has expanded its course offerings to include parenting skills. The parenting class builds a bridge between home and work life, but on another front Motorola seeks to re-establish boundaries that earlier it helped to blur. For example, only a few years ago Motorola taught basic reading and writing skills, but leaders for the firm now believe communities and governments should take responsibility for making people ready to learn and allow businesses to focus on training relevant to the business.

From 1990 to 1995, Motorola saw a 26% annual rise in earnings and a total 139% increase in productivity measured by employee sales. Part of this increase is training-related, but Motorola leaders believe productivity also improves with work environments that stimulate and satisfy employees. Internal culture is monitored and developed by using employee focus groups to measure perceptions of employee satisfaction, morale, and company culture. Employees are encouraged to establish support groups among themselves, and they are protected from arbitrary decisions by practices in place. For example, after 10 years with the company, employees are 'Galvanized', meaning they cannot be fired unless the decision is reviewed by top managers. The Participative Management Program (PMP) also is part of Motorola's efforts to develop a clear corporate culture; this program is based on an assumption that the employee is knowledgeable about the job performed and the best source of knowledge on how to solve job-related problems. The PMP combines financial resources, management leadership, and employee creativity and competence based on three principles:

1 *Employees' behaviors are a consequence of how they are treated. Employees are treated as though they are intelligent, learning, involved, and responsible.*
2 *Every employee needs and expects to live in a rational world. Under the PMP, management is open to competent influence and the rationality of all its decisions is subject to challenge.*
3 *Every employee's effectiveness depends on how acutely aware he or she is of Motorola's and his or her job demands. (Robinson, 1991, p. 83)*

By encouraging employees thoughtfully to challenge managers' decisions or to ask managers for explanations traditionally unshared with employees invites managers and laborers to cross boundaries and barriers that traditionally separated them. An additional boundary is crossed when team members and managers are asked to learn from and teach each other. According to Robinson, the payoff from shared learning is that employees become resources for creative ideas and offer alternative solutions to challenges faced. For example, when Motorola managers considered moving US jobs abroad to cut manufacturing costs, they first asked employees for their ideas. Employees created a plan for building the product at a lower cost and a higher quality level than international competitors, and in the case of a radio-paging product were successful in exporting it to Japan where consumers are known to be particularly demanding.

Motorola's culture also is dynamic and capable of including new entrants to the workforce around the world. For example, after Motorola managers realized that 1980 US census projections meant there would be more women and minorities in the nation and in the workforce, they established ambitious goals for hiring more women and members of minority groups. Mindful that population concentrations differ throughout the world, Motorola attempts to mirror the local population in its hiring practices. For example, if African-American electrical engineers are 4% of the nation's population, then Motorola's goal is to assemble a group of electrical engineers among whom are at least 4% African-Americans. Further, Motorola intends not only to hire from among many groups but also to retain these and other employees. Retention is made possible by tying diversity goals to managerial evaluations. For example, succession planning requires top managers to supply the names of three people most likely to replace them in this order: the person most likely to be tapped if an emergency arose; the person who could be groomed for the job in the next three to five years; and the minority or woman employee closest to being qualified for the position. Managers then are expected to provide opportunities for this third person to gain the experience needed for advancement. The program's success is demonstrated by Motorola's female heirs apparent: women now are the first- or second-slot successors for 75 of the company's 300 top jobs. African-American David Wooldridge, Jr heads sales for Motorola's navigation technology, following in the footsteps of another mentor: his father heads Motorola's Marketing Institute. These visible successes demonstrate the changing face of Motorola, and the knowledge and experiences these people bring to top management will contribute to additional learning at the top that can be translated into bottom-line performance and the ability to hire additional women and minority group employees. In addition to being evaluated on succession plans that include people 'not like us,' managers also monitor and quantify quarterly results of minority hiring associated with internships, flexible work programs, scholarships, partnerships, and community involvement.

The serious nature of the global challenges Motorola faces sometimes are offset by light-hearted competition among employee groups from around the world. Annually, Motorola stages an Olympics-style internal quality event to showcase the best of 3,000 worldwide employee teams. During the event, these teams compete for gold medals in quality, explaining how they speed the product to market cycle, eliminate defects, or achieve important goals.

These various efforts have contributed to Motorola's success in markets, but the real test of Motorola's commitment to them is that training investments continued to increase in 1996 and 1997 even in the face of slower sales growth for Motorola products. Motorola has retained plans to double its education efforts, intending that all employees will study 80–100 hours a year at company expense by the year 2000. According to the head of Motorola University, this education will help workers exercise the type of inventiveness and adaptability needed to compete worldwide, but the problem is time. Many Motorola employees already work 60-hour weeks, and the question is 'How do we stay competitive without killing everybody' (Grant, 1995)?

Sources: Adapted from Grant, Linda. (1995, May 22). A school for success: Motorola's ambitious job-training program generates smart profits. *US News and World Report*, 118(20), 53–56; Himelstein, Linda. (1997, Feb 17). Breaking through. *Business Week*, pp. 64-70; Motorola sponsor. (1996). p. 1, http://www.mot.com/sponsor; Robinson, John W. (1991). Updating and optimizing Adam Smith. In Mary Ann Smith and Sandra J. Johnson (Eds), *Valuing differences in the workplace*, pp. 81–83. Alexandria, VA: American Society for Training and Development.

PART I   LABOR GLOBALIZATION

The previous chapter reviewed three aspects of economic globalization: trade in goods and services, foreign direct investments, and global capital. This chapter looks at the fourth dimension of economic globalization: labor. As was true for other segments of the global economy, global labor is difficult to describe, measure, and compare. Job creation, human and job migration, and national education and organizational training are a few universal challenges for managing human capital in a global economy, but managers necessarily respond to these challenges with incomplete information since globalization is in its infancy. Within the firm, these global challenges translate into business-level concerns about working conditions, wage rates, and worker participation in corporate governance (Applebaum and Henderson, 1995), and to challenges of hiring from a global labor pool. The chapter opens with a look at features of work on a global scale, including demographics of the global labor force, types of employment, sectoral employment, and work hours, compensation, conditions, inequities, and unemployment.

GLOBAL WORK
Demographics of the global labor force

According to 1995 World Bank statistics (Twice the workers, 1995), the global workforce numbers 2.5 billion men and women between ages 15 and 64, an increase of 100% over 1965. Only 380 million workers live in high-income countries, and in 1993, 1.4 billion lived in countries with annual per capita incomes below $695. Many of the latter work in unpaid or underpaid jobs in the agricultural sector or at home. Additional information on the global workforce appears in Figure 6.1, which shows that most of the world's workers are employed in the agricultural sector, fewer in services, and far fewer in industrial production. The following look at this global labor force demonstrates variation in where and how people work.

Views of laborers

Like capital and equipment, labor traditionally has been viewed as a productive factor. A dominant concern among firms has been to maximize labor productivity in the same ways that capital and equipment productivity are maximized. Managerial interests in efficiency throughout most of the twentieth century have stimulated labor standardization schemes, but these are not universally applicable today. For example, as demands increase for high-quality and low-price goods, there also is a growing need for variations in offerings. These variations prevent universal standardization of factory labor, although

312

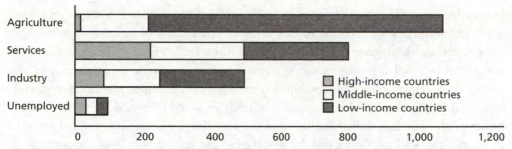

Agriculture
Services
Industry
Unemployed

High-income countries
Middle-income countries
Low-income countries

0   200   400   600   800   1,000   1,200

Note: Data are projected for 1995 from a sample of countries from each income group.

FIGURE 6.1 *The world's labor force by sector and country income level* (Twice the workers – and twice the productivity. (1995, Aug./Oct.). *World Bank Policy Research Bulletin*, 6(4): 1, after World Bank. (1995). *World Development Report 1995*. New York: Oxford University Press).

mechanization and improved machine technologies are making it more efficient to retool for smaller, more specialized production in batches. Growth in service industries also creates needs that are difficult to standardize. For example, services like credit card trans-actions, airlines, travel routes, or health care are by definition unique for most customers, and these variations make it difficult to create 'rules' for how to provide these services. Even if it were possible to create rules to cover any contingency, there would doubtless be too many for people to remember. Additionally, success in providing services is diffi-cult to prescribe because it incorporates intangibles like warmth, sincerity, or personal concern. Finally, unlike production work that can be measured in a quantitative sense, it is difficult to measure service productivity. Thus, quality concerns for products and services have made it more difficult to standardize human inputs and to measure human outputs. With these factors in mind, it becomes easier to understand why labor is diffi-cult to describe in a global world.

PHYSICAL LABOR

Scientific management systems identified the 'one best way' to exploit and measure manufacturing productivity, allocating decisions to managers who organized work. Although the systems for winning compliance differ, consensus-style Japanese manage-ment systems and co-determination in Western Europe both tend to involve workers more in work decisions than has the US system.

KNOWLEDGE-BASED LABOR

As industrial economies shift economic reliance from primarily production to greater reliance on services, human knowledge becomes an important component of work. In the Information Age, the knowledge component of labor has become critical for many firms and many newly recognize that every organizational participant can contribute to the knowledge base. Scientific management made no such assumptions. Managers set standards and workers were expected to follow them. The success of Japanese-style management systems and co-determination in Western Europe led US firms to adapt in the 1970s and 1980s by involving manufacturing workers in business issues, using techniques like quality circles and concepts like total quality management. Traditional animosity between labor and management in the US made it difficult for workers to view these changes in a positive light, but they did show that employee knowledge was an underutilized resource in many organizations. To rectify this imbalance, and to satisfy growing organizational demand for information, the focus has now shifted such that workers worldwide are increasingly viewed as sources of knowledge, once considered the exclusive preserve of managers.

The important and growing role knowledge plays in organizations makes it more difficult to describe the global workforce along boundaries that emphasize divisions like management/labor, blue-collar factory workers/white-collar managers/pink-collar clerical workers, or brawn/knowledge workers. In a globalizing world, labor assumes some amount of management roles, generalists and specialist skills are needed from many, and knowledge is a critical component of almost any job. For individuals, blurring boundaries and shifts are exemplified by the growing demand for people to manage projects and people, for managers to empower and lead, for leaders with vision and an eye to detail. Growing awareness of world pressures to be many things at the same time creates similar conditions worldwide that include demands for increased productivity, managing self and others individually and in teams, and a growing sense that someone, somewhere wants your job. These pressures were exemplified by Motorola concerns that workers already working long hours may find it difficult to invest additional time in themselves and in learning. These examples suggest that traditional boundaries of employment that once seemed clear within nations now are less so as organizations and work conditions respond to global business priorities. The review of work conditions to follow demonstrates the parameters of work found throughout the world.

Formal and informal work sectors

In many developing and transitional economies, many, if not most, economic activities are not reported officially. This work is part of the informal work sector – part of a 'gray,' 'shadow', or underground economy where work is performed for cash or barter for food, shelter, and other basics. Throughout history, some work has traditionally been underreported, e.g., agricultural labor, or unreported, e.g., crime. However, according to a study reported by *The Economist* (Light on the shadows, 1997), Linz University professor Friedrich Schneider's recent examination of unreported economic activity in advanced economies showed that the shadow economy in these nations has grown three times as fast as the reported economy since 1960. There are several reasons for the rapid pace of growth in the shadow economy in advanced economies, including high tax rates on individuals and organizations, the changing structure of advanced economies from manufacturing to service industries, and growing regulation of labor and markets. High tax burdens may discourage individuals from declaring earnings, and intangible services make it hard for the government to count productivity or pay. Finally, constraints on labor or on markets may encourage people to operate outside the legal work sector. For example, bans on evening or Sunday sales encourage Germans to shop at open-air, cash-dependent markets; government restrictions on imports create product demands often satisfied in Asia with night markets; and bureaucratic hurdles that make it difficult to obtain US work permits may induce illegal immigration. The latter forces workers to operate outside government mechanisms such as social security, insurance, and taxes, but also forces many into low-pay jobs where there are few safety precautions and little job protection for workers.

Whether the result of legal or illegal activity, and whether occurring in advanced or developing economies, wages are lower and working hours longer in the informal sector than in the formal sector (Bosch, Dawkins, and Michon, 1993, p. 18). In developing economies, most labor is performed in the informal sector, usually as self-employment or service labor (Dicken, 1992). Because the informal sector is neither organized nor monitored, it is impossible to determine wages, work hours, or other conditions of work. However, some inferences can be made: the relative size of the informal sector is greatest in developing economies; it is populated primarily with women, children and illegal immigrants; and the actual number of hours worked by people in developing economies is vastly under-reported. For example, the UN estimates that women's unpaid work amounted to $11 trillion in 1995. These underestimates of actual productivity thereby understate overall and comparative economic and social health of developing economies and thus of the world. A different picture of world economic productivity would doubtless emerge if unpaid work were included in national accounting systems like GDP. For example, $11 trillion in women's unpaid labor alone would boost world GDP to $40 trillion.

Although the amount of unpaid labor is high, paid labor is growing in its centrality to most economies and many lives. Transitions to market economies, the perceived importance of economic wealth, and the growing number of women in the formal work sector are three major sources of expansion in the paid global labor market. Interestingly, the size of the labor force is shrinking in the industrialized countries, where low birth rates and longevity have reduced the working population, and growing in the developing world, where population growth is greatest. In China, over 45% of the 1996 population was under age 26. The expanding role of paid labor is drawing worldwide attention to variations in work conditions, and to reasons for differences in compensation, work hours, and other employment factors. A look at these variations provides a context for understanding why global businesses are under scrutiny today. The following analysis necessarily examines work in the formal sector, but in view of unreported informal labor and variable reports on work in the formal sector, information provided should be considered more as a general guideline or range than a definitive statement of global work activities. The flaws with these data make it difficult for business managers to plan, but we recognize that one challenge of globalization is to work with incomplete data under conditions of uncertainty.

WORK IN THE FORMAL LABOR
Work in business organizations
Multinational firms employ only about 3% of the global labor force, including 61 million employed in the industrialized countries and 12 million in the developing economies. In the developing economies, only 15% of an estimated 1.4 billion workers have wage contracts, and most of them work in urban industrial firms and in service employment. The tourism industry is a particularly big employer of wage workers in the developing economies because hotels and restaurants require many workers, for greeting, cleaning, and maintenance jobs, and most of them are unskilled. In the middle-income economies (those that are neither rich nor poor) 46% of the working population of 660 million work in industrial and service employment. Finally, among the rich industrial nations, paid labor is concentrated primarily in service industries. Industrial work comprises only 27% of paid labor in the rich, industrialized nations where 60% of the labor force are in service industries; they number 218 million. These figures suggest that there is tremendous room for industrial job growth in the developing economies, whereas the industrialized economies have greatest demand for service work. Although service work often is viewed as low-wage labor for enterprises like restaurants or hotels, it is important to recognize that professions like accounting, consulting, engineering, medicine, teaching, and computing also are part of the service sector. It is these jobs that are contributing most to service growth in the industrial economies. In summary, few work for the MNEs about which we know most, and most work for small, family- or privately owned enterprises about which we know little. Yet, as we have seen in Chapter 3 and will see again later in this chapter, pressures on the larger multinational enterprises are also creating pressures on smaller firms to conform to global employment standards. Although most of these smaller firms have limited reach beyond their own geographic area, their operations are nevertheless being shaped by global actions to improve labor conditions.

Work in not-for-profit organizations
Businesses are not the only entities that provide jobs or otherwise engage in business activities, and worldwide there is an increase in the number of paid and unpaid jobs generated outside the business sector. This includes the governmental sector, as well as not-for-profit

organizations. The impact this has on business policy and practice is that organizations other than those in the business sector now shape the dialogue for organizational purpose and employee action. According to *The emerging sector* (Salamon and Anheier, 1994), the nonprofit sector is a major economic force in seven countries studied that range from the highly industrialized US and UK to agriculture-based Ghana and India. In these seven countries, the nonprofit sector employs 11.8 million workers, accounts for one out of every 20 jobs, one out of eight service jobs, and provides operating expenditures of $601.6 billion US (472.6 billion ECU) – the equivalent of 5 percent of the countries' GDP. More-over, employment in the nonprofit sector in these study countries exceeded the combined employment of the largest private company in each country. Because they are not estab-lished to earn profits and are more likely established to meet social needs, these firms are far more likely to accommodate persons rather than seek short-run efficiencies when selecting, developing, and retaining employees. Given the numbers reported above, the first job for many is likely to be in a nonprofit organization, and experiences there may establish expected standards for work carried into later jobs in for-profit firms.

Hours of work

According to Bosch, Dawkins, and Michon (1993), 'agreement on international working standards were reached within the framework of the ILO [the Geneva-based International Labor Organization is part of the UN] after the First World War and in the first decades after the Second World War' (p. 1). Although few countries officially ratified the various ILO conventions on work hours, vacations, or working age, by the 1960s most of the industrialized countries (except Japan – see Box 6.1) adopted laws for a standard working week of 40 or slightly more hours per week. These laws or statutory limits often are not observed in practice. For this reason, the European Union adopted a working-hours direc-tive in 1993 that outlined limits for work hours, holidays, breaks, rest periods, and shift work. This was deemed important because statutory limits and actual hours worked varied widely within EU nations, and these variations made it difficult for firms to harmonize work hours in plants throughout the EU. For example, in the Netherlands the statutory limit for hours worked in a week is 50, but people there work less than 35 hours on average; the statutory limit in Greece is 40 hours, but actual work weeks are closer to 45. These differences create inefficiencies for firms intending to operate in both Greece and the Netherlands and made the EU less seamless than promised. The 1993 EU directive set a maximum of 48 hours in the work week, requires one complete day of rest per week, and ruled that annual holidays must be four weeks starting in 1999.

Cross-national comparisons of work hours per week can be deceptive since they do not reflect total number of weeks worked per year. For example, vacation benefits usually are five to six weeks in Europe but only one to two weeks in the US and Japan.

Additionally, mandated holidays and the number of free days vary from a 1995 low of 5 paid holidays in the US to 10 holidays and 11 free days in Italy. Accordingly, yearly working averages may provide a more accurate comparative measure of differences in national work practices.

BOX 6.1:   JAPAN'S HARD-WORKING WORKERS

Japanese workers are granted as little as one paid week vacation per year, but even at that, many workers do not use their vacation days. The Japanese government compensates for this behavior by creating national holidays; they now have more national public holidays than any other industrialized country, including Children's Day, Ocean Day, Becoming Adult Day, and Vernal Equinox Day.

Source: Sapsford, Jathon. (1994, Nov. 29). What about taking a day off to think up another day off? *The Wall Street Journal*, p. B1.

A longitudinal examination of yearly work averages reveals that industrialization reduced the annual average hours of work over time. In 1870, work hours per person totaled just under 3,000 hours for most people in what are now industrialized economies. By 1979, annual hours worked per person in those economies were almost halved, ranging from a high of 2,129 hours per year in Japan to a low of 1,451 in Sweden.

By 1995, the average working hours per year in the Netherlands was 1,400 hours, Germany was 1,649 hours, US workers toiled an average of 1,904 hours, Japanese workers averaged 1,888 hours as compared to much higher 1992 figures for the Sudan (2,374), Zambia (2,250), Peru (2,218), India (2,164), and Venezuela (2,042) (*World Labour Report*, 1994, p. 108). In many developing economies the work week absorbs almost all waking hours throughout the year. In the following section, we look at work hours in developing economies and look at some of the reasons for differences in number of hours worked.

As compared to the industrialized world, normal working hours in developing economies are longer on a weekly and annual basis. Many developing economies permit long work days and work weeks of $5\frac{1}{2}$ to 6 days are typical. Reasons are the absence of regulations specifying otherwise, individual efforts to increase revenue, and family need to work long hours to meet subsistence level needs. Examples from the *World Labour Report* (1994) in Table 6.1 illustrate the differences between working hours in the developed and the developing world. Based primarily on studies of developed economies, Bosch, Dawkins, and Michon (1993) observed several trends in work hours prior to 1990:

TABLE 6.1   Normal working time in the manufacturing sector, 1992

Country	Hours worked per week	Annual days leave	Normal annual hours worked
Bolivia	43	15	2007
Colombia	48	15	2189
Germany	37	30	1667
India	48	17	2164
Nepal	48	17	2184
New Zealand	40	15	1880
Portugal	42	22	1898
Romania	40	15	1911
Sudan	48	5	2374
Switzerland	41	24	1865
Tunisia	40	5	1968
United Kingdom	39	25	1777
United States	40	12	1912
Zambia	45	5	2250

Source: World Labour Report. (1994). Geneva: ILO. Based on selected data found in Table VI. Real wages and hourly compensation costs, and working time, p. 108.

1 white collar workers work fewer hours than blue collar workers;
2 male dominated white collar sectors like banking, finance, insurance, and real estate, have shorter working hours than female dominated sectors like retail and blue collar sectors like manufacturing;
3 the overall pattern has been toward fewer working hours, but greater variations between countries suggest that harmonization is less;
4 in all countries reviewed there was a 20 year increase in part-time work explained mainly by women's workforce participation;
5 lifelong working hours are highest in Japan and the US and lowest in Western Europe where collective bargaining and government regulations limit work time.

Economic integration in many developing economies is expected to move jobs from the informal to the formal sector where hours and other conditions of work are more easily observed. World sentiment is toward standardization of humane work conditions, and global firms are under pressure to play a role in establishing those conditions. These dual pressures should cause working hours to fall in economies where work hours currently are more than 40 hours per week.

FULL- VS PART-TIME WORK

Growing female labor-force participation is one factor fueling growth in part-time work, but other factors such as inability to find full-time work and personal choice also affect the amount of time individuals work. In the industrialized economies, full-time work has dropped in the last 15 years with fully 23.8% of British workers and 21.4% of Japanese workers describing their jobs as part-time. In the developing world, part-time employment also is high, fueled by limited numbers of jobs in the paid labor force. Some patch together a living by working two and even three part-time jobs because they cannot find suitable full-time work.

Compensation

Compensation has three components. The first component is direct pay or the amount an employee receives as an hourly or salary wage. Managers typically are paid a salary and are expected to work as many hours as necessary to complete their jobs; laborers are more frequently paid an hourly rate, receiving additional pay per hour of overtime work. In the US, pay typically is about 70% of annual compensation, but in other countries the reverse is more nearly true. A second component of compensation is incentives such as profit sharing or bonuses. In some sectors and many nations, bonus pay represents a significant portion of annual pay. Top US managers, for example, can earn millions in annual bonuses. In Singapore, Indonesia, and Thailand salaried workers typically receive a thirteenth month of pay as an annual bonus, and a vacation bonus is typical in Western Europe. In Mexico, workers must be paid for 365 days a year; they expect a month's pay premium at Christmas, an 80% monthly bonus in addition to paid vacation time, and a year-end bonus based on punctuality. These examples show the mix of direct and bonus pay can vary widely from country to country. Finally, the third component of compensation is benefits or indirect pay in the form of health insurance, educational rebates, vacations, holidays, and the like. Total compensation per hour varies across the world and in ways we might expect: advanced economies pay more compensation per hour than developing economies. Specifics appear in Table 6.2, which shows that highest compensation worldwide in 1995 paid for manufacturing jobs was in Germany, where hourly cash and benefits averaged $31.88, as compared to $17.20 in the US, $5.82 in Taiwan, $1.59 in Malaysia, 30 cents in Indonesia, and 25 cents in India. Table 6.2 also shows how relative wage rates changed between 1985 and 1995. For example, the US offered the world's highest manufacturing wage rate in 1985 but was fourth behind Germany, Japan, and France by 1995. By 1997, relative wage rates had changed yet again. According to Morgan Stanley figures reported in *The Wall Street Journal* (The outlook, 1998), average manufacturing wages declined in many industrialized nations between 1995 and 1997, but they increased in the US from $17.19 to $18.17 per hour. Over the same period, declines were evident in Germany where hourly wages went from $31.85 to $27.81; Japan where they went from $23.66 to $19.01; and France which saw an hourly wage decline from $19.34 to $16.91.

For managers benefits also can include perquisites or 'perks' like cellular telephones,

TABLE 6.2   Hourly compensation worldwide

| | Hourly labour costs in manufacturing ($) | |
	1985	1995
Germany	9.60	31.88
Japan	6.34	23.66
France	7.52	19.34
United States	13.01	17.20
Italy	7.63	16.48
Canada	10.94	16.03
Australia	8.20	14.40
Britain	6.27	13.77
Spain	4.66	12.70
South Korea	1.23	7.40
Singapore	2.47	7.28
Taiwan	1.50	5.82
Hong Kong	1.73	4.82
Brazil	1.30	4.28
Chile	1.87	3.63
Poland	NA	2.09
Hungary	NA	1.70
Argentina	0.67	1.67
Malaysia	1.08	1.59
Mexico	1.59	1.51
Czech Republic	NA	1.30
Philippines	0.64	0.71
Russia	NA	0.60
Thailand	0.49	0.46
Indonesia	0.22	0.30
China	0.19	0.25
India	0.35	0.25

Source: Sliding scales. (1996, Nov. 2). *The Economist*, p. 17, using data from Morgan Stanley.

chauffeurs, housing allowances, or similar inducements. As was true for salaries and bonuses, benefits vary widely on a global basis. For example, US CEOs earn about 160 times more than the average worker in their firms, but Japanese CEOs only earn about 10–20 times more than the average in their firms. Table 6.3 and Figure 6.2 illustrate this point. Table 6.3 compares what an engineer earns in salary, benefits, and perquisites in six nations, showing considerable worldwide variation. Figure 6.2 looks only at salary comparisons for laborers, managers, top managers, and CEOs in seven nations to show the same pattern of wage gaps between workers and top managers, but it also shows a much greater gap between higher and lower paid managers in the US than elsewhere. This gap illustrates why US managers are motivated to work hard to get to the hierarchical peak of their organizations; the payoffs are quite astounding.

A comparison among these few nations shows that total compensation varies widely along multiple dimensions. Other sources identify several universals. Wages are higher

	Britain	Canada	France	Germany	Italy	Japan	USA
Manufacturing	$26,084	$34,935	$30,019	$36,857	$31,537	$34,263	$27,606
White-collar	$74,761	$47,231	$62,279	$59,916	$58,262	$40,990	$57,675
Managerial	$162,190	$132,877	$190,353	$145,626	$219,573	$185,437	$159,575
CEO	$439,441	$416,066	$479,772	$390,933	$463,009	$390,723	$717,237

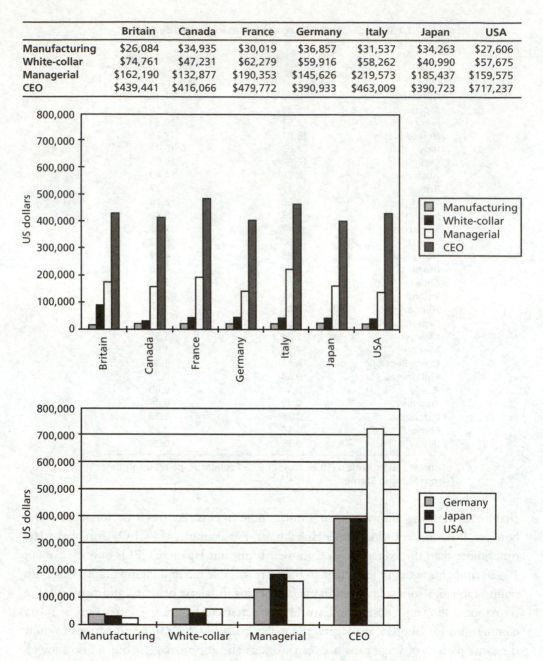

FIGURE 6.2 *Comparative compensation* (Bennett, Amanda. (1992, Oct. 12). Managers' incomes aren't worlds apart. *The Wall Street Journal*, p. B1).

TABLE 6.3 Engineering compensation

Nation	Pay[a] (US dollars)	Bonus	Vacation days	Holidays	Perquisities[b]
Belgium	35,000	3 weeks salary	4 weeks	12	Car, phone, possible expense account
Britain	25,000	Christmas bonus	3–5 weeks	8–12	Car, phone
Hungary	10,000	Not expected	3 weeks	8	Car, hard currency, travel abroad
Japan	30,000	$1/2$–2 times salary	2 weeks	20	Transportation, expenses
South Korea	19,000	Spring, fall, New Year bonus	3 days	19	Car pool or car; expense account
US	32,000	Not usual	2 weeks	9	None except for top managers

[a] For an electrical engineer.
[b] For managers and often salespeople.
Source: Cronin, M.P. (1992, Apr.). A globetrotting guide to managing people. *Inc. Magazine*, 56(3):122.

in the industrialized world than in the developing economies; they are higher for dominant groups than for women and minority groups; in the manufacturing sector they are rising in the developing economies and falling in the industrial economies; knowledge workers earn premiums throughout the world. Support for these perspectives appear below.

WAGES ARE HIGHER IN THE INDUSTRIALIZED WORLD THAN IN THE DEVELOPING ECONOMIES

In the manufacturing sector, highest hourly wages are found in the industrialized countries and lower wages are more usual for developing countries. Table 6.4 compares wages in the global textile industry, and it shows significant hourly wage differentials between textile industry workers in the developed and the developing economies. For example, in 1992 a Danish textile worker was compensated at 28.71 Deutschmarks per hour as compared to .42 Deutschemarks per hour for a worker in Vietnam's textile industry. This table further shows that except for Hong Kong and Taiwan, textile workers in the developing world earn less than 10% of wages for similar work in Denmark, Germany, or northern Italy. Hourly wages (including non-wage costs) for all sectors in 1994 averaged highest for West Germany ($27.29) as compared to $17.10 in the US, $14 in Britain, and $5 in Mexico and Hong Kong. Indonesian workers averaged $.23 per hour.

WAGES ARE HIGHER FOR MEN THAN FOR WOMEN AND MINORITY GROUPS OF MEN OR WOMEN

Women are paid less for their work than men almost universally. Some part of wage differentials for women and men can be attributed to the following factors:

TABLE 6.4   Hourly wage comparisons in the international clothing industry, 1992

Economy	Average hourly wage including social costs	
	Deutschmarks	Index[a] (%)
Developed economies		
Austria	18.14	66
Denmark	28.71	105
France	15.81	58
Germany[b]	27.30	100
Italy (North)	27.77	102
Italy (South)	18.53	68
Portugal	6.00	22
Spain	10.44	38
Switzerland	25.06	92
Turkey	5.50	20
United Kingdom	13.77	50
United States	11.92	44
Developing economies		
Dominican Republic	0.94	3
Hong Kong	5.25	19
India	0.52	2
Jamaica	1.27	5
Malaysia	1.44	5
Mexico (United States-border)	2.53	9
Morocco	1.81	7
Sri Lanka	1.54	6
Taiwan	5.74	21
Tunisia	2.66	10
Vietnam	0.42	2
Central and Eastern Europe		
Former Czechoslovakia	1.72	6
Estonia	0.96	4
Poland	1.87	7
Slovenia	3.33	12

[a] Germany = 100.
[b] Including only the western states of the Federal Republic of Germany.
Source: Adapted from *World Investment Report*. (1994). New York: UN, UNCTAD, p. 207, after Jungknickel, Rolf. (1994). Globalization and the international division of labor: The role of technology and wage costs. In W. Sengenberger and D. Campbell (eds), *New international division of labour: Globalization and the localization of work*. Geneva: International Institute for Labour Studies.

1 Women dominate part-time work.
2 Women take temporary absences from work to care for family members and accumulate fewer years of work experience.
3 Women are concentrated in agriculture, sales, and other sectors where pay is traditionally low.
4 Women are subject to wage discrimination.

Among the 10 nations the UN rated high on gender equity (*Human Development Report*, 1995), equitable wages have not been achieved for women. The female-to-male weekly wage ratio ranged from 80–90% in Australia, Denmark, France, New Zealand, Norway, and Sweden; other countries in Western Europe had ratios of roughly 65–75%. Women in the US earn about 63% of what men earn for comparable work, and in Japan the figure is about 61%. In the US, the annual median income reported for female managers who were white, African-American, and Latino was less than that paid to white male managers; the respective figures were 64%, 65%, and 61% earnings as compared to white male managers. Increased availability of this information and political activity favoring equity suggests that organizations worldwide will be expected to correct apparent pay inequities.

Female entrepreneurs

Many women who face pay inequities or other barriers to paid work are establishing their own businesses. In industrialized nations, female entrepreneurs have created small to large service and manufacturing firms, but in the developing economies women more typically create small businesses, some of which are so small they are known as 'micro'-enterprises. These small enterprises range from services to manufacturing and they often employ only a few people. At the same time, they often alleviate family poverty and provide a mechanism for many to move from the informal to the paid work sector.

Initial funding for many businesses established by women in developing economies originally came from voluntary organizations like the Grameen Bank, Women's World Banking and Accion International, and self-help entities established to improve women's lives by lifting them and their families out of poverty. Inspired by the success of these organizations, more established entities like the World Bank and other lending institutions and the US Agency for International Development also have begun loaning small amounts of money to female entrepreneurs. The overall findings are that women are better at repaying loans than are men and less likely to waste or loot development money. Further, women also are critical in the fight against poverty because they use their earnings to fund education for their children, to provide health care for family members, and to maintain the home. Thus, these entrepreneurs provide a bridge to development not only with the businesses they create but in how they use the profits from business and in how their lives are used. According to *The Wall Street Journal* (Carrington, 1994), studies of loans to female entrepreneurs in developing economies yielded the following findings:

- A World Bank study in the Ivory Coast found that its project to introduce more effective farming methods was run by men and for men with few results, perhaps because women did most of the agricultural work. When women were provided with the funds, the response was positive and yielded crop increases.

- A UN program called Unifem extended credit to women in small silk-weaving businesses that gave young women an alternative to earning income as sex workers.
- CARE, Niger, helped establish women's savings groups because lending institutions typically do not lend to women. Members of the groups each contribute small amounts of money weekly that are then loaned to members. For example, some borrowers might buy seed for planting. The loans are repaid with interest, creating a larger loan pool for subsequent borrowers.

In Russia, where 75% of the unemployed are women, business loans have been critical to helping women join the paid labor force. By mid-1997 women had received about half of the $300 million the European Bank for Reconstruction and Development had thus far loaned, using this money to establish businesses. Their successes have not only provided work and stimulated local economies, but also attracted loans from for-profit venture capital and banking enterprises. In some cases, the small firm grows to become a successful, large enterprise. For example, in 1992 Russian entrepreneurs Tatyana Zeleranskaya and Irina Koroleva launched a successful FM radio station in Moscow, creating a homey atmosphere by playing music by Russian bands, focusing on family and health issues rather than politics, and offering call-in shows. By 1997, the station was the eighth largest in Russia with an estimated 2 million listeners each 19-hour day (Kiskovsky and Williamson, 1997). The technology of micro-enterprise loaning to the poor pioneered in El Salvador, Bangladesh, the Dominican Republic, and other nations also has found its ways to industrialized nations with similar effects. In the US, micro-business lending programs and training for women and the poor are credited with stimulating local and regional development, even helping some escape from welfare rolls. In February 1997, the US held a Microcredit Summit further to explore the benefits of microbusiness lending as a means of alleviating poverty. Although lending for micro-enterprises initially stimulated growth in agricultural, and arts and crafts industries, the concept has expanded to include services such as telecommunications. For example, in 1997 Muhammad Yunus, the founder of Grameen Bank, funded a project with partner businesses from Norway, Japan, and the US to put at least one cellular telephone in each of Bangladesh's 65,000 villages by 2003. This service not only provides a means of outside communication for the poor, but also alleviates surging demand for the government to install new telephone lines. Villager Laili Begun was one of the first to try this experiment. She borrowed $430 for a cellular phone which she repays at about $3.50 per week from profits generated on calls charged at about 10 cents per minute that cost her about 8 cents (Saeed, 1997). Yunus himself established his bank with a $26 personal loan in 1977 but by 1998 was loaning nearly $500 million a year to poor people worldwide and enjoying a 98% repayment rate. Almost 95% of these loans are granted to women, a practice initially resisted in Pakistan but later embraced (Batsell, 1998).

WAGES ARE RISING AND FALLING ON A RELATIVE SCALE

Wages in the manufacturing sector are rising in the developing economies. This is a direct result of economic growth in those nations fueled by changes in government policies, trade output, and increased FDI. Where exports have risen rapidly, wages also have increased by 3% per year (Twice the workers, 1995). The rapid job and wage growth in developing nations is offset by slow to no growth in manufacturing wages in the industrialized world. Among G-7 countries, real growth rates of total compensation per employee fell from 2.5% between 1961 and 1978 to 1% between 1988 and 1994 (*World Economic and Social Survey*, 1995, p. 235).

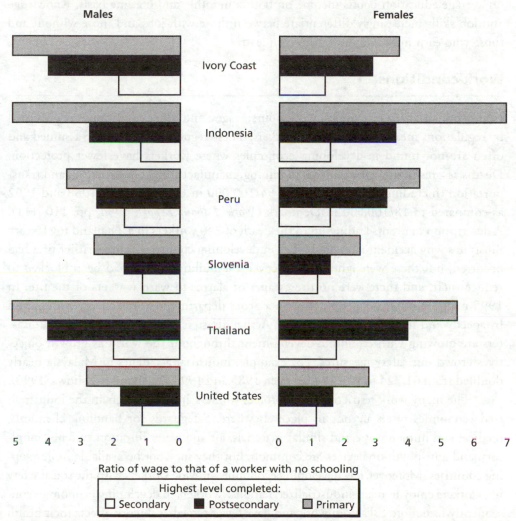

Note: Wage premiums to education for male and female workers. Ratios are derived from statistical estimates that control such variables as age. Data are for 1986 except Thailand (1988–9) and Slovenia and United States (1991).

FIGURE 6.3 *By how much does education raise wages?* (*Human Development Report.* (1995). p. 39. New York: Oxford University Press).

EDUCATED WORKERS EARN PREMIUMS THROUGHOUT THE WORLD
Skilled workers in the industrialized world now earn about 60 times more than the world's poorest group of Sub-Saharan African farmers (*World Development Report*, 1995). Worldwide, there is a positive relationship between education and wages, although the magnitude of this relationship varies. Educated workers command higher premiums with high labor demand and low supply, and lower rewards are available where higher education is the norm. For example, Figure 6.3 shows that in the US, where educated workers are fairly abundant, the return to education is lower than in Thailand, where educated workers are scarce and demand is high. Nevertheless, according to the US Census Bureau, on average education boosts income on both a monthly and lifetime basis. Knowledge and job skills increasingly differentiate between those with jobs and those without and those who earn most and those who earn least.

Work conditions

In the industrialized economies, work hours, wages, and other conditions are governed by regulations meant to protect the workers. These regulations cannot be assumed and often are not found in developing economies where workers have fewer protection. Deaths as a result of work accidents in mining, manufacturing, construction, and transportation (including commuting) were 94/100,000 in Egypt between 1988 and 1992 as compared to 18/100,000 in Denmark (*World Labour Report*, 1994, pp. 110–111). A description of events leading up to the death of 240 workers in a Thailand toy factory illustrates why accident rates are higher in developing countries. Three earlier fires had occurred, but these were ignored. Moreover, the building's exits had been blocked to reduce theft, and there were no fire escapes or alarms to warn workers of the fire. In 1995 many hundreds of people died in a Seoul department store collapse brought on by speedy and inadequate construction. Actual disasters like these and potential disasters are growing with economic development throughout the world as growth objectives crowd out safety measures. For example, industrial accidents in Malaysia nearly doubled from 61,724 to 121,104 between 1985 and 1990 (Thailand fire shows, 1993).

The many work restrictions that protect workers and consumers in the industrialized economies often are not in place elsewhere. Safeguards for handling chemicals, medical and human waste and similar materials, air and water filtration systems, monitors, and anti-pollution devices are common, but they may not be available in developing countries. Moreover, few developing economies provide workers with the social safety net workers enjoy in many industrialized nations. Workers in developing economies consequently face more risks from work and have fewer remedies if work affects their health or well-being. Workers in developing economies also are vulnerable to abuse from owners, managers, and co-workers, and corporal punishment, withheld wages, or verbal haranguing also have been reported to worker rights advocates.

Inequities

WORKING CHILDREN

Mandated schooling in the industrialized world decreased the numbers of children below 16 who work for pay, and there is a similar effect in the developing economies where schooling is universal and mandatory. In the absence of alternatives for children, where enforcement regulations against child labor are nonexistent or weak, or where economic pressures are high, children often work for pay or for food and shelter. The 1997 Oslo, Norway conference on child labor brought together organizations and individuals to create a global strategy against exploitation and abuse of an estimated 250 million working children worldwide. In 1993, the International Labor Organization (ILO) reported an increase among working children throughout the industrialized countries (An evil unbearable, 1993), but for the most part child labor occurs in developing economies. According to the United Nations Children's Fund (UNICEF), over one in four children between ages 5 to 14 works in developing economies, and many are not attending school (Experts work, 1997). Child laborers often work to contribute to family income, sometimes in factories but more often as independent laborers. Thousands of street children from Nairobi to Brazil and Turkey to India have little choice but to work. The ILO recognizes that children in many nations face limited choices but they nevertheless oppose child labor under three conditions: when it is a daily necessity that deprives the child of education and other social skills; when the work is dangerous, such as coal mines in Columbia, or tanneries in Cairo where chemical products are used; and when the work exploits the child, such as forced labor and debt bondage or the child prostitution found almost worldwide.

Child labor is frequent among children who have been uprooted by immigration, and children often are victims of enforced labor that violates ILO recommendations. In Thailand, 'child searchers' kidnap or buy children from poor families and put them up for sale to private households, restaurants, or factories; in the Dominican Republic, children are sent to work in sugar plantations as virtual slaves; in Brazil, poor rural families are encouraged to send their children to the city for high wages, but the children often are charged for travel and food expenses, make low wages, and enter a form of debt bondage.

Child labor has implications for global firms because many subcontractors hire children, particularly for consumer product industries like textiles, furniture, and athletic shoes. The global community then pressures global enterprises to be change agents. For example, 1997 work stoppages and a riot against PT Hardaya Aneka Shoe Industry, Indonesia and labor strikes against Vietnamese manufacturer Sam Yang focused not on these local firms but on the contractor, Nike. It was Nike Corporation that was in the news, Nike managers who hired Andrew Young, former US ambassador to the UN, to conduct a fact-finding mission to Nike subcontractors, and Nike managers who doubtless breathed a sigh of relief when the protests were settled. Based on these experiences, companies like Nike might be expected to impose stricter standards on subcontractors to prevent further bad press and thereby introduce standards more typical for advanced than developing economies. In the case of Nike, the firm has a labor-practices code, and this was reviewed to improve cultural sensitivity in plants where abuses were reported. Solutions to labor disputes often require creativity. According to Oxfam representative, Caroline Lequesne, an impact of retailers' human rights policies in Bangladesh has been that children displaced from textile work have little choice but to take dangerous jobs or prostitute themselves (Human rights, 1995). Levi Strauss adopted a role businesses usually do not play, and resolved this dilemma for a subcontractor by retaining under-age workers and paying them to attend an on-site school until they reached the legal working age of 14 (Zachary, 1994). Because it is more traditional for families or governments to fund education, Levi's example demonstrates that businesses in a global world are taking on roles less usual for the business sector. Having paid the educational costs for these children, Levi's assumed a responsibility that traditionally falls on families and/or the government sector.

WOMEN

Among those countries providing gender-based statistics, the United Nations annually reports that no country treats its women as well as it treats its men. The gender gap this represents is reflected in a 'Gender-related Development Index' (GDI) measuring 146 countries' achievements including comparable life expectancies, education, and income for men and women. The *Human Development Report* (1997) rates Canada tops in the GDI, followed by Norway, Sweden, Iceland, and the US. Among developing economies with high GDI scores are Barbados, Uruguay, Trinidad and Tobago, South Korea, Costa Rica, and Thailand. The 1997 report also contains a 'Gender Empowerment Measure' (GEM) that examines women's access to professional, economic, and political opportunities. According to the GEM ratings reported in 1997, Norway, Sweden, Denmark, and Finland were highest in providing these opportunities to women.

   Differential treatment for women includes poor access to basic safety, security, nutrition, or health care resources; unequal pay; and limited access to educational and promotional opportunities. Women in business worldwide frequently have limited access to professional and managerial jobs. In Europe, for example, women constitute 41% of the workforce, but hold only 29% of all managerial jobs, 2% of senior management jobs, and less than 1% of jobs on boards of directors (Out of the typing pool, 1996). There is evidence of some progress in the US: Table 3.6 above shows there are a growing number of female executives employed by US firms. A report on a Catalyst study (Women hold more seats, 1996) showed that women held 10.2% of corporate board seats on Fortune 500 firms in 1996 in the US (626 out of 6,123 seats). However, another report (Lublin, 1996) of a Catalyst study surveying 461 senior female managers and 325 male chief executives showed that more than 60% of women in management positions hold staff support positions in areas such as human resources management and public relations which traditionally do not offer potential advancement to top levels of management. In 1994, Aslanbeigui, Pressman, and Summerfield's collected review of economic transformations in developing economies of Eastern Europe, Asia, Latin America, and Africa concluded that in economic transformations studied 'women have been over-represented among the losers or under-represented among the winners' (p. 2). Nancy Adler and Dafna Izraeli's (1994) collected evidence of successful female managers from Asia, the Middle East, Africa, Europe, and North America demonstrates that, once allowed opportunity, women contribute to organizational successes.

MINORITY STATUS

Visible and invisible signs of diversity also are the basis for wage and work inequalities and other forms of discrimination. In the US, black Americans historically have had fewer educational or work opportunities than Caucasians, and the same is true for blacks in Brazil and South Africa. For example, although blacks and mixed color people represent 45% of Brazil's population, less than 1% enroll in the nation's largest public university. Over 50% of the unemployed in South Africa are native blacks, and among black Americans, particularly those concentrated in urban areas, as many as 30% are unemployed. Ethnic Chinese often own many resources but encounter discrimination throughout Southeast Asia; Indian shop owners are viewed with suspicion throughout Oceania; and in Japan there is discrimination against natives with Korean heritage. Anti-Turkish sentiment in Germany is largely a reaction to religious differences between Christians and Muslims that also pit the French against Algerian immigrants and British against Pakistanis. Members of these minority groups who then succeed also tend to be viewed more as an exception than as evidence that people given a chance will succeed. Self-made Japanese billionaire Masayoshi Son, founder of Softbank, is billed as the Japanese Bill Gates, but he is a member of Japan's Korean minority group. This example and the example of Sumitomo Bank of California (Box 6.2) show that minority groups often have an unrealized business potential for expanding the range of participation in business.

For organizations like Sumitomo Bank of California, the costs of real or perceived inequalities occur when people object to unequal treatment. These objections can come from individuals or from organizations. For example, a California advocacy group called the Greenlining Institute filed a complaint against Sumitomo of California citing lending practices and the makeup of the workforce. Many new workers are unwilling to be treated as second-class citizens in organizational or national life, and use legal or other means to retain ethnic or cultural identities. Failure to attend to a growing sense of group dignity and identity may be costly to organizations. An example from the US is the growing number of Equal Employment Opportunity (EEO) complaints coming from immigrants. These complaints entail both legal fees and time from human resource managers and other

---

BOX 6.2: SUMITOMO BANK OF CALIFORNIA

Chartered in California in 1925 to help Japanese immigrants, Sumitomo Bank of California expanded its niche during the 1980s to accommodate investors from Japan who wanted to participate in commercial real estate deals in California. But Sumitomo of California has faced challenges in attracting customers whose heritage is not Japanese. Located in a state known for its ethnic diversity, Sumitomo has faced increasing pressure to expand lending and hiring to Hispanic and African-American people. Barriers to success lie not only with the bank's past traditions but also with traditional practices and expectations among potential customers. An example is found in African-American branch manager Craig Samuels who is finding few customers in a predominantly black neighborhood. Visits to black business owners revealed that the Japanese-only image of the bank had created false beliefs, including assumptions that no one at the bank spoke English. Among existing Japanese-American customers, some wondered why a black man had been promoted to branch management, even calling for a replacement. For the bank and for Samuels, it becomes evident that replacing old assumptions is a barrier to creating businesses responsive to today's needs.

Source: Sharpe, Rochelle. (1996, Dec. 30). Stuck in a niche: Japanese bank in US built for one minority is pressed to aid another. *The Wall Street Journal*, pp. A1, A4.

personnel. In 1996 global firms Mitsubishi and Astra were accused of sexual harassment in the US, leading to legal action, and early in the 1990s Japanese women followed the lead of US women and refused to permit sexual harassment (*seku hara)* at work. Complaints against *seku hara* in Japan now total 400 per year as compared to zero prior to 1985, and many firms are writing new policies to outline expected behavior at work (Morrow, 1993). The International Labor Office reported in December 1992 that its survey of 23 nations revealed that between 15 and 30% of women said they had experienced sexual harassment at work. These examples illustrate that equity issues once contained within countries now have become global issues, and they frequently are played out in the workplace.

Unemployment

An economic downturn has its greatest effect on those employed in the formal sector. Self-employed workers, unpaid family workers, or independent workers may experience a slowdown or reduction in labor, but generally they remain employed (Comparable rates of unemployment, 1993). Comparative unemployment data in Table 6.5 show that unemployment is quite high in both the industrial and the developing economies. Unemployment rates are high in parts of Eastern Europe. Reported unemployment for 1994 was a low of 3.2% in the Czech Republic, 10.6% in Romania, 11.1% in Hungary, 13.4% in Bulgaria, 14.1% in Slovakia, and 16.9% in Poland. The rate of unemployment in EU countries in 1995 ranged from a low of 7.8% in Sweden to a high of 24.4% in Spain. These national averages can mask differential rates of unemployment within nations. Data from Australia, for example, showed that in May 1995 overall unemployment stood at 7.5% for people born in Australia; 7% for immigrants from predominantly English-speaking countries; and 12.2% for people from non-English-speaking backgrounds (Working nation, 1995).

The International Labor Organization expects unemployment to persist and even increase in many EU countries because job creation is on the decline in Europe. This is not to say that European firms are not creating jobs, but as we will see when we look at job migration, many of these firms are drawn to nations where labor costs are far lower than in Europe. Table 6.6 anticipates that job migration out of Europe will continue to produce unemployment. For example, by January 1997, German unemployment had risen to 12.2%, boosted by structural factors such as high taxes, high wages and regulations that make it difficult to fire employees once hired, by job migration to lower wage countries, and by growing productivity among retained workers.

TABLE 6.5   Unemployment rates

	Official unemployment rates (%) 1992
Spain	24.4[a]
Morocco	15.4
Sri Lanka	13.3
Belgium	12.7[a]
France	12.2[a]
Italy	11.9[a]
Germany	10[a]
Australia	9.5[a]
Netherlands	9.5[a]
UK	8.2[a]
Turkey	7.8
Egypt	6.9
Bolivia	5.8
US	5.8
Chile	4.4
Switzerland	3.8[a]
Japan	2.8[a]
South Korea	2.4

[a] Data for 1995 from *World Employment Report*. (1995). Geneva: ILO, UN; *ILO Yearbook of Labor Statistics*. (1992, 1993).

TABLE 6.6   High unemployment forecasts (%)

Country	1996	1997	2000
Spain	22	22	23.7
France	11	12	14.0
Italy	10.5	12.4	13.2
Belgium	9.4	13.7	11.8
Australia	7.6	8	11.7
Canada	9.4	9	11.5
UK	8.1	6.7	9.4
Germany	8.7	11.4	8.2
Netherlands	8.5	6.0	6.8
US	6.8	4.6	5.8
Japan	3.2	3.5	2.8
Switzerland	4.0	5.1	1.3

Source: forecast from Zachary, G. Pascal. (1995, Feb. 22). Study predicts rising global joblessness. *The Wall Street Journal*, p. A2, after *World Employment Report*. (1995). International Labor Organization: Geneva: ILO, UN. 1996 data from *World Economic Outlook*. (1995, Oct). p. 95. Washington, DC: IMF; 1997 estimates are derived from government reports published in business periodicals.

Two observations can be made about unemployment: in developing economies, unemployment is lowest in nations where economic integration and global participation rates are high; in the industrial economies, nations with comprehensive social security nets are those where unemployment persists.

In combination, these unemployment figures outline major global challenges. Job flight from the industrialized world has the potential to create a downward spiral as fewer workers support more welfare recipients. In many parts of the developing world, high population growth is outstripping job creation. To quote Dicken (1992, p. 423), the concern is in the question: 'Where will the jobs come from' to support the world? For many in the developing world, the answer is to follow jobs via migration.

GLOBAL MIGRATION

The sense of boundarylessness evident in the global economy also applies to labor. In a world with fewer boundaries, people physically move to find work. According to William Johnston (1997), growing demand for a skilled world labor force will have the following effects:

1 Women will enter the workforce in greater numbers, particularly in the developing economies that have traditionally absorbed few paid female workers.

2　The average age of the world workforce will rise, particularly in the industrialized nations that are producing few new workers.
3　Demand for skilled labor will increase the number of people worldwide with high school and university educations.

Johnston believes that nations demanding labor and those supplying labor can complement one another, but acknowledges that social impediments will offset economic imperatives to impede free flows of labor worldwide. When these flows are impeded, another approach to matching global supply and demand for labor has been for firms to relocate their operations abroad. In these cases, jobs migrate in search of labor. We will examine both forms of migration in the following section, then examine perspectives on each that illustrate advantages and disadvantages.

People in search of jobs

Migration of people has attracted most attention from those studying global labor forces. Both internal migration, like moving from the farm to the city, and external migration across national borders are fostered by economic aspirations and by conflict. Conflict is a growing reason for both internal and external migration. One in 130 persons in the world is a displaced person, and 80% of them are women and children. According to the UN High Commission on Refugees, violent ethnic conflict, atrocities, and persecution had made refugees of 50 million people by 1997. Most of these refugees are displaced persons within their own nations; their plight is particularly keen because no worldwide agency or international convention governs treatment of internal refugees, although several keep watch over refugee patterns between nations. The UN Council on Refugees, which monitors displaced persons leaving their own countries, reports that economic motives are the primary force behind immigration today. Over 23 million refugees fled their home countries in 1993 to seek opportunity in other countries; this is compared to 8 million global refugees in 1980.

According to a report by the Population Reference Bureau (Martin and Widgren, 1996), about 125 million people now live outside their country of birth or citizenship – this number is about equal to Japan's population of 122 million and it totals about 2% of the world's population. About half of these migrants settle in nations where industry is growing, and over a third are found in only seven of the world's most industrialized nations: Germany, France, the UK, the US, Italy, Japan, and Canada. According to Martin and Widgren, oil-rich nations also have attracted many migrants, and in the Middle East as much as 60–90% of the labor force are migrants. In the following sections, we explore how these migrants have been received as they relocate abroad.

IMMIGRATION TO WESTERN EUROPE

The number of economic immigrants has increased throughout Europe in the latter half of the twentieth century, particularly in the last 20 years. By 1985, the foreign-born population in Europe was 23 million, representing 4.7% of the total population (*World Development Report*, 1995). Immigrants to Western Europe, particularly from Africa, Asia, Eastern Europe, and Turkey, have arrived in large waves since 1985, increasing the international populations of many of these countries, and over 10 million 'non-Europeans' from the Middle East, Africa, the former Yugoslavia, and Russia now live in Western Europe (O'Mara, 1992). The direction of immigrant flows by 1992 is shown in Figure 6.4. By 1990, the foreign population as a percentage of total population was 5% in Austria and Sweden, 8% in Germany, and a whopping 16% in Switzerland. The children of immigrants in Western Europe comprised about 10% of the population of Europeans younger than 20, and this population was growing by about 400,000 per year (A generation at risk, 1990).

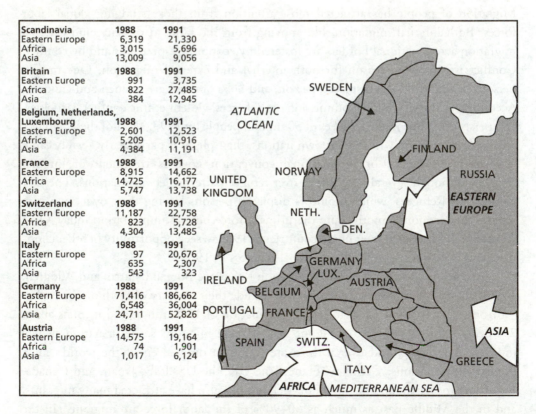

	1988	1991
Scandinavia		
Eastern Europe	6,319	21,330
Africa	3,015	5,696
Asia	13,009	9,056
Britain	**1988**	**1991**
Eastern Europe	991	3,735
Africa	822	27,485
Asia	384	12,945
Belgium, Netherlands, Luxembourg	**1988**	**1991**
Eastern Europe	2,601	12,523
Africa	5,209	10,916
Asia	4,384	11,191
France	**1988**	**1991**
Eastern Europe	8,915	14,662
Africa	14,725	16,177
Asia	5,747	13,738
Switzerland	**1988**	**1991**
Eastern Europe	11,187	22,758
Africa	823	5,728
Asia	4,304	13,485
Italy	**1988**	**1991**
Eastern Europe	97	20,676
Africa	635	2,307
Asia	543	323
Germany	**1988**	**1991**
Eastern Europe	71,416	186,662
Africa	6,548	36,004
Asia	24,711	52,826
Austria	**1988**	**1991**
Eastern Europe	14,575	19,164
Africa	74	1,901
Asia	1,017	6,124

FIGURE 6.4 *The immigrant waves reaching Europe: origins of asylum-seekers in Europe in 1988, before the Berlin Wall collapsed, and in 1991 (The Seattle Times.* (1992, Nov. 26). p. A3, using data from the United Nations High Commission for Refugees)

IMMIGRATION TO THE US

The US also has experienced a significant influx of immigrants in the last two decades. Immigrants represent about 8% of the population, and almost 8.8 million legal immigrants will be admitted to the US through the 1990s. Among the advanced economies, the US admits about half of all legal immigrants, and 85% are from developing economies. In contrast to earlier immigrant groups to the US who came primarily from Europe, recent immigrants to the US are principally from Mexico, Latin America, and Asia. Many of the latter are less inclined to become citizens than were earlier immigrant groups, although in the wake of anti-immigrant sentiment and federal rules barring welfare and other benefits to noncitizens, citizenship applications among immigrants jumped from about 300,000 in 1990 to an estimated 1.8 million for 1997.

IMMIGRATION TO OTHER INDUSTRIALIZED NATIONS

Labor shortages in industrializing countries like Japan and South Korea have attracted over two million men and women from East and Southeast Asia to these nations (Pura, 1992), and like immigrants to most of the industrialized world, they also are would-be laborers in search of economic and political opportunities.

IMMIGRATION TO DEVELOPING AND NEWLY DEVELOPED ECONOMIES

Inflows of foreign workers increased throughout the industrialized economies in the late 1980s and illegal immigrants have been granted amnesty in many countries, including the US, France, Italy, and Spain. The attention these and legal immigrants have drawn in the industrialized world might suggest that immigrant flow is in a single direction, but this is not the case. There are two main movements of economic immigrants: many move from the developing world to industrialized countries, but more than half of the global flow of migrants is now between developing economies. South Africa, Thailand, and Hong Kong are a few nations with net inflows of immigrants. As a percentage of population, foreign-born immigrants in 1985 were 34% of Gulf Cooperative Council states and 16% of Oceania (*Human Development Report*, 1995, p. 65). Following the 1994 elections in South Africa, some estimated that as many as two to eight million illegal immigrants were living there. Ethnic and tribal wars in East Africa encourage this, but many more arrive as economic immigrants to South Africa's relatively more buoyant economy. In Asia, economic immigrants find it relatively easy to cross national borders, legally and illegally. For example, in Kuala Lumpur most construction laborers are legal immigrants from India. The economic downturn in Malaysia beginning in 1997 halted some building projects and led to difficult decisions about how further to employ these Indian immigrants.

Demand for more knowledge workers also is increasing immigration into developing and newly developed economies. In South Korea, for example, the number of foreigners in white-collar jobs is growing rapidly to satisfy demands for world-class managers. Korean *chaebols* like LG and Samsung hire entry-level and executive managers, assigning them to Korea where they are expected to gain organizational experience useful in Korean subsidiaries throughout the world. The demand for foreign professionals in South Korea doubled in 1996, attracting scientists, researchers, professors, technicians, and language instructors (Foreign bodies in South Korea, 1996). In view of 1997 restructuring in South Korea, this demand may ease, but in the long run demand will increase because of gains made with restructuring.

FEMALE IMMIGRANTS

Many more immigrants than in the past are women. In 1996, about 50% of Asian overseas workers were women, up from less than 15% in 1976. Eighty percent of Sri Lankan overseas workers are women, most as housemaids in the Middle East. Reasons for women to become immigrants are limited opportunities in home countries; active family encouragement to send home hard currency earned abroad; and government facilitation of immigration to reduce job pressures in the home country. These female immigrants often are the victims of abuse (UN panel to tackle abuse, 1996). The Philippine Overseas Workers Welfare Administration reported receiving more than 10,000 complaints from overseas workers in 1994; most were from women reporting abuses from mistreatment to rape to virtual slavery (Wallace, 1995). Female migration also has the potential to increase immigrant birth rates in the host country since it is usually young women who migrate and many will marry or remain in host countries.

ILLEGAL IMMIGRATION

Illegal immigrants also have increased in numbers. US officials estimate 2,000 people per month transit through Bangkok alone to enter the US illegally; they come from Thailand, China, India, Pakistan, Bangladesh, Sri Lanka, and even Nigeria to work in US sweatshops and brothels. The $200 a month jobs they might have worked in in their own countries are then filled by illegals from Burma or China (Sherer, 1995). According to the International Centre for Migration Policy Development, about 300,000 people are smuggled into Europe each year. Many economic immigrants turn to organized crime to gain entry to other countries. Triads in Asia are responsible for illegally smuggling mainland Chinese to jobs all over the globe, and Mexican smugglers known as 'coyotes' charge their human cargo $300–600 US to cross the border into the US where work is available. The cost of transit often makes illegal immigrants virtual slaves in the informal sector.

RESPONSES TO IMMIGRANTS

Anti-immigrant sentiment is increasing almost worldwide, fueled by concerns over jobs and cultural identity. Unlike political immigrants of earlier decades, many economic immigrants plan to return to their home countries, and they are less likely to assimilate to the host culture. In Luxembourg, for example, over 30% of the total population of less than 400,000 are foreigners, including many Portuguese with hopes of returning to Portugal. Few of these immigrants speak local languages, and most eat at Portuguese restaurants, drink Portuguese wine, watch television soccer between Portuguese teams, and shop in Portuguese markets (Little Luxembourg, 1994). The borderless world of the EU that makes it possible to create a Portuguese section of Luxembourg also permits foreigners to vote, votes that could reshape the essential nature of the duchy.

Immigration is self-generating, with most immigrants settling where earlier immigrants paved the way (Simai, 1994). At least for the short term, this makes it easier for immigrants to adjust to their new lives, but may delay assimilation into a host culture. According to one source, fear of foreigners has replaced fear of the cold war in much of Western Europe (Newman, 1993), and many Western European countries have virtually closed their doors to immigrants and refugees. France instituted a near 'zero immigration' program; Denmark and Sweden instituted visa requirements for Bosnians not coming directly from the war zones; and it has become virtually impossible for asylum-seekers to enter the Netherlands without a job or a sponsor. Germany changed its refugee policy to return asylum-seekers to their last safe haven, and although it has taken in more foreigners than other European countries (7 million), its 1913 imperial citizenship law makes it virtually impossible for immigrants to become citizens. Japan, Hong Kong, and other nations throughout Asia also are making it more difficult for immigrants to remain in those countries. Anti-immigrant groups claim newcomers consume disproportionate shares of welfare and social programs in host countries; that higher birth rates among immigrant groups create pressures on education and similar institutions; that immigrant concentrations create environmental pressures; that immigrants disrupt host cultures. Global labor market pressures also are fueling anti-immigrant sentiment. Growth slow-downs and actual job losses in the industrialized world make people sensitive to newcomers, and there are fears that immigrants will take jobs from natives.

Proponents believe many immigrants take jobs natives do not want or cannot do, pay more into social systems than they take out, or bring important knowledge and skills to their new homes. For example, fully a third of the 65,000 temporary professionals with US work permits are university teachers and researchers, most with PhDs; a third of all US Nobel prize winners have been foreign-born; and US businesses run by foreign-born immigrants include Intel and McKinsey Consulting. Born in Hungary, New York-based George Soros has generated billions with global investments. Home countries face long-run threats to their own development when immigration robs nations of their best and brightest citizens.

Although many immigrants become citizens of new nations, improved technologies in travel and communications and growing business opportunities combine to create transnational entrepreneurs who develop business interests that span two or more nations. Overseas Chinese and nonresident Indians exemplify this approach because as groups both have established many businesses that span nations and transcend them when developing businesses. The profile of Halpin Ho illustrates this point (Box 6.3). However, economic and political immigrants from many nations besides China and India also return to their homeland to develop business opportunities.

BOX 6.3:   TRANSNATIONAL ENTREPRENEURSHIP

The Ho family left Myanmar (Burma) in the mid-1960s after their businesses were nationalized. This Chinese-Burmese family lost everything and the family split up for years, with some making a new start in Thailand. Success followed success, and by 1995 the Ho Group controlled gem and real-estate businesses in Thailand. Son Halpin Ho expressed fears about returning to Burma, but overcame them in 1991 to work with partners to built a lakeside hotel, develop the Myanmar Fund listed in Dublin, and create a multimillion dollar commercial center further to stimulate investment in his country of origin. His view is that 'if I can make a contribution to my country, I will make my mark in history.'

Source: Mark, Jeremy. (1995, Sept. 7). Burmese family returns from exile with keys to unlock reclusive nation. *The Wall Street Journal*, p. A12.

Jobs in search of labor

Globalization is making it possible for firms from developing economies to enter global markets. Often, their competitive advantage is low-cost labor. In response, firms operating in the industrialized economies have downsized within their nations of origin to outsource or create jobs in low-wage countries. The impact on the manufacturing sector has been greatest: manufacturing employment in the US fell by 1.4 million between 1978 and 1990 (Kapstein, 1996), and Germany alone lost over 500,000 jobs in 1995–6 when firms relocated to or established new jobs in lower wage countries. According to Frederick Studemann (1994), in a survey of 10,000 companies published by the Federation of German Chambers of Industry and Commerce, 3,000 said they expected to shift production facilities abroad between 1994 and 1997 because high labor costs and shorter working hours were making it difficult for the firms to compete.

The lower costs of labor combined with improved distribution systems reduces barriers to moving jobs almost anywhere in the world. Thomson Consumer Electronics employs three times as many people in Asia as in France, and most of Fila's textile output is subcontracted in Asia with only 10% remaining in Italy. Other examples of manu-facturing job relocation include the following:

- US medical-products giant Baxter Healthcare generates $10 billion in annual revenues, selling more of its examination and surgeon's gloves abroad than in the US. Baxter's efforts to remain price-competitive led managers to move production from a low-wage facility in the US South to even lower wage Penang, Malaysia, where it also could be closer to rubber supplies.
- Daimler–Benz added a passenger car plant to its existing truck plant in Mexico in 1995, and planned to build a new plant in Alabama to produce all-activity vehicles, half of which will be shipped to Europe.
- In 1989–90 Siemens Components Ltd shifted almost all of its semiconductor assembly work from Germany to Southeast Asia.

Service as well as manufacturing jobs also have migrated, although some jobs have stayed within a country by shifting them from low-pay jobs to even lower paid workers. For example, some US states now pay prisoners to answer tourists' telephone questions, a practice adopted also by for-profit companies. Jamaican service centers process data for everything from credit card applications to airline reservations; Irish laborers proofread technical manuals and process insurance claims; and Indian, Chinese, and Bulgarian soft-ware programmers write code for firms located anywhere in the world. Migration of service sector jobs calls into question assumptions often made about why organizations move jobs abroad. Although producing goods in a low-wage country can be accom-plished with low- to semi-skilled workers, service firms rely on knowledge-based assets. This need shifts emphasis away from what people can do in a physical sense to what they know, and managing these knowledge workers may require a different set of skills than managing production workers. Further, a need for knowledge workers can reshape job migration from low- to high-skill nations where education is greatest, and so future shifts from production- to knowledge-based work may return jobs to the industrialized nations or provide comparative advantage to small nations with an educated workforce. The example of Iceland illustrates the latter point (see Box 6.4).

Professional work once was somewhat protected from job migration, but crum-bling borders of several types have increased pressure here as well. Boeing Corporation hired about 300 Japanese engineers through a subcontractor for its 777 airplane project, and has hired thousands of Taiwan and Russian engineers. The primary reason for hiring abroad is that many of the countries with which Boeing deals will not purchase airplanes without these or similar hires. Other firms gain access to skills unavailable in the domes-tic workforce or save on professional wages. For example, wages of a software code-writer in Russia are about a fifth of what a US worker would earn (Zachary, 1995). A critical

---

BOX 6.4:   OPPORTUNITY IN ICELAND

The island nation of Iceland, located near the Arctic Circle, is a knowledge-based economy second to few worldwide. Iceland developed the hydropower to produce and export aluminum and ferro-sulfates; its fishing fleet catches almost as much fish as the French with only one-tenth of the labor; and it is the world leader in developing electronic tools for the fishing industry. Per capita income is among the highest in the world, pollution and crime are nominal. Moreover, Iceland offers a good university, four theater companies, dozens of magazine and book publishers, television and radio states, countless restaurants and cultural events, and up-to-date medical care.

Source: Passell, Peter. (1994, June 26). A little economy that can. *The New York Times*, p. E5.

---

shortage of programmers has stimulated a worldwide labor hunt to fill jobs. In order to hire for the 190,000 high-tech jobs open in the US in 1997, employers were sending recruiters to Brazil, Russia, China, the Philippines, India, and elsewhere. However, worldwide growth in demand for programmers makes it harder to hire programmers and US firms have to compete with firms from Israel, India, and Europe, among others, for employees (Baker, 1997).

Labor cost advantages of relocation can be ephemeral or short-lived. Our review of compensation earlier in this chapter showed that direct hourly wage rates do not reflect actual costs of labor in some developing economies. High benefits and bonuses, a need to train and educate a poorly developed workforce, and lower workforce productivity all boost the actual costs of labor. In Asia, a chronic shortage of service workers and local managers forces firms to train people in-house and then sees them leave to take better paying jobs elsewhere. In Thailand, Japanese car makers Toyota, Nissan, and Honda found that a quarter of their local managers quit annually for a rival job when economic growth was high (Asia's labor pains, 1995). Additionally, the rapid rate of development in some countries offers only a temporary advantage. For example, low labor costs in South Korea quickly rose with increased labor demand, and South Korean firms subsequently achieved cost advantages by manufacturing in Eastern European countries where wages were lower than in South Korea. Further, economist Dani Rodrik (1997) argues that economic globalization and political liberalization of trade making it possible for businesses to hire cheap labor worldwide may disrupt social contracts and cultural norms within domestic economies. For example, prohibitions on child labor within a country are violated when companies from that nation substitute child labor abroad for domestic hires from the adult workforce, resulting in social backlash against businesses. Although Rodrik does not advocate protectionism, his thesis is that social forces will create political remedies if businesses fail to recognize the link between their activities and social contracts with nations and with workers.

The preceding sections outlined reasons and ways labor has become more global. They demonstrate growing opportunities for some, and losses for others. Many believe the losses associated with globalization of labor will outweigh the gains, and that global competition for jobs can only be a 'race to the bottom' where the world is worse off at the finish line (Korten, 1995). Others believe the net result will be greater prosperity for all (Naisbitt, 1992). In theory, when wages and working conditions are similar around the world, then off-shore sourcing for labor advantage is not possible; in this way trade benefits all if there are no wage borders (Larudee, 1994). The World Bank concludes that either of these alternatives could be realized for global labor (Figure 6.5). In the divergent scenario of slow growth, wage gaps will grow and there will be rising wage inequality within and between regions. In the convergent scenario, inequality falls across most countries and in most regions, spurred by increased demand for low-skilled workers in the developing economies, and by skill improvements in the industrial world. Either scenario assumes that skilled workers will be favored. According to the World Bank, the scenario realized depends on whether the developing and transition economies:

(a) are successful in establishing market-based growth trajectories that generate rapid demand for labor and raise workforce productivity;
(b) take advantage of global change;
(c) are successful at government levels in creating frameworks that complement informal and rural labor markets; avoid bias toward wealthy insiders; and create an effective system of industrial relations in the formal sector;
(d) succeed in economic integration without also incurring large or permanent costs to labor.

GLOBAL LABOR CONVERGENCE

Convergence implies equity, although Korten (1995) notes that convergence can be either upward or downward. According to the United Nations *Human Development Report* (1994), worldwide prosperity is impossible without equity, and 'the concept of one world and one planet simply cannot emerge from an unequal world' (p. 21). The unanswered question is: Who or what entity is responsible for achieving employment equity? Some, like Paul Hawken (1993), believe that businesses are the only entities of

Wages (US dollars)

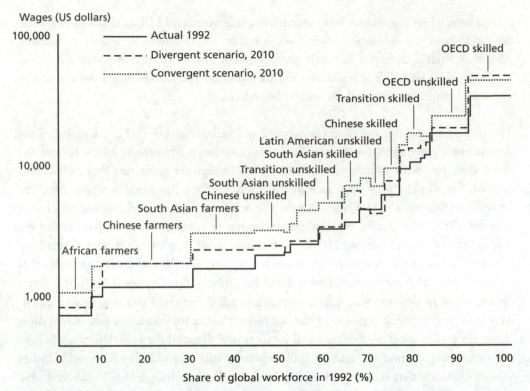

Note: Wages are in 1992 international prices, scaled logarithmically. Each group's share of the global workforce is indicated by the length of its horizontal line segment. Unlabeled line segments represent groups accounting individually for less than 2.5% of the global workforce (10% in total). The scenarios as depicted use 1992 workforce shares, not those projected for 2010. *Transition* refers to the formerly centrally planned economies of Europe and Central Asia.

Figure 6.5 *Two scenarios: wage convergence/wage divergence* (Will wages converge? (1995, Nov.). *Development Brief*, p. 1, for details see *World Development Report, 1995: Workers in an integrating world*. (1995). New York: Oxford University Press)

sufficient size to facilitate the sort of change that would have to occur to achieve job equity. Mihaly Simai (1994, pp. 194–195) believes governments can reduce inequities by improving human resources in the following ways:

(a) promote the quality of the labor force and human resources with educational systems, retrain labor force, promote scientific awareness and progress;
(b) create sociopolitical and economic conditions favoring economic development such as improved working conditions and support for basic human rights.

Enhancing labor quality

Earlier we saw that economic returns to education for the individual are almost immediate. Gregory Mankiw (1995) estimates that two-thirds of all national labor incomes result from improving workers' skills. Worldwide demand for skilled workers is creating new awareness among nations of the need to educate beyond basic skills. Many nations have targeted education as a primary means of labor force improvements. In the industrialized world where skilled and knowledgeable workers are concentrated, the average worker has completed 11 years of education compared with 5 in China and Mexico. Mandatory school attendance is from 5 to 11 years in the developing countries, and from 8 to 11 in the developed economies. Industrial countries have 85 scientists or technicians and 19 university graduates for every 1,000 people; average for the developing countries is 9 scientists and 1 graduate per 1,000 (You ain't seen nothing yet, 1994). Many nations provide more educational benefits for males than for females, but others have begun to invest in education for all potential workers.

Educational differentials have provided an advantage for industrial countries, and rapidly rising educational levels in the developing world are fostering economic development. High educational attainment in India attracts foreign firms to knowledge workers; an enclave of computer software development has developed in Bangalore. The local economy is stimulated via wages, but this form of job migration also increases globalization when computer software developers use their skills to establish new software firms capable of competing domestically, regionally, or worldwide. For example, Arvind Agarwalla's Fact Software International Pte was established in India with a software program that enables businesses to update accounting information on a real-time basis. Mr Agarwalla designed the software during his spare time, then marketed it in Singapore where computer use was more advanced. Fact quickly grew; its 1995 revenues were $2.6 million with offices in four nations and 130 employees. Agarwalla noted that it is not unusual for Indian engineers and scientists to contribute to technological breakthroughs, but it is unusual for them to own the technology (Mark, 1995). Thus, by providing education to its own citizens, India contributes to globalization and to its own welfare.

Other developing economies also are investing in education, often reshaping their traditions to do so. In Malawi, laws were relaxed to make primary education accessible, and Indonesia's commitment to *wajib belajar* reinforces the responsibility all Indonesians have to gain as much knowledge as possible. According to the US Labor Department's Consumer Expenditure Survey, spending on education rises faster than any other sector as income increases (Mandel and Farrell, 1993). This trend may be one reason for growing international enrollment in universities spanning the globe. The Chilean example appearing in Box 6.5 also shows that the shorter term benefits of education affect economic development and may in turn reshape the nation's commitment to education.

BOX 6.5:   CHILE'S SOCIAL SPENDING

According to a 1996 IMF report, Chile's economic development has been accompanied by social spending that increased from 55 to 61% between 1990 and 1995; most of this spending went into health, education, and housing. Rather than producing a drag on economic development, this social spending accompanied high economic growth for Chile. Meanwhile, Chile's illiteracy rate has been reduced to less than 5%, and the poverty rate was cut by 30% in four years. Having witnessed the link between education and economic development, in 1996 Chile passed legislation calling for an increase in funding to build more schools, update the curriculum, and improve teacher training.

Source: Chile boosts social outlays. (1996, Nov. 18). *Business Week*, p. 34.

Improving work conditions worldwide

UNIVERSAL CODES OF CONDUCT

National practices vary on issues ranging from child labor, to working hours and safety conditions, prisoner treatment, and ethnic and gender equity. Not all nations recognize human rights established by common code. In 1948 the United Nations adopted a Universal Declaration of Human Rights to create 'a common standard of achievement for all peoples and all nations' (see Appendix I). In the mid-1970s the International Covenant on Economic, Social and Cultural Rights and the International Covenant on Civil and Political Rights also were adopted. By 1997 the European Convention on Human Rights had been incorporated in domestic laws in every Western European country.

Increased political activity on the part of nongovernmental groups, e.g., Human Rights Watch, Amnesty International, greater social responsibility on the part of both business and governmental entities, and increased access to information continue to define human rights as an issue of global proportions. According to Amnesty International's annual report, in 1993 at least 112 governments tortured or abused their civilians; more than 100,000 people were jailed without charge or trial in 53 countries; 63 countries imprisoned political opponents; and countless thousands around the world were victims of political homicide. While these examples might appear to be extreme ones, they represent only the tip of an iceberg recorded by the US State Department's Annual Reports on Human Rights. An electronic search via Internet 'gopher' links to the Economic Development Information Network/EDIN facilities reveals that the depth and breadth of human rights violations is immense and growing for the 198 countries listed in the database. The growing sense of immediacy surrounding human rights in 1995 led the United Nations to institute a 'Human Rights Hotline' for fax transmissions of abuse reports.

The global basket of human rights issues is necessarily large to encompass many and diverse concerns such as child labor, working hours and safety conditions, prisoner treatment, and ethnic and gender equity, to name but a few. Jack Donnelly (1993) looked at workers' rights, racial discrimination, women's rights, and torture to examine global and regional norms and procedures for them from 1945 to 1985. As Table 6.7 shows, many rights are honored more in rhetoric than in regulation. For example, forced labor in the form of debt bondage is on the increase, and workers involved rarely are able to erase the debt associated with travel to work, housing, and food. Increases in forced labor result from economic need coupled with limited education among the world's poor. In Brazil the problem of enforced labor increased 20% between 1993 and 1994, leading a diverse group of organizations to launch campaigns such as DISQUE-ESCRAVIDAO (DIAL-SLAVERY) for reporting labor abuses. This is the climate in which business enterprises operate today. In view of failures among voluntary and governmental organizations to win lasting improvements in human rights, there is growing worldwide pressure for business organizations to play a bigger role in alleviating human rights abuses.

At the global level, workers' rights are governed primarily by norms providing standards with exemptions and procedures that promote and monitor more than enforce. Government's role in improving work conditions and introducing human rights revolves around its desire and ability to introduce laws and enforce regulations. In the industrialized economies, formal mechanisms include regulations that protect workers, but in the developing economies few have passed regulations to improve work conditions or enhance human rights. China's stance has been to resist outside political pressures, viewing it as a corruption of national norms. Other nations fear they will lose jobs if they raise labor standards, or that opening the door to human rights issues will force undesirable changes. Throughout Asia, many fear that human rights agendas are yet another way for US politics to extend their global reach. These and other concerns retard government enthusiasm for introducing the stricter labor standards found in industrialized countries.

LABOR UNIONS

Upward convergence in labor conditions is an aim of global labor unionization, and it is a perspective that brings labor or trade unions full circle to their early nineteenth-century roots. In response to abuses fostered by the shift from craft to industrial production, laborers in affected countries joined forces both nationally and internationally to win fair and safe conditions of work. However, the common international voice of labor was almost quenched by the nationalism of two world wars, causing unions to develop more within nations than among them, and resulting in cultural variations that define laborer/manager relationships today. For example, the fierce individualism and desire for autonomy

TABLE 6.7 Changes in international human rights regimes, 1945–1985

	1945	1955	1965	1975	1985
Global regime					
Norms	None	Declaratory	Strong declaratory	Promotional	Strong promotional
	None	Guidelines	Strong guidelines	Standards with exemptions	Standards with exemptions
Procedures	None	Weak promotion	Promotion	Strong promotion	Strong promotion/ weak monitoring
Regional human rights regimes					
European regime	None	Implementation	Implementation/ enforcement	Enforcement	Enforcement
Inter-American regime	None	Declaratory	Weak promotional	Promotional	Strong promotional/ enforcement
African regime	None	None	None	None	Declaratory
Asia and the Middle East	None	None	None	None	None
Single-issue regimes					
Workers' rights	Promotional	Promotional/ implementation	Promotional/ implementation	Promotional/ implementation	Promotional/ implementation
Racial discrimination	None	None	Declaratory	Declaratory	Strong promotional
Women's rights	None	Declaratory/ promotional	Declaratory/ promotional	Strong promotional	Strong promotional
Torture	None	None	None	Weak declaratory	Strong declaratory

dominant among US industrialists created an 'us versus them' mentality in US labor/management relationships. In Germany, the post-world war approach of co-determination acknowledged common interest among owners and laborers to ensure a high quality of life, bringing both to board directorship to monitor short- and long-term labor/management concerns. Postwar unionism in Japan also has been one of partnership between management and labor, whereas US labor negotiations remain adversarial in many cases. At about 14.5% of all employment in 1995, US labor union membership is relatively small.

According to Jeremy Brecher and Tim Costello (1994), the challenges of globalization create social challenges that transcend the workplace and can only be addressed by a labor movement that promotes the interests of all workers, including workers who are not union members. According to these authors, 'trade unions must reach out of the workplace and into the community by building coalitions with environmental, community, religious, women's human rights, farm, and other people's organizations' (p. 160) to become partners in improving job conditions rather than competitors for jobs worldwide. These authors recommend that labor movements worldwide can build on past successes and forge new ones by engaging corporations with real, worker-designed workplace solutions to problems jointly faced. An example of this type of approach appeared in the opening case when Motorola found a win/win solution by soliciting worker alternatives to relocating production abroad. Not only did the workers find a better way to reduce costs, they were able to enhance quality and to retain and even create jobs. Inasmuch as many union traditions developed within nations, a major barrier to transnational labor unionism is likely to be the view that jobs 'belong' to one nation or another. Like other entities, labor unions and collective bargaining units within nations find it difficult to trade short-term losses for themselves against longer term benefits for all workers worldwide, and this is an impediment to transnational bargaining for labor unions (Prahalad and Doz, 1987).

Cross-national entities like the International Labor Organization provide a voice for transcending national barriers to realize worldwide work standards, and their voice can be strengthened by regulations others create. For example, development of transnational work councils for European corporations in the European Union may prove valuable in demonstrating that the interests of both labor and management can be met with collaborative arrangements.

TRANSNATIONAL ORGANIZATIONS

Transnational voluntary groups like the International Labor Rights Education and Resource Fund, Human Rights Watch, the Clandestine Commission on Unions, and Amnesty International are only a few among the many that have increased global awareness of human rights. Their advocacy for human rights includes direct action and pressure on national governments to facilitate change. More recently, the scope of these groups has expanded to combine political and economic pressures. For example, the

Lawyers Committee for Human Rights and the Robert F. Kennedy Memorial Center for Human Rights lobbied for introduction of a voluntary code of business conduct for US firms introduced by the US President in 1996. Finally, direct consumer pressure on business organizations has caused the latter also to restructure their work processes.

Pressure on nations to reshape work conditions raises concerns over national autonomy and control. Agitation for global codes also has ramifications for global firms as they weigh tradeoffs of autonomy and control, between patriarchy and partnership, between equality and the inequity inherent in most traditional management structures. Pressures to manage these tensions have led to organizational challenges for managing a global workforce. The following section examines how organizations are managing these challenges.

PART II   ORGANIZATIONAL ACTION

The organizational challenges for assembling a global workforce are numerous. Human resource systems established to select, develop, train, compensate, or retain homogeneous domestic workplaces are stretched to accommodate the growing diversity of a global workforce. As the preceding review of work conditions revealed, global political action is redefining assumptions of work, reshaping expectations of workers and managers, and creating new demands for organizations. In the following sections we will focus on how global organizations work with and develop the global workforce.

STRUCTURES
Structuring business ethics

The field of ethics judges specifically human ends and the relationship of means to those ends, and it is concerned with the study of moral judgment. Business ethics attempts to recognize the relationship of acts to the good of the individual, the firm, the business community, and society. Ethical decisions, then, are necessarily based on moral judgments about what is 'right' or 'good,' and, as we explored in Chapter 4, conclusions about what is 'right' or 'good' tend to vary widely over time and according to individual as well as cultural perspectives. The challenge of business ethics lies in asking business enterprises and the people who run them to develop a hierarchy of what is good or 'right' to do. Although business activities transcend borders readily, principles are not so easily transferred, and hence there is a growing need to establish ethical principles of business that also transcend national boundaries.

The activities and tradeoffs to be made in achieving organizational objectives are the subject of studies in business ethics. There may be some who believe that profit-seeking supersedes ethical behavior, and that lying, cheating, or stealing are all acceptable if a profit is made. Certainly we all hear and read stories about people whose behaviors are both unethical and profitable. However, the vast majority of organizations and individuals easily recognize the difference between these behaviors and ethical practices. The more important challenge in an emerging global business world is that although we all have a stake in the outcome of global business activities, we do not similarly share the same definition of what constitutes 'good.' Because ethics is grounded in a moral philosophy that tends toward absolute right and absolute wrong, many business managers find it difficult to understand how they can use ethics in business decision-making that are less absolute and more frequently relative to a situation (Stark, 1993).

CODES OF BUSINESS ETHICS

Companies increasingly realize that they cannot easily adopt one or more sets of business principles for overseas markets and others for their domestic market. In practice, many face the challenge Levi's faces abroad: it is difficult to initiate changes in other cultures. Skeptics might argue that social responsibility is just another way for organizations to manipulate the public. However, while some undoubtedly continue to view social responsibility as a public relations vehicle, others worldwide are acting to move social responsibility initiatives away from manipulation and influence of the public and toward serious dialogue and debate between the business world and its critics (Steinmann and Lohr, 1992).

Some organizations incorporate ethics as part of their vision statements. For example, McDonald's describes social responsibility in terms of its belief system:

> We believe that being a good corporate citizen means treating people with fairness and integrity, sharing our success with the communities in which we do business, and being a leader on issues that affect customers. (McDonald's Corporation Investor Review, 1992, p. 7)

Other organizations encourage their employees to learn professional standards to avoid legal challenges based on ethical missteps (Siconolfi, 1995). Finally, many business leaders have instituted formal organization codes of ethics: Fiat and Motorola are two examples among global firms. According to one survey, 93% of Fortune 1000 firms contacted reported having a code of ethics (Instilling ethical values, 1992), and 71% of large UK firms also report operating under a code of corporate ethics (Webley, 1992). Others report different findings: 60% of US companies and 30% of European companies have formal codes of ethics (Naisbitt, 1992). In 1996, the five major South Korean *chaebols* adopted a code of conduct urging respect for local workers. Joanne Ciulla (1991) observed that most companies research other corporate codes held at centers like the Ethics Resource Center in Washington, DC, or the Institute of Business Ethics in

London, modeling their own codes along similar lines organized beneath the following topics:

> ... employee conduct, community and environment, customers, shareholders, suppliers and contractors, political interest, and innovation and technology (p. 75)

before writing their own, and hence these codes can be quite similar.

Ethical codes do not ensure success, but they may prevent failures. Their existence makes it less likely that leaders or managers will unwittingly guide the firm into an ethical morass, or that individuals will bring their own ethics to bear when acting on behalf of the firm. This is particularly important at a global level because cultural differences in beliefs and values do lead to cross-cultural differences in behaviors. An argument in earlier chapters is that business leaders have created organizational hybrids by combining features from various theories. In the case of codes of ethics, firms create hybrids that reduce global uncertainties by structuring expectations. Levi Strauss and Reebok reduced the potential for human rights violations or public outcry by outlining specific codes for operational behavior, and many other firms similarly are acting alone or in alliances to structure business codes of ethics. Codes like these, whether they are internal to the firm or represent a global coalition within or across industries provide a way for global enterprises to bring structure to global uncertainties.

A GLOBAL CODE OF BUSINESS ETHICS

Leaders of global businesses and from other walks of life collaborated to create a global code of ethics intended to provide structural order amidst the occasional chaos of dynamic global markets. This document, known as the Caux Round Table (CRT) Principles for Business (1995) was launched in 1994 and has since been translated into many languages and introduced around the world. The CRT Principles speak to business responsibilities, including responsiveness to stakeholders as well as shareholders; efforts to create justice and world community; and business behavior conforming to the spirit as well as the letter of the law. A noteworthy feature of the CRT Principles is that they reflect efforts to create a hybrid founded on two basic ethical ideas: the shared existence and common good of *kyosei* representing Japanese cooperation, and the more Western notion of individualism reflected in an emphasis on human dignity.

Potential advantages of this global code of ethics are several. Like company codes, they reduce the potential for serious missteps and can reduce operating uncertainties. Second, a common code of ethics worldwide makes it possible for all firms to operate according to the same principles; this produces the 'level playing field' upon which many organizational leaders prefer to play. A global code of ethical standards provides a means for standardizing within- and across-firm behaviors as well. For example, the individual or cultural differences that sometimes lead to ethical breaches are less likely to occur with a standard code of ethics. It is relatively easy to see that business efficiency within the firm can be improved by having single rather than multiple sets of standards, and across-firm benefits occur when standards assure consumers of quality levels. Worker protection in all industries is improved, and workplace disasters may be averted. A third incentive for adopting a global code of business ethics is that such codes are needed and are possible in a world that is interdependent on many other dimensions of business activities.

Limits for ethical codes

Despite what appear to be compelling reasons to adopt codes of business ethics, there are limitations as well. Since global rules are likely to emerge from a negotiation process, they are unlikely to reflect values and habits consistent for all cultures. To the extent that global codes of ethics are developed by firms from the Westernized countries, they may not incorporate ethical concerns for other nations. Further, global ethics may be viewed as a 'seal of approval,' and thus represent an end-point to developing global ethics rather than the beginning-point they should be. Global ethics, like other standards, can respond to but rarely anticipate change. Accordingly, organizations may hide behind global codes when conditions change unless there are reasons to keep codes current.

Structuring the human rights agenda

Business incentives to improve working conditions and human rights emerge from public demand, pressure from transnational nongovernmental groups, from government demands, and from business activities. Improved access informs the world of human rights issues and abuses and increased political activity on the part of nongovernmental groups identifies firms perceived to be in violation of human and other rights. These pressures are one force for bringing human rights onto the business agenda. Richard DeGeorge (1993) suggests that other entities will impose rules unless businesses take the initiative to create them for themselves; he suggested they could base their own codes on 'Seven Principles of Business for Multinationals':

1 Multinationals should do no intentional direct harm.
2 Multinationals should produce more good than harm for the host country.
3 Multinationals should contribute by their activity to the host country's development.
4 Multinationals should respect the human rights of their employees.
5 To the extent that local culture does not violate ethical norms, multinationals should respect the local culture and work with and not against it.
6 Multinationals should pay their fair share of taxes.

7 Multinationals should cooperate with the local government in developing and enforcing just support institutions.

HUMAN RIGHTS CODES

Although relatively few people work for multinational enterprises (MNEs), these firms have been the subject of most efforts to pressure business change. First, multinationals draw this attention because of their global scope. Those that are identifiable – particularly consumer product firms – are reluctant to be dragged through the global court of public opinion or to lose sales because of real or imputed bad labor practices. Second, about 60% of the growth in MNE payrolls occurred in developing countries between 1985 and 1992 (Twice the workers, 1995) where most labor violations occur. Third, in developing economies with a large informal economy, jobs created by MNEs or by foreign firms of any size make them major employers for the formal sector. Fourth, as we saw earlier, annual revenue for some MNEs is larger than for nations; this provides firms with considerable economic and political clout. Unilever's sales network in India, for example, has collected more demographic information about India's population distribution than has the Indian government. Finally, as has been demonstrated elsewhere, many workers in the developing nations have high expectations of foreign firms. These are some of the factors that combine to draw attention to how global business giants and their smaller companions relate to workers on a global scale.

Many businesses have played a role in improving worldwide work conditions and standards. Although MNEs pay lower wages in developing countries than in the industrial world, they usually pay higher wages than domestic firms, and they tend to export high labor standards abroad. Additionally, they may provide better work conditions or benefits. For example, in Thailand, wages from a foreign firm often are 10% or more higher than domestic firms of equivalent size, and the propensity of foreign firms to offer health care benefits caused Thai firms to provide similar benefits to retain and attract desirable workers.

Many business leaders believe morality and profits are served by acting ethically in business. Companies like the Body Shop and Esprit have based their global reputation on this approach, and successful firms such as Merck, Sony, and Hewlett-Packard similarly report subordinating financial returns to objectives that are more social in nature (Collins and Porras, 1995). The Body Shop, for example, strives to provide effective cosmetic products without the hype typical for the cosmetics industry, and to extend a down-to-earth approach to the way they do business as well as the business they do. According to founder Anita Roddick:

> We take care in the manufacture of our products to minimize damage to the environment. Our Fair Trade policy establishes trading partnerships with

indigenous people in the developing world. And we actively campaign for human rights and a ban on animal testing in the cosmetics industry. We wish to leave the world a better place, and in better shape, than we found it. (1996 Body Shop catalogue)

Taking a clear position on social responsibility forces business leaders to weigh the benefits of profits and social goods, and a choice for the latter means affirmative actions for firms. Evidence of human rights violations caused Levi Strauss to introduce new terms of association with business partners in 1993, becoming one of the first multinationals to adopt guidelines covering worker treatment and the environmental impact of production. These guidelines covered suppliers and subcontractors who might otherwise use child labor or force employees to work unacceptable hours. Levi's later withdrew from China and Myanmar (Burma) in reaction to human rights violations. Shoe producer Reebok introduced 'Human Rights Production Standards.' The company reported its new standards resulted in local change when Reebok threatened to withhold orders from Chinese contractor Yue Yuen International Ltd. The latter firm moved 800 workers out of unsafe dormitories and agreed to pay for workers' new two-hour daily commute (Smith, 1994). In taking on a human rights agenda, organizations find that new guidelines for behavior necessarily change other habits. For example, Levi's now hires private inspectors to monitor human rights in its manufacturing plants around the world. Starbucks Coffee Company of Seattle found that an aspiration to improve the quality of life in coffee producing countries involved more than a statement of commitment. The Starbucks experience described in Box 6.6 shows that considerable managerial resources are needed to create what became the document ('Starbucks Commitment . . . To Do Our Part').

Less than 5% of US retailers have initiated efforts to reduce human rights violations, but many are well-known firms, including Wal-Mart, Sears, Reebok, Nordstrom, Nike, Liz Claiborne, and Eddie Bauer, and most initiate these changes because of customer preference. Celebrities who endorse these and other products also pressure firms to be socially responsive. Consumers in Europe have agitated for improved global work standards. IKEA recently decided not to sell carpets unless they could be certified as made without child labor. C&A, a Dutch store chain, has agreed to establish a code of conduct to help abolish child labor. A new group including German rug-importers and a number of charities recently launched Rugmark, a trademark signalling that no children were involved in the making of the rug (Human rights, 1995). The Rugmark label is the first 'human rights' seal of approval, and lobbyists reportedly were pressing for its adoption in the US. Similarly, in Indonesia, many textile producers now attach labels reading 'not produced by child labor.'

These same human rights initiatives that make global retailers' products attractive to consumers may create problems and challenges for those whose rights are protected.

> **BOX 6.6:   STARBUCKS COMMITMENT . . . TO DO OUR PART**
>
> In an October 1995 speech, Starbucks senior vice president Dave Olsen described the six-month process that yielded a four-page document stating Starbucks beliefs, coffee mission, goals and action plans to improve the lives of people in coffee producing countries. The document involved more than a product; it caused top managers to 'explore our own values and beliefs' and examine past actions as well as involve themselves in 'a lot of soul searching to come to an understanding of how we can live up to our sense of responsibility to make a difference in the world.' Olsen described this process at an Economic Justice Forum held at Seattle University. Following his explanation of the many top management discussions and deliberations involved in creating this document, a member of the audience promptly asked Olsen: 'Why haven't you done more?' This example illustrates the pressure many MNEs face to be more and more socially responsible.

Representatives of many nations, including China, Malaysia, and Indonesia, claim that human rights programs organized by Westernized firms represent a form of protectionism with 'social correctness' as the rallying cry. According to Benn Steil (1994), social correctness in the European Union is a form of protectionism; by imposing their systems of labor relations and workplace regulations, socially correct nations raise competitors' production costs and thereby protect their own higher priced labor markets. Finally, businesses that support human rights often become targets of social action groups. The example of Phillips-Van Heusen Corporation in Box 6.7 shows how firms can be caught between the need to keep costs low and a desire to improve labor standards worldwide.

Structuring knowledge work

Many structural mechanisms also have been proposed to improve technology transfer and organizational functioning in a global setting. In the case of knowledge transfer, James Quinn, Philip Anderson, and Sydney Finkelstein (1996) conclude that organizations based on professional intellect will continue to use hierarchical structures, but professional knowledge required by service industries like airlines, health care, brokerage, and the like may require different structural forms. These forms will leverage intellect by removing hierarchical layers and pushing responsibility to the point of contact with customers. According to these authors, the spider's web form of the Internet allows information to wander freely, and it can be adapted to organizations (Figure 6.6). The free flow of information among subsidiaries and units in multiple locations in the same

> ### BOX 6.7: PHILLIPS-VAN HEUSEN CORPORATION
>
> Globalization of the textile industry has touched off fierce competition for low-wage labor in an industry with traditionally low wages and poor working conditions. Companies like Phillips-Van Heusen (PVH), manufacturer of brand name products like Izod and Gant, have been caught between simultaneous demands for low costs and the desire to improve working conditions and pay. PVH chief executive Bruce Klatsky recognized that the firm had to import from lower wage countries, but at the same time he took unusual steps to improve labor conditions. For example, in Guatemalan plants, PVH has contributed more than $1.5 million to improve nutrition and schools in the villages where workers live; offers subsidized lunches and free on-site health care for employees; provides school supplies for workers' children; equips sewing workers with ergonomic chairs; and pays higher wages than could be earned for similar jobs in Guatemala.
>
> Yet PVH Guatemala is the target of human rights activists who claim PVH's shirt-making operation is paying wages below the poverty line, hires contractors that use underage workers, and intimidates union organizers. CEO Klatsky, who sits on the board of human rights advocacy group Human Rights Watch, views these attacks as unfounded and unfair. Human rights advocates acknowledge that PVH has worked hard to improve working conditions in Guatemalan plants, but claim that more progress can and should be made.
>
> *Source*: Bounds, Wendy. (1997, Feb. 24). Critics confront a CEO dedicated to human rights. *The Wall Street Journal*, pp. B1, B7.

organization can be harnessed around single problems or challenges, but as Quinn and others note, its success depends on individual identification with the problem at hand and a sense of interdependency. In a globalizing world, the network applies not only to organizations, but can be used to describe how dissimilar organizations coalesce around issues of common concern such as human rights or work conditions.

PROCESSES
Defining knowledge work

Existing systems of deploying human labor have led to some amount of organizational rigidity that many believe can be overcome by expanding the information and knowledge base of the organization. Because knowledge rests with individuals, a new emphasis on

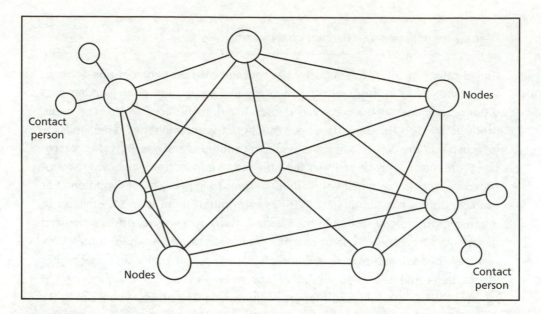

FIGURE 6.6 *Spider's web organizations* (Quinn, J.B., Anderson, Philip, and Finkelstein, Sydney. (1996). Leveraging intellect. *Academy of Management Executive*, 10(3): 21)

knowledge work has led to definitions of what it means to be a knowledge worker. Nuala Beck (1995) described the knowledge worker as a person in one of three employment groups:

(a) professionals such as physicians, attorneys, accountants, university professors with specialized training or credentials;

(b) engineering, scientific, and technical workers with specialized skills;

(c) top managers.

Beck's definition of the knowledge worker focuses on prior investments in education or professional training, but many who are not classified as knowledge workers according to Beck nevertheless contribute to knowledge creation in organizations. Thus, knowledge workers probably can be described more broadly as those for whom thinking is an important part of their work. Organizational intellect is one basis for rapid adaptation in a global world, and organizations seek ways to transfer knowledge quickly throughout the organization. Leif Edvinsson (Stewart, 1994), Skandia's director of intellectual capital, indicates that intellectual capital comes from human assets, who are the source of innovation and renewal, and from structural assets, such as information systems and managerial focus, that make individual intellectual capital accessible to the group or organization.

Learning

According to Peter Drucker (1994), knowledge knows no boundaries, and it – rather than land, labor, or capital – will increasingly be the critical resource for nations, companies, and individuals. Charles Handy (1994) similarly observes that qualities of service work involving intellect make labor inputs less the property of the firm and more the property of the worker. Much of what is known about the learning process focuses on individual learning, but increasingly the focus also is on how individual knowledge can be shared throughout the organization. This focus on organizational learning identifies how individuals learn and disseminate information to create a shared pool of organizational intellect. This intellect is more than just information, data, or knowledge; it includes making meaning of information via direct and indirect modes of communication. Between individuals, for example, an indirect mode of communication could be a slight frown. In learning organizations, the frown would be noted and perhaps lead to a frank discussion; the open dialogue around the frown then becomes a building block for organizational learning.

Learning processes provide a way to think about how intangibles such as learning and knowledge can best serve organizations. The learning organization described by Peter Senge (1990) derives its advantages from continual learning on the part of individuals that becomes transferable to the organization as a whole. In *The fifth discipline*, Senge describes the learning organization in terms of the following basic ingredients:

(a) systems thinking: looking at how the company really works;
(b) personal mastery: being open to others and their ideas;
(c) mental models: recognizing thought patterns and how they aid or impede action;
(d) shared vision: forming a plan that everyone can agree on; and
(e) team learning: making it possible for everyone to work together to realize the shared mission.

We can apply the learning organization model to global demands for human rights initiatives to show how learning occurs and what needs to happen next in learning organizations. Let's take the example of a profit-maximizing global carpet distributor. This firm avoids human rights issues by subcontracting labor in the developing world. Word of this practice gets out, a citizen outcry against child labor is raised, and the industry creates a Rugmark label that becomes a 'seal of approval' for sales. Sales of non-Rugmark carpets plummet before top managers of our distributor issue a statement describing a newly adopted code to comply with Rugmark standards. But how do they then alter existing mental models that made previous practices possible? If assumptions about how to do business are not made transparent, they will continue to direct the behavior of some as others change. Differences in behavior may be ignored or dysfunctional when people are not open to each other. In the end, the result may be little learning and a seldom-practiced written code of ethics. Conversely, when there is open dialogue and discussion, authentic individual and organizational learning can occur.

Many believe that organizational ability to learn is the critical factor for surviving or thriving in the global marketplace. Ikujiro Nonaka and Hirotaka Takeuchi (1995) view the knowledge creation process as a spiral that operates at multiple levels to share internal and external information. Socialization among internal participants in the form of meetings, one-to-one communications, social gatherings, and teamwork are a few of the networks through which organizational knowledge passes and is transformed to create additional knowledge. Although knowledge generation is a critical concern for most companies, many US organizations find it difficult to leverage knowledge. Nonako and Takeuchi believe this occurs because of Western emphasis on the analytical nature of explicit knowledge. Conveying explicit information up or down organizational levels reinforces facts, but it does not enhance understanding. The latter comes more frequently from implicit or tacit knowledge, information that is difficult to convey in a patterned or written order, and is instead portrayed in symbol, metaphor, or analogy.

Nonaka and Takeuchi believe that in Japanese firms implicit knowledge-sharing occurs mainly at the group level, whereas in the West explicit knowledge results from individual actions (see Figure 6.7). Thus, heavy reliance on facts and reports conveys information, but little about how the job was done or what could be done differently. The collective or group nature of implicit knowledge means that everyone must think about how a task is accomplished and all are contributing to and absorbing knowledge – this is one reason given for why Japanese companies have been so successful with innovations. US firms are best known for invention, and may underutilize the power of collective knowledge. Ikujiro Nonaka has been a standard-bearer for a new understanding of implicit knowledge and information, and in that role he demonstrates why both invention and innovation are important to global firms. Interestingly, Nonaka not only became the dean of the department of knowledge science at Japan's Advanced Institute of Science and Technology in Hokuriku, but also the first ever professor of knowledge at the University of California, Berkeley.

Many business leaders and academics believe the knowledge-based firm is the key to the future (Burrows, 1994). Olivetti leaders believe that the winning information technology company of the 1990s will be a learning company that moves rapidly on a global scale because it is managed by a network of alliances where individuals working in teams are at the core. Other global organizations use information technologies to disseminate knowledge worldwide. Coca-Cola, Young & Rubicam, and Coopers & Lybrand are among those that have created the position of Chief Knowledge Officer (CKO)

Japanese organization	Western organization
• Group-based	• Individual-based
• Tacic knowledge-oriented	• Explicit knowledge-oriented
• Strong on socialization and internalization	• Strong on externalization and combination
• Emphasis on experience	• Emphasis on analysis
• Dangers of 'group think' and 'overadaptation to the past success'	• Danger of 'paralysis by analysis'
• Ambiguous organizational intention	• Clear organizational intention
• Group autonomy	• Individual autonomy
• Creative chaos through overlapping tasks	• Creative chaos through individual differences
• Frequent fluctuation from top management	• Less fluctuation from top management
• Redundancy of information	• Less redundancy of information
• Requisite variety through cross-functional teams	• Requisite variety through individual differences

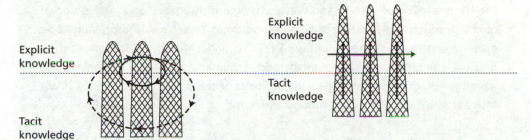

FIGURE 6.7 *Japanese- and Western-style organizational knowledge creation* (Nonaka, Ikijuro, and Takeuchi, Hirotaka. (1995). *The knowledge-creating company: How Japanese companies create the dynamics of innovation*. Oxford: Oxford University Press, p. 199)

responsible for facilitating information flows among and between units. This office makes better use of internal and external information, but free flow of information challenges many traditional assumptions about knowledge resources. Knowledge, like other sources of traditional power, has been viewed as a scarce resource, but knowledge-based systems treat it as a shared resource. Computer-based networks, for example, provide access to information previously shared only among a few. As many or all gain access to the same information, power derived from access to information erodes. Managers and workers become more equal; organizations become more democratic; and expectations grow for organizations to be community members. The role of knowledge manager has taken on a different flavor in advertising firm Saatchi and Saatchi, as the example in Box 6.8 shows.

Auditing processes

IMPLEMENTING ETHICAL CODES
Organizational processes to develop or audit information systems or ethics policies have proved difficult to create. Organizations simply have limited experience with how these

> **BOX 6.8:   WHAT DOES IT MEAN TO BE DIRECTOR OF KNOWLEDGE MANAGEMENT AND CONSUMER INSIGHTS?**
>
> ---
>
> Myra Stark's title is a new one in advertising and every other industry, and she is defining the role by directing and managing pursuit of all kinds of knowledge. Ms Stark jets around the world to confirm consumer trends. For example, she observes that polenta has gained popularity in both the US and New Zealand, Internet cruising creates a state of mind where adults are no longer totally conscious of their surroundings, and boundaries of many types are blurring. Three examples: neutriceuticals combines food and health products; spirituality has reasserted itself in the US as a blend of Eastern and Western religious traditions; and localization of global products is evident when foie gras becomes 'New York Hudson Valley foie gras' or calamari becomes 'Montauk [NY] calamari.' Although Ms Stark's title is unusual, combined need for creativity and consumer information endemic to the advertising industry has yielded a 'department of the future' at ad agency TBWA International, and a 'director of mind and mood' at Foote, Cone & Belding.
>
> *Source*: Ono, Yumiko. (1997, Feb. 28). Saatchi's 'Manager of Knowledge' keeps track of what's trendy. *The Wall Street Journal*, p. B5.

processes can or should operate. Firms with formal codes of ethics often find it difficult to operationalize them at lower organizational levels, sometimes because employees remain unconvinced that top managers mean what they say. According to Jane Sasseen (1993), Europeans have frequently viewed codes of ethics as public relations tools or as expensive luxuries available only to large firms, but repeated business scandals demonstrate that businesses brought to public account can quickly lose a reputation built over years or decades.

Researchers also find that ethical codes have not yet been fully operationalized at lower levels. A study of young, junior-level managers in the US found that many firms view ethical behavior only as staying within the law, and the young managers were discouraged from overinvesting in ethical behavior (Badarocco, 1995). Similarly, a comparative study of senior executives in the US, the UK, Germany, and Austria revealed that companies tend to address substantially more ethical issues in written policy statements than in training (Schlegelmilch and Robertson, 1995).

ACCOUNTING FOR INTELLECT

Knowledge-based assets may be as high as three to four times book valuation of the firm (Handy, 1990), and they represent a knowledge bank composed of employee skills and abilities, customer or client lists, and so on. These assets are not owned by the organization in the same ways as bricks and mortar, and the organizational value they reflect is difficult to measure as tangible results cannot easily be derived from such intangible inputs.

MANAGERIAL COMPETENCIES FOR A GLOBAL WORLD
Staffing

Managerial staffing abroad traditionally has been accomplished in three ways: sending an expatriate manager from the headquarters staff; hiring a host-country national; or hiring third-country nationals – managers whose citizenship differs from that of the firm and of the nation. According to Heenan and Perlmutter (1979), the choice of which manager to hire reflects four orientations toward foreign subsidiaries:

- An *ethnocentric* approach to staffing retains control at headquarters, important decisions are made in the home country, and key posts are held by expatriates.
- A *polycentric* approach staffs subsidiaries abroad with host-country nationals who have some decision autonomy, but few of these managers are promoted to jobs at headquarters.
- A *regiocentric* approach employs a wider pool of managers within a geographic region like Asia or Latin America, employing host-country and/or third-country nationals. Although these managers have some degree of decision-making autonomy within their regions, they are seldom brought into jobs at headquarters.
- A *geocentric* approach to staffing identifies and selects the best person for the job regardless of nationality.

As Table 6.8 shows, company philosophy favoring one or another form of centrism is likely to affect more than staffing decisions. The underlying philosophy of the firm also influences where major decisions are made as well as decisions about the type of training managers receive prior to working abroad. The geocentric approach to staffing can result in hiring a third-country national. Zeira and Harari (1977) studied third-country nationals and concluded that most are part of a competent and mobile group of managers with high adaptability and an open disposition to new cultures. This third-country national often carries dual citizenship or was born in one country and raised in another. Because they have lived within two cultures, bicultural managers are likely to have developed sensitivities to cross-cultural differences that are otherwise difficult to acquire.

Rapid globalization also might create reasons for combining these staffing strategies. For example, few in Eastern European transitional economies were familiar with

TABLE 6.8   Staffing philosophy

Organizational philosophy	Decision source	Manager/training options
Ethnocentric Parent values and interests guide strategic decisions	Centralized at HQ	Home office expatriate; training differentiates host from home culture
Polycentric Strategic decisions tailored to countries where company operates	Decentralized	Local or third-country nationals; value-free culture training
Regiocentric Blends its interests with those of divisions	Shared decisions	Nationals from the region training to assimilate/acculturate
Geocentric Develops a global strategy oriented toward standardization and global products	Centralized; favors wholly owned subsidiaries	Parent, local, or third-country national within firm; training focuses on organizational culture

profit-motivated business behaviors in 1989 and firms often sent third-country European nationals to manage and teach national locals. In developing economies, managerial experience may be limited and this too might be a reason to send expatriates or third-country managers. Many of the 'common-sense' assumptions made when selecting managers have not been borne out by experience. For example, hyphenated Americans, e.g., Chinese-Americans, often face barriers in countries of heritage because they are not perceived as being 'real' Americans or 'real' Chinese. In this case, an ability to bridge cultural borders can seem to work against managerial success. Firm strategy also is a reason for selection decisions. For example, Coca-Cola defines its strategy as multilocal, and therefore prefers to select local managers who are responsive to and knowledgeable about local customs and needs. At the same time, Coca-Cola also sends parent-country nationals abroad for management assignments when they can provide a needed skill and to develop their international knowledge. Knowledge transfer frequently is viewed as one of the most important functions of the expatriate manager (Ondrack, 1985), and this is one reason Colgate-Palmolive and other firms send expatriates abroad. Knowledge also is transferred by sending local nationals to headquarters on temporary assignments. For example, Rockwell International's Allen Bradley Company Division brings host nationals to the US for training. Similarly, Unilever found that hiring local managers provided a good perspective on India, but that to do their jobs well the Indian managers also needed to be exposed to the principles of Unilever's culture. In summary, managerial staffing decisions depend on the objectives deemed most important to organizational leaders at a given time. In global firms comprised of many businesses and serving many markets, the selection approach may be a hybrid combination of ethnocentric to geocentric approaches.

Matching jobs and skills

In September 1996, Ernst and Young LLP held a roundtable discussion for chief executives of multinational companies to explore some of the challenges of managing across borders. These managers provided suggestions for managing cross-cultural differences from a distance, and they included the following:

- form an advisory council of senior executives in each country to guide the country managers on cultural issues;
- facilitate a global communication network between managers to foster teaming and idea sharing;
- rotate headquarters-based managers into international assignment and bring non-HQ managers to work at headquarters;
- develop common ethics and principles worldwide (Donlon, 1996).

According to Kenichi Ohmae (1990), achieving success with global managers also will require alterations in structure because 'no company can operate effectively on a global scale by centralizing all key decisions and then farming them out for implementation' (p. 87). Further, there is an increasing need to build a cadre of truly international (Ondrack, 1985) and global managers (Adler and Bartholomew, 1992; Bartlett and Ghoshal, 1992).

Most international management research concentrates on US expatriates managing wholly owned subsidiaries abroad. A successful domestic track record has been an important selection criterion for multinational firms expatriating US personnel, but scholars observe that technical skills do not always foster managerial success abroad. Rosalie Tung (1987) suggested four factors that predicted expatriate success, including: (a) technical competence on the job; (b) personality traits or relational abilities; (c) environmental variables; and (d) family situation. Later work conducted by Stewart Black (1988) showed that expatriate success also can be associated with individual adjustment to the job and with interacting with others. This and other work led Black, Mendenhall, and Oddou (1991) to argue that five sets of factors shape expatriate success, including: (a) individual variables; (b) job variables; (c) organizational culture variables; (d) organizational socialization variables; and (e) nonwork categories. Parker and McEvoy (1993) suggested these factors could be categorized as (a) individual, (b) organizational, and (c) contextual, such as, having a family or country assignment.

Studies of non-US managers revealed different experiences for them than have surfaced in research on US expatriates (André, 1985; Zeira and Harari, 1977), and research on women managers abroad similarly shows that women do not necessarily fit profiles based on US male experiences (Adler, 1987; Parker, 1991). Finally, a study that compared wholly owned subsidiary expatriate managers with international joint venture managers found the latter viewed adaptability as more important to their jobs than did the former (Parker, Zeira, and Hatem, 1996). These studies support a conclusion that factors affecting success abroad extend far beyond technical skills, and that individual differences of gender, nationality, context, and organizational form can affect performance success for both the manager and the organization managed. Growing diversity of people and organizational forms involved in global business suggests there will be few universals to follow when selecting managers, but it may be safe to assume that any approach to managerial staffing requires attention to host-country response lest the firm be viewed as ethnocentric, and to the technical and managerial skills set needed for the particular assignment abroad. Further, according to chief executives, firms need a common set of principles and ethics to guide these managers throughout the world.

Training for knowledge work

The rapid pace of global change has created demand for people with specialized technical and managerial skills, and people with these skills might be said to have a comparative advantage over others. Many global leaders believe that technical skills in combination with people skills represent an important knowledge set, but there may be greater emphasis on the ability to learn than on current knowledge. Firms increasingly expect nations to invest in education sufficient for employment. According to vice president James Austgen, Motorola is phasing out its basic-skills programs because they no longer feel they can train people to be trainable (Avishai, 1996). As the opening case indicated, Motorola spends about 4% of its total wage bill on training, emphasizing proficiency in scientific and technical disciplines and people skills. Leaders believe that the knowledge worker will be more than a repository of technical knowledge; he or she must be able to access that knowledge and transfer it to other people.

In industries where intellectual capital is the main currency, firms are forging new territory to acquire the people they need. For example, following Deutsche Bank's purchase of Morgan Grenfell in 1989, the renamed Deutsche Morgan Grenfell irritated competitors by hiring over 200 bankers from rival firms over the next seven years. This practice stood in sharp contrast to traditional banking practice. Microsoft and IBM both sponsor training programs in China to develop people they need and supply state-of-the-art computer resources for use. Decisions about how to manage these and other employees is another staffing challenge for the global enterprise.

In Chapter 4, culture was depicted as an iceberg where information such as values and beliefs are hidden from immediate view, and training was shown to reveal hidden dimensions of culture by providing specific knowledge about other cultures and introducing underlying reasons for why and how cultural norms differ. We saw that the length and breadth of training varies widely in international firms. According to Magoroh Maruyama (1992), not all Japanese firms train extensively and some provide only two weeks' notice before sending their employees abroad. Matsushita, on the other hand, provides training of six months or more for the foreign assignment, and some South Korean firms establish 'culture houses' where employees live and speak like natives of the country where they will work. In view of growing demands for knowledgeable workers, global firms can be expected to follow Motorola's lead to increase training investments. Similarly, nations also may be motivated to invest in educating their populace.

Leadership for teaching and learning

A unique feature of Peter Senge's work on the learning organization is an emphasis on everyone being both a learner and a teacher. This represents a profound change from traditional management principles which more clearly allocate the job of thinking and teaching to top or middle managers. Leaders must be designers but they also have to be stewards to the learning process to help others see the bigger picture of the organization and its direction in a larger context. Stewardship, like managing, involves taking responsibility for the affairs of others, but the word has meaning beyond its definition. It also assumes one is a guide and a helper rather than merely a director of events.

Based on interviews with leaders in six continents, Charles Farkas and Philippe De Backer (1996) concluded there are only five approaches to leadership for the chief executive officer (CEO) which are:

1 *Strategic*: the CEO is the top strategist responsible for vision and an outline for implementation.
2 *Expertise*: the CEO focuses organizational attention as champion of a specific, often proprietary form of expertise.
3 *Box*: the CEO develops rules, regulations, procedures, and values to control behavior and outcome within defined boundaries.
4 *Change*: the CEO acts as a radical change agent to transform bureaucracy.
5 *Human assets*: the CEO manages success through promoting program, principles, and policies in support of the organization's human resources.

The human assets approach was the most popular, practiced by 30% of those interviewed, including global leaders at PepsiCo and Gillette, and it requires a chief executive who manages for success through people, and an emphasis on teamwork, building leaders, and genuine forms of empowerment.

Incentives

Evidence provided earlier in this chapter showed compensation practices differ worldwide. These differences raise issues of fairness and create inequalities that can be disruptive when they are perceived to be unfair. Unequal treatment may undermine employee loyalty to organizations, and force continual revisions of compensation systems. There is a need for sufficient continuity to ensure fairness and yet a competing need to respond to dynamic change as it occurs. According to a Western model, workers are believed to be motivated by pay incentives, but this may not be a worldwide phenomenon, as is demonstrated by the experience of Finnish paper and power equipment firm A. Ahlstrom, (Box 6.9).

BOX 6.9:   INCENTIVE PAY AT A. AHLSTROM

Incentive pay did not improve low employee morale at the 400-employee Ahlstrom Fakop plant in Poland, but morale and sales both increased in 1993 when the firm offered to maintain staffing at current levels if the plant met sales targets. This suggests that leaders assess what does motivate employees before investing in schemes that may not work.

In some cases, internal incentives are either absent or insufficient to retain employees.

INCENTIVES FOR KNOWLEDGE WORKERS

Knowledge workers create special challenges for compensation programs for the following reasons:

1 The duration of projects varies from weeks to years, but many compensation systems are annual.
2 Performance targets cannot be set because the nature of knowledge work often is discovery and exploration.
3 The impact of a knowledge worker's performance sometimes is not apparent until well beyond the event.
4 Knowledge workers often operate in teams that make it difficult to establish individual input (Incentives and knowledge workers, 1989).

Although the work produced by knowledge workers may belong to the organization, the ability to create that work remains the worker's property. To foster ongoing development of this human capital, organizations often need to create a workplace where people want to be, and that may be thought of as one dimension of compensation. For example, if part of the pay-off from work is intellectual stimulation, then the work should provide such stimulation as a main incentive. Thomas Stewart (1997) believes that retaining the knowledge worker also comes from stimulating economic self-interest among employees. Stock ownership plans or gain-sharing bonuses provide this motivation, causing the organization and the employee to develop mutual interests in successful performance. Often found in the computer industry, stock ownership plans have made many employees rich. The down side is that some of those made rich by firm stock holdings may leave the firm. Many of Microsoft's early millionaires are retiring before 40 to spend their financial and intellectual capital elsewhere. In the Seattle area, results have included an explosion in philanthropic giving, rising costs of housing when money is no object, and volunteerism that benefits the community rather than Microsoft *per se*.

Intelligent careers

Organizational learning processes require changes in the way organizational participants transmit and create knowledge and intellect, and these changes have in turn altered ways of thinking about careers. In his book *The intelligent enterprise*, James Brian Quinn (1992) argues the firm must focus on developing and managing intangibles through three core knowledge competencies: culture (knowing why), know-how, and networks (knowing who). Michael Arthur, Priscilla Claman, and Robert DeFillippi (1995) believe these competencies are relevant also to individuals planning an intelligent career. The organization's culture involves knowing why some projects are important and others are not or knowing why things are done as they are. Know-how relates to important skills and abilities and knowing who relates to the networks to which an individual belongs. In combination, these three competencies distinguish the individual career. It is therefore important for the individual to examine these competencies, and the authors suggest this becomes possible by asking questions about new and old paradigms shaping organizations (Table 6.9).

Organizations are unlikely to adopt the new paradigms suggested by Arthur, Claman, and De Fillipi without retaining some characteristics of existing paradigms. In view of labor globalization and the growing need for employees who can adapt to different situations when forging a career, it is important for individuals first to clarify their own goals and career paradigm preferences and then gauge the extent to which a potential employer favors one approach over the other. For example, some firms may be arranged as a hierarchy but expect individuals also to make decisions within specified parameters. Interviews then are a reciprocal process where both organization and individual assess potential fit for employment.

TABLE 6.9   Principles behind the new vs old career paradigms

Old career paradigm	New career paradigm
A formal, static contract creates an implied trade of job security for employee compliance	Rewards are exchanged for specific task performance, and contracts can be renegotiated as conditions change
Employees usually are expected to work for only one firm; the firm specifies jobs to be done and provides training to meet their needs and interests	Employees do not expect to work for only one firm in a career; employees become responsible for training and self-development each thinks will enhance a career
A hierarchically organized firm concentrates expertise and strategic direction in top management at corporate headquarters	Strategic thinking becomes dispersed and businesses gain more freedom to pursue their own objectives
Firms are viewed as autonomous, stand-alone entities in competition with other firms	Firms begin to share interdependence with regional and/or broader industry groups
Corporate allegiance generates fairly permanent groupings within the organization with project goals subordinate to corporate needs	Project allegiance is introduced; assignments change over time and project outcomes become more important

Source: Adapted from: Arthur, Michael B., Claman, Priscilla H., and DeFillippi, Robert J. (1995). Intelligent enterprise, intelligent careers. *Academy of Management Executive*, 9(4): 13.

In summary, a globalizing world of work offers almost limitless potential for opportunity, but choosing among these opportunities becomes yet one more challenge for the individual. Finally, despite the guidelines suggested here and elsewhere, there are no hard and fast 'rules' for global work. Worldwide changes in technology, in organizations, in culture, and in other aspects of work generate jobs that did not previously exist in diverse locations. Recognizing, weighing, and selecting from among these and other opportunities are only a few of the challenges for work in a global world.

| APPENDIX | THE UNIVERSAL DECLARATION OF HUMAN RIGHTS |

PREAMBLE

Whereas recognition of the inherent dignity and of the equal and inalienable rights of all members of the human family is the foundation of freedom, justice and peace in the world,

Whereas disregard and contempt for human rights have resulted in barbarous acts which have outraged the conscience of mankind, and the advent of a world in which human beings shall enjoy freedom of speech and belief and freedom from fear and want has been proclaimed as the highest aspiration of the common people,

Whereas it is essential, if man is not to be compelled to have recourse, as a last resort, to rebellion against tyranny and oppression, that human rights should be protected by the rule of law,

Whereas it is essential to promote the development of friendly relations between nations,

Whereas the peoples of the United Nations have in the Charter reaffirmed their faith in fundamental human rights, in the dignity and worth of the human person and in the equal rights of men and women and have determined to promote social progress and better standards of life in larger freedom,

Whereas Member States have pledged themselves to achieve, in co-operation with the United Nations, the promotion of universal respect for and observance of human rights and fundamental freedoms,

Whereas a common understanding of these rights and freedoms is of the greatest importance for the full realization of this pledge,
Now therefore,

The General Assembly

Proclaims this Universal Declaration of Human Rights as a common standard of achievement for all peoples and all nations, to the end that every individual and every organ of society, keeping this Declaration constantly in mind, shall strive by teaching and education to promote respect for these rights and freedoms and by progressive measures, national and international, to secure their universal and effective recognition and observance, both among the peoples of Member States themselves and among the peoples of territories under their jurisdiction.

ARTICLE 1

All human beings are born free and equal in dignity and rights. They are endowed with reason and conscience and should act towards one another in a spirit of brotherhood.

ARTICLE 2

Everyone is entitled to all the rights and freedoms set forth in this Declaration, without distinction of any kind, such as race, colour, sex, language, religion, political or other opinion, national or social origin, property, birth or other status.

Furthermore, no distinction shall be made on the basis of the political, jurisdictional or international status of the country or territory to which a person belongs, whether it be independent, trust, non-self-governing or under any other limitation of sovereignty.

ARTICLE 3

Everyone has the right to life, liberty and the security of person.

ARTICLE 4

No one shall be held in slavery or servitude; slavery and the slave trade shall be prohibited in all their forms.

ARTICLE 5

No one shall be subjected to torture or to cruel, inhuman or degrading treatment or punishment.

ARTICLE 6

Everyone has the right to recognition everywhere as a person before the law.

ARTICLE 7

All are equal before the law and are entitled without any discrimination to equal protection of the law. All are entitled to equal protection against any discrimination in violation of this Declaration and against any incitement to such discrimination.

ARTICLE 8

Everyone has the right to an effective remedy by the competent national tribunals for acts violating the fundamental rights granted him by the constitution or by law.

ARTICLE 9

No one shall be subjected to arbitrary arrest, detention or exile.

ARTICLE 10

Everyone is entitled in full equality to a fair and public hearing by an independent and impartial tribunal, in the determination of his rights and obligations and of any criminal charge against him.

ARTICLE 11

1 Everyone charged with a penal offence has the right to be presumed innocent until proved guilty according to law in a public trial at which he has had all the guarantees necessary for his defence.

2 No one shall be held guilty of any penal offence on account of any act or omission which did not constitute a penal offence, under national or international law, at the time when it was committed. Nor shall a heavier penalty be imposed than the one that was applicable at the time the penal offence was committed.

ARTICLE 12

No one shall be subjected to arbitrary interference with his privacy, family, home or correspondence, nor to attacks upon his honour and reputation. Everyone has the right to the protection of the law against such interference or attacks.

ARTICLE 13

1 Everyone has the right to freedom of movement and residence within the borders of each State.

2 Everyone has the right to leave any country, including his own, and to return to his country.

ARTICLE 14

1 Everyone has the right to seek and to enjoy in other countries asylum from persecution.

2 This right may not be invoked in the case of prosecutions genuinely arising from nonpolitical crimes or from acts contrary to the purposes and principles of the United Nations.

ARTICLE 15

1 Everyone has the right to a nationality.

2 No one shall be arbitrarily deprived of his nationality nor denied the right to change his nationality.

ARTICLE 16

1   Men and women of full age, without any limitation due to race, nationality or religion, have the right to marry and to found a family. They are entitled to equal rights as to marriage, during marriage and at its dissolution.

2   Marriage shall be entered into only with the free and full consent of the intending spouses.

3   The family is the natural and fundamental group unit of society and is entitled to protection by society and the State.

ARTICLE 17

1   Everyone has the right to own property alone as well as in association with others.

2   No one shall be arbitrarily deprived of his property.

ARTICLE 18

Everyone has the right to freedom of thought, conscience and religion; this right includes freedom to change his religion or belief, and freedom, either alone or in community with others and in public or private, to manifest his religion or belief in teaching, practice, worship and observance.

ARTICLE 19

Everyone has the right to freedom of opinion and expression; this right includes freedom to hold opinions without interference and to seek, receive and impart information and ideas through any media and regardless of frontiers.

ARTICLE 20

1   Everyone has the right to freedom of peaceful assembly and association.

2   No one may be compelled to belong to an association.

ARTICLE 21

1   Everyone has the right to take part in the government of his country, directly or through freely chosen representatives.

2   Everyone has the right of equal access to public service in his country.

3   The will of the people shall be the basis of the authority of government; this will shall be expressed in periodic and genuine elections which shall be by universal and equal suffrage and shall be held by secret vote or by equivalent free voting procedures.

ARTICLE 22

Everyone, as a member of society, has the right to social security and is entitled to realization, through national effort and international co-operation and in accordance with the organization and resources of each State, of the economic, social and cultural rights indispensable for his dignity and the free development of his personality.

ARTICLE 23

1   Everyone has the right to work, to free choice of employment, to just and favourable conditions of work and to protection against unemployment.

2   Everyone, without any discrimination, has the right to equal pay for equal work.

3   Everyone who works has the right to just and favourable remuneration ensuring for himself and his family an existence worthy of human dignity, and supplemented, if necessary, by other means of social protection.

4   Everyone has the right to form and to join trade unions for the protection of his interests.

ARTICLE 24

Everyone has the right to rest and leisure, including reasonable limitation of working hours and periodic holidays with pay.

ARTICLE 25

1   Everyone has the right to a standard of living adequate for the health and well-being of himself and of his family, including food, clothing, housing and medical care and necessary social services, and the right to security in the event of unemployment, sickness, disability, widowhood, old age or other lack of livelihood in circumstances beyond his control.

2   Motherhood and childhood are entitled to special care and assistance. All children, whether born in or out of wedlock, shall enjoy the same social protection.

ARTICLE 26

1   Everyone has the right to education. Education shall be free, at least in the elementary and fundamental stages. Elementary education shall be compulsory. Technical and professional education shall be made generally available and higher education shall be equally accessible to all on the basis of merit.

2   Education shall be directed to the full development of the human personality and to the strengthening of respect for human rights and fundamental freedoms. It shall promote understanding, tolerance and friendship among all nations, racial or religious groups, and shall further the activities of the United Nations for the maintenance of peace.

3   Parents have a prior right to choose the kind of education that shall be given to their children.

ARTICLE 27

1   Everyone has the right freely to participate in the cultural life of the community, to enjoy the arts and to share in scientific advancement and its benefits.

2   Everyone has the right to the protection of the moral and material interests resulting from any scientific, literary or artistic production of which he is the author.

ARTICLE 28

Everyone is entitled to a social and international order in which the rights and freedoms set forth in this Declaration can be fully realized.

ARTICLE 29

1   Everyone has duties to the community in which alone the free and full development of his personality is possible.

2   In the exercise of his rights and freedoms, everyone shall be subject only to such limitations as are determined by law solely for the purpose of securing due recognition and respect for the rights and freedoms of others and of meeting the just requirements of morality, public order and the general welfare in a democratic society.

3   These rights and freedoms may in no case be exercised contrary to the purposes and principles of the United Nations.

ARTICLE 30

Nothing in this Declaration may be interpreted as implying for any State, group or person any right to engage in any activity or to perform any act aimed at the destruction of any of the rights and freedoms set forth herein.

Hundred and eighty-third plenary meeting.
10 December 1948.

Source: Langley, Winston E. (Ed.). (1992). *Human rights: Sixty major global instruments*. Jefferson, NC: McFarland, pp. 2–6.

KEY CHAPTER CONCEPTS

Informal or Shadow Work: The informal work sector is not counted in GDP estimates, and conditions of informal work go unreported, but it is believed that hours of work are longer and wages are lower than in the formal work sector.

The Growing Role of Paid Labor: Paid labor is growing in its centrality to most economies and many lives, spurred on by transitions to market economies, the perceived importance of economic wealth, and a growing number of women in the formal work sector.

MNEs Employ Few Worldwide: Multinational firms employ only about 3% of the global labor force; 61 million are employed by MNEs in the industrialized countries and 12 million in the developing economies. Thus, most paid labor is provided by small, place-bound firms.

Growth in Employment in Non-Business Sectors: There is a worldwide increase in the number of people working outside the business sector for government and nonprofit organizations. The first job for many may be for nonprofit organizations, and these experiences may establish expected standards for work likely to have a spillover effect on for-profit firms.

Work Week Standards: By the 1960s most of the industrialized countries (except Japan) conformed to a harmonized standard working week of 40 or slightly more hours per week. People in the developing economies tend to work more hours per week and annually than people in the industrialized nations.

Part-Time Labor: The number of people who work fewer than 40 hours per week is growing, in part because there are more women in the paid labor force and women are less likely than men to work at paid jobs on a full-time basis.

Formal Sector Work Improves Labor Standards: Economic integration in many developing economies is expected to move jobs from the informal to the formal sector where hours and other conditions of work are more easily observed and legislated. World sentiment is toward standardization of humane work conditions, and global firms are under pressure to play a role in establishing those conditions.

Human Rights Initiatives Worldwide: Human rights initiatives encompass many and diverse concerns such as child labor, working hours and safety conditions, prisoner treatment, and ethnic and gender equity. Human rights abuses affect businesses because they reduce labor productivity, violate individual autonomy, and reduce loyalty to the firm.

Business activities in support of human rights result in organizational alterations. A primary shift is for organizations to view themselves more as community members than autonomous actors.

Business Ethics Defined: Business ethics attempts to recognize the relationship of acts to the good of the individual, the firm, the business community, and society. The challenge of business ethics lies in asking business enterprises and the people who run them to develop a hierarchy of what is good or 'right' to do in a world where there are few absolutes.

Three Incentives for Developing Business Codes of Ethics: Three incentives for developing an ethical code of conduct are: (a) organizational leaders believe that doing right is the right thing to do for either moral or business reasons; (b) convergence among firms and other segments of societies has for the first time created a desire for agreement on ethical frameworks and behaviors; and (c) codes provide one means for clarifying and directing ethical business activities.

Growing Demand for Global Codes of Ethics: Reasons for businesses to cooperate in creating a global code of ethics include the following: (a) maintaining or creating the opportunity for business activities; (b) all firms should be operating according to the same principles – this produces the 'level playing field' upon which many organizational leaders prefer to play; (c) ethical codes are needed and are possible in a world that is interdependent on many other dimensions of business activities; (d) they reduce operating uncertainties; and (e) growing interest in this topic on the part of public citizens and government officials suggests that if businesses don't develop such codes, they will be developed by other bodies that may be unfavorable to business interests.

Four Challenges to a Global Business Ethic: There are four challenges inherent to developing a global code of ethics. First, since global rules are likely to emerge from a negotiation process, they are unlikely to reflect values and habits consistent for all cultures. To the extent that these rules are developed by firms from the Westernized countries, they may not incorporate concerns for much of the world. Second, global ethics may be viewed as an end point rather than a beginning point for developing global ethics. Third, organizations may hide behind global codes, claiming that the absence of rules means that all behaviors are acceptable as conditions change. Finally, a global code of ethics also may serve to depress innovation, since some will hesitate to act in the absence of clear guidelines, but guidelines will never keep pace with globalization.

Knowledge Work Defined: Knowledge is a growing component of labor worldwide, and its importance is linked to a growing service sector and demand for greater variation in industrial production. Knowledge workers are those for whom thinking is an important part of their work. Knowledge work is a critical resource for companies, but unlike tangible resources, knowledge is difficult to measure and value as a firm asset.

The Learning Organization: The learning organization is one that can leverage individual and organizational knowledge so that everyone is a learner and everyone a teacher. Organizational learning philosophies affect leadership, followership, teamwork, and evaluation systems. Emphasis on learning also has implications for career planning.

From Ethnocentrism to Geocentrism: The tendency to think of one's own culture and business practices as 'best' is ethnocentric. Philosophies of management that are ethnocentric tend to lead to centralized decision-making, including hiring expatriate managers to work abroad. Competing philosophies of management such as geocentrism require a different stance on decision-making and managerial hiring where learning can occur.

REVIEW AND DISCUSSION QUESTIONS

1   Many organizational leaders have been taught to think that incentive pay motivates employees to achieve company goals. What are the cultural explanations you can offer for when incentive plans fail to achieve desired results? What does this say about the universality of incentive pay systems?

2   What benefits can organizations realize by subscribing to human rights initiatives? What are the possible costs to them?

3   *The Global Enterprise Project*: To what extent does the firm you're studying employ a global labor force? Where are employees located? How does the firm manage cultural differences evident around the world? Look particularly at compensation systems and benefits.

4   To what extent should business organizations be held accountable for social injustice? The following description challenges you to make decisions that weigh human rights against business interests.

It's easier when someone else decides

Oriental carpets are very popular throughout the world, but they are expensive. Human rights groups argue that among the most expensive are carpets hand-woven in developing economies by very young children of less than 10 or 12 years of age. Their nimble, delicate, and small fingers facilitate tying the fine knots that go into making the carpets. But human rights advocates are protesting this practice of using child labor by boycotting stores in the US and other industrialized countries to stop the import of such carpets. Store owners argue that these are high-quality carpets that last more than 100 years and often have an impressive creative value; they have been a preferred item for the buyer who is looking for value. Merchants add that selling the carpets is contributing to economic development in those countries where they are manufactured. Furthermore, they argue that many of the rugs are crafted on home-based looms and by participating in their creation, children are important contributors to family income and welfare. Further, merchants selling the rugs argue that human rights groups should not dictate the destiny of millions of lives based on practices that are widespread, acceptable, and economically valuable to other countries.

Source: Adapted from: Rajib N. Sanyal and Joao S. Neves, Trenton State College.

Assume the roles of the advisory board for the company selling the carpets in industrialized countries. Evaluate the arguments, economic and social, for continuing to merchandize the carpets. Additionally, consider the negative repercussions that could occur when merchants decide not to merchandize the carpets. How does this example illustrate some of the paradoxes we must manage in global business environments?

REFERENCES

Adler, Nancy J. (1987). Pacific Basin managers: A *Gaijin*, not a woman. *Human Resource Management*, 26: 169–191.

Adler, Nancy J., and Bartholomew, Susan. (1992). Managing globally competent people. *Academy of Management Executive*, 6(3): 52–65.

Adler, Nancy J., and Izraeli, Dafna N. (1994). *Competitive frontiers: Women managers in a global economy*. Oxford: Blackwell.

André, R. (1985). The effects of multinational business training: A replication of INSEAD research in an institute in the United States. *Management International Review*, 25, pp. 4–15.

Applebaum, Richard P., and Henderson, Jeffrey. (1995). The hinge of history: Turbulence and transformation in the world economy. *Competition and Change*, 1(1): 1–12.

Arthur, Michael B., Claman, Priscilla H., and DeFillippi, Robert J. (1995). Intelligent enterprise, intelligent careers. *Academy of Management Executive*, 9(4): 7–22.

Asia's labor pains. (1995, Aug. 26). *The Economist*, pp. 51–52.

Aslanbeigui, Nahid, Pressman, Steven, and Summerfield, Gayle. (1994). *Women in the age of economic transformation*. London: Routledge.

Avishai, Bernard. (1996, July 29). Companies can't make up for failing schools. *The Wall Street Journal*, p. A10.

Badarocco, Joseph. (1995, Winter). Business ethics: The view from the trenches. *California Management Review*, pp. 8–28.

Baker, Stephen. (1997, July 21). Forget the huddled masses: Send nerds. *Business Week*, pp. 110–116.

Bartlett, Christopher A., and Ghoshal, Sumantra. (1992, Sept./Oct.). What is a global manager? *Havard Business Review*, pp. 124–132.

Batsell, Jake. (1998, Jan. 30). Advocate says tiny loans save lives. *The Seattle Times*, pp. C1, C4.

Beck, Nuala. (1995). *Shifting gears: Thriving in the new economy*. New York: HarperCollins.

Black, J. Stewart. (1988). Work role transitions: A study of American expatriate managers in Japan. *Journal of International Business Studies*, 19: 277–294.

Black, J. Stewart, Mendenhall, Mark, and Oddou, Gary. (1991). Toward a comprehensive model of international adjustment: An integration of multiple theoretical perspectives. *Academy of Management Review*, 16: 291–317.

Bosch, Gerhard, Dawkins, Peter, and Michon, François. (1993). *Times are changing: Working time in 14 industrialized countries*. Geneva: International Institute for Labour Studies, ILO.

Brecher, Jeremy, and Costello, Tim. (1994). Global village or global pillage. Boston, MA: South End Press.

Burrows, Brian. (1994). The power of information. *Long Range Planning*, 27(1): 142–153.

Carrington, Tim. (1994, June 22). Gender economics. *The Wall Street Journal*, pp. A1, A6.

The Caux Round Table Principles for Business. (1995). Minneapolis, MN: *Business Ethics*.

Collins, James, and Porras, Jerry. (1995). *Built to last: Successful habits of visionary companies*. New York: HarperBusiness.

Comparable rates of unemployment. (1993). *World of Work – U.S.*, 5: 16.

Ciulla, Joanne B. (1991, Fall). Why is business talking about ethics? Reflections on foreign conversations. *California Management Review*, pp. 67–86.

DeGeorge, Richard T. (1993). *Competing with integrity in international business*. New York: Oxford University Press.

Dicken, Peter. (1992). *Global shift* (2nd ed.). New York/London: Guilford Press.

Donlon, J. (1996, Sept.). Managing across borders. *Chief Executive*, p. 58.

Donnelly, Jack. (1993). *Universal human rights in theory and practice*. Ithaca, NY: Cornell University Press

Drucker, Peter. (1994, Nov. 8). *The age of social transformation*. Teleconference via satellite from Washington, DC.

An evil unbearable to the human heart. (1993). *World of Work – U.S.*, 4: 4–5.

Experts work to eradicate use of child labour. (1997, Oct. 29). *New Zealand Herald*, p. A8.

Farkas, Charles M., and De Backer, Philippe. (1996). *Maximum leadership*. New York: Henry Holt.

Foreign bodies in South Korea. (1996, Dec. 14). *The Economist*, p. 66.

A generation at risk. (1990). *ILO Information*, 18(1): 7.

Handy, Charles. (1990). *The age of unreason*. Cambridge, MA: Harvard Business School Press.

Handy, Charles. (1994). *The age of paradox*. Cambridge, MA: Harvard Business School Press.

Hawken, Paul. (1993). *The ecology of commerce*. New York: HarperBusiness.

Heenan, D.A., and Perlmutter, Howard V. (1979). *Multinational organization development*. Reading, MA: Addison-Wesley.

Human Development Report. (1995). New York: Oxford University Press.

Human Development Report. (1997). Cary, NC: Oxford University Press.

Human rights. (1995, June 3). *The Economist*, pp. 58–59.

ILO Yearbook of labor statistics. (1992). Geneva: ILO.

ILO Yearbook of labor statistics. (1993). Geneva: ILO.

Incentives and knowledge workers: Oil and water? (1989, Summer). *Briefings*. College Park, MD: Newsletter of the Forum for College and University Governance.

Instilling ethical values in large corporations. (1992). *Journal of Business Ethics*, 11(11): 863–867.

Johnston, William B. (1997). Global work force 2000: The new world labor market. In

Heide Vernon-Wertzel and Lawrence H. Wortzel (Eds), *Strategic management in a global economy*, pp. 368–381. New York: John Wiley.

Kapstein, Ethan B. (1996, May/June). Workers and the world economy. *Foreign Affairs*, 75(30): 16–37.

Kiskovsky, Sophia, and Williamson, Elizabeth. (1997, Jan. 30). Second-class comrades no more. *The Wall Street Journal*, p. A12.

Korten, David. (1995). *When corporations rule the world*. San Francisco, CA: Berrett-Koehler.

Larudee, Metrene. (1994, Sept./Oct.). Who gains from trade? *Dollars & Sense*, p. 29.

Light on the shadows. (1997, May 3). *The Economist*, pp. 63–64.

Lublin, Joann. (1996, Feb. 28). Women at top still are distant from CEO jobs. *The Wall Street Journal*, p. B1.

Little Luxembourg sees a big problem. (1994, Mar. 31). *The Wall Street Journal*, p. A11.

McDonald's Corporation Investor Review. (1992).

Mandel, Michael J., and Farrell, Christopher. (1993, June 14). Jobs, jobs, jobs – eventually. *Business Week*, pp. 72–73.

Mankiw, Gregory. (1995, Sept.). *The growth of nations*. New York: Brookings Institution, Brookings Papers on Economic Activity.

Mark, Jeremy. (1995, May 9). Small Asian firm breaks into ranks of Western-dominated software firms. *The Wall Street Journal*, p. A16.

Martin, Philip, and Widgren, Jonas. (1996). International migration: A global challenge. Washington, DC: Population Reference Bureau.

Maruyama, Magoroh. (1992). Changing dimensions in international business. *Academy of Management Executive*, 6(3): 88–96.

Morrow, David J. (1993, Nov. 7). Women exposing sex harassment in Japan. *The Seattle Times*, p. D9.

Naisbitt, John. (1992). *Global paradox*. New York: William Morrow (reports a study of European companies conducted by the Institute of Business Ethics in Britain).

Newman, Barry. (1993, July 8). Flooded by refugees, Western Europe slams doors on foreigners. *The Wall Street Journal*, pp. A1, A8.

Nonaka, Ikujiro, and Takeuchi, Hirotaka. (1995). *The knowledge-creating company: How Japanese companies create the dynamics of innovation*. Oxford: Oxford University Press.

Ohmae, Kenichi. (1990). *The borderless world: Power and strategy in the interlinked economy*. New York: HarperBusiness.

O'Mara, Richard. (1992, Nov. 26). Europe forgets why millions want in. *The Seattle Times*, p. A3.

Ondrack, Daniel. (1985, Fall). International transfers of managers in North American and European MNCs. *Journal of International Business Studies*, pp. 1–19.

Out of the typing pool, into career limbo. (1996, Apr. 15). *Business Week*, pp. 92–94.

The outlook. (1998, Jan. 26). *The Wall Street Journal*, p. A13.

Parker, Barbara (1991). Employment globalization: Can 'voluntary' expatriates meet US hiring needs abroad? *Journal of Global Business*, 2(2): 39–46.

Parker, B., and McEvoy, G. (1993). Initial examination of a model of intercultural adjustment. *International Journal of Intercultural Relations*, 17: 355–379.

Parker, Barbara, Zeira, Yoram, and Hatem, Tarek. (1996). International joint venture managers: Factors affecting personal success and organizational performance. *Journal of International Management*, 2(1): 1–29.

Prahalad, C.K., and Doz, Yves L. (1987). *The multinational mission: Balancing local demands and global vision*. New York: Free Press.

Pura, Raphael. (1992, Mar. 5). Many of Asia's workers are on the move. *Wall Street Journal*, p. A10.

Quinn, James Brian. (1992). *The intelligent enterprise*. New York: Free Press.

Quinn, James Brian, Anderson, Philip, and Finkelstein, Sydney. (1996). Leveraging intellect. *Academy of Management Executive*, 10(3): 7–27.

Rodrik, Dani. (1997). *Has globalization gone too far?* New York: Institute for International Economics.

Saeed, Hasan. (1997, Apr. 3). Cellular phones to link villages in Bangladesh to outside world. *The Seattle Times*, p. A11.

Salamon, Lester M., and Anheier, Helmut K. (1994). *The emerging sector*. Baltimore, MD: Johns Hopkins University Institute for Policy Studies.

Sasseen, Jane. (1993, Oct.). Companies clean up. *International Management*, pp. 30–31.

Schlegelmilch, Bodo B., and Robertson, Diana C. (1995). The influence of country and industry on ethical perceptions of senior executives in the U.S. and Europe. *Journal of International Business Studies*, 26(4): 859–881.

Senge, P. (1990). *The fifth discipline: The art and practice of the learning organization*. New York: Doubleday.

Sherer, Paul M. (1995, Nov. 2). *The Wall Street Journal*, p. A7.

Siconolfi, Michael. (1995, Feb. 21). Wall Street gurus are hitting the books again. *The Wall Street Journal*, pp. C1, C22.

Simai, Mihaly. (1994). *The future of global governance*. Washington, DC: United States Institute of Peace.

Smith, Craig S. (1994, Aug. 16). Reebok compels Chinese contractor to improve conditions for workers. *The Wall Street Journal*, p. A10.

Stark, Andrew. (1993, May/June). What's the matter with business ethics? *Harvard Business Review*, pp. 38–48.

Steil, Benn. (1994, Jan./Feb.). 'Social correctness' is the new protectionism. *Foreign Affairs*, pp. 14–20.

Steinmann, Horst, and Lohr, Albert. (1992, Apr.). A survey of business ethics in Germany. *Business Ethics: A European Review*, pp. 139–141.

Stewart, Thomas A. (1994, Oct. 3). Your company's most valuable asset: Intellectual capital. *Fortune*, pp. 68–74.

Stewart, Thomas A. (1997). *Intellectual capital*. New York: Doubleday/Currency.

Studemann, Frederick. (1994, Apr.). Germany: Shaken and stirred. *International Management*, pp. 45–47.

Thailand fire shows region cuts corners on safety to boost profits. (1993, May 13). *The Wall Street Journal*, p. A13.

Tung, R.L. (1987). Expatriate assignments: Enhancing success and minimizing failures. *Academy of Management Executive*, 2: 117–126.

Twice the workers – and twice the productivity. (1995, Aug./Oct.). *World Bank Policy Research Bulletin*, 6(4): 1–6.

UN panel to tackle abuse of women working abroad. (1996, May 28). *Seattle Times*, p. A7.

UNHCR by numbers. (1997, Jan. 12). http://www.unicc.org/unher/un&ref/numbers/numbers.htm

Wallace, Charles P. (1995, June 30). Filipinas face rampant abuse in overseas jobs. *The Seattle Times*, p. A14.

Webley, S. (1992). *Company values and codes: Current best practices in the United Kingdom.* London: Institute of Business Ethics.

Working nation: works for everyone. (1995). *Women & Work*, 16(2): 1–4.

Women hold more seats on Fortune 500 boards. (1996, Dec. 12). *The Wall Street Journal*, p. A8.

World Development Report 1995: Workers in an integrating world. (1995). New York: Oxford University Press.

World Economic and Social Survey. (1995). New York: United Nations.

World Employment Report. (1995). Geneva: ILO, UN.

World Investment Report. (1994). New York: UN, UNCTAD.

World Labour Report. (1994). Geneva: ILO.

You ain't seen nothing yet. (1994, Oct. 1). *The Economist*, pp. 20–24, The Global Economy Survey.

Zachary, G. Pascal. (1994, July 28). Exporting rights. *The Wall Street Journal*, pp. A1, A5.

Zachary, G. Pascal. (1995, Feb. 2). US software: Now it may be made in Bulgaria. *The Wall Street Journal*, p. B1.

Zeira, Yoram, and Harari, E. (1977). Genuine multinational staffing policy: Expectations and realities. *Academy of Management Journal*, 20(2): 327–333.

Chapter 7

Global Political and Legal Environments

ONE CHILD SMILES

Operation Smile International is a transnational voluntary group organized to provide recon-structive surgery around the world to children with facial deformities such as cleft lips and palates, tumors, and burn scars. This story is of one small child in a very big world whose life changed because of one man and one transnational organization.

Only one person knows where Li Meng Fang's life began, or what the circumstances were surrounding her birth. In 1990, Li Xing Shan, a poor farmer, who was scavenging for bottles and cans to sell for scrap, found the baby on a garbage heap. The box holding Meng Fang contained a bottle of milk and a scribbled message that said: 'Please have mercy.' The plea for mercy doubtless came because the child's palate and lip were cleft, and according to local super-stition the cleft lip is an evil omen. After feeding the child, the farmer returned her to the box for other scavengers to find. Days later, the farmer returned to the dump, finding the baby still there, but too weak even to cry. Determined not to let her die, he took the baby home.

The government's family planning policy allowing only one child did not permit another child in the farmer's family. Further, the farmer's wife and the other villagers could not under-stand why the farmer would risk government penalties for a deformed baby. Finally, forced to choose between the child and his life among his friends and wife, Li Xing Shan made a painful decision. He and the baby he had rescued became two of the 150 million itinerant Chinese wandering China who beg when they cannot eke a living from scraps scavenged from garbage dumps. Li lived in fear that someone would take the child from him.

In November 1993, Li and his rescued child appeared in Shantou, China, just another stop on a 3,000-mile odyssey from nowhere to nowhere. Gathered among other travelers one night, Li heard that a voluntary medical group was repairing cleft palates at a local hospital. He and Meng Fang slept at a construction site across from the hospital that night, waiting for the doors to open. It was the last day for medical screening, and in fact the surgery schedule had already been filled, but when people heard the story of Meng Fang, they made room for the child. Two days later, Meng Fang's cleft was repaired in an operation that took less than an hour, and in just a few more days all traces of what had been a deformity had begun to disappear. Said Li: 'Nobody wanted her and we spent our lives in hiding, but I promised myself that one day I would get her lip fixed. I never dreamed that I would have the opportunity.'

Li Xing Shan had too few resources to pay for cosmetic surgery for his much-loved child, but the surgery she experienced made it possible for Meng Fang to become a productive member of society rather than an outcast. Acting collectively to provide resources of time and money and medical skills, transnational voluntary groups like Operation Smile do more than provide direct services. They train local medical personnel committed to performing the same voluntary services, and they help local volunteers establish reasons and ways to provide services like cleft repairs that government cannot or will not provide. They work with pharmaceutical firms to raise funds, and they rely on businesses to participate in fund-raising and promotion to continue the work others begin. In 1998, funds committed by Computer Associates and Microsoft Corporation's founder were released to develop a 'Smile Train' initiative in China. Funding from these donations makes it newly possible to purchase equipment that can be moved as needed by train throughout China, eliminating international and internal travel costs for the equipment, and reducing the per-child costs of cosmetic surgery. Finally, they do the work they came to do: give one child the smile she needs to light up the world.

Source: Operation Smile International brochure. (1996). Norfolk, VA: OSI.

PART I GLOBAL PRESSURES ON POLITICAL DECISIONS

The fall of the Berlin Wall in November 1989 signaled the end of a political era dominated by a Cold War that had simmered between the USSR and US since the close of World War II in 1945. For some, this event and later dissolution of the Soviet Union signaled a worldwide shift toward market economics that has had a profound affect on political and legal systems within nations. This chapter outlines ways free markets have shaped political and legal concerns within, between, and among nations worldwide.

The chapter begins with an introduction to the basic functions of government, then examines how globalization has led to reshaped roles and responsibilities among government leaders in nations. Globalizing systems of trade governance including trade alliances and trade agreements are reviewed, as are globalizing systems of governance relating to human development and justice. Roles of intergovernmental organizations, nongovernmental organizations, and businesses in achieving global economic and social justice also are examined because roles traditionally allocated to government or to business are increasingly performed by nongovernmental organizations. The example of Operation Smile International (OSI) in the opening case demonstrates how one voluntary organization plays roles often assumed by governments and how businesses also help OSI to perform their work. A major challenge businesses face in a changing political environment is risk exposure; theories and practices of risk management examined include political, financial, and corruption risk for the firm. The chapter concludes with a look at how managers cope with the psychological and personal risks increasingly manifest at work. Topics explored include stress, conflict, and violence management.

THE ROLE OF GOVERNMENT

Culture is the pattern of shared values developed to cope with common problems, including the problems of common defense and common survival. The network of political and legal arrangements that constitute a government are an important mechanism for meeting common needs for defense, survival, and development. Governments can be informal or formal and they can rely on custom or on law to fulfill their mission, but today most governments are organized around sovereign and independent nation-states defined by geographic boundaries. Within these national borders, parallel and complementary political and legal systems often coexist, encompassing national, regional, state, or municipal objectives. Political systems for these nation-states often differ on two important dimensions: who makes decisions, and how resources ensuring defense and development are distributed.

Decision-making in nations

In a democracy, decisions are distributed among the populace. A direct form of democracy occurs when people meet to represent their own interests, but population size of most nations makes this rare in practice. Instead, most democratic nations adopt a representative democracy where voters elect political representatives to participate in decisions of government. Decisions in other government systems such as communism, socialism, absolute monarchies, or dictatorships can be centralized in the hands of a powerful few in a command system. In the former Soviet Union, the few in command were top members of the Communist Party. Either type of system influences how resources are managed.

Resource distribution in nations

Philosophical differences in how to use resources for the common good lead to practical differences over use of productive resources like land, factories and equipment, raw materials, labor and capital. Most of these resources are finite or limited, and government leaders decide how to allocate them. In a command form of government, the government owns most productive assets, and so it is government leaders who decide how they will be used. In the former Soviet Union, for example, the Communist Party dictated not only which goods would be produced and where, but also assigned workers to jobs where they were needed. In a free market, many if not most productive resources are held in private hands.

In the absence of income-producing activities like gambling in Monte Carlo and Las Vegas or oil production in Saudi Arabia that generate government incomes, most governments gain access to the operating income they need via taxation levied against private resources, including taxes on personal income, on sales, on property, or on corporate profits. Regardless of the sources, government revenues typically are used to support government operations, build a defense system, or redistribute them for the common good. Among projects believed to serve a common good are welfare and other social support programs, road or infrastructure projects, education, food subsidies, and even business development programs. Schemes to redistribute resources vary widely by nation and this affects tax rates and the amount and extent of government spending. For example, corporate tax rates, like individual tax rates, vary by country, ranging from a 1996 high of 59% in Germany to about 40% in the US and a little more than 30% in Sweden. However, according to an *Economist* article (The tap runs dry, 1997), globalization in two spheres may make it more difficult for nations to tax corporations. First, Internet technology allows almost all organizations to cross commercial borders, and few mechanisms exist to monitor these sales. Second, multinational enterprises

TABLE 7.1   Tax freedom day in selected countries, 1995

Singapore	March 4
USA	April 11
Japan	April 12
Australia	April 25
Britain	May 9
Canada	May 12
Germany	May 23
Netherlands, France	June 12
Belgium	June 17
Sweden	July 3

(MNEs) as well as smaller firms increasingly earn more of their revenues abroad, and they may find it advantageous to report greatest profits in nations where tax rates are low.

Individuals also are increasingly global, and they too may be motivated to work in nations where individual tax rates are low. In 1994, individual tax revenues in the most industrialized countries (including income taxes, consumption, and social security contributions) ranged from a high of 50% in Sweden, where infrastructures and social supports are strong to a low of 23% in Turkey, where there are fewer social support systems and fewer roads or programs supported by government. For individuals, the most meaningful comparative measure of taxation is 'tax freedom day,' or the day each year when the nation's demand for individual taxes is met. As Table 7.1 illustrates, some governments levy more individual taxes than others.

Implementing governmental decisions

Whatever the form of government, national governments make decisions and manage resources for the common good by legal and regulatory means. On the domestic scene, government regulates what businesses can and cannot do through laws; redistributes resources through taxation and welfare plans; and collaborates with businesses and others to promote economic growth and social development. The effects of regulations on business activities range from the mundane, such as whether a limited liability company is designated by Ltd, as in Britain, Gmbh, as in Germany, or Inc., as in the US, to the powerful, e.g., government-directed industrial policy. Business laws also establish standards, e.g., safety, professional licensing, or minimum wage, affecting how work is accomplished. For example, government leaders can protect future resources or provide public goods through regulatory means, perhaps protecting future air quality by setting air emissions standards. Except for those few nations where governments interfere in almost no ways with the market, most governments correct market imperfections and manage business and individual behavior through regulations, policies, rules, and standards. Within nations, legal arrangements that enforce government decisions are based on common and shared understandings among people as to what is good, right, acceptable, or fair, and three types of legal systems are most in use today:

- A *civil law* system strives to outline the law in specific terms, encoding common understandings of what is fair or good in written law that then is applied by the courts. Nations organized under civil laws include most countries in Western Europe except those in the British Commonwealth, and fewer countries in East Asia, including Japan, South Korea, and Taiwan.
- Laws in a *common law* system are somewhat more broadly described than in a civil law system, and it is therefore up to the courts to interpret these laws by applying them to situations that are brought forward for court decisions. The common law system as we know it originated with William the Conqueror in 1066 in an effort to create one set of common laws for England, and it is still practiced in the British Commonwealth, in the US, and in most countries settled by Anglo-Saxons.
- Many countries follow *religious law*. For example, many Islamic countries follow Sharia or the laws of Islam, which define individual behavior as well as social relations, business relations, and community life. The ideological basis of these relations is found in the Qur'an (or Koran as it is often spelled in English); this tome spells out expectations for Islamic life. Less well-codified or unwritten religious laws also direct beliefs and behaviors among some tribal groups, such as animists who believe the soul is the principle of life and may be found in all natural objects. Magic, fate, luck, and signs also are a part of animist religions.

Among the challenges of global diversity is that individuals and companies from varied nations are not easily able, nor always willing, to alter their behaviors to fit with laws they may not understand or recognize in another nation. This leads to conflict within and between nations. For example, animist traditions among Aborigines often conflict with Australian common law, and differences between Islamic religious law and civil or common law become more evident as nations interact. The US, for example, is a litigious society, as witnessed by the fact that about a third of the attorneys in the world practice there, and their propensity to sue over differences in business practices creates a challenge for managers from abroad. The legalistic orientation typical for the US is now being taken global as those attorneys increasingly practice law for companies doing business globally.

International roles for national governments

National opinions of what is good or right or fair in practice and in law commonly are not shared among nations or at a global level, and so regulations, rules, policies, standards, and practices developed for domestic markets are adapted or supplemented for international interactions. This can result in trade negotiations between nations that produce one set of rules for domestic businesses and another for businesses from other countries. Policies affecting cross-border business include trading conditions, regulations, standards, taxation of foreign imports, and others. For example, governments often protect domestic producers or policies from outsiders by means of trade controls such as tariffs, quotas, subsidies, customs valuations, standards, licensing, reciprocal agreements, or restrictions of services. Despite considerable rhetoric, most nations today have trade controls. Japan does not import apple or pear root stock; Australia does not import apples from New Zealand; the European Union provides subsidies to agriculture and other industries; and textiles is one among many industries protected by US tariffs and import quotas. These practices increasingly are being re-examined because globalization has meant that economic and social prosperity within almost every nation are ever more tied to the fate of other nations.

Economic integration and greater interdependence in other spheres have led to global agreements reducing the scope and even the focus of domestic policy activities. This is causing leaders within nations to turn their attention outward as well as inward. The following section examines six major changes among national governments resulting from globalization.

RESHAPED ROLES FOR NATIONAL GOVERNMENTS IN A GLOBAL WORLD

Increasing interdependence among economies and blurring sectoral boundaries are making it more difficult for nations autonomously to manage fiscal and monetary policy; telecommunication breakthroughs distribute resources national governments once controlled; and many conflicting demands now tug at national leaders. In response, government leaders are reshaping their roles to ensure survival, prosperity, and defense in a global world. Important examples include privatization, deregulation, industrial policies, and government supports for business.

Privatization

Government entities worldwide are divesting themselves of productive factors they once owned or controlled. This process of privatization has occurred for three principal reasons:

1 Many developing nations are growing too rapidly for the governmental sector to keep pace. Governments keep up by allowing the private sector to perform some roles normally reserved for government.

2 Government downsizing in the industrialized world includes contracting with private vendors for work previously done by government workers, such as garbage removal services or prison management. This is the government equivalent of outsourcing.

3 Governments all over the world are divesting infrastructure businesses like telecommunications and selling government-owned companies either outright or in shared ventures to improve the quality of services offered.

Until recently, many industries in European countries were owned by the government, but almost all have begun to privatize. France is privatizing its telecommunications industry; Germany announced plans to abolish its postal monopoly by 2003 and open mass mailings to competition as early as 1998; and Great Britain has divested itself of Rolls-Royce and British Airways, among others. The costs are high for establishing and maintaining capital-intensive industries like airlines, railroads, and telecommunications links in a global world, but so are the stakes; if the world is global, then travel and communication will be every nation's link with that global world. Nations fearful of being left behind in these industries are reducing restrictions that have kept them in government hands, and more of them are being moved to the private sector. As a first-mover in wide-scale privatization, Chile proved that economic development could follow privatization, and became the model for privatization now being implemented not only in Latin America but worldwide. For example, in 1993 alone Argentina made a public stock offering in oil and gas giant YPF; Brazil sold a major steelmaker to a group of banks; Jamaica sold sugar plantations to the Sugar Company of Jamaica; Mexico sold Television Azteca to the Salinas Pliego and Sabo families; and Panama sold its fruit juice company to a Colombian extractor. Since then, hundreds of similar deals have been made throughout the region, including Colombia's sale of automaker Colombiana Automotriz to Mazda and Sumitomo. Telecommunications industries also have been privatized in full or in part since 1987 from Latin and Central America to include Argentina, Chile, Peru, Mexico, Venezuela, countries in the Caribbean such as Cuba and Jamaica, and industrialized countries such as Canada, Germany, and the Netherlands. Worldwide sales of state-owned enterprises numbered 2,700 in over 95 countries between 1988 and 1993, and total value of privatization sales in 1994 was just less than $80 billion. As shown in Table 7.2 privatization of services such as telecommunications and utilities totaled about $36 billion in 1994. By 1996, the global value of privatization had risen to $88 billion; however, most privatization in advanced nations has taken place in part or in full and the world now is witnessing

TABLE 7.2   Privatization, by industry, 1994

Industry	Volume ($ millions)	% of total
Telecommunications	13,975.6	17.4
Power utilities	11,573.7	14.4
Energy	10,611.2	13.2
Tobacco	7,775.7	9.7
Insurance	7,482.1	9.3
Banking	4,465.6	5.6
Vehicles	2,094.7	2.6
Steel	1,899.1	2.4
Mining	1,661.5	2.1
Coal	1,497.4	1.9

a shift in privatization from the advanced economies to countries outside the OECD. Developing economies sponsored only about 17% of privatization revenues in 1990, as compared to about 22% in 1996. Government divestment of these organizations is expected to be a more efficient use of scarce resources because businesses are believed to extract value more efficiently than do politicians.

In some cases, privatization has been followed by social upheaval and led to face-offs between businesses and other interests. Because privatization typically permits new competitors to enter formerly protected industries, many in those industries fear for their jobs, often because private purchasers streamline organizations made unwieldy under government management. As firms are reshaped to generate profits in the private sector, they can expect to run afoul of labor and citizen groups more accustomed to having a say in the organization's destiny. In these cases, business organizations often have found it difficult to conduct business with an eye toward profits. That is, layoffs, restructuring, and even job redesign have been resisted, and businesses and governments face challenges in managing these changes.

Eroding public confidence in government

The government/business relationship has been reshaped by factors other than privatization. For example, in mainland China flourishing capitalism may be causing people to view the government sector as irrelevant. According to a *Wall Street Journal* report, business opportunities beginning in 1978 have made money more important than the Communist Party to many Chinese, resulting in a drop in party membership and less attention to party dictates (Kahn and Brauchli, 1994). The Chinese government also has less control over individuals as a result of free enterprise because people who work for themselves do not have to conform to government dictates. For example, Chinese people now are less inclined to obey laws forbidding early marriage, and they are earning sufficient income from the private sector to pay fines for choosing to have second and even third children (Tofani, 1994). This example not only illustrates the growing role of business enterprise in private lives, but also shows growing interdependence among political entities, business entities, and social and cultural norms.

The transition to market economics in Eastern Europe also has created a crisis of leadership reflected in elections that vacillate between communist and democratic leadership. According to a 1996 Open Media Research Institute study, voters in Eastern Europe hold contradictory opinions. Most think economic reform has occurred too slowly, but few want reform to include personal hardships (Paradox explained, 1995). Finally, demands for government downsizing in the industrialized world also indicate declining belief in government's ability to solve important problems. In the US declining belief in 'big' government is manifested in calls for less federal government and more autonomy at state and local levels. These examples from around the world reflect growing demand for finding new solutions to problems governments once were expected to resolve.

Revamping welfare

Many industrialized nations have developed social welfare systems to redistribute resources. These systems are under review in many nations for two major reasons: welfare funds are perceived to be a growing financial burden; and in many nations people believe these programs do not function well. For example, annual costs of welfare were 14.9% of GDP in Eastern Europe and 16.3% in OECD countries between 1985 and 1990. Throughout the industrialized world, many believe that welfare is drained by those who do not need it. There is decreased willingness among some politicians to fund welfare programs, and increased public agitation to revise welfare programs. For example, a White Paper released in Britain in 1994 called for reducing or abolishing welfare benefits for recipients who refuse to participate in job training programs, and the Netherlands also has revised disability rules such that fewer people can qualify for long-term benefits. Interestingly, countries with a strong social net are rolling back these systems at the same time that developing economies have begun to invest more resources in charitable activities amidst citizens' call for intervention to aid the elderly, the poor, children, and others in those nations. These countervailing forces suggest that many national governments face new roles in shaping welfare systems. Another countervailing force is found in industrialized economies where conservative calls for reductions in social welfare are being countered by calls for fewer programs serving business interests such as government subsidies, supports, and programs like the Overseas Development Program in the US.

Industrial policy

Few nations have sufficient resources to develop in all desired directions simultaneously, yet national leaders have growing incentives to do so. Japan, Indonesia, and South Korea are among several nations that have addressed the problem of scarce development resources by means of industrial policies targeting specific industries. For the most part, industries targeted are capital-intensive, often those that are growing quickly, but always those with the potential to add greatest value or return to investments. Industries targeted via industrial policy often include telecommunications, aircraft, automotives, and computers.

Industrial policy is most frequently used to describe overt governmental action. Japan's MITI and South Korea's support of industrial groups called *chaebols* are clear industrial policies, and other nations also develop a national plan to outline how and where industrial growth will occur. Figure 7.1 describes the 10 industries Indonesia's government has targeted for development. It also is important to realize that industrial policy can exist even when it is not formalized as official policy. For example, from its early beginnings as a republic in 1787, the US federal government's interest in economic growth for the nation was developed via tariff laws and subsidies to promote manufacturing (Schnitzer and Nordyke, 1983). The existence of these mechanisms is evidence of an industrial policy, although in the US this policy is defined more by political lobbying on behalf of specific industries than as a cohesive national plan.

Deregulation

Regulations introduce reliable standards of conduct for business and industry. Some industries – particularly those that serve a common, national good – have been heavily regulated, and some remain so. Because existing laws and standards emerged primarily to serve national interests, most tend to reflect cultural beliefs and assumptions that may be more relevant to nations than to the world. In some cases, these national regulations make it difficult for firms from these nations to participate in global industries. For example, the Glass–Steagall Act prevents US firms from combining commercial banking and securities underwriting, but a major source of global growth in this industry has been integration along these lines. Thus, the nation's laws retard global participation, and proponents of Glass–Steagall repeal argue that firms cannot operate under this law if they are to be global.

Governments in many nations are deregulating formerly regulated industries to permit national firms to enter global markets. For example, the US airline industry is deregulated, and the European Union has set a 1997 target date for full airline deregulation. This is one way national leaders prepare their nations to participate in global

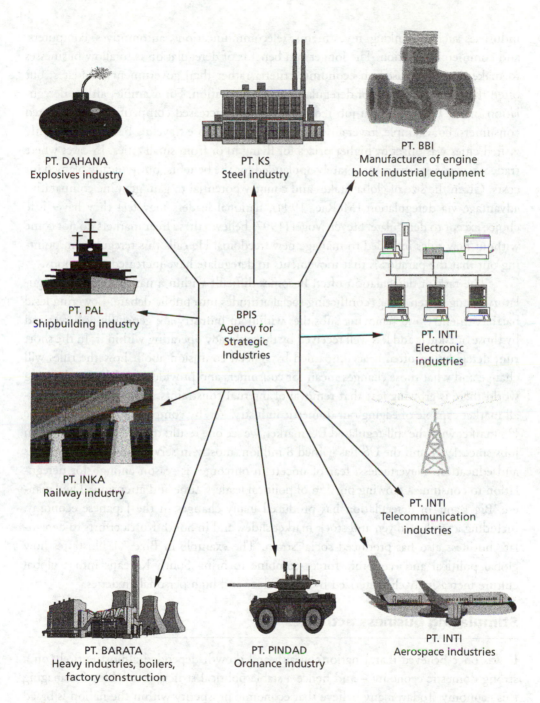

FIGURE 7.1 *Indonesia's Agency For Strategic Industries* (*IPTN Annual Report*). (Industri Pesawat Tetbang Nusantra Annual Report. (1992). Jakarta: Government Printing Office)

industries such as banking, investments, telecommunications, automotives, computers, and commercial aviation. The longer run benefits of deregulation is to allow businesses to make decisions based on economic criteria rather than government mandates, but often there are social costs of deregulation within a nation. For example, airline deregulation in the US resulted in job redundancies and increased competition that affected consumers. For example, lower airline ticket prices for those traveling between frequently visited cities was offset by higher prices for flying to or from small cities. In cases where tradeoffs occur, government is rarely applauded for the benefits, but typically blamed for costs. Given the size of global stakes and country potential to gain genuine comparative advantage via deregulation (McRae, 1994), national leaders may feel they have little choice except to deregulate. Steven Vogel (1997) believes these freer markets do not come without new rules intended to manage new freedoms. He calls this reregulation, pointing out that the paradox is that movements to deregulate have increased regulations.

The task of deregulation often becomes difficult within a nation because a regulatory change often brings conflicting social attitudes into public debate. Lowering legal barriers to entry and removing subsidies within an industry are generally well received by those outside it and less well received by those already operating within it. In the short run, deregulation often is accompanied by general confusion about how the rules will change and what those changes mean for consumers and providers, and in a globalizing world there is growing fear that removal of internal constraints will result in a free-for-all market capable of edging out domestic industry. Yet, by comparing the relatively free US market with the still-regulated EU market, we see one result: the EU has lost 5 million jobs since 1991 and the US has gained 8 million, mostly in service jobs requiring skills and education. Nevertheless, fear of uncertain outcomes is reason enough for deregulation to consume a growing portion of political leaders' time and attention. The Japanese 'Big Bang' of deregulation has produced many changes in the Japanese economy, including a weakened yen and stock market slides, and in South Korea efforts to deregulate business also has produced social strain. The example in Box 7.1 illustrates how global political and economic forces combine to bring South Koreans into a global culture increasingly characterized by uncertainty and high personal anxieties.

Stimulating business activities

It was once believed that a nation's wealth and growth depended almost entirely on a strong domestic economy – and hence a stable political structure capable of managing this economy. Today, many believe that economic prosperity within the nation is based on free national markets fully exposed to global economic interests. For example, the Heritage Foundation study of living standards and free markets concluded that countries with the highest standards of living also had the highest levels of economic freedom

---

BOX 7.1: ECONOMIC REFORMS IN SOUTH KOREA

Chapter 1 outlined some of the social and business problems South Korea has faced following economic growth. But these problems have not deterred government leaders from introducing changes they believe will ensure the nation's place in the global economy. Abolition of laws prohibiting outside ownership exceeding 10% will doubtless lead to a wave of mergers and acquisition. Labor law changes proposed are expected to allow Korean firms to discontinue lifetime employment and seniority-based promotion. South Korean workers may recognize the need for laws that make Korean companies more global, but many are themselves reluctant to change a system that predictably hires and promotes individuals over a lifetime. Governmental decisions intended to make Korea more global also foster global concerns for Korean workers: greater uncertainty, less stability, and a rapid pace of change for which outcomes are not clear.

(*Index of Economic Freedom*, 1997), and, conversely, nations with least economic freedoms also had the lowest standards of living. Further, the authors believe there also is a link between political freedom and economic freedom. This latter point is much in debate worldwide. Some believe political freedoms follow economic freedom, and many in Asia believe that political emphasis on personal freedoms in the US has sacrificed the public good for personal rights. For example, Kishore Mahbubani, a representative of Singapore's foreign ministry, believes an excess of democracy in the West coupled with individual fulfillment have led to family breakdown, a press that destroys respect for institutions, and general inability to manage national progress. Further, economic progress in Asia for nations that are not democracies, such as Malaysia and Indonesia, gives reason to re-examine the link between political freedoms and national wealth in a globalizing world.

If a nation's ability to create wealth does not depend on its form of government, then many more nations can be part of the global economy given world diversity of government structure. Further, the example of Mauritius shows that national wealth can be based on international and global trade more than on a nation's ability to leverage its natural assets internally. This 720 square mile island nation prospers by concentrating on clothing exports and tourism made possible by improved world telecommunications, transportation and distribution networks. For Mauritius and for other nations, reasons to expand beyond domestic markets are many, including slow domestic growth, a desire among developing economies to gain a foothold in stronger economies, and growing opportunities for business worldwide.

STIMULATING EXPORTS

Stimulating commercial development outside the nation has become one of the highest priorities for national governments. Whereas national leaders once concentrated the bulk of their energies on stimulating local or domestic business activities, they now also seek to stimulate export opportunities and attract inward-bound foreign direct investment (FDI). Both efforts require mechanisms to support business activities.

Among efforts national governments make to encourage exports are reduced constraints on exports, government-sponsored trade missions, subsidies for new businesses, and centers for export assistance. Many regional, state, provincial, and local authorities also provide resources to stimulate export activities. For example, although the US economy is more closely tied to foreign markets than five years ago by virtue of an increase in merchandise and commodity exports from 5.5% to 8.4% of GDP from 1989 to 1995, individual states such as Washington, Texas, Vermont, and Louisiana export more than 15% of their gross GDP. Thus, these states have a greater incentive to stimulate export activities because they are more dependent on exports than states like Wyoming or New Mexico. Export sales earn income for domestic firms and often create jobs, but because they rely on foreign buying power and economic cycles, many national, regional, or state politicians seek also to attract investments of fixed assets because once invested the latter are not easily withdrawn.

ATTRACTING FOREIGN DIRECT INVESTMENTS

Foreign direct investments in plant and equipment are encouraged by means of a broad array of mechanisms, including tax rebates, industrial site development, reduced utility rates, promises for streamlined government controls, worker training, currency translation protections, and even protection from import competition. According to a UN report titled *Incentives and direct foreign investment* (UN Division, 1995), government programs to attract FDI are becoming so competitive that many are overbidding for new businesses. For example, a combination of incentives cost Britain about $120 million US to attract a South Korean electronics firm, and this amounted to about $30,000 in incentives per job created. Attracting BMW to Spartanburg, South Carolina, required about $110,000 in incentives per job created, and France paid about $57,000 in incentives for each job created at a Mercedes-Benz Swatchmobile factory in 1995. In some cases, tax incentives burden local communities by eroding the tax base even as an influx of workers consume government services including free education. In some cases, firms use incentives, then relocate elsewhere or leave the community within a few years. Overall, the UN report suggests that global cooperation may be necessary if excesses in incentives offered are to be reduced or managed.

Foreign direct investment also occurs when equities or bonds attract foreign buyers. The number of foreign stock exchanges is increasing, foreign ownership of security transactions and government bonds is growing more common in the industrialized countries (The world economy, 1995), and there has been a relaxation of restrictions on foreign ownership of companies. All contribute to greater interdependencies among economies and national governments. France's decision to lift limits on non-EU offers for French firms is an example, and from Hungary to China, the transition economies all are making it easier for foreigners to own half or more of firm assets or equities.

The preceding section showed how national governments are increasingly engaged in challenges new to them, including privatization, eroding public confidence in government, revamped welfare systems, industrial policy, deregulation, and growing involvement in stimulating business growth. All of these roles expand the emphasis of government to an outward as well as an inward focus, and all involve national government leaders in global as well as domestic politics.

PRESSURES TOWARD GLOBAL GOVERNANCE

The purposes of domestic governance remain the same in a global sphere: national development and national defense. National ability to achieve these goals is made more difficult in the global sphere because existing systems of global governance are imperfect and additional systems must be introduced in response to global changes in many spheres.

Defense

With some exceptions, the collective defense motivation that spawned NATO and similar agreements evaporated with the Cold War, and entities like this are being scaled down. Defense cutbacks permit reductions in government expenditures and can reduce tax levels. This is a boon for development because military spending contributes less to world trade than does the private sector spending that replaces it (Global defense cuts, 1993). According to a 1992 International Monetary Fund report, a 20% cut in military spending worldwide could produce a long-run increase in consumption amounting to as much as $150 billion in the industrialized world and $40 billion in the developing countries. Thus, a world that conducts its wars on economic turf provides additional opportunities for all economic competitors in the world marketplace, including smaller nations. As the role of government shifts from defense, it should be possible for all to develop economically.

This possibility has not been realized in the many nations where defense budgets are increasing. Between 1985 and 1992 when NATO expenditures and defense spending were decreasing in the West, total defense spending increased by 63% in South Korea, 36% in Singapore, and 31% in Malaysia. By 1995, Thailand had purchased 28 Russian combat jets and six Sikorsky helicopters from the US; Indonesia acquired 40 German patrol boats and transports; and the Philippines acquired missiles from the US, armed vehicles from Britain, and fighter planes from Italy (The hot spots, 1996). Border disputes, ethnic conflict, and ongoing differences between religious and political rivals are fueling defense spending for smaller nations, and these examples show that for many nations internal defense remains a high priority. In advanced nations the shift is from defense to business which affects more than spending priorities; however, it is reshaping the role of embassies as well as revising assumptions about what kinds of training are most relevant to them. Box 7.2 illustrates this point.

BOX 7.2:   US EMBASSIES ABROAD

Traditional US embassy emphasis on safeguarding national security is being sidelined by growing commercial advocacy. This is shifting the role of foreign-service officers dedicated to commercial affairs. Once seen as holding 'dead end' jobs, commercial attaches now are on the fast track to embassy promotions. Stimulated by awards that grant $5,000 to the ambassador and foreign-service officer who do the most for business, ambassadors and other embassy personnel are spending more of their time with businesses and less with politicians. As US Ambassador to Malaysia, John Wolf was honored for helping McDonnell Douglas Corporation win a $700 million order for jet fighters. Worldwide, ambassadors and embassy employees spend more time than in the past attending economic conferences, lobbying on trade issues, and attending grand openings of new US business ventures.

Source: Steinmetz, Greg, and Greenberger, Robert S. (1997. Jan. 21). Open for business: US embassies give American companies more help overseas. *The Wall Street Journal*, pp. A1, A8.

At the global level, common defense needs include defense against acts of military aggression and also against growing worldwide terrorism and global criminal activities. Both are growing in scope and number. Table 7.3 illustrates some of the acts of military aggression in 1996, and these are only a few among hundreds of defense flash points that flared worldwide.

Table 7.3 does not list disputes in Asia in 1996, including armed disputes between Tamil rebels and the government of Sri Lanka, Khmer Rouge guerrilla action in Cambodia, insurrection in Myanmar (Burma), Indonesia, and Bangladesh, submarine aggression on the part of North Korea, or China's claim of Mischief Reef in the Spratley Islands. Also missing are Tupac Amaru's occupation of the Japanese Embassy in Peru, a

TABLE 7.3   Acts of aggression, 1996

Aggressor	Target
Syria redeployed troops and equipment in	Lebanon
The US launched cruise missiles at	Iraq
Groups opposed to a Western presence in Saudi Arabia	bombed US installation at Khobar Towers
Turkey sent military units to	Cyprus to counter what they saw as a military buildup
Libya's Gadhafi sent troops to quell Islamic dissidents	in eastern mountains of Libya
In Algeria there was	internal violence over a vote banning political parties based on creed or race
Northern Ireland's IRA	bombed British Army headquarters in Lisburn
Basque separatist	bombs in Spain
In Zaïre, clashes between the army and ethnic Tutsis threatened to draw in	Rwanda's troops and engulf refugee camps; hundreds of thousands returned to Rwanda

peacekeeping force in Haiti, rebel movements in Southern Mexico and Nicaragua, and a continuing list of internal and external armed conflict almost worldwide. Though none are global in scope, each conflict dims hopes for global peace and justice. What distinguishes many of these conflicts is they are motivated more by ethnic, religious, and cultural differences than political ones. Moreover, the nature of war has changed in this century. Whereas in World War II the ratio of casualties was 5 civilians to 95 combatants, that ratio now is reversed. Increasingly, women and children are the victims of armed combatants who use murder, rape, and starvation as weapons of war.

At the business level, warfare improves opportunities for arms dealers and mercenaries, but provides limited or uncertain opportunities for other businesses. Accordingly, few businesses locate in war zones. On the other hand, terrorists and global gangs and crime lords operate readily in war zones and are moving their activities to the peaceful business sphere, and in the process reshaping traditions of business conduct and managerial practices.

GLOBAL GANGS AND CRIME

Following ratification of the North American Free Trade Alliance (NAFTA) by Canada, the US, and Mexico, US firms reported that goods were newly subject to truck-jackings in Mexico, where 85% of goods are transported by truck (Smith, 1995). Trains also are subject to highjackings in Mexico. These local gangs are joining forces globally as Chinese Triads, Japanese *yakuza*, the Sicilian and Russian Mafias, drug cartels, and pirates enlarge their worldwide presence. Chinese Triads, some with as many as 180,000 members worldwide, operate not only in Asia but smuggle weapons and people throughout the world, using local street gangs to penetrate new markets. Organized crime in Russia has established outposts in 29 countries outside the former USSR, and the Russian Mafia is responsible for most of the counterfeit US dollars held in Russian hands. Japanese *yakuza* have been accused of playing a major role in doubling of stock and land prices in Japan (How the mob, 1996). According to the UN *World Drug Report* (1997), total world revenue from illicit drugs is about $400 billion annually – about 8% of total trade. Examples shown in Figure 7.2 illustrate that global gangs are deriving opportunities from reduced barriers of globalization, and are often threatening to legitimate commercial activities.

Interestingly, and like legitimate global enterprises, these global gangs are moving away from the rigid structure of Italy's Cosa Nostra and Colombian drug cartel's centralization toward the same sort of global thinking and local action characteristic of other types of global enterprises. Because their niche is illegal and illicit businesses, activities conducted by global gangs highlight a need for individual nations to join forces to curtail them. According to Diego Gambetta, author of *The Sicilian Mafia* (1996), part of the success of Italy's Mafia occurred because the weak Italian government was unable to enforce business contracts or property rights. The atmosphere of distrust that resulted created a subsequent need for protection which was supplied – for a price – by the Mafia. In other words, the Mafia grew in Italy to provide protections that the government was not providing. Application of Gambetta's hypothesis in the global sphere creates an argument for curtailing global gang activity with strong global standards of law. The interaction between gangs, business activities, and government are illustrated by the death of Vladislav Listyev (Box 7.3).

Common commercial interests

Governmental leaders have joined forces in formal and informal associations to stimulate and standardize commercial activities in two ways: they are part of trade alliances to share commercial benefits; and they have joined forced to create rules capable of ensuring compliance and accountability in world markets (Hormats, 1994). Trade alliances will be explored below, followed by an examination of trade agreements made to establish and enforce global trade policy.

TRADE ALLIANCES
The role of creating national economic advantage increasingly is met via economic and political links to create trade alliances more powerful than any single nation acting alone. Trade alliances meet multiple needs in addition to those of free trade: they provide a means for group members to influence world trade; they provide a defense against other

1 Some $750 million to $1.5 billion in money is laundered through Australia annually

2 Chinese gangs in Hong Kong account for 40% of the world's counterfeit card losses of between $700 million to $1 billion per year

3 About $10–20 billion is laundered through Hong Kong annually

4 In 1995, some 10% of nonperforming loans or $3.5 billion in Japan's banking system were held by members of criminal gangs

5 Illegal immigration from China produces $2.5 billion in annual gang revenue

6 Over 1 million people are smuggled yearly, 20% from China

7 Burma and Laos produced about 65% of the world's opium in 1994

8 Afghanistan produces some 30% of the world's supply of opium poppies

9 Over 200 Russian crime groups operate in 29 countries outside the former Soviet Union

10 Hungarians act as middlemen to sell Russian oil to sanctioned nations

11 The Sicilian Mafia manages a far flung network for gambling, drugs, and prostitution

12 Up to $1/2$ of illicit drug use in the United Kingdom is financed by crime

13 Nigerian syndicates distribute half of the world's heroin

14 Some 40% of the heroin seized going into the US is brought there by Nigerian drug traffickers

15 Police report more than 70 international drug syndicates were operating from South Africa by the beginning of 1995

16 Russian gangs operating in Canada netted $7 million in gold robberies in 1994

17 New York-based Chinese gangs smuggle 100,000 illegals into the US annually

18 Polish gangs based in Chicago steal autos, move them to Baltimore, and then ship them to Poland for resale

19 In 1994, Russian gangs were responsible for $1 billion in medical fraud in California

20 The Juarez, Mexico cartel annually ships 100 tons of illegal drugs into the US, generating $200 million in profit per week

21 In Colombia, gang kidnappings for ransom are part of an estimated $200m a year industry

22 Colombia cultivates 50,000–80,000 hectares of coca, sufficient to produce 80–500 tons of cocaine per year

FIGURE 7.2 *Gangs and global crime*

BOX 7.3:   INTERDEPENDENCE AND DEATH

The death of Russian television journalist and executive Vladislav Listyev in March 1995 exemplifies relationships among business, government, and gang activities. Listyev had been made executive director of Ostankino TV channel – the state-owned channel infamous for corruption. Characterized by both bad journalism and bad pay, independent producers had traditionally been allowed to siphon off most of the advertising revenue. But central government control over the station had begun to slip, and competitors had entered the market to create a model for quality television news providing a more balanced approach, e.g., to the Chechnya war, than the government provided. Losses at Ostankino forced restructuring, and Listyev was appointed to the job. His first move was to temporarily stop showing ads. With ad costs of $30,000 per minute and ad receipts of $8 million a month, someone put out a contract on Listyev's life. Was it the Russian Mafia, the government, competitors? Who will decide how the rules of business will be conducted in a globalizing world?

Source: Gutterman, Steve A. (1995, May). Anchorman's staying points to ad scandal. *Advertising Age*, p. 44.

trading blocks; and they create the unity needed to overcome costly cross-border in-efficiencies (GATT and FTAs, 1992). Trade alliances have assumed new importance for the global century, developing at many levels to include economic alliances and special arrangements like foreign economic zones and city-states within nations; industry alliances such as OPEC (the Organization of Petroleum-Exporting Countries) and regional economic alliances such as the EU and ASEAN. Examples of Trade Alliances and Agreements appear in Table 7.4.

Four types of regional trade alliances

There are four types of regional trade agreements, differentiated by the degree of trade commitment:

1   A *free trade area* encourages trade among member nations by eliminating trade barriers such as tariffs or quotas. Even while enjoying internal trade freedom, each member nation retains authority over all trade policies with nonmembers. The North American Free Trade Agreement (NAFTA) created free trade for members Mexico, the US, and Canada. Reduction of trade barriers between

TABLE 7.4   A sample of trading groups

EFTA (European Free Trade Association) is a limited free industrial trade association of Finland, Sweden, Norway, Iceland, Switzerland, and Austria.

MERCOSUR countries of Argentina, Brazil, Paraguay, and Uruguay formed a common market in 1994; total 209 million people with combined GNP of $655.5 million (http://www.americasnet.com/mauritz/mercosur); the Andean Pact includes Bolivia, Columbia, Ecuador, Peru, and Venezuela with 97 million people and a combined GNP of $122.5 million in a custom union (http://www.iadb.org).

ASEAN (Association of Southeast Asian Nations) formed in 1967 to strengthen regional cohesion and self-reliance and emphasize economic, social, and cultural cooperation and development. Members include Brunei Darussalam, Indonesia, Malaysia, the Philippines, Singapore, Thailand, and Vietnam (http://www.asean.or.id).

NAFTA (North American Free Trade Agreement) between the US, Canada, and Mexico is scheduled to eliminate all trade barriers and investments between the three countries within five years of 1994 founding; Chile was invited to join NAFTA in 1994 (http://www.sunsite.oit.unc.edu or http://www.iep.doc.gov/border/nafta.html).

Mexico and the US puts no constraints on how either partner deals with Germany, for example.

2 A *customs union* also eliminates internal trade barriers among members, and in addition the members agree to common external trade policies toward those who are not members.

3 A *common market* moves member countries one step beyond the customs union. Agreement on internal and external trade policies now is complemented by removing restrictions on productive factors such as capital, technologies, and labor. However, some restrictions may remain. For example, within the common market framework of the European Economic Community, medical doctors and others governed by licensing standards were not granted the option of practicing medicine anywhere in the EEC.

4 *Economic integration* incorporates all the features of a common market, and in addition member nations link economic policies to create common fiscal and monetary policy, a common currency, a common system of taxation, and supporting mechanisms to enhance economic union. Because economic issues are embedded in political, cultural, and other issues, it is important to recognize that full economic integration requires other forms of integration as well.

Whether initiated as trade unions or as mechanisms for full economic integration, most trade agreements have regional roots, often among contiguous nations. Although leaders of nations involved in trade associations acknowledge the shared interest they pursue through association with others, it often is difficult to exploit shared interests because of cultural, political, or other differences. Development of the European Union illustrates this point.

The European Community becomes the European Union

European nations held both political and economic sway over most of the world at the dawn of the twentieth century. Belgium's colonies were in the African Congo; Germany's in East Africa and Libya; and France held vast sections of Southeast Asia and North Africa; the Netherlands had colonized Indonesia, Malaysia, and what is now Sri Lanka; and Britain claimed Burma, India, most of Southern Africa, Anglo-Egyptian Sudan, Nigeria, and many Caribbean islands as colonies. The British Empire covered 40% of the globe, giving geographic scope to the cliché 'the sun never sets on the British Empire.' Britain's 1988 agreement to return Hong Kong to mainland China brought the former empire almost full circle in the colonialization processs. Britain's wealth and strength, like that of the other strong nation-states in Europe, had come from military might to control colonial resources.

Colonial days were largely over by the close of World War II, an end brought about by many factors, not least that former colonies objected and colonists had little remaining military strength to disagree. Thus, many Western European nations faced a post-1945 future without the colonies that had contributed to their former economic and political strength. The nations of Western Europe were exhausted by wars, and they faced a threat to what little political strength remained because of Cold War politics. Sandwiched between the US and the USSR, European nations recognized they were the likely site for any third war. Separately and independently, many in these nations recognized they had but two options:

(a) to reassert the balance of nation-state powers that they had been before the war, or

(b) to develop some sort of common voice to generate collective economic power for Europe.

The predominant desire to return to nation-state status was outweighed by the high costs of autonomy, and a confluence of events and concerns that made a collective scheme more attractive. The Marshall Plan required European nations to create a common plan for aid distribution; NATO had developed as a common defense plan for Europe; and all of Europe had reason to find ways to contain and control extreme forms of nationalism in Germany. The Council of Europe formed to consider issues of nationalism versus federalism, and discussions following led to the Treaty of Paris, which established the 1952 European Steel and Coal Community to develop the coal-rich Saar Valley in Germany. This alliance between France, Germany, Belgium, the Netherlands,

Luxembourg, and Italy removed customs duties and quotas on coal and steel among the six participating countries. The success of this alliance was followed by other agreements, and the 1957 Treaty of Rome establishing the European Economic Community.

Original EC members were France, Germany, Italy, and the Benelux countries. Britain did not participate in the Treaty of Rome, remaining outside the EC until 1973. Ireland and Denmark also joined the EC in 1973, followed by Greece in 1981, and by Portugal and Spain in 1985. Sweden, Finland, and Austria joined the EEC in 1995, but Norwegian voters decided against membership in 1994. By 1997 10 countries from Eastern Europe had submitted EU membership applications, including Poland, Hungary and the Czech Republic. Turkey has been seeking admittance for over a decade.

Over the years, the terms Economic Community and European Economic Community have been used interchangeably to refer to this common market arrangement, and so it may seem that the European Union (EU) also is just another term for the same entity. This is not the case; Box 7.4 makes some distinctions that may be useful. The Maastricht Treaty of December 1991 officially established the European Union, 'marking a new stage in the process of creating an ever closer union among the peoples of Europe' defined by objectives that include the following:

- to promote economic and social progress which is balanced and sustainable, in particular through the creation of an area without internal frontiers, through the strengthening of economic and social cohesion and through the establishment of economic and monetary union, ultimately including a single currency;
- to assert the EU's identify on the international scene;
- to strengthen the protection of the rights and interests of the nationals of its member states through the introduction of a citizenship of the Union.

This stage of EU development represents a significant step up from the free movement of goods, capital, and labor characteristic of a common market. As the EU moves toward full integration in the years ahead, European nations will continue to struggle with the interests, objectives, and cultures that each participating nation brings to it. Objectives of common currency, a common competitive policy, common transportation policies, and full economic integration intended to launch European firms into the global marketplace in some instances have been delayed by national preferences, and lack of agreement about how to deal with new members. At the same time, according to an EU survey of its roughly 370 million citizens, many have begun to think of themselves as Europeans first and citizens of nations second. These results are shown in Figure 7.3.

Other regional trade agreements such as Mercosur and ASEAN began as customs

> **BOX 7.4:   A EUROPEAN GLOSSARY**
>
> The European Economic Community (EEC) came into being on January 1 1958; original members were Italy, Germany, France, Belgium, Luxembourg, and the Netherlands. Nations that later joined the EEC are Denmark, Britain, Greece, Ireland, Portugal, and Spain.
>
> The European Union came into being as part of the 1991 Maastricht Treaty; members are the 12 nations of the European Economic Community, Sweden, Austria, and Finland, with a 1996 combined population of about 370 million.
>
> In 1996 there were 12 current applicants for EU membership, including Switzerland, Turkey, Cyprus, and many former communist countries such as Hungary, Poland, the Czech Republic, and Latvia. The population estimate for these 12 nations is 179 million.
>
> The European Council is the EU's political arm; the European Commission is the executive branch appointed by national governments; the Council of Ministers is the EU's top law-making body.
>
> EMU or European Monetary Union is the EU's effort to achieve monetary and economic union. The circulating currency will be the euro but it will not be introduced until after economic integration of the EU in 1999.

unions, and time will tell if they too find it more useful to move toward full economic integration in Asia and Latin America.

GLOBAL TRADE AGREEMENTS

As differentiated from trade alliances, which emphasize common benefits for members, the two trade agreements explored below represent efforts to establish common policies that improve every nation's ability to trade openly and freely. The longer-standing World Trade Organization will be examined first, followed by a look at the Asian Pacific Economic Consensus (APEC), because the latter agreement illustrates changes occurring in global political arrangements.

From GATT to the WTO

An important step toward globalization of business rules was taken by politicians who established the General Agreement on Trades and Tariffs in 1947. GATT's charter was

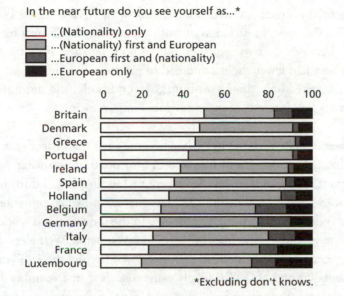

In the near future do you see yourself as...*

☐ ...(Nationality) only
▨ ...(Nationality) first and European
▨ ...European first and (nationality)
■ ...European only

Britain
Denmark
Greece
Portugal
Ireland
Spain
Holland
Belgium
Germany
Italy
France
Luxembourg

*Excluding don't knows.

FIGURE 7.3 *Who are we?* (More or less European Union. (1995, Aug. 26). *The Economist*, p. 46, using Eurobarometer data)

to set rules of commercial behavior by which the 23 signatory nations would abide. The founding meeting was followed by trade negotiation meetings and agreements among member nations conducted in 'rounds' of talks that could last years, including the founding Geneva Round, the Tokyo Round of 1973–9, and the most recent Uruguay round, which began in 1987.

GATT agreements were expected to harmonize trade practices worldwide and therefore make it possible for companies from many nations to participate in world economic growth. The national motivation to participate is that most of the world's largest traders are GATT members, including the US, the nations of Western Europe, and Japan. Initial participation and compliance with GATT rules were helpful in reducing tariffs, but over time GATT proved less than successful, for reasons such as the following:

1 There were many exceptions to GATT agreements, leading to constant conflict over special status advantages.
2 The mutual monitoring system established to bring complaints of violations to GATT was being circumvented by voluntary bilateral agreements that

represented restraints on trade inconsistent with GATT intent. For example, Japan's self-imposed restriction on auto exports to the US may have reduced strains between the two countries, but without Japanese imports, US consumers had fewer choices and had to pay more for autos.

3 GATT covered only about two-thirds of world trade, and did not cover industries and interests of growing global importance

For these and other reasons, GATT had become a less than effective organization by its 1987 meeting. Many thought of it as a forum for political posturing, joking that the group's acronym stood for the General Agreement to Talk and Talk. Efforts to improve the group's relevance were bolstered by the 1987 Uruguay round when provisions were introduced to cover industries of growing importance to the industrialized world: agriculture, intellectual property, and services like banking and investments. Wrangles over if and how these and other issues would be decided continued well beyond the 1987 meeting.

The Uruguay round of GATT finally came to a close in December 1993. Its provisions covered many important industries and issues for world trade not previously covered by GATT, including agriculture, intellectual property, and services, as well as textiles and direct investments abroad. It also sought to remedy a major GATT weakness by creating a dispute resolution process that did not foster separate bilateral agreements. The latter was one of the features of a newly constituted GATT to be called the World Trade Organization. Other features that distinguish the WTO from GATT are as follows:

- The WTO is an institution with a director general and resources available to pursue trade goals; GATT was an agreement with few institutional mechanisms.
- The WTO rules are binding; GATT rules were guidelines with weaker enforcement mechanisms.
- Trade disputes can be brought to the WTO, whose members rule on their findings; resolution of the first formal dispute was in 1996, and the ruling went against the US.
- Like GATT, the WTO cannot force member nations to do anything; however, part of dispute resolution allows for retaliation against members who do not comply with rulings.
- The WTO mandates equal representation of members; under GATT any powerful country could (and did) block adverse rulings with a veto.

Not without difficulty, Uruguay round GATT proposals were approved by member nations, and GATT became the World Trade Organization on January 1, 1995. By the close of 1997, the WTO counted 126 member nations. Another 30 nations seek WTO membership, and most of these come from current or formerly communist countries, including China and Russia. The main feature of the WTO is that it provides a single set of *enforceable* commercial rules intended to be global in impact and establish free trade policy. Elimination of tariffs and industrial subsidies for all industries will not be fully realized until the end of a 10-year phase-in process. However, long-enjoyed food subsidies will be eliminated sooner in the industrialized countries. According to the World Bank, agricultural subsidies alone annually translate into hundreds of billions of dollars worldwide, with 70% of the EU total budget going to agricultural subsidies. Subsidies in the US support many industries including sugar, tobacco, and textiles.

US Budget Office estimates are for worldwide tariff decreases of 30–40%. All countries will replace nontariff measures (quotas and export subsidies) with tariff measures, and this is expected to reduce hidden or disguised tariffs on goods and services. Rule changes are expected to add $1 trillion to the US in the coming decade because of the benefits associated with free trade; and the U.S. Budget Office estimates that GATT agreements will represent a $744 billion dollar tax cut to the world. The World Bank estimates the annual gain in world trade by 2005 could equal $260 billion per year in 1992 dollars, with a greater gain in developing countries than industrialized countries. Worldwide commercial rules emerging from this political sphere of activity have affected virtually all other spheres of interest. The example in Box 7.5 shows the effect on telecommunications.

As the example of telephone liberalization demonstrates, WTO rules may provide benefits to some, but also hardships for others. At least in the short term, there are likely

---

BOX 7.5:   LIBERALIZATION IN TELECOMMUNICATIONS

In February 1997 69 nations reached agreement to lower telephone rates worldwide and pursue other efficiencies that could improve telecommunications services and lower costs to save more than $1 trillion for worldwide consumers by 2010. According to the agreement, many monopolies on telephone services would be expected to open their markets, and the likely stampede of stronger competitors into newly opened markets will not come without threats to firms located in these nations. Liberalization of telephone regulations also is expected to foster many more cross-border alliances in the already actively cooperative telecommunications industry.

Source: WTO annual report 1997. (1997, Dec.). Geneva: WTO Publications.

to be winner and loser companies, industries, and even nations as consumers 'win' from lower prices due to tariff elimination. Consumers in other nations will 'lose' from reductions in subsidies. Sub-Saharan Africa and other agriculture-based nations are expected to be particularly hard hit on every score. WTO rules will deny them:

- favored access to selling agricultural goods in Europe;
- access to food as lower subsidies lead to higher prices worldwide;
- agricultural sales, unless they can shift from commodity to high-quality, specialty producers; there are few resources available to do this.

Finally, although the WTO illustrates growing desire to liberalize world trading, actual steps toward progress are impeded by different priorities for progress. For example, European nations favor an end to limits on profit repatriation, many Asian countries prefer that the WTO focus first on manufactured goods, and US priorities are for improved labor conditions and less business corruption. This exemplifies the main problem of reaching global agreement among nation-states; each is more interested in achieving their own goals first.

APEC

Twelve nations with common interests in Asia-Pacific trade first met in 1989 to discuss the common possibilities for their future. The Asian Pacific Economic Cooperation (APEC) forum now counts 18 member nations, including Japan, South Korea, China, Taiwan, Papua New Guinea, Indonesia, Malaysia, Burundi, Australia, Mexico, Canada, and Chile. APEC meetings held in Indonesia in November 1994 focused attention on Asia to showcase developing and newly developed Asian countries' rise in influence from producing 4% of world economic output in the 1960s to 25% in the 1990s. Sources of that productivity are shown in Table 7.5. As a group, APEC members account for 41% of world trade, 52% of world GDP, and 38% of the world's people. Fifty-four percent of all US trade goes to/from APEC countries and 24% comes from Washington state alone.

Several factors make APEC an unusual form of trade arrangement. First, inclusion of members from outside the region such as Chile, Australia, and the US as well as many Asian countries makes it a global rather than a regional group. This geographic scope collects nations from many cultures which have different histories of economic development and different forms of government. Second, in counting both Taiwan and China as members, APEC has shown that economic interests can be used to bridge political differences. Third, APEC intends to be nonexclusive by extending the benefits of negotiated agreements to nonmembers as well as to members. Finally, APEC is 'a wholly new model of regional economic cooperation: a steady ratcheting up of trade liberalization

TABLE 7.5 Pacific Rim trade: statistics on APEC members

Country	Exports ($ billions)	Imports ($ billions)	Per capita GDP (US = 100) 1996
Australia	44.1	43.6	18,500
Brunei	2.3	2.0	9,000
Canada	133.9	125.3	20.970
Chile	10.0	9.2	6,326
China	92.0	104.0	1,838
Hong Kong	145.1	149.6	21,500
Indonesia	38.2	28.3	2,601
Japan	360.9	240.7	19,920
South Korea	81.0	78.9	10,000
Malaysia	46.8	40.4	7,191
Mexico	50.5	65.6	8,200
New Zealand	10.3	9.4	15,502
Papua New Guinea	1.3	1.6	1,972
Philippines	11.1	17.1	2,172
Singapore	61.5	66.4	16,736
Taiwan	85.0	77.1	10,600
Thailand	28.4	37.6	5,018
US	449.0	582.0	23,220

Source: Adapted from: Asia-Pacific Forum finds focus: Trade. (1994, Nov. 14). *The Wall Street Journal*, p. A8, using data from Central Intelligence Agency World Fact Book, Statistics New Zealand and Penn World Tables.

between the regional and global levels' (Bergsten, 1994). All these factors define APEC as a hybrid global entity assembled from ideas taken from regional trade alliances and from ideas about global trade policy; they demonstrate that trade agreements intended to be global can be discussed by disparate partners who need not be located in the same region; and they demonstrate that economic connections have become more important in some instances than geographic boundaries. APEC also demonstrates how difficult it is to create hybrids; neither an agreement nor an alliance, APEC remains a group in search of a way to define itself as something other than a consensus.

In summary, the experiences of the European Union, APEC, and the WTO illustrate how trade alliances and agreements have come to play roles in global governance. Many more trade agreements similarly exist to expedite trade and economic development. These agreements and alliances provide a way for participant nations to retain some control over their own destiny, but all also require that member nations give up some degree of control over their own economic and political destinies. Although achieving national advantages is the charge of national government leaders, this charge is an impediment to developing global political or legal agreements on trade. An example from the US illustrates this point: The US Justice Department seeks to protect the interests of

US consumers and companies by prosecuting foreign firms for corporate collusion, in effect, extending US law to other nations. Similarly, passage of the Helms–Burton Act extends political reach through businesses by imposing sanctions on foreign firms that trade with Cuba. These examples from the US illustrate the tensions nations face to balance between worldwide trade agreements and their own policies, laws, and political preferences.

Even with overriding common trade goals, there are no guarantees that trade alliances and agreements will work. Politicians often answer to a national electorate or ruling bodies which may fail to re-elect unless rulings are favorable to them. In effect, trade alliances and agreements demand that nations act against their own self-interest in some instances, but politicians may pay the price. Thus, to be truly global, trade alliances require a new definition of what constitutes self-interest (Prestowitz, Tonelson, and Jerome, 1991).

Historical development of nation-states suggest few will be willing to sacrifice national interests to common and global interests. And, if unwilling to compromise national interests to meet goals they do share in common, national governments may be even less willing to compromise those interests for the good of people not represented at the bargaining table. This is the problem of market imperfections taken to the global level: Who will look after the global public good? By definition, only the 'haves' are well represented in trade alliances based on market principles. The interests of the 'have nots' increasingly are represented by interest groups functioning on a variety of levels in response to growing global public opinion favoring intervention to alleviate human suffering and promote worldwide justice (Watson, 1995). Thus justices other than economic ones also are pursued on a global level, and this too alters the context for governance.

GLOBAL GOVERNANCE FOR THE PUBLIC GOOD

The 1995 Commission for Global Governance concluded that there are five basic international public goods that a global governance system should provide for:

- a systematic financial system to smooth worldwide volatility;
- an open system for trade, technology transfer, and investment with acceptable dispute mechanisms;
- infrastructure and institutions to reach agreements on common systems like weights and measures or aviation and communication systems;
- protection of the global commons and a framework to promote sustainable development;
- equity and social cohesion through economic cooperation that includes

international development assistance and disaster relief. (Commission on, 1995, p. 150)

Balancing commercial and public goods

The first two points above establish needs for supranational or global rules of conduct to facilitate global trade; both are met in large part by trade alliances and agreements described earlier. Many environmental or equity concerns have not been addressed by these alliances, however, even as the global ramifications of equity and environment concerns are growing, fueled by increased awareness of ethnic conflict, human rights violations, and environmental degradation. The urgency of these issues has drawn many into the public sphere. Among organizations playing a role are educators, not-for-profit enterprises, arts organizations, religious organizations, trade unions and organizations, and professional societies. At the global level, most strive to achieve balance between what often are competing interests of economic and human development needs. Among these, three forces for these interests will be examined: intergovernmental cooperative agreements (IGOs), nongovernmental organizations (NGOs), and noncoordinated political action.

INTERGOVERNMENTAL COOPERATIVE AGREEMENTS (IGOs)

Cooperative agreements among nations provide important means for resolving trade and other issues. Both formal and informal types of intergovernmental organizations (IGOs) have developed to address these issues. Formally constituted IGOs like the UN or the OECD tend to operate according to a charter that includes well-defined objectives and membership; whereas informal types of IGOs like the G-7 can be more responsive to emergent needs, and accommodate fluid membership and changing objectives. For example, growing trade between the US and EU countries amounting to about $40 billion per year made it more important to reduce the growing costs of trade due to expensive certification or inspection requirements and cumbersome paperwork trails. A partial solution was negotiated in May 1997 with a draft document called a Mutual Recognition Agreement (MRA) which accepts industrial and regulatory standards of these nations for products ranging from pharmaceuticals to appliances and telecommunications equipment.

According to Mihaly Simai (1994), the network of IGOs has expanded considerably since the turn of the century, counting only 30 then, 123 by 1950, and several hundred by the 1990s. Further, some nations are more inclined to be involved in IGOs than others; as of 1990 the average number of IGOs each nation participated in was 30, but the US had participated in 140 and France had participated in 270. The IGOs described below are those that focus on human development issues rather than on trade organizations described earlier or defense IGOs like NATO.

Formal IGOs

The United Nations and the OECD were almost alone in their post-World War II roles as nongovernmental actors shaping the international and global governance system. How each came into being and its promised or realized functions require examination.

Organization for Economic Cooperation and Development

The OECD was founded as the Organization for European Economic Cooperation, part of Marshall Plan mandates for Europe to develop a plan for administering redevelopment aid. Forced to develop a common plan accommodating the many divergent interests of postwar Europe, the group was successful in developing an overall perspective on conflicting views of business, government, and society in meeting the same collective needs. In 1961, the OEEC became the OECD, a forum for the world's 24 most industrialized countries to assist them in formulating policies for promoting economic and social welfare. The OECD also provides a means for harmonizing aid support to developing countries. A major concern for the 1970s was the divide between the industrial Northern hemisphere, where wealth and most of the world's productive resources are concentrated, and the agrarian South, whose nations are poorer. The OECD's major function since the early 1990s has been to develop the basic points to be resolved and addressed by future multilateral trade negotiations, including closer relationships between trade policy and competition, investment, technology and innovation, and environmental policies (U.S. International Trade Commission, 1994).

Latin American Economic System

The Latin American Economic System headquartered in Caracas, Venezuela, is a regional intergovernmental organization funded by 27 member countries in Latin America and the Caribbean, and like some other IGOs, it sponsors studies of economic and trade issues of common interest to its members.

The United Nations

Also founded in the postwar era, the United Nations charter begins 'We the peoples of the United Nations . . .'. According to the Commission on Global Governance (1995), this introduction to the charter represented a hope for people of the world to unite and take ownership for meeting common needs and goals. During the celebration of its fiftieth year in 1996, this hope and other unrealized ambitions for the United Nations drew far more attention than its successes.

The United Nations was established by Allied nations to provide institutional guarantees against future armed conflict and develop a system to oversee world peace and cooperation. Founding principles for collective security spoke not only to the need to contain armed conflict but also the need for universal human rights and fundamental freedoms all should share. The developing Cold War focused greatest attention on defense issues. The United Nations' strongest members retain veto power over any decision, and the UN lacks enforcement ability. Both of these are reasons to argue that the UN will reflect changes in world order more than it will create them (Thakur, 1995).

The UN is an umbrella-type organization housing many operations under three related systems: the General Assembly; the Bretton Woods institutions such as the World Bank and the IMF; and specialized agencies such as the UN Conference on Trade and Development (UNCTAD), which houses the Division on Transnational Corporations and Investments. The Security Council responds to armed conflict, and the specialized agencies pursue human development initiatives with four agencies: the International Labor Organization (ILO), which oversees work conditions; the World Health Organization (WHO); the Food and Agriculture Organization (FAO); and the UN Educational, Scientific and Cultural Organization (UNESCO). Programs and funds organized by the UN include many affecting business activities throughout the world, including the Population Fund, the World Food Programme, the Environment Programme, and the High Commissioner for Refugees. Finally, the UN sponsors many more specialized and technical agencies, such as the International Telecommunications Union, which sets global telecommunications standards.

BOX 7.6: THE FOOD AND AGRICULTURE ORGANIZATION (FAO)

FAO predictions show that agricultural production must expand by 75% by 2025 to match population growth, but current figures are not reassuring: the global grain harvest, for example, has increased only by 2.3% since 1990 but population has grown by 10%. Reasons for the current crisis include: agricultural collapse in Russia after 1989; government alliances like the WTO that have cut subsidies to agriculture; poor weather in the US and Russia; and dietary substitutes in China. Global weather patterns, cultural change, and governmental decisions demonstrate the interactions among global environments. These shifts create challenges that increasingly must be resolved by global organizations. Responding to growing fears of worldwide food shortages, the FAO met in Rome in fall of 1996 to search for new approaches to helping economically poor nations to grow, buy, or otherwise get more food.

Source: McLaughlin, Martin. (1997, May 3). The hungry seventh of the world. *America*, pp. 14–18.

Informal IGOs

Informal IGOs are task or focus groups of government representatives who meet periodically to discuss ideas and issues of multilateral concern. The G-7 and G-10 are informal IGOs that meet to discuss economics, and draft policies expected to enhance worldwide economic development. The growing importance of groups like these is underscored by recent founding of the G-6 comprised of the US, Japan, China, Hong Kong, Singapore, and Australia. These nations met for the first time in February 1997 to establish a group small enough to respond rapidly to financial crises, to help deregulate financial markets in Asia, and to stabilize exchange rates. This type of cooperation is viewed as particularly important for easing China into world financial markets.

Most criticisms of IGOs have centered on UN actions or inactions, but many note that the failures of the UN have been offset by successes, including containment of conflict, advancement of human rights, global conferences on population and women's issues (Commission on, 1995; Simai, 1994). General criticisms of IGOs other than the UN have been that separate emergence has resulted in competing and parallel groups unorganized by formal designs or structures (Simai, 1994). As will be shown by the example of efforts favoring women's rights, absence of an organized structure is not necessarily a bad thing.

NONGOVERNMENTAL ORGANIZATIONS (NGOs)

Entities other than government-sponsored ones also play a role in shaping the terms of global trade, business activities, and political action, and many entities other than for-profit businesses sustain national and global wealth. For example, many educational institutions attract significant foreign investments from abroad, religious institutions collect and disburse funds globally, and non-profit hospitals as well as medical services of many kinds also are increasingly global.

A 1994 Johns Hopkins study of the nonprofit sector in 12 countries (the US, UK, France, Germany, Italy, Hungary, Japan, Brazil, Ghana, Egypt, Thailand, and India) demonstrated that other sectors in the economy can have a powerful influence on the economy (Salamon and Anheier, 1994). While the nonprofit sector can comprise a wide array of organizations, five common features define organizations in this sector: (1) they are formally constituted; (2) they are separate from the government; (3) they do not seek profits; (4) they are self-governing; and (5) their labor is to a significant extent voluntary.

While the Johns Hopkins study found the US housed the largest nonprofit sector in both absolute and relative terms, it is important to recognize that the number of nonprofits in many developing economies was found to be quite high. Egypt reported over 20,000 nonprofits, while Brazil counted over 200,000. Even Hungary, a land of about 10 million people which was almost devoid of nonprofits in 1989, had about 20,000 nonprofits by 1993 that were accounting for 3% of all service jobs. If, as these data suggest, nonprofit activity is high in developing economies, then we might expect that development in these nations will occur with workers whose work experience often is based on principles and practices consistent for the nonprofit sector. This dynamic could play an important role in shaping how employees expect businesses to act when operating globally.

In summary, these nongovernmental organizations (NGOs) are primarily voluntary groups organized to address concerns viewed as low priorities among governments and most businesses, and they too shape both economic and political interests. NGO objectives range from prevention, such as Save the Whale or the Sierra Club, to rescue or protection, sponsored by Amnesty International, Human Rights Watch, or Médecins Sans Frontières/Doctors Without Borders, to charitable institutions, such as Save the Children or Operation Smile International, to development, such as L'Arche or Habitat for Humanity. According to the International Classification of Nonprofit Organizations found in Appendix B of the Salamon and Anheier book (1994, pp. 118–121), nonprofits can be grouped into 12 categories, each of which has many subcategories. The 12 major categories include groups sponsoring culture and recreation, social services, environment, law, religion, business and professional associations and unions, and international activities. Subgroups for the latter include exchange/friendship/cultural programs, development assistance associations, international disaster and relief organizations, and human rights and peace organizations, to name a few. Unlike charitable groups of earlier decades, NGOs emphasize self-help and empowerment to meet present and future needs. For example, the description of Operation Smile in the opening case for this chapter illustrates that people involved with the organization not only work directly with children to make cosmetic repairs, they also train medical personnel who share their desire to provide these services in their own locales.

The contemporary NGO movement originated in the 1970s in developing countries like Bangladesh, the Philippines, Rhodesia (now Zimbabwe), and Indonesia, but rapidly spread worldwide to number in the hundreds of thousands in the developing and developed economies alike. Lester Salamon (1994) identifies worldwide growth in NGOs and their impact on global governance as a 'global associational revolution' powered by multiple factors, including the following:

- The perceived crisis in the welfare state suggests that government is not capable of managing all the social problems it faces.
- Rapid economic development has created an immediate need for services that governments cannot satisfy.
- Global environmental crises cannot wait.
- Improved literacy and a communication revolution make it possible to organize and mobilize groups of people worldwide.

Global NGOs often coalesce around issues important more to global survival than to country or industry concerns. Others function to find or force ways for businesses to serve a common good. Many thousands of these groups exist today; they cover a broad range of interests and activities too numerous to review here. However, examples below taken from a single page of the *Yearbook of international organizations, 1995–96* provide some insight (Table 7.6).

Transnational efforts to achieve a common good interacted successfully with business and government interests worldwide when anti-apartheid groups represented by Reverend Leon H. Sullivan urged economic sanctions and mass corporate exit from South Africa in 1983. These activities eventually led to the Sullivan rules for doing business with South Africa, and based on them many firms ceased operations there, including IBM, Firestone Tire and Rubber, CPC International, Xerox Corp., and Eastman Kodak. This example provides reasons to believe that activities other than those directly sponsored by the government also can influence politics and business and human development throughout the globe. Student boycotts forced many firms to withdraw from politically repressive Myanmar (Burma) in 1996; and consumer actions have led to worldwide labor reforms in textile and shoe production.

Often, going global brings NGO leaders face-to-face with conflicting demands. For example, Greenpeace seeks to save the earth but sometimes engages in illegal acts to accomplish its ends and the Missionaries of Charity (Box 7.7) serve many in overpopulated nations but maintain opposition to birth control.

TABLE 7.6 Nongovernmental organizations: a sample

Organizational name	Location
African Network for Prevention and Protection Against Child Abuse and Neglect	Nairobi, Kenya
Amnesty International	London, England
Arab Organization for Human Rights	Cairo, Egypt
Avocats sans frontiers	Brussels, Belgium
Caribbean Association for Feminist Research and Action	St Augustine, Trinidad–Tobago
CBF World Jewish Relief	London, England
Committee Against Torture	Geneva, Switzerland
Equal Earth	Benenden, England
Foundation Against Trafficking in Women	Utrecht, Netherlands
Hot Line Asia	Hong Kong
Human Rights Watch	New York, USA
International Centre for Trade Union Rights	Prague, Czech Republic
International Entente Against Violence in Sport and Fair Play	Monaco
International Fund for Animal Welfare	Crowborough, England
International Peace Research Association	Bonn, Germany
Physicians for Human Rights	Boston, MA, USA

Source: Yearbook of international organizations, 1995–96, p. 928, Societal Problems/Maltreatment (out of about 150 entries on the page). Paris: K.G. Saur.

BOX 7.7:   MISSIONARIES OF CHARITY/THE GLOBAL GOOD

The Missionaries of Charity are best known because of their leader, Mother Teresa, who founded this religious order in service to the poor. Priests, religious brothers, 3,000 religious sisters, and tens of thousands of ancillary workers have built and staffed schools, homes for orphans, AIDS sufferers and the destitute in 500 centers operating in more than 100 countries. This religious organization joins many other voluntary organizations in serving global needs to meet human as well as economic development goals.

NONCOORDINATED POLITICAL ACTION: THE CASE OF FEMALE EQUITY

One effect of shared knowledge among women has been united voices on those factors that particularly affect women's opportunities to prepare for and perform jobs in the paid labor force. Another source of unity is common efforts to fight problems occurring in most countries, such as violence against women or female illiteracy. Many organizations work to improve female opportunity, including IGOs, NGOs, and governmental agencies sponsored by individual and joint alliances. These are in no way organized into a tightly knit global force and yet global progress is being made on behalf of women.

Political action on behalf of women's status is occurring in myriad ways, including an increased number of women in public offices, the increased power of nongovernmental organizations devoted to issues affecting women, and the increased activities of professional and social groups. The 6,000 individual firms that belong to the National Association of Women Business Owners (NAWBO) in the US enhance awareness about and opportunities for women business owners through radio programming and lobbying activities that partially contribute to domestic legal change such as the passage of the Women's Business Ownership Act (1988). By drawing attention to female-owned businesses and the difficulty these businesses face in obtaining loans, professional organizations help the business world to recognize and resolve problems. Creative solutions then can be shared worldwide through low- or no-cost telecommunications.

Through sponsorship of international women's conferences, the United Nations and nongovernmental organizations have provided a platform for carrying information about women's status worldwide. Within many countries, nongovernmental organizations provide critical resources for women, including birth control information, education, health, and safety. Often these organizations operate in tandem with government programs, but in other cases they provide services that the government is unable or unwilling to offer women. Religious groups also have played a role in raising awareness of women's roles worldwide. For example, in 1993 representatives for 20 of the worlds' religions, including the Dalai Lama, the World Council of Churches, and most major Protestant sects, signed a document of core values that calls for an end to discrimination against women worldwide.

Women also have made clear progress in political life. In 1997 women held 13% of parliamentary seats, and 6% of cabinet posts worldwide (*Human Development Report*, 1997). In the 1970s, three women had major roles in running modern countries, but by the 1990s 25 women had been elected heads of state or government. Many of these women were the first females to hold high office in their countries. For example, in 1997 Jenny Shipley became the first female prime minister in New Zealand. As of 1994, there were 300 women ministers in 142 countries. The increased number of women in elected offices has been accompanied by a growing number of those women who work to improve women's status or opportunities. Chief among them in recent years include many who have moved on to other work, including Gro Harlem Brundtland, former PM of Norway, Mary Robinson, former President of Ireland, Benazir Bhutto, former PM of Pakistan, Violeta Chamoro, former President of Nicaragua, and Eugenia Charles, former PM of Dominica. Among the goals of these women has been to generate political action to improve opportunities for women as well as for men.

In addition to capturing national offices, individuals who work on behalf of women's issues also are taking leadership roles in political parties. Strong support for women's issues and concerns leads to increased voting among women. For example, the political party Women in Russia won over 8 percent of the vote in parliamentary elections in Russia in 1994. Many believe this occurred because Russian women perceive their opportunities will not improve except by attending to women's issues and concerns. Examples such as these show that women voters can achieve change through a unified vote, they demonstrate that women will coalesce around important issues, and they suggest that political leaders will increasingly promote issues important to most women such as education, human rights, poverty, and security. At the global level, by 1998 women were at the helm of some of the world's most influential development agencies, taking charge of UNICEF, the World Health Organization, the UN High Commission on Refugees, the World Food Program, the Population Fund, and the Human Rights Commission. When appointed European Commissioner for fisheries, consumer affairs, and human rights, Emma Bonino assumed some of these responsibilities for Western Europe.

Examples such as these show why political leaders are more concerned about women's issues, and how women voters achieve power with a unified vote. Although based on only a few of the many global efforts underway to advance female equity and opportunity, these examples show that activities pursued by individuals and by organizations within nations are altering social and business norms on a worldwide scale. They suggest that an overriding value pursued in myriad ways is an appropriate way to implement change, and they show such changes can come about even without the boundaries provided by a formal coordinating mechanism.

INTERNATIONAL STANDARDS

The broad perspective taken by many alliances, IGOs, and NGOs contains ideals for action, but realizing these ideals requires implementing mechanisms. International standards have been developed by many organizations, including government bodies, IGOs, NGOs, and professional organizations. The rules and regulations suggested by these groups are important tools and techniques for smoothing international differences in product standards, work conditions, and technical specifications. The importance of these types of standards cannot be overstated since they cover virtually all aspects of product development, manufacturing, distribution, and even recovery. For example, worldwide compliance with 'built for reuse' standards in the automotive industry would require that the recyclable amount of all products be specified.

Many of the difficulties in setting standards are illustrated by examples taken from the EU. Because Brussels classifies carrots as fruit, for example, any rule governing EU fruit requires a ruling for how to handle carrots. The number of perforations in a fold of toilet tissue, grams of tobacco in a cigarette, and even the size of a strawberry are subject to classification. In the latter case, an EU ruling specifying strawberries had to be bigger than 22 mm in diameter eliminated smaller Swedish strawberries from the retail market. These examples illustrate the level of detail involved to create the millions of technical specifications for trade within a regional alliance; millions could become billions in the global sphere.

Even prior to economic convergence, many international bodies had been established to develop standards. Some are chartered by trade alliances, like the European Commission, and others are associated with IGOs, such as the International Telecommunications Union chartered by the UN. Still others are developed by professional associations, but their reach is extended by support from others. For example, ISO 9000 was developed by one group but its aims have been forwarded by support from the European Union, which adopted these standards to facilitate economic unification and provide a universal framework for quality assurance.

ISO 9000

ISO 9000 specifies global quality standards for manufacturing. Developed by the International Organization for Standardization, ISO 9000 has thus far been a successful, albeit costly, attempt to harmonize world quality standards and quality monitoring systems. These standards were not required by government but instead were member-initiated and developed with various groups of professionals working to articulate common standards. ISO 9000 is a series of five international standards and guidelines first published in 1987 that specify how firms can comply on quality management and quality assurance; the standards were revised in 1994. These standards are generic, but they are not prescriptive and can thereby apply to all industries, including services and industrial production. Companies seeking compliance engage in a series of internal and external quality audits to identify challenges and help leaders know what to correct in order to qualify for ISO 9000 certification. Often, companies decide to seek ISO qualification because their buyers demand it of them. This process requires that participating firms define appropriate quality standards, document processes, and adhere to both. Leading an ISO process requires a manager able to learn from and listen to others; Figure 7.4 demonstrates steps to follow and skills needed. ISO 14000 standards for environmental management systems also have been developed; these include a definition of management's environmental responsibility, record keeping, organizational structures, and auditing as well as performance evaluation and life cycle assessment.

International accounting standards

An international committee of accountants, financial executives, and equity analysts revised international accounting standards (IAS), making it possible to use a single set of accounting procedures worldwide. The implications for worldwide adoption of this system are immense since it is costly to maintain different accounting systems. Common accounting standards would also facilitate similar interpretations of economic performance results worldwide and so would stimulate worldwide investments in equities.

BUSINESS ACTIVITIES

Business organizations also have incentives to play roles more usually played by government. Coalitions of businesses can successfully pressure national governments to ease trade restraints, as occurred to lift the US embargo on Vietnam. Participating firms made their case on two fronts. First, without diplomatic ties US firms could not provide attractive development financing through the Overseas Private Investment Corporation or the US Export–Import Bank. Hence, US firms were losing contract opportunities to competitors from Korea, France, and other nations. Second, Vietnam's entry into the Association of Southeast Asian Nations (ASEAN) could have created a conflict if the US refused to recognize a member of an association with which it does have diplomatic relations.

Some fear that growing influence of business in government spheres will displace national governments. Richard Barnet and John Cavanagh (1994) argue in *Global dreams: Imperial corporations and the new world order* that a few hundred corporations will become world empires in the twenty-first century to operate as shadow governments. According to these authors, the emerging empires would be those companies that dominate (a) media and entertainment, (b) consumer marketing, (c) global manufacturing, and (d) global finance. These corporations' economic dominance would lead them to

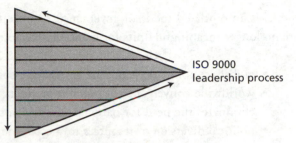

Observe
Listen
Ask questions
Document findings
Develop clear objectives
Disseminate the objectives
Participate in an exemplifying role
Listen some more
Ask more questions
Repeat the process

ISO 9000
leadership process

FIGURE 7.4   *ISO 9000 leadership process* (Badiru, Adedeji. (1995). *Industry's guide to ISO 9000*, p. 10. New York: John Wiley and Sons Inc.)

BOX 7.8:   BARINGS BANK COLLAPSE LEADS TO RECOMMENDATIONS

In the aftermath of the Barings bankruptcy described in the opening case for Chapter 5, central banks from 12 major countries acted in concert with the Bank for International Settlement to draft a global plan for calculating and managing risk exposure within banks. Whether these rules will be used remains to be seen; Barings itself did not follow guidelines already in place to reduce derivatives' risks.

Source: Bettering Basle: Risk management. (1995, Dec. 9). *The Economist*, pp. 76–77.

---

work together to allocate wanted and needed resources worldwide, and they could thereby gather more economic and political clout than many, if not most, nations. The authors of *World dreams* examined five companies they believe will typify the new world order: Bertelsmann, Philip Morris, Ford Motor, Sony, and Citicorp, but many other companies are of sufficient size and influence to affect governments, including Exxon, Siemens, Unilever, or Nestlé. Moreover, political clout also may be exercised by privately owned businesses, as is the case in many nations where wealth is held by nuclear or extended families.

ARE NATION-STATES IRRELEVANT?

National governments' roles are changing in a globalizing political environment. Loss of autonomy and in some cases loss of political clout, greater economic interdependence, and diminished confidence in world political leaders lead some to argue the nation-state model is an outdated mode of governance. Ohmae (1995) contends that nation-states are no longer meaningful units for managing economic activities, asserting that:

- global economic decisions are beyond the control of nation-states;
- worldwide convergence of tastes in products like cola beverages or blue jeans eliminates the need for national governments to protect their markets;
- political diversion of resources to special interests makes nation-states wealth destroyers instead of wealth creators.

In spite of progress toward global governance plans and programs covering trade issues from investments to human rights, there is little reason to expect global unity on a myriad of other governance issues. If not a global system of government, then, what is proposed as an alternative to nation-states? Four options are presented below.

The European Union's director of science and technology, Richard Petrella, predicts government in the future will be managed by 'international metropolitans' or *city-states* that can work in tandem with the transnational companies controlling capital. The current cooperation pact between Lyons, Milan, Stuttgart, and Barcelona provides the model for cities that manage their economic development with relative political autonomy (Drozdiak, 1994).

Ohmae (1995) argues *region states* will emerge as boundary-spanning economic zones. Comprised of about 5–20 million people, region states would be geographic units large enough to provide an attractive market for consumer products and offer economies of services and infrastructure, but small enough to share economic and consumer interests. These interests can extend beyond geographic territory to include informal agreements (Box 7.9) and 'virtual' association.

Virtual states also represent a possible option for organizing common interests. Gottlieb (1994) believes it is possible to create states without territory as a way for different groups within the same area to pursue separate interests, arguing that an international order limited to territorial states can expand to accommodate nations that are not organized territorially. Kurds located in many nations, for example, could use technology to create a common governance structure without relocating. If nations can be formed around ideals rather than around territory, then the world will not only become more complex, but will permit more opportunities for small cultural groups to pursue economic interests through a common and worldwide governance structure. Tonn and Feldman (1995) have identified technological breakthroughs as a means for creating cyberspace governments or 'virtual' governments able to perform public services without national boundaries.

This look at the changing roles national leaders play in domestic and global settings clarifies the need to reconsider traditional political/economic relationships. This

BOX 7.9:   GOVERNMENT BY INFORMAL AGREEMENT

Because Somalia could not reach agreement on consociation, a decentralized state based on clan affiliation rather than on territory, or any other form of government, the result has been no government at all. Rather Somalia operates under a loose set of agreements between clans on areas of common interest such as health, education, and currency. Although far from perfect, this system represents an improvement over prior strife in Somalia, and it suggests that under some circumstances it is possible for clans and tribes to share common services but retain group autonomy.

Source: A society without the state. (1995, Sept. 16). *the Economist,* pp. 50–51.

introduction to national and global governance issues illustrates that nations and other governmental entities face multiple demands. Nations that seek the benefits of global trade want to retain national sovereignty, yet have little choice but to involve themselves in collective action. Decision-making now is distributed at the global level not just among the superpowers but among all. This distribution almost guarantees disputes. There is the need for stability nationally and the need for change globally, but the two are intertwined. Global organizations also face dual demands for stability and change. Their preferences for autonomy are difficult to realize in a global world where alliances are a norm. Yet the external alliances that allow for opportunity also require power-sharing. Just as individual countries demand a greater voice in global decisions, consumers also demand a role in corporate governance. Managing these multiple and competing objectives requires exposure to risks that few organizations are well prepared to meet.

PART II   ORGANIZATIONAL ACTIONS/MANAGING RISK

The possibility of risk is embedded in most situations, especially new or unaccustomed ones. Mihaly Simai (1994) defines international risks as 'important, potentially disturbing and destablizing factors or acts originating with, or generated by, various actors on different structural levels, and having spillover consequences for other members of the international community' (p. 258). This definition is unique in identifying risk as coming from different structural levels and resulting in spillover effects. The following examinations of political risk and foreign currency exchange risk, corruption risk, and personal risk show many different actors have expanded business risk, and demonstrates how global organizations are managing the spillover effects of long-standing and relatively new forms of risk.

POLITICAL RISK

Much of the business literature defines international political risk narrowly as risks to company resources because of political decisions. Growing awareness that political systems are interdependent with other national systems led to recognition that political risk includes social as well as political decisions, events, or conditions that could cause investors to lose money or opportunities (Howell and Chaddick, 1994). Political risk has been assessed by private organizations such as Political Risk Services, Business Environment Risk Intelligence, and the Economist Intelligence Unit. These groups measure activities such as societal conflict or exchange controls to build indices of country risk. *The Economist*'s index of risk, for example, incorporates measures of bad neighbors, Islamic fundamentalism, authoritarianism, war/armed insurrection, ethnic tension, urbanization pace, and generals in power (Countries in trouble, 1986).

Llewellyn Howell and Brad Chaddick (1994) compared data produced by published and private sources to find that existing measures of risk generally are poor predictors of specific outcomes. Based on their research, they concluded that individual factors of regional hostility and authoritarian government were better predictors of potential problems than indices combining all risk events.

Processes and structures for assessing political risk

Organizations assess risks by creating internal systems for risk analysis, via projections based on published risk analyses, and on reports purchased from independent risk assessment corporations. For example, Citibank established a Market Risk Policy Committee to oversee market risk and provide a check and balance for their business risk management process (*Citicorp Annual Report*, 1995, p. 34). Although it has become customary to build sophisticated, multivariate models of risk, Howell and Chaddick's (1994) research suggests that a simple approach might be as effective. This advice is counter to the bigger-is-better assumption for model building.

Business–government alliances represent another way to reduce organizational risk. In partnership with governments, businesses induce government commitment to their interests, but at the same time they relinquish total decision control. Organizations also manage political risk by taking a longer run view of the risk. For example, following the near collapse of Mexico's economy in 1995, Acer and Ford both chose to absorb short-term risks by cutting prices to remain in the market. Many firms made similar decisions as a currency crisis swept through Asia in 1997. For example, because the CEO of McDonald's International viewed problems in Asian economies as temporary setbacks, he said McDonald's intended to stay in Asian markets. Further, *The Wall Street Journal* (Can the US weather, 1998) quoted Jim Cantalupo as saying:

> We've been through similar situations before in Latin America . . . and we've learned that you have to stay the course. In Brazil we've survived seven economic reform plans, five currencies, five presidents, two constitutions and 14 finance ministers. Today in Brazil, McDonald's is the unchallenged market leader. In the past three years, our same-store sales have doubled – in an economy that very recently was described in the same dire terms used to characterize conditions in some Asian markets today. (p. A22)

CURRENCY EXCHANGE RISK

According to Kim and Kim (1993), three types of currency exchange fluctuations create potential risks for firms:

1 Translation or 'paper' exposures occur when financial information is translated for financial purposes from the accounting practices and currencies of one country to another. For example, Coca-Cola lost $13 million on currency translation in 1988, gained $20 million in 1989, and lost $500,000 in 1990.

2 Transaction exposure involves real losses or gains arising from transaction settlements involving exchange rates. The parent company for Swatch watches experienced a currency loss of 140 million francs ($123 million) in 1995.

3 Exposure to changes in the economic situation of nations represents an economic exposure over the lifetime of the enterprise.

Processes and structures for managing currency exchange risk

Many forms of economic exposure can legitimately be considered political risk factors, and paper losses or gains may be difficult to manage, but the real concern for global firms is transaction exposure to currency exchange gains and losses. The vacillating value of the US dollar in world markets together with a propensity to use dollar-denominated transactions increases this exposure. For firms like Nestlé, Unilever, and Coca-Cola whose revenues and profits come primarily from outside their home countries, currency transactions can represent volatile source of losses and gains. Firms manage this volatility in a number of ways:

- Over four-fifths of company treasurers manage currency risk with hedging strategies that use financial instruments to guarantee exchange rates (see also Box 7.10).
- Bartering also provides a means for reducing exchange rate risk.
- Sony's overseas sales are 97% in foreign currencies and it promotes currency swap agreements among their units to minimize risk.
- Motorola uses a currency netting system to collect and disburse cash payments among Motorola companies and their suppliers (Holland, 1994).
- Wedco Technology, which custom-grinds plastics and other materials for companies in the US and Europe, hedges against currency risk by billing in dollars; it also forces customers to supply their own raw materials so Wedco can avoid currency risks for imports.
- Currency exchange risk also can be hedged with short terms for payment, or buying forward contracts from banks that lock in exchange rates.

CORRUPTION RISK

Corruption is defined as operating without honesty or integrity. In the business arena, corruption encompasses a broad range of activities ranging from bribery, counterfeiting, smuggling, tax evasion, business irregularities like insider trading or kickbacks, price-fixing, fraud, and extortion. The economic costs of these various forms of corruption are many, including misuse of productive factors, possible reductions in returns to shareholders, diminution of reputation for firms identified as corrupt, or reduced morale among workers. According to a 1996 study of crime and corruption

---

BOX 7.10: HEDGING CURRENCY EXCHANGE EXPOSURE

One way to avoid currency exposure is to locate production facilities in local markets, but even then interdependencies among units of the same worldwide firm may lead to currency exchange exposure. For example, although products for Siemens' medical technology division contain about 70% of local products in the U.S., Siemens faces a risk for the remaining 30%. According to a *Wall Street Journal* report, this exposure amounts to a reduction of 3–4 million marks for every 1 pfennig rise in the mark against the dollar.

Source: Roth, Terence. (1995, Mar. 9). In Europe, strengthening of currencies is causing headaches for many exporters. *The Wall Street Journal*, p. A14.

in Thailand, illegal activities there may almost equal the Thai national budget (see Box 7.11).

Economic gains from corruption range from large to paltry. Relatively small amounts of money are involved when a speeding driver pays off police or a building inspector overlooks minor defects for a bribe, but in China, where *guanxi*, or business connections, are important, costs to grease the wheel of business were estimated to average 3–5% of operating costs in 1992 (The destructive costs, 1993).

A study conducted by the Political and Economic Risk Consultancy of Hong Kong (How corrupt is Asia? 1995) asked 95 North American, European, and Australian corporate managers to assess corruption in Asian countries. Even without considering the pattern of preferential treatment accorded family and friends in Asia, participants reported that bribes and payoffs are a way of life in many Asian countries. On a scale of 1–10, China and Indonesia tied for most corrupt with a score of 7.31. A belief that everything is negotiable may be one reason managers rated Indonesia high on corruption. For companies doing business there, one concern is whether their presence implies responsibility for corruption that does occur (see Box 7.12). Singapore was shown to be least corrupt with a score of 1.19 (well below the 2.12 average respondents assigned to their own countries), demonstrating that corruption is not critical to economic development. Further, this difference demonstrates the diversity found among Asian countries on this and other business practices.

Although reports of corruption often focus on Asian nations, corruption is widespread, even among nations that have worked particularly hard to eradicate business and political corruption. Moreover, corrupt practices vary worldwide and the reasons for corruption also vary. Whereas corruption in Asia and Eastern Europe tend to enrich

---

BOX 7.11:   CATEGORIES OF CORRUPTION IN THAILAND AND THEIR ECONOMIC COSTS

According to a December 1996 study reported in the *Wall Street Journal*, researchers at a top Thai university concluded that drug trafficking, contraband arms trading, diesel oil smuggling, trafficking in women for prostitution and in human labor, and certain forms of illegal gambling contributed $24–34 billion in economic activity per year between 1993 and 1995. The biggest contributor to underground activity was prostitution, which employs 150,000–200,000 workers and many ancillary workers.

Source: Sherer, Paul M. (1996, Dec. 3). Economic value of crime in Thailand may equal state budget, study says. *The Wall Street Journal*, p. A17.

> **BOX 7.12:   VENTURE RISK IN INDONESIA**
>
> Hughes Aircraft, Sumitomo Bank, British Petroleum, Siemens, Merrill Lynch, and Kia are only a few of the many global enterprises that have entered Indonesia by means of ventures with members of the Suharto family. Many wonder what will happen to these Suharto-aligned firms now that President Suharto, 75, is replaced. Will firms allied with the family be held accountable for corruption found in Indonesian business and government, or will they be viewed as victims who had little choice but to cooperate with the family or stay out of Indonesia's booming economy?
>
> *Source*: Engardio, Pete, and Shari, Michael. (1996, Aug. 19). The Suharto empire. *Business Week*, pp. 46–50.

individuals, particularly greedy bureaucrats, corruption in Western Europe and the US more usually advances business interests. In recent years, tougher laws on business practices and stronger enforcement efforts have revealed many cases of business corruption in Western Europe where the cost of bribery appears to be escalating. According to Udo Mueller, president of the General Accounting Office in the German state of Hesse, 'In the 1950s, you might have won the contract by taking the responsible official out for a couple of lunches. Now you need to pay for his holiday and a fur coat for his wife' (Germany catches the European disease, 1995, p. A10). Legal sanctions against bribery in Western Europe introduce different costs. For example, in response to growing concerns about corruption among industrial economies, the 29 members of the Organization for Economic Cooperation and Development (OECD) agreed to ban bribery as a means for companies to win business. Further, the bill called the Convention on Combating Bribery of Foreign Public Officials in International Business Transactions asks signatory governments to draft laws barring bribery and introduce legislation by April 1998 to criminalize bribery of foreign officials in international business. As the examples in Box 7.13 show, business corruption too frequently occurs in OECD countries.

The 1995 bribery conviction of a Lockheed Martin vice-president (listed in Box 7.13) is particularly ironic because it was Lockheed's bribery of Japanese officials that led to introduction of the US Foreign Corrupt Practices Act (FCPA). Since 1977 when the FCPA was introduced, it has had a considerable effect on US businesses doing business worldwide. Features of the FCPA include:

- No employee of a US firm can corrupt foreign officials, politicians, or political candidates with bribes.

BOX 7.13:   CORRUPTION IN OECD NATIONS

- Pierre Suard, was ordered to step down as head of telecommunications giant Alcatel Alsthom, and later indicted for overbilling France Telecom.
- Adam Opel AG was accused of taking kickbacks; three senior officials resigned.
- The US Department of Justice filed 15 criminal counts against North Carolina auto dealer Rick Henrick, claiming he had bribed excecutives at American Honda from 1981–1992. Two of Honda's top US sales executives received 5-year prison sentences for trading favors with dealers.
- Giancarlo Parretti and Florio Fiorin bribed Credit Lyonnais bankers to loan them $2 billion.
- Five officials of Fininvest were arrested on charges of bribery and false accounting in 1996.
- In 1995, Siemens was embroiled in alleged bribery cases in Spain and Italy.
- Also in 1995, Volkswagen's Jose Ignacio Lopez de Arriortua was accused of industrial espionage by former employer General Motors (the suit was settled out of court, but VW agreed to pay $100 million in damages to GM, and Lopez was not allowed to work for VW for three years).
- Mario Conde was accused of using questionable accounting practice to inflate former employer Banesto's profits.
- In Japan, investor Ryuichi Koike reportedly took payoffs from Nomura Securities.
- Three executives from Takashimaya, Japan's oldest department store were arrested for bribing a gang leader; Daimaru also admits giving hush money to the same individual.
- Canada's Bre-X fraud led to stock losses of over $3 billion.
- The president and former vice-president of Cumberland Packing Company (maker of Sweet n' Low) pleaded guilty to fraud charges involving illegal political campaign contributions.
- A former vice-president of Lockheed Martin Corporation was found guilty of bribing an Egyptian official to win aircraft orders.

- Firms must keep detailed records of their actions, and they must provide reasonable assurance to show that all transactions were within the law.
- Facilitating payments are allowed when paid to lower level employees or clerks to speed up duties they would have performed. An example would be a 'grease' payment to a customs official to clear a delivery sooner rather than later.
- Offences can lead to fines of up to $1 million and/or five years in jail.

The preceding review of corrupt behaviors in nations with and without legal sanctions against them suggests that business corruption is almost universal. However, corruption appears to be greater under circumstances where rules have recently changed, where market capitalism is a relatively new phenomenon, and where friendship and other relationships are the traditional basis for business. Corruption is less when business behavior is clearly defined in written form or according to commonly shared values, and where there are legal or industry sanctions against corruption accompanied by strict enforcement policies. Finally, corruption is likely to be less if public awareness has the potential to damage the firm's reputation and its subsequent opportunities.

Although economists once argued that bribes and other forms of corruption removed barriers to business, many now believe that the economic and social costs of corruption are dysfunctional, and business leaders believe that it hurts their interests. Moreover, corruption is contrary to free market principles that encourage equality of access and information. Businesses are themselves involved in finding ways to reduce corruption. Their efforts include voluntary alliances, individual actions, lobbying efforts for stronger legal sanctions, and business pressures.

Managing corruption risks

STRUCTURING VOLUNTARY ALLIANCES
Business/academic alliances

Transparency International is a German-based group of business leaders and academics dedicated to reducing corruption by asking that businesses and governments act in more transparent, open, and honest ways. Funded in part by European aid agencies and large multinational firms, Transparency International believes corruption will be reduced as political and economic competition within countries increases and as institutional reforms such as pay raises for civil servants are adopted. In some parts of Mexico, for example, a norm for police bribery results in abnormally low public wages for police. These institutional mechanisms give police little choice but to take bribes. According to a study of the relationship between low wages and corruption, economists Caroline Van Rijckeghem and Beatrice Weder (1997) found evidence of less corruption in countries where public employees are paid relatively well, and they concluded that if public servants' pay were to go from 100% to 200% of a manufacturing worker's wages, the corruption index for the nation would drop one point.

This is one approach to fighting corruption. Transparency International also sends teams of managers to developing countries to help them devise programs for fighting corruption, and they also expose relative corruption in nations by means of their international index for corruption. This index is based on data reported by other groups such as Hong Kong's Political and Economic Risk Consultancy, the *World Competitiveness*

Report and similar surveys. Countries rated in the 1997 report are ranked from most to least corrupt (see Figure 7.5). These results show the most economically developed nations are least corrupt.

Business/government alliances

These alliances also have emerged to improve integrity in the worldwide business environment. The Australian Transaction Reports and Analysis Center (Austrac) illustrates how concepts of boundarylessness have aided and deterred corruption. Austrac technicians and engineers borrowed a US Air Force computer program to detect military warheads, converted it to a money-tracking system called ScreenIt, and used it to capture a Chinese trader operating from a US base to launder money and defraud banks worldwide (Fialka, 1995).

THE STRUCTURE OF LEGAL REMEDIES

The 1977 Foreign Corrupt Practices Act outlined above is an example of national legislation to outlaw corrupt behavior. US threat of prosecution under the FCPA is real, and it is believed to be a deterrent to corruption for most US businesspeople. In 1996 and in late 1997 it adopted a proposal for OECD nations to criminalize payments made to political or business representatives to win contracts and other work. The Organization of American States signed an anti-corruption agreement in March 1996, and the United Nations adopted a resolution against corruption in December 1996. The 1997 *World Development Report* confirms earlier studies showing that corruption is negatively correlated with both investment and growth; the World Bank declared its intention to revoke loans to government enterprises when bribes are used to allocate business opportunities; and after concluding that high levels of corruption hurt a country's ability to attract capital, the International Monetary Fund (IMF) issued 1997 staff guidelines that involve the IMF in governance issues like the use of public funds, and asks staff to raise corruption issues with government officials. Finally, the IMF bailout of South Korea and Indonesia in 1997 and 1998 included demands that these countries restructure and engage in more transparent business transactions.

Government leaders also have acted to reduce corruption. In the Philippines, for example, President Fidel Ramos has led by example, making elimination of corruption one of his highest priorities. Improved economic conditions in the Philippines suggest the payoff for cleaning up corruption is improved economic growth. Alternatively, governments that permit corruption destroy citizen trust in government and affect people's willingness to be honest and obey laws (Melloan, 1995). Finally, wide-scale privatization of many industries has reduced government control over these enterprises, thereby limiting opportunities for corrupt government officials to benefit from payoffs and bribes.

CREATIVE PROCESSES

The enforcement teeth of the FCPA may have deterred US firms from offering outright bribes, but they have found ways to compete for contracts against those who do use bribes or other corrupt practices. At the same time, it is not entirely clear whether corruption does in fact cost US firms. According to a survey of 250 of the top 1,000 US companies, only 30% of respondents believed they had suffered losses due to the FCPA and among those the majority reported only 'somewhat of a decrease in business' (Pines, 1994, pp. 208–209). Yet, according to a 1995 US Department of Commerce report covering an eight-year period (Foreigners use bribes, 1995), US firms lost half of 200 international deals attributable in part to more aggressive payments on the part of competitors. More than $1 trillion in overseas capital projects are expected to be bid in the next decade, suggesting that US firms will be increasingly motivated to find alternatives to corruption. Some of those alternatives include funding scholarships and training, providing small fees to reimburse for out-of-pocket costs, trips to the US for purposes of student development or relationship-building, and the following:

- Union Texas Petroleum Holdings, Inc. of Houston formed a petroleum joint venture with Pakistan's government, offering to spend more than $200,000 a year to train government personnel.
- Hewlett-Packard offers Chinese journalists the equivalent of $12 to pay taxi fares for them to attend HP news conferences.
- Boeing is spending more than $100 million to train Chinese workers to use its technology.
- IBM donated $25 million in hardware and software to 20 Chinese universities.

Alternatives to corruption also are emerging from countries where corruption is believed greatest. According to a *Wall Street Journal* article, Russian firms found that straightforward reporting and a commitment to honesty led to increased investor confidence and rising share prices. China's experiments include honoring prior commitments as a way to build business confidence and attract FDI. In both countries, these changes in operating behaviors suggest adjustments in management thinking from short- to longer run returns on investments. These organizations appear to be adopting practices from market economies, just as the examples above show US firms are adapting to concepts of *guanxi* and still staying within the law.

PUBLIC SANCTIONS

Because China and Russia are counted as nations with the most corrupt business practices, both have incentives to improve their performance records. It is difficult to attract new business when reports of corruption are rife. Additionally, both nations have applied for World Trade Organization membership, and may be more highly motivated than at any other time to be viewed favorably by the world business community. China's government has lost credibility among its own entrepreneurs for favoring inept party bureaucrats who set up businesses, and this represents a risk to party officials who depend on public support and tax revenues (Pennar, 1993). At least one source believes that bribery and corruption are an inevitable result of, and even essential to, China's emergence from a totalitarian society (Yin, 1994).

RESPONSES TO CORRUPTION

Richard DeGeorge (1993), author of *Competing with integrity in international business*, suggests a number of strategies for dealing with corruption, five of which are listed here:

1 Do not respond in kind by adopting the very practices you find unethical.
2 Decision-makers may have to use moral imagination to respond when there are no specific rules for response.
3 Be ready to act with moral courage.
4 Seek joint action with others and work for ethical change.
5 Be prepared to pay a price and sometimes a higher price for responding ethically to a nonethical opponent (pp. 114–121).

Ettore (1994) suggests that US managers can prepare for overseas assignments not only by learning about the culture, but also by performing a due diligence investigation of everyone who will work for the company as an agent, distributor, representative, or partner by examining their reputation, and particularly their reputation for honesty. He recommends entering into specific written contracts to outline employee responsibilities as they pertain to company policies and the FCPA, and encourages managers to be sure that people understand company policies and views towards bribery.

MANAGERIAL COMPETENCIES FOR A GLOBAL WORLD: CONFLICT AND RISK

Responses to organizational forms of risk described above call for organization alterations in existing processes, structures, and personnel. Teams linking suppliers and buyers, networks for currency exchange cooperation, and educational programs represent ways each aspect of organization experiences change. Top and middle managers designing these changes face resistance among their peers and from external markets when the status quo is disrupted, and often middle or supervisory managers who announce or implement change encounter employee resistance to it. Resistance to these changes and efforts to overcome them are increasingly a part of managers' lives, resulting in personal risks such

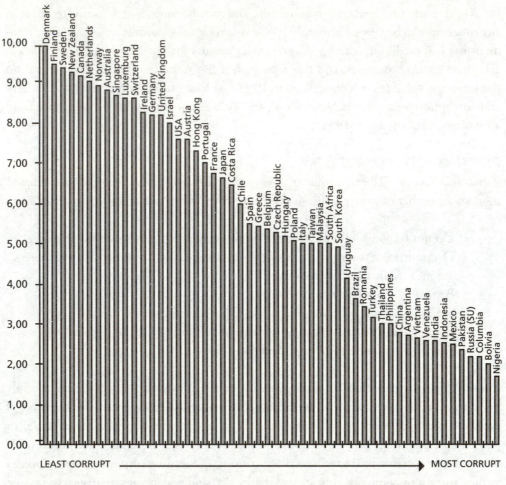

FIGURE 7.5 *Corruption perception index, 1997* (Transparency International and Johann Graf Lambsdorff, Göttingen University. http://www.gwdg.de/~uwvw/rank-97.jpg)

as stress and conflict. Managerial risk takes many forms. Below we will explore three forms of risk the global manager faces: psychological risk from stress, physical risk arising from conflict and violence at work, and physical risk attendant on being an international representative of business abroad. Neither stress nor conflict is inherently negative. In fact, both are believed necessary to induce desired action or create desirable results. However, taken beyond optimal levels, both stress and conflict can result in dysfunctional consequences such as substance abuse, noncompliance, or escalating violence at work.

Personal risk

MANAGING STRESS FROM WORK

Stress is a normal and natural part of life and work. Some degree of workplace stress moti-vates and energizes work productivity, and many believe that a moderate amount of stress produces highest levels of personal productivity. Figure 7.6 illustrates these relationships, and shows that too much stress can produce brown-out or lower productivity or even lead to burn-out or collapse of the person and an inability to work. Worldwide work-related stress is growing, exacerbated by the potential for working every hour of the week, a growing sense that hard work is the only way to sustain jobs, growing pressure to do more with less, and almost constant demands to learn new skills. These demands for new skills often are related to computer technologies, but other examples follow.

Bullet train projects like those at Yokogawa not only reduce manufacturing time, they cause teams of designers, managers, and producers to work faster, smarter, and more. Worldwide travel for top managers also has increased. For US managers, business travel increased 20% between 1990 and 1995, and travelling time was condensed. Five years ago, most business trips abroad were five days, but today 25% of business travelers return home within 24 hours (Miller, 1996). This pace provides constant exposure to the stress of new cultures and new experiences, but also increases personal demands. These and other changes introduced at every organizational level can produce stressors that create anxieties and disrupt many workplaces. Persons experiencing these stressors in the

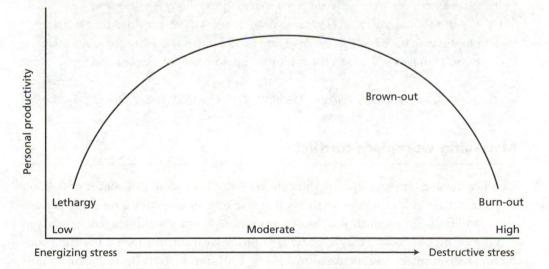

FIGURE 7.6 *The stress curve* (adapted from: Kreitner, Robert. (1982). Personal wellness: It's just good business. *Business Horizons*, 25: 32)

445

brown-out and burn-out stage can experience family estrangement, overwork, indulge in drug and alcohol abuse, or generate dysfunctional workplace conflict. Whereas these symptoms of stress have more traditionally been viewed as personal problems requiring personal solutions, increasingly organizations are assuming responsibility for stress reduction. Evolving Systems Inc. is a software developer with a mission to provide an excellent work environment that fosters employee growth and job satisfaction. It aims to reduce workplace stress for engineers who work long hours by hiring an 'office mom' to make sure employees eat regularly, to host holiday and birthday parties, water the plants, and make sure sick workers get the care they need. Others firms have provided an office concierge to help workers manage their personal needs when at work such as getting laundry done, arranging for car repairs, purchasing theater tickets, and the like. The examples in Box 7.14 illustrating assistance for business travelers shows how other firms aim to reduce the strain of frequent employee travel.

BOX 7.14: STRESS REDUCTION FOR TRAVELERS

Hewlett-Packard provides a toll-free telephone number for traveling executives to facilitate family contacts; executives can use the number even to read bedtime stories to their children.

American Family Insurance provides an on-site convenience store for travelers to pick up last-minute travel items like hosiery, shaving cream, and snacks.

Price Waterhouse flies its consultants home from wherever they are in the US because executives were believed to be spending too many weekends away.

An informal policy at Electronic Data Systems (EDS) provides time off for employees who have been on the road for four or more days; this reacquaints them with their families and allows them to catch up on personal errands and tasks.

Source: Laundry and dog-walking. (1996, Nov. 1). *The Wall Street Journal*, p. B9.

Managing workplace conflict

Conflict involves disputes that are difficult to resolve because of differences of opinion or practice, and at least one study shows that executive time spent on resolving personality conflicts is on the increase. Accountemps, a temporary staffing agency, surveyed executives in 1986 to find they spend 9% of their management time on resolving conflicts. The percentage had increased to 13% in 1991 and to 18% by 1996. In a global world with greater diversity, differences of opinion and conflict are inevitable but not necessarily dysfunctional. Leonard Greenhalgh (1986) suggests a framework for conflict

TABLE 7.7   Conflict diagnostic model

Conflict dimension	Resolution difficult	Resolution easier
Issue at question	Matter of principle	Divisible issue
Size of the stakes	Large stakes	Small stakes
Interdependence of parties	Zero sum	Positive sum
Continuity of interaction	Single transaction	Long-term
Structure of the relationship	Fractionalized, with weak leaders	Cohesive, with strong leaders
Third party involvement	No neutral third party	Trusted, powerful third party
Perceived events to this point	Unbalanced; one party feels more harmed	Balanced; equal harm

Source: Greenhalgh, Leonard. (1986). Managing conflict. *Sloan Management Review*, 27(4): 45–51.

diagnosis capable of recognizing the cross-cultural dimensions of conflict. As shown in Table 7.7, conflict is more difficult to resolve when it is a matter of principle. In the global workplace, conflicts over religious practices have proved particularly challenging. For example, Sanyo Electric Company banned headscarves (*hidjabs*) at its Jakarta subsidiary. Where once they might have kept silent, the women affected marched to the Indonesia House of Representatives to protest the behavior of the company. Headscarves also were the focal issue in French higher education when student Soumaya Bourachdi filed suit seeking her professor's apology for ejecting her from a class after she refused the choices offered: remove the *hidjab* or leave the class. Cultural clashes like these throughout the world focus attention on profound differences in principles being played out in workplace conflict.

Greenhalgh's list of seven conflict dimensions identifies sources of conflict difficulties, and suggests methods for achieving positive outcomes from conflict. If parties are interdependent, for example, then a win/lose approach to resolution is less likely to succeed than an approach in which all parties win. An example of a win/win solution is to provide a nonsectarian space for employees to pray and sufficient flexibility in the work schedule to allow work/religion balance. Organizations may relinquish absolute control over workers' activities but gain a loyal and committed workforce. An additional benefit is that all employees and not just the ones with particular work/religion needs benefit from increased autonomy, and this reduces dysfunctional internal competition.

Managing violence at work

The likelihood that managers will confront violent forms of conflict increases with the presence of global and local gangs and terrorist groups who routinely use violence. For example, the president of Fuji Photo was murdered in 1994 after he scorned gangs, and in the summer of 1996 Sanyo Corporation paid $2 million in kidnap ransom money to win the release of Mamoru Konno, president of Sanyo's Video Component Corporations in Mexico. According to Control Risks Group, foreigners in Mexico once were exempt from kidnappings, but they now are viewed like anyone else – as sources of ransom payoffs. These external threats are increasingly met with security measures ranging from lessons in evasive driving for top management chauffeurs, hiring bodyguards, providing preventive training, and even buying kidnap and ransom insurance. The combined costs of these protections are significant: according to some accounts, US businesses were spending over $200 million annually in 1994 to protect their top-level employees (Royal, 1994). Businesses with high international exposure train people in risk avoidance or how to identify sources of greatest risk. According to a 1996 *Wall Street Journal* report, agencies like Control Risks Group in London and Air Security International in Houston scan news sources from around the world to prepare daily databases on terrorism and global criminal activities (Dahl, 1996).

Violent solutions to workplace challenges also may be growing among employees. According to a review of media reports in the US, workplace violence has increased there, exacerbated by three factors: (a) changes in an individual's social support system; (b) shrinking labor market opportunities; and (c) changing societal values (Allen and Lucero, 1996). According to Bemsimon (1994), violence appears to occur more frequently in organizations when stressors such as heavy workloads, understaffing, layoffs, restructurings, and other forms of change are present.

Bemsimon notes that indicators of a stressful workplace include persistent and widespread complaints about working conditions, labor/management conflict, frequent grievances and injury claims, and high absenteeism. A review of workplace murders reported in newspaper articles dating back to 1986 led Allen and Lucero (1996) to propose that organizational aggression is triggered by perceived or real aversive treatment like firing or layoff, will be preceded by exhibitions of anger, resentment, or frustration, and will be targeted at the person perceived to be most responsible for the aversive treatment. They further suggest steps management can take to reduce workplace violence. These include:

- fair treatment of all employees, including clear expectations and performance feedback;
- supervisory training for those closest to employees;
- employee assistance efforts to help employees deal with difficult transitions;
- termination practices that are fair and extend assistance to the employee in finding other work;
- a security system limiting workplace access, especially for those who have been recently fired or made redundant.

This review of organizational responses to risk explored challenges firms face with increased interactions between global political events and organizations. Many of these risks are new ones with which managers have little experience, and all reflect increased variety of actions and beliefs associated with greater workplace diversity. Some of the challenges managers face may require accommodation more than change, and this too increases the uncertainties and dissonance associated with managing today. The evident need for balance between flexibility and stability also is the challenge nations face in an increasingly globalized political/legal environment.

KEY CHAPTER CONCEPTS

Government Defined: The network of political and legal arrangements that constitute a government are an important mechanism for meeting common needs for defense, survival, and development. The purposes of domestic governance remain the same in a global sphere: national development and national defense. National ability to achieve these goals is made more difficult in the global sphere because existing systems of global governance are imperfect and additional systems must be introduced in response to global changes in many spheres.

The Changing Role of National Governments: Economic integration and greater interdependence in other spheres have led to global agreements reducing the scope and even the focus of domestic policy activities. This is causing leaders within nations to turn their attention outward as well as inward. Internal shifts include privatization, eroding public confidence in government, revamped welfare systems, industrial policy, deregulation, and growing government efforts to stimulate business growth.

Reaching Global Political Resolutions: An enormous number of resources are needed to reach global resolutions, and because of the widespread impact such resolutions are likely to have on nations, political representatives see it as imperative to involve themselves in the world business community. Thus, individual nations and individual organizations may find themselves joining forces to find solutions to global business challenges of the twenty-first century.

A Shift in Defense Spending: Since the end of the Cold War, fewer resources have gone into global defense systems like NATO. While the industrialized nations have channeled defense resources to private uses, many developing economies are spending more on defense.

A Shift in Targets for Military Aggression: Military aggression is more localized than global, and armed conflict over ethnic and religious differences is in a growth mode. Military aggression increasingly targets noncombatants as victims.

Growth in Global Gang Activity: Growth in global gang and crime activity refocuses global defense from military to commercial protection. Global gangs are reshaping business tradition and practices.

Proliferation of Trade Alliances: Trade alliances and agreements are increasing in number and scope, expanding beyond regions to encompass diverse members, and expanding beyond cultural and political boundaries of nations to enhance full economic integration.

The Expanding Role of IGOs and NGOs in Global Governance: Globalization of commerce highlights the link between economic justice and social justice. Demands for achieving balance between these two types of justice are growing, and entities like intergovernmental cooperative organizations (IGOs) and nongovernmental organizations (NGOs) increasingly act to achieve this balance on a global scale.

New Units of Governance?: Globalization has stimulated growth in forms of government other than the nation-state, including international metropolitans, region states, and virtual states.

Growing Risk: Businesses and other entities increasingly face risk related to change in the global political/legal sphere. Their leaders must manage political risk, financial risk, and corruption risk at the organizational level. At the personal level, global leaders and employees must manage psychological and physical forms of risk.

REVIEW AND DISCUSSION QUESTIONS

1 This chapter asserts that the borders of business, government, and society are blurring. Use the example of a transnational organization like Operation Smile to prove this point. Library research on a transnational voluntary organization, business, or IGO also can be used to illustrate these points.

2 How are alliances like the EU similar to and different from alliances like the WTO? Relying on material provided here or found elsewhere, describe the defining characteristics of each entity to make your points.

3 Examine the features of the World Trade Organization. Does the WTO represent a threat to national sovereignty? In what ways do you think it does or does not do so.

4 The traditional argument in support of government ownership of services like telecommunications, banking, or commercial air and train travel is that these industries are important to national defense. In view of almost worldwide privatization of these

industries, how do you think nations expect to provide for their defense? Does privatization create risk for nations in a global world?

5   What political risks do you see for nations as leaders deregulate, privatize, and encourage exports and attract FDI? Will some nations be more at risk than others? Why or why not?

6   Among the hundreds who attended the Japanese Embassy holiday party in Peru were diplomatic and commercial representatives and their families. All were seized and 75 were held hostage by guerrilla group Tupac Amaru, whose members hoped to trade their hostages for jailed comrades. Months later, Peruvian armed forces stormed the occupied embassy; all of the guerrillas were killed, but all but two hostages were released unharmed. In what ways does this event and its aftermath illustrate challenges in global defense? How does it illustrate organizational and personal risk for people representing commercial interests worldwide?

7   Indonesian leaders have been accused of repression and constraints on trade, including corruption, yet Indonesia's economy continued to grow. Contrast these findings against claims that democracy and economic freedoms are linked. Do business corruption or political repression affect nations in ways that might not be immediately reflected in economic growth activity? What might be longer run effects of corruption on economic growth?

8   *The Global Enterprise Project*: Demonstrate ways it is evident that the firm is responsive to a globalizing political environment; this section can include benefits/costs of trade pact participation, responses to rules and regulations with specific countries or worldwide, or lobbies to alter firm or industry environments. Examine the results of deregulation or privatization for leaders in your firm.If you have not selected a firm to study, look at firms in the banking or telecommunications industries for examples. What do organizational leaders have to say about the effects of deregulation and privatization on their operations? Do they see these forces as opportunities, threats, or both?

REFERENCES

Allen, R.E., and Lucero, Margaret A. (1996). Beyond resentment: Exploring organizationally targeted insider murder. *Journal of Management Inquiry*, 5(2): 86–103.

Barnet, Richard, and Cavanagh, John. (1994). *Global dreams: Imperial corporations and the new world order*. New York: Simon & Schuster.

Bemsimon, H.F. (1994). Crisis and disaster management: Violence in the workplace. *Training and Development*, 28: 27–32.

Bergsten, C. Fred. (1994). APEC and world trade. *Foreign Affairs*, 73(3): 20–26.

Can the US weather Asia's storm? (1998, Jan. 5). *The Wall Street Journal*, p. A22.

Citicorp Annual Report. (1995). New York: Citicorp.

Commission on Global Governance. (1995). *Our global neighborhood*. New York: Oxford University Press.

Countries in trouble. (1986, Dec. 20). *The Economist*, pp. 69–72.

Dahl, Jonathan. (1996, Aug. 5). Psst . . . Private tips safeguard business trips. *The Wall Street Journal*, p. B1.

DeGeorge, Richard. (1993). *Competing with integrity in international business*. New York: Oxford University Press.

The destructive costs of greasing palms. (1993, Dec. 6). *Business Week*, pp. 133–136.

Drozdiak, William. (1994, June 5). Five centuries later, 'city-states' are back. *Washington Post*, p. A3.

Ettore, B. (1994, June). Why overseas bribery won't last. *Management Review*, pp. 20–24.

Fialka, John. (1995, May 8). Computers keep tab on dirty money. *The Wall Street Journal*, p. B7B.

Foreigners use bribes to beat US rivals in many deals, new report concludes. (1995, Oct. 12). *The Wall Street Journal*, pp. A3, A8.

Gambetta, Diego. (1996). *The Sicilian mafia*. Cambridge, MA: Harvard University Press.

GATT and FTAs: No longer foes. (1992, Oct.). *International Business*, pp. 6–14.

Germany catches the European disease. (1995, July 13). *The Wall Street Journal*, p. A10.

Global defense cuts could be a big boon to living standards. (1993, Sept. 24). *The Wall Street Journal*, p. B5A.

Gottlieb, Gidon. (1994). Nations without states. *Foreign Affairs*, 73(3): 100–112.

Greenberger, Robert S., and Brauchli, Marcus W. (1994, Nov. 11). U.S. has lost some of its clout in Asia. *Wall Street Journal*, p. A10.

Greenhalgh, Leonard. (1986). Managing conflict. *Sloan Management Review*, 27(4): 45–51.

Holland, Christopher P. (1994, Fall). The evolution of a global cash management system. *Sloan Management Review*, p. 38.

Hormats, Robert D. (1994). Making regionalism safe. *Foreign Affairs*, 73(2): 97–108.

The hot spots Clinton skipped over. (1996, Apr 29). *Business Week*, pp. 56–57.

How corrupt is Asia? (1995, Aug. 21). *Fortune*, p. 28.

How the mob burned the banks. (1996, Jan. 29). *Business Week*, pp. 42–47.

Howell, Llewellyn D., and Chaddick, Brad. (1994, Fall). Models of political risk for foreign investment and trade. *Columbia Journal of World Business*, 29(3): 70–91.

Human Development Report. (1997). Cary, NC: Oxford University Press.

Index of economic freedom. (1997). Kim R. Holmes, Bryan T. Johnson, and Melanie Kirkpatrick (Eds). Washington, DC: The Heritage Foundation and Dow Jones & Co.

Kahn, Joseph, and Brauchli, Marcus W. (1994, Dec. 19). Low Marx: China's communists face serious threat. *The Wall Street Journal*, pp. A1, A10.

Kim, Suk H., and Kim, Seung H. (1993). *Global corporate finance*. Miami, FL: Kolb Publishing.

McRae, Hamish. (1994). *The world in 2020*. Boston, MA: Harvard Business School Press.

Melloan, George. (1995, Nov. 13). Political corruption: The good, bad and ugly. *The Wall Street Journal*, p. A15.

Miller, Lisa. (1996, May 31). Pace of business travel abroad is beyond breakneck. *The Wall Street Journal*, p. B1.

Ohmae, Kenichi. (1995). *The end of the nation state*. New York: Free Press.

Paradox explained. (1995, July 22). *The Economist*, p. 52.

Pennar, Karen. (1993, Dec. 6). The destructive costs of greasing palms. *Business Week*, pp. 133–137.

Pines, David. (1994). Right of action. *California Law Review*, 82: 185–229.

Prestowitz, C.V., Jr, Tonelson, Alan., and Jerome, Robert W. (1991, Mar./Apr.). The last gasp of GATTism. *Harvard Business Review*, pp. 130–138.

Royal, Weld F. (1994, Dec.). Passport to peril? *Sales & Marketing Management*, pp. 74–78.

Salamon, Lester. (1994). The rise of the nonprofit sector. *Foreign Affairs*, 73(4): 109–122.

Salamon, Lester M., and Anheier, Helmut K. (1994). *The emerging sector*. Baltimore, MD: Johns Hopkins University Institute for Policy Studies.

Schnitzer, Martin, and Nordyke, James. (1983). *Comparative economic systems*. Cincinnati, OH: South-Western Publishing.

Simai, Mihaly. (1994). *The future of global governance*. Washington, DC: US Institute of Peace.

Smith, Geri. (1995, May 22). Pinatas on 18 wheels. *Business Week*, p. 62.

The tap runs dry. (1997, May 31). *The Economist*, pp. 21–23.

Thakur, Ramesh. (1995). The United Nations in a new world order. In Kanti P. Bajpai and Harish C. Shukul (Eds), *Interpreting world politics*, pp. 162–189. New Dehli: Sage.

Tofani, Loretta. (1994, Nov. 4). Chinese becoming their own bosses in many respects. *Seattle Times*, p. A19.

Tonn, Bruce E., and Feldman, David. (1995). Non-spatial government. *Futures*, 27(1): 11–36.

UN Division of Transnational Corporations and Investments. (1995, Apr.). *Incentives and direct foreign investments*. New York: United Nations.

U.S. International Trade Commission. (1994, Mar. 27). *The year in trade 1993*. U.S. Government Printing Office.

Van Rijckeghem, Caroline, and Weder, Beatrice. (1997, May). Corruption and the rate of temptation: Do low wages in the civil service cause corruption? Washington, DC: IMF Working Paper.

Vogel, Steven. (1997). *Freer markets, more rules*. Ithaca, NY: Cornell University Press.

Watson, Adam. (1995). The prospects for a more integrated international society. In Kanti P. Bajpai and Harish C. Shukul (Eds), *Interpreting world politics*, pp. 130–138. New Dehli: Sage.

World Development Report 1997: The state in a changing world. (1997). New York: Oxford University Press.

World drug report. (1997). Cary, NC: Oxford University Press.

The world economy survey. (1995, Oct. 7). *The Economist*, p. 9.

Yin, X. (1994, Apr.). China's gilded age. *The Atlantic Monthly*, pp. 42–53.

Chapter 8

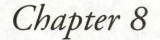

Global Industries and Tasks

ABB GOES GLOBAL

The 1987 merger between Swedish engineering firm Asea AB and Swiss competitor BBC Brown Boveri created ABB Asea-Brown Boveri, a firm that by 1997 had become a giant in global markets for electric power generation, high-speed trains, and environmental controls systems generating annual revenues of more than $35 billion. The transformation of these two nation-based firms into one global firm was led by Percy Barnevik. The opportunities and threats ABB Asea-Brown Boveri faced in a globalizing world included the following:

- **Global economy:** *World trade barriers had begun to fall, making it easier for competitors to cross national boundaries; economic growth in the industrialized countries was a motivator to invest in developing economies where business practices were varied.*
- **Industry globalization:** *Borders of individual industries had begun to blur as the electric industry moved toward electronics and power generation became linked with environmental protections; firms worldwide were entering capital-intensive industries, introducing different approaches to managing competition and generating greater competition in formerly protected nations and industries.*
- **Global politics:** *Formerly protected industries in European nations were losing these protections with cross-border mergers in the European Community; Asea's Swedish base could erode in the face of increasing foreign competition and there was a need for a pan-Nordic as well as a national presence; business decisions, e.g., labor costs and conditions, within many European nations were bound by national politics and long-term relationships that constrained business choice.*
- **Technological change:** *The growing capital-intensive nature of power generation*

and high-speed trains emphasized technological abilities of firms.

- **Global culture**: *National pride powered many business decisions in Europe and national preference had supported nation-based firms, but many wondered if national pride would remain relevant in a European context, particularly with increased price competition.*
- **Natural environment**: *Environmental pressure, particularly in Europe, encouraged short-run cost investments; there was growing demand for environmentally sensitive operations and for environmental accountability.*

Among the challenges ABB faced as a global firm was to integrate worldwide functions to benefit from global scope and yet develop a world-class technology responsive to local needs in the countries where the company operates. The vision and strategy Barnevik developed illustrate only two of the organizational processes many global enterprises review as they go global. For example, a 1988 meeting among key managers resulted in a policy 'bible' that articulates a philosophy of remaining customer-driven in all aspects of the business, outlines values for creating a global culture, and provides guidelines for overall behavior. One value is that it is better to be generally right with respect to speed than to be exactly right. Why? Because it takes a great deal more time to be exactly right, and that time might cost the firm advantages to be gained from being first to market. Adopting processes like vision also meant adapting existing structures and creating a workforce responsive to a globalizing world.

Barnevik created a decentralized and very flat structure for the organization that moved operational decision-making, authority, and responsibility into the lowest organizational levels. In this flat structure, less than six jobs stand between the CEO and the shop floor. In terms of its effect on people, these processes and structural changes resulted in job reductions at the highest levels of the organization and job additions at lower levels. This was accomplished by consolidating executive jobs so that only about 250 global executives lead over 200,000 employees worldwide. At the top of the organization are eight executives of differing nationalities: US, Swedish, Danish, Swiss, and German. Another aspect of top executive diversity is that the backgrounds for executive committee members include computer science, business administration, research, marketing, and engineering. At lower levels, ABB has added over 100,000 jobs, mainly through joint ventures and acquisitions. This flat structure is combined with a matrix design that delegates global product strategy and performance decisions to business-area managers, e.g., decisions for the worldwide robotics business, and yet there also are national managers to retain a local focus, e.g., Robotics Indonesia. This formula for structuring an organization violates many traditional management principles such as chain-of-command, decision centralization, and headquarters' control, but Barnevik believed the advantages outweighed the risks. For example, global purchasing decisions reduced costs and better communication occurred as a result of the reduced hierarchical levels of the flat structure. Additionally, the national and functional diversity found in ABB's executive committee has become important when dealing with customers, suppliers, and government representatives from the over 140 countries where the firm does business. Although ABB deviates from traditional management principles on many dimensions, Barnevik subscribed to the principle of clearly defined organizational purpose.

In early 1996, Barnevik was voted the most admired manager in Europe, yet by the fall of that year he was no longer CEO of ABB Brown Bovieri. Acting on investor worries that Barnevik had become too central to the success of the firm, he became board chairman and was replaced as president and CEO by Swede Goran Lindahl. Effective from April 14, 1997, Barnevik became the new chairman of Investor, a giant holding company controlled by Sweden's Wallenberg family. Although Investor's companies are principally based in Sweden, Barnevik's declared plan is to take the firm global.

Source: The ABB of management. (1996, Jan. 6). *The Economist*, p. 56; Guyon, Janet. (1996, Oct. 2). ABB fuses units with one set of values. *The Wall Street Journal*, p. A12; Redding, Gordon. (1995, Feb.). ABB – The battle for the Pacific. *Long Range Planning*, pp. 92–94; Reed, Stanley. (1996, Oct. 28). Percy Barnevik passes the baton. *Business Week*, p. 66.

PART I   EVOLVING INDUSTRIES AND TASKS

The task environment usually refers to day-to-day activities or concerns for a business such as manufacturing a good or providing a service, dealing with customers, or negotiating with lenders (Fahey and Narayanan, 1986). With globalization, customers, lenders, and inputs for goods and services can be located a world away from the focal firm, and this distance makes it more difficult for managers to keep up with events that affect even their daily tasks. Similarly, the events and activities shaping industries are occurring less in domestic markets and more at a global level. Distance from events affecting them impedes managers' ability to remain current or to anticipate industry change affecting firm success or survival. This chapter examines globalization of task and industry environments, explores which industries are globalizing and why, and looks at practical and theoretical suggestions for creating structures and processes and developing people to ensure organizational success and survival in a global industry.

GLOBALIZATION OF INDUSTRIES
Defining an industry

Just as boundaries of nation-states, economies, and cultures are increasingly permeable, industry boundaries also are blurring. In publishing, textbooks are being replaced and supplemented by CD-ROMs and educational software in the 'edutainment' industry. Optical fiber technology replaces thin telephone wire and coaxial cables for television to create 'infotainment.' Pharmaceutical and cosmetics industries overlap to produce 'cosmeceuticals,' and natural foods and pharmaceuticals blend to create 'neutriceuticals.' These examples illustrate the merging, melding, and reshaped borders for existing industries from which new industries emerge and old ones may be redefined, and they redefine important tasks for businesses.

A second impact of globalization on industry structure is called disintermediation or side-stepping of traditional industry structures or organization to accomplish tasks (Prahalad and Hamel, 1994). For example, individuals once were forced to use brokers to buy or sell stocks; now via the Internet they can trade on their own accounts. Similarly, retail sales can be purchased via the Internet rather than in retail establishments or tickets purchased without an agent. These and similar instances of disintermediation allow new and often innovative competitors to enter existing industries, forcing current participants to rethink how they operate their businesses.

A third important industry change attributable to globalization is integration across organizational boundaries. Cross-border mergers, acquisitions, and strategic alliances include collaborative arrangements between businesses from multiple countries, governments and not-for-profit organizations partnering with businesses, and cooperation among firms that are rivals in one line of business and competitors in another. On a national level European and US firms compete in the computer industry but collaborate to produce a new computer chip, and IBM and Apple compete in the personal computer market but collaborate in the lab to develop a non-DOS platform for personal computers. Some believe activities like these represent the death of competition as we know it (Moore, 1996), arguing for coopetition involving win/win solutions (Brandenburger and Nalebuff, 1996). In view of industry border permeability, increased collaboration among and between firms, and mergers and acquisitions, the term 'competitive' environment may no longer be entirely accurate for the global marketplace. Accordingly, this chapter uses the more general term 'industry/task' environment to describe what is sometimes referred to as the 'competitive' environment of business.

In many if not most cases, industry and task environments are characterized by rapid change, greater uncertainty, and multiple challenges for business managers. New industries develop almost overnight, existing organizations must shift their tasks quickly to respond, and competitors learn to collaborate and compete simultaneously. Accordingly, a globalizing industry environment creates demands for balancing among multiple and seemingly competing objectives.

Industry variety

Managers find it difficult to track change in all industries because industries differ. Almost intuitively we recognize significant differences between industries. A comparison of the nuclear power industry with pet foods shows these differences. The high cost of investing in nuclear power makes it difficult for new firms to enter this industry. As a result, nuclear power plants often are fully or partially government-owned, sales of services are to industrial users, planning occurs with a long lead time, and there are few competitors and few substitute products. The pet food industry is organized by the private sector, product sales are to consumers' owners whose fickle tastes demand constant innovation in relatively short product planning cycles. The costs of producing pet food are relatively low, competitors can be many, and there are many substitutes. Differences in buyers, suppliers, the nature of competition, availability of substitute products, and entry barriers to the industry are five characteristics used to distinguish between one industry and another. In practice, managers tend to focus on those industries in which they operate to identify critical historical variables for the industry. For example, outcomes for global corn processors like Archer Daniels Midland are dependent on weather patterns and firms in this industry look first at the natural environment, whereas businesses in the machine tool industry look first at economic indicators. The important point is that managers of every firm must recognize where their greatest external dependencies lie. Additionally, because the boundaries and barriers of industries have the capacity to shift as new industries are created, managers also must recognize where future dependencies lie. Thus, it is not enough to remain fixed on history or the present; it also is important to monitor the entire global horizon to identify trends likely to have future impact on the firm.

Often trends that change industries begin outside them. For example, 'hubbing' practices developed for the airlines have altered wholesale and food retailing by shipping goods to large, regional warehouses from which they can be distributed to individual stores. This technique reduces the costs of inventory for each store, saves on shipping costs, and requires computer programs to queue and dispatch merchandise expeditiously. In the global personal computer industry Acer's Stan Shih adopted the 'fast food' concept of McDonald's to deliver his product. These examples illustrate that successful managers must be intimate with the particulars of their own industries but also familiar with activities and practices in other industries. They must be future-oriented, but neither should they ignore the past. When assessing industry history or current conditions, most managers use a technique popularized by Michael Porter in the early 1980s.

COMPETITIVE STRATEGY

In his successful book *Competitive strategy*, Michael Porter (1980) offered industry analysis as a tool to identify the potential for earning above-average profits from an industry. Five industry characteristics important to this analysis are shown in Figure 8.1. Once the industry is analyzed and competitor moves analyzed in the same way, the focal firm can identify the competencies it has for the industry and develop appropriate competitive moves consistent with these competencies. At the heart of all this is the industry analysis itself.

Rivalry

The degree of rivalry in an industry establishes parameters for action. Competition in domestic and international business has been placid in some industries and fierce in others. In the soft drink beverage industry, Coca-Cola and PepsiCo have been consistent and fierce competitors within the domestic US market, taking it on the road to expand internationally. Prior to 1989, a long-standing agreement between PepsiCo's chairman and the Russian premier made it almost impossible for Coke to participate in Soviet markets, but when entry was possible Coke wasted no time or effort, pouring $1.5 billion into Eastern Europe to gain a foothold against Pepsi products (Nash, 1995). Marketing money spent in Eastern Europe, head-to-head combat over bottling in Latin America, and continued competitive warfare in established markets are evidence that Coke and Pepsi remain committed rivals worldwide. The type of fierce rivalry that Pepsi and Coke maintain shapes the industry, making it more volatile, more difficult to predict, and more prone to cost-cutting and pre-emptive strikes that keep competitors off

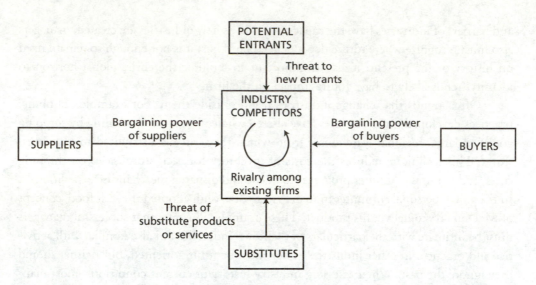

FIGURE 8.1 *Five forces of industry competition* (Porter, Michael E. (1980). *Competitive strategy.* New York: Free Press, p. 4)

balance. These conditions of rivalry make it difficult for other soft drink beverage firms to predict or plan for the industry, and may well be a deterrent to new entrants.

Barriers to industry entry

High initial costs, existing brand loyalty, economies of scale, government actions that limit entry, or access to distribution channels all create opportunities for existing firms that makes it difficult for new firms to enter the industry.

Availability of substitutes

The availability of substitute products or services makes it more difficult for firms within an industry to earn above-average profits. If they raise prices, sales may go to substitute products, making the industry less attractive than one with few or no substitutes.

Buyer or supplier power

The relative strength or bargaining power of buyer or supplier groups shape the firm's ability to set prices autonomously. For example, if buyer groups purchase large volumes of a firm or industry's output, they can command better prices than when buyers are dispersed or uninformed.

Competitive strategy in a global world

The volatility of globalization makes it more difficult to conduct an industry analysis than it was when firms operated in domestic or boundaried international markets. First, industry participants span the globe, and there are many more activities to monitor globally. Although managers have access to many sources of information, these sources may not present or interpret information in ways accessible to managers worldwide. Information abundance may motivate managers to attend only to their own industries, but this could be an impediment to recognizing ideas and synergies arising in other industries. Additionally, the set of competitive activities firms conduct based on an industry analysis views the world from the perspective of the firm rather than from the perspective of the customer (Keen and Knapp, 1996). Even if the firm does direct attention toward customers, this can be problematic since global customers are not cohesive and their interests can change rather rapidly. Further, when competitors within an industry come from around the world, they are less likely to know or honor industry conventions developed over time. This creates volatility in many industries, and makes it difficult for firms to plan. Jeffrey Pfeffer (1994) believes that these and similar weaknesses with industry analysis are not an argument against strategic analysis; they simply show that as conditions change, so too must the tools adapt to assess them. In summary, industry analysis provides a framework for organizations to assess historical and current industry factors, but there is a growing need as well to analyze industry globalization and assess organizational competencies with an eye toward future globalization of industries.

Reasons for industry globalization

Worldwide integration within and across global environments also is affecting industries. Throughout the 1980s, capital, knowledge, and technological breakthroughs were more accessible worldwide than had previously been the case; this made it possible for firms from around the world to enter industries previously closed to them. At the same time, slowing economic growth in the industrialized nations increased the desirability of selling products and services elsewhere; businesses that expanded worldwide carried with them new options and suggested unexplored opportunities. For a variety of reasons, including industrial policies within nations, large and small organizations from all over the world began to enter industries previously dominated by Western or Japanese firms. Together, the collective activities of these myriad firms have reshaped the nature of many industries, making many more global in scope. Development and production of the Mazda Miata automobile (Box 8.1) provides an example of the global nature of the automotive industry, but many other industries similarly finance, design, produce, and sell worldwide.

Growing incidence of industry globalization led theorists to argue that industry-specific events occurring in one country were likely to be replicated in other countries, and firms faced an industry environment where economic forces were dominated not by single nations but rather by worldwide collective economic forces (Bartlett and Ghoshal,

> **BOX 8.1: THE MIATA MX-5**
>
> Financing for the Miata came from Tokyo and New York; it was designed in California but the first prototype was created in Worthing, England. The automobile is assembled in Michigan and Mexico using advanced electronic components invented in New Jersey and fabricated in Japan. It is sold primarily in the US, but its success there encouraged sales growth worldwide. Technological, economic, and cultural tastes on a global scale have combined to produce global demand for this sporty little car.

1992). Focus necessarily turned to an examination of the effects economic and other forces such as politics, technology, and culture had on firms, and efforts began to define characteristics of a global industry.

Defining a global industry

According to Michael Porter (1986), globalization of industry competition had become more the rule than the exception by 1986, and he defined a global industry as one offering competitive advantage to firms that could integrate activities on a worldwide basis. In Porter's view, linkages among domestic industries combined structural forces of industry into a single global competitive arena. Measures of globalization could include the amount of industry factors shaped outside domestic markets, a high industry–trade ratio measured by percentage of trade contributing to industry revenues (Porter, 1980) ranging from about 30 to 55% (see Roth and Morrison, 1990, footnote 2), or a percentage of a firm's sales derived from abroad. The latter is most frequently used to reflect industry globalization because these type of data are relatively easy to obtain. A 1989 study of 433 chief executives' views on globalization showed that despite growing revenues from international operations, few were deriving more than a modest percentage of revenues from abroad (Anders, 1989). For example, only 13% of 1988 revenues from North Americans polled were from abroad as compared to 33% of European revenues and 18% of Japanese revenues. This study showed that industries with largest revenues from abroad also were those with big research and development budgets like aerospace; those characterized by heavy capital spending such as automotives or consumer electronics; or those with strong consumer demands such as blue jeans. At the time of this study, packaging, financial services, and retailers did not view their industries as having potential for globalization. Today that picture is much changed.

The definition of globalization was expanded in an article by Steven Kobrin (1991) which used intrafirm flows of resources or the flow of information, funds, people, and other resources internationally but within the firm, to measure degrees of integration on a global scale. Using product measures from 1982 data, Kobrin discovered that intrafirm flows accounted for 25% of international sales for 10 industries that have been thought of as global industries (Table 8.1).

Comparisons between the 1982 data and 1986 data Kobrin collected showed dramatic increases in global integration for many of the industries listed in Table 8.1. In the last decade greater integration of the type measured in Kobrin's study has also occurred. Kobrin notes that firms are the vehicle for cross-border integration of technology, production, and economic activity, but argues that the true global forces are technology and economic activity themselves.

Kobrin's work provides a useful way to think about global industries. The global integration within and across national and sectoral borders he describes is shaped not within single sectors but through interrelationships between global technology, global industries, global culture, and other environments. Subsequent to Kobrin's study, services as well as manufacturing industries have gone global. Advertising, consulting, engineering, commercial air travel, and retailing are a few among many industries that are now global, containing many firms definable as global enterprises. Industries ranging from data processing to leisure and tourism, forest products, chemicals and steel are by virtue of sales more global than domestic, and smaller industries such as watches, copiers, pet foods, cereals, and athletic shoes also have gone global. Well-known as well as little-known participants in global industries appear in Table 8.2.

TABLE 8.1   Intrafirm activities by industry, 1982

Industries for which intrafirm activities account for >25% of sales	%
Motor vehicles	44
Communications equipment	40
Electronic components including semiconductors	39
Computers and office machinery	38
Farm machinery	34
Photographic equipment	32
Engines and turbines	30
Scientific instruments	29
Optical goods	27
Industrial chemicals	26

Source: Kobrin, Steve. (1991). An empirical analysis of the determinants of global integration. *Strategic Management Journal*, 12 (Special Issue): 17–31.

TABLE 8.2   Global industries and participants

Advertising	Saatchi & Saatchi, Havas, Omnicom, WPP Group, Dentsu, McCann-Erickson Worldwide
Automotive tires	Bridgestone, Groupe Michelin, Goodyear, Sumimoto Rubber, Continental AG
Athletic shoes	Nike, Reebok, Adidas, Fila, Diadora, Puma, K-Swiss
Beer	Heineken, Guinness, Anheuser Busch, Fosters, Kirin, Millers, Interbrew Labatt, San Miguel
Confections	Cadbury Schweppes, Mars, Hershey, Nestlé, Jacobs Suchard, Haribo, Hahtamaki
Container shipping	Evergreen Marine, Hyundai, Cosco, GP Livanos, Sea-Land Service, Nippon Yusan Kaishe Line, Hanjin
Cosmetics	L'Oréal, Estée Lauder, Avon, Shiseido, Body Shop, MAC, Hard Candy
Motorcycles	Suzuki, Harley Davidson, Piaggio, Honda, Aprilia Moto
Petroleum refining	Royal Dutch/Shell, PEMEX, British Petroleum, Imperial Oil, Texaco
Photographic equipment	3-M, Kodak, Fuji, Casio, Epson
Publishing	Thompson, Dow Jones, Reed Elsevier, Bertelsman, Quebecor
Retailing	IKEA, Carrefour, Marks & Spencer, Makro, Hudson's Bay, Ito-Yokada, Royal Ahold, Wal-Mart
Video games	Nintendo, Sega, Sony, Philips, Mattel

Source: Global 500. (1996, July). *Fortune*

DIAGNOSING INDUSTRY GLOBALIZATION

In his book *Total global strategy*, George Yip (1995) outlines four factors that drive industry globalization. An examination of these four factors may help managers of worldwide businesses assess the degree of industry globalization in their businesses.

Market globalization can be assessed by examining: (a) common needs of end use customers worldwide; (b) national and multinational global customers who search the world for suppliers but use the purchased product or service either in one country or in many; (c) ease with which marketing can be transferred worldwide; and (d) lead countries where the most important product or process innovations for the industry are located. By assessing these four elements of market globalization, managers are able to see when consumer tastes converge; when buyers consolidate their buying; when marketing can be used globally; and where they need to invest to be part of a developing global industry.

Cost globalization drivers depend on the economies of the business and so can vary by industry. For example, global economies of scale are a cost globalization driver when they can only be realized with sales in many countries rather than one. As the costs of computer circuits drop, for instance, firms must compete on cost and can only achieve lower costs by producing on a worldwide scale. Other cost globalization drivers include global economies of scope, experience curves, sourcing efficiencies, favorable logistics, fast-changing technology, high product development costs, and differences in country costs. In Chapter 6 we saw that differences in the cost of labor were a major factor influencing job migration, and in Chapter 2 (Box 2.7) we saw how Ford expects to reduce development costs by producing a global car.

Yip's *government globalization* drivers are similar to factors we reviewed as part of the global political/legal environment in Chapter 7. These include: favorable trade policies that make it desirable to expand into new nations; compatible technical standards; common marketing regulations; host government concerns; and government-owned competitors and customers. For example, the potential for globalization of an industry can increase when a government-owned entity is a competitor because government actors can marshall resources and may subsidize industries to take them global. The aerospace industry began to globalize with subsidies from the multiple nations that joined to establish Airbus.

Competitive globalization drivers for Yip are very similar to those identified in our Chapter 5 examination of the global economy. Central themes include: economic integration via increased exports and imports; competitors from many nations; increased economic interdependence among countries; and increased rivalry on a global scale. These reflections of globalization are occurring across industries of every kind and in every sector. Whether classified as product or service industries; noncyclical products like shampoo or cereal purchased on a regular basis or cyclical ones like heating oil purchased for cold weather; consumer nondurables whose value is depleted relatively fast or durables like automobiles that last many years; or as basic or value-added industries, all are increasingly global. Basic industries like chemicals, food, and textiles, as well as extractive industries such as oil, aluminum, or coal that are commodity or near-commodity products, now see prices determined by worldwide availability. As developing countries seek out 'value-added' industries, manufacturers in the industrialized world simultaneously surrender some of their profits or offer additional product value to retain buyers. Thus, prices for value-added products are likely to decline as more business participants enter the market and as additional technological efforts lower costs and improve quality and access simultaneously. The personal computer industry is one where costs have declined with increasing quality, making the product price-accessible to many more people worldwide. As value-added industries like this one globalize, businesses offering lower prices also may see their profits decline.

GLOBAL INDUSTRIES AND FIRMS

In Chapter 2, a global enterprise was defined as one that draws resources such as capital or labor from a global pool, views the world as home, establishes and maintains a global presence, pursues a global strategy, and transcends external and internal boundaries. According to the 1995 *World Investment Report*, heightened business competition can be expected as companies from fast-growing emerging economies become multinationals. Differences among these firms led to diverse business practices that have transformed industries and organizations within them. Size and orientation toward business were shown to be two among many ways global enterprises differ. Organizations like ABB and General Electric draw resources and staying power from being big, but act small to remain alert to customer demand. The fluid structure of many smaller firms allows them to act quickly, and technological changes facilitate access to information and capital once available only to larger firms with significant research capabilities. Firms of every type and from every part of the world now cross boundaries of size, economies, and other boundaries to participate in business. This process is unfolding very quickly because all companies now need access to global technology, capital, components, and even labor just to survive in their own home markets. According to Kang Hyo Jim, executive director of Samsung, 'We see globalization as a survival strategy.' Increased industry participation and the importance to participants of being global makes it imperative to look at many rather than a few examples when assessing global industries.

Large multinationals

About 40,000 firms are identified as transnational companies; collectively these firms generate more than $5 trillion in annual sales from 250,000 affiliates abroad (*World Investment Report*, 1995). In 1994, these firms accounted for two-thirds of global trade in goods and services; operate in industries ranging from low to high value-added production and from products to services. Many are global. In August 1997, *Fortune* magazine produced a list of industries defined as global because they contain the 500 firms with highest worldwide earnings in the previous year. These global industries are shown in Table 8.3. Missing from this list are global industries whose firms collectively also generate billions in revenue, such as apparel, textiles, jewelry, toys, tires, and sporting goods. Also missing are firms that do not report their financial results. Examples of firms operating on a global scale in the following sections look at these as well as publicly owned multinational enterprises (MNEs) to paint a broader picture of industry globalization.

Ownership of many large global firms is public, and financial results and organizational decisions are reported widely, just as shown in Table 8.3. Large privately held firms also are the subject of public inquiry when their activities are global or products are globally known, e.g., Henkel or Benetton. Many of these large worldwide enterprises grew because of access to capital, using it to merge, acquire, or expand globally to achieve economies of scale and scope. These cross-border transactions make it difficult to know exactly who owns whom, contributing to a sense that many firms are associated less with a nation than with the world. The capital advantage many larger firms had as they expanded worldwide up to the 1990s may be eroding as entrepreneurs find it possible to enter markets with little more than a personal computer and a link to world markets. In the wake of deregulation around the world, and standardization of commercial rules, larger firms also may lose the knowledge advantage they once had as repositories of

TABLE 8.3 Global industry leaders, 1997

Global industry *Fortune* Global 500 (1997)	Industry revenues (no. of firms counted) (1996)		Largest firm in the industry (1997)	Global 500 rank (1996)	Sales in $ millions for largest firm (1996)
Aerospace	130,346	(8)	Lockheed Martin	112	28,875
Airlines	97,488	(7)	AMR	208	17,753
Banks: commercial and savings	1,252,970	(69)	Bank of Tokyo-Mitsubishi	41	46,451
Beverages	53,200	(4)	Coca-Cola	196	18,546
Building materials; glass	44,299	(3)	Saint-Gobain	205	17,862
Chemicals	275,002	(14)	El DuPont De Nemours	55	36,689
Computers, office equipment	251,575	(9)	IBM	15	75,947
Diversified financials	82,825	(5)	Fannie Mae	120	25,054
Electronics; electronic equipment	809,741	(26)	General Electric	12	79,179
Energy	55,024	(3)	Rao Gazprom	146	32,554
Engineering; construction	199,916	(13)	CIE Générale des Eaux	81	32,429
Entertainment	69,725	(6)	Walt Disney	195	18,739
Food	250,795	(12)	Unilever	31	52,067
Food and drug stores	455,010	(27)	Metro Holding	62	36,568
Food services	42,332	(2)	PepsiCo	86	31,645
Forest and paper products	88,650	(7)	International Paper	169	20,143
General merchandisers	361,744	(14)	Wal-Mart Stores	11	106,147
Health care	29,983	(2)	Columbia/HCA	174	19,909
Hotel, casinos, resorts	24,233	(2)	Japan Travel Bureau	293	14,061
Industrial & farm equipment	149,144	(9)	Mitsubishi Heavy Industries	103	27,899
Insurance: life & health – mutual	449,964	(19)	Nippon Life	18	72,575
Insurance: life & health – stock	287,554	(16)	ING Group	64	35,913
Insurance: property & casualty – mutual	53,748	(2)	State Farm Group	49	42,781
Insurance: property & casualty – stock	461,927	(20)	Allianz Holding	28	56,577
Mail, packaging & freight delivery	173,528	(8)	US Postal Service	29	54,402
Metal products	33,653	(4)	Pechiney	341	12,742
Metals	193,277	(14)	Nippon Steel	110	27,178
Mining, crude-oil production	61,584	(3)	Pemex	97	28,429
Motor vehicles & parts	1,177,545	(27)	General Motors	1	168,369
Petroleum refining	991,388	(31)	Royal Dutch/Shell Group	6	8,887
Pharmaceuticals	160,547	(10)	Novartis	95	29,310

TABLE 8.3   Continued

Global industry Fortune Global 500 (1997)	Industry revenues (no. of firms counted) (1996)		Largest firm in the industry (1997)	Global 500 rank (1996)	Sales in $ millions for largest firm (1996)
Publishing, printing	49,183	(4)	Bertelsmann	273	14,728
Railroads	100,526	(7)	East Japan Railway	148	22,318
Rubber & plastic products	45,476	(3)	Bridgestone	203	17,999
Science, photo, control equipment	41,320	(3)	Eastman Kodak	245	15,968
Securities	75,109	(4)	Merrill Lynch	121	25,011
Soaps, cosmetics	57,910	(3)	Procter & Gamble	65	57,910
Specialist retailers	71,475	(5)	CostcoCos	178	19,566
Telecommunications	533,350	(22)	Nippon T&T	14	78,321
Tobacco	95,541	(3)	Philip Morris	30	54,553
Trading	1,120,886	(22)	Mitsui	3	144,943
Utilities	288,921	(14)	Tokyo Electric Power	43	44,735
Wholesalers	120,540	(9)	Franz Haniel	226	16,757

Source: Global 500. (1997, Aug. 4). *Fortune*, pp. F1–F30. Also available at: www.pathfinder.com/fortune500/500list.html

regulatory standards in most of the world. Additionally, liberalization of commercial rules in the developed and developing countries alike makes it easier for enterprises of any size to enter markets. Finally, globalization has exposed the following weaknesses of large, multinational firms:

1 Deregulation and lower trade barriers have reduced the value of relationships multinationals cultivated with government leaders.
2 The spread of modern management techniques has reduced the monopoly position of large multinationals on management wisdom.
3 Large, bureaucratic organizations find it difficult to adapt rapidly to change (Who wants to be, 1995).

Hidden champions

As compared to MNEs rarely is as much information available or sought from firms whose activities are less in the public eye. According to Hermann Simon's book *Hidden champions: Lessons from 500 of the world's best unknown companies* (1996), firms whose activities are little known publicly have worldwide market shares of 50%, 60%, and even 90%. Examples include Mabuchi of Japan, and Johnson Electric of Hong Kong which command 40% and 25% respectively of the small motor market worldwide, or Hauni from Germany, which dominates 90% of the market for high-speed cigarette-makers. Simon believes that to some extent these firms adopt management practices that are contrary to current management wisdom. For example, most have authoritarian leaders who delegate day-to-day management, they avoid alliances and outsourcing in favor of internal strengths, and they engage in limited professional marketing. At the same time, Simon finds these firms are aggressively globalizing, highly dependent on their human resources, and pursue extreme innovation. Finally, he argues that hidden champions are firms capable of the both/and approach that has been a theme throughout this text. For example, hidden champions innovate on both product and process technologies, and their leaders often are authoritarian in terms of core values yet participative in terms of implementation. Other examples of both/and approaches among hidden champions appear in Table 8.4.

Privately held global enterprises

Each year, *Forbes* magazine compiles a list of personal and family fortunes estimated at $1–10 *billion* US. Some family names are familiar but more are not because many share a sentiment expressed by billionaire Robert Ng: 'We like to keep a low profile'(Mao, 1994, p. 158). Mars Inc., Levi Strauss, Sainsbury, Guess?, Domino's Pizza, Deloitte & Touche, and Hallmark Cards are a few among many privately owned global firms. And, like large publicly held firms, leaders of closely held firms have their eyes on global

TABLE 8.4   The hidden champions' both/and philosophy

Aspect	Both . . .	And
Market	Narrow: product, technology	Wide: world, regional
Driving force/innovation	Customer-driven	Technology-driven
Strategy	External opportunities	Internal resources/competencies
Innovation	Product	Process
Time horizon	Short-term: efficiency (doing the right thing)	Long-term: effectiveness (doing the thing right)
Competitive advantage	Product quality	Service/interaction
Creation of value-added	Core activities in-house	Outsourcing of noncore activities
Job turnover	High: early in the selection phase	Low: long-term personnel
Leadership	Authoritarian in core values, goals	Participative in details, process

Source: Simon, Hermann. (1996). *Hidden champions: Lessons from 500 of the world's best unknown companies*, p. 273. Cambridge, MA: Harvard Business School Press.

growth. For example, Kim Woo-choong, founder of Daewoo, asserts that the firm's goal 'is to become a company without borders' (Asami, 1995). Their growth patterns and the resources they employ can differ from those used by publicly owned firms. Levi Strauss, for example, sold and then repurchased equity shares from the market because answering to shareholders did not allow the decision latitude important to Levi's longer run, socially responsive view of business.

Family-owned business enterprises

Family ownership of firms is quite common among ethnic Chinese, in Africa, in Europe, and throughout Central and Latin America; it is not all that unusual among firms operating in the US. Family ownership allows broad latitude for management practices, and this increases diversity of business objectives in the global sphere. Family-held businesses can assume a longer planning horizon than firms under pressure to produce quarterly profits. Since personal and family ties tend to endure over the lifetime of the firm, profit-taking on each deal is less important than firm survival based on profits over the long run, and because many ethnic Chinese depend on personal ties to conduct business, trust is more important than written agreements.

Over 900 Chinese multinationals have 4,600 foreign affiliates in 130 countries (*World Investment Report*, 1995), and many thousands more are domestic and regional business participants. Overseas Chinese are major investors in China, contributing over $1.2 billion by 1997, and Chinese business owners also are responsible for much growth in Indonesian's economy. For example, according to one estimate, of the 140 major business conglomerates that account for the majority of Indonesia's gross national product, 110 are controlled by ethnic-Chinese families (As good times roll, 1997). Indonesia is not the only Asian nation where overseas Chinese have achieved business success. They dominate commercial life in the region; nine out of every ten of the region's billionaires are overseas Chinese; and they control two-thirds of retail trade in the region (Inheriting the bamboo, 1995). The Fujitsu Research Institute (cited in Ziesemer, 1996) estimates that in five nations the majority of all companies' ownership is held by people whose heritage is Chinese, including 81% of publicly traded companies in Thailand and Singapore, 73% in Indonesia, 62% in Malaysia, and 50% in the Philippines. Finally, according to Sterling Seagrave (1995), overseas Chinese contribute $450 billion to GDP in their nations, a figure about equal to China's 1994 GDP. However, as Murray Weidenbaum (1996) and others (Kao, 1993; Tanzer, 1994) have noted, this 'bamboo network' must change to remain successful in a globalizing world. Peter Drucker (1994) believes challenges for the overseas Chinese multinational will include the following: (a) the founders are aging, and successors have grown up in a different world; (b) in order to grow, the multinational will have to engage in joint ventures with all manner of foreigners; and (c) growth is impeded by relying on clan membership alone; multinationals will grow by hiring and maintaining talented people, regardless of their family connections. Some may find these to be new challenges, but others learned them long ago. For example, in the early 1970s Liem Sioe Liong of Indonesia's Salim Group broke with Chinese tradition by hiring Filipino Manuel Pangilinan to set up the Hong Kong investment arm. Pangilinan subsequently developed First Pacific Co. Ltd, a trans-Asia conglomerate that earned over $120 million after tax in 1994 for the Liem family (Tanzer, 1995). Similarly, Hong Kong-based Patrick Wang operates Johnson Electric by empowering workers in Shenzhen and Hong Kong to work directly with customers. This approach has been particularly difficult to teach in mainland China because it requires a shift towards capitalist thinking that lionizes the customer.

A challenge for family-owned business under any circumstances is to acquire professional management skills appropriate to tasks faced. Hiring relatives often means selecting among those available rather than seeking those who are best qualified. Moreover, even when managerial talent is available within the family, aging leaders with familial preferences may not recognize it. The world is changing quickly, and a leader guided more by family interests than by externalities may not be as quick to gauge and respond to environmental changes. Growing uncertainties of globalization may increase family strife and disrupt the firm.

Overt conflict is unusual among ethnic Chinese, but it may increase as younger family members become educated outside their own countries. In some cases, the level of parental authority becomes a problem for the children. Charlene Wang established First International Computer Inc. (FIC) in the 1980s because manufacturing personal computers and motherboards did not interest her industrialist father. Sometimes family ownership of businesses restricts growth to those industries most congruent with family resources, whether human or financial. Family-style management practices among ethnic

Chinese traditionally have placed limits on the types of businesses families can pursue, and they are concentrated in industries like real estate, trading, shipping, hotels, textiles, and toys. Growing desire to expand into high value-added industries like automotives has altered traditional family ownership. For example, Indonesia's Raja Garuda Mas Group financed expansion in the pulp and paper products industry by consolidating factories under Asia Pacific Resources International Holdings. Following the consolidation, billionaire founder Sukanto Tanoto took the company public and subsequently raised $150 million on equity while maintaining 60% family ownership (Asia, 1995).

When family-owned firms are forced to raise capital on global markets, management practices are subject to external review. In Italy, many managers did not stand up to scrutiny, leading to the ouster of Giovanni Agnelli from Fiat, Carlos De Benedetti from Olivetti, and the Ferruzzi family from top jobs at agrochemical firm Ferruzi SpA – all in 1996. Whether these changes signal a breakdown of the family ownership system or will lead to tighter fiscal controls within firms remains to be seen.

Still another challenge for family-owned firms arises from the original means for acquiring family wealth. In many developing economies, this wealth resulted from relationships with the government. When that government is overturned, as occurred in the Philippines when Ferdinand Marcos was ousted, many who previously benefited from the regime's largesse fall into disfavor. With privatization and deregulation occurring in many countries, and an increased call for economic freedoms worldwide, more families whose wealth is seen as a legacy of a corrupt past regime may be at risk.

Small to medium size global enterprises

Like larger firms, these smaller firms and their leaders grow by capitalizing on opportunities emerging from global change. Although large firms are more typically involved in global business than smaller firms, the latter also shape global industries. Many small to mid-size firms have become leaders in business globalization, often by transcending 'traditional' rules of business. Examples include the following:

- Industrie Natuzzi SpA, grew from 1980 sales of 6 billion lira to become a world market leader in leather furniture. The unusual twist is Natuzzi's chairman crossed Italian labor boundaries by maintaining a nonunion labor force. Manufacturing has never lost a day of work in strike-prone Italy, and its founder even convinced his workers to halve their customary four-week vacation to meet a backlog of orders (Bannon, 1994).
- Smaller German firms were the first to establish a strong presence in Eastern Europe, creating 5,000 joint ventures in the Czech Republic by 1994 as compared to 600 ventures initiated by US firms; they transcended geographic boundaries as well as psychological boundaries remaining from Nazi occupation.

- Small enterprises have helped fuel an export increase for the US from $348 billion in 1986 to $696 billion in 1994. As compared to about 11% of small US firms exporting in 1992, about 24% of such firms were believed to be involved in exporting in 1994, providing a variety of products and services ranging from horsefeed to cholesterol-testing equipment to satisfy worldwide awareness of personal health. As many as 87% of US exports are from small firms employing less than 500 people (Holstein, 1992). In 1995, small firms exported more manufactured goods than did large firms, with fast growth more likely among small businesses involved in exporting (Barrett, 1995). The size barrier is less important to globalization than it once was perceived to be.

- Smaller firms also are pioneering organizational and even societal changes that make it possible for enterprises to survive in global markets. Following 1995 wage hikes, the 2.5 million small and medium-size German companies known as the *Mittelstand* began to shave labor costs. The *Mittelstand* employs 80% of those in the private sector, represents two-thirds of GNP, and earns 40% of sales on German exports. Internal boundaries transcended include voluntary wage reductions or increases in the number of hours worked. According to Heinz Greiffenberger, owner of strip-steel maker J.N. Eberle, 'if we don't change the system, we will all suffer' (Miller, 1995, p. 54). Contrary to prior practice where family members automatically moved to management positions, many of these smaller firms now are hiring professional managers; some are even raising capital by selling shares in the firm. Outward-oriented boundary-spanning includes overseas expansion, stepping up the pace of offshore production where wages are cheaper, and challenges to the German wage settlement.

Like their larger counterparts, leaders of small firms also find that the constantly shifting parameters of industry competition create opportunities for new markets and boundary transcendence. The changing political agenda in many countries has reduced restrictions and stimulated business start-ups. Additionally, improvements in information technology have facilitated worldwide matches between investors and people with business ideas. Furthermore, these technological improvements decrease some of the uncertainties associated with start-ups by providing more information to entrepreneur and investor alike. Hence, it becomes possible for banks and other more conservative lending institutions to run credit checks and otherwise reduce their perceived risk in making loans. Information technology also makes it possible for those who have been excluded from business to join the world of business activities on their own terms. For example, information technology allows native Indians in the Amazon basin to decide which goods they will sell, where and to whom, instead of being economically 'captured' by firms with greater capital or other resources.

Small firms traditionally challenge conventional management practices with their creativity. While some of these managerial challenges are reshaping how work is organized, others alter external relationships. For example, in the US small firms increasingly are raising equity capital not via underwriters but by selling shares directly to the public, and high-tech entrepreneurs are raising less capital from venture capital firms and more from family and friends called 'angels'. These practices expand and stretch options for raising capital in the US, but they also demonstrate how US practices are borrowing practices such as linking friendship and business which has been more traditionally practised in other parts of the world.

Consistent with Porter, earlier definitions of the global enterprise suggest that, whether large or small, this firm's worldwide presence increases its vulnerability to worldwide events. For example, worldwide sales of a consumer disposable shields the firm from domestic or regional downturns but exposes it to global risk. If the firm's critical input must be acquired from a world market, an overall increase in the price of that input will affect firm costs worldwide and presumably reduce sales globally. Finally, the same opportunities that attract small firms to a market also attract larger firms, particularly as markets globalize.

SURVIVAL OVER THE LONG RUN

The life of most firms is relatively short; for US multinationals life expectancy is 40–50 years, and most small firms in the US fail within one year of founding. Further, according to Stratix Consulting Group, both Japanese and European firms have an average life expectancy of less than 13 years (How to live long, 1997). There are relatively few reviews of long-lived firms, but among those described in this section, success characteristics appear to be a clear strategy, luck, and investments in people. Among companies known as *Les Hénokiens* shown in Table 8.5, surviving firms often operate in industries like confections, alcoholic beverages, textiles, and construction supplies that chance to have remained important in every period of human history. Candidates for *Les Hénokiens* must meet three conditions of membership: (1) the companies they own have done business for at least 200 years; (2) members are direct descendants of the founders; and (3) the company enjoys sound financial health. *Les Hénokiens* translated to English is 'the Enochites' after the Old Testament biblical figure Enoch who lived 365 years.

According to Arie de Geus, author of *The living company* (1997), long-lived firms are those that meet four conditions: (1) their financial affairs are managed conservatively; (2) they are sensitive to their external environment and adapt appropriately; (3) they have a strong sense of cohesion around a common goal set and are able to convey common values to succeeding generations of employees; and (4) they show internal tolerance that fosters creativity and camaraderie. Unlike 'economic' companies that expend their energy in achieving high economic returns over short time periods, the returns for de Geus's

TABLE 8.5 *Les Hénokiens* 22

Founded in	Name	Headquarters	Businesses
718	Hoshi	Japan	Hotels
1460	Barovier & Toso	Italy	Glass products
1526	Beretta Corporation	Italy	Firearms
1551	Codorniu	Spain	Sparkling wines
1568	Poschinger Glashütte	Germany	Glass products
1613	Mellerio dits Meller	France	Jewelry
1637	Gekkeikan Sake Company Ltd	Japan	Liquors
1639	Hugel & Fils	France	Vineyards
1664	Friedr. Schwarze	Germany	Liquors
1679	Viellard-Migeon & Cie	France	Metal products
1680	Tissages Denantes	France	Textiles
1685	Maison Gradis	France	Wine
1690	Delamare Sovra	France	Wood products
1733	Fratelli Piacenza	Italy	Textiles
1745	Daciano Colbachini & Figli	Italy	Bells
1755	Marie Brizard & Roger International	France	Liquors
1757	Lanificio G.B. Conte	Italy	Textiles
1760	Griset	France	Metal products
1762	F. V. Möller	Germany	Metal products
1770	Silca	Italy	Keys and key-making equipment
1779	Ditta Bortolo Nardini	Italy	Distilleries
1783	Confetti Mario Pelino	Italy	Candies

Source: Tagliabue, John. (1994, Oct 30). This business club is the real old boys' network. *The New York Times*, p. 4.

'living companies' are not correlated with maximized financial returns nor with country or industry. But they survive. Thus, survival over the long term may depend on more than good fiscal performance including a clear vision of both internal and external capabilities and needs.

DIAGNOSING INDUSTRY FUTURES

Gary Hamel and C.K. Prahalad (1994) believe that the historical look at industries provided by industry analyses are insufficient today. Technological, demographic, regulatory, and other changes occurring worldwide have the potential to transform industry boundaries and create new space for firms. Thus, managers must not only diagnose the past and the present, they must create a vision of the future. Hamel and Prahalad argue that current emphasis on restructuring and re-engineering processes in many firms is analogous to turbocharging an old engine when what many firms need is to build an entirely new engine. According to Hazel Henderson (1996), whole industries and sectors could disappear with globalization. Those based on technologies that cannot be sustained, such as fossil fuels or those that pollute or create disposable products, will be less desirable than those that are sustainable over time. Examples of the latter include pollution control, natural foods, waste recycling, and reuse and other sectors shown in Table 8.6. Henderson's outline in this table provides one example of how industry leaders can think about future industries, a process that often begins with asking why- and 'what if'-type questions. Jorma Ollila, CEO of Nokia, believes these questions will not be asked unless the CEO understands each business – otherwise the CEO will end up reading reports based on financial criteria rather than developing an understanding of where the future lies. In other words, for managers and employees alike, envisioning the future begins with hands-on knowledge of the organization and its businesses. Ticketmaster Corporation sells seats to sporting and entertainment events, but a change in the airline industry has caused Fredrick Rosen of Ticketmaster to ask: Why does it have to be the same way? If airlines can reclaim ticket sales previously made through independent agents, Rosen reasons that Ticketmaster's instant connections can be used also to sell airline tickets, sea and ski travel packages, or coordinate parking, restaurant, and show tickets. The importance of this kind of 'what if?' thinking at Intel is described in Box 8.2.

TABLE 8.6   Restructuring industrial economies

Obsolescent sectors (unsustainable, entropic)	Emerging sectors (sustainable, low entropy)
Industries, companies based on heavy use of nonrenewable energy and materials	Industries, companies based on efficient use of energy and materials and human skills
Bureaucratic, large, less flexible	Entrepreneurial, small, flexible
Nonrecyclable products, packaging	Recyclable products, remanufacturing
Military contracting	Conservation, innovation
Products involving toxic, nonbiodegradables, polluting materials, throwaway items	Fuel-efficient motors, cars, mass transit
Planned obsolescence	Solar, renewable energy systems
Chemical pesticides, inorganic fertilizers	Communications, information services
Heavy farm equipment	Infrastructure, education, training
Polluting, inefficient capital equipment, process machinery, processing systems	Space communications satellites
Extractive industries with low value-added	Peacekeeping, surveillance of treaties
Fossil fuels, nuclear power generation	Efficient capital equipment, processes
High-tech, hospital-based medical care	Restorative industries, reforestation, desert greening, water-quality management
Highly processed foods	Health promotion and disease prevention
Advertising encouraging waste and polluting practices	Organic agriculture, low-till systems
Shopping center developers	Integrated pest management
Speculative real estate development	Pollution control, cleanup, and prevention
Large, fuel-inefficient vehicles	Natural foods
Monoculture farming	Waste recycling and reuse
Hardwood and tropical forest products	Community design and planning
Capital- and energy-intensive tourism	'Caring' sector
	Eco-tourism

Source: Henderson, Hazel. (1996). *Building a win-win world: Life beyond global economic warfare*, p. 37. San Francisco, CA: Berrett-Koehler; original source was *Paradigms in progress* © 1989/91 Hazel Henderson.

BOX 8.2: INTEL'S PARANOID THINKING ALTERS STRATEGY

Until the mid-1980s, Intel's core business was designing and manufacturing memory chips for computers, but the industry changed in 1984 when Japanese firms entered with high-quality, low-price competitive products. Memory chips were abundant and Intel was losing money. According to Intel chief Andy Grove, he asked then-CEO Gordon Moore what he thought a new CEO and president would do. The answer was to get out of the computer-memory business, and that is exactly what Intel did, even though Grove himself felt the idea was far-fetched and even paranoid. However, the shift from memory into microprocessor production led to development of the 386 chip, which became an industry mainstay and made Intel an industry giant in microprocessors. According to Andy Grove, Intel made this decision at what he called a 'strategy inflection point' where the whole life of the business was about to change because fundamental forces acting upon it were undergoing fundamental change. In this case, history now shows those fundamental changes in the chip industry included: global industry change as competitors from other nations entered markets previously dominated by one or a few nations; global technological change hinging on microprocessor breakthroughs; global economic change creating a computer-buying middle class; and global political change leading to commercialization of the Internet and growing demand for computers to access its offerings.

Source: Adapted in part from: Grove, Andrew S. (1997). *Only the paranoid survive*. New York: Currency Doubleday.

CHALLENGES OF GLOBALIZATION FOR INDUSTRIES

The 'big picture' view of global industrialization recommended by Hamel and Prahalad includes looking at relationships between business and government and among businesses. The following sections examine those relationships, showing how shifts and reshaping of relationships have redefined views of industries and organizations operating in them.

The global field for competition: do nations or firms compete?

Business activities have played a role in shaping industries, but national governments also have shaped industries through industrial policy, subsidies, regulations, patents, trademarks, and other mechanisms. The active role many governments have played in shaping industry environment for firms in domestic and international markets raise an important question for industry globalization: Is it nations or firms that compete in global markets?

NATIONS COMPETE

In the bordered world of international expansion, development of the nation and development of domestic businesses were viewed as complementary activities. In the US and Western Europe subsidies for tobacco, corn, and sugar support agricultural industries, and tariffs protect textile and apparel goods. In contrast, South Korea, Indonesia, and Japan have used industrial policies to support some industries and suppress others. The perceived role these policies and programs play in shaping industries has itself shifted with globalization. For example, following Japanese inroads into world auto and electronic markets in the 1970s, many felt that MITI, Japan's industrial planning group, had played a powerful role in these successes. Similar industrial policies were called for in other countries, an implicit argument favoring nation-to-nation forms of competition to fight the force of MITI. Richard Nelson (1992) observed that enthusiasm for MITI waned as Japanese firms reached and defined technological frontiers, but ideas of government-managed trade relationships persist. Introduction of a national industrial policy defines those industries the government intends to support. This support may include government infusions of cash for industry research and development, special advantages for firms operating in targeted industries, or possibly tariffs or other forms of protection for the industry in the domestic setting. With industrial policies, national governments concentrate and stimulate business investments in targeted industries but they may at the same time deter interest in industries important to the future. Thus, industrial policies generate benefits but also have their costs.

Historical experience with trade across national borders created systems that reinforce belief in nation-to-nation competition. Global measures of competitive ability frequently rank nations on past, present, or future competitive abilities. Until 1996, the World Economic Forum and the International Institute for Management Development (IMD) jointly published an annual *World Competitiveness Report* ranking nations according to eight criteria: domestic economic strength, international activity, government policy, financial markets, infrastructure, management, science and technology, and people. In 1996, the World Economic Forum and IMD produced separate reports using different criteria, but both continued to rank nations according to their competitiveness. Union Bank of Switzerland produces annual assessments of nations' future competitiveness, and on occasion *The Economist* has done the same. According to the IMD, the US, Singapore, and Hong Kong were the three most competitive nations in the world from 1995 to 1998. Other rankings are shown in Table 8.7.

TABLE 8.7   National competitiveness rankings, 1995–1997

World ranking	1995	1996	1997
United States	1	1	1
Singapore	2	2	2
Hong Kong	3	3	3
Finland	18	15	4
Netherlands	8	7	5
Norway	10	6	6
Denmark	7	5	7
Switzerland	5	9	8
Canada	13	12	9
New Zealand	9	11	10
Japan	4	4	11
Britain	15	19	12

Source: International Institute for Management Development (IMD). Also see: Garelli, Stephane. (1997). Work competitiveness yearbook executive summary, http://www.imd.ch/wcy/approach/summary/html

Business researchers compare business activities by nation more than by industry to produce categories like those shown in Table 8.7and in Chapter 3 where we compared US, European, Japanese, and other management styles. The relative ease provided by national comparisons encourages this practice, and clear national differences in politics, economics, and national sentiment make this approach logical. At the same time, national comparisons tend to obscure differences between firms from the same country, and they reinforce notions of national competition that may be irrelevant to borderless firm-to-firm forms of competition. Moreover, inasmuch as nations raise revenues on domestic business operations, government leaders may have little incentive to redefine competition among 'stateless' firms. The debate in the US was best expressed by former Labor Secretary Robert Reich, who described 'American' companies as those from any nations providing high-skill jobs for Americans in America, and chief White House economist Laura Tyson, who at the same time asserted that the economic fate of nations remains tied to the success of domestically based organizations.

Michael Porter (1990) argued that nations became more important as a result of global competition, with national competitiveness a central preoccupation of governments and industries throughout the world. Porter believes that popular views of what influences national competitiveness such as cheap and abundant labor or government policy provide insight into firm competitiveness but that none provide sufficient aid to managers. Instead, he proposed that national competitiveness stems from four industry determinants such as the availability of productive factors, demand, proximity of related or support industries, and firm strategy, structure, and rivalry consistent with national norms. Working from a different perspective, Hamish McRae (1994) concludes that nations have been increasingly able to imitate one another because innovations can cross national borders within days and weeks. Accordingly, he believes that the best predictor of a nation's economic success will not be technological achievement but a nation's creativity and social responsibility. The latter are somewhat more difficult to measure than specific technological achievements, giving force to earlier arguments that intangibles more than tangibles will produce challenges for organizations operating globally.

ONLY FIRMS COMPETE

Economist Paul Krugman (1994) argues that a national focus on industrial policy creates trade wars that harm everyone in their single-minded pursuit of 'winning' when world trade is not and need not be played as a 'zero-sum' game. He further argues that thinking in terms of national competitiveness leads to bad economic policies that hinder rather than help nations. Further, government money used to protect failing industries is wasted; and thinking in terms of national competitiveness could lead to protectionism. Krugman believes that the real pain of job losses or downsizing could blur issues of competitiveness, and perhaps divert government attention from policies that have important long-term implications for nations. In summary, Krugman believes the business of government is to govern, and it is businesses that should compete.

Competition, cooperation, and coopetition

Some US organizations are calling for governmental protections of industries, often arguing that government intervention will create a 'level playing field' to compensate for worldwide differences in business practices. Since business organizations usually prefer less rather than more governmental influence on business activities, calls for government protections represent something of a paradox for free market adherents. These businesses may be wed to the notion of winning at any cost – even if it means bringing in 'Big Brother' government to facilitate the win. Writing in *The winner-take-all society*, Robert Frank and Philip Cook (1995) observe that defining competition as win/lose has created a star system in some societies that have national implications since stars are few and far between. Achieving this status is impossible for most, and dysfunctional at the national level when firms export jobs to remain the lowest cost producer; when students vie for limited spots at 20 star academic institutions; when all feel inadequate unless they have attended 'star' institutions, earned outstanding grades, taken jobs at the limited number of 'star' firms, and distinguished themselves with stellar careers. The disappointment sure to follow for the billions of people and millions of firms that cannot be stars often is externalized and blame laid at the feet of government, managers, and other people who impeded the would-be star's trajectory, while the real failure lies with the winner-take-all philosophy.

The star system makes it difficult for US firms to embrace anything other than a sole survivor, competitive stance within industries. This stance is reflected by a research tradition recommending wholly owned subsidiaries as the first or most preferable mode of entering new markets. However, firms with cultures that also nurture relationships may be better able to accommodate options beyond short-term wins and losses, and firms that survive and thrive globally may be those that develop sustainable competitive advantages from activities based less on a 'winner take all' mentality and more on one that can blend competition with cooperative practices. According to an early article on the topic, Perlmutter and Heenan (1986) observed that whether they were large or small, few firms could achieve industry leadership or be competitive globally without some set of global strategic partnerships (GSP) in their portfolios. However, they observed that diverse backgrounds and cultures characteristic for global partnerships could lead to challenges in six areas:

1 *Mission*: Each must be convinced the other has something they need and commit to a win/win sense of mission.
2 *Strategy*: Must be clearly articulated to avoid intolerable overlaps between cooperation and competition.
3 *Governance*: Observing that US firms historically harbor a belief in power over parity, they point out that the latter is the appropriate approach for collaborative arrangements.
4 *Culture*: The partners must be willing to shape a common set of values while also retaining national identities.
5 *Organization*: Requires new organizational patterns capable of blending best practices of partners.
6 *Management*: Unitary management methods must be adopted to reduce potential disputes.

Others are less enthusiastic about alliances. Porter (1990) views strategic alliances as risky and unstable arrangements inevitably dominated by the stronger partner. Losses associated with strategic alliances often point to industries where alliances have failed to produce expected results. Television in the US provides one example. Once the bastion of television production, by 1994 the US had lost the capacity to manufacture televisions. Some believe the industry was undermined when RCA licensed color TV technology to a number of Japanese companies in the 1960s who copied the product, innovated, and successfully drove RCA and other manufacturers from the market. Early experiments with cooperation in global markets favored partnerships between firms not otherwise competing. Backward or forward integration with suppliers and buyers to create just-in-time inventory systems are an example of alliances between noncompetitors.

FROM EITHER/OR TO BOTH/AND OPTIONS WITH COOPETITION

Despite evidence of successful cooperative arrangements, leaders at many firms feel their own position in an industry is compromised by collaborating with competitors. This is in sharp contrast to the view that coopetition can include both competitive and cooperative elements. Dowling et al. (1996, p. 155) call these relationships 'multifaceted' when a supplier, buyer, and/or partner is also a major competitor. Examples include: (a) vertical cooperation between buyers and suppliers in direct competition, such as occurs between IBM and Intel when the latter supplies IBM with microprocessor chips and also competes in a variety of markets; (b) when buyers or suppliers are in indirect competition, as was the case in Apple/Microsoft connections when the former bought software from Microsoft, but also filed a lawsuit against the Windows platform; and (c) as partners in competition via a joint venture, research consortium, or licensing agreement as a way to pool resources against other competitors. For example, the 1986 alliance between Canon and Hewlett-Packard captured 70% of the US market in laser printers and provided a barrier to other entrants. Although the latter arrangement was still operating in 1998, the partners remain intense rivals in other areas such as ink-jet technology. Intense rivalry also can alter abruptly as seemed to happen in 1997 when Microsoft announced its intention to invest $150 million in former arch-rival Apple. In other quarters, coopetition is based on game theory arguments suggesting new mindsets and new games capable of changing industry and organizational strategy from win/lose to win/win (Brandenburger and Nalebuff, 1996).

According to James Moore's *The death of competition* (1996), product superiority and industry dominance are no longer the driving force behind organizational success. Instead, what matters is a form of systematic leadership that integrates technologies and develops new markets. Growth then comes through cooperation as well as competition cast in the win/lose mold. Some global organizations can accommodate both competition and cooperation with partners at the same time, but firms doing both simultaneously face challenges of two types. The first challenge is externally when partners act on different expectations for what it means to combine cooperation and competition, and the second occurs internally when managers cannot adopt behaviors appropriate for both competitive and cooperative interactions.

PART II   ORGANIZING FOR GLOBAL BUSINESS

The preceding sections of this chapter defined and described global industries, outlining some of the global and national challenges for thinking about industries and firms in them. Businesses previously identified as members of an industry or strategic group now encounter shifting boundaries for global industries that require constant review of industry parameters and redefinition of business activities. Demands to be many things simultaneously creates a paradox for organizational leaders who compete as autonomous actors more than as representatives of nations but also are expected to cooperate with former and current competitors. This creates challenges for employees and challenges for processes and structures combined to derive advantages from both autonomy and interdependence.

PROCESSES
Creating a sustainable advantage

The continued existence of any business organization is to provide a product or service for which people will pay, and this depends on creating and sustaining a real or perceived advantage for customers. Given cultural, political, economic, and technological differences worldwide, it may be more difficult to create a sustainable advantage globally than to create a similar advantage within a single or related markets. One of the challenges for thinking about global organizations is that many are corporations with dozens or more businesses operating in different industries. For some sustainable advantage is corporate, and for others it is found at the business level. For example, the Disney Corporation is a single entity defined by a clear corporate culture encompassing diverse entities such as Touchstone Pictures and Disney World. These two businesses operate in different industries, e.g., film and amusement parks, but they share most attributes of the Disney culture. For Disney, sustained advantage has come from an intangible but strong organizational culture that others have been unable to imitate. By contrast, Unilever does not have a strong cultural identity, and this permits individual businesses like Dove soap or Calvin Klein perfume the autonomy each needs to create separate sustainable advantages. For global firms, the important issue is not where sustainable advantage is found, but rather that it can find an exploitable advantage at some level.

Whether defined at corporate, business, or even operational levels, sustainable advantage is what distinguishes a firm from others providing the same products or services; it generates positive economic returns and/or aids survival. Doing either over time requires an advantage others will find difficult to copy. For example, although much has been written about what Disney does and how it does it at its theme parks, none have been able to copy the unique set of attributes that provide the Disney Corporation with a sustained advantage. However, as the Boeing example in Box 8.3 shows, corporations can, and do, revise their views of what makes them unique.

Chapter 4 looked at organizational and global culture and showed that many global organizations develop sustainable advantage by concentrating on a few core values. These core values can be developed at the corporate or the business level. Interviews with top managers reported in that chapter showed core values are usually few in number and are

---

BOX 8.3: REDEFINING CORE COMPETENCIES

The Boeing Corporation traditionally protected technologies associated with wing and nose sections of its airplanes. These two protected technologies were believed to be the inimitable, core competencies of the firm. More recently, Boeing leaders believe their sustainable advantage is the ability to integrate massive amounts of data.

---

a simple statement intended to direct organizational attention throughout the organization. Core values typically focus in three ways: (a) on what the firm does well, e.g., customer service, learn, innovate; (b) on qualities it uses to create advantages, e.g., integrity, honesty, social responsibility, trust, loyalty; or (c) on how it achieves advantage, e.g., teamwork, personal responsibility, rapid response, generating win/win solutions.

SUSTAINABLE ADVANTAGE BASED ON ABILITIES

As a source of sustainable advantage, an orientation toward customer service is particularly useful for the global firm providing services or products to worldwide buyers who differ. The philosophy of customer service shifts attention from what organizational participants think they know about customers to what customers know about themselves. Internal stakeholders are asked to view the business through the customer's lens to ask: Who are our customers? What are their needs and expectations? How are they satisfied? How do we know? Asking the customer to answer these questions reduces the potential for erroneous assumptions such as: the customer is just like me; the customer will buy what we make; the customer will never change. Like a customer service orientation, organizational learning skills also move attention away from the self to ask: What can I learn from this interaction? How can my knowledge enhance organizational learning? Focus on innovation causes all to ask: How can I do this differently and better? What is possible that I do not now see? In every case, core values directed toward what the organization does best cause individuals to think outside the parameters they bring to work, and to focus on the past to think about how past experiences can be constraints for the future.

SUSTAINABLE ADVANTAGE BASED ON INTANGIBLE QUALITIES

Basing sustainable advantage on intangible qualities like honesty and integrity also begins with the individual in relationship to the organization. It causes people to clarify how they define honesty or integrity and focuses attention on how the organization defines the same attributes. Deriving sustainable advantage from qualities depends on organizational leaders who provide clear definitions of qualities sought. Without them, individuals are more likely to operate from personal rather than organizational codes of behavior. For this reason, organizations often distribute their values in written form, often as belief, vision, or commitment statements. These statements can be created for any or every organizational level. For example, according to public statements, the overall mission for the Boeing Corporation is to be the number one aerospace company in the world and among the premier industrial concerns of quality, profitability, and growth, but each subunit and division such as Boeing Computer Services and Boeing Support Services also publishes a statement of its mission as well.

SUSTAINABLE ADVANTAGE BASED ON HOW ADVANTAGE IS ACHIEVED

This type of advantage comes from defining tasks such as how work is accomplished whether through teamwork, personal responsibility or some combination, what is to be accomplished, and timeliness. Knowing what to do and how to do it directs individual activities, but a further advantage is to help people know where to turn when help is required. For example, at W.T. Gore and Associates, individuals define their own jobs and so each must decide what is important and how to do it. Additionally, Gore employees independently make important decisions except for those 'waterline' decisions that could sink the metaphorical ship, and it is up to the individual to decide which are waterline decisions. Other organizations like McDonald's and KFC succeed because their task technology is highly standardized. When employees at the latter firms face a unique challenge, they might be expected to turn to standard operating manuals or to experienced others before making a personal judgment.

Writing in 1988, George Stalk, Jr described time as a source of sustainable advantage, arguing that competitive advantages associated with time include efficient management of production time, of product development and introduction time, and of sales and distribution time. Increased attention paid to 'fast' teams and 'fast' companies in the business press suggests that a growing number of organizations are basing their sustainable advantages on time.

Core competencies

In contrast to the singular qualities described above, core competencies usually combine the various and most important ways an organization achieves advantage. These core, or most important, competencies can vary from firm to firm. Three to five core competencies usually are identified, and for all firms they represent the basis of an organization's strength. Core competencies can be derived for corporations as links among many businesses, or they can be defined for single-product businesses within the corporation. In Rubbermaid, a company that derives 14% of annual profits from new products, core competencies include innovation and an ability to change in a firm that introduces an average of one new product per day; in a hospital core competencies might be managing patient flow and providing outstanding medical care; and rapid information retrieval combined with accuracy and honesty might be the core competency of a newspaper or a data retrieval firm. In many firms, the combination of qualities important to sustainable advantage must be reviewed constantly to reinforce and adapt them. For example, Pharmacia instituted a group called 'Personal and Business Culture' to develop corporate principles expected to sustain and articulate firm identity (Hedlund and Rolander, 1990), but Viacom assembled a core of 20–25 executives from its various divisions, including Paramount, Blockbuster, MTV, and Showtime, who meet every four to six weeks to strategize and find ways to generate synergies among the divisions; these executives meet in person to develop relationships and synergies executives believe can only be made through personal contact.

Among the more important choices firms make today are to remain domestic or go global. Choosing to go global would usually entail expansion of plant or equipment or a merger or acquisition. In these cases, decisions for attaining global sustainable advantage depend on finding a match between what the industry needs and what the firm can supply. Table 8.8 suggests that firms with the specific competencies listed in

TABLE 8.8   Fostering fit: matching global demands with business competencies

	Cultural	Economic	Political	Technology	Natural
Response to customer needs; customer relations & service; marketing appeal, skills; reputation; sales force knowledge or skills	X				
Access to efficient or low-cost productive factors; vertical integration; operating efficiencies; superior financial resources; lower cost financing		X			
Patents, licenses, copyright; government support; industrial policy			X		
R&D factors; product line; manufacturing technology				X	
Proximity to customers; access to distribution channels; physical distribution capacity					X

Source: Adapted from: Yip, George S. (1995). *Total global strategy*, p. 240. Englewood Cliffs, NJ: Prentice Hall.

the left-hand column would find a match when global industry demands depend most on one or another global environment. For example, a firm responsive to customer needs is likely to learn more about those global needs by looking first at globalization of culture.

Global strategy processes

STRATEGY DEFINED

Strategy is the limited set of important, nonroutine, nonprogrammable decisions that guide overall organizational direction. Chapter 3 described the five organizational levels requiring strategic attention. Enterprise strategy defines organizational purpose, e.g., to earn maximum profits, to provide family benefits, to improve society, and it is most often derived from founders who conveyed their enterprise strategy via explicit statements or behaviors that implicitly convey the firm's purpose. Corporate-level strategies identify which businesses the firm will presently pursue and in the future, and business-level strategies describe how each business will compete. Competitive choices are many, including quality or service objectives, profitability, market share, competitive position, technological leadership, or some combination among these and other business-level strategic objectives. At the operational and individual levels where strategy is implemented, major concerns are developing functional, unit, team and individual processes, people, and structural goals consistent with strategy achievement. Enterprise, business, operational and individual strategies are relevant to all firms; corporate-level strategy is more usual for firms that have many separate businesses in the same corporate portfolio. Firms best able to coordinate among strategy levels are those best able to sustain overall advantage in a global market.

FAILURES AND SUCCESSES WITH STRATEGIC PLANNING

Strategic management was an outgrowth of battle strategies used in World War II, and most US firms modeled their top-down, command and control linear thinking along military lines. Strategic planning along these lines was a popular business level tool throughout the 1970s, but it languished in the mid-1980s. Criticisms of strategic planning included paralysis by analysis and emphasis on single-point historical analysis and number crunching that neglected complex organizational concerns in an increasingly turbulent environment (Wilson, 1990). Further planning at the business level provided insight on performance achievements, but proved insufficient as a means of pulling these together into a corporate whole.

According to Henry Mintzberg (1994), strategic planning failed as practiced because it described visions and elaborated existing strategies instead of creating the future-oriented visions most firms needed. By 1996, strategic planning was back (Strategic planning, 1996), reshaped to include line and staff from many functions and incorporate customer and supplier interactions, and redefined to focus on organizations as complex entities working in cooperation and competition to anticipate and shape industry change. This latter approach to strategy crosses internal boundaries of rank and external boundaries to include many in the strategic planning process and so may be better suited for the borderlessness of globalization than were more military models of strategic planning.

BUSINESS-LEVEL COMPETITIVE STRATEGIES

Michael Porter (1990) defined a global industry as one 'in which a firm's competitive position in one country is significantly affected by its position in other countries or vice versa' (p. 18). Porter's emphasis here is on business level strategies and how businesses compete, and his points are that firms are affected by competitive actions they take and by activities that are largely outside their control. Firms are affected by more than competitive events in a converging world in which cultural, technological, political, and other global events all affect the firm. Although in 1990, it was believed that firms could choose to go global or remain domestic, growing interdependence in many global spheres makes it nearly impossible for firms to survive without interacting on a global level. In the aerospace industry, for example, access to capital, labor, and sales depend on global rather than domestic economies, global rather than domestic politics.

Stephen Kobrin (1991) recognized that industries like automotives, microelectronics, and telecommunications were being forced toward globalization, but he also observed that transnationality or globalization is inherent for firms operating in industries too small to survive or thrive except on a worldwide basis. For example, high research and development investments at Merck Pharmaceuticals only can be justified with worldwide sales. This concept of forced globalization also can be applied to smaller firms and to those that appear to be local. For example, a US-based entrepreneur uses the Internet to sell industrial music CDs worldwide. The domestic market is simply too small for him to thrive, but by taking a global approach, he is able to establish a retail CD sales channel for the relatively small industrial music industry. Even neighborhood restaurants that give every sign of being local interact at a global level to purchase food made globally available through advances in food production and distribution. For these local businesses and for the purposefully global corporation, a critical strategic challenge is to develop internal systems that are responsive to a global industry, but at the same time remain alert and responsive to the shifting customs, preferences, and needs of individual nations or regions. In other words, organizations must pay attention not only to what is global or what is local, but to both. The challenge of this dual approach will be examined in the following section on the global strategy process.

WORLDWIDE INTEGRATION STRATEGY

One option available to firms in globalizing industries is to design and produce to a cross-national standard (Porter, 1990) with a worldwide integration strategy. In industries where products can be standardized to appeal on a global scale, some can enjoy integration strategies that standardize products and/or services on a worldwide scale. Ford is pursuing this strategy with its world car, and Fiat similarly has achieved economies of scale by producing its model 178 called Palio in Brazil where it has met with great success. Following the April 1996 launch of Palio in Brazil, over 250,000 autos were sold; this is nearly twice the sales record for any new car in Brazil. According to Kobrin (1991), worldwide global integration involves 'rationalization that may entail standardization of product, centralization of technological development, or the vertical or horizontal integration of manufacturing' (p. 19). Further, it can involve more than interdependence among units; for large MNEs it also may involve dependence of subsidiaries on the multinational system for information, technology, capital, products, and management. C.K. Prahalad and Yves Doz (1987) believe that pressures toward strategic coordination and global integration of activities critical to worldwide integration strategy for the corporation include the following:

1 Multinational customers can readily switch suppliers because they can find lower price producers.
2 The presence of multinational competitors makes it more important to centralize information gathering and strategic decision-making.
3 An investment-intensive business can best leverage investments on a worldwide scale.
4 Control over quality, cost, and new product development in technology-intensive industries usually means there will be few production facilities and these are easier to coordinate centrally than many production facilities.
5 Pressures for cost reductions motivate firms to seek efficiencies via low-cost labor or large plants that provide economies of scale.
6 If the product responds to a universal need, it is easier to adopt a worldwide production standard.
7 A need for access to specialized raw materials or energy can dictate centralized manufacturing appropriate to integration.

Later we will see how organizations with many businesses attempt to coordinate among them; the following discussion is directed toward business-level decisions for single or related products in a single industry.

The business-level worldwide integration strategy is analogous to Porter's (1980) cost leadership strategy, drawing its strength from reducing costs across an entire product line, and is supported by functional activities subject to industry constraints, e.g., economies of scale, favorable raw material supplies, location. The benefits of integration provided by a worldwide integration strategy often are offset by costs associated with a greater need to coordinate, many reporting requirements, reduced morale among managers with limited autonomy, or a product that does not fully satisfy customers anywhere (Yip, 1995). Ford Motor Company's Mondeo (also known as the Contour) uses delayed differentiation to adapt to varying customer tastes. For example, the smoother exterior lines Europeans prefer can be added at the end of the assembly process. Delayed differentiation, or introduction of variations late in production, is one way a firm can produce to a global integration standard but remain responsive to individual markets. In some cases, however, demands for variation exceed a firm's ability to achieve it through limited, end-process adjustments. In these cases, a multilocal strategy responsive to local tastes may be more appropriate.

MULTILOCAL STRATEGY

Customer preference and differences among countries are two factors driving what can be thought of as a multilocal strategy. According to George Yip (1995), a multilocal strategy treats competition in each country or region on an individual basis. Pressures toward this approach focus primarily on differences in customer preferences, distribution channels, government regulations, or market structure (Prahalad and Doz, 1987) that preclude global integration. The multilocal strategy is analogous to Porter's (1990) differentiation strategy which also adapts products or services to differing customer demands. Primary emphasis on differentiation in style or quality increases variety and costs, but global pressures will force businesses in most cases to keep costs close to those of competitors.

At the corporate level, a multilocal strategy provides benefits of increased managerial autonomy but can be offset by duplication when design, production, and marketing are needlessly independent. Ford, for example, centralized design when it realized that not one of 400 parts for a similar car were interchangeable internationally. Global managers also observe that many cross-cultural assumptions of difference between customers are changing with global lifestyle changes and exposure to similar stimuli. Advertisers find success with global ad campaigns and producers find their assumptions may be outdated. For example, sales of large GE refrigerators in Japan soared in 1995 because women working outside the home had little time to shop daily and the high price of the yen made GE's products cheap relative to the Japanese currency. Slow growth in Japan's economy has made consumers sufficiently price conscious to try new products, reducing commitment to Japanese-made products. These examples from Japan illustrate that consumer perceptions leading to demands for customized and locally responsive products depend on more than single variables.

BOX 8.4:   COCA-COLA'S WORLDWIDE STRATEGY SHIFTS

The ubiquitous red can and Coca-Cola logo are found worldwide, and one of the best-known products worldwide is original Coke. Global integration in production and marketing of Coke does not mean that Coca-Cola pursues a worldwide integration strategy in all its product lines. In Japan, for example, Coca-Cola sells original Coke and also offers products that are not offered worldwide, including an Asian tea called Kochakaden, a coffee drink called Georgia, and a fermented-milk beverage called Lacta. As recently as 1990, Coca-Cola sold 90% of all colas in Japan, but competitive entry from firms operating worldwide and fickle Japanese consumers combined to make Japan the world's most competitive soft-drink market in 1997, forcing Coca-Cola to develop new brands based on local tastes.

Source: Shirouzu, Norihiko. (1997, Jan. 20). For Coca-Cola in Japan, things go better with milk. *The Wall Street Journal*, pp. B1, B8.

MIXED STRATEGIES

Roderick White and Thomas Poynter (1990) believe maximum strategic advantage may come from combining different perspectives to create a mosaic of advantages for the same business. Global standardization to achieve an advantageous cost advantage, for example, could be combined with differentiated ad campaigns that adjust marketing mix to local situations. Coca-Cola's strategy is to pursue worldwide integration for its main products, but as the example in Box 8.4 shows, the company also will develop products in response to local tastes. White and Poynter note that organizations able to combine these strategies are unlikely to follow conventional management prescriptions. Interestingly, the mosaic they suggest is analogous to Porter's (1980) focus strategy, suggested for firms that can neither be industry-wide low-cost producers nor achieve comprehensive differentiation. The suggested approach for a focus strategy is to select a narrower strategic market and concentrate on serving the distinctive market; this concentration allows differentiation or cost leadership in the chosen markets, including portions of a product line, particular customer segments, limited geographic area, particular distribution channels, or a combination of these. Empirical research on focus strategies found them difficult to distinguish from cost and differentiation strategy *per se*, but many argue that focus is most appropriate to smaller firms. It also may be relevant to larger firms now made smaller in world markets.

Used to describe global firms, mixed strategies may emerge from looking at strategic intent in global industries. For example, Table 8.9 matches the extent of a firm's

TABLE 8.9   Global presence and strategy combine to influence the relationship between a business and its industry

		EXTENT OF GLOBAL PRESENCE	
		High	**Low**
STRATEGY	**Worldwide integration**	**Shape:** Coca-Cola Acer Natuzzi	**Experiment:** IPTN Unimarc Trading Doc Martens
	Multilocal	**Adapt:** Nestlé Unilever	**Opportunistic:** Hansons PLC Ticketmaster Fiat 178

global presence with its strategic business approach to define the firm's position vis-à-vis industry futures. Firms like Coca-Cola with high global presence and a worldwide integration strategy for the Coke product formulate activities intended to shape the industry. Though smaller than Coca-Cola, Acer and Industrie Natuzzi also pursue worldwide strategy in most product lines, with purposeful intent to reshape their industries. Size and industry are less important descriptors of all than their common intent to transform the industry. Other firms with less global presence also pursue a worldwide integration strategy, experimenting to test industry parameters, often with a single product. For example, Indonesia's IPTN was created to produce mid-size aircraft in the US, Chile's Unimarc Trading is a major player in the farm-raised salmon industry, and Doc Martens sells unisex boots worldwide. All are experimenting in existing industries, but none appear to have reshaped their industries. Firms organized around a multilocal strategy for most lines of business and with high global presence include Nestlé and Unilever; these large organizations and smaller ones pursuing the same strategy can be viewed as adaptive to industry change, perhaps made so by their experience in adapting to local tastes. Finally, firms with a multilocal strategy but with low global presence like Hanson PLC, the Fiat 178 auto, or the industrial music retailer described earlier can be characterized as opportunistic in the industry, a position they can take because their presence in multiple domestic markets keeps them attuned to opportunities. Table 8.9 shows that many firms are clustered in the upper left quadrant with an intent to reshape their industries. Firms that operate within industries to experiment, adapt, or seize opportunity also have the potential to reshape industries, but this is not their primary intent. This matrix identifies four types of opportunities for global industry participation, and at the corporate level it may provide a useful way to think about strengths and weaknesses of singular approaches like worldwide integration that make it hard to see opportunities other than those sought.

Revolutionizing industries

Whatever their size or strategy, global firms often take unconventional approaches to their industries, developing strategic innovations that change the rules of the competitive game in a particular industry (Hout, Porter, and Rudden, 1982). Deutsche Morgan Grenfell has changed the rules of global banking by raiding employees from other firms, and Suisse Bank similarly is breaking away from conservative Swiss banking to invest in riskier opportunities in Eastern Europe. Nike reshaped the trainer/sneaker market by creating shoes for athletes, and Reebok followed with athletic shoes for women. Richard Branson has done the almost unthinkable by introducing Virgin Cola to the highly rivalrous global soft-drink beverage market, and Sam Walton revolutionized marketing by fixing consumers' attention on price alone. This and other industry revolutions result from someone, somewhere questioning the industry status quo.

According to Gary Hamel (1996), except for industry leaders with an unassailable position, most businesses have a larger stake in revolution than in the status quo. He proposes nine ways firms can revolutionize their industries.

Reconceive a product or service:
 (a) radically improve the value ratio by 500% or more, like Hewlett-Packard did in the printer industry and IKEA did for furniture;
 (b) separate function and form, as the security industry did by using the credit card industry's magnetic stripe idea to authorize entry to rooms, buildings, copiers;
 (c) achieve joy of use, as Trader Joe's did by making grocery shopping surprising and fun;

Redefine market space:
 (d) push the boundaries of universality to identify new opportunities: the single-use camera is accessible to children who were not users of other types of cameras; Domino's Pizza is popular in Japan with squid and other offerings;
 (e) strive for individuality to respond to needs people have to feel special: Levi Strauss now uses computer measurements to manufacture personalized jeans;
 (f) increase accessibility via telephone, expanding hours, or location such as locating fast foods in buildings where people work;

Redraw industry boundaries:
 (g) rescale industries, making local services national or national ones global, or the reverse to create micromarkets for standardized goods like bakery products or microbrew beers;

(h) compress the supply chain by removing steps from processes, e.g., cut out the cost of shipping paper worldwide with electronic media to transmit information;

(i) drive convergence between industries, a process grocery stores have fostered by offering prepared meals equivalent to those available in restaurants.

According to Hamel, true industry revolutionaries do not care what industries they are in because existing boundaries are not meaningful. What is more meaningful are emerging industries that create tomorrow's advantages.

PEOPLE
Managerial competencies for a global world: guiding strategy

Top managers have traditionally guided organizational purpose. Although the role of guide remains important, how one guides and who is guided has changed. Where once the top leader answered to owners, and shared a vision only with those at the top, he or she increasingly answers to many organizational stakeholders and involves others in the process. The others involved cross line and staff boundaries, shifting the CEO role from decision-maker to inspiration for the global strategic planning process (Lorange and Probst, 1990).

According to Kenichi Ohmae (1982), a top manager's strategy-making involves rational analysis to stimulate the creative process but the basic thought process is more creative and intuitive than rational. Similarly, Henry Mintzberg (1994) observes that strategic thinking calls for synthesis more than analysis, and relies on thinking outside the boundaries of past events. Mintzberg observes that analytical thinkers tend to be favored by large, bureaucratic organizations, but intuitive thinkers are favored in more flexible and project-oriented organizations. Involving both in strategic thinking is important but difficult. Either/or thinking is a barrier, and a second barrier is how the organization defines nontraditional thinking. For example, pre-1988 IBM accommodated diverse thinking by hiring people they described as 'wild ducks,' but they avoided the 'crazy' ducks. Yet the crazy ducks in organizational life often are those with penetrating insights and revolutionary ideas who also are prone to ideas that just seem loony. A need for diversity of thought at top levels calls for people 'not like us' also to fit with corporate culture, requiring internal tradeoffs.

Gary Hamel and C.K. Prahalad (1994) argue that shifts in the rules of an industry require industry insight from the senior management team. Yet their work with senior managers showed they devote less than 3% of their energy to developing a corporate perspective on the future, spending most of their time on operations management and too little on assessing and planning for future opportunities. They believe that initiating this process requires that the senior management team spend 20–50% of their time over a period of several months to develop a forward-looking view of their industry, and then revisit this view regularly to develop additional industry foresight. According to Hamel (cited in Reimann, 1994) the basic foundation for promoting foresight includes:

(a) a restlessness with the status quo;

(b) a boundless curiosity with issues that are outside the industry;

(c) a willingness for top managers to listen and speculate rather than judge;

(d) a childlike innocence making it possible to ask basic questions;

(e) an inherent eclecticism that brings diverse groups of people together from different functions, geographies, or positions;

(f) a capacity for thinking in the abstract;

(g) a bias for contrarianism because people who create the future usually are those who don't play by existing rules;

(h) liberal use of metaphors and analogies from other industries;

(i) genuine empathy with human needs.

Introducing many forms of diversity among those involved in the strategic planning process is one way to incorporate alternative modes of thinking. This explains why many organizations seek input from line and staff employees as well as from suppliers and buyers. Accommodating diversity in thinking may involve shaping the culture of 'who we are' relative to others. At Turner Broadcasting, employees may not use the word 'foreign' because it creates a false sense of 'us' and 'them' when all are perceived as neighbors in the same world. Earlier we saw that some few global firms are hiring women at the top. Others are introducing diversity to strategic thinking by hiring from nations other than headquarters. Some examples appear in Table 8.10. Still, diversity in top management groups and among those formulating strategy is limited and a boundary that remains to be crossed in most global organizations.

Competitive advantage through people

Jeffrey Pfeffer (1994) believes traditional sources of success such as product and process technologies, protected or regulated national markets, access to financial resources, and economies of scale provide fewer advantages than they once did. This elevates the importance of organizational culture and capabilities created from managing people well. Organizations find many ways to derive sustainable advantage from people, and so none will use exactly the same criteria. Yet Pfeffer identified 16 interrelated practices that often help companies achieve sustainable advantage through people. Among the practices listed

TABLE 8.10   Who is where? Globalization at the top

Business	HQ	Top executive manager	Nationality
L'Oréal	France	Lindsay Owen-Jones	Welsh
Heinz	US	Tony O'Reilly	Irish
Ford	US	Alex Trotman	Scottish
Schering	Germany	Giuseppe Vita	Italian
McKinsey	US	Rajat Gupta	Indian
Nestlé	Switzerland	Helmut Maucher	German
Barclays	UK	Martin Taylor	US
Sotheby's	UK	Diana Brooks	US
First Pacific	Indonesia	Manuel Pangilinan	Filipino
Pharmacia & Upjohn	Sweden; US; Italy	Fred Hassan	Naturalized US; native of Pakistan
Rubbermaid	US	Wolfgang Schmitt	German
Pearson PLC	UK	Marjorie Scardino	US
Goodyear Tire & Rubber	US	Samir Gibara	Egyptian

in Table 8.11 are some that contrast with current practice in some firms, e.g., provide employment security or pay high wages, and others, like efficiency in cross-utilization and cross-training, that reinforce it.

Pfeffer believes that achieving sustainable advantage though people and human resource practices is more enduring than a new piece of equipment to improve economies

TABLE 8.11   Sixteen characteristics for achieving sustainable advantage through people

1 Employment security
2 Selectivity in recruiting – choose the right people in the right way
3 High wages – you get what you pay for
4 Wage compression – reduce gap between highest and lowest paid employees
5 Incentive pay – shared gains have to be viewed as 'fair'
6 Employee ownership
7 Information sharing
8 Participation and empowerment
9 Teams and job redesign
10 Training and skill development
11 Cross-utilization and cross-training
12 Symbolic egalitarianism – provide ways to signal outsiders and insiders that there is comparative equality
13 Promotion from within
14 Long-term perspective
15 Measurement of practices
16 An overarching philosophy

Source: Pfeffer, Jeffrey. (1994). *Creating sustainable advantage through people*, pp. 30–59. Boston, MA: Harvard Business School Press.

of scale, but in contrast to activities like the latter, sustainable advantage through people also takes time to achieve. This longer time horizon is more easily achieved in family- or privately owned firms less answerable to stockholder demands for short-term profits. Global organizations also need to take this longer run view to develop the knowledge- or customer-oriented workers they need, but face difficult tradeoffs with stockholder demands for short-term profitability. Pfeffer also believes that external barriers to achieving sustainable advantage through people include national and even world veneration for the wrong heroes, and economic theories and models that emphasize neoclassical principles like agency theory and transaction costs. The latter's emphasis on opportunism, for example, fosters distrust within and between organizations. Making heroes of people who have made money or claimed fame based on layoffs and 'lean and mean' behavior suggests people are an expendable resource. Internal barriers include using language that undermines rather than develops employee confidence or loyalty, e.g., thinking of others as foreigners. Finally, Pfeffer suggests heroes, theories, and language used within a firm should be integrated and consistent with a desire to build advantages through people. Managing these intangibles may be more important to sustaining advantage than a short-lived economic advantage, but is difficult for analytical managers who prefer to manage concrete and tangible assets.

GLOBAL STRUCTURE

Leif Melin (1992) observes that international business research on structure has looked primarily at how businesses achieve fit between structure and strategy. He believes this approach overemphasizes linear thinking, and fails to account for important processes like learning. Further, he notes that firms can best expand beyond domestic bases by adopting a dynamic and complex view of organizations incorporating heterogeneity and diversity. As Table 8.12 indicates, the amount of diversity organizations incorporate increases when firms expand beyond domestic bases. For example, insular domestic firms might choose to ignore cultural interactions; multidomestic firms tend to recognize but minimize them, multinational firms assimilate them. Finally, global firms often view cultural interactions as a source of organizational advantage. Table 8.12 also shows how a firm's orientation toward its world also define its strategy, structure, and other cultural behaviors.

The following look at structural adaptation among global firms shows diversity among them. Patterns of convergence first reflect a propensity for trading off between centralization and decentralization. There appears also to be greater centralization of decision authority at top levels in some European firms and distribution of decision-making at lower levels of Pacific Rim firms described. Among US firms, there appears to be a trend toward centralizing functions that eliminate structural duplication.

TABLE 8.12 Strategy, structure, and cultural behaviors appropriate to firm presence abroad

	Domestic	Multidomestic	Multinational	Global
Strategies for expanding beyond domestic markets	None	Country-specific; locally responsive	Integrated worldwide	Locally responsive and integrated worldwide
Structure	Centralized hierarchy	Decentralized hierarchy	Centralized hierarchy	Networks and linkages
Managers	Local	Host-country nationals	Expatriates and third-country nationals	A diverse mix
Cultural perspective	Parochial	Culturally relative	HQ-oriented	Culturally synergistic
Nature of cultural interactions	Ignored	Recognized but minimized	Assimilated	Source of organizational advantage
Dynamics of cultural interaction	Cultural dominance	Cultural adaptation when necessary	Cultural accommodation	Cultural synergy, collaboration; learning

Source: Adapted from: Adler, Nancy and Bartholomew, Susan. (1992). Academic and professional communities of discourse: Generating knowledge on transnational human resource management. *Journal of International Business Studies*, 23(3): 551–569.

Internal adjustments of structure

Examples from European firms:
- In 1996 Deutsche Bank announced a new structure, moving away from management with a board of peers and toward a more centralized management structure with a clearly identifiable and responsible CEO; board members are responsible for a single business within four global operating divisions.
- Asea-Brown Boveri organized a lean matrix structure, placing only one layer of people between the top level and 1,300 operating units. Only 175 people work in Geneva headquarters.
- IKEA flattened its structure by delegating more responsibilities to subsidiary managers; decisions previously had been centralized in Sweden.

Examples from US firms:
- Ford Motor Company merged engineering and research and development divisions worldwide.
- In 1996 Coca-Cola changed its management reporting structure, after which all six global operating divisions reported to the president.

- Levi's selected a flatter structure to focus on brands and tie activities directly to the consumer.
- Whirlpool merged national designers and researchers into pan-European teams to work closely with US designers.

Examples from Pacific Rim firms:

- In 1992 Honda's internal 'Honda Way' system of consensus management and distributed decision-making was revamped to centralize decisions at the top level, allowing top managers more time to develop a broad view of global change.
- Sony eliminated product groups, replacing them with eight independent companies targeted toward specific product categories and customer bases such as consumer audio visual products, broadcast products, and mobile electronics.
- Samsung altered its entire structure to distribute decision-making authority among managers throughout the organization.

Theoretical models suggested for global restructuring include internal and external adjustments. The following are examples of internal adjustments.

INTERNAL NETWORKS

Ram Charan (1991) believes that as compared to traditional corporate structures, networks have the ability to muster the speed, focus, and flexibility needed to succeed in a dynamic world. Based on his studies of networks in 10 large companies, including DuPont and CIGNA, Charan concluded that internal networks are relatively permanent structural arrangements intended to deliver on some aspect of corporate strategy. They are developed by senior managers to create a boundary-spanning structure composed of a select group of managers – usually no more than 100 nor fewer than 25 – whose skills and abilities are drawn from across the company's functions, units, geography, and existing hierarchy. A major purpose of this network is to transcend borders of functional or departmental interests, but other objectives include empowering managers to talk openly, building trust, and improving the quality of decisions by including more people in decisions that affect them. Finally, and quite unlike the static nature of a traditional hierarchy, internal networks are dynamic because they permit information flows and decisions to travel in appropriate directions.

SHAMROCK ORGANIZATION

Charles Handy, author of *The age of unreason* (1991), *The age of paradox* (1994), and other books, argues that a shamrock form of organization more responsive to the process-centered nature of organizations is likely to replace traditional hierarchical pyramids (Figure 8.2). At the core of the business and in the center of the shamrock is a small,

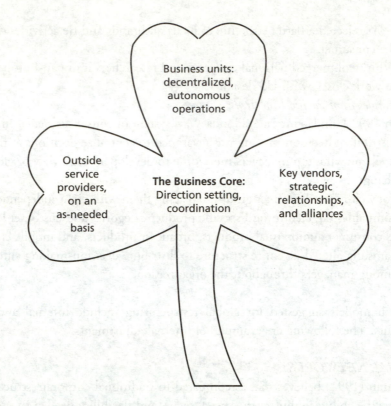

FIGURE 8.2 *The shamrock organization* (Handy, Charles. (1991). *The age of unreason.* Boston, MA: Harvard Business School Press)

central group of managers and technical staff whose skills represent the firm's core competencies. The three leaves of the shamrock are connected through their interactions with people in the business core. The top petal includes decentralized and autonomously operating business units; the right petal includes strategic vendors such as suppliers or companies and individuals who perform contractual work peripheral to the core, e.g., janitorial services, and the left petal includes temporary and outside service providers, most of whom work for the company on a contract or as-needed basis.

HORIZONTAL STRUCTURE

Combined examples from theory and practice appearing above reinforce organizational commitments to being fiscally efficient and also sufficiently flexible to pursue developing opportunities in a global marketplace. Many firms are achieving both by creating structures capable of responding to both cost and differentiation advantages associated with worldwide integration and multilocal strategies. Roderick White and Thomas Poynter (1990) believe a horizontal structure makes it possible to respond to multiple and competing demands of worldwide integration in some lines and local responsiveness in others. As shown in Figure 8.3, the horizontal structure is found when opportunities for globally based advantages are many and locally based advantages also are many. Characteristics of the global horizontal structure include the following:

1 Lateral decision processes bring together those most affected by decisions to collaborate on key issues that facilitate product flow, develop and adjust overlapping programs that deploy resources, and share information and knowledge.
2 Horizontal networks purposefully break traditional vertical reporting relationships, causing functions like marketing, sales, or manufacturing to operate as discrete units; lateral processes like teaming across functions provide flexible linkages that can be established as needed.
3 Common decision premises able to cross differences of geography or nationality are needed to facilitate congruent decision-making and usually depend on a strong and shared sense of corporate purpose.

The horizontal structure White and Poynter describe overcomes some of the challenges of mixing multilocal and worldwide integration strategies because it focuses attention where it is needed and when. The glue that ensures flexibility is a strong sense of shared values. Matsushita instills these values by bringing worldwide managers and supervisors

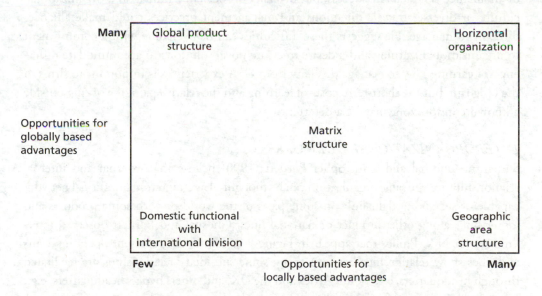

FIGURE 8.3 *Structural orientations* (White, Roderick, and Poynter, Thomas. (1990). Organizing for world-wide advantage. In Christopher Bartlett, Yves Doz, and Gunnar Hedlund (Eds), *Managing the global firm.* London: Routledge, p. 97)

505

to its training center in Osaka, Japan, where they spend several weeks studying the company's history and philosophy before visiting factories to see how the philosophy is implemented. Dow also trains its managers in company philosophy. Horizontal structure represents a change in more than reporting relationships; it also requires process-oriented top managers, employees who share information and other resources, and personal flexibility responsive to changing demands.

Alterations in external structural arrangements

In addition to changing internal structural forms, some organizations are restructuring external relationships with other firms. Large South Korean *chaebols* have broken with tradition to sustain and develop small supplier firms; Japanese *keiretsu* and government leaders have loosened their hold on business activities in Japan; and businesses throughout the world have put aside exclusive 'go it alone' thinking to forge linkages such as strategic alliances, international joint ventures, and joint marketing campaigns. The example of IBM's 1996 restructuring (Box 8.5) illustrates how internal and external restructuring occur simultaneously, often raising new questions and concerns.

Arvind Parkhe (1991) believes competitive advantage depends not only on internal restructuring but also on structuring global strategic alliances (GSA) with other firms. According to Parkhe, diversity in reciprocal strengths and resources that lead to formation of an alliance can facilitate success, but diversity of societal, national, and organizational culture or diverse strategic directions and management practices could make alliances difficult to manage. He suggests these difficulties can be overcome with a commitment to organizational learning and a desire to create novel solutions to accommodate differences. Learning how to manage diversity from GSA experiences is important to firms in the long run, but the short-term costs of learning and the relative pain of working outside a known comfort zone may be a deterrent.

INTERORGANIZATIONAL NETWORKS

Sumantra Ghoshal and Christopher Bartlett (1990) believe that external and internal relationships for the same organization can be thought of as an interorganizational network capable of sustaining tight links in some parts of the world or with some products and looser links along other product or national lines. Ghoshal and Bartlett observed interlinkages for N.V. Philips that appear in Figure 8.4. The circles represent operating units and lines show relationships between them; some subsidiary relationships are facilitated through headquarters, e.g., South Africa and the UK, and others bypass headquarters, e.g., Japan and US. These different linkages were intended to accommodate differences between Philips' operating units, which range from single-function operations responsible only for research and development to large, fully integrated companies responsible for R&D,

BOX 8.5:   IBM ALTERS INTERNAL AND EXTERNAL STRUCTURAL RELATIONSHIPS

IBM products traditionally were sold through a special IBM sales force called 'blue suits' because organizational culture at IBM traditionally reinforced blue suits as the norm. But many traditions are changing at IBM to make it a more global company. Globalization of the computer industry has produced thousands of independent distributors who have a broader reach than a single firm can offer. Like many other firms, IBM found it could sell more computers through distributors than through 'blue suits' alone. Accordingly, IBM restructured the firm, selecting Lucio Stanca for a new position to oversee 'direct' worldwide sales like catalog and on-line offering and coordinate all distributors that sell IBM products (except personal computers). This change represented an alteration in external relationships as the boundaries between IBM sales agents and distributors become less clear. Within IBM, these and other realignments are expected to eliminate overlapping responsibilities and make people more accountable for sales and service. CEO Louis Gerstner hopes thereby to end internal competition for resources and recognition between IBM units located in various countries. If these internal boundaries can be reduced or eliminated, IBM can better use resources to grow globally. In early 1998, Gerstner appointed Linda Sanford general manager of Global Industries, making her responsible for 17,000 people who sell to IBM's top 20,000 customers. This executive shuffle indicates IBM, like many other firms, continues to search for people, structure, and processes appropriate to a global world.

Source: Ziegler, Bart. (1996, Dec. 13). IBM revamps global units, sets one brand. *The Wall Street Journal*, p. A3 [http://www.ibm.com].

production, and marketing. Evidence of similar differentiated networks in large MNEs from all over the world, including Procter & Gamble, Unilever, Ericsson, NEC, and Matsushita, led Ghoshal and Bartlett to argue that convergence toward patterns of linkages in many businesses may be reflective of broader and global societal changes. Each of the firms in Ghoshal and Bartlett's study has continually revised and restructured various businesses in response to globalization. For Ericsson this has meant downsizing in their Information Systems unit and for Philips it has meant over six years of restructuring in Philips Electronics including moving its headquarters from Eindhoven to Amsterdam.

Having looked at organizational structures, people, and processes affected by global industry change, we can conclude that changes in this global environment also have created uncertainties. Many global firms have responded to these uncertainties with

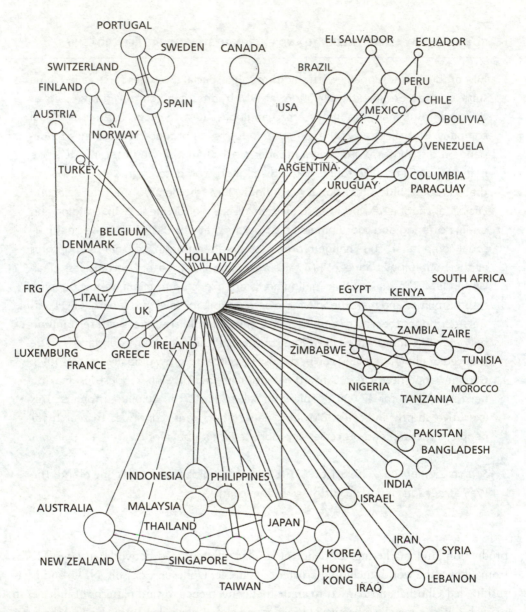

FIGURE 8.4 *Examples of interlinkages for N.V. Philips* (Ghoshal, Sumantra, and Bartlett, Christopher. (1990). The multinational corporation as an interorganizational network. *Academy of Management Review*, 15(4): 605)

incremental change; others show a willingness to adopt mechanisms untested by experience; others have embraced and even stimulated industry change; and still others have adopted mechanisms successful for other firms. For example, firms in the Pacific Rim seem to be trying to improve decision autonomy just as firms in the US and Europe are trying to centralize it. Structural arrangements to accommodate industry change frequently emphasize fluid networks and linkages adaptive to differing needs. Strategic management processes in many firms cross boundaries of function and role to encourage strategic thinking across the organization. The type of strategic planning recommended requires synthesis and intuition more than analysis, and senior managers willing to devote time and personal resources in three directions: reflections on the past, analysis of the present, and visions of the future with respect to global industries and tasks. Diversity of people needed to plan strategically is at the structural level complemented by diversity in goals when organizations compete and cooperate. All of these changes put greater emphasis on intangibles like organizational culture, learning, intuition, and envisioning and therefore the results of suggested changes will take more time to achieve and be more difficult to measure than tangible and known parameters.

KEY CHAPTER CONCEPTS

Defining Task and Industry Environments: The task environment usually refers to day-to-day activities or concerns for a business such as manufacturing a good or providing a service, dealing with customers, or negotiating with lenders, whereas the industry environment includes those activities that influence any firm in the industry.

The Five Forces Framework: Michael Porter's 'Five Forces' for analyzing industry competition have proved popular as a way to assess industries, but a global sphere requires additional tools to assess activities affecting the growing number of global industries.

Diverse Business Participants Increase Complexity: Management of firms in global industries has increased in complexity as new entrants from many countries such as small, family-owned, and private firms as well as large MNEs participate in global industries.

Industry Boundaries are Shifting: Technological, demographic, regulatory and other changes occurring worldwide have the potential to transform industry boundaries and create new space for firms. Thus, managers must not only diagnose the past and the present, they must create a vision of the future.

Access to Resources Worldwide: Globalization of capital, knowledge, and technology made each more accessible worldwide than had previously been the case, and these forces for globalization made it possible for firms from around the world to enter industries previously closed to them. The diverse mix of traditional and new competitors, large and small, from many nations and for various reasons stimulated experimentation that has reshaped many industries.

Four Measures of Industry Globalization: Four factors can be assessed to measure the degree of industry globalization: these are market globalization, cost globalization, government globalization, and competitive globalization.

The Costs of Competition: The 'winner-take-all' mentality of competition as a zero-sum game can create dysfunctions for organizations and for nations when people strive to 'win' at all costs. Awareness of this dilemma has led some to argue for 'coopetition' that fosters both competition and collaboration.

Creating Sustainable Advantage: Creating sustainable firm advantage in a global world increasingly depends on organizational clarity about what the firm is trying to do and with what skills and abilities. Whether these are defined as core values, mission, distinctive competencies or some other concepts, the underlying theme is that the organization must have a clear focus that is well communicated among internal and external constituents.

Strategy Defined: Strategy is the limited set of important, nonroutine, nonprogrammable decisions that guide overall organizational direction. Strategy-making occurs at multiple levels. At the business level it answers the question: How shall we position the business in its industry?

Global Strategic Options: The strategic decision often has been viewed as a choice between a worldwide integration or multilocal strategy. The former concentrates on integrating functions worldwide while a multilocal strategy concentrates on localizing strategies to specific markets. Many argue that these two types of strategies also can be blended to develop integration on some organizational dimensions and localization on others. Mixed or hybrid strategies often are found, reflecting leaders' awareness of the need to be efficient and locally responsive at the same time.

Strategic Innovations: Whatever their strategy or size, global firms often take unconventional approaches to their industries, developing strategic innovations that change the rules of the competitive game in a particular industry. Firms revolutionize their industries in myriad ways, including reconceiving the product, redefining markets, and redrawing industry boundaries.

People as a Critical Source of Sustainable Advantage: Many view people as the greatest source of comparative advantage not only for firms but for nations because product and process technologies, protected or regulated national markets, access to financial resources, and economies of scale provide fewer advantages than they once did. This elevates the importance of organizational culture and capabilities created from managing people well.

Dual Challenges of Diversity and Efficiency: Many large would-be global firms have restructured in response to globalization, but there is no clear pattern – no 'one best way' to restructure for global success. If there is any single lesson, it is that firms are trying to integrate and achieve efficiencies wherever possible without losing the flexibility they need to be responsive to diversity and to change.

Structural Integration: Many of the structural responses to globalization involve integration – crossing borders between functions of the organizations and across borders that more traditionally exist between organizations, their buyers and suppliers, their competitors, and others.

The Value of Abstract Thinking: Managers with insight are needed to forge new links and see new industry opportunities; these managers often are abstract thinkers, but many are empathetic to others and can therefore see the same events from new perspectives.

REVIEW AND DISCUSSION QUESTIONS

1   Think for a moment about the factors that helped fast food restaurants to grow in the industrialized world. What are some of these factors? Are they the same factors fueling growth for fast foods in the developing world? Do you think certain groups of people will adopt fast food habits, e.g., younger, in different parts of the world, earlier than other groups? Why?

2   Ben and Jerry's and Häagen-Dazs both are competitors in the premium ice cream market, but the two firms have very different competitive motives. Identify the different motives, and then describe how these differences in motives can be used to explain different actions on the part of the two organizations.

3   Competition on a global sphere raises the question of whether it is nations, firms or both that compete globally. Second, many firms find that they can successfully cooperate and compete in global industries; this approach to managing global strategy is called coopetition. Develop a four-cell box to present arguments for and against competition and collaboration for either nations or businesses.

4   US managers typically receive their rewards based on short-term results like quarterly returns on equity or annual returns on profits. Is this type of reward system consistent with competition in a global world?

5   What is meant by blurring boundaries of industry? What is it that is blurring and why is this blurring occurring? What are the longer run effects of blurred industry boundaries for managers within firms?

6   Will globalization make it more or less possible for small firms to participate in

business? In what ways does globalization create similar challenges for any size firm? What are key differences between large and smaller firms that make each more and less adaptive to globalization?

7   Non-profits as well as global gangs play a role in reshaping global business activities. In what ways do these and other entities, e.g., government, play roles in shaping business activities and industry conditions?

8   *The Global Enterprise Project*: What are global industry revenues and where does your firm rank quantitatively as compared to other firms in this industry? What is the firm's competitive stance? How rivalrous is it and with what firms? What are its major strategies/approaches to competing in the global market? Does it compete to win with wholly owned subsidiaries or collaborate via joint ventures or other strategic alliances? How does the firm view the industry shaking out in the future?

REFERENCES

Anders, George. (1989, Sept. 22). Going global: Vision vs. reality. *The Wall Street Journal*, pp. R20–21.

As good times roll, Indonesia's Chinese fear for their future. (1997, June 5). *The Wall Street Journal*, p. A18.

Asami, Hiroko. (1995, July 17). Asia. *Forbes*, p. 144.

Asia. (1995, July 17). *Forbes*, p. 141.

Bannon, Lisa. (1994, Nov. 17). Natuzzi's huge selection of leather furniture pays off. *The Wall Street Journal*, p. B4.

Barrett, Amy. (1995, Apr. 17). It's a small (business) world. *Business Week*, pp. 96–101.

Bartlett, Christopher, and Ghoshal, Sumantra. (1992). *Transnational management*. Boston, MA: Irwin.

Brandenburger, Adam, and Nalebuff, Barry. (1996). *Co-opetition*. New York: Doubleday.

Charan, Ram. (1991). How networks reshape organizations – For results. Reprinted in James Champy and Nitin Nchria (Eds), *Fast Forward*. (1996), pp. 15–38. Cambridge, MA: Harvard Business School Press.

de Geus, Arie. (1997). *The living company*. Boston, MA: Harvard Business School Press.

Dowling, Michael J., Roering, William D., Carlin, Barbara A., and Wisnieski, Joette. (1996). Multifaceted relationships under coopetition. *Journal of Management Inquiry*, 5(2): 155–167.

Drucker, Peter. (1994, Dec. 20). The new superpower: The overseas Chinese. *The Wall Street Journal*, p. A14.

Fahey, Liam, and Narayanan, V.K. (1986). *Macroenvironmental analysis for strategic management*. St Paul, MN: West Publishing.

Frank, Robert H., and Cook, Philip J. (1995). *The winner-take-all society*. Cambridge, MA: Free Press.

Ghoshal, Sumantra, and Bartlett, Christopher. (1990). The multinational corporation as an interorganizational network. *Academy of Management Review*, 15(4): 603–625.

Hamel, Gary. (1996, July/Aug.). Nine routes to industry revolution. *Harvard Business Review*, pp. 72–73.

Hamel, Gary, and Prahalad, C.K. (1994). *Competing for the future*. Boston, MA: Harvard Business School Press.

Handy, Charles. (1991). *The age of unreason*. Boston, MA: Harvard Business School Press.

Handy, Charles. (1994). *The age of paradox*. Boston, MA: Harvard Business School Press.

Hedlund, Gunnar, and Rolander, Dag. (1990). Action in heterarchies: New approaches to managing the MNC. In Christopher Bartlett, Yves Doz, and Gunnar Hedlund (Eds), *Managing the global firm*, pp. 15–46. London: Routledge.

Henderson, Hazel. (1996). *Building a win-win world: Life beyond global economic warfare*. San Francisco, CA: Berrett-Koehler.

Holstein, William J. (1992, Apr. 13). Little companies, big exports. *Business Week*, pp. 70–72.

Hout, Thomas, Porter, Michael, and Rudden, Eileen. (1982, Sept./Oct.). How global companies win out. *Harvard Business Review*, pp. 98–108.

How to live long and prosper. (1997, May 10). *The Economist*, p. 59.

Index of Foreign Billionaires. (1994, July 18). *Forbes*, pp. 152–218.

Inheriting the bamboo network. (1995, Dec. 23). *The Economist*, pp. 79–80.

Kao, John. (1993, Mar./Apr.). The worldwide web of Chinese business. *Harvard Business Review*, pp. 24–36.

Keen, Peter G.W., and Knapp, Ellen M. (1996). *Every manager's guide to business processes*. Boston, MA: Harvard Business School Press.

Kobrin, Stephen. (1991). An empirical analysis of the determinants of global integration. *Strategic Management Journal*, 12 (Special Issue): 17–31.

Krugman, Paul. (1994). Competitiveness: A dangerous obsession. *Foreign Affairs*, 73(2): 28–44.

Lorange, Peter, and Probst, Gilbert. (1990). Effective strategic planning processes in the multinational corporation. In Christopher Bartlett, Yves Doz, and Gunnar Hedlund (Eds), *Managing the global firm*, pp. 144–163. London: Routledge.

McRae, Hamish. (1994). *The world in 2020: Power, culture and prosperity*. Boston, MA: Harvard Business School Press.

Mao, Phillipe. (1994, July 18). Hong Kong and Macau. *Forbes*, pp. 158–159.

Melin, Leif. (1992). Internationalization as a strategy process. *Strategic Management Journal*, 13: 99–118.

Miller, Karen Lowry. (1995, Apr. 10). The Mittelstand takes a stand. *Business Week*, pp. 54–55.

Mintzberg, Henry. (1994, Jan./Feb.). The fall and rise of strategic planning. *Harvard Business Review*, pp. 107–114.

Moore, James. (1996). *The death of competition*. New York: HarperBusiness.

Nash, Nathaniel C. (1995, Feb. 26). Coke's great Romanian adventure. *The New York Times*, pp. F1, F10.

Nelson, Richard. (1992, Winter). Recent writings on competitiveness: Boxing the compass. *California Management Review*, pp. 127–137.

Ohmae, Kenichi. (1982, July 1). Beyond the myths: Moving toward greater understanding in US–Japan business relations. *Vital speeches*, pp. 555–557.

Parkhe, Arvind. (1991). Interfirm diversity, organizational learning, and longevity in global strategic alliances. *Journal of International Business Studies*, 22(4): 579–601.

Perlmutter, Howard V., and Heenan, David A. (1986, Mar./Apr.). Cooperate to compete globally. *Harvard Business Review*, pp. 136–152.

Pfeffer, Jeffrey. (1994). *Competitive advantage through people*. Boston, MA: Harvard Business School Press.

Porter, Michael E. (1980). *Competitive strategy*. New York: Free Press.

Porter, Michael E. (Ed.). (1986). *Competition in global industries*. Boston, MA: Harvard Business School Press.

Porter, Michael E. (1990). *The competitive advantage of nations*. New York: Free Press.

Prahalad, C.K., and Hamel, Gary. (1994). Strategy as a field of study: Why search for a new paradigm? *Strategic Management Journal*, 15(5): 5–16.

Prahalad, C.K., and Doz, Y.L. (1987). *The multinational mission: Balancing local demands and global vision*. New York: Free Press.

Reimann, Bernard C. (1994, Sept./Oct.). Gary Hamel: How to compete for the future. *Planning Review*, pp. 39–43.

Roth, Kendall, and Morrison, Allen J. (1990). An empirical analysis of the integration–responsiveness framework in global industries. *Journal of International Business Studies*, 21(4): 541–564.

Seagrave, Sterling. (1995). *Lords of the Rim*. London: Bantam.

Simon, Hermann. (1996). *Hidden champions: Lessons from 500 of the world's best unknown companies*. Boston, MA: Harvard Business School Press.

Stalk, George, Jr (1988, July/Aug.). Time – the next source of competitive advantage. *Harvard Business Review*, pp. 41–51.

Strategic planning. (1996, Aug. 26). *Business Week*, pp. 46–52.

Tanzer, Andrew. (1994, July 18). The bamboo network. *Forbes*, pp. 138–145.

Tanzer, Andrew. (1995, Dec. 23). Inheriting the bamboo. *Forbes*, pp. 48–50.

Weidenbaum, Murray L. (1996). *The bamboo network*. New York: Martin Kessler Books.

White, Roderick, and Poynter, Thomas. (1990). Organizing for world-wide advantage. In Christopher Bartlett, Yves Doz, and Gunnar Hedlund (Eds), *Managing the global firm*, pp. 95–113. London: Routledge.

Who wants to be a giant? (1995, June 24). *The Economist*, Multinational Survey, p. 4.

Wilson, Ian. (1990). The state of strategic planning: What went wrong? What goes right? *Technological Forecasting and Social Change*, 37: 103–110.

World Investment Report. (1995). New York: UN, UNCTAD.

Yip, George S. (1995). *Total global strategy*. Englewood Cliffs, NJ: Prentice Hall.

Ziesemer, Bernd. (1996, June). The overseas Chinese empire. *World Press Review*, p. 29 (reprinted from Wirtschaftswoche, Feb. 29, 1996).

Chapter 9

Globalization of Technologies

AFRICA ONE AND OTHER LINKAGES: BUSINESS ACTIVITIES AFFECT MORE THAN BUSINESSES

The Africa One project initiated by telecommunications giant AT&T through its submarine systems business promises to provide African countries with a basic broad band transmission system that can carry other telecommunication systems as they develop, e.g., wireless telephones or interactive computer services. This network is expected to cost between $2 to $3 billion for underwater fiber-optic cable around the African continent with gateway links among and between African countries and the world. In its initial phase, which is expected to be completed in 1999, the project would link 41 coastal countries and islands of Africa with 21,000 miles of undersea fiber-optic cable. Later, satellite and existing microwave and fiber-optic connections would be used to link up landlocked countries. While African leaders would like their countries to be hooked to these technologies, the costs for building appropriate infrastructure are prohibitive. According to Severin Kaombwe, acting director of the Southern Africa Transport and Communications Commission, 'It would take an investment of $14 billion just to get telephone penetration in the southern African region as high as the 10% penetration in South Africa.' Moreover, there are other reasons the project will be costly. For example, once telecommunications networks are in place, Africa will have to embark on a massive education campaign, because 90% of the population in Sub-Saharan Africa has never made a telephone call, much less worked at a computer. AT&T's initial involvement in the project was to pursue both business and social goals motivated by a 1993 appeal from the International Telecommunication Union for firms to help bridge the technological gap between Africa and the rest of the world. By 1995, in addition to Africa One, NYNEX had proposed its FLAG project to link the African continent via a cable running from Japan to the UK, and France's Alcatel had proposed a 9,000 mile cable under the Mediterranean through Morocco and along Africa's west coast to Cape Town, South Africa. By late 1995, AT&T's undersea cable unit had linked up with Alcatel Alsthom to lay the undersea cable, but by mid-1997 AT&T had sold its submarine systems business to Tyco International.

This example demonstrates increasing interdependence between business activities and both political and cultural dimensions of life, and it demonstrates the rapid pace telecommunications firms maintain. Should the communications cable for Africa prove successful, the resulting need for telephones and roadways in response to growing opportunity will doubtless affect every aspect of life throughout Africa. Thus, business activities shape social expectations which in turn generate new demands for enterprises involved in business activities. Business activities occurring in developing economies also have the capacity to alter telecommunication traditions. For example, China and South Korea have led an effort to install a submarine telecommunications cable between the US and the Asian mainland. The cable is expected to handle telecommunications increases of 60% between South Korea and China, but also facilitates growing links between the two countries and the US. The new cable would sidestep the existing TPC-5 fiber-optic line between the Asian mainland and North America which was part of a joint project between AT&T and Kokusai Denshin Denwa Company (KDD), Japan's government controlled telecommunications firm. AT&T and KDD also are discussing the possibility of collaborating with China on the new cable line, but AT&T is hedging its bets with a separate China venture in case political considerations cause KDD to withdraw or be excluded from the project. These big players in telecommunication industries are actively investing in new projects not just in Asia but worldwide. KDD and AT&T are partners in several telecommunications alliances, including Fiber-optic Link Around the Globe (FLAG) and the Asia Pacific Cable Network Links (APCN) consortium that includes Alcatel. Acting without partners, KDD gained 1997 US Federal Communications Commission permission to offer connections between the US and major regions of the world, including open circuits through the US to France, Belgium, Hong Kong, Russia, and Mongolia among others. The link between technologies and culture demonstrated by the Africa One project; the link between politics and laying of a trans-Pacific fiber-optic cable; the link between companies – all these are reflective of changes in telecommunications industries and technologies.

Sources: AT&T enters the race to wire Africa. (1995, May–June). *Africa Report*, p. 9.; Revzin, Philip. (1995, June 9). Info-highway builders seek to change African nations' development priorities. *The Wall Street Journal*, p. B5B.

PART I   A TECHNOLOGICAL REVOLUTION

Technological advances in almost every sphere of endeavor are important factors driving globalization; and the explosion of technological breakthroughs in telecommunications industries has made it possible for information and innovations rapidly to cross national borders and boundaries of time and space. A cursory review of recent breakthroughs reveals a tendency to focus most on 'high' technology and on what variously is called the Information Age, the Knowledge Revolution, and the Information Revolution. In this chapter, we look at both 'high' and 'low' technologies to assess the impact of technology transfer throughout the world, and examine opportunities and threats for businesses. The chapter begins with a broad definition of technology, describes how processes of technological discovery have changed in a globalizing world, and considers how changes associated with what we will call the Information Revolution have stimulated and been stimulated by still other changes in many spheres of human activity. This examination of the many technologies contributing to globalization recognizes opportunities provided even as it examines the challenges raised for existing and future political, economic, and social systems.

HISTORICAL TRENDS IN WORK TECHNOLOGIES

When applied to practical issues, the science of basic invention and discovery becomes new technologies – new products and new processes put to practical use. Technological breakthroughs of almost every kind punctuate known history, and many of these breakthroughs have brought about revolutionary changes in how work is accomplished. Invention of the wheel doubtless represented a product breakthrough as profound for its time as assembly-line processes introduced by the Industrial Revolution changed life thereafter. Spyros Makridakis's (1989) historical review of technological development identified five factors characteristic of technological developments over time:

1 Throughout history, the manual work of humans has been supplemented, substituted, or amplified by a variety of means. A similar supplement/substitute/amplify pattern also has occurred for mental work, but much later in time than for manual work.
2 Innovations and breakthroughs often occur in clusters.
3 The rate of innovation has increased markedly during the last 200 years, particularly due to the Industrial Revolution.
4 In every age, there have been considerable spin-offs from technology to all areas of personal and family lives.
5 The importance of technology has increased over time.

Below these characteristics are set in a historical context, thus permitting an examination of similarities and differences between the Information Revolution and the earlier Industrial Revolution.

Work is aided by technology

When a human first used a stick to dig more than half a million years ago, the technology of the tool was born. As the body of knowledge about tools spread among early people – necessarily by direct word of mouth or demonstration – innovations occurred to improve on original implements such that they became more complicated and more specialized. These tools improved human quality of life by making it easier to hunt, gather food, carry water. Breakthroughs such as irrigation systems, large-scale commerce, and the many other innovations in Table 9.1 illustrate that each had the potential to improve life quality for people. Technology has provided an endless stream of innovations from the days of cave dwellers to present, and every phase of history has been impacted in some way by the advancement of technology. Further, these technological innovations have occurred not only in the product sphere about which we know most; process innovations also have continually changed how work is organized, completed, and evaluated, and new processes of thinking have affected how people conceptualize their world.

Technological breakthroughs in work processes and recent inventions in many fields such as digital electronics serve the same purpose: they can make our lives easier. The continuing shift from labor to knowledge work in the advanced economies has generated a shift away from physical prowess and toward intellect – an individual asset that can be continually renewed and is rarely strained or hurt as are the muscles used in manual labor. Many of the process technologies to support knowledge work are only now being discovered.

Innovations often occur in clusters

Innovations occur in clusters largely because a single but profound technological breakthrough often causes people to rethink traditional assumptions about how work can be accomplished. Having seen one change, people not only imitate, but innovate, adding features to and finding new uses for technological advances. Early advances in technology were dispersed only when people traveled. For example, although communication in written form was enhanced over 500 years ago when Johann Gutenberg first used moveable type to print a Christian Bible, distribution of written knowledge remained limited until most people could read and write. Thus, the process technology of reading was limited until educational technologies were developed. Nor could printed books be easily distributed; in the absence of mail and other distribution systems, it took people traveling

TABLE 9.1   Historical innovations and breakthroughs

Epoch	Approximate time (years from 1988)	Innovation/Breakthrough	Consequence/Reason
		TECHNOLOGY	
A	1,750,000	Primitive tools	
B	100,000	Making and using gear for hunting	• Extending human capabilities
	40,000	Making and using weapons	
	5500	The wheel	
D	4000	Bronze and other metals	
	3500	Boats and sailboats	
	800	The clock, compass and other measurement instruments	• Reducing and/or making manual work easier
E	600	Gunpowder	
	500	The printed book	
	350	Mechanical calculators	• Facilitating and/or making mental work easier
	210	Engines	
F	180	Railroads	
	150	Electricity	
	130	Image and sound reproduction	• Improving comfort and/or speed of transportation
	90	Telecommunications	
G	85	Airplanes	
	70	Automobiles and roads	
	60	Mass-produced chemical products	• Increasing speed and/or availability of telecommunications
	45	Nuclear weapons	
	40	Computers	
	35	Mass-produced home appliances	• Improving quality of arts and entertainment
	35	The transistor	
H	30	Extensive use of fertilizers	
	30	Artificial satellites	• Improving material quality of life
	25	Lasers	
	20	Microtechnology (microchips, bio-chemistry, and genetic engineering)	
	20	The moon landing	
		EXPLOITING NATURE'S RESOURCES/CAPABILITIES	
	400,000	Hunting	• Decreasing dependence on the environment
A	300,000	Harnessing of fire	
	150,000	Shelter	
	20,000	Permanent settlements	
	20,000	Domestication of animals	• Exploiting nature's capabilities
C	15,000	Agriculture	
	10,000	Using animals for transportation and labour	
	3500	Irrigation systems	
D	3000	Harnessing wind power	• Using nature's resources
	2000	Using horses for transportation and labour	

TABLE 9.1 Continued

E	800	Using the energy of falling water	
F	180	Using coal and oil for energy	• Adapting to changes in the environment
H	45	Nuclear energy	

SOCIAL AND INTELLECTUAL HUMAN ACHIEVEMENTS

A	1,500,000	Social organization to care for children	• Better mastery of environment
	500,000	Language	
	400,000	Immigration	
C	20,000	Religion	• Need for socialization
	7000	First cities	
	5500	Alphabet	
	5000	Abacus	• Need for knowledge
D	3500	Money for transactions	
	3000	Number system	
	2500	Arts, philosophy, sciences	
	2500	Democracy	• Drive toward equality
	500	Scientific experimentation	
E	500	The discovery of the new worlds	
	475	*The Prince* by Machiavelli is written	
	400	Large-scale commerce	• Desire for achievement
	300	Scientific astronomy	
	300	Mathematical reasoning	
	210	Discovery of oxygen (beginning of chemistry)	
	200	French and American revolutions	
	150	Babbage's failed computer	• Appreciation of arts
F	150	Political ideologies (communism, capitalism)	
	120	Foundations of genetics	
	100	Financial, banking, and insurance institutions	
G	80	The theory of relativity	• Desire to reduce future uncertainty
	50	The concept of the computer is demonstrated mathematically	

MEDICINE

D	2500	The doctor as a healer	• Curing disease
E	500	Therapy based on sound medical reasoning	
	300	Drugs with real medical value	• Prolonging life expectancy
	90	X-ray	
	55	Antibiotics	• Providing better diagnostics
H	30	Oral contraceptives	
	20	Tissues and organ transplants	• Preventing unwanted pregnancies
	10	The CT (CAT or body) scan	

A = The emergence of human domination; B = The first hand-made tools to extend human capabilities; C = The beginning of human civilization; D = The foundation of modern civilization; E = The foundations of modern science and society; F = The start of the Industrial Revolution; G = The Industrial Revolution; H = Spin-offs of the Industrial Revolution, the start of the Information Revolution. *Source*: Makridakis, Spyros. (1989). Management in the 21st century. *Long Range Planning*, 22(2): 37–53.

one-by-one or via slow ships to spread this technology worldwide. It was nearly 400 more years after invention of moveable type before communication pioneers sent a telegraphic message to create the first telephone exchange in 1878 and lay the groundwork for what now is a global system for rapid communication.

Communication efficiencies as well as the introduction of steam engines from the 1760s to the 1830s ushered in a new age of growth in product and process technologies representing a leap in technological innovations called the Industrial Revolution. The years from 1880 to 1930 to follow were shaped by the spread of electrical power, mass production in the industrial countries, and a new age for work in those countries.

The rate of innovation changes with the Industrial Revolution

Two hundred and fifty years ago, each of the many parts needed to assemble a watch were individually crafted by a master watchmaker, an assistant, and one to three apprentices; the time involved to produce a watch was about a month, and its estimated cost in 1994 US dollars was $10,000 (Makridakis, 1989). This system of production was called a 'craft' system because it took one or more workers to create an individually crafted product. The continued existence of watch-making, paper production, furniture-making, and other arts and crafts within geographic regions depended heavily on the expertise of the craftsperson and his or her willingness to train others in the trade. The number of jobs thereby created from this mode of production was necessarily limited by the teaching skills of the craftsperson and the limited demand for products made costly by the amount of human labor required for production.

No previous change in history had quite such a revolutionary effect on work as introduction of steam power in the 1770s. Changes brought about by the steam engine, whether large or small, profoundly altered the nature of work as well as daily life. One of the most important technological breakthroughs that resulted from steam power was that goods could be mass-produced in a factory process. Steam-powered machinery made it possible to manufacture in batches rather than single items, thus moving many crafts into industrial production. This shift in how work could be accomplished eventually led to a massive movement of people from agrarian work on farms to industrial work in towns and cities.

The organization of labor also changed. Assembly work enabled producers to reduce costs and generate more affordable goods for a wider range of buyers. But factory production also created challenges for business enterprises. As the number of people working in assembly increased, so did the need for ways to organize work, and assembly work was standardized and regulated. For example, factory work required laborers to work simultaneously and this meant that all had to arrive at the same time rather than at individually convenient times. This brought about demand for punctuality among workers, and caused people to become more attentive to time. Moreover, owners recognized that efficiency was improved if everyone completed the same tasks in the same ways, and so workers were discouraged from innovating. Thus, work was not only standardized but routinized so that many people could be trained for the same job. One effect was that the specialized knowledge of the craftsperson was no longer central to the production process. Additionally, responsibility for deciding how and when the job was to be completed shifted from the individual craftsperson to the owner whose job it became to organize the workplace.

Eventually, as assembly work grew in popularity and as organizations grew in size, factory owners found it impossible or impractical to coordinate and control all organizational functions. Increasingly, owners hired professional managers to help them make or enforce decisions. These managers not only saw to it that workers arrived on time, they also established rewards and punishments, allocated resources, and otherwise accomplished the many activities now identified as traditional management tasks: plan, organize, delegate, and control the work of others. Although it might not seem so today, replacing owners with professional managers represented a revolutionary change in management. This change is chronicled by Alfred Chandler in his fascinating book *The visible hand* (1977), so named because its author showed how management practices within business enterprises came to replace the 'invisible hand' of market mechanisms in coordinating economic activities. Whether as owner or as professional employee, the manager's challenge included reshaping worker attitudes toward work. The example in Box 9.1 shows how business needs shaped cultural and social values toward work.

In the early phases of industrialization, goods could not be distributed much beyond nations or regions because few distribution systems were in place. Early constraints on business such as these together with high demand conditions and growing competition in local and regional markets caused factory owners and managers to focus much of their attention on factors internal to the organization, particularly managing people and production. The propensity to focus on internal concerns was well ingrained, and changed little, when steamships and railroads made international expansion possible. Often this expansion involved acquiring raw materials in developing economies, adding value in the manufacturer's nation, and then selling finished goods at home and abroad.

Technological spin-offs to personal and family life

The shift from craft to assembly work also transformed individual lives. Having taken jobs in factories, people working for cash had need to purchase goods like food that previously had been self-produced. This created challenges but also provided benefits many sought. For example, many could afford mass-produced items like pocket watches that

BOX 9.1:   WORK RESHAPES BEHAVIORS

At the dawn of the Industrial Revolution, industry required disciplined workers, but English workers proved themselves to be transient, restless, and often absent, especially at the beginning of the week. Further, when at work, people preferred to work intensely for periods of time and then to slack off, but this was contrary to assembly work demands for steady routines. Work rules were imposed to instill discipline, including threats of dismissal, fines, and even beatings. Rewards such as payment based on results of work and subcontracting for group labor often were used to motivate adults. Finally, work was equated with moral values, and play with sloth and lack of Christian character. According to some, the drive to morally uplift the working class was linked more to the need for factory discipline than to any real concern for working-class souls.

Source: Pollard, Sidney. (1963, Dec.). Factory discipline in the Industrial Revolution. *Economic History Review*, Second Series, 26(7): 254–271.

previously had been available only to the rich. These and similar symbols of new affluence doubtless led many to prefer assembly labor over agricultural work. This revolution ushered in an era of increasing demand for goods and services, and may have been the birth of a consumer society where people acquired goods more wanted than needed.

Other changes resulting from industrialization affected where and how people lived and worked. In order to produce in mass, people assembled around factories, creating cities as they abandoned village and farm life. Thus, one result of the Industrial Revolution was creation and expansion of urban areas. Urbanization also generated a massive change in individual lives and a reorganization of social/cultural units. The relative autonomy and variety of agrarian labor was replaced by assembly labor where jobs and time were standardized and regulated. As has proved true under conditions of globalization, behavioral changes in one sphere of life or in one aspect of work did not lead to an overnight alteration in attitudes or behaviors in other spheres. Culture changes at a slower pace than technology changes. For example, just as all members of the family – including children – contributed to farm work, so they all initially worked for pay in factories. Accordingly, it was not unusual for children as young as 9 or 10 years old to work six-day weeks, toiling in factories for 12–16 hours at a stretch. While this practice is held in low regard in the advanced economies today, seen in the context of time and place it is less surprising. Finally, it is important to recognize that standardization and regularization of factory work meant that the worker became a cog, and a replaceable cog at that, in the industrial process. Thus, while there were benefits associated with factory work, there were also costs. An individual cost of mechanization was loss of autonomy. Because factory workers were hired less for their minds than their ability to complete repetitive tasks efficiently, employees and employers alike sacrificed or ignored the organizational potential of individual innovation and of what we now call knowledge work.

FIVE CHANGES RESULTING FROM INDUSTRIALIZATION

Daniel Rodgers (1978) believes the Industrial Revolution brought about five changes to society between 1750 and 1830. These included the shifts from agricultural to industrial economies and urbanization in the Western world that were explored above. Additionally, this earlier revolution led to

(a) unprecedented population growth;
(b) an unprecedented high standard of living, and doubling of average life span in developed countries;
(c) continuous technological introduction and change that created a sense of constant change, and more change coming.

Viewed as constant and almost unstoppable, much as technological breakthroughs of globalization are viewed, the changes occasioned by the Industrial Revolution also were viewed with alarm. Having witnessed the social disruptions brought about by urbanization, industrialization, and labor standardization, many felt that machines would diminish or replace human labor. The most extreme form of reaction came from a group called the Luddites who attacked mechanical textile looms in a vain attempt to preserve weavers' jobs. Rapid government action quickly quelled the brief-lived Luddite movement, but the name lives on among those who question the efficacy of technological change or try to impede its progress. Today's neo-Luddites often are those who call for a return to a simple life less cluttered with 'things' that people want but do not need. Others believe that just as industrial machinery made workers another cog in the wheel of progress, computers can reshape humans along machine-like lines, causing them to substitute that which is most human for automaton-like behaviors. According to Stephen Talbott (1995), when people link into computer networks, important human qualities may be lost.

Others cannot legitimately be called Luddites, but they do concern themselves with where technology is taking humankind and whether it is anywhere people should want to go. Futurists, for example, suggest that unintended, unknown, and delayed consequences of technologies may prove more important in the long run than the intended effects. Table 9.2 illustrates how third-, fourth-, and fifth-order consequences of a new

TABLE 9.2   The effects of television technology

First order	Second order	Third order	Fourth order	Fifth order	Sixth order
People have a source of entertainment and enlightenment in their homes	People stay home more, rather than going out to where they would meet others	Residents of a community meet less often and do not know each other well	As strangers, community members find it difficult to unite on common problems; individuals are isolated and alienated from neighbors	Isolated from others, family members depend more on each other for satisfaction of most psychological needs	Inability to satisfy psychological demands of the family may lead to frustrations taken out on each other; divorce or abuse may follow

Source: *The art of forecasting*. (1993). Bethesda, MD: World Future Society.

technology such as television have the potential to diminish rather than enhance quality of life in a global community.

The pace of technological change is increasing

Digital electronics, miniaturization, telecommunications, computers, robotics, artificial intelligence, genetic engineering, low-flying satellites, and laser conductors are only a few among many product technologies revolutionizing relationships today between people and organizations worldwide. Medical breakthroughs from birth control to disease control bring more people to the workplace; product and process breakthroughs constantly alter the nature of their work; and information-based technologies have made people and information a critical resource for organizations. By 1994 the time-piece that took artisans a month to craft for a price equivalent to $10,000, 200 years earlier could be manufactured for less than $1 in under a minute.

Technological breakthroughs are accelerating at a rate directly proportional to falling technological barriers worldwide. Corporations are racing to take advantage of this trend and many are finding opportunities. One opportunity is that organizations can hire skilled and educated workers from around the world. International Data Solutions, for example, scans case and client files for US law firms and transmits them in digital form via satellite to the Philippines. There, workers organize and index the documents for ready retrieval by a computer network in the US. International Data employs two full time employees in Virginia, and up to 3,000 Filipinos. 'With the Information Superhighway revolution, this trend is accelerating dramatically,' says International Data

President Kenneth R. Short. 'It really doesn't matter where the work is done as long as quality, price, and service are right' (Engardio, 1994a, p. 119). Accelerating speed of change also is altering industry organization; examples from the telecommunications industry illustrate this point (Box 9.2).

BOX 9.2: USA GLOBAL LINK PARTNERS WITH PT INDONESIA SATELLITE

Only a few years ago, costly international calls and computers created an opportunity to develop a telecommunications niche called telephone call-back services. For example, call-back customers to the US can pay lower rates by dialing a US number, then hanging up. The computer then returns the call to provide a phone line billed at domestic rather than international rates; savings can be as much as 50%. Now, however, growing telecommunications competition worldwide has caused the price of long-distance calling to fall, thus reducing customer costs and niche player's opportunities. As a result, one of the major US call-back service providers, Global Link, has joined forces with Indonesia's main telephone company, PT Indonesia Satellite, to install telephone switches in Germany and Japan to create a hybrid service linking switches with leased fiber-optic cables worldwide. This allows both companies to participate in the global telecommunications market, not just as call-back providers but also within domestic service areas.

Source: Schenker, Jennifer L. (1996, June 24). USA Global Link aims to change focus from the 'call-back' phone business. *The Wall Street Journal*, p. A9B.

SIMILARITIES BETWEEN THE INDUSTRIAL AND INFORMATION REVOLUTIONS

The greatest similarities between these two revolutions are that both have generated profound changes in how human labor can be organized, and both have stimulated discussion of the role work and organizations play in human life. In the Information Age, reorganization of the work environment has led to challenges for traditional notions of work and organization that were a direct result of the Industrial Revolution. Specific challenges to traditional organizational practices include the following: organizations should be hierarchically organized; low-cost labor is low-skill labor; or managers should make all the important decisions. Additionally, as occurred in the Industrial Revolution, the Information Age has generated questions relating to the purpose and social function of business enterprises.

Changes in work organization

Like the Industrial Revolution, the Information Revolution is producing changes in how work is organized. For example, just as the Industrial Revolution caused people to abandon work at home to assemble products in factories and offices, the Information Revolution makes it possible for people to 'telecommute' and thus accomplish work from home or other locales. Despite evident benefits of telecommuting, including greater freedom to live where one wants or eliminating travel time to work, second- and third-order outcomes of telecommuting may include reduced human contact and social isolation. Slow or uncertain mail systems that deter communication can now be avoided with facsimile telephone communication, and among those nations linked to the Internet another means of rapid communication is e-mail. From a perspective in advanced economies where many have resources like telephones and personal computers, it is easy to forget that people in developing economies may not have similar access. In fact, over half the world's people have never used a telephone and 80% do not have a phone in their homes; only about 7% of the Latin American population have access to a telephone, and as the opening case demonstrates, few in Africa have access to telephones. In many developing economies, changes brought about by the Information Revolution accompany those brought about by industrialization. People newly introduced to telephones also are introduced to fax capabilities, CAD/CAM (computer aided design/computer aided manufacturing) design, computerization, and other icons of the Information Age at the same time.

The rush to accumulate wealth worldwide has created a consumer society anxious to experiment with new products and services. Improved telephone technology extends the reach of business activities to many more homes, businesses, and nations. In the process of reaching out in this way, organizational participants find that new markets generate new ways of accomplishing work. For example, marketers find that newer telephone users are more receptive to telemarketers. Improvements in information management make it possible to produce goods in response to individual demands, to tailor products to smaller and smaller buyer groups such as DINKs (double income, no kids), and to segment and target micro-instead of mass markets. For example, CNN Marketing and American Express teamed up to profile 10% of the latter's Italian users, using that information for a direct mail campaign to 300,000 Italians who fit the profile. This saved American Express the costs of a mass mail appeal bound to be less successful. For most organizations, and particularly those that are large and established, these opportunities do not come without change. Any internal change intended to make the firm adaptable to global markets – whether initiated as an alteration in structure, processes, or people – is bound to affect all three internal dimensions of organization.

Changes in work relationships

The Information Revolution has the capacity also to change many work relationships. For example, as information becomes more important to organizations, status and organizational power can increasingly be gained through access to information the organization wants and needs. The ability to acquire this information may depend less on traditional training or tenure, and more on intuition or creativity. If this is the case, then it may be possible for young people with limited training to take managerial roles that once were reserved for people more seasoned by prior work experience. Further, it is probable that workplaces increasingly will be populated with people who come from diverse backgrounds and approach organizational challenges in diverse ways. There is already evidence of a shift from exclusive use of hierarchical organizations to flatter or 'horizontal' structures in some organizations, and many firms employ people all over the globe. Contrary to the popular notion that low wages mean low-skill workers, many lower cost workers in the developing economies are as well educated for their work as people in the industrialized world, if not more so. The example of software development in Bangalore – India's Silicon Valley – illustrates this point (Box 9.3).

Within organizations, information technology also has brought about changes in how work is accomplished. More people now work with computers for some part of their day, and internal as well as external communications increasingly occur via the Internet. In the example in Box 9.4, Chrysler's experience with an intranet set up as a private

---

BOX 9.3: INDIA'S SILICON VALLEY

The $485 million in software work produced annually in India represents only a tiny portion of the $85–150 billion estimated annual worth of the software industry, but it represents 125,000 jobs for software engineers, many of whom are located in Bangalore near the southern tip of India. Educational attainment in India is highly valued, but until recently, few Indian software engineers could apply their skills globally. Advent of the Internet has transferred current software expertise throughout the world, including Bangalore, and a shortage of software engineers in the US sends firms there on a search for talented workers. According to one estimate, as many as 75 Fortune 500 companies have started contracting with India for software development, including Nordstrom and Microsoft.

Source: Bjorhus, Jennifer. (1996, Sept. 15). A byte of India. *Seattle Times*, pp. E1,E2.

internal model of the Internet shows that change can provide opportunities but often is difficult to implement.

BOX 9.4:   CHRYSLER'S INTRANET

Intranets are private, scale models of the Internet's World Wide Web, and they allow employees to communicate internally, rapidly, and at reduced costs. In addition to paper saved by using electronic messaging, benefits also allow a broader scope of information sharing, and time and money savings. According to Zona Research, business investments in intranets could rise five-fold from $2.6 billion in 1996 to $13 billion in 1999. Chrysler's experience with an intranet demonstrates there are opportunities and there are costs. Their intranet system proved to be a cheaper, faster, and more convenient way for managers to communicate with staffers and reduce burdensome paperwork. For example, when large-car-platform program manager Ken Nestico recognized a way to save $2 per car, he immediately sent an e-mail action letter authorizing the cost saving. At the other end of the e-mail, the engineer in charge somehow missed seeing the message and Chrysler missed two to three months of savings before the oversight was discovered. The moral of this story is that habits such as paying most attention to paper directives are not easily overcome in an established organization. This example shows that cultural changes often need to accompany technical changes to implement a successful change initiative.

Source: White, Joseph B. (1997, May 13). Chrysler's intranet: Promise vs. reality. *The Wall Street Journal*, pp. B1, B7.

ALTERATIONS IN THE WORK/SOCIAL LIFE MIX

As was true for the Industrial Revolution, many fear the Information Revolution will foster undesirable changes in work and social life. For example, the advantage of constant communication provided by fax, telephone, and the Internet also can tether a person to work, reducing the amount of time available for rest, social, or family life. Within the US, many stockbrokers located on the West Coast now find it desirable to rise at 5 a.m. to participate in the opening of the New York Stock Exchange and work through the evening until the Tokyo exchange opens. In other industries, a customer service orientation means staffing stores, medical clinics, and social services for 24-hour, 7-day weeks. In the US, the benefit to consumers of all-day, every day retailing is offset by personal costs to sales clerks working these hours, often through weekends and holidays. Thus, a customer service orientation can produce greater strains for employees.

With telecommuting, borders between work and non-work are blurred, and there are possible sacrifices of personal and professional privacy. Not only can employers look into telecommuters' computers, but businesses can look into household patterns via interactive television/computer networks, and Internet links have the potential to develop individual profiles based on websites visited. These and similar challenges have caused many worldwide to feel that technological advances in information also have costs.

DIFFERENCES BETWEEN THE REVOLUTIONS
Increased reliance on intangibles

Unlike the land, labor, and capital factors so important to economic growth during the Industrial Revolution, the driving force behind the Information Revolution is an intangible: information and, more specifically, knowledge. According to Richard Saul Wurman (1991), the supply of information available in a weekday edition of the *New York Times* contains more information than the average person was likely to encounter in a lifetime in seventeenth-century England. The amount of information available had been doubling every five years, but now may be doubling every two years. A quick glance over Table 9.3 reflects how much personal and professional lives have changed just since 1983. Given the ever-increasing amount of information available to us in an average day, what may be most amazing is that we actually get anything more done than just take it in.

In view of information abundance, it is important to distinguish between data and the sort of information needed to generate knowledge. Data are the collection of facts like numbers, names, or values; these can be derived from experiments, but without interpretation, they have no inherent meaning. Moreover, as we saw when we looked at different GDP calculations in Chapter 5 on global economy, data are not always reliable or may not always mean what we think they mean. Moreover, the same data can be manipulated to argue for different points of view. When data are processed, manipulated,

TABLE 9.3   Information Age change

Increase in number of computers in US offices between 1983 and 1994: 25,000,000
The number of days for World Wide Web pages to double since 1995: every 53 days
Percentage of US people who say they do not have time to do all they want: 51%
Average Internet hours per week per US Internet household in 1996: 6.3
Hourly wage paid to Internet information guides: $100
Increased number of fax machines in US offices and homes between 1987 and 1994: 10,000,000
Annual weeks of time lost per US executive retrieving misplaced information: 6
The average number of e-mail messages sent every day in the US: 150 million
Increase in worldwide mobile phone subscribers between 1990 and 1995: 77 million
Increase in international telephone calls between 1990 and 1996: double to 62 billion minutes

or analyzed, the result can be information or its counterpart, disinformation, i.e., false information intended to mislead. Finally, information is the collection of all these facts or data derived from study, experience, or experiment and allows one to become more informed. Weighing this information to decide if it has value and assessing that value is the basis of knowledge creation. Students, for example, are bombarded with facts and data, making it essential for them to weigh and assimilate information into meaningful wholes that advance their knowledge. According to futurist Michael Marien (1997), the Information Revolution is having a negative effect on our thinking as information devoted to entertainment and commercial interests squeezes out information that could contribute to a better quality of life, stronger communities, and more useful knowledge. Nicholas Negroponte (1995) further notes that growing digitalization is likely to mean that every item of data ever recorded can be made accessible anytime and anywhere. What this means is that in a world where it is increasingly important to be informed, we face data overload. This information overload may have contributed to public reports attributing the explosion of TWA flight 800 in June 1996 to a US military mistake. A credible public figure believed he had been provided with accurate data, but it was later revealed the bogus report had been posted only on the Internet and then by an anonymous source. This example illustrates how important it has become to identify reliable sources of information. Doing so may become an important part of the knowledge creation challenge in the years ahead. Many will want to acquire skills for bringing information together at an ever-increasing rate to create knowledge; doing so is the result of and the input for the next phase of the Information Revolution.

Speed of change

As compared to the Industrial Revolution, when technological change unfolded over many decades, the Information Revolution is unfolding much more rapidly. In technology-dependent industries like computers, pharmaceuticals, or bio-engineering, revolutionary changes are introduced not over decades but sometimes in months and even weeks or days. According to a survey of 200 US firms conducted by the Product Development and Management Association, products are faster to market not only because designers can communicate quickly via electronic links but also because manufacturing speeds are quicker. For example, Hewlett Packard reported that in the 1980s it took four years to design and manufacture a new ink-jet printer, but by 1996 development time had been reduced by 40%. Supercomputers and sophisticated software have reduced the need for expensively equipped biology labs or wind tunnels. Thanks to better instruments, more powerful simulations, and faster searches of scientific journals, 'we can do five times more in the labs than we did 15 years ago,' according to Joe A. Miller, Jr, senior vice-president for R&D at DuPont Co. At their desktops, today's scientists and engineers have more sophisticated software than their predecessors who built atomic power plants and rockets in the 1960s.

Potential for new equalities

Unlike the Industrial Revolution, the Information Revolution has made it possible for many to assume an equality that was never before possible. For example, despite whatever personal or hierarchical differences there might be between a manager and an employee, both often are privy to the same information. Further, according to Peter Drucker (1994), the higher up the ladder one goes in knowledge work, the more likely it is for men and women to be doing the same work. Thus, knowledge becomes an equalizer in terms of work performed and may also be an equalizer in terms of pay and other work opportunities. This equalization process has made it possible for human rights groups to gather information that governments have long been able to suppress, and for television and similar forms of entertainment to suggest new possibilities for gender, ethnic, and other forms of equality worldwide. Information sharing is yet another way that equality can be enhanced, and this form of sharing is creating many opportunities for individuals and business and challenges for the nations where they live.

Use of the term 'Information Revolution' to characterize contemporary change has drawn greatest attention to information technologies as a source of globalization. But other technologies also are developing rapidly worldwide, and they too have the capacity to change life as we know it. In 1995 and 1996, the most visionary technology experts at Battelle Laboratories were asked to identify top technologies for the next decade that would provide a benefit and a value to end users, offer businesses opportunities for a competitive advantage, and support a company's business goals. Giving proof to the argument for rapid technological change, the results of these 'top 10' lists below show that changes occurred in just one year's time; changes are shown in parentheses in the following list (Millet and Kopp, 1996; Oleson, 1995):

1 Genetaceuticals combining genetic research and pharmaceuticals (also ranked no. 1 in the 1995 survey, but then labeled genetic mapping).
2 Personalized computers (super materials were ranked no. 2 in 1995).
3 Multi-fuel vehicles capable of running on different fuels depending on geographic location and running speed of the vehicle (ranked no. 9 in 1995 when no. 3 was high-density energy sources).
4 Digital High Definition Television (HDTV) (also no. 4 in 1995).
5 Electronic cash (miniaturization was no. 5 in 1995).
6 Home health monitors (smart manufacturing was no. 6 in 1995).

7 Smart maps and tracking devices (anti-aging products held the seventh position in 1995).
8 Smart materials (analogous to super materials ranked no. 2 in 1995).
9 Weight control and anti-aging products and services.
10 Never-owned products are those products that become obsolete so rapidly, e.g. personal computers, that people lease rather than buy them (edutainment was no. 10 in 1995).

The preceding list of technologies for 2006 is targeted primarily at users in advanced and industrial economies. In Sub-Saharan Africa, where many go hungry every day, there's little likelihood of pent-up demand for weight control products or anti-aging remedies. More appropriate technologies there may be those that address challenges of resource scarcity or degradation; ways to renew exhausted land or procedures that curb diseases that mutate and re-emerge ever more resistant to scientific advances; and low-tech products that meet important daily needs. An important observation is that businesses are attending to the latter needs as well as to needs of consumer societies, responding to both through technological breakthroughs. According to founder Kono-suke Matsushita's enterprise strategy, 'the mission of a manufacturer should be to overcome poverty, to relieve society as a whole from misery, and bring it wealth' (Kotter, 1997, p. 109), a mission Matsushita has worked to realize by improving productivity and lowering costs to make more products cheaper and thus more accessible to everyone in the world.

The technological breakthroughs needed in much of the world may come from looking at existing problems in new ways; from combining new technologies with old ones; and from cross-industry fertilization in knowledge creation. Using all these approaches to technological innovations is most likely to lead to new products capable of improving the quality of all lives. Technological opportunities also arise from looking at present challenges with new eyes. For example, interest in technological improvements in bicycles was revived in 1995 when Owens Corning invited top design and engineering universities worldwide to undertake a Global Design Challenge to engineer a bicycle with glass-fiber components for less than $100. The Kangaroo design submitted by students from the University of São Paulo was declared a winner because of its adaptability to multiple uses and users worldwide. For example, the seats and handlebars can be adjusted to accommodate 95% of the world's population in terms of height and weight. Since the bicycle is the primary mode of transportation worldwide and is environmentally sustainable, this kind of breakthrough can be applied worldwide. BayGen also combined old and new technologies in 1995 with the wind-up radio (Box 9.5).

BayGen's wind-up radio provides one way to manage challenges people face.

BOX 9.5:   BAYGEN'S OPPORTUNITY

Earlier in this chapter, we noted that 80% of the world's population does not have an in-home telephone, and over 50% have never used a telephone. Most are located in Africa where other technologies such as electricity and radio also are limited. At the same time, more advanced technologies elsewhere highlight the plight of many Africans caught in the middle of ethnic conflict and strife. In response to this dilemma, a South African firm called BayGen began producing a wind-up radio able to produce sufficient electricity to receive short wave, AM, and FM signals for about 40 minutes. This device provides a communication break-through for developing economies and many war-torn sections of Africa, yet it operates much like a wind-up gramophone, is simple to use, inexpensive, and needs no batteries or plugs. Although far from high-technology, the self-winding radio represents an important technological breakthrough to link isolated people. Further, its discovery came more from looking to historical technologies of the gramophone than to current and promised telecommunications technologies.

Sources: McNeil, Donald, G. Jr. (1996, Feb. 16). This $40 crank up radio lets rural Africa tune in. *New York Times*, p. A1; Strassel, Kimberley A. (1997, July 15). Low-tech, windup radio makes waves. *The Wall Street Journal*, p. B1.

Remediation technologies also are needed in African and other nations to correct water, soil, and air degradation, and other, perhaps simple technologies also are needed to improve recycling efforts or avoid creating new landfills. These technologies call on con-temporary breakthroughs, but also may use existing technologies or turn toward older breakthroughs to examine them in new ways. For example, lightweight insulation from transparent aerogels has long offered the promise of temperature-retention because a single inch of aerogel provides the same amount of insulation as 10 inches of fiberglass. Discovery of a new process technology provides a way to produce aerogels safely and in a cheap continuous process rather than the more expensive batch process of the past. Similar breakthroughs have made it possible to replace metal in automobiles with cheaper, stronger, and lighter plastics and ceramics materials; to absorb oil spills with sawdust; to eliminate the odor of pig manure by mixing it with peanut shells. These high- and low-tech solutions to age-old challenges only scratch the surface of today's techno-logical revolution.

BREAKTHROUGH TECHNOLOGIES OF THE INFORMATION REVOLUTION

Most of the scientists who ever lived are living today, and their contributions to knowledge are shown in Figure 9.1. According to the *Encyclopedia of the future* (Kurian and Molitor, 1996), these scientists are doubling the pool of scientific information every 12 years. These facts suggest great knowledge potential for meeting both high- and low-technology challenges. Many scientists have contributed to the basic science of discovery that laid the groundwork for the Information Revolution while still others devote their energies to finding applications leading to the many products spawned by this revolution. The revolutionary changes introduced by new or improved products like computers, satellites, or laser optics have in turn led to a need for technological breakthroughs in the processes by which we accomplish tasks or produce goods. Whereas earlier we looked at the Information Revolution in a general way, in the following section we examine information-based technologies further to explore how they are changing work and personal lives.

The rapid rate of technological change has produced many product and process innovations in a relatively short period, and many have occurred during your lifetime. Because changes have occurred so rapidly, you may view technological breakthroughs and change not only as inevitable but as natural events to which we must adapt. Many would argue with this point of view, particularly those who believe that technological changes create social disruptions. Disruptions might occur in the family as children and younger adults begin to speak a language older family members don't share. Words like 'bit' or 'byte,' 'RAM and ROM,' that you use naturally may have little or no meaning for others, but as important as the words, the technology itself remains foreign and inaccessible to those who did not grow up with computers. Not only might they feel the Information Age is leaving them behind, but they might also feel that by embracing information

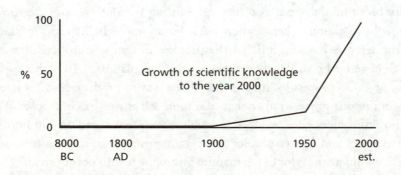

FIGURE 9.1 *Growth of scientific knowledge* (Merrifield, Bruce. (1994, Apr. 4). Wharton School. *Fortune*, p. 75)

technology young family members reject beliefs and traditional values. As all of us watch more television, or spend more time interacting with a computer, there is less time to engage in traditional family activities. Thus, some believe that information technology represents a disruption of the established social system. Similarly, in the workplace, we tend to interact less with one another on a face-to-face basis and to interact more via computer, fax, and other forms of distant contact. All of this means changes not only in the social structure, but changes also in how the organization is structured, and how work is accomplished.

Computers and digital electronics

According to Makridakis (1989), today's technological revolution began in the 1940s when the concept of the computer could be demonstrated mathematically. Since then computerization has been at or near the heart of technological revolutions occurring almost worldwide. Digitalization or translation of signals into 0s and 1s readily understood by computers and other digital devices represents a breakthrough over analog devices because digitalization makes it possible to generate, process, store, and transmit text, graphics, or sound from one digital device to another (Burrus and Gittines, 1993). Telephones previously able only to transmit sound can through digitalization also transmit graphics, video images, and text.

Computer concepts were first applied in 1944 with the technological breakthrough offered by an automatic sequence machine, a lumbering behemoth that absorbed more space than a typical US house of 2,200 square feet but had less computing power than today's standard scientific pocket calculator. By 1952, the first commercial electronic computer was made available. Soon called mainframes, the enormous computers available for business use usually were housed in isolation to protect them from dust or unexpected jolts and cool the tremendous heat they generated. However, so great was general interest in computers that the isolation rooms often had many windows for the curious to observe these unique machines.

THE DATA PROCESSING ERA OF COMPUTER USE

Using Richard Nolan's Stages Theory of business demand for information services, Bradley, Hausman, and Nolan (1993) characterized this early stage of computer use in businesses as the Data Processing Era (DP). Spanning 1960–1980, the DP Era was dominated by mainframes that improved organizational efficiencies. Many of these efficiencies were difficult to achieve initially because computers were new to organizations and required new ways of thinking and acting. For example, early mainframes read data from computer cards punched with the requisite array of 0s and 1s on a specialized machine. The cards then were ordered and submitted to the computer for batch processing, but woe betide the user who accidently mispunched a critical card or submitted cards out of sequence; the computer would terminate the job and spit the cards back for reordering or corrections. Owing to the relatively high cost and training needed to use them in the DP Era, computers were adopted primarily within industries that processed vast volumes of information, e.g., banking, where computers handled repetitive tasks easily and efficiently. It took about 10–15 years for firms to assemble enough automation equipment and sufficient learning to realize economies, and most of these economies were achieved by laying off factory and clerical employees engaged in repetitive work. The layoffs associated with this early era of computerization, and the challenges faced in learning to use computers, led to worries that computers would displace people or interfere with ordinary human activity. The latter concern was fueled by frequent claims that 'the computer ate it' when something went wrong at work, and by popular fiction and films. For example, the film of Arthur C. Clarke's book *2001: A space odyssey* depicted 'HAL' as a thinking computer that shut down human life-support systems to prevent harm to him. Box 9.6 provides an update on the 'HAL' image.

BOX 9.6:   HAPPY BIRTHDAY, HAL

According to the filmed version of Arthur C. Clarke's book *2001: A space odyssey*, HAL was 'born' on January 12, 1997. In honor of HAL's birthday, artificial intelligence (AI) leaders were asked to comment on how close people are to creating a real-life HAL for the year 2001. AI is a field that explores the extent to which computers can simulate human thought processes. Many of these AI experts believe that real-life computers have advanced in graphics and networking far beyond those HAL could achieve. At the same time, most conclude that, unlike the fictional HAL, computers cannot reason nor can they engage in the complex thought processes that distinguish people from machines.

Source: Stork, David. (1997). *HAL's legacy: 2001's computer as dream and reality*. Boston, MA: MIT Press.

Although the DP Era of computer use in organizations has passed, mainframes remain important but they are no longer the physical behemoths they once were. Today's mainframes are far smaller machines that provide significantly more computing power. Used to manage tasks involving millions of calculations like those required by the weather service or to model nuclear explosions, a 1996 IBM mainframe could perform 3 trillion numerical calculations per second. These supercomputers not only operate at high speed, they also offer vast improvements for data storage. This kind of data storage is essential for organizations that process data, and computers can provide storage space on disk that is almost impossible to realize otherwise. For example, in 1995 IBM announced that laboratory tests had demonstrated a new world record for magnetic-data storage density of 3 billion bits, which was nearly five times the density of the most advanced disk available. By 1997, the lab capability for hard disk storage stood at 11.6 billion bits which would fit 725,000 double spaced typed pages (the equivalent of about 12 books) on each square inch of disk. In paper, the same information would rise to form a stack 241 feet high or taller than a fifteen-story building. The visual view of the transition from Data Processing to Micro to Network Eras represented by Figure 9.2 suggests that these technological developments occurred over a relatively short period of time to move work from an industrial to an information-based economy.

THE MICRO ERA

The first miniaturized computer using transistors rather than vacuum tubes was available in 1960 but Intel's 1971 introduction of a second-generation microprocessor was what made the personal computer or PC possible. As distinguished from the DP Era, which replaced repetitive work with computers, the Microcomputer Era leveraged the work of professionals and incorporated microcomputers directly into firm products and

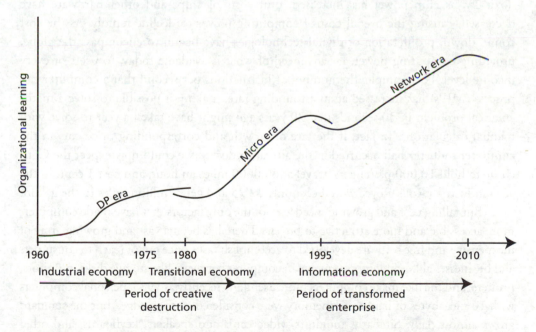

FIGURE 9.2 *Nolan's stage theory of computer use in business* (Bradley, Stephen. P., Hausman, Jerry A., and Nolan, Richard L. (1993). Global competition and technology. In *Globalization, technology and competition*, pp. 3–33. Boston, MA: Harvard Business School Press). (© 1992 Richard L. Nolan)

services. Products ranging from automobiles to toys to credit cards were not only manufactured with the use of microcomputers but some, like autos, were themselves equipped with microcomputers. Like the DP Era, microcomputers also replaced workers, particularly professionals working in the middle of the organization; this included engineers and middle managers as well as administrative secretaries and other support personnel. Further, post-1975, the microcomputer became accessible to individuals and to smaller, resource-poor organizations. Worldwide personal computer sales experienced growth averaging about 21% per year from 1991 to 1995, and 25% in 1996, but fell to about 16% in 1997. Personal computers have become increasingly accessible because of what has been called 'Moore's Law.'

MOORE'S LAW

In 1965, Intel's Gordon Moore predicted that the computing power of chips would double every 18 months. He revised the prediction in 1975 when it became clear that computer chip power had doubled roughly every two years. This pace of change has been made possible by succeeding waves of technological breakthroughs. For example, an important announcement in 1997 was that IBM had found a way to substitute copper for aluminum and thereby improve chip speed by 40% and reduce costs by 30%. Paradoxically, as chip power has increased, unit costs of chips and other hardware have decreased, causing the overall cost of computing power to decline rapidly. As the cost comes down, proliferation of digital technologies have begun to encompass the globe, providing computing power, far advanced of what is available today, to users of every income level. For example, the number of instructions per second that a computer can process (MIPs) has increased at an astounding rate, making it possible to solve a mathematical problem in 30 seconds that 20 years ago might have taken a year to solve with manual calculations. In fact, if the rate of growth and corresponding price cuts in the computer industry had occurred in the aircraft industry, we could now expect the Concorde to hold 10,000 passengers, travel at 60,0000 miles an hour, and cost 1 cent; in the auto industry a Rolls-Royce would cost only $2.75 and get 3 million miles to the gallon.

But falling cost and growing speed are not the only factors that have made computers more accessible and more attractive to buyers. There has been a vast and growing array of inexpensive and free software developed to accomplish tasks once out of reach to consumers and businesses alike, and improvements in computer hardware like storage disks, monitors, printers, and the like make computers more useful. As recently as 1985, personal computers with 10 megabytes of hard drive memory were considered 'cutting edge,' but the standard grows almost daily. Similarly, monitors, video cards and speakers, keyboards, and other components of computers are daily becoming both more sophisticated and less costly.

No one knows for sure how many transistors can fit on a tiny bit of silicon, but the number continues to grow. For example, in one decade, the number of components on a chip doubled each year from 1 in 1960 to 1,000 in 1970. Since then the number of components has doubled every 18 months, reaching 1 billion in 1992 (Morrison and Schmid, 1997). An interesting factoid of computer technology is that the average consumer of today now wears more computer power in the form of a wristwatch than existed in the entire world before 1950. More remarkably, the cost of producing exponential computer power has gone down, despite the tremendous increase in computer capacity.

THE NETWORK ERA

According to Bradley, Hausman, and Nolan, (1993), the third or Network Era of computer use at work evolved for two reasons: to meet combined demands for automating repetitive work and leveraging professional work and a need to support smarter products and services. Local area networks (LANs) to link teams of engineers electronically within the same firm expanded to create internal and external networks of scientists, consumers, government officials, and others; even computers within automobiles now are networked internally and in some other cities they can be linked externally as well, to directional devices.

Changes in how computers were used and who used them also affected development of industries related to computerization. Some of these effects appear in Box 9.7.

BOX 9.7: TECHNOLOGICAL CHANGE REDEFINES INDUSTRIES

In the 1960s the computer industry was populated entirely by mainframe producers, but introduction of the personal computer in 1977 divided this industry into two. Subsequent technological development further divided hardware and software industries, and entire new industries emerged. For example, software originally was an undifferentiated market but markets developed for communication software, personal finances, business spreadsheets, and the like. More recently, business activities have again redefined industry environments for both hardware and software. For example, Microsoft Corporation developed Internet software to participate in the telecommunications industry, and also is linking telecommunications and entertainment in a business called DreamWorks that includes top managers of visual entertainment.

Home use of computers

In the US, computers for home use were popularized by Apple Computers. Apple machines were almost exclusively used in US schools, and were an early means of introducing children to this new technology. Children took a matter-of-fact approach to computers, found them to be fun, and often agitated for home purchase of machines they used at school. Home use stimulated by Apple also was nurtured by other global enterprises. For example, Vtech Holdings Ltd offered computer-based educational toys in response to growing recognition of a need for computer skills among children. In 1996, Vtech's share of US computer-based educational toys reached 70%, even though the firm is headquartered in Hong Kong, and hires design teams in China. Part of its success is due to talented engineers in China who work for salaries of about $5,000 US per year as compared to about $40,000 for US-based engineers.

Growing evidence of home use for computers motivated IBM to introduce a personal computer in 1981; the PC was targeted at business and home use, and ran on a DOS operating system that made a first fortune for Microsoft Corporation founders. Growth in business and home use continued in the US, powered in part by exponential growth in the computing power of chips that made computers more than toys. An array of home business software, from spreadsheets to personal financial management to retirement planning, fueled home use, and business adaptation also expanded because computers had become relatively easy to operate.

Home use of the PC followed the same post-1980 trajectory as business use, progressing rapidly from stand-alone microprocessors to a more networked approach. Sales of personal computers to households began to grow in 1993, stimulated primarily by falling prices and by growing awareness of the important role computers had begun to play in education, in business, and in connecting people to the world via the Internet and other media. Enhancements in video technologies formerly available only on televisions or with special, stand-alone game boxes were folded into computer technology, making the computer a multi-use product.

Almost one-third of US households owned computers by 1995, and according to market research firm Computer Intelligence (a unit of Softbank Corporation of Japan) 40% of US households were using computers by 1996. This boom in home use went global in about 1995, stimulated by price drops and by growing availability of foreign-language software. Since fewer households abroad own computers, they represent a vast opportunity for growth in PC sales worldwide. According to a study by Link Resources reported in the *Wall Street Journal* (Foreign markets, 1995), foreign sales are expected to be more than double US sales by 2000, going from 33.4 million units sold to 72.3 million. At the same time, US sales also are expected to grow from 24.7 to 44.4 million units between 1995 and 2000 (Martin, 1996) (Figure 9.3). PC prices outside the US as well as inside continue to fall, and like US consumers, households throughout the world also are rushing to meet educational, entertainment, and at-home work objectives. For example, high-capacity disk drives like CD-ROMs make it possible to acquire low-cost software libraries to support education and work at home. Materials ranging from telephone directories to dictionaries, almanacs, census information, thesauruses, and encyclopedias all can be part of a home reference library. In addition to providing video and

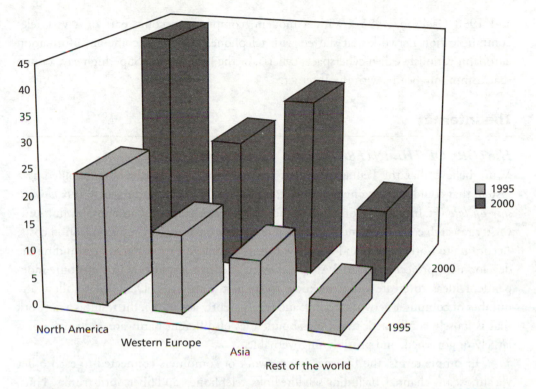

FIGURE 9.3 *Personal computer shipments in millions* (Martin, Michael H. (1996, Oct. 28). When info worlds collide. *Fortune*, p. 131)

sound, CD-ROM versions of library references provide a low-cost and timeliness advantage with which the book publishing industry cannot compete: they are updated every three months or less as compared to three years for most encyclopedias in book form at one-tenth the cost of a book version (Tapscott, 1996).

Building the guts of this digital world, the hardware, software, and microprocessors, will realign the computer and information industries. Advances are introduced so rapidly that video games available to children often have the graphics power of a 1980s vintage Cray supercomputer. It is expected that by the year 2010, the same device will fit in the palm of your hand and deliver photo-perfect images on a razor-thin display. By then, too, the transmission speeds of optical fibers will have jumped a hundred-fold, enabling a strand of glass thinner than a human hair to carry a full-length movie in a fraction of a second.

Although the computer is powered by ordinary electrical lines, it becomes networked to other machines and to most of the services described above through telephone lines reached through internal or external modems. Once able to transmit data only at a speed of 300 bits per minute, the standard went from there to 28,800 bits and growing, and this is one reason modem sales are expected to grow at 17% worldwide between 1994 and 1998 (Jackson, 1995). With a modem, computers become part of a vast tele-communication network that started with telephones and has become an information autobahn variously called cyberspace, cyberia, or the Information Superhighway, a route that commonly begins with the Internet.

The internet

HISTORY OF THE INTERNET

Many believe that the Pentagon project that fostered the Internet was intended as a system that could survive a nuclear attack, but according to the authors of *Where wizards stay up late* (Hafner and Lyon, 1996), the Internet was primarily an effort to link university research computers and scientists and save a little money in communication costs. According to Katie Hafner and Matthew Lyon, the collegial atmosphere surrounding the development project called ARPANET allowed scientists worldwide to contribute independent ideas to create what we know today as the Internet. Designed to allow any number of computer networks to link and transparently act as one, the result is a network that is loosely configured, transcends boundaries of different hardware and software, is largely ungoverned, and possibly ungovernable.

In simple terms, the Internet is a network of computers connected to each other via almost any channel, including satellite links, telephones, and fiber-optic trunks. Thus, the Internet is a network of networks. Connections to these networks are not visible to the user, but they make it possible to send and receive electronic mail (e-mail); transfer files from home computers to remote servers and vice versa; gather news; peruse research findings; and otherwise engage in activities that bridge traditional boundaries of time, place, and even propriety. Any form of information transferred via the Internet is sent in the form of compressed digital packets of 0s and 1s that go from their source to a router that then sends each to its destination address. The route taken depends not on geographic proximity but rather on line availability so that two messages from the same person can take different routes to arrive at the same destination. Figure 9.4 illustrates in simplified form relationships that are invisible to users.

ACCESS TO THE INTERNET

Beginning at a workstation or computer equipped with a modem, the Internet user dials into a host computer linked to the Internet. Once linked to the Internet, the personal computer transcends the limits of its own software by means of a common Internet protocol called TCP/IP (Transmission Control Protocol/Internet Protocol) that serves as a bridge to information available worldwide. Host computers or servers can service a few or many thousands of users, but most are maintained by commercial services or large institutions such as universities and governments. These servers typically store news and

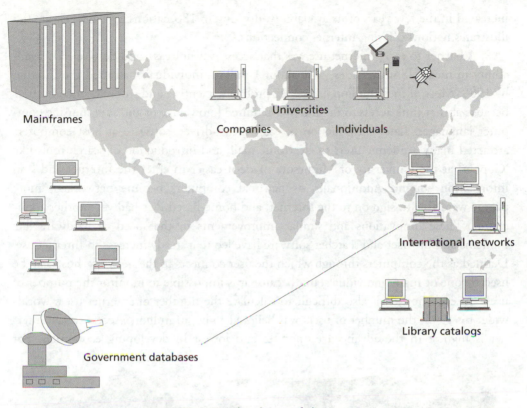

Mainframes

Universities

Companies

Individuals

International networks

Government databases

Library catalogs

FIGURE 9.4 *The shape of the internet*

reference material, private electronic messages, and public collections of messages on what are known as public bulletin boards. Servers also can contain large documents, graphics, or computer programs made available to all users.

Some of the most popular servers initially were located at colleges and universities throughout the world; these servers were popular because educational institutions usually provide access to the Internet at no direct cost to the individual user. However, several fee-for-service vendors saw an opportunity to attract users outside academic circles, and as commercial restrictions on the Internet have been relaxed, even more commercial entities have popped up to provide fee-based access to the Internet. Popular commercial hosts in the US include America Online, CompuServe, and Prodigy; fee-paying users in Japan often access the Internet via PC-Van or Nifty-Serve; Europeans also tap into CompuServe. Any of these or other commercial services provides easy-to-use menu-driven software to connect to servers and navigate through the material they contain and into the Internet. Further, front-end software packages called browsers make accessing tools and services relatively easy for the user. International connectivity to the Internet has increased in the few years of its availability, drawing in 186 nations by 1996. Figure 9.5 illustrates nations offering Internet connections.

A barrier to early Internet use was that access was not easy, and despite early availability in most US universities, only about 1 million individuals had used the Internet by 1988. Most of these million users were probably scientists and students of computers because at that time access to the Internet required knowledge of and skill in using computer languages. Later introduction of easy, menu-driven software at host computers attracted many academic users to electronic mail, and introduction of search tools like 'Gopher' at the University of Minnesota made it easier to enter the Internet and find information sought. Additionally, as personal computers became networked, more people were able to sign on to the Internet, and home-based PCs had yet another application. These innovations and similar improvements in the speed of hardware like modems and browser and searcher software have led to a steady increase in Internet use. Defined as the computers through which the user connects to the network, hosts can be used by one or many individuals, but because it is impossible to monitor the number of users on each host, it is also difficult to calculate the number of Internet users worldwide. By 1998, the number of users was believed to be 50 million. Access to the Internet is highest in the advanced economies and lowest in developing economies. For

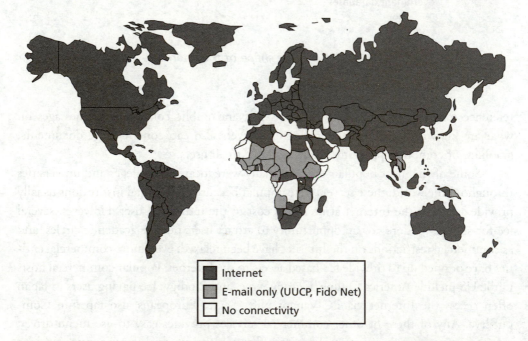

- Internet
- E-mail only (UUCP, Fido Net)
- No connectivity

FIGURE 9.5 *International connectivity* (Copyright © 1997 Larry Landweber and the Internet Society. Unlimited permission to copy or use is hereby granted subject to inclusion of this copyright notice.) www.ISOC.org/infosvc/map.gif

example, Finland offers one server per 25 citizens, while India has 1.2 million per server; these relationships are shown in Table 9.4. However, this can change rapidly. In the six months between July 1996 and January 1997, Indonesia experienced an 85% increase in Internet hosts, Malaysia almost 200%, and the world 30%.

About 60% of host servers are located in the US and the highest absolute number of Internet users also are there, encouraged by higher sales of computers in the US and an English-language standard among browsers, servers, and users. Among the 23.4 million estimated Internet households, over 60% are in the US as compared to about 16% in Europe, 14% in Asia and the Pacific, and about 10% elsewhere. However, according to estimates generated by Jupiter Communications, the number of Internet households will triple to 66 million by the year 2000, and include a higher percentage of both European and Asia/Pacific households for 25% and 15% respectively of the total (In search of, 1997).

With the introduction of instant on-line translators, the English-language bias originally evident on the Internet could be reduced. For example, in Europe and in Asia, it is increasingly common for homepages to offer language alternatives. Interestingly, the motivation to provide translations from English to non-English comes from business: in many countries there are not enough English readers to support English-only Internet

TABLE 9.4 Internet hosts per person, 1996

Country	Number of persons/server
Finland	25
US	50
Australia	60
Canada	70
Netherlands	90
Singapore	125
Britain	130
Germany	180
Israel	185
Hong Kong	310
Japan	470
Taiwan	850
South Africa	930
Brazil	8,000
Thailand	15,000
South Korea	15,550
Indonesia	87,000
China	561,000
India	1,200,000

Source: Martin, Michael H. (1996, Oct. 28). When info worlds collide. *Fortune*, p. 132.

services but translating devices remove this impediment to selling subscriptions or on-line memberships.

THE WORLD WIDE WEB COMES TO THE INTERNET

Post-1993 growth in Internet use was stimulated by both a technological breakthrough and a political change – permission to use the Internet for commercial purposes was granted in 1995. The technological breakthrough of HTML (hyper text markup language) made it possible to create direct links to related subjects and to send and retrieve graphic images and sound – this innovation created the World Wide Web (WWW). Thanks to HTML, while cruising the Web, one can listen to a song performed by a favored performer, dissect a frog on-line, view a video clip from the latest movie or review photos taken from the Hubble Space Telescope, find a copy of *Aesop's Fables*, check out legislation pending worldwide, download immigration forms from almost any nation, search the holdings of thousands of libraries, or read hundreds of publications.

The Web component of the Internet also was created in service to research. In this case, creator Tim Berens-Lee, working at the European Particle Physics Laboratory (CERN), created HTML to provide researchers with a tool to publish their findings electronically. Like TCP/IP, HTML is a shared protocol recognized and used throughout the world, and it adds another layer of 'bells and whistles' to Internet use. Introduction of the Netscape Navigator in 1994 further stimulated Internet use, making it easier to log onto the WWW and find interesting or worthwhile sites available throughout the Internet whether in graphic or prose form alone. Microscoft introduction of its Explorer also stimulated web use. Additionally, Web searchers like Lycos, AltaVista, and Yahoo in English have enhanced user ease because they group similar sites. For example, Yahoo's index to Business and Economy points the user to business homepages.

User interest in the graphics and sound available via the WWW have almost eclipsed an important contribution HTML made to research: it can forge 'hot' links to like subjects. An example can be traced through the homepage supporting this text (http://www.seattleu.edu/~parker). Once inside this homepage, users can point and click at underlined titles to instantly be transported to those sites. For example, the heading called 'Global Politics' has direct links to the headquarters of many trade alliances, including the World Trade Organization, APEC, the European Union, NAFTA, and MERCOSUR; to intergovernmental cooperative organizations such as the United Nations and the OECD; and to nongovernmental organizations such as the International Chamber of Commerce. A link to any one of these on-line entities provides still other 'hot' links to similar organizations. In this way, one can go careering into cyberspace, following link after link after link.

Almost since its inception, the thousands of researchers, government agencies, and universities already connected to the Internet, and new users representing newspapers, television stations, libraries, politicians, record companies, art galleries, catalog houses, and individual users have set up what are called websites. This system provides access to a stunning amount of information stored on thousands of computers around the world, and it bears witness to recognizing the difference between information and data. Home-pages such as 'Mind the Cat' or 'My New Car' are in a different league from pages that provide links to Human Rights Organizations or global business enterprises. The World Wide Web that incorporated these features also provided a way to make commercial ventures attractive and it offered a method for advertising goods and services, but the commercial aspect of the Web remains in its infancy. Nevertheless, a business crowd has been attracted to the Web, causing the number of available address sites to dwindle. In response, the Internet Society – the self-governing entity that sets standards for the Internet – created new domain names for business and other uses in 1997. These are shown in Table 9.5. However, by early 1998 growing demand called for still more business domains.

The commercial potential of the Web has attracted many users and many more vendors. A shift from largely academic to commercial use of the Internet becomes evident when looking at diverse indicators. Computers in educational institutions were the largest single group of hosts until October 1994 when commercial sites earned that crown. Second, the number of homepages for commercial sites continues to grow: 100 million websites are expected to be available by 2000 (Planet Internet, 1995). Many new websites are under construction; many more are of limited value; and some developed since 1994 are now defunct. For example, according to Web crawler AltaVista, nearly 5 of the total 30 million websites AltaVista indexed had not been updated between early and late 1996, and 75,000 had not been touched since 1994. Like the Internet, growth of the WWW component has as much hype and hope as reality and much work remains

TABLE 9.5   World Wide Web domains, 1998

Business use:	
original domains for business users	.com
	.org
domains added in 1997:	
(a) for businesses and firms	.firm
(b) for stores	.store
(c) for entities providing information services	.info
Educational use:	.edu
Military use:	.mil
Government use:	.gov
Activities on the Web:	.web
Cultural and entertainment activities:	.arts
Recreational activities:	.rec
Individual or personal listings:	.nom

to be done to make this resource altogether useful. For academic researchers, the WWW is in many cases less useful than other Internet sources supported by universities, research institutes, and libraries. Publishers worldwide that recognize the gap between World Wide Web potential and realization are quickly gearing up to close the gap between publishing in 'hard' or paper copy and 'soft' electronic publication. The Simon & Schuster example illustrates one approach (Box 9.8).

BOX 9.8:   SIMON & SCHUSTER'S DIGITAL FUTURE

In 1996 Simon & Schuster generated 25% of its revenue from electronic publishing of CD-ROMS, videodiscs, or via the World Wide Web, but Chairman Jonathan Newcomb plans to double the percentage of electronic revenue by 2000. At the heart of Newcomb's plan is a Corporate Digital Archive expected to make it possible to organize literally everything into databases searchable anytime, anywhere. The advantage of a computer-based data storage system becomes evident when compared to older technologies. For example, locating an appropriate photograph for a textbook traditionally involved researchers in weeks of work searching through multiple archives by hand, then sending the resulting photograph for preparation, and finally customizing the photo for the text. With digital archiving, the search is a single search of integrated databases, instant retrieval, and the ability to customize and thereby use the same photo for multiple uses. The obvious cost savings for a fully integrated digital archive will improve publishing efficiencies, but digital archives also offer a source of new revenue to others who similarly seek a faster, easier, better way to sell photos and information around the world.

Source: Verity, John W. (1996, Dec. 23). A model paperless library. *Business Week*, pp. 80–82.

THE INTERNET AS INFORMATION DISTRIBUTOR

Information can be easily transmitted through the Internet, and this ease of transmission has led to unexpected and undesirable effects in many sectors. For example, Intel executives acknowledge that the growing reach of the Internet was a contributing factor to wide-scale media coverage of a mathematical flaw in the original Pentium chip. The story of this chip and the role Internet information played in discovering the flaw is an interesting one that illustrates the power of the Internet to shape information, business decisions, and development of computer-based industries. Despite 24-hour testing that *Business Week* (Hof, 1994) referred to as 'the most exhaustive ever done on a computer chip,' Intel discovered after it released the Pentium chip that it had a flaw: a floating decimal point affecting some high-precision division problems. The flaw was broadcast via the Internet, picked up by print news media, and soon became common knowledge among consumers. Accustomed to working with technical people and scientists rather than with consumers, and aware that the flaw was of limited scope, Intel originally offered to replace chips only for people affected by the flaw. Public outcry was immediate and harsh, and again the Internet played a significant role as the forum for consumer opposition. Eventually, Intel executives made a $500 million decision to replace all Pentium chips. Messages on the Internet immediately proclaimed David's victory over the Intel Goliath. From this experience, Intel learned the important role the Internet could play in making world news out of what would have been a non-event in prior years, the difference between expectations of technical and consumer users, and the need to stand behind their 'Intel Inside' product.

The potential for equal access to opportunity created by information technologies is balanced by fears that those without access to the Internet will become the cyberspace equivalent of highway 'road kill,' creating a new divide between those who have information and those who do not. The advantages of easy access to information also may be offset by the loss of privacy (Forrester and Morrison, 1992), and information thus gained can be used to harm rather than help. Problems with 'peepers' reading one's private mail, or 'hackers' obtaining banking and credit information are now obvious.

INTERNET ABUSE

The same Internet opportunities available to ordinary users are also available to pranksters, hackers, and thieves, and all three of these groups have discovered new opportunities on the Internet. Microsoft Corporation was the victim of one such prank in December 1994 when an authentic-looking but bogus Associated Press news wire story appeared on the Internet – datelined Vatican City – to announce that the Vatican had agreed to be acquired by Microsoft Corporation 'for an unspecified number of shares of Microsoft common stock.' This bogus news item was fully developed to include a new organizational structure naming Pope John Paul II the senior vice-president for the new Religious Software Division and a plan to license electronic rights to the Bible and offer on-line holy sacraments (Lewis, 1994). This and similar prankish behavior is possible because the Internet permits messages to be sent anonymously.

Anonymity also is a refuge for hackers, who prowl throughout the Internet looking for the electronic equivalent of an unlocked door or an unguarded vault. Groups of hackers have been known to break into computer systems run by the Sprint Corporation and IBM, warning corporate America to get out of cyberspace. Hackers who illegally and unethically use the Internet may challenge or amuse themselves, but hacker activities also have threatened national as well as global security. For example, hacker attacks on US Defense Department computers were estimated to be 25,000 in 1995, compromising national security and costing millions. Because of the serious threat they pose, apprehended hackers now face vigorous legal prosecution and lengthy prison sentences if convicted of computer hacking. The example in Box 9.9 of the attack on the National Weather Service illustrates the global reach offered by the Internet.

BOX 9.9:   ATTACK ON THE NATIONAL WEATHER SERVICE

Computer manager John Ward knew that hackers had penetrated the National Weather Service's computers, and because these computers handle about 95% of computations that go into national weather forecasts, he also knew they had to be stopped before harm was done. Because airlines depend on the Weather Service for guidance, a compromised Weather Service system would undermine US air travel. But despite months of effort, the hackers remained active. Ward discovered the hackers' port of entry was through an MIT computer, and so he installed an alarm system to alert him and the FBI whenever the hackers entered either the MIT system or the Weather Service computer. Often, the hackers used the latter as a launching pad to jump into other computer networks and steal more passwords. The case broke when MIT computer managers observed unusual activity on a computer telephone account and traced it through a local telephone call to Denmark. There, Danish police helped track down the hackers, seven young men between the ages of 17 and 23. Full details of the arrest were not released, but the Danish police reported surprise because they believed hacker attacks in Denmark were coming from the US rather than the reverse. According to their own careful records, the hackers had put together a global network of computers and telephone lines to reach computers in Israel, Brazil, and Japan as well as 32 different systems in the US.

Source: Fialka, John. (1994, Oct. 10). The latest flurries at weather bureau: Scattered hacking. *The Wall Street Journal*, pp. A1, A6.

As increasing numbers of individuals and businesses sign onto the Internet, the volume of illegal activity associated with the Internet also has increased. In 1995, a 28-year-old Russian computer hacker demonstrated the increased vulnerability of banks to worldwide computer links when he and associates stole $400,000 and illegally transferred $11.6 million from Citibank. According to a *Wall Street Journal* account of the event (Carley and O'Brien, 1995), the transfers were stymied by an alert Buenos Aires investment company official who happened to be looking at his computer screen when he observed unauthorized transfers from Argentina through Citicorp computers in New

York to unknown accounts in San Francisco. Arrests followed from Russia to the Netherlands, Tel Aviv, Britain, and the US. To forestall future break-ins, businesses are developing or purchasing new software to plug security gaps or prevent misuse of Internet links. Firewall software is developed to detect phony messages or keep out viruses meant to do mischief; safe software practices including authentication of copies of Web browsers and other programs; and codes and forms of data encryption also are suggested as ways to protect information.

CYBERSPACE GOVERNANCE

Perhaps needless to say, Internet use by pranksters, hackers, and electronic thieves has raised many issues around Internet governance. Cyberspace governance is difficult to achieve because the Internet is not subject to the laws of any one country; it exists separate from the rules and regulations associated with geography and with traditional laws of nations. Accordingly, governments have found it difficult to keep out unwanted cyber visitors or to limit use to legal, moral, or ethical ends. For example, although national regulations allowed Germany to block CompuServe on-line 'newsgroups' judged to be pornographic, in fact German citizens still can gain access to these and similar resources through other Internet providers or by dialing into CompuServe via long-distance to other countries. Table 9.6 showcases some of the challenges the Internet poses for national governments. In response to nations' efforts to curtail Internet use, the Internet Society has attempted to develop standards of use. Additionally, in 1996, 16 computer industry and telephone companies formed to lobby governments worldwide to ensure open access free of security breaches. Called the Global Internet Project, organizational members including AT&T, MCI, IBM, Sun Microsystems, British Telecom, and BBN Corporation seek to inform members of worldwide legislation intended to curtail Internet freedoms.

The Internet has provided many opportunities and embodies many of the challenges organizations and individuals confront with new and untried technologies. This breakthrough technology already has transformed many modes of communication. For example, fewer people use telephones as their exclusive mode of personal communication. According to a January 27, 1997, *Business Week* note, in 1992 only 2% of the US population used e-mail, but the percentage of users had climbed to 15% by 1996 (p. 6); in 1997 Forrester Research reported that consumer/home use of e-mail in the US had skyrocketed from 10 million to 150 million messages per day to an average of 2.7 messages per person per day (Auerbach, 1997). According to Forrester Research estimates, by 2005 over 170 million e-mail users will send 5 billion messages daily, averaging 29.4 messages per person/per day! Although the computer was the original building block for the Internet, newer technologies make it possible to use televisions rather than computers to access the Internet, send and receive e-mail, and otherwise communicate worldwide. One of these technologies is called the information appliance.

TABLE 9.6   Internet use and national priorities

Use	National priorities
Saudi Arabian hackers debate topics from atheism to pornography via telephone connections to Internet servers in other countries	Saudi government fears it will lose control over political dialogue and public mores
Nongovernmental agencies use the Internet to rally support for their causes	Malaysian authorities examined financial and other records of local NGOs to examine the link between them and foreign subversives
BurmaNet lobbies businesses to discourage operations in Myanmar (Burma)	Myanmar (Burma) collects e-mail addresses of BurmaNet users
English-language dominance on the Internet	The French Association for the Defense of the French Language and the Future of the French Language sued Georgia Tech Lorraine to translate its Internet site into French; the settlement allows English language courses
Cyberspace freedoms	Singapore Broadcasting Authority plans to hold access providers responsible for material appearing on the Internet, encouraging providers to block access to sites like Playboy Enterprises' homepage
China/Taiwan struggles	Website http://www.taiwanese.com/protest lists anti-Chinese protests around the world, provides addresses for protesting China policies
Information sharing	Grass-roots movement worldwide use the Internet to share information, e.g., the Association for Progressive Communications created a homepage for the UN Fourth World Conference on Women

The information appliance

For most people the personal computer is the point of access to the Internet, but a limitation is that not all homes have PCs. However, in the US almost 100% have television (Ziegler, 1996), and this represents an exploitable opportunity. Oracle's NC or networked computer is a stripped-down version of a computer that can be used with the television. Other examples of TV/PC combined technologies include a Net TV introduced by both Sony and Philips, and Sega's Saturn gamebox, which is a cartridge that permits access to the Internet through the television set. The cost of this technology is about the same as that of a color television.

Telecommunications technologies

TELEPHONES

Modes of information transmission witnessed few technological breakthroughs until this century. The spread of postal service worldwide was one earlier breakthrough, followed by the first telegraph message in 1794 transmitted from Paris to Lille. However, the telephone was not invented until 1876, and the first transatlantic telephone service was not inaugurated until 1956. One reason telephone technology developed slowly is that this mode of communication was accomplished by sending electricity through copper wires. These wires typically are strung above ground or buried beneath it, a costly process when there were many miles to cover. Further, in a world organized around nations operating in relative autonomy and isolation as compared to today, there was limited reason to develop communication links between countries. Often there was also too little national economic development to warrant the cost of installing telephone lines within countries. For example, in many developing economies, telephone access is limited to 1% or less of the population. According to the International Telecommunications Union (ITU), 71% of the world's current telephone lines are in countries with only 15% of the world's people. But that may be changing, stimulated not only by business initiatives such as the Africa One project described in the opening case for this chapter, but also by a growing desire worldwide to be part of the global marketplace.

Today, many of the same technological factors and cost conditions that have fueled growth in computer industries also are stimulating growth in telecommunications. According to *The Economist* (1990, Dec. 22), a three-minute transatlantic call from New York to London was billed at $230 in 1930; at $49 in 1969; and at $2.33 in 1990 (all figures adjusted to 1990 dollars). Today that same call costs less than $2, and according to a 1995 report published by the World Bank (Forge, 1995), the call in 2005 will be enhanced with video capabilities yet cost only a few cents per *hour*.

Despite falling costs for long-distance calls, and perhaps enhanced by a rising number of overall calls, the global telecommunications market is expected to expand from a total of $460 billion in 1993 to as much as $1.1 trillion in 2000; details on this growth are reported in Figure 9.6. This growth potential is partially due to the limited number of telephone lines now available for home or business use in developing economies. The average number of telephone lines in wealthier economies is one for every two persons as compared to 13 lines for every 1,000 people in India and 11 per 1,000 in Sub-Saharan Africa.

The Africa One project described in the opening case would do much to increase the ratio of telephones to people throughout Africa, enhancing the potential for individual communication and for business opportunities. At the same time, these technologies also have the potential to disrupt societies currently based on person-to-person

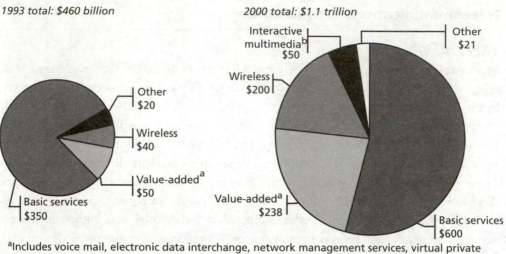

1993 total: $460 billion

2000 total: $1.1 trillion

Interactive multimedia[b] $50

Wireless $200

Other $21

Other $20

Wireless $40

Value-added[a] $50

Value-added[a] $238

Basic services $350

Basic services $600

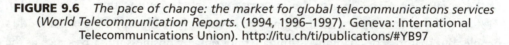

[a]Includes voice mail, electronic data interchange, network management services, virtual private networks, and outsourcing.
[b]Capacity large enough for two-way transmission of voice, video, and data signals.

FIGURE 9.6 *The pace of change: the market for global telecommunications services* (*World Telecommunication Reports.* (1994, 1996–1997). Geneva: International Telecommunications Union). http://itu.ch/ti/publications/#YB97

communication and agricultural rather than industrial development. In much of the rest of the world, telecommunications technologies are capable of transmitting information almost instantaneously throughout the world, and they make it possible for people and businesses to communicate 24 hours a day, seven days a week. These info-links provide instant access to information for business transactions such that the world's stock markets operate almost continuously and financial services have become readily available worldwide. For example, a credit card approval for an American Express card in Paris moves information across 46,000 miles of telephone and computer lines, but the transaction itself can be completed in only a few seconds. These telecommunications breakthroughs have been facilitated by breakthroughs in still other technologies and also by worldwide industry deregulation. The example in Box 9.10 illustrates how World Trade Organization agreements are expected to facilitate global telecommunications.

FIBER OPTICS

Telephone communication through copper wires is being enhanced by fiber-optics technologies. First introduced in 1952 by scientist Narinder Kapany, fiber optics' original use was to explore the interior of the human body. The fiber-optic cable used in telecommunications is a bundle of glass strands protected by a metal casing. When activated by electricity, a laser light traveling through glass strands the size of a single hair give off light pulses that travel at the speed of light. The high-frequency signals on which they travel allows them to carry more information than copper wire. Unlike copper, which can be costly and generates heat, the glass fibers used in this technology are manufactured

BOX 9.10:   TELECOMMUNICATIONS DEREGULATED

According to the World Trade Organization, global trade in information technology products amounts to about $600 billion. The combined value of domestic
and international revenue generated in basic telecommunications services also is
about $600 billion per year. Both figures are expected to grow as the result of two
1997 WTO agreements. In February 1997, 69 nations agreed to liberalization of
telecommunications services that could reduce the average cost of an international
call from $1.00 to 20 cents per minute even as it doubles or triples the revenues
for global communications firms. In March of the same year, 40 governments
agreed to begin cutting customs duties by the following July on information technology products to meet a goal of eliminating all duties on these products by 2000.
The latter agreement enhances prior pacts on computers and together the two
agreements cover about 90% of world information technology trade in computers,
semiconductors, software, and similar products and telecommunications services.

Source: WTO Annual Report. (1997). Geneva: WTO Publications.

from common beach sand. Further, glass fibers are lightweight, are not affected by
electrical or radio interference, and can carry information long distances. Finally, and
probably most important for the Information Age, fiber optics can carry far more information than copper wire in much less space. For example, a conventional 3 inch cable
of copper wires can carry 14,400 telephone conversations as compared to a half inch
thick fiber-optic cable which can transmit 3.5 million conversations.

The added capacity of fiber-optic cables means that a single fiber can handle thousands of telephone calls simultaneously. The increased carrying capacity of fiber optics
also creates the potential for interactivity among televisions, computers, and other modes
of communication. Thus, fiber optics also can replace coaxial television cables as well as
copper telephone wires. Today, fiber optics are transforming telecommunications, blurring borders between industries like cable TV, telephone, and computers that once were
viewed as separate and distinct industries.

Fiber optics show so much promise and, relatively speaking, are so much less expensive than previous technologies that they are being used to leap-frog older and existing
technologies in many developing economies. For example, all of the 300,000 lines
Vietnam plans to install annually will use fiber-optic technologies. Unlike US consumers,
Brazilian consumers now can bank at home thanks to leap-frogging into computer-based
technologies at home and in banks (McCartney and Friedland, 1995). Demand for
breakthrough telephone technologies such as these also are fueled by the rush to

capitalism witnessed throughout the world. Telephones, fax machines, and similar communications technologies have made it possible for people throughout the world to participate in the global economy. Evidence of growing worldwide use of telephones is indicative of growth in business within economies; China alone is expected to add 35.5 million telephone lines between 1993 and 2000 (Engardio, 1994b). According to the ITU (World Telecommunication, 1996/97), overseas calls also doubled from 23 to 47 billion minutes between 1988 and 1993, and increased to 60 billion by 1995, doubtless fueled by business, by globalization of education and business travel, increased tourism, and falling prices in long-distance telephone rates.

WIRELESS TELEPHONE TECHNOLOGIES

The demand for telephones also has fueled demand for wireless instruments. Cellular telephones, which originally relied on low-frequency radio transmissions long in use among police and rescue workers, now are a growing segment of the telephone market. These mobile phones communicate first with a base station or 'cell,' which assigns a private radio channel for callers and then transmits the call to a telephone network which completes the connection. If the mobile phone moves outside the range of one base station, another station picks it up without any interruption or awareness from the user. Originally broadcast at low frequencies of around 800–900 megahertz, cellular phones now are going digital on higher frequencies that require more base stations but can transmit three times the information of an analog network. These digital forms of mobile phones are relatively new, but catching on fast because of speed and privacy advantages. One result is developing world battles for setting the standard. For example, in digital cellular phone technology the European standard GMS vied for supremacy over the US entry of digital time division multiple access (Arnold, 1996).

Wireless telecommunications technologies have been particularly popular in developing economies like China and Hungary where the wait for telephone lines remains long and existing telephone lines often are far less efficient than what mobile telephones offer. Because of insufficient telephone lines to satisfy business and consumer demands, China and Hungary advanced directly to cellular phone technology. Similarly, in Prague the Komercni Banka leap-frogged from paper-based accounting to a client-server network through which it could tap into worldwide currency trading networks. Leap-frogging technologies becomes possible because it is far cheaper to build radio towers for transmitting signals than it is to string copper or fiber-optic lines, and in cities built hundreds of years ago, it is difficult to retrofit ancient buildings and crowded streets with telephone lines. Additionally, mobile phones have provided a way for grid-locked commuters to make use of the time they spend in their cars in congested cities like Bangkok, Beijing, and Los Angeles. Satellites also have facilitated wireless communication.

SATELLITE TRANSMISSIONS

Telephone communications via satellite is in its infancy, but it too is a rapid-growth industry. The Soviet launch of Sputnik in the 1950s touched off the information component of the Cold War as the US, Russia, China, and other countries vied to be premier powers in transmitting information about each other via satellite. Government-sponsored monopolies dominated the field for geosynchronous earth-orbiting satellites (GEOs), and hundreds of these powerful and expensive satellites continue to circle the planet today at distances in excess of 22,000 miles from the surface. Military and scientific use continues to be the *raison d'être* for most GEOs and for medium-range satellites, but many discoveries made with these satellites have led to civilian use and commercial applications. For example, 24 global positioning satellites orbiting 11,000 miles from earth all emit the same signals at exactly the same time. When four or more of these signals are picked up by the same portable receiver, the information can be used to calculate latitude, longitude, and altitude within about 330 feet or 100 meters. Commercial use of GPS locating systems was revealed by a United Airlines' test which used GPS position coordinates to land a Boeing 737-300 in the exact same location 110/111 times at a NASA test field (reported by the Boeing Corporation in their internal newsletter, October 21, 1994). In April 1996 GPS technology was released to consumers in the form of hand-held receivers expected to prevent hikers, bikers, and mountain climbers from losing their way in rough terrain; the price was $200. Similar technology is being developed for boaters' use for communication and rescue. Furthermore, in response to dual pressures to increase profits and reduce pesticide use, about five percent of US farmers are using GPS systems in their work. Satellites map the terrain when farmers drive over their soil and this information is then fed into computers to produce precise calculations for the amount of seed, fertilizer, or herbicides needed on each square yard of soil (Carton, 1996).

The distances covered by GEOs and medium earth-orbiting satellites described above require ground equipment to support them, often to handle the delays and garbled messages that occur when information travels over vast distances. As a result of the costs involved with ground equipment, relatively few commercial ventures had the fiscal or political resources needed to launch their own satellites, and satellite technology rested largely in the hands of governments. (An exception was AT&T's launch of its Telstar satellite in 1962.) More recently, however, businesses have launched low earth-orbiting satellites (LEOs) which have proved commercially feasible because their transmissions can be relayed directly to hand-held devices like cellular telephones or laptop computers. The beams of LEOs cannot reach as far as GEOs, so their practical use can only be exploited by a constellation of satellites to cover the globe. These LEOs are expected to offer both voice and video communications. Other LEO satellites such as Globalstart, ICO Global Communications, Odyssey Telecommunications International, and Motorola's Iridium are limited to voice communications.

Like cellular phones, voice communication satellites provide a way for many nations to introduce telephones without laying costly land lines. Further, satellites do not require even the radio towers that cellular telephony uses to transmit radio beams. Thus satellites are expected to be more useful than cellular technology in providing service to underserved nations where there are few telephones in use. One instrument used is called a global mobile personal communications system (GMPCS), and it is a portable and affordable personal telephone that is fairly low in cost and therefore more accessible to people around the world. Commercial access offered through Iridium, Globalstar, ICO Global, and Odyssey will continually be enhanced by improvements in the power, capacity, and switching capabilities of communications satellites, making GMPCS transmissions ever more efficient and reliable, and the commercial possibilities are great. Market estimates for GMPCS devices range from 5.2 million in 2002 to 34.9 million by 2010 (Borzo, 1996).

Television broadcasts via satellite also are fueling growth in the worldwide satellite market. According to a Merrill Lynch study of this market (cited in Activate the money star, 1997), world satellite operators earned $4.5 billion from direct-to-home satellite TV in 1996, but stand to see an increase to $16.3 billion by 2002. This potential may explain why businesses from so many industries have invested in some segment of the home entertainment industry.

In examining the greater promise of the Information Revolution for some than for others we see the greatest flaw of information technology: it has zero inherent capacity to right existing wrongs or to prevent future ones. As in other fields, technology development reflects the interests of the developer. Thus, ASCII characters are English-language characters; many computer games have greater appeal for boys than for girls; computer icons of file folders or thumbs up represent Western, and more particularly US, cultural experiences; and the format of games and programs reflects a Western bias for action, linear thinking, and self-determination (Goulet, 1977; Magnet, 1994). Box 9.11, for example, illustrates that Western cultural traits such as self-determination and individual initiative are built into much available technology.

The preceding review of global changes in information technologies provides strong support for those who argue that technological change is powering globalization, particularly in industries like telecommunications. Global technological changes also have an impact on many other spheres of endeavor. In medicine, for example, information-based technologies make it possible to share health care information globally, to detect life-threatening conditions, to transplant human organs, to extend and improve the quality of health care, and even to clone living organisms. Information-based technologies make it possible for medical care to be more efficiently conducted, making medicine more like business than it has been in the past. For this and other industries, the world of their business is being reshaped; a review of changes in the

BOX 9.11:   WESTERN CULTURAL TRAITS BUILT INTO TECHNOLOGY

- Computer logic is based on a procedure and manner of problem-solving that applies logic in a linear fashion.
- Individual initiative in taking action is viewed as integral and essential to the application of technology.
- Personal self-worth and social status are determined through one's work and material achievements using technology.
- Self-determinism is the key to making technology work.

Source: Goulet, Dennis. (1977). *The uncertain promise: Value conflicts in technology transfer*. New York: North America Inc.

banking industry, pharmaceuticals, cosmetics, automotives, or any other globalizing industry would show all have been affected in similar as well as different ways by digitalization and the Information Revolution. An example of change for the telecommunications industry between 1985 and 1995 appears in Figure 9.7. Prepared by Northern Telecom (Nortel) President and CEO Jean C. Monty, this figure shows that while some changes are specific to the industry itself, more are held in common with any globalizing industry: a shift from a domestic to a global orientation; a shift from distinct and regulated market segments to convergence and overlapping among markets; a shift from stability to a dynamic environment; and a growing need for customer orientation and customer service.

PART II   ORGANIZATIONS AND TECHNOLOGY

In the coming years, the entire information industry is likely to be further restructured, although no one can say just how. Building the guts of this digital world, the hardware, software, fiber optics, and microprocessors, will realign the computer and information industries. Questions raised by the future of technologies start with: Will the world go wireless or be encased in fiber optic? Will the PC gobble up the functions of telephones, video games, and television, or will phone companies win that race? No one can answer these questions with certainty, and this means that business leaders in telecommunications and technology-dependent companies must make decisions under conditions of uncertainty. For Ricoh Company, the decision includes combining their traditional technology of copiers and printers with digital media to create more productive offices. For

1985	1995
STRUCTURE AND SCOPE	
Telecommunications ⟶	Global communications
Home country	World
Franchise monopolies	Near full service competition
MARKETS	
Market segments separated ⟶	Convergence of telephony, computers,
by regulation and technology	cable TV, broadcasting, and publishing
COMPETITION	
Stable ⟶	Dynamic and fast-paced
NETWORK INFRASTRUCTURE	
Copper, radio ⟶	Fiber, ATM, radio, satellite, coax
Data and voice separate	Integrated voice, data, video, and wireless
Services may vary by territory	Consistency of global alliance service offerings
NETWORK MANAGEMENT	
Hardware-driven ⟶	Focus on platforms, software, and services
NETWORK INNOVATION	
Technology-driven ⟶	Pulled by market demands
CUSTOMER NEEDS	
Deploy digital ⟶	Demanding more bandwidth
Reduce costs	Improved cost performance
	More mobility
	New services
CUSTOMER SERVICE	
Driven by what's offered ⟶	Driven by customer needs
EQUIPMENT SUPPLIERS	
Large ⟶	First-tier and sub-components
Nation-based	Global and local
CUSTOMERS	
Telecom operators ⟶	New operators
	New service providers
	New telco structures
	Cable TV companies
PRODUCT CYCLES	
Slow time-to-market ⟶	Rapid time-to-market

FIGURE 9.7 *Industry power shift* (Monty, Jean C. (1997, Jan.). Northern Telecom: The anatomy of a transformation. *Northern Telecom*, p. 4)

Matsushita Electric it means digitalizing products but maintaining 'analog' or person-to-person relationships with customers.

Nortel CEO Monty tries to anticipate pending change to stay ahead of the technology curve changing his industry. As shown in Table 9.7, Nortel redefined core businesses, emphasizing the newly integrating nature of digital networks. Further, its market position shifted from one based on technological leadership to being a 'global resource.' Finally, the number of research labs increased, expanded from 3 to 16 nations, and included an almost four-fold increase in R&D employees. According to Mr Monty, the percentage of knowledge workers also increased from 42% to 66%, and as Table 9.7 shows, revenues per employee increased as Nortel's earnings became increasingly international.

TABLE 9.7   Northern Telecom's transformation, 1985–1995

	1985	1995
Core business	Design and manufacture of telecommunications equipment	Design, deployment, and integration of digital networks
Market positioning	Technology leader	Global resource for digital network solutions and services
Customers	Operating companies, large communications users, distributors	Wide range of network service providers, public and private enterprises
Employees		
US	21,972 (47%)	22,410 (35%)
Canada	21,338 (46%)	21,263 (33%)
International	3,239 (7%)	20,042 (32%)
	46,549	63,715
Research and development		
Spending	$429*m*	$1.6*b*
Labs	14	38
Country locations	3	16
Employees	4,900	16,500
Manufacturing plants		
Canada	25	15
US	15	4
International	5	19
	45	38
Revenues		
US	$2.9*b* (67%)	$5.4*b* (50%)
Canada	$1.1*b* (25%)	$1.1*b* (11%)
International	$320*m* (8%)	$4.2*b* (39%)
	$4.2*b*	$10.7*b*
Revenue per employee	$90,227	$167,935

Revenues by product line		*Revenues by network business*	
Digital switching	50%	Public-carrier networks	40%
PBXs, CPE, subscriber apparatus	30%	Enterprise networks	30%
Transmission equipment	13%	Broadband networks	10%
Cable and outside plant	6%	Wireless networks	15%
Other services	1%	Other	5%

Source: Monty, Jean C. (1997, Jan.). Northern Telecom: The anatomy of a transformation. *Northern Telecom*, p. 24.

Technological competence in both product and process has been a critical success factor for businesses in most industries, and developing new technologies and sustaining existing technologies remain important challenges for business enterprises. Yet, many fail to recognize the opportunities until another firm has exploited them. For example, like Henry Ford's auto, which consumers could order in any color so long as it was black, for the first decade firms manufacturing personal computers provided consumers only with grayish computer cases, grayish monitors, grayish printers. However, Taiwan-based firm Acer saw the need to satisfy a broad range of customer needs by offering computers in colors matching walls, furniture, or preferences, including an environmentally sensitive PC. In the following sections, we explore how this and other businesses have met the challenges of technological change with adaptations in organizational processes, structures, and people.

The ability to innovate and further develop and apply new technologies is fundamental to building strength and power for many companies operating in the global marketplace. These strengths lead to strategic advantages critical to business success and survival. Tomorrow's processes and products will inevitably propel others into industry leadership unless today's leaders remain technologically astute. Interestingly, information technologies like computerization and the Internet invented primarily in developed economies now make it possible for developing economies and firms from them to participate in additional technological breakthroughs. Thousands of Israeli scientists and entrepreneurs, for example, are successful contributors to breakthroughs in advanced computer design, electric auto fuel, data networking, medical imaging, and electronic cash transfer. Companies like digital printer Indigo or voice imager Vocal-Tech are only two of many Israeli companies founded on the strength of technological discovery and innovation. And Israel is not alone in being a new source of technological breakthroughs located in a developing economy. The equivalent to California's Silicon Valley or Massachusetts' Highway 128 are springing up around the world in support of the computer industry, including the Silicon Forest in Seattle, a Multimedia Super Corridor in Malaysia's high-tech zone, India's Silicon Valley near Bangalore, the Silicon Glen in Scotland, the Silicon Fen in Cambridge, England, and similar development areas in Singapore, Taiwan, Argentina, and Brazil. In China Silicon 'Alleys' are located in the Zhongguancun area near Beijing University where university graduates, students, and professors are developing high-tech companies.

The growing domain for scientific research and development experienced in the computer industry also applies to other industries; as Figure 9.8 shows, transportation, biotechnical, computers, and environmentally sensitive technologies are being developed not only in the industrialized nations but in developing economies as well. Many of the dominant national players in technology have had to cede ground to newer entrants, and others have responded by altering their focus. Intel, for example, no longer views the US as the most dynamic market for high tech as more of its revenues come from outside the US (55% in 1995). These shifts in industry participants and in where they focus their organizational energy make it imperative to look at how organizations are responding to sweeping global change. At a national level, it is crucial to examine how well educational systems prepare students to be globally adept. Since mathematics is the foundation of digital advances, nations with a workforce well versed in that discipline, including China, India, and the nations of Southeast Asia, could turn their homelands into formidable technology powers. The description of Malaysia's Multimedia Super Corridor (Box 9.12) shows that becoming a superpower in the technological realm may result from combining 'best' practices worldwide.

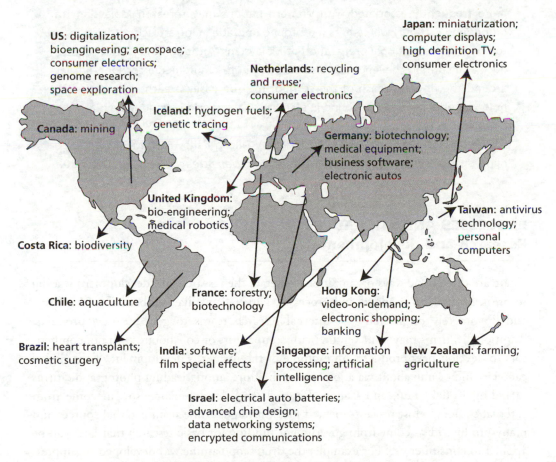

FIGURE 9.8 *Some technology hot spots*

BOX 9.12:   MALAYSIA'S MULTIMEDIA SUPER CORRIDOR

In the 1980s Malaysia emulated Japan to move beyond agricultural and extractive industries to develop value-added industries like automotives and electronics, but national strategy to become a multimedia superpower is drawing Malaysian attention further eastward to California's Silicon Valley and beyond. A 10 by 30 mile multimedia corridor located south of Kuala Lumpur is expected to include: a futuristic city where 'smart' technologies like cards process virtually all transactions; a new government capital re-engineered into a paperless bureaucracy; and a multimedia university around which will gather companies eager to operate in a high-technology environment. Unlike current practices, foreign workers in the corridor would find it easy to obtain work visas, and computer users would be permitted options not available in censorship-prone Malaysia. This experiment with freedoms more frequently associated with Western nations may threaten Malaysian traditions and certainly will require a profound upgrade in infrastructures from roads to power to educational preparation of Malaysians. Although the plan is to introduce and contain challenges to tradition within the multimedia corridor, borders around the physical reach of the corridor may be easily breached by high-technology media increasingly found in all parts of the world beyond Malaysia.

Source: Wysocki, Bernard, Jr. (1997, June 10). Silicon Valley East: Malaysia is gambling on a costly plunge into cyber future. *The Wall Street Journal*, pp. A1, A10.

PROCESSES AND STRUCTURES
Research and development

There are three basic ways organizations generate the research and development leading to breakthroughs in products and processes. Larger firms like Rubbermaid, 3M, Sony, and Toyota rely on in-house or internal research teams to generate new products. Additionally, firms may joint venture with competitors or collaborate with noncompetitors to develop new products. An example of the former is development of the digital camera which came about via a joint research effort among leading photographic firms including Kodak, Fuji, and Canon. Research and development also can come from external sources. Most process-oriented breakthroughs come from external sources and many product ideas come from government funding for basic research that later can be applied to consumer use. For example, the drug scopolamine was developed to suppress air sickness for astronauts but later became available for ordinary travelers. In many nations, a significant amount of research and development is government sponsored, provided in the form of funds for research labs or in tax breaks or similar cost reductions for firms engaged in research and development, particularly in industries like computers, aerospace, and pharmaceuticals that are perceived to be research-intensive.

With regard to stimulating change, General Electric Chairman Jack Welch asks: 'Are you regenerating? Are you dealing with new things? When you find yourself in a new environment, do you come up with a fundamentally different approach? That's the test. When you flunk, you leave [the industry]!' (Peters, 1994). This pretty well sums up the attitude it takes to stimulate technological breakthroughs. The need for continuous breakthroughs occurs because new products and processes can be copied by others, and because the pace of invention is rapid. In turn, this calls for organizational efforts to engage all members of the organization – from top to bottom – in the process of innovation. For many organizations, like Northern Telecom, research and development of new products, services, and processes are vital to the very health and future of the corporation. Nortel has increased its R&D budget almost four-fold in the past decade, and others similarly invest heavily in research. In the pharmaceuticals industry, R&D traditionally is the single most expensive endeavor for firms. In 1995, Merck alone spent $13.25 billion on R&D.

The environment of R&D often drives people to approach product development much like a religion. Product development and the teams of people that spend their lives in the trenches must believe that the products they are developing will best all other products. These teams must also believe in the premise that they will produce the next generation of a product fast enough to make yesterday's product obsolete.

Technology transfer

Research and development of new products, services, and processes is vital to the health and future of many global enterprises, and the relative ease and rapid speed with which information can be transferred makes it possible for firms to transfer new technologies around the world. Technology transfer is defined as the transfer of systematic knowledge for the manufacture of a product, for the application of a process, or for the rendering of a service, and does not extend to the mere sale or lease of goods (*International code*, 1981). An example of a technology transfer occurred when the Ford Motor Company built an assembly plant in Hermosillo, Mexico, where technology products such as robotics and manufacturing processes were moved from the US. Many companies, especially multinational and global firms, are dependent on technology transfers to stay competitive. Motorola is one of those firms, and the example in Box 9.13 shows how efforts to focus and transfer technology led to an abrupt departure from the past.

BOX 9.13:   MOTOROLA RESTRUCTURES

Semiconductors or computer chips are the 'guts' of computer systems. Motorola's approach to selling chips traditionally has been to produce chips and then sell them to different markets. But in May 1997, Motorola changed its approach to find out what customers want and produce it in 30 versus 90 days. This reversal required changes in production processes to stress cycle time, but also has brought about a structural change in the semiconductor sector. Existing relationships with buyers are the basis of five new market-oriented groups, including wireless communications, transportation (supplying to the auto industry), networking and computing systems, semiconductor components, and digital consumers. The first four groups will be based in Texas, but digital consumer products will be based in Hong Kong, providing another boundary for Motorola to transcend in efforts to remain a global force in the semiconductor industry.

Source: Hardy, Quentin, and Takahishi, Dean. (1997, May 28). Motorola revamps its chip group to speed delivery. *The Wall Street Journal*, p. A14.

Protecting intellectual property rights

For many firms, a concern is not just staying ahead technologically, but protecting their ideas in a global marketplace. Reverse engineering, unlicensed borrowing, and outright stealing threaten the investments firms make in R&D to produce a new product or service. Many firms vigorously defend their technologies at the global level by endorsing stronger intellectual property rights. Like corruption, intellectual property risk is widespread and occurs in part because of national differences in defining property. According to US government definitions, intellectual property refers to a broad collection of rights relating to human inventiveness and creativity. It comprises two main branches: first, industrial property, covering inventions, trademarks, and industrial designs; and, second, copyright.

A *patent* is a governmental grant of a property right to the inventor of a product or process which is new and has utility – that is, it has industrial application. A patent provides the inventor, or the inventor's successor in title, with exclusive rights that generally preclude others from making, using, or selling the invention. A Uruguay Round agreement requires that a patent must be valid for a minimum of 20 years from the filing date of the application.

A *trademark* is any word, symbol, design, or device used to identify a product.

Service marks involve similar descriptors to identify a service. The purpose of a trademark or service mark is to identify goods put on the market, thereby distinguishing them from other goods and services, and to indicate their source or origin. To a large extent trademarks have become a guarantee of quality. GATT agreements provide that initial registration of a trademark must be valid for a period of at least seven years with indefinite renewals.

Copyright usually refers to 'literary and artistic works.' US copyright law enumerates eight broad categories of protectible subject matter: literary works (which include computer software); musical works, including accompanying words; dramatic works, including accompanying music; pantomimes and choreographic works; pictorial, graphic, and sculptural works; motion pictures and other audiovisual works; sound recordings; and architectural works. US law, consistent with the Berne Convention and GATT agreements, protects a copyrighted work for the term of author's life, plus 50 years.

Common global policies on intellectual property have not emerged, in large part because many of the products they cover are evolving faster than rules can be written. Although GATT outlined an Agreement on Trade-Related Aspects of Intellectual Property Rights, most nations have yet to clarify how they will implement these rights. Further, focus on issues of intellectual property is not just a question of protections for industrialized nations and their firms. For example pharmaceutical firms, cosmetics, even toothpaste industries face growing allegations that they exploit indigenous people by using the latter's knowledge of local plants without proper reimbursement. Following the 1992 Convention on Biological Diversity, Merck was one firm to take action, agreeing to pay $1 million to Costa Rica's National Institute of Biodiversity, to collect plants, insects, and microbes; they further agreed to pay royalties for discoveries made based on the Institute's help with research.

Products ranging from pharmaceuticals to entertainment to computer software are especially vulnerable to intellectual property risk, as are trademarks for many established consumer products. In developing economies, it is not unusual to see look-alike products on grocery and pharmacy shelves; sometimes the resemblance to an existing product is not just similar, it is identical. For example, in China, texts, popular magazines, videos, and music often are faithfully reproduced to such high standards that it is difficult to know the product is a fake. In Indonesia, Thailand, Vietnam, and other countries, roadside vendors offer brand knockoffs of watches and other jewelry at less than $10. Figures released by the International Federation of the Phonographic Industry sets the value of 1994 pirate retail sales of sound recordings at $2.25 billion or 6% of total sales. Pirating losses for books and pharmaceuticals also reach billions per year. Biggest losses are in the computer software industry: the Software Publishers Association estimates $8 billion of its retail sales are lost to pirates worldwide. Three common forms of software piracy are 'softlifting' or copying a licensed version for others; 'hard disk loading' is unauthorized loading of software onto hard disk by hardware dealers; and 'bulletin board piracy' is illegal transmission and posting of copyrighted software to computer bulletin boards (Software piracy, 1995). In 1996 more than 225 million business applications were pirated, leading to lost sales of over $11.2 billion worldwide (Business Software Alliance, 1998). Figure 9.9 indicates that piracy rates vary worldwide, but it also shows that a higher percentage of users purchased rather than pirated business software between 1994 and 1996. Reasons for this are described below.

Processes and structures for managing intellectual property risk

Figure 9.9 shows a decrease in pirating that is attributable in large part to actions businesses have taken. These include price decreases that make products more accessible,

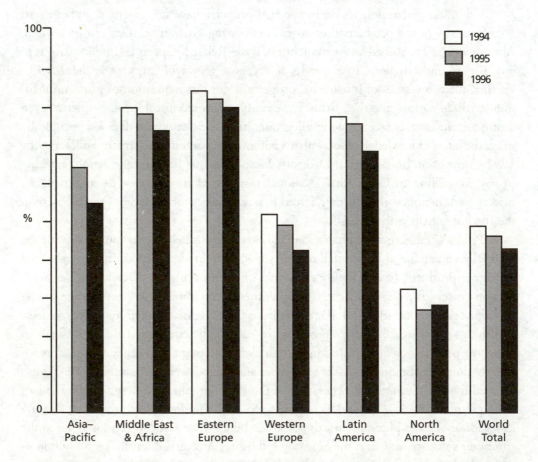

FIGURE 9.9 *Business software piracy rates, 1994–1996* (1998, Jan. 5). 1996 BSA/SPA piracy study results. piracy/96 TABLES.HTM

features that make legitimate copies easier to identify, better servicing networks, and information and education campaigns.

- The Business Software Alliance formed by Aldus, Ashton-Tate, Lotus, Microsoft and WordPerfect now includes software producers worldwide who increase public awareness of piracy and promote the benefits of using nonpirated software.
- Stream International Inc. has introduced previously nonexistent distribution channels into countries to make legitimate products available and price-competitive.
- Efforts to protect the software itself often fail and have been replaced with efforts to distinguish the original from copies. These efforts include Microsoft's use of holograms and a Certificate of Authenticity required from original equipment manufacturers.

Total/continuous quality improvements

Total quality management (TQM) and other continuous quality improvement programs were among the earliest process-oriented changes shared worldwide. Practiced in Japan following World War II, TQM principles developed to include: taking a long-term view; empowering those closest to the work to make decisions; management by facts; reductions in product variability; removal of waste; and continuous improvement. In theory, all organizational members similarly embrace these principles to achieve continuous improvements and produce 'zero defects.' This group of theories can be thought of as hybrid because they emphasize long-term gains and short-term efficiency, they involve equal participants in the process, and they call for both quantitative and qualitative skills.

Well suited to Japanese firms where lifetime employment and consensus decision-making were the norm, principles variously known as TQM, CQM (continuous quality management), CQI (continuous quality improvement) and other acronyms initially proved less beneficial for US firms where there were clear status differentials between managers and workers and where it was possible to eliminate workers to achieve quality goals. Failure to adapt TQM principles to new settings led to initial failures in TQM programs, and a general sense that what worked for Japan could not work elsewhere. In an article titled 'Top managers and TQM success: One more look after all these years,' Thomas Choi and Orlando Behling (1997) concluded that the 1990s had not been good to TQM, citing studies reported in the US and in Britain that showed TQM programs had not produced expected results. Other initiatives using TQM have illustrated how important it was to adapt TQM programs to the firm and its culture and to adapt other firm procedures like inventory, supply management, and rewards system to TQM.

Successful adaptations of TQM processes have led TQM programs to innovations such as return on quality which ensures that quality sought is the quality customers want. Rapid change in most industries requires organizations to continuously monitor and improve on their core competencies, but managers cannot do this alone. Organizational processes like culture make it possible for every employee to understand, act on, and improve core competencies. Effective information systems, teams, and learning processes also help to accomplish this goal.

Re-engineering processes

Continuous improvements enhance existing processes, whereas, as pioneered by Michael Hammer and James Champy (1993), re-engineering discards existing processes to begin anew. Among the ideals of re-engineering are ones shared with other theories: emphasize hybrids that blend centralized and decentralized structural forms; move decisions to those most affected by them; and perform process steps in a natural order such as beginning with the customer's needs rather than telling customers what they need. Consistent with traditional bureaucracy, re-engineering favors a top-down approach to the change process, and seeks to minimize overlap in functions, but runs counter to it in reducing checks and controls. Work need not be performed at an office, but can instead be distributed, often by means of telecommunications.

Writing in 1995, James Champy's *Re-engineering management: The mandate for new leadership* acknowledged the revolution re-engineering was intended to spur had not occurred. According to Champy, part of the problem was widespread belief among employees that re-engineering was a prelude to layoffs or plant closings. However, Champy believes that most of the problem was underestimating the impact re-engineering would have on people, and he suggests re-engineering be organized around and managed according to five core processes:

(a) mobilizing people around initiatives;
(b) enabling the workforce to accomplish change;
(c) defining objectives;
(d) measuring performance; and
(e) communicating to employees throughout the organization.

For US firms, effective redesign efforts appear to be associated with three requirements, including a commitment to total redesign as an economic imperative rather than a good idea, a clear strategic vision and accompanying process and structural changes to support it, and a managerial philosophy suited to the chosen strategy and structure (Miles, Coleman, and Creed, 1995). A study of re-engineering efforts in some of the most important Swiss and German firms in chemical, auto, manufacturing, and engineering industries also showed successful efforts to re-engineer businesses result in re-engineering of the entire management process (Ruhli, Treichler, and Schmidt, 1995). These findings are consistent with assertions throughout this text that organizational leaders prepared to adapt one aspect of internal organization also should prepare to adapt others. At the same time, and as the example of Levi Strauss illustrates (Box 9.14), re-engineering is not a panacea.

BOX 9.14:   RE-ENGINEERING AT LEVI STRAUSS

Levi's Robert Haas hoped to become an industry leader in service to retailers, but the project got away from Haas and from Levi, becoming a huge, complex, technologically sophisticated failure costing $850 million. According to Stratford Sherman's analysis, the problem with this re-engineering effort was not the desire to reduce delivery time, nor the purchase of state-of-the-art computer systems. It was that Levi's vaunted 'openness and honesty and respect for one another's opinions cannot alter the fact that none of them really know what they are talking about.' In other words, re-engineering cannot succeed without knowledge of what is to be done and why.

Source: Sherman, Stratford. (1997, May 12). Levi's: As ye sew, so shall ye reap. *Fortune*, pp. 104–116.

Innovation

Organizational leaders at companies like 3M and Rubbermaid believe that innovation or constant development and refinement of products and processes is the source of strategic advantage. Many also believe that innovation is the basis for a nation's strategic advantage as well, and they would therefore argue that it remains important for national governments to invest in efforts that stimulate national innovation. However, Hamish McRae (1995) predicts that the rapid transfer of information and goods across nations will make it possible for nations to imitate one another in a matter of days so that creativity and social responsibility will be the best predictors of a nation's economic success rather than innovation *per se*. Both creativity and social responsibility are processes more than products, suggesting that nations may need to stimulate these processes as much as they seek to stimulate product development in the interests of stimulating national wealth.

Organizational motivations to innovate are several, including desire to maintain established market share in an industry, to be part of a changing industry, or to create new opportunities for the organization. Often organizations become alert to the need to innovate because of changes in buyer habits. For example, in nations where a growing number of women begin to work outside the home, typically there is a decrease in the number of times people shop for groceries and a growing need for larger refrigerators. Additionally, more meals will be purchased rather than prepared at home. Retailers alert to the first change have countered its effect by offering ready-made meals and making it easier for shoppers to consolidate their shopping. Businesses also can anticipate changes that will require a new or revised product or service – responsive organizations will be those that supply buyers with what they want before they know they want it. Club Med has developed interest in adventure traveling by establishing outposts in ever more exotic locations, and conversion of the Star Clipper, a nineteenth-century sailing ship, into a high-tech cruiser has attracted people to new cruising experiences.

As we saw earlier, innovation can result from an internal research and development effort, alliances, and national investments in research and development. For example, intensive US space R&D during the Sputnik era resulted in products businesses later adapted for consumer use such as powdered fruit juice and the freeze-dried food now popular for hiking and camping trips. Almost 96% of national R&D traditionally has been conducted by wealthy industrialized nations such as Japan, the US, Germany, France, and others in Western Europe. However, according to the 1996 *World Competitiveness Report*, national R&D spending in South Korea and Taiwan had increased to the same level as many European countries. A US National Science Foundation report titled *Asia's new high-tech competitors* concluded that newly developed and developing Asian nations invest in efforts to upgrade the technological base, using four approaches: expanding expenditures on R&D; improving education; attracting FDI; and making the home country more attractive to home-country engineers and scientists.

Organizations innovate internally in two ways – through product or process technologies introduced. Innovative products often emerge from research labs, but they are not isolated there. In many organizations ideas that lead to new products can come from any person who asks: Could it be done another way? Encouraging people to ask this and other questions is part of the challenge of stimulating learning, stimulation partly due to changes in processes that cause people to approach their work in new or different ways. For example, reassigning work from the individual to the team is a process innovation when it encourages many to engage in thinking. Training also can stimulate innovation, particularly training that encourages people to examine their assumptions about how work is or should be accomplished or how a product is or can be used.

Although many have argued that bureaucratic organizations tend to depress innovation with their rigidity, in practice this is not necessarily the case. For example,

Minnesota Mining and Manufacturing (3M) is a highly structured organization and also one that is well known for product innovations. This suggests that large hierarchically organized firms as well as small or horizontally organized ones can build innovations into existing structures. At 3M, one way this has been achieved is that people are encouraged to innovate and take risks. All technical people are encouraged to spend 15% of their work time on personal projects. But when those projects are not successful, their sponsors are not punished. This sends a signal showing that failures are a natural and expected part of risk-taking. Internally, innovative ideas often are brought to production by 'idea' champions – people who believe in the ideas enough to invest time and energy in seeing them developed. In *Winning through innovation*, Michael Tushman and Charles O'Reilly III (1997) argue that successful innovation is difficult to sustain because of both structural and cultural inertia within organizations. That is, over time organizations develop structures, processes, and systems to manage work, but changing them is costly because employees resist change. This cultural inertia of how things are or should be done often proves more intractable than structural change, but Tushman and O'Reilly believe inertial resistance can be overcome if organizational leaders emphasize constant learning. Although their focus is on innovation, the thesis these authors present reinforces themes presented throughout this book: changes in one part of an organization necessarily involve change in other parts of organizations, and changes in processes and people often are more difficult to effect than structural change.

PEOPLE
Creativity

Innovation often is stimulated by creative thinking on the part of people who are willing to think 'outside the box' and put forward ideas others might consider far-fetched or just plain wrong. In *Jamming: The art and discipline of business creativity*, John Kao (1996) argues that the only way for businesses to generate new ideas is to hire creative people and then give them an environment where they are free to develop their ideas but also directed toward focusing on tasks and working with others. According to the Center for Creative Leadership, organizational stimulants to individual creativity include providing the six elements described below:

(a) freedom in deciding what work to do or how to do it;
(b) challenge to work hard on important projects;
(c) resources needed to do the work;
(d) encouragement from a supervisor who is a good work model, who sets appropriate goals, who supports and has confidence in the work group;

(e) work group supports such as diverse skills, people who communicate well, are open to new ideas, constructively challenge on another's work, are committed to their work, and trust and help each other;

(f) organizational encouragement in a culture that supports creativity and communicates a shared vision of the organization.

Factors that depress creativity include: (a) organizational impediments such as internal political problems, harsh criticism of new ideas, destructive forms of internal competition, avoidance of risk, and overemphasis on the status quo; and (b) workload pressure such as unrealistic expectations, too many distractions, or extreme time pressures (KEYS, 1995). In summary, creative people need other creative people, they require organizational structures that allow flexibility but also provide direction, and processes that facilitate rather than impede the innovations that often emerge from creativity.

Although creativity may come naturally to some people, individual intelligence as well as training also have a role to play in helping people express creativity. Mr Kao, for example, appears to be a person with natural creative gifts: in addition to having been an executive producer in the film business, he played piano for Frank Zappa, has a passion for multimedia, and owns his own creative consulting firm. His intelligence is reflected by academic accomplishments that include a PhD in psychiatry and an MBA. However, he attributes his own ability to cross traditional boundaries not to academics or work experience but to his Chinese-American background and to a father who combined Chinese- and Western-style medicine. Mr Kao's example suggests that creativity may be stimulated by diversity, and that people provide strong models for others to develop their own creative potential.

According to James Higgins, author of *Escape from the maze* (1997), personal creativity is stimulated by taking nine steps:

1 Accept innate creativity by consciously trying to use imagination and intuition.
2 Unlearn how not to be creative by breaking habits of predictable thinking developed in the past.
3 Expand personal problem-solving styles; for example, people who are intuitive should practice being rational and vice versa.
4 Use creativity techniques such as brainstorming.
5 Practice thinking more in pictures and visual images than just in words.
6 Learn when to think because both vigorous exercise and sleepiness tend to turn off internal mental censors that program out creativity.
7 Think in new ways by looking for solutions in unfamiliar places and using multiple techniques.

8 Keep a creativity record, perhaps a notebook to preserve ideas.

9 Face complexity by realizing that few problems have simple answers.

Computer work

Throughout the world, there are increasing demands for college-educated people with computer skills. In the US, for example, between 1984 and 1993, the percentage of jobs for college graduates requiring computer skills rose from 42% to 67%. According to a 1994 *Business Week* report, the percentage of workers using a computer on the job was just under 60% for college graduates and more for those with post-graduate college education. With the exception of Sweden, the Netherlands, and Finland, computer use at home and work are lower in Western Europe than in the US. For example, Microsoft estimates that more than 90% of US white-collar workers use computers as compared to 55% of their counterparts in Western Europe (Europe's technology gap, 1997). This gap may grow because of an increased disparity in information technology investments. For example, in 1992 the European information technology market was about equal in size to that of the US, but by 1998 the US market was about 50% larger. Additionally, Europe is estimated to be several years behind on Internet use as well (Moschella, 1998). The success of their own Minitel computer system may be one reason French people have not embraced the Internet. The gap between US and Japanese executives' use of computer is wider: 37% of Japanese executives report they seldom use a computer; and only 8% believe they must use one as compared to 64% of US executives (Vital signs, 1995). Cultural variations, economics, and politics all play a role in these differences. For example, slower economic growth in Europe and Japan as compared to the US and tariff and similar barriers can impede computer sales from abroad. Finally, the face-to-face relational approach to business practiced in Japan may constrain electronic communication there, whereas, tall hierarchical structures and status differentials demonstrated by a phalanx of secretaries may dissuade French executives from using computers themselves. On the contrary, in the US, downsizing has eliminated many secretarial positions and computers support autonomy and efficiency motives encouraged among US managers.

Nevertheless, in advanced and developing economies, information technology is expected to create many of the new jobs from 1992 to 2005, with computer engineers, scientists, and systems analysts in greatest demand. The bad news is that information technology also will phase out jobs, particularly for those who do not have a college education and those with degrees who do not know how to use computers (Sager, 1994). In view of plummeting chip prices and enhanced computer capabilities, even smaller, less wealthy companies are demanding that all prospective employees be computer knowledgeable. In Western Europe, smaller firms often use computers frequently as compared to lower use among larger firms.

Many wonder if this ambitious sweep of technology is carrying us into a new age of work. Have businesses and workers of the world embraced the vast potential of computers and telecommunications and broken free of age-old constraints like geographic location and national borders? As with most things, positive changes in our lives rarely come without a potential for negative side-effects. Technology is no exception. Along with championed positive effects of technologies, it also is important to review examples of the negative potential for these technological advancements. According to pamphleteer Jerry Mander (1995), the costs of technology often are masked by early enthusiasm for technology; this comes with a caution to be mindful that most of what we know about technology comes from its proponents; negative attributes are slow to emerge; and an individual technology is only one piece of a larger web of technologies whose second- and third-order effects are unpredictable. For these reasons, it is important that people acquire computer skills but also develop other technical and personal skills to improve their adaptability to what will certainly be growing technological change.

Skills like computer literacy already are in demand globally, but what other skills will be needed for the years ahead? How is one to prepare for a future that offers so few certainties? Managing or working with people who are not just like you may mean acquiring new managerial skills, while work in a global industry could require additional technical or practical skills. Finally, changes brought on by information technology and globalization in other spheres require a change in thinking about organizations, employment, teams, and work itself. Michael Arthur and Denise Rousseau (1996) believe boundarylessness also will redefine careers from a hierarchical progression of advancement to a sequence of experiences that may or may not be related or progressive. While the latter approach to careers allows for a degree of freedom unusual today, it also creates uncertainties for those who prefer linearity.

Managerial competencies for a global world: enhancing knowledge

Interviews with executives and results of a career questionnaire completed by members of the International Association of Corporate and Professional Resources were used to identify the knowledge, skills, and abilities important to shaping a successful managerial career in the twenty-first century. Study authors Brent Allred, Charles Snow, and Raymond Miles (1996) grouped these success characteristics into five categories:

1 As in the past, managers will begin their careers with a technical specialty, but will need stronger computer literacy skills than today and must be able to interpret and use a broad array of data.
2 Future managers must not only have multicultural and international

experience, they also must have cross-functional expertise that allows them to be both managers and technical experts.

3 Future managers will be collaborative leaders, and will be part of both temporary and permanent groups over the span of a career.

4 Future managers will not only need to manage their careers and their time at work, they will need to balance career and personal demands rather than rely on bosses to allocate time and tasks.

5 Flexibility will be the most important individual trait for successful managers, but integrity and trustworthiness are part of this equation as well.

In review, managerial competencies leading to successful careers are those that require balance and call for a sense of personal priorities. For example, without a clear view of personal and professional priorities, individuals can easily lose desired balance between personal life and work or become flexible at the cost of personal or professional integrity. Additionally, given infinite opportunities to acquire computer knowledge, it becomes possible to spend every moment learning and few moments managing. In summary, among the career competencies needed for the information age is the ability to develop self-knowledge and the capacity to develop, manage, and fulfill goals that are as much personal as professional. Doing this shifts the career development burden from the organization, where once there may have seemed to be 'one best way' to shape a career, to the individual, creating an opportunity and a challenge for lifelong learning and successful managerial careers that take many different forms.

KEY CHAPTER CONCEPTS

The Industrial and the Information Revolutions: Introduction of steam power in the 1770s had a revolutionary effect on work; the same revolutionary impact for the Information Age was stimulated by computerization. Changes of the Industrial Revolution included work shifts from agricultural to industrial economies, population shifts from rural to urban areas, unprecedented population growth, an unprecedented high standard of living as well as doubling of average life span in developed countries, and continuous technological introduction that created a sense of constant change. These same conditions are evident in the Information Revolution.

Technological Revolutions Change Every Form of Organization: Technological breakthroughs of almost every kind punctuate known history, and many of these breakthroughs have brought about revolutionary changes in how work is accomplished. Technological revolutions also have had a profound impact on social and family life. In the Information Age, these impacts are an increasing rate of change, a growing sense of job insecurity, and blurring boundaries between work and personal life.

Information Intangibility as a Driving Force for Wealth Creation: Unlike the land, labor, and capital factors so important to economic growth during the Industrial Revolution, the driving force behind the Information Revolution is an intangible: information, and, more specifically, knowledge. Whereas the Industrial Revolution tended to standardize and routinize work, the Information Revolution has reintroduced variety in work and shattered many assumptions about the importance of routine.

Information Isn't Always Useful: Information abundance, even overload, makes it critical to distinguish between data and the sort of information needed to generate knowledge.

Three Stages of Business Use of Computers: Businesses adopted computers in three distinct phases: as data processors, as microcomputers, as networked information systems. The networked connectivity of computerization that spawned the Internet is an emerging phase of computer use.

Personal Computers Are Global: Plummeting prices and growing computer power made computers adaptable to most businesses' uses and to many home uses worldwide. Sales growth in personal computers (PCs) is increasingly powered by purchases outside the US.

The Internet as a Symbol of Boundarylessness: The Internet symbolizes the computer-based equivalent of boundarylessness: it is ungoverned, operates night and day around the world, is accessible to many, often free, and provides a knowledge-based window to the world. Easing of regulatory restrictions on the Internet in 1995 brought a flood of business uses to the Internet, including the graphics/text/video combinations offered by the World Wide Web.

Transformation of Telecommunications Industries: Telecommunications industries and firms in them have been transformed as it becomes more nearly possible to communicate worldwide at little cost.

Technology as a Source of Economic Development: Satellite systems and wireless telephone technologies are making it possible for developing economies to leap-frog intermediate steps when adopting telephone technology.

Innovation as a Source of Strategic Advantage: The ability to innovate constantly is expected to provide an organization with the potential to create and sustain a strategic advantage. However, providing the climate for innovation and creativity requires rethinking existing processes and supporting structures, and stimulates the need to select and nurture creative people.

582

Change Processes Require Changes in Organizational Structure and Orientations: Continuous quality improvement programs and process re-engineering have proved to be two useful ways to stimulate innovation, but neither can be achieved without accompanying alterations in organizational structures and processes.

Boundaryless Careers: These are less frequently managed by organizations and more usually managed by individuals who can choose many paths to shape a successful career. Few of these paths to success are available without knowledge of computers, an ability to work with others, and self-knowledge.

REVIEW AND DISCUSSION QUESTIONS

1   Chapter 1 weighed assessments of the positive and negative effects of globalization. Using information technology as the example, weigh the positive and negative effects of this technology at four levels: global, national, business, personal. Provide at least two examples of a positive and two examples of a negative for each level.

2   According to a *Business Week* article titled 'The technology paradox' (1995, March 6, pp. 76–84), the new rules of business such as making money by giving things away, teamwork, mass customization, are challenging the 'rock-solid principles of commerce of decades past' (p. 77). Identify three examples from this chapter that you believe are challenging business traditions; explain the tradition and describe how businesses are moving away from or adapting each of the three traditions you have identified.

3   Perhaps more than other sources of globalization, technological changes are causing organizations to collaborate and cooperate as well as compete. Find examples from the chapter that prove this point and explain why technological change has produced cooperation among businesses.

4   Technological change of one type generates still other changes when business leaders examine underlying assumptions. The following example illustrates that those changes can be negative as well as positive. After you have read the Sara Lee example, assess the firm: Is it oriented toward an Industrial Age or an Information Age? What traditional managerial assumptions did Sara Lee managers make that reflect the 'one best way' of scientific management? What approach would you take if you faced the same type of situation?

Sara Lee's bakery in New Hampton, Iowa, began to produce croissants and hand-decorated cakes in the 1980s. Consumers particularly wanted croissants with forward curling tips, and at times employees raced one another to produce as many as 100 croissants per minute. But there were problems. Employees had to twist their wrists more than before while reaching over conveyor belts, and that – together with standing on concrete floors all day – led some number of employees to complain about shooting pains in their arms, numb and tingling fingers, and aching wrists. At first, workers' complaints were dismissed because local doctors could not diagnose a problem. Increased numbers of complaints by 1986 caused Sara Lee management to recruit a hand surgeon from 100 miles south who visited the bakery to time worker wrist actions per minute, measure table heights, and photograph worker movements before suggesting ways employees could work without using awkward postures. The bakery made the suggested changes, including slowing down the fast workers and adding an additional worker to the line. But the program was a flop. Workers were confused by technical terms, and worried when so many of their colleagues underwent surgery for what was now diagnosed as carpal tunnel syndrome. Further, workers objected to driving so far to see the doctor – especially since they were not paid for the four- to five-hour round trip, sometimes through ice and snow. Finally, for this and other reasons, workers at the Sara Lee factory called a strike that lasted for two weeks in March of 1990.

Source: Rigdon, J.E. (1992, Sept. 28). The wrist watch: How a plant handles occupational hazard with common sense. *The Wall Street Journal*, pp. A1, A9.

5   How would you feel about having other people, e.g., your boss, your parent, your friends, read your private e-mail notes? How would you feel about others – even strangers – gaining access to information about your financial assets? What cultural, political, economic or other reasons can you find to explain why you feel as you do?

6   The content of the chapter focused primarily on information technologies, but many other technologies also are having a profound effect on people and organizations. Select a 'breakthrough' technology outside the field of information technology (IT); possibilities include AZT medicine for AIDs, cloning, organ transplants, genetic engineering, and others on the list of 'top 10 technologies' for this chapter. Choose one breakthrough technology and outline three ways it has, could, or will change work life in terms of organizing work; what we do when at work; how we accomplish tasks; how we interact with others. Map out first-, second-, and third-order effects of these technologies on the quality of human life.

7   *The Global Enterprise Project*: Demonstrate the firm's responsiveness to technological progress within or outside its industry; this section might include reference to research and development programs, to intellectual property protection, to technology transfer, to teamwork, to re-engineering, or to how the firm has adopted other technologies, e.g., hardware or software.

REFERENCES

Activate the money star. (1997, May 3). *The Economist*, pp. 56–59.

Allred, Brent B., Snow, Charles C., and Miles, Raymond E. (1996). Characteristics of managerial careers in the 21st century. *Academy of Management Executive*, 10(4): 17–27.

Arnold, Wayne. (1996, Sept. 16). Cracking the code. *The Wall Street Journal*, pp. R18, R21.

Arthur, Michael B., and Rousseau, Denise M. (1996). A career lexicon for the 21st century. *Academy of Management Executive*, 10(4): 28–39. (Arthur and Rousseau also are editors of and contributors to *The boundaryless career*. New York: Oxford University Press, 1996.)

Auerbach, Jon G. (1997, June 16). Getting the message. *The Wall Street Journal*, p. R22 (Special Report on Technology).

Borzo, Jeanette. (1996, Nov. 11). ITV seeks satellite standard. *Info World*, pp. TW1–2.

Bradley, Stephen P., Hausman, Jerry A., and Nolan, Richard L. (1993). *Globalization, technology, and competition*. Boston, MA: Harvard Business School Press.

Burrus, Daniel with Gittines, Roger. (1993). *Techno trends*. New York: Harper Business.

Business Software Alliance. (1998). Overview: Global software piracy report: Facts and figures, 1994–1996. http://www.bsa.org/piracy/96REPORT.HTM

Carley, W.M., and O'Brien, T.L. (1995, Sept. 12). How Citicorp system was raided and funds moved around world. *The Wall Street Journal*, pp. A1, A6.

Carton, Barbara. (1996, July 11). Farmers begin harvesting satellite data. *The Wall Street Journal*, p. B4.

Champy, James. (1995) *Reengineering management*. New York: HarperBusiness.

Chandler, Alfred. (1977). *The visible hand: The managerial revolution in American business*. Cambridge, MA: Belknap Press of Harvard University Press.

Choi, Thomas Y., and Behling, Orlando C. (1997). Top managers and TQM success: One more look after all these years. *Academy of Management Executive*, 11(1): 37–47.

Drucker, Peter. (1994, Oct. 17). The continuing feminist experiment. *The Wall Street Journal*, p. A14.

Engardio, Peter. (1994a, Nov. 18). High-tech jobs all over the map. Special issue: 21st century capitalism. *Business Week*, pp. 112–120.

Engardio, Peter. (1994b, May 18). Third world leapfrog. *Business Week*, pp. 48–49.

Europe's technology gap. (1997, Mar. 17). *Fortune*, pp. 26–27.

Foreign markets give PC makers a hearty hello. (1995, Sept. 15). *The Wall Street Journal*, p. B3.

Forrester, Tom, and Morrison, Perry. (1992). *Computer ethics: Cautionary tales and ethical dilemmas in computing*. New York: McGraw-Hill.

Forge, Simon. (1995). *The consequences of current telecommunication trends for the competitiveness of developing countries*. Washington, DC: World Bank.

Goulet, Dennis. (1977). *The uncertain promise: value conflicts in technology transfer*. New York: North America Inc.

Hafner, Katie, and Lyon, Matthew. (1996). *Where wizards stay up late*. New York: Simon & Schuster.

Hammer, Michael, and Champy, James. (1993). *Re-engineering the corporation*. New York: HarperBusiness.

Higgins, James M. (1997). *Escape from the maze*. Winter Park, FL: New Management Publishing.

Hill, G. Christian. (1997, Jan. 27). Global PC sales growth slowed to 11% in 4th quarter as US rate fell to 16%. *The Wall Street Journal*, p. B14.

Hof, Robert D. (1994, Dec. 19). The 'lurking time bomb' in Silicon Valley. *Business Week*, pp. 118–119.

In search of the perfect market. (1997, May 10). *The Economist*, Electronic Commerce Survey, pp. 3–5.

International code of conduct on the transfer of technology. (1981). New York: UN.

Jackson, James. (1995, Spring). It's a wired, wired world. *Time*, Special Issue on information technology, pp. 80–82.

Kao, John. (1996). *Jamming: The art and discipline of business creativity*. New York: HarperBusiness.

KEYS: New survey measures creativity in the workplace. (1995). *Issues and Observations*, 15(3): 2, 9. KEYS: Assessing the Climate for Creativity by the Center for Creative Leadership from the work of Teresa Amabile and Stan Gryskiewicz, published by the Center for Creative Leadership, Greensboro, NC.

Kotter, John. (1997, Mar. 31). Matsushita: The world's greatest entrepreneur (book excerpt). *Fortune*, pp. 105–111. (Excerpt from the book *Matsushita leadership*. Boston, MA: Free Press, 1997.)

Kurian, George Thomas, and Molitor, Graham (Eds). (1996). *Encyclopedia of the future*. New York: Macmillan Library Reference.

Lewis, P.H. (1994, Dec. 31). And the spoof begets a news release, and another. *The New York Times*, p. 29.

McCartney, Scott, and Friedland, Jonathan. 1995, June 29. Catching up: Computer sales sizzle as developing nations try to shrink PC gap. *The Wall Street Journal*, pp. A1, A11.

McRae, Hamish. (1995). *The world in 2020*. Boston, MA: Free Press.

Magnet, Myron. (1994, June 27). The productivity payoff arrives. *Fortune*, pp. 79–84.

Makridakis, Spyros. (1989). Management in the 21st century. *Long Range Planning*, 22(2): 37–53.

Mander, Jerry. (1995). *Four arguments for the elimination of television*. New York: Quill.

Marien, Michael. (1997, Jan./Feb.). Top 10 reasons the Information Revolution is bad for us, *The Futurist*, pp. 11–12.

Martin, Michael. (1996, Oct. 28). When info worlds collided. *Fortune*, p. 131.

Miles, Raymond E., Coleman, Henry J., Jr, and Creed, W.E. Douglas. (1995). Keys to success in corporate redesign. *California Management Review*, 37(3): 128–145.

Millet, Stephen, and Kopp, William. (1996, July/Aug.). The top 10 innovative products for 2006. *The Futurist*, pp. 16–20.

Morrison, J. Ian, and Schmid, Greg. (1997). *Future Tense: The business realities of the next ten years*. New York: William Morrow.

Moschella, David. (1998, Jan. 12). Spotlight on Europe, *Computerworld*, p. 97.

Negroponte, Nicholas. (1995). *Being digital*. New York: Knopf.

Oleson, Douglas. (1995, Sept./Oct.). The top 10 technologies. *The Futurist*, pp. 9–13.

Peters, Tom. (1994, Aug.). How life really works. *Quality Digest*.

Planet Internet. (1995, Apr. 3). *Business Week*, pp. 118–124.

Rodgers, Daniel. (1978). *The work ethic in Industrial American 1850–1920*. Chicago, IL: University of Chicago Press.

Ruhli, Edwin, Treichler, Christoph, and Schmidt, Sascha. (1995). From business reengineering to management reengineering – a European study. *Management International Review*, 35(4): 361–371.

Sager, Ira. (1994, May 18). The great equalizer. *Business Week*, pp. 100–107.

Software piracy report. (1995). http://www.bsa.org/bsa/docs/94prpt.html.

Talbott, Stephen L. (1995). *The future does not compute*. Sebastopol, CA: O'Reilly.

Tapscott, Don. (1996). *The digital economy*. New York: McGraw-Hill.

Tushman, Michael L., and O'Reilly, Charles A., III. (1997). *Winning through innovation*. Boston, MA: Harvard University Press.

Vital signs. (1995, Sept./Oct.). *World Business*, p. 8. (Sources cited were Fuld & Company and Fujitsu Research Institute.)

World Competitiveness Report. (1996). Geneva: Institute for Management Development.

World Telecommunication Development Report. (1996/97). Geneva: International Telecommunications Union.

Wurman, Richard Saul. (1991). *Information anxiety: What to do when information doesn't tell you what you need to know*. London: Pan.

Ziegler, Bart. (1996, Mar. 28). Up and running. *The Wall Street Journal*, p.R6.

Chapter 10

Globalization of the Natural Environment

THE BODY SHOP: BUSINESS FOR A SUSTAINABLE FUTURE

The Body Shop International was founded to produce soaps and lotions from natural ingredients, but its goals soon expanded to include social objectives. According to founder Anita Roddick, the Body Shop's greatest achievements have been to alter the way cosmetics are sold by promoting self-esteem for consumers and eliminating sex and hype from cosmetics; to spearhead a campaign against the use of animal testing in the industry; and to make the industry more aware of environmental issues such as wasteful packaging. Social action is central to both the company's and Roddick's view of business roles in a global world. Body Shop themes of self-care, self-renewal, and environmental renewal identified with Roddick also are shared not just with customers but with other businesses in the cosmetics industry. Interestingly, this industry that has traditionally catered to women is causing both men and women to rethink many roles and existing assumptions about self-esteem, personal relationships, sex roles, and roles consumers and organizations play in sustaining present and future natural resources. Cosmetics producer Make Up Artists (MAC) pushes the boundaries of gender by employing a transvestite spokesperson; Japan's Shiseido defines beauty as inner and spiritual well-being as well as a matter of physical attributes; Avon has provided work opportunities for millions, most recently in China and Latin America; and all cater to the growing diversity of color and cosmetic use worldwide.

The Body Shop symbolizes many of these changes because founder Anita Roddick was among the first in the Western world to attract media attention for successfully combining business with personal politics. Since its founding in 1976, the Body Shop grew from a single store in Brighton, England, to become a global force for natural cosmetics. Sales in 1996 were $906 million and there are over 1,400 shops in 46 countries. The Body Shop also became a force for social issues: Roddick helped Greenpeace launch a save-the-whales campaign in 1985, *and subsequently campaigned publicly for causes backed by Amnesty International, Friends of the Earth, and Survival International. She also became an advocate for ethical business relations with indigenous people. The Trade Not Aid program initiated in 1987 provides a means for the Body Shop to implement its principles in Fair Trade Guidelines that seek to do the following:*

- *an aim to respect people's rights to control their own resources, lands, and lives;*
- *to pay special attention to minority groups, women, and people who are socially and economically marginalized;*
- *to respect all environments and trade in renewable natural materials;*
- *to benefit the primary producer and treat trading partners with respect and integrity;*
- *to create successful and sustainable trade links and encourage small-scale community economies that can be easily duplicated.*

According to Body Shop descriptions, the organization's members believe in the power of community economic initiatives to change lives, and they believe that by trading with these communities and encouraging economic initiatives, the firm can create jobs to support sustainable development, including buying ingredients and accessories, e.g., beads, sisal scrubs. By 1995 the Body Shop had trading pacts with producer groups worldwide providing direct and indirect employment for marginalized groups in Brazil, Mexico, Nepal, India, Nicaragua, Ghana, Bangladesh, Zambia, and South America.

The Body Shop also has a waste management policy characterized by a Reduce, Reuse, Recycle philosophy; when waste is created, the Body Shop aims to dispose of it by the safest and most responsible means possible. One way the firm pursues this policy is to encourage customers to reuse containers, and by offering to recycle any Body Shop packaging customers return. Within the firm, much work is accomplished by teams, including the Values and Vision group, established to wage campaigns against injustices wherever they occur worldwide, and the Community Trade team, which tries to ensure that the company pays reasonable prices to suppliers. According to Roddick, 'The fact that we are honorable and honest is more important than somebody maximizing stockholder profits' (Kochan, 1997, p. 46).

Sources: Body Shop publications; Kochan, Nicholas. (1997, Jan./Feb.). Soap and social action. *World Business* (a publication of KPMG/Peat Marwick), pp. 46–8; Wallace, Charles P. (1996, Apr. 15). Can the Body Shop shape up? *Fortune*, pp. 118–121.

PART I ONE EARTH, ONE WORLD FOR BUSINESS

Many believe that the fundamental source of economic wealth is greater productivity – lowering the amount of input needed for the same output – and there is abundant evidence to show that as worldwide productivity has grown, so too has grown the financial wealth of many individuals, business enterprises, nations, and the world. These productivity increases rely on acquiring, efficiently exploiting, and continually developing productive factors such as capital, technology, raw materials, natural resources, and labor. Most advanced economies continue to prosper because they are able to improve productivity over time; the example of labor illustrates this point. According to a 1997 study sponsored by the OECD (Pilat, 1997), labor productivity among OECD nations was highest in the US for 1960, 1985, and 1995. In contrast, although labor productivity in West Germany grew to 86% of US productivity in 1985, it fell to 81% of US productivity by 1995, dragged down by higher wages that necessarily increased production costs. In other countries such as Britain and Japan, labor productivity grew in all three time periods, contributing to greater prosperity for nations involved. Comparisons of productivity growth are shown in Table 10.1, where value added per hour of labor is compared to the US standard of 100.

In these and other countries, efforts to induce productivity gains also have produced costs – costs of 'hot' money that increases economic vulnerability of nations, costs of depleting natural resources, costs of increased stress for people who feel they must work more hours, travel more, and compete harder to win or retain jobs. These costs of productivity growth increasingly have become the responsibility of businesses, but they also are borne at least partially by nations. National development requires investments in education so that the national workforce can attract and retain businesses, but many nations do not provide universal or low-cost educational opportunities. Taking on the costs of education will certainly mean reducing current government spending in some

TABLE 10.1   Labor productivity in OECD nations, 1960, 1985, 1995, measured by value added per hour worked

	1960	1985	1995
United States	100	100	100
West Germany	56	86	81
Japan	19	69	73
Britain	45	60	70

Source: Pilat, Dirk. (1997). *Labour productivity levels in OECD countries: Estimates for manufacturing and service sectors.* OECD Economics Working Paper no. 169.

other quarter, or require tax hikes that are unpopular in every country. Similarly, national leaders seeking economic development must weigh the long-run social costs to the nation if they allow natural resources of land, raw materials, and labor to be degraded or depleted.

ECONOMIC GROWTH AND ENVIRONMENTAL PROTECTIONS

Even with evidence that free market economic development has improved the quality of human life, we also see these improvements have had unexpected and undesirable effects. Many people today face increased threats to their personal security; free markets have created inequalities; and there is continued concern about the tradeoffs thus far made between economic development and the long-term quality of human life. In view of these and similar concerns, some argue that headlong economic development must be replaced with a new global business ethic called 'sustainable development,' or development that ensures a viable future for the generations that succeed us.

Sustainable development, like many other global constructs, has been viewed from multiple perspectives. Box 10.1 illustrates that these perspectives vary: some emphasize biological minimums (sustaining life); others call for improvements in quality of life; and still others describe tradeoffs among competing goals of biological and economic systems. Regardless of the view taken, all definitions of sustainable development force us to think about obligations to the future – to consider roles businesses as well as individuals, voluntary organizations, and governments play in ensuring a quality future. In contrast to principles of economic development along free market lines, proposals for sustainable development typically call for fundamental changes in how life is organized. For example, market-based economics acknowledge there are likely to be rich and poor, but sustainable development calls for a greater degree of economic equity in the world. Creating better economic opportunities for poorer people and poorer nations requires a change in economic systems, and attendant changes in businesses because they have been the chief forces for spreading market-based economics.

Although globalization has expanded trade and investment, and it has helped reduce poverty in countries like India, opportunities for the world's poorest people are shrinking, the gap between them and the wealthy is growing, and the technologies available for change often are not appropriate. In announcing these and other results of the *Human Development Report* (1997), report coordinator Richard Jolly calls on all nations and all financial and international agencies to do more than cheer the virtues of globalization. Instead, he urges partnerships among all sectors on a global scale to redefine notions of world cooperation (Globalization leaving, 1997).

How these and related objectives might be achieved is a topic for debate all over the world, and it may be many years, if ever, before global agreement is reached.

BOX 10.1:   REPRESENTATIVE CONCEPTIONS OF SUSTAINABLE DEVELOPMENT

Improving the quality of human life while living within the carrying capacity of supporting ecosystems (World Conservation Union, United Nations Environment Programme, and Worldwide Fund for Nature, 1991, p. 10).

Sustainability is a relationship between dynamic human economic systems and larger dynamic, but normally slower-changing ecological systems, in which (a) human life can continue indefinitely, (b) human individuals can flourish, and (c) human cultures can develop; but in which effects of human activities remain within bounds, so as not to destroy the diversity, complexity, and function of the eco-logical life support system (Costanza, Daly, and Bartholomew, 1991, p. 8).

Sustainability is an economic state where the demands placed upon the environment by people and commerce can be met without reducing the capacity of the environment to provide for future generations. It can also be expressed as . . . leave the world better than you found it, take no more than you need, try not to harm life or the environment, and make amends if you do (Hawken, 1993, p. 139).

Sustainability is a participatory process that creates and pursues a vision of community that respects and makes prudent use of all its resources – natural, human, human-created, social, cultural, scientific, etc. Sustainability seeks to ensure, to the degree possible, that present generations attain a high degree of economic security and can realize democracy and popular participation in control of their communities, while maintaining the integrity of the ecological systems upon which all life and all production depends, and while assuming responsibility to future generations to provide them with the where-with-all for their vision, hoping that they have the wisdom and intelligence to use what is provided in an appropriate manner (Viederman, 1994, p. 5).

Source: Gladwin, Thomas N., Kennelly, James J., and Krause, Tara-Shelomith. (1995). Shifting paradigms for sustainable development: Implications for manage-ment theory and research. *Academy of Management Review*, 20(4): 877 (the refer-ence list records the citations).

Accordingly, the option of sustainable development explored here is offered not because it is the best or only option, but because it illustrates the nature of the debate around economic growth and environmental preservation and describes some of the challenges businesses face as they are asked to achieve both.

Principles of sustainable development

Just as definitions of sustainable development vary, so too do the suggested principles vary; the following are likely to be particularly relevant to businesses and to management practices:

1 Tensions between economic growth and environmental protection and regeneration have to be resolved.
2 Poor nations cannot nor should they necessarily imitate the production and consumption patterns of rich nations.
3 Lifestyles in the rich nations must change.
4 Maximization of income must be replaced with the expansion of opportunities for people.

Each principle of sustainable development listed above presents a challenge to many traditional business practices. For example, due to market imperfections, economic growth throughout the world has emphasized development at the cost of the natural environment. Recent attention to old growth forests, to air and water quality, and to other aspects of the natural environment suggests that economic growth often has resulted in environmental sacrifices. Sustainable growth advocates believe that current rates of economic growth will quickly consume all the world's natural resources, leaving nothing for future generations to enjoy. Devastation of the rain forest, the growing roster of extinct or endangered animals, oil spills, and nuclear disasters each provide a glimpse of a future bereft of many natural resources we now enjoy or depend upon. For example, in 1997 when Japanese tanker *Grace Diamond* hit a reef in Tokyo Bay, reporters commented on the oil slick foreground against the backdrop of Mount Fuji. The bay not only handles one-fifth of Japan's shipping, but also has been home to pleasure craft, and many towns along the coast depend on the bay's fish. This and similar oil spills damage natural beauty, threaten the livelihoods of people who depend on the sea, and disrupt business as well.

Given a competitive business environment, and a world population anxious to join the world economy, business organizations are caught somewhere between the proverbial 'rock and a hard place.' Businesses unwilling to compromise the natural environment may themselves lose profit opportunities or perhaps fail to thrive in the market, while those that take active steps to preserve the environment may be accused of imposing their own values on host countries anxious to develop economically. For example, although an international treaty is now in effect to require double-hull tanks on oil carriers, the *Grace Diamond* spill in Tokyo Bay occurred because owner Nippon Yusen had commissioned the ship before the treaty went into effect. The tradeoff between fiscal and environmental costs is further clarified by a look at the various perspectives represented by logging in the Pacific Islands. There is growing evidence that tropical rain forests in the Pacific Islands are being destroyed by logging and farming practices. Logging companies are benefiting from this practice, as are the owners of the islands, whose profit-maximizing behaviors are accelerating deforestation. From the perspective of logging and landowners, forest removal is good. From the perspective of environmentalists, deforestation might be considered bad because trees help to produce breathable air. From the perspective of the global citizen, deforestation might also be considered bad if it destroys the only means of income available to Pacific Islanders, throws them as immigrants into a world employment market for which they are ill prepared, or helps contribute to ozone depletion. The example in Box 10.2 shows that development can occur without also taking on challenges of depletion and dependence.

BOX 10.2:   SUSTAINABLE DEVELOPMENT IN FIJI

Montfort Boy's Town School in Fiji is linking five different micro-industries to use waste from each as a key input to another and at the same time linking students' education to the country's need for a more productive, less polluting economy. Sludge currently discarded by a large Fijian brewery is a potential source for five new enterprises, including growing fresh mushrooms and vegetables, feeding chickens and fish, and providing fuel for electric power. Not only does the Fijian project meet local needs, it shows how a poor farming community can adopt sustainable agricultural principles rather than adopt agri-business principles that might introduce problems such as pollution, job loss to mechanization, or heavy export dependence.

Source: Kane, Hal. (1997, July/Aug.). Eco-farming in Fiji. *World Watch Magazine*, p. 169.

Resolving tensions like these represents a critical global challenge for businesses. Part of the challenge is that many people who live in developing economies *want* to adopt the production and consumption patterns of industrialized nations. Having seen television and similar evidence of material goods in the industrialized world, many see only the financial benefit in the land or raw materials they trade to get or produce consumer products. Ironically, even as some argue that lifestyles in the rich nations must be altered to consume less, many in developing economies advocate the opposite change: they want to adopt the habits of materialism consistent with a consumption-based society. Given a world that wants consumer goods, why should a business organization refuse this business? Thus, one of the challenges of sustainable development is to manage the paradox of economic growth against protection and regeneration of the natural environment. Many argue that this requires emphasis on using renewable resources, limiting or eliminating waste, and reducing impact on the natural environment.

A balancing act

This balancing act between economic development and sustainable growth was the issue explored when delegates from 170 nations met at the United Nations Conference on Environment and Development (UNCED) held in June 1992; this meeting sometimes is referred to as the Rio Summit. Delegates' tasks were to weigh the benefits and costs associated with a worldwide move toward economic development. They considered issues of population, poverty, pollution, and consumption that also will be reviewed in this chapter. The following five main agreements emerged from the Rio Summit; they demonstrate the global nature of environmentalism and recognize the global link between environmentalism and economic development activities:

1 The *Rio Declaration* articulated principles tying economic growth to environmental issues.
2 A *Biodiversity Treaty* aims to protect endangered species and better share profits from use of global genetic resources.
3 The *Climate Change Treaty* called for voluntary reductions of carbon dioxide and other gas emissions leading to the threatened 'greenhouse effect' of global warming.
4 The *Statement of Forest Principles* recommended protecting forests against development-related damage.
5 *Agenda 21* provided an 800-page nonbinding recommendation for how to carry out the Rio principles.

EARTH SUMMIT PROGRESS

Meeting again in 1997, the Earth Summit reviewed progress over the past five years to find that despite declining fertility rates in many nations, poverty has grown; one third of the world's population lives in countries that have moderate to severe access to fresh water; a total of 34 million acres of forest continue to be lost each year to cutting and burning; and worldwide annual carbon dioxide emissions rose from 5.9 billion tons in 1990 to 6.2 billion in 1996. Overall, the report did not paint an encouraging picture of global environmental progress. Events later in 1997 provided even greater cause for concern. Fires raging out of control in Indonesia from late July cast a blanket of smoke across Indonesia, Malaysia, Singapore, the Philippines, and other nations. The net result was not only trees and peat consumed by the fires, but human effects from smoke inhalation, and business effects that included work lost to smoke-induced illness and revenues lost to tourist cancellations. The Third Conference of Parties to the UN Framework Convention on Climate Change (commonly known as the Kyoto Conference) held in December 1997 also demonstrated little progress on reducing greenhouse gases. For example, the US continued to contribute most to air and ozone degradation. In an effort to correct these problems, the Kyoto Conference established clearer and legally binding targets on emissions of carbon dioxide and other greenhouse gases, and initiated a Clean Development Mechanism to globalize efforts to limit greenhouse gas emissions. Progress on these and similar initiatives is in part impeded by the fact that there are opposing views on globalization of the natural environment. This debate was made global at the 1992 UN Conference and it continues in subsequent discussions of the environment. Although oversimplified, this has been described as the 'boom' and 'doom' debate, terms adopted for the discussion below because they represent the extremes of the environmental argument.

THE COMING 'BOOM'

Some believe that concerns about natural resources are unfounded. For example, one argument is that technological breakthroughs of every kind will be the source of sustainable development, and that technology will make it possible for all the world's people to live in relative affluence. Julian Simon (1981) often represents this point of view, and he believes that environmental concerns are pointless because technology, free markets, and human creativity will make the world a better place. Writing in *A moment on the earth*, Gregg Easterbrook (1995) argues that the age of pollution in the Western world is almost over, citing pollution controls on gas-powered vehicles as one example of how the tide is turning. His argument is that economic development leads to improvements in environmental usage, and it is a perspective many share. Further, Easterbrook argues that the natural world is far more resilient than many think, and he calls for 'eco-realism' among those concerned about environmental use. To one degree or another, these and other authors conclude that checks and balances in economic systems can be trusted to develop new technologies if old ones fail. For example, if fossil fuels reach depletion, businesses will find it profitable to develop alternative forms of energy. This school of thought represents a 'boom' mentality or a belief that rapid growth in economic development will produce the technology needed to solve environmental problems businesses help create. In other words, continued desire for economic growth will motivate business people to solve the problems they create. In Box 10.3, Michael Zey represents a 'boom' mentality in his outline for a new 'Macro-industrial Era.'

BOX 10.3: THE MACROINDUSTRIAL ERA

Reaching the first truly global era will require total involvement of every nation and alliance; all will benefit from the extension of human domination in six separate dimensions:

- *Time* will be extended to improve human lifespan and increase the amount of time each person has to make a unique contribution to society; superfast communication links will transfer information rapidly but superfast transport will enhance human contact; robotics and emerging technological developments will make it possible to complete more, faster.
- *Space* will extend outward into the atmosphere and downward into the oceans and earth.
- *Scarcity* will be overcome with technology that can turn out huge quantities of goods using fusion energy rather than fossil fuels; food will be abundant because of biotechnology and genetic engineering. The same technologies that enhance quantity will improve *quality* as well to produce smart technologies, enhance human intelligence, and allow nonscientists to participate in scientific and technological breakthroughs.
- *Scope* will be global as more of the world's population participates in producing and consuming goods; all countries will be equal contributors to human progress because they can exchange the information and labor that will raise quality of life worldwide.
- *Size* will be redefined in terms of what is large and what is small. The concept of huge will expand to include projects and buildings such as Malaysia's 30-mile wide Super Corridor, create irrigation projects that can move entire bodies of water, or build habitable stations underground or in outer space. Small will include nanotechnologies, making it possible to develop computers and machine parts as small as atoms and molecules.

Zey reasons that the answer to pollution is economic growth, providing evidence that shows poor nations invest in cleaner air and water once they develop economically.

Source: Zey, Michael G. (1997, Mar./Apr.). The Macroindustrial Era: A new age of abundance and prosperity. *The Futurist*, pp. 9–14.

'DOOM' APPROACHES

Paul Erlich, author of *The population bomb* (1969), represents an opposing view to the 'boom' argument; he believes that overpopulation, overcrowding, and industrial means of production will inevitably lead to starvation or make immigrants of millions of environmental refugees. According to Erlich, environmental impact (I) is equal to population (P) multiplied by consumption or evidence of affluence (A), then multiplied again by technology (T), or I = PAT. As the equation expresses, technology is in this view part of the environmental problem rather than its solution. Lester Brown, lead author since 1992 of the annual publication *Vital signs*, and president of the Worldwatch Institute, is one among many who also believes that industrial production is on a collision course with the earth's natural limits. Observable acceleration of economic, cultural, and political globalization described in earlier chapters puts greater demands on the natural environment, leading to concerns about food, air and water quality, fuel and other natural resources, emissions and global warming, to name a few. According to Paul Hawken (1993), technological breakthroughs that make it possible to extract more of the world's resources faster have hastened environmental decline rather than helped economic growth.

Although economists often view economic growth as providing the answer to most problems, more are weighing the tradeoffs between rapid growth and the natural environment to rethink this position. Some join Erlich in expressing concerns about the carrying capacity of the earth. In contrast to Michael Zey's argument for economic growth described above, economist Herman Daly, writing in *Beyond growth: The economics of sustainable development* (1996), argues that economic growth cannot be sustained at present levels. Further, he asserts that economic growth has increased environmental costs faster than it has increased the benefits of production. The result is that the world now is poorer rather than enriched by growth in economic development. Economists studying this tradeoff have developed a field called 'ecological economics' that calls for re-evaluating economic principles and shifting taxation away from income and toward resource use. For example, oil refiners would pay pollution taxes on each gallon of gasoline produced. This and other practices would provide incentives for businesses and other resource users to reduce use and waste of resources like air that are 'free' to most industrial producers but will be costly or impossible to replace once depleted or degraded. According to Colin Hutchinson (1992), there should be no contest when firms make the strategic choice between a sustainable future and an unsustainable future because the latter is a method of global suicide for humans.

The challenge for most of us is that we cannot know where the truth lies. Information abundance enables proponents of almost any position to produce empirical evidence supporting their views. As we saw in Chapter 9, information technologies produce access to data, but what they cannot provide for us are the skills to decide whose information best predicts the future. Those associated with the 'boom' school deride predictions of 'doom,' claiming that environmentalists like Rachel Carson or Paul Erlich are alarmists whose most dire predictions did not materialize. For example, in 1962 Rachel Carson predicted the American robin would become extinct within a decade, but it is very much present in the US today. Erlich predicted in the 1970s that hundreds of millions of people would die of starvation; it didn't happen. What has happened is that many animals whose demise was not expected are now gone or at risk; tens of millions of people did die of starvation. These facts suggest that some predictions have not been as dire as expected, but this is hardly consolation for the millions who have starved, for a world forced to carry on with fewer birds, fewer animals, and limited diversity in species. The bottom line for people on this debate is that the cost of being wrong about 'the coming boom' is extremely high. Moreover, the rapid pace of industrial growth worldwide reduces the margin of error over time, making it newly possible for environmental systems worldwide to erode simultaneously. Error could mean degradation of the planet such that it is impossible for life or a reasonable quality of life to be sustained. Because the cost of being wrong about the future is so high, many reason that it is imperative for businesses, governments, and individuals to act together and individually to preserve and develop natural resources now. This argument is based on the assumption that higher short-run costs, including education, training, and development of environmentally friendly products and services, should be measured against the longer run costs of waiting until it is too late to make a difference.

GROWTH VERSUS ENVIRONMENT: THE BUSINESS DEBATE

The 'growth versus environment' debate that occurred between nations at the 1992 Earth Summit also appears in the business literature. For example, authors Noah Walley and Bradley Whitehead (1994) point out that the economic costs of ambitious environmental goals are real, asserting that 'talk is cheap; environmental efforts are not.' While these authors do not suggest that businesses should return to earlier environmental strategies of ignoring, fighting, or frustrating environmental regulations, they do believe that increasingly complex environmental challenges also will increase the business costs of environmental sensitivity, making it less feasible for organizations to go 'green.' They argue there will be few win/win solutions for environmental challenges, an argument that contrasts with the experiences and strategies of firms like DuPont that continue to invest in environmentalism, and with futurists like Hazel Henderson (1996) who believe win/win solutions are not only possible but imperative to human and business survival. Michael Porter and Claas van der Linde (1995) suggest that the debate described above arises from framing the debate in either/or terms such as ecology versus the environment. They believe a more appropriate approach is to view environmental improvement and business success as complements rather than competitors. Their study of industries such as pulp and paper, paint and coatings, electronics manufacturing and others most affected by environmental regulations showed that the costs of meeting environmental regulations can be minimized and even eliminated with innovations. Contrary to traditional arguments that regulation increases costs, these findings suggest that the innovations resulting from regulation enhance quality and actually reduce business costs. Additionally, the up-front costs of correcting past habits can be less than those estimated. For example, retreat from CFC technology was less costly to firms producing CFCs than had been anticipated.

W. Edward Stead and Jean Garner Stead (1996) provide another reason for businesses to be part of the balance of competing interests of environment protection and industrial growth. They believe that couching the debate in terms of either one or the other stimulates a win/lose approach to challenges that can only be managed with the understanding that 'economic success and ecosystem survival are both worthy and necessary goals for individuals, organizations, society and Nature' (p. 131). This approach allows opponents to find common ground on which they can cooperate to create synergies that have the potential to satisfy each. The balance of this chapter describes environmental challenges, further explores tensions between proponents for growth and environmentalism, and describes how organizations like the transnational Worldwatch Institute (whose mission statement appears in Box 10.4) and businesses like the Body Shop (see the opening case) are responding to these and related challenges.

BOUNDARYLESSNESS AND ONE EARTH

In crossing boundaries of time and space and nations, we come to recognize that the earth itself is boundaried, and although it is possible to colonize outer space or develop subterranean communities, neither provides a guarantee for expanding the physical boundaries of our world. In sharing one earth, we live in a complex worldwide ecosystem where activities in one part of the world increasingly affect some or all of the world. In earlier chapters, we reviewed many ways business activities cross boundaries of nations, time, and space. With equal ease, disease, pollution, and environmental degradation also can cross traditional borders. Examples of these are reviewed below to provide insight into the state of the world.

The global commons

At a global level, we must be concerned for those resources held in common because they sustain life – global commons such as air and water whose future depends not on one nation or one business but on the activities of all. The waters of every ocean represent an important global common. Water absorbs and stores heat for the earth, provides

---

BOX 10.4:   MISSION STATEMENT FOR THE WORLDWATCH INSTITUTE

The Worldwatch Institute is dedicated to fostering the evolution of an environmentally sustainable society – one in which human needs are met in ways that do not threaten the health of the natural environment or the prospects of future generations. The Institute seeks to achieve this goal through the conduct of interdisciplinary nonpartisan research on emerging global environmental issues, the results of which are widely disseminated throughout the world.

The Institute believes that information is a powerful tool of social change. Human behavior shifts either in response to new information or new experiences. The Institute seeks to provide the information to bring about the changes needed to build an environmentally sustainable economy. In a sentence, the Institute's mission is to raise public awareness of global environmental threats to the point where it will support effective policy responses. The Institute's outlook is global because the most pressing environmental issues are global. Given the earth's unified ecosystem and an increasingly integrated global economy, only a global approach to issues such as climate change, depletion of the stratospheric ozone layer, the loss of biological diversity, degradation of oceans, and population growth can be effective.

Source: Worldwatch Institute. (1997, June 19). http://www.worldwatch.org

---

abundant energy and food resources, and provides a means of access among many nations. Almost 70% of the earth is water. While boundaries can be drawn around nations, no nation can draw a boundary around the world's common water resources. Yet many operate independently in their use of the ocean and fresh water – often in the name of business and individual self-interest – and this has led to problems all necessarily share.

WATER

Fresh water is crucial to human existence, and 90% of all fresh water on the planet is held in common in Antarctica, which is owned by no country but by all. According to some, fresh water will become so scarce in the next 50 years that it may replace oil as the prime trigger for international conflict (Indiana Center, 1994). A 1996 UN report released at the International Conference on Managing Water Resources for Large Cities and Towns concluded that ensuring adequate water supply worldwide has become a major problem because of growing population, urbanization, and environmental degradation. The same report revealed that water lost through leakage or theft in Kenya was sufficient to supply the nation's largest city, and in China over 300 cities face chronic water shortages. An estimated 20% of urban dwellers in developing economies must purchase water because they have no access to clean water, amounting to as much as 35% of monthly income for a poor family in Khartoum, Sudan. Dirty water also contributes to disease and early death, causing 80% of disease in the developing world and killing 10 million people annually.

AIR

Air similarly has been thought of as a 'free' global common, but its continued availability depends on current use. According to reports generated following the Berlin UN Climate Conference in April 1995, global warming due to ozone thinning in the atmosphere is expected to cause as much as a .5 meter rise in sea levels by 2100, and this will displace the 95 million people who live on affected land. Ozone thinning has been blamed on CFC use, but the problem of thinning goes beyond a single source to demonstrate complex ecosystem relationships among trees and other green plants, water, and air. For example, scientists have found that the ocean helps to destroy methyl bromide, the chemical that depletes ozone in the earth's atmosphere. Global warming is expected to cause ecosystems to disappear, deserts to expand, and storms to become more violent and frequent – all within your lifetime. According to the United Nation's Intergovernmental Panel on climate change humans are a major force for these changes. Some of the anticipated changes are shown in Box 10.5

Writing in 1993, Paul Hawken provided a chilling report on utilization of the global commons within the US and beyond. According to him:

> We know we have decimated ninety-seven percent of the ancient forests in North America; every day our farmers and ranchers draw out 20 million more gallons of water from the ground than are replaced by rainfall; the Ogalala Aquifer, an underwater river beneath the Great Plains larger than any body of fresh water on earth, will dry up within thirty to forty years at present rates of extraction; globally we lose 25 billion tons of fertile topsoil every year, the equivalent of all the wheat fields in Australia. (p. 3)

Disruption of species

An example of ecological disruption due to industrialization is that plants and animals, as well as the diseases and insects they carry, can travel more easily worldwide. According to the World Resources Institute (1996/97), in each decade between 1995 and 2015

BOX 10.5:   UN INTERGOVERNMENTAL PANEL ON CLIMATE CHANGE, 1996

The evidence reviewed suggests a discernible human influence on global climate which have and will have the following effects:

- The amount of carbon dioxide in the atmosphere has increased 30% since about 1750 (preindustrial era).
- Since the late 19th century, global mean temperatures have increased between .3 and .6 degrees Celsius (half to 1 degree F); they will rise by 1.5 and 4 degrees C (2 to 6 degrees F) by 2100
- Higher temperatures will lead to severe droughts and floods in some parts of the world.
- Sea levels have risen an average of 1.0 to 2.5 millimeters per year over the past century; they will rise .5 meters by 2100.
- Improvements in energy efficiency of 10% to 20% are feasible at little or no cost.

Source: Intergovernmental Panel on Climate Change. (1996, Jan.). IPCC Second Assessment Synthesis of Scientific-Technical Information Relevant to Interpreting Article 2 of the UN Framework Convention on Climate Change 1995. Geneva: UN Environment Program.

somewhere between 1% and 11% of the world's species will be committed to eventual extinction. Habitat destruction and deliberate destruction are two major forces threatening species; a third is introduction of new species from elsewhere. For example, after 23 years, embargoes against Washington state apples have been lifted by Japan, Argentina, China, Israel, Russia, and Vietnam, and increased liberalization of embargoes against fruit, vegetables, and meat is expected following World Trade Organization agreements. While trade liberalization does not mean that these products will carry disease or insects, it does allow both to cross borders more readily than in the past. The challenge created is to local or regional subsystems with no immunity or defenses against newcomers.

Available evidence shows that migrating plants and animals have disrupted existing ecosystems. Often, when introduced to new surroundings, these visitors from afar overwhelm defenseless plants and animals there, even driving some into extinction. For example, the island of Guam had no snakes until they hitchhiked in via aircraft 30 years ago. Now brown tree snakes are so prevalent on the island that they have killed off virtually all species of birds and many other animals as well. Moreover, these snakes have interfered with industrial production, causing over 1,200 power outages on the island since 1978. Increases in air travel serving tourist and business interests also increase the potential for similar migrations to occur with similar and devastating effects on local flora and fauna. Complex interactions among parts of the ecosystem like these often become known only as disaster looms.

Zebra mussels traveling on Russian ships clog intake pipes in the Great Lakes of the US, at an annual cost of $500 million, while European green crabs introduced in San Francisco Bay in 1990 have consumed the East Asian clams once residing there. The Rainbow jellyfish entered Black Sea waters in 1982 in the ballast water of a ship and has eaten plankton, fish eggs, and the larvae of existing mussels and oysters there, and continues to spread rapidly. Not only do these marine hitchhikers affect the local fauna, but they increase business and environmental costs where shipowners are asked to pay part of the tab for the damage done and as indigenous species are destroyed. Along with their destruction goes the livelihoods of people who depended on these indigenous animals. The propensity of animals like these to travel on ships or by air is nothing new, but what is new is the number and growing effects of these cross-border hitchhikers.

Theo Colborn, Dianne Dumanoski, and John Peterson Myers (1996) believe that human species are threatened also by air- and food-borne chemicals that interfere with reproductive hormones. According to them, DDT, PCBs, dioxin, and hundreds of other synthetic chemicals mimic the human hormones estrogen and testosterone. When introduced to humans through food ingestion or via air-borne particles, these and similar synthetics have the potential to disrupt endocrine counts. Although the authors acknowledge that wheat, garlic, and hundreds of other foods also act like human hormones, they believe that in thousands of years humans have adapted to these natural hormones. Rapid introduction of synthetics makes it less possible that humans can adapt, and the result may be lowered fertility rates, increasing cancer, or effects like those found among adult rats exposed to synthetics in embryo; some die, those that live can be easily stressed. Neither the positive nor the negative effects of these synthetics are known, but it is clear that they are being introduced rapidly. Among the negative longer term effects is that irreparable damage could occur.

In summary, the same boundarylessness that many believe provides a benefit to businesses as they cross national boundaries also is available to disease. In crossing the boundaries of known science to produce synthetics, scientists may be providing an opportunity or a threat. Finally, there is the issue of biological diversity. If particular species of plants and animals are not well suited to the introduction of new influences, e.g., snakes that prey on birds, then they disappear. Similarly, if synthetics in the air affect specific types of people, the latter may disappear. The result is a shrinking gene pool of animals, plants, and people less able to adapt and thus more vulnerable to future disease or other influences. This reduction in variety threatens species survival.

Natural disasters

Even without human intervention, nature easily is able to affect business activities. This was demonstrated in January of 1995 when an earthquake in Kobe, Japan, closed the city's port, the fourth largest in the world, handling 12% of the country's exports. On the other side of the world, February flooding in the Netherlands prevented thousands of vessels from traveling on the Rhine River link between Rotterdam – the world's largest port – and the industrial centers of eastern France, Germany, and Switzerland. The resulting ban on shipping disrupted almost 60% of the commercial freight between the Netherlands and Germany that normally moved along the rivers, and according to estimates Dutch barge operators were losing about $6 million US a day for every 24 hours they could not travel on the Rhine (Simons, 1995). These natural disasters demonstrate business and human dependency on existing natural resources, and bolster the argument that protection and development of natural resources is an important business activity.

Globalization of disease

Diseases that afflict both people and plants also are going global. For example, the A2 strain of potato virus recently migrated from central Mexico to US potato fields, devastating crops, and costing farmers millions of dollars (Winslow, 1995). The only previous global migration of the fungus occurred in the 1840s, but with increased trade – and particularly increased agricultural trade due to commercial rules fostered by alliances such as NAFTA, the EU, Mercosur, and the World Trade Organization – the spread of agricultural disease could increase.

Like the potato fungus, the HIV virus also has gone global, becoming one of the first human diseases in the era of globalization to be spread via worldwide integration. Although estimates vary, the Global AIDS Policy Coalition estimates that 30.6 million people are infected with HIV, a figure that may more than double by the turn of the century; 16,000 new cases occur each day. About 1.7 million died from AIDS in 1995, and 4.7 million became infected with HIV, including over half a million children born with HIV. HIV is spreading quickly in the developing economies, often carried by migrant workers and long distance truck drivers. According to a 1997 World Bank report (Confronting the spread, 1997), AIDS is a generalized epidemic in many nations, including Sub-Saharan Africa and possibly Central and Eastern Europe where the incidence of AIDs is exploding. Over 40 developing nations have concentrated epidemics confined to specific geographic areas, but in large areas of China, India, and Pakistan, infection is at a nascent stage and has infected less than 5 percent of people who engage in very high AIDs risk behavior. Thus, efforts to combat AIDs on a worldwide scale require local adaptations as well as global campaigns. Author Laurie Garrett examines the spread of AIDs and other lethal epidemics in her book *The coming plague: Newly emerging diseases in a world out of balance* (1994) to argue that disease is interconnected with individuals, societies, and governments. For example, in the developing economies, AIDS might have been spread because well-meaning help-givers reused needles for vaccinations, and it is clear that AIDS has spread in many nations because government leaders have been unwilling to acknowledge or treat the disease.

AIDs has now reached near-epidemic proportions according to the World Health Organization's Global Program on AIDS, and it continues to spread because it has followed different patterns attributable to cultural habits. For example, since 1987 Thailand has witnessed a 23% increase in AIDS among those who are within the age of reproduction because (a) cultural norms have led to development of a large sex industry, (b) it has been culturally acceptable for single and married men to patronize sex workers, (c) there is a growing trend to delayed marriage, and many young people have moved to the cities where they have opportunities to experiment sexually, and (d) there is a belief that AIDS is a problem among specific groups, but not for the general population (Brown and Xenos, 1994).

Because people erroneously believe that AIDS does not afflict the general population, the HIV virus has spread rapidly in Asia, hastened by increased demand for goods transported over land and sea by truckers and seamen who themselves carry the virus. National boundaries opened to commerce by trade alliances improve access to consumer goods and also improve the potential for this disease. In still other countries, AIDs is viewed as a shame on the family, and this leads those with HIV exposure to deny the disease and avoid testing for it, allowing it to spread. In Japan, for example, disclosure of AIDs can lead to loss of one's job, social isolation, and even family rejection. The worldwide impact of AIDs is considerable: entire generations of African adults have been wiped out by the disease leaving grandparents to raise children, and no one to support either financially. The incidence of AIDs in Africa is rising and by 1997 totalled 14 million in Sub-Saharan Africa. The costs of AIDs in Africa are not only human, but also affect African economies as indicated in Box 10.6. According to studies conducted by the International Food Policy Research Institute, AIDS weakens economies by shifting resources away from production and education and toward health care, and because its greatest effect is on healthy young adults, the economy loses productive members of society. The greatest effect may be on the poor because AIDS deprives them of the main resource they bring to the economy: their labor (International Food Policy Research Institute: http://www.cgiar.org/ifpri). Although it is much in the news, AIDs is only one of several global disease threats for humans. There may be as many as 300 million carriers

BOX 10.6:   AIDS IMPACT ON ECONOMIES

- In 1993 Thailand, each death from peak-earning AIDS sufferers equalled $22,000 in lost future earnings.

- Death stemming from AIDS killed about 10% of Uganda Railway employees in the mid-1990s, creating an annual 15% turnover of workers.

- Tanzanian losses of teachers to AIDS is projected to be 14,460 by 2010, and 27,000 by 2020.

- In developing economies, adults with AIDS experience an average 17 episodes of illness before death. The costs often deplete household savings.

- In Sub-Saharan Africa as many as 40 million or 16% of children may be orphans by 2010.

- Treatment for AIDS during 1993 in Thailand – excluding expensive drugs – amounted to 50% of income for the average family.

- In Tanzania, orphaned children are more malnourished than others, and orphaned older children are dropping out of school to care for younger ones.

- Life expectancy in Zimbabwe in 1997 was 22 years less than it would have been in the absence of AIDS.

Sources: Barnathan, Joyce. (1993, Feb. 22). The AIDS disaster unfolding in Asia. *Business Week*, pp. 52–54; Brown, David. (1994, Nov. 29). World Bank targets AIDS as economic threat. *The Seattle Times*, p. A9; Buckley, Stephen. (1995, Mar. 17). African AIDS epidemic creating a society of orphans. *Washington Post*, p. A41; Confronting AIDS: Public priorities in a global epidemic. (1997). World Bank, http://www.worldbank.org/aids-econ/confront/press-1/index.htm

of Hepatitis B which annually kills over 2 million worldwide; tuberculosis claims 3 million deaths per year; pneumonic plague may become a global killer; and even flu viruses like the 1997–98 chicken strain threaten to rapidly spread worldwide.

World population

According to the organization Zero Population Growth (http://www.zpg.com), it took 4 million years for humanity to reach a population of 2 billion in 1927, but it will take a mere 70 years to triple. World population is estimated to stand at 5.7 billion people; growth to 8.3 billion is expected in less than 30 years. While 77% of the world's people were living in the developing world in 1990, 83% will live in the developing world by

2025. The presumed carrying capacity of the earth has been estimated at between 4 and 16 billion; the lower estimate has already been exceeded, the upward estimate could easily be reached within 50 years. Finally, according to the United Nations, world population is likely to double in the next two decades to include 11 billion people. UN predictions for the six largest populations in 2050 are given in Table 10.2.

In his article 'The tragedy of the commons,' environmentalist Garrett Hardin (1968) asserted that unlimited population growth is likely to have dire results as more people are needed to produce and they in turn consume and ultimately degrade commonly held, life-sustaining resources. A contemporary example of this phenomenon occurs in Sub-Saharan Africa. Tribal groups and nomadic families earn income by reducing trees to readily saleable charcoal; more family members equal more earnings, but as more are born and work, more air is polluted, and fewer trees are left to provide a positive environmental effect. The eventual loss of all trees in an area forces relocation and may stimulate greater population growth because families need still more productive members. If this process is repeated, the downward spiral of resource use and degradation and the upward spiral of population growth continues until environmental devastation of the life-sustaining commons is global as well as local.

DIFFERING POPULATION CHALLENGES

In an increasingly populous world, population growth represents a different challenge for developed and developing economies. In the developed world of advanced and industrialized economies, there is below-zero or zero population growth (ZPG). That is, births there are fewer than those needed to replace the current population. As early as 1976 some industrialized countries experienced population decline where deaths outpaced births (Carlson, 1986). From 1990 to 1994, fertility rates for Italy were 1.3, for Japan they were 1.7, and for the US they were 2.1 (The politics of population, 1994). More recent figures appear in Figure 10.1. Interestingly, US fertility rates are higher than elsewhere in the industrialized world because of higher birth rates among African- and Hispanic-Americans; many of the latter are immigrants. Because most industrialized

TABLE 10.2 Highest six estimated populations for 2050 (millions)

Nation	1996	2050
India	945	1,533
China	1,232	1,517
Pakistan	140	357
USA	269	340
Nigeria	115	337
Indonesia	200	300

nations are at or below ZPG, these nations face challenges for sustaining demand and production as domestic markets shrink. They will continue to view immigration as a way to grow, but may also view it as a threat to national culture, as was shown in our review of global labor migration in Chapter 6.

In the developing economies, the population challenge is exploding growth, with estimated average fertility rates in Africa – the world's poorest continent – approaching 6 births per family. The impact of a population explosion on the world is great because most population growth comes from nations where there already are many, many people and few resources to sustain them. For example, the estimated population of India is 945 million, and the average Indian family has 3.8 children. At these rates, population growth for India will double in about 22 years. This is a staggering population growth rate for a country only beginning to develop economically, but this pattern is evident in many of the world's other economically least advantaged nations (as shown in Figure 10.1). So great is population growth in the developing economies that as many as 98% of all births worldwide are expected to take place there by the year 2050.

Population growth can represent growth in the number of consumers and associated expansion of business opportunities, but in the developing world this scenario has not yet been achieved. First, there is the problem of economic development: these countries remain poor when compared to the advanced economies, and population increases also put a strain on developing economies, to provide food, shelter, and health care to citizens. Many argue that providing these basic resources to people delays a country's ability to invest its resources in economic development. A second strain on developing economies occurs because so few members of the population are well enough educated to play an active role in economic development. Moreover, few receive the type of health care they need throughout their lives to be productive members of society. That is, many citizens in the developing world are net recipients of national goods rather than contributors in the form of labor, taxes, etc. This occurs because they remain illiterate, poorly prepared for work by limited food or health care, and untrained for labor in a world requiring more, not fewer, knowledge workers. One proposed solution to the 'problem' of world overpopulation is to find ways to reduce births, and suggested means are but two: provide birth control, or provide education for girls and women. Ironically, birth control methods, particularly abortion, have proved useful only in reducing the numbers of female babies born. In South Korea, India, China, and Taiwan abortions of female fetuses has already seriously unbalanced the male to female ratio of births, creating a disequilibrium bound to produce global consequences. For example, by 2000 China could have 70 million single men (Abortion in Asia, 1996). Despite the availability of birth control devices, population growth continues, showing birth control has not been altogether successful in reducing births. Conversely, education does appear to lead to lower birth rates.

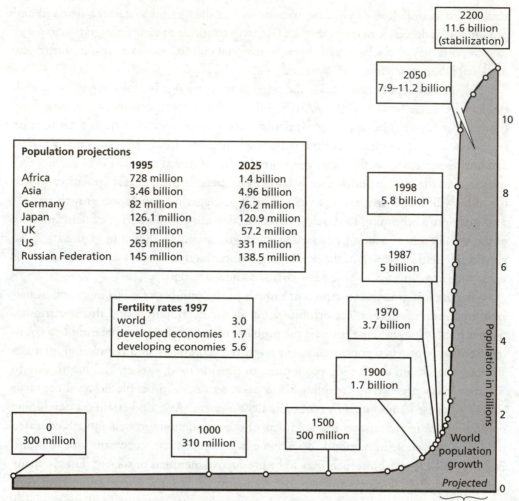

Population projections

	1995	2025
Africa	728 million	1.4 billion
Asia	3.46 billion	4.96 billion
Germany	82 million	76.2 million
Japan	126.1 million	120.9 million
UK	59 million	57.2 million
US	263 million	331 million
Russian Federation	145 million	138.5 million

Fertility rates 1997
world	3.0
developed economies	1.7
developing economies	5.6

2200
11.6 billion
(stabilization)

2050
7.9–11.2 billion

1998
5.8 billion

1987
5 billion

1970
3.7 billion

1900
1.7 billion

1500
500 million

1000
310 million

0
300 million

World population growth

Projected

Population in billions

0 100 200 300 400 500 600 700 800 900 1000 1100 1200 1300 1400 1500 1600 1700 1800 1900 2000 2100 2200

Years

FIGURE 10.1 *Population growth*
Source: Politics of population. (1994, Sept. 1). *The Seattle Times*, pp. A1, A14;
Population Reference Bureau (1998, Jan. 31). www.prb.org; UN Population Division.
(1998, Jan. 31).

According to findings presented in Cairo at the 1994 UN Conference on Population and Growth, every year of schooling a woman gets decreases her fertility rate. In Sub-Saharan Africa, for example, a study of 15 nations showed that increased schooling equates with fewer children (Ainsworth, 1994). More educated people tend to be better consumers of birth control information and devices, and education provides opportunities for work outside the home that is facilitated when fewer children require in-home care. In addition to curbing population growth, education also provides a means for

614

nations to develop economically as women move out of the unpaid labor force and gain skills for paid labor. Finally, education of women offers greater potential for economic development in many nations because worldwide it is women who are least well educated. For example, in 1994 two-thirds of the world's 960 million illiterates were women. Thus, many argue that education is the primary means for achieving lower population growth, with the added benefit that education for girls and women simultaneously improves the potential for economic development.

Industrialization

The industrial model of economic growth has been a driver for worldwide economic integration and for integration of culture, politics, industries, technologies, and the natural environment. Factories that produce pollutants also create jobs and a standard of living that individuals as well as nations seek, even as they gather people into densely populated areas where urban problems of garbage and water treatment as well as noise pollution may occur. Industrialization is a mixed blessing in improving world prosperity measured by economic wealth at the same time that it increases the potential for ecological disruption and an attendant decline in quality of life. For example, Western observers estimate that a 1994 oil leak in Russia's Komineft pipeline network in western Siberia poured millions of gallons of crude oil into water, but because the pipeline is important to their livelihood, Russians will not consider abandoning it and say it is too expensive to fix. One result of these and similar industrial activities is that many areas of the ocean are degraded; tons of litter and other pollutants are dumped into the sea each day; and overfishing as well as pollution has reduced the number of fish and other aquatic organisms. Without a healthy ocean, we cannot expect healthy air, yet industrialization often pours pollutants into the air and they are blown around the world to create effects we cannot anticipate or do not measure. Often, this pollution occurs not in industrialized countries but in developing economies that can least well afford additive miseries and high costs to human life. However, as the example in Box 10.7 shows, the global reach of television technology has stimulated citizen awareness of environmental threats, causing them to expect more social and environmental responsibility from businesses.

Diseases of affluence including circulatory disease, heart failure, and lung cancer have become the leading causes of death in the industrialized world, brought on by increased wealth and changes in consumption habits. In Chapter 1, we saw that mainland Chinese are migrating to cities to join an industrial labor force, and one result is that the leading cause of death in China now is lung disease due to industrial pollutants. Diseases of affluence found more in the industrialized countries will doubtless follow, including heart disease and other diseases usual when diets include higher fat and protein levels. According to the World Health Organization, diseases of affluence are catching

BOX 10.7:   CITIZENS, MEET CAPITALISM

Globalization of capitalism together with traditional Russian skepticism of almost everything has made many wary of business motives. This has created unusual citizen-initiated demands for Amoco Oil in Novy Port, Russia. The following example illustrates one challenge business enterprises face when citizens are well informed by television, historically cautious about promises, and motivated to avoid environmental mistakes of the past.

Novy Port is a town of 1,000 residents located on top of the largest untapped oil field in the world. While the citizens of Novy Port recognize the advantages that could accrue to them if the oil field is developed, they also are aware of the environmental costs. The legacy of environmental damage to air and water that occurred under Soviet management is visible, underscored by a high cancer rate believed to result from environmental damage. Now that television has exposed Novy Port citizens to the world 'people are beginning to understand the concepts of a market, rights and potential profit'. Having already invested tens of millions of US dollars in the area, Amoco has yet to drill the first hole, and its representatives remain tied up in local meetings answering questions like, 'How much money are you going to earn from all this?' Novy Port citizens, like citizens in many parts of the world, are acting to assure themselves that private enterprise will not exploit them in future. Oil companies British Petroleum and Arco gain permission to drill oil wells in places like Siberia and Alaska by guaranteeing that they will build schools and airports or act as stewards of the environment.

As in Novy Port, many view business organizations with some degree of suspicion or skepticism. In some cases these suspicions may be based more on perception than on past behavior, but perceptions also shape actions. Sectors other than business in both the developing and industrialized world also bring pressure to bear on business enterprises. How, then, is an organization involved in global business expected to operate in a world that both welcomes and rejects its activities? This is a challenge facing most if not all business enterprises today, and the diversity of responses to the same business activities has led many business leaders to re-evaluate and perhaps for the first time explicitly consider their worldwide autonomy. This has broadened the arena for discussion of governance for worldwide business activities.

Source: Specter, Michael. (1994, Nov. 27). In the defiled Russian Arctic, hope is a US oil company. *New York Times*, p. A1.

up with infections as global killers. By 1995, smoking alone was responsible for three million adult deaths worldwide.

The preceding reviews of boundarylessness across the global commons and the spread of disease show existing resources are decreasing, being degraded, or taking different shape – perhaps leading to less environmental diversity. Growth in population and in economic development are hastening the pace of environmental use. W. Edward Stead and Jean Garner Stead (1996) place people and industrialization at the center of what they have called 'The Issue Wheel' (Figure 10.2) for the world's ecosystem. This figure shows that population growth and unlimited economic growth are acting together to foster rapid increases in both production and consumption. Growing demands quickly deplete and pollute resources, and world industrial output will have to double, triple, or even quintuple to meet the needs of the world's citizens. Seventy percent of the world's resources are consumed by people living in industrialized nations, but economic growth in the developing world will increase competition for these resources. As it is, many people in developing countries are destroying their natural resources in order to survive, cutting down trees to produce industrial energy, consuming and polluting air and water to produce goods, or selling their resources to earn the dollar a day that supports 1.3 billion lives worldwide. Industrialization and population growth in the developing world could increase pollution and resource use in these countries such that they have fewer rather than more resources with which to develop. Before the year 2000 in Asia alone environmental needs associated with economic growth are estimated to require $80 to $100 billion to provide the foundation for acceptable water infrastucture; $50 billion for scrubbers and other devices to produce clean power; and billions more to handle sewage, noise, and trash (Moffat, 1996).

As developing economies industrialize to feed their populations, and assuming business as usual, pollution will increase. As it is, seven industrialized countries (including the US) account for about 45% of human-caused greenhouse gas emissions, and other forms of pollution affecting water and land quality also are concentrated in the industrialized countries and will increase with worldwide industrialization. This in turn leads to acid rain, global warming, human health problems, climate changes, species loss, and other environmental effects shown at the edge of the environmental issue wheel. If, as suggested, growth in population and economic development are at the center and the two interact to increase the velocity of environmental degradation, then world approaches to resolution should focus on controlling population and/or managing economic growth. Pressures to do either tend to focus attention outward toward what 'they' should do rather than inward to what 'we' can do.

As described by David Korten (1995), the challenge is that 'representatives of rich countries condemn the population growth of the poor and refuse to discuss overconsumption and inequality', just as 'representatives of poor countries condemn

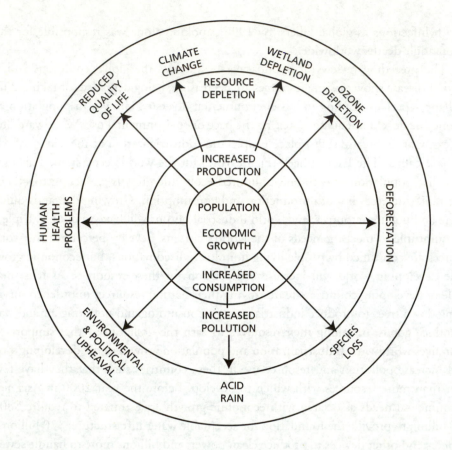

FIGURE 10.2 *The issue wheel* (Stead, W. Edward, and Stead, Jean Garner. (1996). *Management of a small planet*, p. 22. Thousand Oaks, CA: Sage)

overconsumption and inequality and refuse to discuss population growth' (p. 33). The scope of these challenges is expressed in comparisons presented in Table 10.3.

Since people, governments, and business all fuel environmental disruption, all also must play roles in reducing negative impacts. These challenges are not local or national, they are global and cannot be managed unless the world acts as one. Because business activities are part of the problem, businesses also are expected to be part of the solution. The following section reviews pressures brought to bear on businesses to participate in finding these solutions to threats against the natural environment.

FORCES FOR ENVIRONMENTAL ACCOUNTABILITY

Many forces now operate to cause the world to act as one with respect to environmentalism. According to Rolf Marstrander (1994), the kind of collaborative activity that has

TABLE 10.3   By the millions

100 million in the US are part of the paid labor force	100 million in China are part of the 'floating' population of displaced farmers without work
100 million people use the Internet	If Internet growth continues at its 1994 pace, 750 million will use it by 2000
The teen population of the US will have spending power equal to $100 billion by the year 2006	100 million children are part of the global labor force
100 million Indian's watch Z-TV	Among Africa's millions, only 1 in 10 has ever used a telephone

led to global environmental regulation represents a new phase of regulation. Earlier phases included reliance on local and domestic communities to regulate industries, followed later by reliance on national governments. Demands for environmental accountability now come from domestic and global regulations and voluntary codes, from consumer demands, from ethical investors, from employees, environmental interest groups, from lenders and insurers (Stead and Stead, 1996), and from the business community itself. For Marstrander, multiple involvements in environmentalism represent a proactive and more global regulatory phase where businesses, government, and society collaborate on a global level to reach agreements that preserve the environment. Some examples of environmental accountability in this global sphere are reviewed below.

Political/legal action

Many nations have industrialized via exploitation of existing natural resources, particularly fossil fuels and trees, and as these resources reach depletion many nation-states have passed rules, regulations, laws, and projects to preserve or protect the natural environment. Green tourism or ecotourism is an example of the latter. According to the non-profit Ecotourism Society, ecotourism is one of the fastest-growing segments of the tourism industry. This segment offers nature-based tours in Tibet; the mountains of Nepal; Kenyan safaris; biodiversity explorations in Costa Rica; and Cambodia has proposed to attract tourists by converting the whole of the country into a world national park. This kind of tourism provides new environmental education opportunities, provides local jobs and income for indigenous people, and creates a reason for preserving the environment for future generations. These and similar projects provide access to cash without compromising natural resources.

In response to growing environmental regulation, the advanced and industrialized nations have made significant progress toward reducing the environmental costs of business within their own borders. According to Stead and Stead (1996), national laws introduced in the US and throughout Western Europe govern many business activities, covering specific environmental problems like air and water pollution or species protection, specific industries like paper pulp or agriculture, and geographic regions that need special protection such as wetlands, forests, or coastal areas. These regulations generally are strictly enforced and violations are punished. In France, for example, manufacturers are required to document the kind of waste they have, where it goes, and how it is disposed of or used; they must receive local approval for waste generated, prove there is no cleaner way to produce their product, and bear costs to take waste to special landfills (The environment is, 1992). Strict enforcement in the Netherlands helped that country become a world leader in environmental technologies.

Environmental norms and laws to enforce them also have emerged from alliances among nations. For example, a mandate entitling a clean environment for all citizens was part of the European Community's 1987 Single European Act, and specific legislation has been passed subsequently to ensure air and water purity and preserve other resources. For example, the European Union voted to ban any cosmetic products tested on animals, effective in 1998. NAFTA's agreement is patterned after EU models, and agreements made with NAFTA also affirm commitment to conservation and protection and to sustainable development that provides for future generations. The 1992 UN Conference on the Environment and Development mentioned earlier in this chapter resulted in commitment among 170 nations to develop regulations and programs to address environmental threats.

German legislation has introduced 'take-back' laws which make it mandatory for manufacturers to take back and recycle the raw ingredients used in their production. These take-back laws reduced the amount of packaging waste by 600 tons, or 4%, during their first two years of operation. Even without similar laws in other countries, this German law establishes a *de facto* global manufacturing standard. Companies from nations outside the EU must comply with these 'green' dictates to participate in business in much of Western Europe, and may use these products as the platform for global standards.

How well have these regulatory pressures addressed environmental challenges? Businesses within these nations claim the complexity and costs of compliance have been high (Stead and Stead, 1996). Further, some nations and individuals view external rules with a jaded eye because they interfere with their own priorities. Evidence of progress on compliance with environmental standards is most evident in the advanced economies where most environmental regulations are found. Progress is less evident among developing economies where regulations are fewer, and there is mixed progress also toward resolving challenges to the life-sustaining global commons. The concentration of ozone-depleting chemicals in the lower atmosphere declined in 1995, but it may take 50 to 60 years to restore the earth's ozone level. This decline is the first since the early 1960s, providing evidence that a 1987 treaty banning products that release chlorine and bromines into the air has reduced their use in the industrialized world.

As indicated earlier, global warming has not improved since the signing of the 1992 Earth Summit; it is in fact worse. Yet little has been done or is being done on a global regulatory scale to halt the energy consumption and pollution contributing to global warming. While government rules and regulations are a deterrent to these activities in the already industrialized nations, in the developing economies the costs of anti-pollution devices often are deemed too high, and developing world governments often serve the interests of economic development by assuming high environmental risks. In Maili Sai, Kirgizstan, for example, radioactive waste from uranium mining was buried or left in open piles under USSR management. A huge mudslide in spring 1994 pushed much of this waste into the Maili Sai river, which flows into one of the most densely populated areas of the former USSR, enters one of Central Asia's chief waterways, and then joins the Aral Sea. But people in Maili Sai have no jobs and few resources to address this local problem that has become a regional and possibly global one. We know about this, we know about Chernobyl, but what other damage has been or is being done to the earth that we do not know about?

At the 1995 follow-up to the Earth Summit, where it was shown how little progress had been made to reduce global warming, the rich industrialized countries asked poorer economies also to cut back on their industrial development; the latter called for more cutbacks among the industrialized countries. The result was no action. This imbalance in results shows that problems of pollution may be reduced through regional regulatory efforts but more global problems may be resolvable only through global approaches. These are difficult to achieve, a fact demonstrated by controversy surrounding greenhouse emission limits at the 1997 Kyoto Conference.

Consumer demands

Jane Goodall (1995) has been an advocate for chimpanzees, and like many she admits to feeling overwhelmed by the countless environmental problems of the world. She asserts:

> We love to point fingers when we try to deal with difficult problems such as the environment, to lay the blame on industry or science or politicians. But who buys the products? We do, you and I, the vast, amorphous general public. Each of our actions has a global impact. (p. 699)

In the interests of sustainable development, many individuals have changed their expectations and buying habits. These 'green' consumers in turn expect more from the businesses that generate products, and green consumers often tend to be those who make their individual and collective wishes known.

Stead and Stead (1996) define green products as those of 'high quality, durable, made with nontoxic materials, produced and delivered using energy efficient processes, packaged in small amounts of recyclable material, not tested on animals, and/or not derived from threatened species' (p. 161). Green consumers range widely from those who buy only when a product meets all of the above characteristics, to those who buy when one or more important attributes are met, to those who say they are green consumers but will substitute green products for lower price products some or all of the time. According to Ottman (1992), only about 25% of US purchasers are consistent green consumers. An eco-labeling program translated as Blue Angel was introduced in Germany in 1977, and, according to Ottman, the label was attached to 3,100 products. Similar national and global schemes may help consumers worldwide identify green products.

Socially responsible investment funds have provided another way for consumers to impress their concerns on business. In the US, popular and successful funds such as Acorn have introduced investment choice. Socially responsible funds generally steer away from products and services that have social or health costs, such as liquor or tobacco, and many investors avoid specific companies because they believe managers are not socially responsible. Although still small in number, the growth in demand for socially responsible funds has made investment counselors more aware of consumer concerns, and these concerns are in turn passed on to firms.

Yet a third way consumers act on environmental and other interests is through 'affinity' purchasing. MBNA America bank issues credit cards which give a dime for each charge to one of 32 charitable or environmental organizations, including the Rainforest Action Network and Global Focus for civil rights and nuclear disarmament. The firm fills a niche that consumers want, although its own pitch is not ideological. They're just providing a service.

Environmental interest groups

These groups have been active in identifying products that are distinctly not green, and they have played major roles in alerting the public to business transgressions and in forcing business accountability for environmental preservation. Local, regional, national, and global groups have played diverse and varied roles in this process. Transnational environmental groups recognized by name include Greenpeace, rainforest activists Survival International, Friends of the Earth, the Worldwatch Institute, Zero Population Growth, and others less well known whose activities range from overt to subtle. According to research on environmental groups influencing business practices, these groups differ on four dimensions:

1 Their philosophies range on a continuum from affective, process-oriented approaches to technological, data-gathering, linear approaches.
2 Their approach to advocacy ranges from low-key to confrontational.
3 They differ on desired end states.
4 They differ according to the degree of professionalism, size, and complexity found in the group. For example, an advocacy group like Greenpeace operates as a large, technically sophisticated global organization, but another advocacy group can be four concerned individuals gathered around a card table in someone's basement (Clair, Milliman, and Mitroff, 1995).

In the interests of advocacy, many of these groups become NGOs, playing roles government does not or will not play. For example, advocacy groups often become the sole source for birth control or family-planning advice.

Business communities

INDUSTRY INITIATIVES

Insurance firms were very much present at the 1995 follow-up to the Earth Summit, aware that their businesses will be bankrupt if global warming results in the natural disasters predicted. For example, a 5 degree average Fahrenheit increase in the US Midwest would turn Kansas into a dust bowl and a 15% increase in hurricane wind speeds would double insured losses. Similarly, banks loaning funds are at greater risk of losses with any increase in natural disasters caused by atmospheric change. The long-term self-interests these industries recognize is one business approach being taken on environmental issues. In taking this longer run view, industries within nations may take on short-term costs. For example, the Canadian Pulp and Paper Association invested $4 billion in new processes that were more socially responsible because they eliminated pollution, but in the short run production costs were higher and had to be balanced against unprecedented global competition from Russia, Mexico, and China where environmental regulations and environmental lobbies are fewer.

ALLIANCES

Alliances among businesses and their employees, among businesses, between business and government, and among business/environmental/government groups are one additional means of addressing global environmental challenges. The latter include groups established within industries such as the chemical industry, within and across nations such as EU environmental standards, and worldwide such as ISO 14000, which specifies global environmental management systems standards. These are described in Box 10.8.

Whether they are created by individuals, consumer or environmental groups, or

BOX 10.8:   ISO 14000

The ISO 14000 series emerged primarily as a result of the Uruguay Round of the GATT negotiations and the 1992 Rio Summit on the Environment which stimulated a commitment to protect the world's environment. The steady growth of national and regional standards created by associations like the British Standards Institution and the Canadian Standards Association fostered interest in environmental management, auditing, eco-labeling, and other standards. Additionally, the European Union sponsors these initiatives and also has introduced regulations calling for environmental responsiveness. ISO formed the Strategic Advisory Group on the Environment (SAGE) in 1991 to consider whether such standards could serve to:

- promote a common approach to environmental management similar to quality management;
- enhance organizations' ability to attain and measure improvements in environmental performance;
- facilitate trade and remove trade barriers.

In 1992, SAGE's recommendations created a new committee, TC 207, for international environmental management standards. The committee and its subcommittees include representatives from industry, standards organizations, government, and environmental organizations from many countries. The new series of ISO 14000 standards are designed to cover;

- environmental management systems;
- environmental auditing;
- environmental performance evaluation;
- environmental labeling;
- life-cycle assessment;
- environmental aspects in product standards.

These standards bring a worldwide focus to the environment and encourage a cleaner, safer, healthier world for all. Further, the existence of standards allows organizations to benchmark their environmental efforts against internationally accepted criteria. Just as occurred in Europe when ISO 9000 quality registration became almost necessary to do business in many sectors, ISO 14000 management system registration may become the primary requirement for doing business in many regions or industries.

ISO 14000 requires an environmental policy to be in existence within the organization, fully supported by senior management, and outlining the policies of the company, not only to the staff but to the public.

Source: ISO 14000 InfoCenter. (1997, June 19). http://www.iso14000.com/index.html

business actions, alliances can function to inform the public and produce pressures for environmental change. Many companies from all over the world are not likely to become environmentally responsive unless they are called to public and global account. The approach toward these firms may drag them to environmental accountability, but that may be necessary to reduce threats to the global commons, to continued quality of life, and even to continued human existence. For example, Pemex's awareness of the costs to it of environmental issues stemmed from protests in Tabasco, Mexico, that blocked the entrance to oil wells (Mexico's Pemex, 1996). In response, the company developed an environmental plan that called for a three-year clean-up of existing problems, including lowering the lead level in gasoline, encouraging purchase of low-lead gasoline, and reducing the sulfur level in diesel fuel.

Data presented earlier in the chapter showed that Earth Summits and environmental agreements emerging from them have had limited success in meeting stated goals. This is not only because these issues are complex, but because national cultures have different orientations toward the business/environmentalism mix. For example, in the US, where individualism and organizational autonomy are held in high regard, environmentalism has been largely a matter of individual choice. While some organizations based in the US are committed to reducing their impact on the environment, others are not convinced that this is a role they should or will play; individualism operationalized as business autonomy lets them make this choice. Sometimes this individualism is deflected by politics. For example, Vice President Al Gore has been a long time spokesperson for environmentalism, but as a representative of the US government at the Kyoto Conference, his personal views appeared to be tempered by US political goals. In his 1992 book *Earth in the balance: Ecology and the human spirit*, Gore outlined five strategic goals to save the global environment, proposing the global equivalent of the postwar Marshall Plan:

(a) stabilize the world population;
(b) rapidly create and develop environmentally appropriate technologies,

especially in fields like energy, transportation and agriculture; rapidly transfer these technologies to developing economies;

(c) establish by global agreement common rules to measure the impact of economic and other decisions on the environment;

(d) negotiate and approve a new generation of international agreements to provide a regulatory framework for environmental action;

(e) establish a cooperative plan for educating the world's citizens about the global environment.

In Japan, cultural collectivity and pride in national development has produced an ambivalent response to environmentalism. On the one hand, Japan boasts of being one of the cleanest industrial producers in the world, and has become the world's largest donor to overseas environmental projects. In contrast, critics argue that economic development has reduced natural habitats in Japan like tidelands, and Japanese firms (among others) have been accused of using lower environmental standards abroad than at home.

In Western Europe, and particularly in European Union nations, a quality of life orientation that extends beyond individual benefits to include a broader community is found in environmental initiatives. The Netherlands 'Green Plan,' for example, requires that building plans specify reuse at obsolescence, provides taxation on autos to fund air quality innovation, and covers monitoring of manufacturing country-wide. As a group, EU nations have committed to cutting their emissions of greenhouse gases by 15% below 1990 levels by the year 2020. Figure 10.3 demonstrates success in reducing emissions throughout most of Western Europe. The network of 'Green' political parties within Europe and high citizen involvement in recycling and reclamation also are evidence of European commitment to quality of collective life values; these values were explored in greater depth in Chapter 4. Finally, this evidence allows us to conclude that if there is to be a global Marshall Plan for environmentalism, that plan will most likely come from Western Europe because it is there that people are most united behind strong environmental standards.

PART II ORGANIZATIONAL COMMITMENTS TO SUSTAINABLE DEVELOPMENT

Paul Hawken (1993) believes sustainable development can be achieved when businesses are organized around three goals:

(a) entirely eliminate waste from industrial production – this would involve

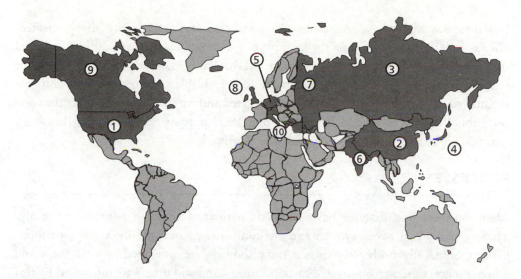

①	US	4.80	⑥	India	0.76
②	China	2.60	⑦	Ukraine	0.61
③	Russian Federation	2.10	⑧	United Kingdom	0.56
④	Japan	1.06	⑨	Canada	0.41
⑤	Germany	0.87	⑩	Italy	0.41

FIGURE 10.3 *Gassing up the world: the world's biggest emitters of carbon dioxide (in millions of metric tons)* (Fialka, John J. (1997, May 27). Global-warming treaty faces host of political clouds. *The Wall Street Journal*, p. A20, using data from US State Department)

shifting current approaches of efficient disposal and recovery of waste to designing systems that have little or no waste to begin with;

(b) change from an economy based on carbon to one based on hydrogen and sunshine;

(c) reverse the pattern of production and consumption to create systems of feedback and accountability that support and encourage resource restoration.

These are challenging goals calling for entirely new or reconfigured approaches to business production and distribution. They may foster win/win solutions, but at the same time may not be possible to achieve without intermediate steps for individuals to rethink relationships between what is production and what is waste. Hawken and others describe how these boundaries have been transcended, and new ways of business exchange created. For example, Hawken recounts the example of Curitiba, Brazil, where garbage collected in slums because streets were inaccessible. Mayor Jaime Lerner created an exchange system, providing bus tokens for separated and recyclable garbage and food chits for organic waste. The city's gains from selling organic and recyclable wastes offset the costs for public transportation and food chits, but the important result was that this was a win/win approach where everyone gained by wasting less.

PROCESSES

Many business organizations have assumed voluntary leadership positions to resolve existing tensions between growth and environment, encouraged by a range of motivations. Some, like Body Shop owner Anita Roddick, are motivated to make the world a better place, others are motivated by opportunity, and still others are motivated by fear of negative public response if they do not act. William Halal (1996) organizes these approaches into three categories of interests: (a) pollution prevention at a profit; (b) recycling, reclamation, and remanufacturing; and (c) progressive phases of environmental management characterized by receptivity and constructive and proactive approaches to environmentalism. As the examples below show, in practice these three approaches overlap, but this is nevertheless a useful organizing framework for describing how businesses participate in developing sustainable systems.

Prevention at a profit

AT&T, 3M, Royal/Dutch Shell, Monsanto, and many other global firms report operating efficiencies from environmental efforts. Cutbacks in air and water emissions, use of less toxic or recycled materials, and waste reduction all have made these firms more cost competitive. Cost reductions in these firms demonstrate that environmentalism often entails greater up-front investments. For example, a Dow Chemicals plant in Fort Saskatchewan, Alberta, Canada, cost 8% more than other ethylene plants to build, but it used 40% less energy and required less maintenance. These were direct cost benefits to the firm. The plant also released 10 gallons of cleaned waste water per minute as compared to 360 gallons/minute for older plants, and so longer term environmental costs for which Dow may not have paid also were reduced. Other examples include the following:

- Lever Brothers, manufacturers of Wisk detergent, decreased the size of the package by creating a concentrate. Additionally, manufacture of the plastics includes 25% or more post-consumer recycled plastic.
- Procter & Gamble, manufacturers of Bold Plus detergent, also decreased the

size of the package and concentrated the detergent, making the box from 100% recycled paper and a minimum of 35% post-consumer use. The consumer is assured that cleaning agents are biodegradable. These two examples illustrate how firms compete to be viewed as 'more green' than the next.

Productive efficiencies made possible from creating more with less have inherent appeals for most businesses. Competitive positioning also is another motivator for environmentalism. In their book *Financing change*, Stephan Schmidheiny, Federico Zorraquin, and the World Business Council for Sustainable Development (1996) show how companies will make more money or lose less by going green, and this appeal is likely to find many adherents in the business community.

Recycling, reclamation, and remanufacturing

Recycling provided an early success for environmentalism as consumers and businesses came to realize that much waste can be reused. In many countries, bottles, cans, and paper used by consumers are recycled for business use; some provide economic incentives to stimulate recycling and others rely more on local or regional commitment. In the Pacific Northwest where many are conscious of the natural environment, Oregon requires a 5 cent deposit on every glass bottle to encourage its return. In Seattle, recycling is voluntary, encouraged by consumer pull more than regulatory push. In turn, this leads to new opportunities for business. Consumers' interest in recycling green waste in Seattle yielded almost triple the expected 13 million tons for the first year of operation, making it possible to establish a composting company powered by Danish equipment that now has become the largest of its kind in the US.

Recycling efforts of every kind are pursued throughout the world, often creating businesses in the developing world with materials deemed useless in industrial countries. US steel and paper wastes are exported for reuse to South Korean and elsewhere in Asia. This form of reuse can be beneficial to the world or merely a means of exporting risk. For example, since 1991, when African and Latin American states banned trade in trash, Asia has become one of the few regions in the world where waste brokers can dump trash. Many medical and toxic wastes are exported because regulatory standards in much of Asia do not similarly protect workers from exposure risks. China's already growing problem with industrial waste has increased with imports of waste from the industrialized world. For example, according to a *Wall Street Journal* report titled 'China becomes industrial nation's most favored dump' (Smith, 1995), a county of eastern Jiangsu province had to shut off water supplies to allow a 150 square kilometer 'black tide' to pass downriver from upstream factories. This was the county's eighth black tide event in seven years.

Growing awareness of environmentalism and improvements in water and air pollution in the industrial economies can lull consumers and businesses into believing that progress outweighs problems. This is not necessarily a shared view. Maneka Gandhi, India's former minister for the environment and forests, may represent a shared sentiment in the developing economies when he concludes that Western industries have dumped harmful or inefficient machinery and products on the developing economies. Writing in 1992, he provided evidence that Indian thermal plants built by Western firms produce at less than 50% of capacity, and that 1,600 dams similarly sponsored by Western concerns create only 2.5% of power but wreak havoc with flooding during the monsoon season. He claims that water pollution in India is in part caused by pesticides sold by firms based in countries that have banned them, and believes that Western cultures of consumption are corrupting values of sustainability long necessary for the developing economies. This view of the industrialized countries is often expressed in the developing world, where large firms are viewed with suspicion even as they provide jobs and economic opportunities.

Industrial ecology uses wastes from one process or company as input for another. In simple form, the sawdust waste from lumber can be recycled as pellets used to fuel milling machinery. More complex and integrated systems of industrial ecology also can be created. The Kalundborg Four in Denmark is composed of a power plant, an enzyme plant, a refinery, and a wallboard plant, all of which use one another's leavings as raw materials. Reclamation projects like these create integrated systems, often beginning by asking 'What can we do with waste?' rather than 'How do we get rid of it?' Other examples include the following:

- Steelcase Inc., one of the world's largest manufacturers of office furniture, stopped sending fabric scrap to landfills in 1991, choosing to process it for use as sound-dampening insulation in the automobile industry. Nearly 40 tons of fabric were recycled during the first six months of the program.
- A Vermont-based company is refurbishing plastics from IBM integrated circuits and Ben and Jerry's four- and five-gallon pails for recycling in non-food packaging applications like organic fertilizer and cat litter containers. The products previously went to landfills.

Remanufacturing processes include efforts to build products engineered for reuse or designed for disassembly (DFD). A primarily goal of DFD is to design and build a product with a long-run view of how components can be rebuilt, reused, or disposed of safely at the end of the product's life. Technological progress stimulates attention because products like computers quickly become obsolete, creating a growing store of products made useless because of technological advances. For example, by 1995, two computers

TABLE 10.4 DFD applications

Industry	Firm and actions	Results
Automotives	BMW and other German automakers estimate 20 million autos will be disassembled for reuse in 2000; 250,000 will be BMWs. The BMW 1991 Z1 Roadster uses plastic side panels that come apart	BMW learned to replace glue or solder with snaps and fasteners to improve assembly and disassembly; the recyclable portion of a car by weight is 80% and the target is 95%
Computers	Siemens Nixdorf's PC41 was introduced in 1993 with 29 assembly pieces vs 87 for its 1987 model	The PC41 can be assembled in 7 minutes and taken apart in 4 compared to 33 for assembly and 18 for disassembly of the 1987 model
Telephones	Northern Telecom breaks down old telephones, puts the insides in a new plastic housing, and sends them out again	The company is moving all design and development to DFD
Engines	Klockner Humboldt Deutz realized ease of engine disassembly spawned many small companies that were rebuilding Deutz engines	Deutz Service International was established to buy back its own engines and remanufacture them
Cameras	Under pressure from environmentalists, Kodak converted disposable cameras to recyclables by using fasteners instead of welding to seal the case	Kodak recycles or reuses 87% by weight of single-use cameras; employs persons with disabilities to disassemble; sold 30 million single-use cameras in 1993

Source: Bylinsky, Gene. (1995, Feb. 6). Manufacturing for reuse. *Fortune*, pp. 103–112.

were made obsolete with every three purchased, and by 2005 the ratio is expected to be one to one. Phenomenal growth in auto sales in Asia create greater world need for recycling. Reasons for adopting DFD include regulations that make the original manufacturer responsible for product waste, buyer pressure for environmentally sustainable products, and manufacturer incentives to reduce the cost of assembly and disassembly. Table 10.4 provides examples that demonstrate reasons for DFD, and although results vary widely, all represent win/win outcomes.

Many firms combine recycling and reuse programs. For example, McDonald's Earth Effort program is an example of an integrative recycling program: it starts with three waste reduction principles: reduce, reuse, recycle. McRecycle USA is a commitment to buy at least $100 million worth of recycled products every year for the building, operating, and equipping of the company's restaurants. Carryout bags are made from recycled corrugated boxes and newsprint, and takeout drink trays are made from recycled newspapers. Insulated concrete blocks made from recycled photographic film are used for building construction, roofing tiles are from used computer casings, and recycled automobile tires are used in play areas. The company worked with the Environmental Defense Fund to cut down on trash, switched from foam packing to paper wrap for sandwiches, and reduced the use of plastic by having tank trucks pump beverage syrup directly into storage vats. Canon, a global firm headquartered in Japan, has established the 'E' Project ('E' for environment, ecology, energy), and their Clean Earth Campaign, a cartridge collection program, is an outgrowth of this concern for the environment. The campaign helps to keep the environment clean by paying to have consumers return used toner cartridges. Portions of the returned cartridges can then be used to create new ones. For each cartridge returned, Canon USA makes a contribution to the National Wildlife Federation and the Nature Conservancy.

Progressive phases of environmental management

In 1990, August A. Busch III expressed a sentiment widely shared among those taking leadership roles in environmental sustainability when he said:

> The world we all share is given to us in trust. Every choice we make regarding the earth, air, and water around us is made with the objective of preserving it for all generations to come.

Organizational leaders who freely assume responsibility for a trust passed on by past generations very often want to preserve that trust for future generations. Often, they do so via leadership roles in environmental initiatives, and in creating organizations characterized by trust. Both aspects of sustainability will be explored below.

A proactive, advantage-driven approach behind environmentalism has been pursued by many global firms. According to reports of a conference on integrating environmental decision-making and profitable results, firms must move from a piecemeal to a comprehensive approach that anticipates standards and ensures regulatory compliance and looks ahead to identify strategic advantages with environmentalism. Five common practices found among environmentally responsible firms are:

(a) corporate values promoting environmental advocacy and a clear mission statement;
(b) a framework to manage environmental initiatives and activities;
(c) process and product designs that are environmentally sensitive;
(d) stakeholder partnerships that focus on the environment;
(e) education initiatives with internal and external stakeholders (Dechant et al., 1994).

DuPont voluntarily decided to abandon $750 billion invested in chloroflourocarbon (CFC) manufacture by 2000, and invest $1 billion in a search for safe alternatives. It collaborates with environmental groups, finds alternate uses for waste products, and has developed and expanded on environmental clean-up services that meet its needs and also help industrial customers to clean their waste.

Total quality management and environmentalism

Chapter 9 described total or continuous quality management as a process aimed at taking a long-term view, empowering those closest to the work to make decisions, management by facts, reductions in product variability, removal of waste, and continuous improvement. By revisiting TQM processes in this chapter, we can see how they can be extended to encompass environmental initiatives. According to Porter and van der Linde (1995), pollution represents resource inefficiencies because it shows that quality has not been built into all phases of the product. These authors also believe that it takes a different kind of thinking to recognize that reducing environmental pollution is as much a part of the quality process as a defect-free product. This kind of thinking requires a shift from the either/or thinking of environmentalism versus quality to the both/and hybrid approach where opposites are found to attract and complement more than they were once believed able to do. Moreover, recognition of pollution as a quality defect shows a need to integrate environmental performance with wider issues of global ecology (Welford, 1993) such as the following:

(a) a specific organizational consciousness of sustainable development;
(b) energy-efficiency focused on minimizing CO_2 and similar emissions and avoiding nuclear wastes;
(c) the need to conserve nonrenewable resources should shape waste minimization, reuse, and recycling;
(d) product design should prioritize use of renewable resources;
(e) sourcing should have no negative impact on biodiversity, endangered habitats, or rights of indigenous people;
(f) overall corporate policy should assess the business's current and future impact on developed and developing economies.

Costs of environmental leadership

Firms whose leaders are exploring or are committed to sustainable development or to putting environmental principles before or equal to profits often encounter opposition and criticism. Body Shop products are not tested on animals and they are available in recyclable containers which customers are offered an economic incentive to reuse. These and other standards established the Body Shop as a principled firm, and this stance brought it into the public eye, where it was attacked, charged, and tried in the press for not living up to its own high principles. Although subsequent investigations revealed allegations against the Body Shop were unfounded or unfair, the firm faces a public now made suspicious because they do not know who to believe. Robert Shapiro faces a similar challenge in his efforts to make Monsanto into a biotechnology powerhouse. Shapiro believes that worldwide population growth will strain the earth's ability to feed people, and is responding by investing in genetic engineering to increase food production. But many are leery of genetic engineering, and this has resulted in bans on allowing genetically engineered products into the EU.

The public also find it difficult to decide whom they should trust and often forces decisions not in their best interests. For example, although McDonald's had invested millions to develop a biodegradable plastic package for burgers that proved less expensive than the environmental costs of producing paper, the public forced them to withdraw the product because they were convinced the plastic was more environmentally harmful (Halal, 1996). In the late 1970s a similar furor erupted in the US over environmental comparisons between disposable versus paper cloths for babies. The evidence against plastic nappies was low biodegradability, but cloth diapers consumed more water and left detergent and chlorine residue in water supplies. Which product was environmentally best remains a mystery, with reality obscured by industry charges and countercharges that provide data but little information. The end result of this and many similar environmental debates is a public made aware but kept ignorant. The environmental challenge for firms is of the 'damned if you don't; damned if you do' variety where there are no winners, only losers. In turn, attacks like these may encourage other businesses to take a middle road rather than the high-profile advocacy role of the Body Shop.

Progressive firms are those that not only take a stand for environmentalism but recognize relationships among easy cost/benefit analyses and the more complex ones that yield fewer clear results. For example, McDonald's will not purchase beef raised on rain forest (or recently deforested rain forest) land; the Body Shop supports causes like Amnesty International; and Canon played a leadership role in forming the Caux Principles for a Global Business Ethic described in Chapter 6. Some firms also have created programs to encourage their employees to be mindful of conservation. For example, timber giant Weyerhaeuser introduced a program called 'Weyerhaeuser Freeways' that gives employees free, unlimited bus or car pool passes, promotes telecommuting, and offers compressed work weeks, guaranteed rides home, expanded transportation between Weyerhaeuser buildings, and even $1 a day to any employee who car pools, rides a bicycle, or walks to work.

PEOPLE
From power to empowerment

Traditional US models concentrate power at the peak of an organization's hierarchical pyramid. According to this model, top leaders and managers derive their power from five sources:

(a) legitimate power or authority from one's position or role in the organization;

(b) authority to distribute rewards that induce behaviors wanted;

(c) authority to dispense punishments that coerce behaviors wanted;

(d) expert power from having a skill, knowledge, or technical ability important to the organization;

(e) referent power from people identifying with and wanting to follow someone because of personal attributes like likability, charisma, or attractiveness (French and Raven, 1960).

The first three sources of power listed above are vested in position, and the last two are found in the person. 'Expert' power in the form of information and knowledge is increasingly important in learning organizations where it is distributed rather than centralized,

---

BOX 10.9:   THE MOST JOY WE CAN HAVE

When David Sun and John Tu sold 80% of US-based Kingston Technologies – the world's largest maker of computer memory products – to Softbank of Japan, they vowed to share the benefits with their employees. At their December 15, 1996 holiday party for employees, these global managers announced their plan: $100 million of the profit to be shared as bonuses with employees. The average bonus per employee will be $75,000 but some will get as much as $300,000. The total amount allocated will be $100 million; $60 million more will be held in reserve for future use. Asked to explain this decision, Tu said: 'They [the employees] are the ones working hard day in, day out. Our attitude toward our employees is, "You deserve this. You deserve more than this."'

Sun said: 'To share our success with everybody is the most joy we can have.'

Source: Miller, Greg. (1996, 15). Holiday bonus for workers: $100 million. *Los Angeles Times*, p. A1.

and the ability to reward, punish, or direct work increasingly is distributed to teams and even to self-managed individuals. As a result, top and middle managers find that their remaining source of power is referent power – being someone the workforce wants to follow. Often this comes from attributes few managers learn in business schools. The example from Kingston Technologies (Box 10.9) suggests the manager others want to follow might well be one who shares more than authority and power, but also financial resources.

Managerial competencies for a global world: the empowering leader

According to George Simons, Carmen Vazquez, and Philip Harris (1993) the transcultural leader is:

(a) a visionary with a broad perspective who has a clear and powerful vision and a long-term outlook;

(b) a communicator of organizational and personal vision, expectations, and responsibilities;

(c) a role model who is personally an empowered high performer;

(d) a realist who recognizes that the person closest to a decision usually has the best view of it;

(e) a delegator who believes in people and their potential and who will assign goal setting to individuals and teams;

(f) a mentor who is accessible to all;

(g) a service-oriented person who sees employees as customers (p. 190).

Robert Moran, Philip Harris, and William Stripp (1993) observe that empowerment tears down the walls between management and labor, becoming a means of transcending internal boundaries of power. Virginia-based AES Corporation has successfully done this by rotating duties, including having stockroom operators plan budgets and control-room operators arrange financial deals. Further, before the start-up phase of each new plant established abroad, AES has every employee at every level participate in a three- to four-month training program where the topic of conversation includes company values and culture. AES now has 27 plants abroad from Argentina to the United Kingdom and Pakistan and all operate with a strong degree of autonomy that includes employee empowerment. Company earnings were $533 million in 1995; profits were $100 million.

Loyalty and trust

Leadership attributes listed above are expected to instill trust and generate loyalty. According to Francis Fukuyama (1995), high trust made it possible for Japanese firms to introduce management techniques like Just-in-Time inventory systems and TQM techniques that successful Japanese firms use in the world market. Fukuyama further argues that nations which create organizational structures that closely monitor and control behavior, as in Italy, France, and China, reinforce low trust levels within the cultures. Fukuyama asserts that the modern corporation was pioneered in the US because of high national trust. Today, national and organizational trust is eroding, hastened by national leaders' inability to protect jobs and by downsizing, 'right sizing,' and restructuring initiatives that eliminate jobs. Growing global competition for efficiencies has made this a global challenge. Many Japanese firms have abandoned lifelong employment practices, European firms are outsourcing jobs, and some US firms export jobs and eliminate them. Conversely, General Motors offered lifetime employment contracts as part of 1996 collective bargaining as an inducement for current workers to vote for reductions that will take place after they retire. The paradox and currently unresolved challenge is how to create loyalty and generate trust from employees without at the same time being loyal to employees. Creating or sustaining trust among employees is particularly challenging for the virtual organization because employees often work on their own, yet their work defines the organization's success. Charles Handy (1995) proposes that trust in the virtual organization requires bonding, but also demands learning and openness to change on the part of managers. He suggests that trust need not be 'blind' trust, but that defining the boundaries of trust aids employers and employees.

According to Frederich Reichheld (1996), employee loyalty creates both customer and shareholder loyalty. This in turn generates additional employee loyalty because firms who are able to hold onto customers and shareholders are ones that can pay higher wages. Further, Reichheld argues that firms like Leo Burnett advertising agency and State Farm Insurance that he deems loyal are those that nurture employees, often because they are vulnerable to losses of key knowledge-sharing employees. Whether initiated at the firm, the project, or by leaders, some firms see loyalty as providing more benefits than costs. For example, firms included in the list of the 100 best companies to work for in America (Levering and Moskowitz, 1998) are successful financially and committed to their employees. The ways that organizations express employee loyalty clearly varies. All stock in TD Industries of Texas is in employee hands, and financial results are reported in monthly meetings. At aerospace company MOOG, there are no strict work plans and no time clocks; Federal Express offers profit-sharing; and the family feeling of work at Smucker's has kept more than 40% of workers longer than 10 years.

STRUCTURING SUSTAINABLE DEVELOPMENT

Business efforts to consolidate environmental demands have led to development of standards, and these standards provide a structured way for individual firms to respond to demands for environmental accountability. Over 80 businesses have signed the CERES Principles developed by the Coalition for Environmentally Responsible Economies. These companies pledge to do the following:

(a) minimize the release of pollutants;
(b) conserve nonrenewable natural resources through efficient use and careful planning;
(c) minimize the creation of waste, and particularly hazardous waste;
(d) use energy wisely;
(e) diminish environmental, health, and safety risks to employees and communities;
(f) sell environmentally safe products;
(g) accept responsibility for environmental harm and make compensation;
(h) disclose potential environmental hazards;
(i) appoint one board member for environmental interests;
(j) produce and publicize a self-evaluation each year.

Business communities also can develop at the local level to negotiate agreements between industries and community members or neighborhoods. The Good Neighbor Project was initiated by the nonprofit Center for the Study of Public Policy to assist localities throughout the US in promoting clean and safe industrial jobs. Workers, plant neighbors, and environmentalists in a Good Neighbor project promote ongoing, incremental improvements and dramatic innovations at local industries, and because of the local approach diverse initiatives have emerged. These include facility and document inspection, new partnerships and institutions, legislative or regulatory initiatives, community organizing, dialogue with a firm's shareholders and insurers, and redirected private and public investment. The DuPont statement in Box 10.10 demonstrates progress made toward articulating environmental goals.

Bioregionally sustainable multinational corporations (BioCorps)

In *Greening business*, Paul Shrivastava (1996) devotes the first 13 chapters to what he calls 'reformist' themes for existing corporations, then presents his vision of 'radically green corporations of the future,' which he calls bioregionally sustainable multinational corporations or BioCorps. These BioCorps will emerge from a context where corporations

BOX 10.10:   DUPONT'S COMMITMENTS

We affirm to all our stakeholders, including our employees, customers, sharehold-ers and the public, that we will conduct our business with respect and care for the environment. We will implement those strategies that build successful businesses and achieve the greatest benefit for all our stakeholders without compromising the ability of future generations to meet their needs.

We will continuously improve our practices in light of advances in technology and new understandings in safety, health and environmental science. We will make consistent, measurable progress in implementing this Commitment throughout our worldwide operations. DuPont supports the chemical industry's Responsible Care & Regulation; and the oil industry's Strategies for Today's Environmental Partnership as key programs to achieve this Commitment.

We will adhere to the highest standards for the safe operation of facilities and the protection of our environment, our employees, our customers and the people of the communities in which we do business.

We will build alliances with governments, policy makers, businesses and advocacy groups to develop sound policies, laws, regulations and practices that improve safety, health and the environment.

Compliance with this Commitment and applicable laws is the responsibility of every employee and contractor acting on our behalf and a condition of their employment or contract. Management in each business is responsible to educate, train and motivate employees to understand and comply with this Commitment and applicable laws.

We will deploy our resources, including research, development and capital, to meet this Commitment and will do so in a manner that strengthens our busi-nesses.

We will measure and regularly report to the public our global progress in meeting this Commitment.

Source: DuPont Homepage. (1997, June 21). http://www.dupont.com

globalize, where there is expanded degradation and ecological risk from industrial activi-ties, and where there will be local social resistance to activities that create environmental problems. In form, BioCorps will be structured as flat organizations where decentralized, participative decision-making will be encouraged. Similar to commitments described for DuPont in Box 10.10, the BioCorps will distribute responsibility for environmental concerns throughout the organization. Moreover, the structure will contain a strong environmental affairs department with access to top management, credible and visible champions for environmental issues within the firm, and a board of directors to oversee environmental performance. This structure will be supported by administrative systems that seek out and respond to environmental demands. Finally, in terms of people, Bio-Corps will be places where employees are viewed as complex and valuable beings working at meaningful labor. Further, work at BioCorps will not only provide opportunities for human creativity and growth, but also allow employees to achieve balance among competing demands of work, family, organizational, and professional life.

Achieving balance between growth and environmentalism at personal, organizational, national, or global levels does not come without business costs. As shown above, some businesses are environmental only when it is cost-free or when mandated by law, others recognize that short run costs may be offset by longer-run gains, others like the Body Shop take a broader view to assume responsibility even at the cost of profits to ensure a viable and equitable future for all people worldwide. Individuals and nations also take the same path, with some actively involved in environmentalism and others following only legal or social mandates. Whatever the level of environmental effort, all contribute incrementally to improving the balance between the closed system of resources that is earth and the open system of business growth made possible by worldwide integration. This book and its exploration of boundarylessness concludes with recognition that boundaries transcended create new awareness of boundaries we didn't know were there. Having seen that business organizations can cross many boundaries, we see also that they are constrained – by time, by money, by an inability to be all things to all people. Economic assumptions of infinite growth may be realizable, but we have seen that these also entail costs – to the earth, to nations, to organizations, and especially to people and other living beings whose future depends more than we realized on decisions made in the interests of business. How those interests are defined in terms of self and community interests, fulfilling economic and quality of life objectives, creating efficiencies and providing meaning – all these and more are the balancing acts all people face as members of an expanding global community.

KEY CHAPTER CONCEPTS

Productivity Creates Benefits and Costs: Worldwide productivity has grown to stimulate financial wealth of individuals, business enterprises, nations, and the world. These productivity increases rely on acquiring, efficiently exploiting, and continually developing productive factors such as capital, technology, raw materials, natural resources, and people. But in many cases, these productivity gains have produced costs to the natural environment.

Four Principles of Sustainable Development: Principles of sustainable development include beliefs that tensions between economic growth and environmental protection and regeneration have to be resolved; poor nations cannot nor should they imitate the production and consumption patterns of rich nations; lifestyles in the rich nations must change; and maximization of income must be replaced with the expansion of opportunities for people.

Boundaries of Earth: The boundarylessness of globalization driven by growth and productivity has run up against the physical limits of the earth. Many argue that technological breakthroughs make the 'boom' of growth almost infinitely possible, but others assert that growth is consuming and degrading resources faster than they can be replaced by any technology. Water, air, and natural resources are being consumed in the interests of fiscal wealth creation and disease and environmental disruption are being spread by them.

Two Challenges to the Earth: Population and Industrial Development: Rapid population growth as much as industrial development are increasing strains on the natural environment to sustain human needs. Thus, the challenges of industrialization and rapid population growth are not isolated at local or national challenges; they are world challenges; that cannot be solved unless the world acts as one. Because business activities are part of the problem, businesses also are expected to be part of the solution, and it may be the global reach of many businesses that allows them to play this role.

Sources of Growing Demands for Environmental Accountability: Growing demands for environmental accountability now come from domestic and global regulations and voluntary codes, from consumer demands, from ethical investors, from employees, environmental interest groups, from lenders and insurers, and from the business community itself.

Ways Individuals Can Be Environmentally Responsive: Becoming 'green' consumers, investing in socially responsible investment funds, and changing consumption habits are three ways individuals can motivate businesses to become environmentally responsive.

Growth in Environmental Advocacy Groups: Environmental advocacy groups are growing in number and in their global clout because they use resources like the Internet to transfer information quickly and inexpensively.

Three Ways Businesses Reduce Environmental Overuse: Alliances inside organizations and between organizations in the same industries or with similar interests have proved useful in effecting changes in organizational consumption patterns. Recycling, reclamation, and remanufacturing are three ways businesses have reduced their own costs and improved their stance on environmentalism.

Common Environmental Practices: Common practices found among environmentally responsible firms are: (a) a mission statement and corporate values that promote environmental advocacy; (b) a framework for managing environmental initiatives; (c) green process and product design systems; (d) environmentally focused stakeholder partnerships; and (e) internal and external education initiatives.

Leadership in Socially Responsive Organizations: Many managers find that traditional sources of power are less viable in a knowledge-based organization, with followership depending more on being someone others want to follow than on more traditional rewards like pay or promotions.

Characteristics of the Empowering Manager: The empowering manager is one who has a vision but who can make decisions and encourage and direct others to task accomplishment. Often, this manager is more a 'servant' than a leader.

Costs of Environmental Sensitivity: Organizations and individuals committed to finding new ways to work with rather than against the natural environment find that fulfilling these commitments can be frustrated by a public with high expectations and limited tolerance for failure.

REVIEW AND DISCUSSION QUESTIONS

1   Would you agree that there are 'global commons'? If so, generate a list of properties for global commons and explain/defend their place in the global schema.

2   What should be the top priorities for countries that have high population growth and low economic development? Should these nations have special priorities for dealing with girls and women? Explain why you would agree or disagree with these special priorities.

3   If knowledge and education are the primary assets for organizations, consider the following: (a) How will traditional management techniques found in your nation have to change? (b) What will employee benefits packages need to stress: Wages or educational subsidies? Wage raises or health care? Time or money? Explain the reasons for your conclusions.

4   In what ways is inequality inefficient at the global, national, and firm levels? When there are inequalities in the firm, are there some that people will accept and others that might be counterproductive? What would these be? What is the basis for acceptable versus unacceptable forms of inequalities?

5   Find an article that appeared in a trade journal or newspaper in the last six months that describes how an organization is responding to environmentalism. Describe at

least three ways the organization is showing environmental responsibility; describe the costs of taking on environmentalism when competitors do not. Use your own words and examples from the article to explain why environmental challenges are global in their impact on businesses.

6   Industrialized nations may be those whose cultures are most aligned with concepts of consumerism and economic development. Less developed economies may not have cultural mechanisms supportive of capitalism. For example, many in Africa are members of tribes and similar social groups whose history is nomadic and agrarian. How can nomadic people stay in control of their own development when the very concept of development is contrary to their culture? If people are unable to antici-pate political, cultural, economic, and technological change, how can they plan for or cope with sustainability?

7   *The Global Enterprise Project*: Demonstrate the firm's responsiveness to globalization of natural resources. In terms of globalization of natural resources, what are the firm's major issues with respect to acquiring and using natural resources? Is it involved in sustainable development? Does it use environmental accounting, pollution con-trols, etc. to protect the environment?

REFERENCES

Abortion in Asia. (1996, Sept. 12). *The Wall Street Journal*, p. A16.

Ainsworth, Martha. (1994). Socioeconomic determinants of fertility in Sub-Saharan Africa. Washington, DC: World Bank Policy Research Dept.

Barbier, Edward. (1987). The concept of sustainable development. *Environmental Conservation*, 14(2): 101–110.

Brown, Lester, Lenssen, Nicholas, and Kane, Hal. (1995). *Vital signs*. Washington, DC: Worldwatch Institute (an annual publication since 1992).

Brown, Tim, and Xenos, Peter. (1994, Aug.). AIDS in Asia: The gathering storm. *Asia Pacific Issues*, p. 16.

Carlson, Allan. (1986, Apr. 13). Depopulation bomb: The withering of the Western World. *The Washington Post*, pp. C1, C2.

Carson, Rachel. (1962). *Silent spring*. London: Hamish Hamilton.

Clair, Judith, Milliman, John, and Mitroff, Ian. (1995). Clash or cooperation? Under-standing environmental organizations and their relationship to business. In Denis Collins and Mark Starik (Eds), *Research in corporate social performance and policy, Supplement 1*, pp. 163–193. Greenwich, CT: JAI.

Colborn, Theo, Dumanoski, Dianne, and Myers, John Peterson. (1996). *Our stolen future*. New York: Dutton.

Confronting the spread of AIDS. (1997, Nov. 3). The World Bank Group press release. http://www.worldbank.org/html/extdr/extme/1513.htm

Costanza, Robert, Daly, Herman E., and Bartholomew, Joy A. 1991. Goals, agenda and policy recommendations for ecological economies. In Robert Costanza (Ed.), *Ecological economics: The science and management of sustainability*, pp. 1–20. New York: Columbia University Press.

Daly, Herman. (1996). *Beyond growth: The economics of sustainable development*. Boston, MA: Beacon Press.

Dechant, Kathleen, Altman, Barbara, Dowining, Robert M., and Keeney, Timothy. (1994). Environmental leadership: From compliance to competitive advantage. *Academy of Management Executive*, 8(3): 7–27.

Easterbrook, Gregg. (1995). *A moment on the earth*. New York: Viking.

Erlich, Paul R. (1969). *The population bomb*. Binghamton, NY: Vail-Ballou.

The environment is good business in France. (1992, Mar.). *Civil Engineering*, p. 66.

Fukuyama, Francis. (1995). *Trust: The social virtues and the creation of prosperity*. London: Penguin.

French, John R.P., and Raven, Bertram. (1960). The bases of social power. In Dorwin Cartwright and A.F. Zander (Eds), *Group dynamics: Research and Theory*, pp. 607–623. New York: Harper & Row.

Gandhi, Maneka. (1992, June). The West sets a bad example. *World Press Review*, pp. 11–12.

Garrett, Laurie. (1994). *The coming plague: Newly emerging diseases in a world out of balance*. New York: Farrar Straus Giroux.

Gladwin, Thomas N., Kennelly, James J., and Krause, Tara-Shelomith. (1995). Shifting paradigms for sustainable development: Implications for management theory and research. *Academy of Management Review*, 20(4): 874–907.

Globalization leaving many poor countries behind. (1997, June 12). New York: United Nations press release on the Human Development Report.

Goodall, Jane. (1995, Dec.). A message from Jane Goodall. *National Geographic*, p. 102.

Gore, Al. (1992). *Earth in the balance: Ecology and the human spirit.* New York: Houghton Mifflin.

Halal, William. (1996). *The new management.* Thousand Oaks, CA: Sage.

Handy, Charles. (1995, May/June). Trust and the virtual organization. *Harvard Business Review,* 40–50.

Hardin, Garrett. (1968). The tragedy of the commons. *Science,* 162: 1243–1248.

Hawken, Paul. (1993). *The ecology of commerce.* New York: HarperBusiness.

Henderson, Hazel. (1996). *Building a win-win world: Life beyond global economic warfare.* San Francisco, CA: Berrett-Koehler.

Human Development Report. (1997). Cary, NC: Oxford University Press.

Hutchinson, Colin. (1992). Corporate strategy and the environment. *Long Range Planning,* 25(4): 9–21.

Indiana Center on Global Change and World Peace Prediction. (1994, Fall). Bloomington, IN: Indiana University.

Korten, David. (1995). *When corporations rule the world.* San Francisco, CA: Berrett-Koehler.

Levering, Robert, and Moskowitz, Milton. (1998, Jan. 12). The 100 best companies to work for in America. *Fortune,* pp. 84–95.

Marstrander, Rolf. (1994). Industrial ecology: A practical framework for environmental management, in Bernard Taylor (Ed.), *Environmental management handbook.* (Chapter 12) London: Pitman Publishing.

Meadows, Donella H., Meadows, Dennis L., and Randers, Jorgen. (1992). *Beyond the limits: Confronting global collapse – envisioning a sustainable future.* Post Mills, VT: Chelsea Green.

Mexico's Pemex says 'redoubling' environmental effort. (1996, May 27). *Wall Street Journal* Interactive. http://www.wsj.com.

Moffat, Susan. (1996, Dec. 9). Asia stinks. *Fortune,* pp. 120–132.

Moran, Robert, Harris, Philip, and Stripp, William. (1993). *Developing the global organization.* Houston, TX: Gulf Publications.

Ottman, J.A. (1992). *Green marketing.* Lincolnwood, IL: NTC Business Books.

Pilat, Dirk. (1997). *Labour productivity levels in OECD countries: Estimates for manufacturing and selected service sectors*. OECD Economics Working Paper no. 169.

The politics of population. (1994, Sept. 1). *The Seattle Times*, pp. A1, A14.

Porter, Michael E., and van der Linde, Claas. (1995, Sept./Oct.). Green and competitive: Ending the stalemate. *Harvard Business Review*, 73(5): 120–134.

Reichheld, Frederick. (1996). *The loyalty effect*. Boston, MA: Harvard Business School Press.

Schmidheiny, Stephan, Zorraquin, Federico, and the World Business Council for Sustainable Development. (1996). *Financing change*. Cambridge, MA: MIT Press.

Shrivastava, Paul. (1996). *Greening business*. Cincinnati, OH: Thomson Executive Press.

Simon, Julian. (1981). *The ultimate resource*. Oxford: Martin Robinson.

Simons, George F., Vazquez, Carmen, and Harris, Philip R. (1993). Houston, TX: Gulf Publishing.

Simons, Marlise. (1995, Feb. 4). Dutch flooding a severe blow for business. *New York Times*, pp. 1, 4.

Smith, Craig A. (1995, Oct. 9). China becomes industrial nations' most favored dump. *The Wall Street Journal*, p. B1.

Stead, W. Edward, and Stead, Jean Garner. (1996). *Management for a small planet* (2nd ed.). Thousand Oaks, CA: Sage.

UN Framework Convention on Climate Change. (1997). Kyoto Conference. UN: Geneva; www.undcp.org/unlinks.html.

US President's Council on Sustainable Development. (1994). *A vision for a sustainable US and principles of sustainable development*. Washington, DC: Author.

Viederman, Stephen. (1994). *The economics of sustainability: Challenges*. Paper presented at the workshop, The Economics of Sustainability, Fundacão Joaquin Nabuco, Recife, Brazil.

Walley, Noah, and Whitehead, Bradley. (1994, May/June). It's not easy being green. *Harvard Business Review*, pp. 46–52.

Welford, Richard. (1993, Winter). Breaking the link between quality and the environment: Auditing for sustainability and life-cycle assessment. *Business Strategy and the Environment*, 2, Part 4. ERP Environment.

Winslow, Ron. (1995, Jan. 1). 'Fungus fatale' poses a threat to potato crop. *The Wall Street Journal*, pp. B1, B5.

World Conservation Union, United Nations Environment Programme, and Worldwide Fund for Nature. (1991). *Caring for the earth: A strategy for sustainable living*. Gland, Switzerland: Author.

World Resources: A guide to the global environment. (1996/97). New York: World Resources Institute.

Index